World Economic and Financial Surveys

WORLD ECONOMIC OUTLOOK
September 2006

Financial Systems and Economic Cycles

International Monetary Fund

Production: IMF Multimedia Services Division
Cover and Design: Luisa Menjivar-Macdonald and Jorge Salazar
Figures: Theodore F. Peters, Jr.
Typesetting: Choon Lee

World economic outlook (International Monetary Fund)
World economic outlook: a survey by the staff of the International Monetary Fund.—1980– —Washington, D.C.: The Fund, 1980–

v.; 28 cm.—(1981–84: Occasional paper/International Monetary Fund ISSN 0251-6365)
Annual.
Has occasional updates, 1984–
ISSN 0258-7440 = World economic and financial surveys
ISSN 0256-6877 = World economic outlook (Washington)
1. Economic history—1971– —Periodicals. I. International Monetary Fund. II. Series: Occasional paper (International Monetary Fund)

HC10.W7979 84-640155
338.5'443'09048—dc19
AACR 2 MARC-S

Library of Congress 8507

Published biannually.
ISBN 1-58906-598-0

Price: US$57.00
(US$54.00 to full-time faculty members and students at universities and colleges)

Please send orders to:
International Monetary Fund, Publication Services
700 19th Street, N.W., Washington, D.C. 20431, U.S.A.
Tel.: (202) 623-7430 Telefax: (202) 623-7201
E-mail: publications@imf.org
Internet: http://www.imf.org

recycled paper

CONTENTS

Tables

Figures

ASSUMPTIONS AND CONVENTIONS

A number of assumptions have been adopted for the projections presented in the *World Economic Outlook*. It has been assumed that real effective exchange rates will remain constant at their average levels during July 5–August 2, 2006, except for the currencies participating in the European exchange rate mechanism II (ERM II), which are assumed to remain constant in nominal terms relative to the euro; that established policies of national authorities will be maintained (for specific assumptions about fiscal and monetary policies in industrial countries, see Box A1); that the average price of oil will be $69.20 a barrel in 2006 and $75.50 a barrel in 2007, and remain unchanged in real terms over the medium term; that the six-month London interbank offered rate (LIBOR) on U.S. dollar deposits will average 5.4 percent in 2006 and 5.5 percent in 2007; that the three-month euro deposits rate will average 3.1 percent in 2006 and 3.7 percent in 2007; and that the six-month Japanese yen deposit rate will yield an average of 0.5 percent in 2006 and of 1.1 percent in 2007. These are, of course, working hypotheses rather than forecasts, and the uncertainties surrounding them add to the margin of error that would in any event be involved in the projections. The estimates and projections are based on statistical information available through end-August 2006.

The following conventions have been used throughout the *World Economic Outlook:*

. . . to indicate that data are not available or not applicable;

— to indicate that the figure is zero or negligible;

– between years or months (for example, 2004–05 or January–June) to indicate the years or months covered, including the beginning and ending years or months;

/ between years or months (for example, 2004/05) to indicate a fiscal or financial year.

"Billion" means a thousand million; "trillion" means a thousand billion.

"Basis points" refer to hundredths of 1 percentage point (for example, 25 basis points are equivalent to ¼ of 1 percent point).

In figures and tables, shaded areas indicate IMF staff projections.

Minor discrepancies between sums of constituent figures and totals shown are due to rounding.

As used in this report, the term "country" does not in all cases refer to a territorial entity that is a state as understood by international law and practice. As used here, the term also covers some territorial entities that are not states but for which statistical data are maintained on a separate and independent basis.

FURTHER INFORMATION AND DATA

This report on the *World Economic Outlook* is available in full on the IMF's Internet site, www.imf.org. Accompanying it on the website is a larger compilation of data from the WEO database than in the report itself, consisting of files containing the series most frequently requested by readers. These files may be downloaded for use in a variety of software packages.

Inquiries about the content of the *World Economic Outlook* and the WEO database should be sent by mail, electronic mail, or telefax (telephone inquiries cannot be accepted) to:

World Economic Studies Division
Research Department
International Monetary Fund
700 19th Street, N.W.
Washington, D.C. 20431, U.S.A.
E-mail: weo@imf.org Telefax: (202) 623-6343

PREFACE

The analysis and projections contained in the *World Economic Outlook* are integral elements of the IMF's surveillance of economic developments and policies in its member countries, of developments in international financial markets, and of the global economic system. The survey of prospects and policies is the product of a comprehensive interdepartmental review of world economic developments, which draws primarily on information the IMF staff gathers through its consultations with member countries. These consultations are carried out in particular by the IMF's area departments together with the Policy Development and Review Department, the International Capital Markets Department, the Monetary and Financial Systems Department, and the Fiscal Affairs Department.

The analysis in this report has been coordinated in the Research Department under the general direction of Raghuram Rajan, Economic Counsellor and Director of Research. The project has been directed by Charles Collyns, Deputy Director of the Research Department, and Tim Callen, Division Chief, Research Department.

The primary contributors to this report are Thomas Helbling, Subir Lall, Kalpana Kochhar, S. Hossein Samiei, Roberto Cardarelli, Florence Jaumotte, Toh Kuan, Valerie Mercer-Blackman, Hélène Poirson, Martin Sommer, Nikola Spatafora, Irina Tytell, and Johannes Wiegand. To-Nhu Dao, Christian de Guzman, Stephanie Denis, Nese Erbil, Angela Espiritu, Patrick Hettinger, Bennett Sutton, and Ercument Tulun provided research assistance. Mahnaz Hemmati, Laurent Meister, and Casper Meyer managed the database and the computer systems. Sylvia Brescia, Celia Burns, and Jemille Colon were responsible for word processing. Other contributors include Ricardo Adrogue, Sergei Antoshin, Bas Bakker, Dan Citrin, Gianni De Nicolo, Roberto García-Saltos, Christopher Gilbert, David Hauner, George Kapetanios, Manmohan Kumar, Michael Kumhof, Luc Laeven, Doug Laxton, Ross Levine, Papa N'Diaye, Christopher Otrok, Arvind Subramanian, Stephen Tokarick, Thierry Tressel, Kenichi Ueda, and Khuong Vu. Jeff Hayden of the External Relations Department edited the manuscript and coordinated the production of the publication.

The analysis has benefited from comments and suggestions by staff from other IMF departments, as well as by Executive Directors following their discussion of the report on August 22 and 23, 2006. However, both projections and policy considerations are those of the IMF staff and should not be attributed to Executive Directors or to their national authorities.

FOREWORD

The *World Economic Outlook* is truly a joint product, primarily with inputs from the Research Department of the International Monetary Fund, but also from the staff of a number of other departments. I thank Charles Collyns, David Robinson (who was with us during the important initial phase of this Outlook), Tim Callen, members of the World Economic Studies Division, and all the IMF staff from other divisions and departments who worked together to bring this *World Economic Outlook* to you.

The world economy continues to be strong, with a third year of significantly-above-trend growth. Growth continues to become more balanced with the United States slowing and the euro area picking up, while Japan's growth is moderating toward trend. A key element to the strong world performance is the extraordinary growth of emerging markets and developing countries.

Much has rightly been made of the strong productivity growth of the U.S. economy over the last decade or so, which has contributed to this purple patch for the world. Far less has been made of the equally impressive productivity growth in emerging markets and developing countries. In Chapter 3, we examine the sources of labor productivity growth in Asia (the primary source of growth in output per capita), and compare it with other regions of the world. Asian labor productivity growth has benefited not just from fast accumulation of physical and human capital but also significant total factor productivity (TFP) growth—growth that typically comes from technological progress and from using the factors of production more efficiently. Indeed, in both China and India, TFP growth exceeds the contribution of physical or human capital accumulation. This extraordinary change has been made possible through an enabling environment that has fostered the development of efficient manufacturing (and in the case of India, services), while encouraging some movement of labor out of low-productivity agriculture.

Given the still high share of employment in agriculture in China, India, and the ASEAN countries, and provided the policy environment continues to be enabling, growth will continue to come from the shift out of agriculture. Given that a substantial population will still be employed in agriculture in the poorer Asian economies for some time, an important objective of policy should be to improve agricultural productivity. Equally important for the richer countries is to improve productivity in the service sector, especially because services will constitute an increasingly important fraction of their economies. For a number of Asian economies, a critical element of any policy mix to improve agricultural and service sector productivity will be opening up these sectors to foreign entry and competition.

Productivity growth, especially when unexpected, has a number of valuable benefits. Other things equal, it reduces unit labor costs, and increases the potential growth rate of the economy. Thus it helps keep inflation under check. It also helps offset the investment and growth consequences of adverse supply shocks. That the world economy has remained robust in recent years despite higher oil and commodities prices is due, in no small part, to the enabling policies that allowed economies to continuously improve productivity.

Robust global growth over the last few years has brought some new policy challenges. For one, unexpectedly high demand for some non-oil commodities may have generated enormous revenues for some commodity producers temporarily, but conditions will change as supply catches up. As Chapter 5 suggests, prospects for non-oil commodities, especially metals, may be different from oil in that there is more likely to be a robust supply response as investment increases to meet the unexpectedly higher demand. Our model, as well as futures prices, suggests that metals prices are likely to decline in the future. Non-oil-commodity-dependent economies should anticipate this risk by being cautious on raising expenditures that are hard to reverse, such as public sector salaries, and instead focus on expenditures that help build diversified productive capacity for the future.

Another risk is that some market-led processes may overshoot when times are good. For instance, widespread productivity growth may have played a role in the emergence of global current account imbalances. The strong productivity growth in the United States, as is well known, certainly made the United States an attractive place to invest in, drawing in capital and producing a counterpart current account deficit in the late 1990s. In addition though, as Chapter 4 suggests, the United States' sophisticated arm's length financial system made it easier for consumers to borrow against future incomes and consume immediately, augmenting the size of the current account deficit. Indeed, the expectation of higher future incomes coupled with accommodative monetary policy and low interest rates may have fueled the U.S. housing boom, which boosted consumption even more as the financial system allowed borrowing against collateral.

Even though emerging markets have experienced strong productivity growth in recent years, many did not have financial systems that could translate this into either higher investment or higher consumption. Their rising incomes were therefore channeled into net savings that helped finance the United States' dissaving. The ability to run current account imbalances therefore has allowed the world to grow faster than it would otherwise have. This is a good thing but it has limits. It is important, therefore, that we bring imbalances down in stable times so that we have room to expand them when future needs arise—this is just prudent countercyclical global policy.

Prudence is especially important when the times are changing. Revisions to U.S. data suggest that productivity growth was not so high as earlier believed. Furthermore, productivity growth has been declining as the expansion matures, and unit labor costs have been accelerating. With tight labor market conditions (including in other industrial countries), and high capacity utilization, inflationary pressures are on the rise. Even as liquidity is being withdrawn, the Federal Reserve has to assess not just how much the economy will slow because of prior rate increases (and their effects via the housing market) and higher energy prices, but also what the potential growth of the economy truly is. It also has to pay attention to the narrowing global output gap. There are risks of both excessive tightening as well as overly gradual tightening.

While growth in the rest of the world is likely to pick up some of the slack of a slowing U.S. economy, it is hard to estimate precisely how much of that momentum is independent of U.S. growth because the world has become so much more closely integrated over the last few years. Our baseline is that world growth will continue to be strong, but that forecast is surrounded by significant risks to the downside.

Policymakers should recognize that some of their country's performance is not just because of their own skills at the helm but because of spillovers from the robust global economy, as well as the benign financial conditions. The emerging protectionism not just in trade, but increasingly in preventing cross-border acquisitions and foreign direct investment, can interrupt the process of global productivity growth that has been so critical to the robust health of the world in recent years. This is why country authorities should strive hard, not just to revive the Doha Round, but even to make it more ambitious. They should work together to sustain the smooth flow of goods, capital, and ideas across borders, not least through the various mechanisms proposed by the IMF's Managing Director in his Medium-Term Strategy to invigorate the quality of the multilateral dialogue. Finally, wherever possible, they should ensure that public policy does not exacerbate imbalances created by the private sector, as well as avoid creating uncertainties where none existed before. Prudent, predictable policy, in this environment of increasing uncertainty, is the need of the hour.

Raghuram Rajan
Economic Counsellor and Director, Research Department

EXECUTIVE SUMMARY

Global Economic Environment

- The global expansion remained buoyant in the first half of 2006, with activity in most regions meeting or exceeding expectations (Chapter 1). Growth was particularly strong in the United States in the first quarter of 2006, although it has slowed subsequently. The expansion gathered momentum in the euro area, and continued in Japan. Emerging markets have grown rapidly, especially China, and low-income countries have also maintained an impressive growth performance, helped by strong commodity prices.
- At the same time, there are signs that inflationary pressures are edging up in some countries as sustained high rates of growth have absorbed spare capacity. Headline inflation in a number of advanced economies has for some time been above central bank comfort zones, pushed up by rising oil prices, but there are now signs of increases in core inflation and inflation expectations, most notably in the United States. In Japan, there is increasing evidence that deflation has finally ended.
- Oil and metals prices have hit new highs. Prices have been supported by tight spare capacity in global markets against the background of buoyant GDP growth, and in the case of oil, rising geopolitical tensions in the Middle East and risks to production in some other large producers (notably Nigeria). Futures markets suggest that oil prices will remain elevated for the foreseeable future.
- Major central banks have responded by tightening monetary policy. The U.S. Federal Reserve continued to raise interest rates through June, although pausing in August; the European Central Bank has raised interest rates further in recent months; and the Bank of Japan ended its zero interest rate policy in July. The U.S. dollar has weakened against the euro, and to a lesser extent the yen, while long-term interest rates have firmed.
- Rising inflation concerns and tighter monetary conditions led to some weakness in advanced-economy equity markets and a series of larger moves in some emerging market asset prices in May–June, although markets have been more stable since July. These moves appear to largely represent corrections after major price run-ups, rather than a fundamental reassessment of economic risks, and seem unlikely to have a major growth impact, although growth in some individual countries may be dampened as their central banks have raised interest rates to calm financial market conditions and head off inflationary pressures.
- Global imbalances remain large. Despite an acceleration in export growth, the U.S. current account deficit is expected to near 7 percent of GDP in 2007. Surpluses in oil exporters and a number of Asian countries are expected to stay high, with China's surplus remaining in excess of 7 percent of GDP.

Outlook and Risks

- The forecast for global growth has been marked up to 5.1 percent in 2006 and 4.9 percent in 2007, both ¼ of a percentage point higher than in the April 2006 *World Economic Outlook.*
- Growth in the United States is expected to slow from 3.4 percent in 2006 to 2.9 percent in 2007, amid a cooling housing market. Growth in Japan will also ease as the cycle matures. In the euro area, the recovery is projected to sustain its momentum this year, although growth in Germany will be reduced in 2007 by the planned tax increase. Among emerging markets and developing countries,

growth is expected to remain very strong, with the Chinese economy continuing its recent rapid expansion.

- The balance of risks to the global outlook is slanted to the downside, with IMF staff estimates suggesting a one in six chance that growth could fall to 3¼ percent or less in 2007. The most notable risks are that inflationary pressures could intensify, requiring monetary policy to be tightened more than currently expected; that oil prices could increase further against the background of limited spare capacity and geopolitical uncertainties; and that the U.S. housing market could cool more rapidly than expected, triggering a more abrupt slowdown of the U.S. economy.
- The potential for a disorderly unwinding of global imbalances remains a concern. A smooth, market-led unwinding of these imbalances is the most likely outcome, although investors would need to continue increasing the share of U.S. assets in their portfolios for many years to allow this to happen. The depth and sophistication of U.S. financial markets has facilitated the financing of recent large current account deficits. However, there remains some risk of a disorderly adjustment, which could impose heavy costs on the global economy.

Policy Challenges

Advanced Economies

- Central banks in advanced economies will need to carefully weigh the relative risks to growth and inflation in the period ahead. The U.S. Federal Reserve faces a difficult situation of rising inflation in a slowing economy, but given the importance of keeping inflation expectations in check, some further policy tightening may still be needed (Chapter 2). In Japan, interest rate increases should be gradual, as there is little danger of an inflationary surge, while the reemergence of deflation would be costly. In the euro area, further increases in interest rates are likely to be needed if the expansion develops as expected, but for now inflation pressures seem broadly contained, and faced with continuing downside risks to growth, policymakers can afford to be cautious in tightening monetary policy further.
- In most of the large advanced economies, fiscal consolidation in the face of aging populations remains a huge challenge. Fiscal consolidation is envisaged in many countries in the coming years, but it is neither ambitious enough nor backed up by clearly identified policy measures. Social security systems need to be put on sounder footings, and effective ways found to contain the inexorable rise in health care costs.
- Structural reforms to improve the business environment and global competitiveness remain essential to bolster growth prospects. In the euro area, faster progress to advance the Lisbon agenda—particularly more open competition in services, more flexible labor markets, and financial sector reforms—remain key to boost productivity growth and improve job opportunities. In Japan, priorities include public sector reforms, steps to enhance labor market flexibility and financial sector efficiency, and reforms to improve productivity in the services sector.
- Chapter 4 examines how differences in financial systems can affect economic cycles in advanced economies. A new index is constructed that characterizes financial systems according to the degree to which transactions are based on long-term relationships between borrowers and lenders or are conducted at "arm's length." The chapter finds that while there has been a general trend toward bank disintermediation and a greater role for financial markets, the pace has differed across countries, and there are still important differences in financial systems. The chapter offers some evidence that such differences in financial systems may affect cyclical behavior. Specifically, in more arm's length systems, households may be able to better smooth consumption in response to changes in income, but their

spending may be more sensitive to changes in asset prices. Corporate investment appears to react more smoothly to cyclical downturns in relationship-based systems, but arm's length systems seem better at reallocating resources in response to structural changes.

- The move toward more arm's length financial systems that has been under way in most countries over the past decade is set to continue, given technological innovations and the removal of regulatory barriers. Policymakers will need to maximize the benefits from this ongoing change, including by implementing complementary reforms to increase labor market flexibility, improve the portability of employee pension plans, and strengthen bankruptcy procedures. Supervisory and regulatory policies will need to keep up with the increasing sophistication of the financial sector, while macroeconomic policy management will need to adapt to reflect possible changes in cyclical behavior.

Emerging Market and Developing Economies

- In emerging market and developing economies, policymakers must adjust to the more challenging global environment by continuing to reduce vulnerabilities and by putting in place reforms that will help sustain the current growth momentum. Recent developments have provided a reminder that emerging market economies remain susceptible to turbulence in global financial markets. Countries at risk include those with still weak public sector balance sheets, large current account deficits, and less well-anchored inflation expectations. In a number of countries in emerging Europe, the increasing reliance on private debt flows to finance large current account deficits is a concern. More also needs to be done in emerging market and developing economies to advance market-oriented reforms, particularly by reducing barriers to competition, to create the climate for vigorous private sector–led growth.
- Chapter 3 analyzes Asia's remarkable growth performance, and focuses on what needs to be done to sustain strong growth in the future. The chapter finds that the favorable policy environment in Asia has been the key to strong total factor productivity growth and rapid accumulation of physical and human capital in the region. Indeed, the importance of establishing a favorable policy environment is the key lesson that late developing countries—both within Asia and in other parts of the world—can learn from the successful early developers such as Japan and the newly industrialized economies (NIEs). Trade liberalization, improved access to education, and steps to promote financial development and encourage entrepreneurship would facilitate the ongoing shift of resources out of agriculture and into industry and services. Efforts to boost productivity growth in industry, and particularly the relatively more sheltered services sector, will also pay important dividends. Policies to encourage increased competition in services include removing barriers to entry, encouraging foreign investment, and streamlining regulations.
- Chapter 5 examines the outlook for prices of nonfuel commodities. These prices—particularly for metals—have risen sharply in recent years, defraying the losses from higher oil import bills for exporters of these commodities. The chapter finds that price increases have largely been driven by strong demand, particularly from China, as well as supply bottlenecks. In addition, the chapter finds that speculative activity does not seem to have been a significant driver leading commodity price movements, although speculators may have played a role in providing liquidity to markets. Metals prices are expected to come down over the medium term as new production comes on stream to meet rising demand. The key policy message for countries that export commodities—particularly metals—is that they should not assume that high prices will be sustained.

Current revenue windfalls should be saved or invested to support future growth in noncommodity sectors, rather than used to increase spending in areas that will be difficult to reverse later.

Multilateral Initiatives

- Joint policy efforts would help to ensure a smooth reduction of global imbalances. An orderly private sector–led adjustment, involving a rebalancing of demand across countries, with accompanying further depreciation of the U.S. dollar and exchange rate appreciations in many surplus countries (notably in parts of Asia and oil producers), remains the most likely outcome. However, there remains a risk of a more disorderly unwinding that would imply a heavy cost for the global economy. The risks of such a disorderly adjustment would be considerably reduced by sustained policy actions across the major players in the world economy involving steps to boost national saving in the United States, including through fiscal consolidation; greater progress on structural reforms in Europe and Japan; reforms to boost domestic demand in emerging Asia (consumption in China, investment elsewhere) together with greater exchange rate flexibility; and increased spending in oil-producing countries in high-return areas, consistent with absorptive capacity constraints, especially in the Middle East, where the large buildup of investment projects already in train is welcome. Taking a joint, multilateral approach may help to advance implementation by providing assurance that possible risks associated with individual actions would be alleviated by simultaneous policy initiatives elsewhere. The present multilateral consultation by the IMF can contribute to this process.
- Efforts are needed to reinvigorate the process of multilateral trade liberalization. The apparent deadlock in the Doha Round is deeply disappointing. Trade liberalization on a nondiscriminatory (most favored nation, or MFN) basis remains the best way to open up new global growth opportunities. The threat of protectionist pressures needs to be firmly resisted.
- High and volatile prices in world energy markets remain a major concern that will require sustained efforts from all sides to address. Increased investment is needed to build up adequate production and refining capacity, while appropriate incentives for consumers would encourage improved energy conservation.

CHAPTER 1

GLOBAL PROSPECTS AND POLICY ISSUES

World output increased briskly in the first half of 2006, and global growth is projected at 5.1 percent for the year as a whole before moderating to 4.9 percent in 2007 (Figure 1.1 and Table 1.1). Nevertheless, inflationary concerns, tighter conditions in financial markets, and further jumps in oil prices to new highs have highlighted downside risks as the global economy enters the fourth year of this current expansion. Other notable sources of uncertainty include the threat of an abrupt slowdown in the U.S. housing market; lingering doubts about prospects for growth in the other advanced economies; and questions about the resilience of emerging market countries in a more challenging global environment. Moreover, large global imbalances continue to prompt concerns, while the potential for protectionist pressures has increased now that the Doha Round seems to be deadlocked. Against this background, policymakers will need to respond flexibly to events and act with foresight to head off potential strains, recognizing the importance of spillovers across countries and the benefits of taking a joint approach to managing global risks and promoting a robust world economy.

Global Economic Environment

The global expansion was broad-based in the first half of 2006, with activity in most regions meeting or exceeding expectations, and recent indicators suggest that the pace of expansion is being maintained in the third quarter (Figure 1.2). Growth was particularly strong in the United States in the first quarter, although it slowed in the second quarter in the face of headwinds from a cooling housing market and rising fuel costs. The expansion gathered momentum in the euro area, notwithstanding a slow start to the year in Germany, and the Japanese economy continued to expand. Growth in China has accelerated even further, emerging Asia and Europe have continued to grow rapidly, and the pace of activity has picked up in Latin America. Middle Eastern oil exporters and low-

Figure 1.1. Global Indicators[1]

(Annual percent change unless otherwise noted)

The global expansion continues above trend, the fourth consecutive year of strong growth, contributing to some pickup in inflationary pressures.

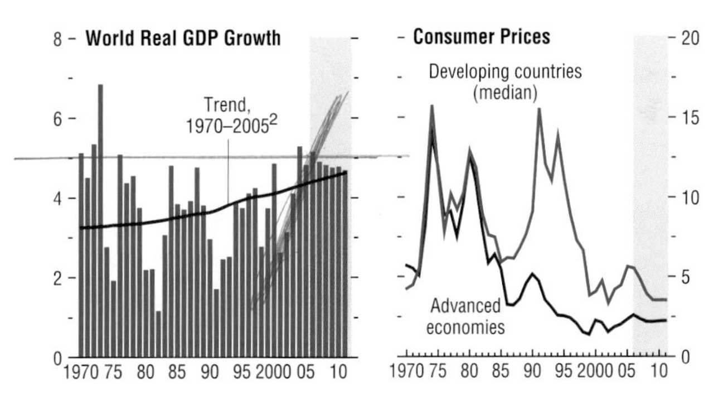

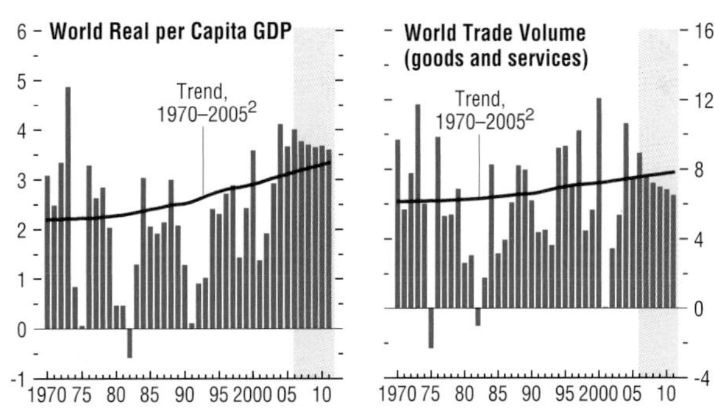

[1]Shaded areas indicate IMF staff projections. Aggregates are computed on the basis of purchasing-power-parity (PPP) weights unless otherwise noted.

[2]Average growth rates for individual countries, aggregated using PPP weights; the aggregates shift over time in favor of faster-growing countries, giving the line an upward trend.

Table 1.1. Overview of the *World Economic Outlook* Projections
(Annual percent change unless otherwise noted)

			Current Projections		Difference from April 2006 Projections	
	2004	2005	2006	2007	2006	2007
World output	**5.3**	**4.9**	**5.1**	**4.9**	**0.3**	**0.2**
Advanced economies	3.2	2.6	3.1	2.7	0.1	–0.1
United States	3.9	3.2	3.4	2.9	—	–0.4
Euro area	2.1	1.3	2.4	2.0	0.4	0.1
Germany	1.2	0.9	2.0	1.3	0.7	0.3
France	2.0	1.2	2.4	2.3	0.3	0.2
Italy	1.1	—	1.5	1.3	0.3	–0.1
Spain	3.1	3.4	3.4	3.0	0.1	–0.2
Japan	2.3	2.6	2.7	2.1	–0.1	0.1
United Kingdom	3.3	1.9	2.7	2.7	0.2	0.1
Canada	3.3	2.9	3.1	3.0	—	–0.1
Other advanced economies	4.6	3.7	4.1	3.7	—	—
Newly industrialized Asian economies	5.9	4.5	4.9	4.4	–0.2	–0.1
Other emerging market and developing countries	7.7	7.4	7.3	7.2	0.4	0.5
Africa	5.5	5.4	5.4	5.9	–0.4	0.4
Sub-Sahara	5.6	5.8	5.2	6.3	–0.6	0.6
Central and eastern Europe	6.5	5.4	5.3	5.0	0.1	0.2
Commonwealth of Independent States	8.4	6.5	6.8	6.5	0.8	0.4
Russia	7.2	6.4	6.5	6.5	0.4	0.7
Excluding Russia	11.0	6.7	7.6	6.4	1.5	–0.2
Developing Asia	8.8	9.0	8.7	8.6	0.5	0.7
China	10.1	10.2	10.0	10.0	0.5	1.0
India	8.0	8.5	8.3	7.3	1.0	0.3
ASEAN-4	5.8	5.1	5.0	5.6	—	–0.1
Middle East	5.5	5.7	5.8	5.4	0.2	–0.1
Western Hemisphere	5.7	4.3	4.8	4.2	0.4	0.6
Brazil	4.9	2.3	3.6	4.0	0.1	0.5
Mexico	4.2	3.0	4.0	3.5	0.5	0.4
Memorandum						
European Union	2.4	1.8	2.8	2.4	0.4	0.1
World growth based on market exchange rates	3.9	3.4	3.8	3.5	0.2	—
World trade volume (goods and services)	**10.6**	**7.4**	**8.9**	**7.6**	**0.9**	**0.2**
Imports						
Advanced economies	9.1	6.0	7.5	6.0	1.2	0.4
Other emerging market and developing countries	16.4	11.9	13.0	12.1	0.1	0.2
Exports						
Advanced economies	8.8	5.5	8.0	6.0	1.4	–0.1
Other emerging market and developing countries	14.6	11.8	10.7	10.6	–0.2	0.2
Commodity prices (U.S. dollars)						
Oil[1]	30.7	41.3	29.7	9.1	14.9	6.2
Nonfuel (average based on world commodity export weights)	18.5	10.3	22.1	–4.8	11.9	0.7
Consumer prices						
Advanced economies	2.0	2.3	2.6	2.3	0.3	0.2
Other emerging market and developing countries	5.6	5.3	5.2	5.0	–0.1	0.2
London interbank offered rate (percent)[2]						
On U.S. dollar deposits	1.8	3.8	5.4	5.5	0.3	0.4
On euro deposits	2.1	2.2	3.1	3.7	0.1	0.3
On Japanese yen deposits	0.1	0.1	0.5	1.1	0.1	0.1

Note: Real effective exchange rates are assumed to remain constant at the levels prevailing during July 5–August 2, 2006. See Statistical Appendix for details and groups and methodologies.

[1]Simple average of spot prices of U.K. Brent, Dubai, and West Texas Intermediate crude oil. The average price of oil in U.S. dollars a barrel was $53.35 in 2005; the assumed price is $69.20 in 2006, and $75.50 in 2007.

[2]Six-month rate for the United States and Japan. Three-month rate for the euro area.

income countries in Africa have also maintained impressive growth rates.

Sustained high rates of global growth have absorbed spare capacity and led to some emerging signs of inflationary pressures. While estimates of potential GDP are always subject to uncertainty, output gaps seem to be closing in much of the world (Figure 1.3), while buoyant demand for fuel and raw materials has contributed to record high prices for oil and other commodities. Headline inflation in many of the major advanced economies has for some time been above central bank comfort zones, pushed up by rising oil prices, but there are now signs of increases in core inflation, in market-based and survey measures of inflation expectations, and in unit labor costs, particularly in the United States (Figure 1.4). In emerging markets, a number of countries—including Argentina, India, Russia, South Africa, Turkey, and Venezuela—are facing price pressures following sustained periods of rapid growth or large exchange rate depreciations.

Against this background, central banks in the major advanced economies have taken steps to tighten monetary conditions. The U.S. Federal Reserve continued to raise the Fed funds rate through June, although pausing in August, seeking to balance inflation concerns against signs that the U.S. expansion is beginning to slow (Figure 1.5). The European Central Bank has raised its policy rate further, and the Bank of Japan has moved away from quantitative easing and in July raised the overnight policy rate from zero to 25 basis points. Central banks in Australia, Sweden, and the United Kingdom have also tightened in recent months. Longer-term government bond yields have increased, although they still remain quite low in real terms relative to average levels over the past 25 years (Figure 1.6).

Since late 2005, the U.S. dollar has depreciated against the euro, and to a lesser degree the yen, partly reversing its appreciation during the previous 12 months (Figure 1.7). The recent depreciation of the U.S. dollar seems to reflect in part perceptions that with the U.S. expansion at a more mature stage, interest differentials

Figure 1.2. Current and Forward-Looking Indicators

(Percent change from a year ago unless otherwise noted)

Industrial production, trade, and confidence indicators suggest that the pace of expansion is well sustained.

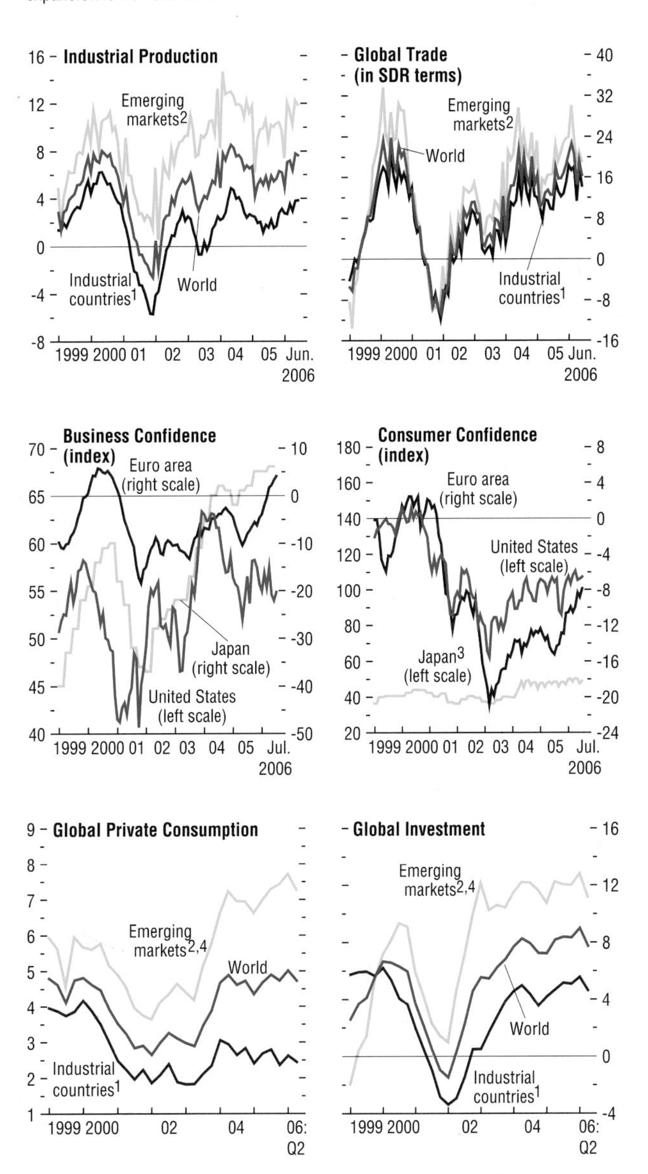

Sources: Business confidence for the United States, the Institute for Supply Management; for the euro area, the European Commission; and for Japan, Bank of Japan. Consumer confidence for the United States, the Conference Board; for the euro area, the European Commission; and for Japan, Cabinet Office; all others, Haver Analytics.

[1]Australia, Canada, Denmark, euro area, Japan, New Zealand, Norway, Sweden, Switzerland, the United Kingdom, and the United States.

[2]Argentina, Brazil, Bulgaria, Chile, China, Colombia, Czech Republic, Estonia, Hong Kong SAR, Hungary, India, Indonesia, Israel, Korea, Latvia, Lithuania, Malaysia, Mexico, Pakistan, Peru, the Philippines, Poland, Romania, Russia, Singapore, Slovak Republic, Slovenia, South Africa, Taiwan Province of China, Thailand, Turkey, Ukraine, and Venezuela.

[3]Japan's consumer confidence data are based on a diffusion index, where values greater than 50 indicate improving confidence.

[4] Data for China, India, Pakistan, and Russia are interpolated.

Figure 1.3. Measures of the Output Gap and Capacity Pressures[1]

Sustained growth has reduced output gaps and lowered unemployment rates. Tighter capacity constraints in commodity sectors have contributed to sharp increases in oil and metals prices.

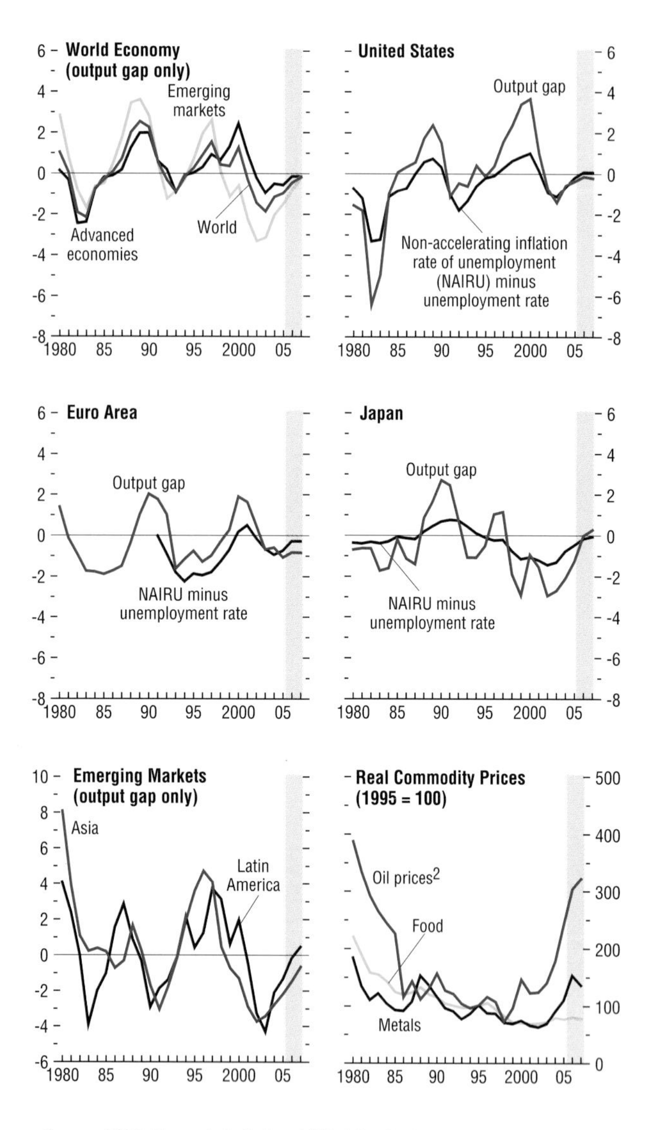

Sources: OECD, *Economic Outlook;* and IMF staff estimates.

[1]Estimates of the non-accelerating inflation rate of unemployment (NAIRU) come from the OECD. Estimates of the output gap, expressed as a percent of potential GDP, are based on IMF staff calculations.

[2]Simple average of spot prices of U.K. Brent, Dubai Fateh, and West Texas Intermediate crude oil.

vis-à-vis the other major currencies are likely to narrow, as well as increased market concern with global imbalances as the U.S. current account deficit has continued to widen and the surpluses in parts of emerging Asia and oil exporters have increased further (Figure 1.8). In real effective terms, the U.S. dollar is now close to its average level since 1980, while the euro is somewhat above its long-run average in real terms, and the yen somewhat below. Volatility in currency markets has also risen back to more normal levels, in part reflecting the fact that monetary policy decisions have become more data dependent and harder to predict.

Rising inflation concerns and tightening by major central banks had a marked impact on financial markets during March–June, 2006. Starting in March, currencies of some countries with particularly wide current account deficits—Iceland, New Zealand, and Hungary—depreciated sharply. There was a more general retreat from equity markets and emerging market currencies in May and June (Figure 1.9 and Box 1.1). Particularly affected were asset prices that had previously risen sharply (such as equities in Colombia and India), and the exchange rates of countries with high current account deficits (such as Hungary, South Africa, and Turkey).[1] With these developments coming on top of already overheated conditions in some countries, a number of central banks in emerging market countries have raised rates to calm financial conditions and to head off inflationary pressures. Since July, however, conditions have been more stable.

The IMF staff's assessment is that these market events should not significantly slow the overall momentum of global activity, although growth in some individual countries (such as Turkey) may be dampened. For the most part, asset price declines seem to have represented corrections after major run-ups rather than a fundamental reassessment of economic risks. It

[1]These developments are examined in depth in Chapter I of the IMF's September 2006 *Global Financial Stability Report.*

is striking that the impact on emerging market external bond spreads was relatively subdued, in part reflecting progress made in strengthening fiscal positions and the buildup of international reserve cushions, as well as recent debt buyback programs that have improved the supply-demand balance in these markets. Welcome progress has also been made in improving the structure of public debt, with increased sales of local currency debt to foreign investors, although some of the wind was also taken from these markets in the recent correction. Nonetheless, recent market pressures have provided a timely reminder of the need for continuing progress to improve public sector balance sheets and to address other vulnerabilities.

Oil and other commodity prices continued at elevated levels in the first eight months of 2006, with petroleum and metals prices reaching new highs (Appendix 1.1). Oil prices have been supported by tight spare capacity in global markets—both in production and refining—against the background of buoyant GDP growth, security concerns in the Middle East, and continued risks to production in some large producers elsewhere (notably Nigeria). Metals prices also have been boosted by strong demand growth, especially in emerging markets, by capacity shortages, and by labor disputes. Prices of food and other agricultural products rose in relative terms in the first part of 2006, although they have not participated in the price boom affecting oil and metals in recent years. Against this background, some commentators have suggested that speculative activity may have contributed to recent price surges, particularly in oil and metals. However, an IMF staff analysis, reported in Chapter 5, suggests that while speculators may have played a role in providing liquidity to markets, speculative position-taking does not seem to have been a significant driver leading commodity price movements.

Outlook and Short-Term Risks

Notwithstanding tightening financial conditions, the baseline forecast for world output

Figure 1.4. Global Inflation

(Annualized percent change of three-month moving average over previous three-month average, unless otherwise noted)

Measures of core inflation and inflation expectations in industrial countries have picked up recently, while the picture in emerging market countries is more mixed.

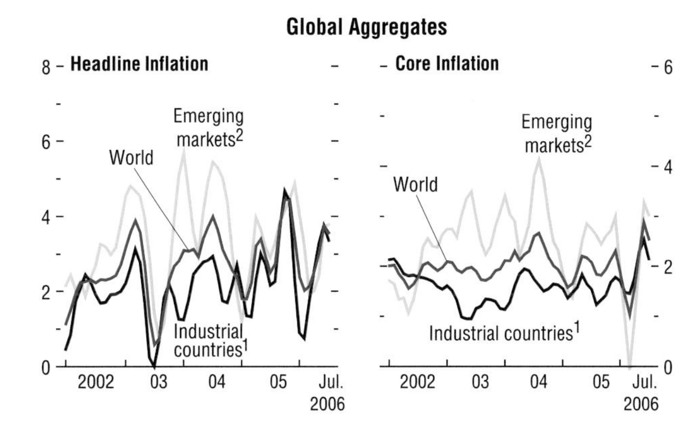

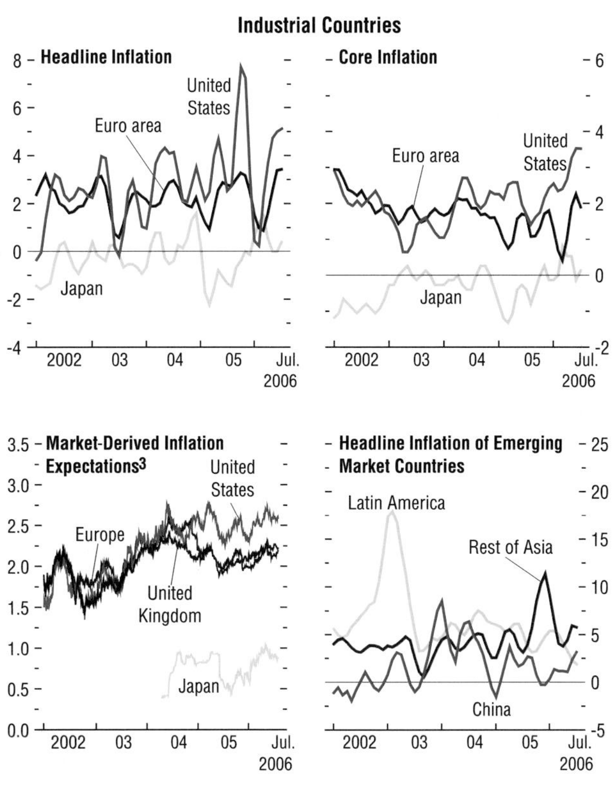

Sources: Haver Analytics; and IMF staff calculations.

[1]Australia, Canada, Denmark, euro area, Japan, New Zealand, Norway, Sweden, the United Kingdom, and the United States.

[2]Brazil, Bulgaria, Chile, China, Estonia, Hong Kong SAR, Hungary, India, Indonesia, Korea, Malaysia, Mexico, Poland, Singapore, South Africa, Taiwan Province of China, and Thailand.

[3]In percent; nominal minus inflation-indexed yields on 10-year securities.

Figure 1.5. Developments in Mature Financial Markets

Short-term interest rates have increased in most industrial countries, while long-term interest rates have also risen.

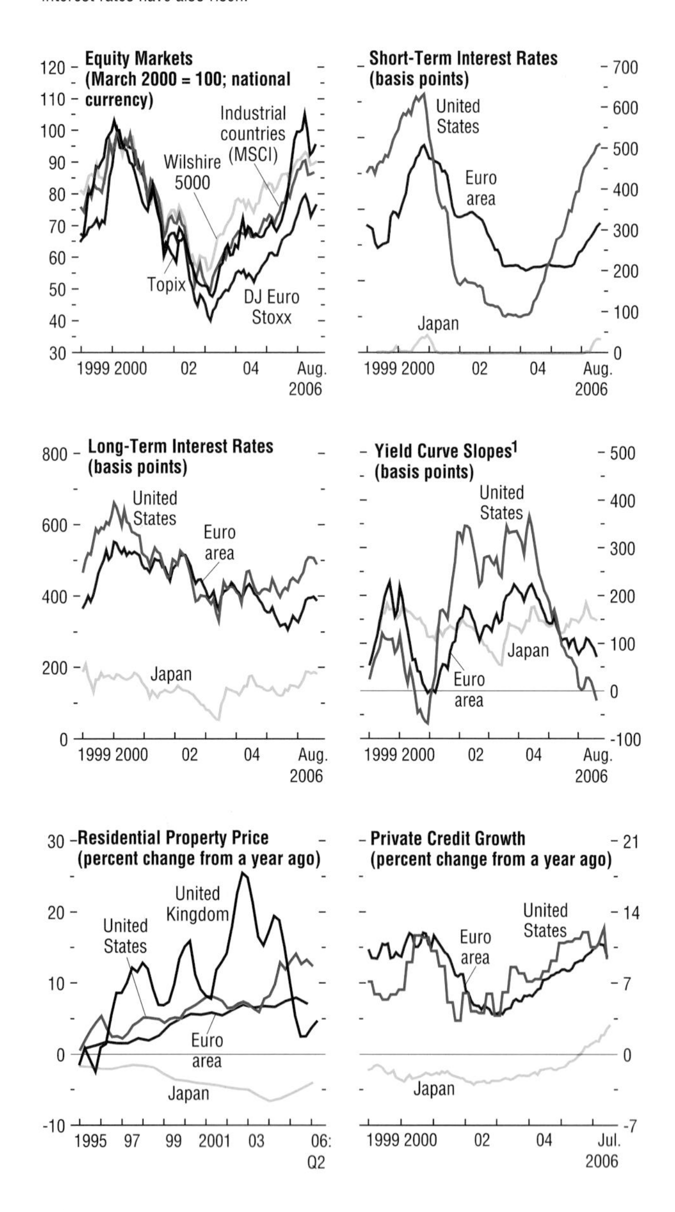

Sources: Bloomberg Financial Markets, LP; CEIC Data Company Limited; Haver Analytics; OECD; national authorities; IMF, *International Financial Statistics;* and IMF staff calculations.

[1]Ten-year government bond minus three-month treasury bill rate.

growth has been marked up to 5.1 percent in 2006 and 4.9 percent in 2007, ¼ percentage point above the April 2006 WEO projection in both years (Figure 1.10).[2] This would be the strongest four-year period of global expansion since the early 1970s. This favorable outlook depends on the view that inflationary pressures will be successfully contained with modest further interest rate increases by the major central banks, that the growth of domestic demand will be better balanced across the advanced economies, that emerging and developing countries will largely avoid capacity bottlenecks, and that global financial market conditions will be more stable now that excessive valuations in some sectors have been reduced. More specifically:

- The U.S. economy would grow 3.4 percent in 2006, before slowing to 2.9 percent in 2007, broadly in line with potential. A cooling housing market would continue to dampen private consumption and residential investment, but corporate investment should be supported by high capacity use and strong profitability.
- Growth in the euro area would rise to 2.4 percent in 2006—its highest rate in six years—before moderating to 2 percent in 2007. Stronger corporate balance sheets have paved the way for higher investment, rising employment, and a better balanced expansion. The slowing in 2007 would largely reflect scheduled tax increases in Germany.
- The Japanese economy would grow by 2.7 percent in 2006, based on solid domestic demand, before easing to 2.1 percent in 2007.
- Growth in emerging markets and developing countries would remain very strong at 7.3 percent in 2006, and slow only marginally to 7.2 percent in 2007. China would sustain growth around 10 percent—an upward revision relative to the April 2006 *World Economic Outlook*—

[2]This forecast is broadly in line with the private sector consensus and projections from other international agencies such as the OECD for 2006, while for 2007 the IMF staff projection for global growth is about ¼ percentage point above the consensus.

while India and Russia would also continue to grow rapidly. Latin American countries would continue to lag, although growth prospects have been marked up in this region.

- Headline inflation in the advanced economies would increase modestly to 2.6 percent in 2006, and start to come down in 2007 as the upward impetus from oil price increases recedes. Inflation pressures would also generally be contained in emerging market and developing countries.
- The U.S. current account deficit would rise further—to 6.9 percent of GDP in 2007—with large surpluses continuing in Japan, parts of emerging Asia, and oil-exporting countries in the Middle East and elsewhere.
- Private capital flows to emerging market and developing countries would slow from the torrid pace of 2005, but with the overall net current account surplus of these countries rising further, the pace of accumulation of international reserves would remain high (Table 1.2).

The risks to this baseline forecast would seem, however, increasingly tilted to the downside, even more so than at the time of the April 2006 *World Economic Outlook*. As reflected in the fan chart for global growth (Figure 1.11), which is based on the past forecasting record and an assessment of the current distribution of risks, in the IMF staff's view there is a one in six chance of growth in 2007 falling to 3¼ percent or less, a significant slowdown compared to the last four years.

Before considering these downside risks in more detail, it is worth highlighting sources of potentially even more rapid growth. These would seem to be concentrated in emerging markets, where growth has been underpredicted by IMF staff in recent years. In China, in particular, investment could be even higher than projected, in part reflecting abundant banking system liquidity, although such an outcome would further increase concerns about a boom-bust investment cycle. More broadly in emerging markets, a return to calmer global financial conditions could presage a resurgence of portfolio inflows, which could foster easy monetary

Figure 1.6. Mature Financial Market Indicators

Interest rates in real terms have risen closer to long-run averages and equity price-earnings ratios are generally below trend, while market volatility has recently increased.

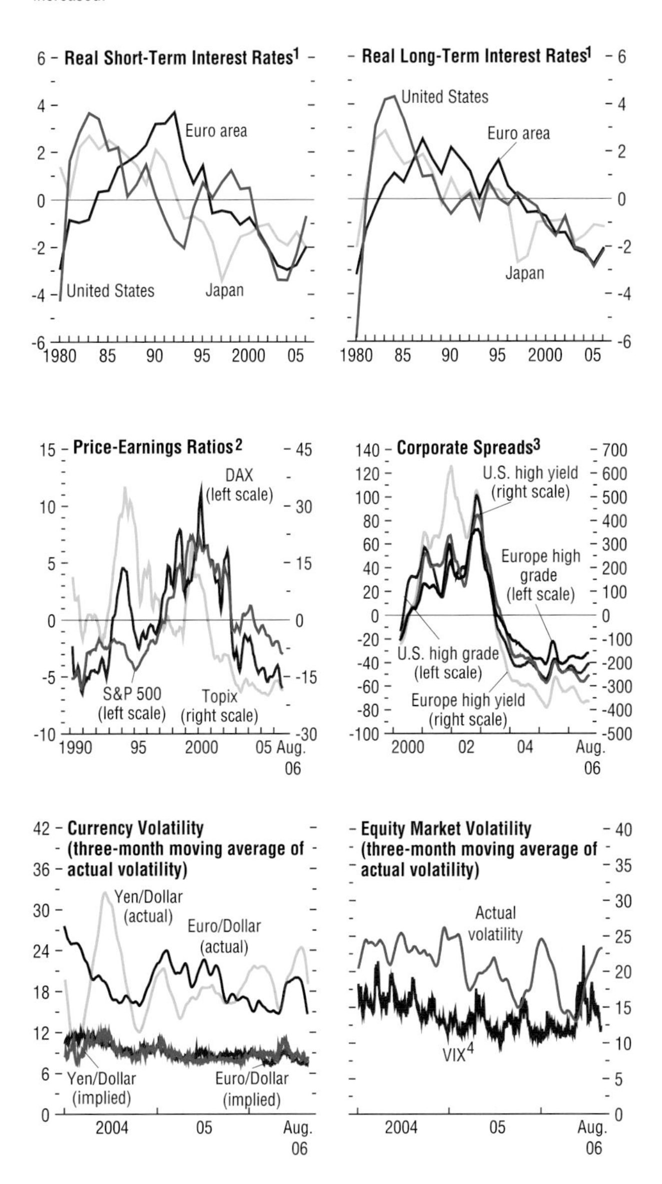

Sources: Bloomberg Financial Markets, LP; and IMF staff calculations.
[1]Measured as deviations from 1980–2006 average.
[2]Twelve-month forward looking price-earnings ratios measured as three-month moving average of deviations from 1990–2006 average.
[3]Measured as three-month moving average of deviations from 2000–06 average.
[4]VIX is the Chicago Board Options Exchange volatility index. This index is calculated by taking a weighted average of implied volatility for the eight S&P 500 calls and puts.

Figure 1.7. External Developments in Major Advanced Economies

The U.S. dollar has depreciated modestly in real effective terms since late 2005, but its current account deficit has remained high. The euro area's current account is close to balance, while Japan retains a sizable current account surplus.

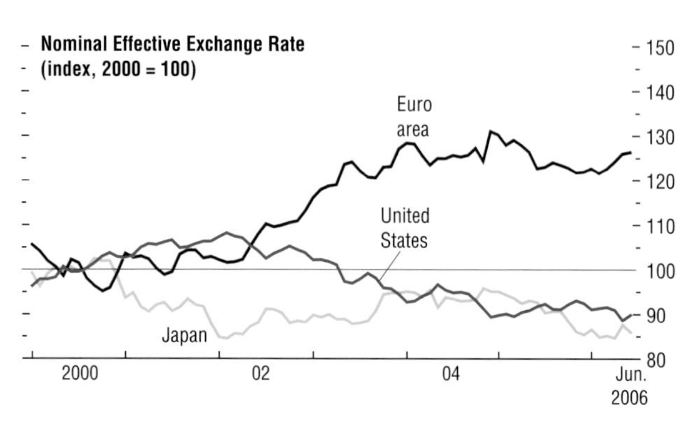

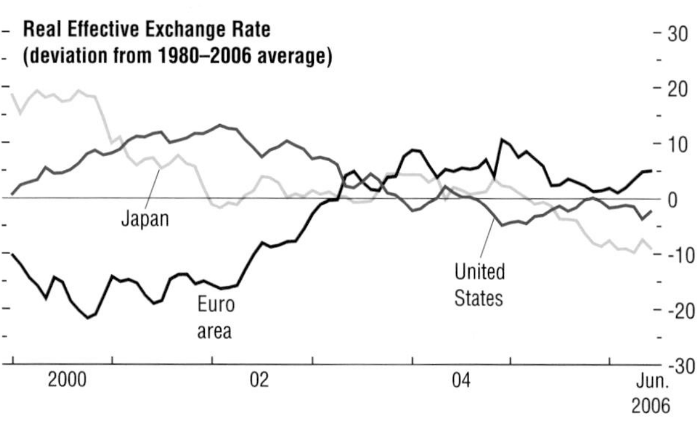

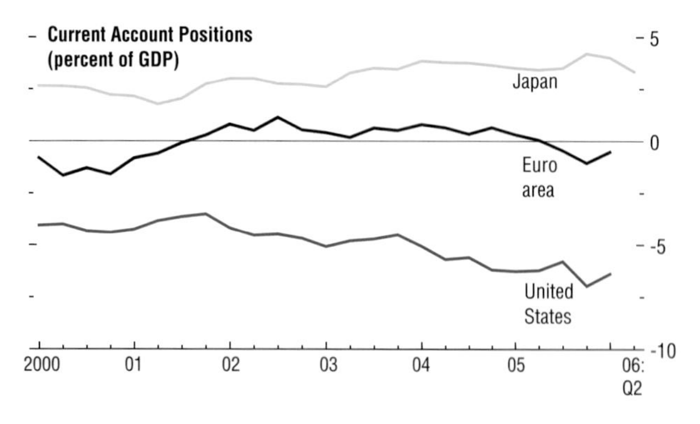

Sources: Haver Analytics; and IMF staff calculations.

conditions, a rebound in asset prices, and a further strengthening of domestic demand. In the advanced economies, the main upside potential would seem to be in business investment, given strong corporate profitability and rising capacity utilization.

Turning now to the downside, markets have been concerned that a continued buildup of inflation pressures in advanced economies could require a more aggressive monetary policy response to cool the growth momentum, particularly in the United States. Clearly, there are risks in this direction coming from tightening capacity constraints and the continuing potential for high headline inflation to seep into price expectations and bolder wage demands. Cost push pressures have risen in the United States in recent quarters, reflecting both rising employee compensation and slowing productivity as the expansion matures, although unit labor cost growth has remained subdued in the euro area and Japan (Figure 1.12).

A related risk to the outlook comes from the continued potential for supply-side shocks in the oil market, which could give a further upward impetus to international oil prices, thus exacerbating inflationary pressures while cooling household demand. In the baseline forecast, the international oil price is expected to average $75 a barrel in 2007, close to the peak reached in early August (see Appendix 1.1). As emphasized in past issues of the *World Economic Outlook*, up to now the global economy has been able to absorb quite well the run-up in oil prices, reflecting that—to a considerable degree—the price increases have been driven by strong demand growth rather than supply constraints, and that central banks have had the credibility to focus on core rather than headline inflation. The decline in energy intensity of global output compared to the 1970s has also played a role in containing the impact of oil price increases. However, with spare capacity remaining at recent very low levels, supply concerns have played a growing role in pushing up oil prices, and a major disruption in a large producer or a further escalation of security concerns in the Middle East could well lead to another upward oil price spike.[3] Over time, investment in new production and refining capacity both inside and outside the Organization of the Petroleum Exporting Countries (OPEC), diversification into alternative energy sources, and increased conservation efforts by consumers responding to price incentives should restore spare capacity to more comfortable levels, but the lags are lengthy, and considerable uncertainty remains about the pace and extent of these responses.

There are also supply-side risks from nonfuel commodity prices. In total, nonfuel commodities represent almost twice as large a share of world trade as fuels and can have an important impact on the global economic environment, both for consumers and the exporters, which (like oil) tend to be in emerging market and developing countries. In fact, for a number of these countries, nonfuel commodity price increases have provided significant terms-of-trade gains or at least offset some of the losses from higher oil import bills (Figure 1.13), while in some countries like Chile government revenues from these sectors are an important share of total revenues.

Chapter 5 of this report discusses the prospects for nonfuel commodity markets in more detail. Its analysis suggests that, as with oil, recent price increases have been substantially driven by a surge in demand, particularly in rapidly growing, large emerging markets like China. This surge in demand has outstripped supply capacity, especially in metals where supply responses are subject to longer lags than in agriculture. However, unlike the petroleum market, nonfuel commodity prices are expected to retreat more rapidly from recent highs as new capacity comes into operation, although not to fall back to earlier levels—in part because higher energy costs have boosted costs of production. Nonfuel com-

[3]Oil options prices suggest that in August 2006 markets put a 10 percent chance on Brent oil exceeding $90 a barrel in December 2006.

Figure 1.8. External Developments in Emerging Market Countries

Movements in nominal exchange rates over the past year have generally moved real effective exchange rates in emerging market countries closer to historical averages. Current account surpluses in China and the Middle East have continued to rise.

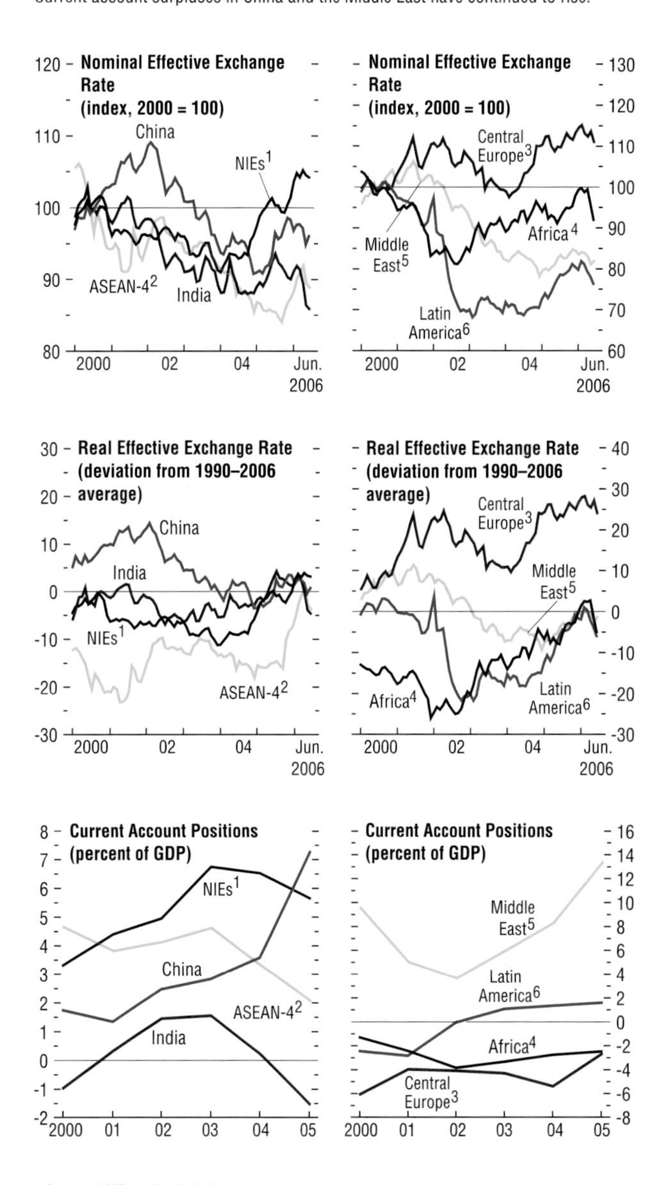

Source: IMF staff calculations.
[1]Newly industrialized economies (NIEs) include Hong Kong SAR, Korea, Singapore, and Taiwan Province of China.
[2]Indonesia, Malaysia, the Philippines, and Thailand.
[3]Czech Republic, Hungary, and Poland
[4]Botswana, Burkina Faso, Cameroon, Chad, Republic of Congo, Côte d'Ivoire, Djibouti, Equatorial Guinea, Ethiopia, Gabon, Ghana, Guinea, Kenya, Madagascar, Mali, Mauritius, Mozambique, Namibia, Niger, Nigeria, Rwanda, Senegal, South Africa, Sudan, Tanzania, Uganda, and Zambia.
[5]Bahrain, Egypt, I.R. of Iran, Jordan, Kuwait, Lebanon, Libya, Oman, Qatar, Saudi Arabia, Syrian Arab Republic, United Arab Emirates, and Republic of Yemen.
[6]Argentina, Brazil, Chile, Colombia, Mexico, Peru, and Venezuela.

Figure 1.9. Emerging Market Financial Conditions

Notwithstanding some recent corrections, asset prices in most emerging markets remain close to peak levels, while sovereign risk spreads are still close to all-time lows.

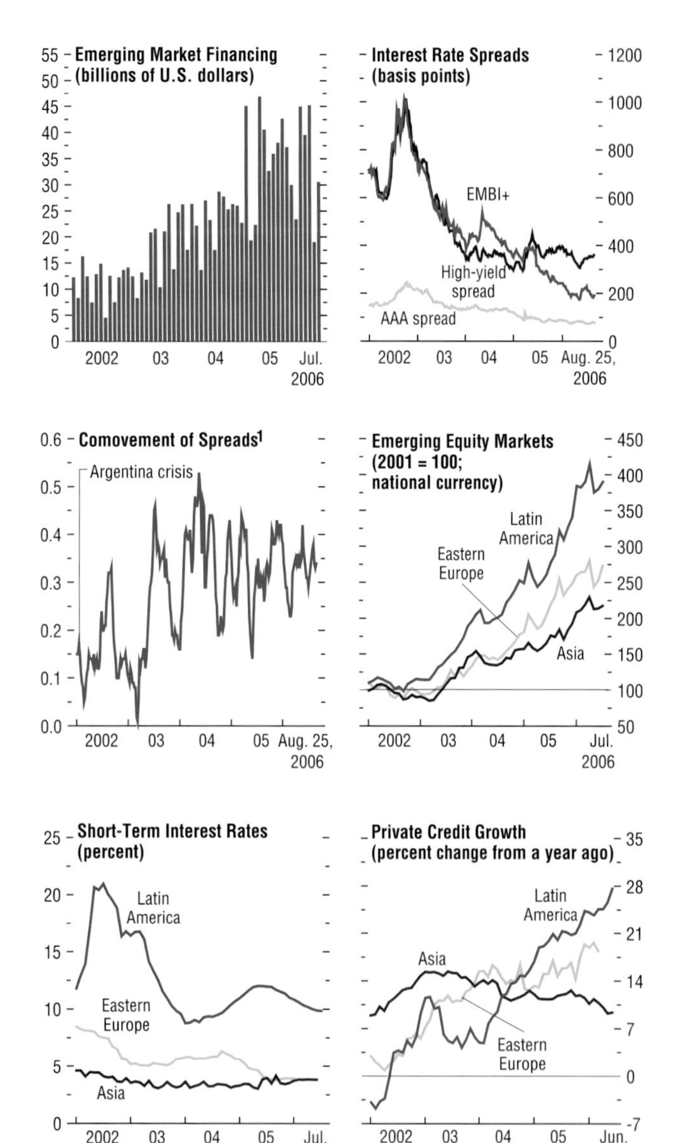

Sources: Bloomberg Financial Markets, LP; Capital Data; IMF, *International Financial Statistics;* and IMF staff calculations.

[1]Average of 30-day rolling cross-correlation of emerging market debt spreads.

modity exporters will thus need to be cautious in managing the uncertain stream of foreign exchange earnings and government revenue from these sources.

A key risk on the demand side is that the continued cooling of advanced-economy housing markets will weaken household balance sheets and undercut aggregate demand. At this point, concerns center on the United States, although other markets, such as those in Ireland, Spain, and the United Kingdom, also still seem overvalued by most conventional measures. In the United States, the April 2006 issue of the *World Economic Outlook* suggested that, by 2005, average home prices had risen around 10–15 percent above levels consistent with fundamentals. Recent data indicate that the market is now softening quite rapidly, with home sales and mortgage applications weakening, housing starts falling, and house price increases dropping. The baseline U.S. growth forecast assumes house price growth will continue to slow, implying a drag on domestic demand from the housing market of approximately ½ percentage point in each of 2006 and 2007. However, if the housing market were to cool more abruptly, IMF staff estimates suggest that this could subtract up to an additional 1 percentage point from GDP growth relative to the baseline. To be sure, house price softening in other countries like Australia and the United Kingdom, coming off larger upward spikes in house prices than experienced in the United States, has been absorbed thus far with relatively mild and brief economic slowdowns. Nevertheless, the concern remains that a sharp adjustment in the housing sector would generate strong headwinds for the U.S. economy.

Other demand-side risks relate to the extent to which expansions in Europe and Japan will be sustained by increasing strength of household demand, reducing reliance on exports and exposure to a slowdown of demand in the United States. Such a rebalancing appears to be under way, but concerns remain, particularly in Europe, where both job growth and wage increases remain modest in the face of slow productivity growth and labor market rigidities. There are also uncertainties related to the ongoing process of fiscal consolidation in these countries; deficit reduction is necessary in the face of upcoming demographic pressures on spending and dependency ratios, but could cause short-term shifts in aggregate demand that are hard to predict. An example is the 3 percentage point increase in the value added tax (VAT) in Germany in early 2007, which is expected to lower GDP by around ½ percentage point in 2007 relative to 2006, but the impact could even be larger. Such fiscal-related uncertainty is also significant in Italy, where the new government is expected to bring in an adjustment package to address its deep-seated fiscal imbalances.

Recent developments have provided a healthy reminder that emerging markets remain susceptible to turbulence in global financial markets, notwithstanding progress in reducing underlying vulnerabilities. Countries particularly at risk would include those with still weak public sector balance sheets and less well anchored inflation expectations. Moreover, recent experience has underlined that a buildup in current account deficits from private saving-investment imbalances and an associated rapid growth of bank credit can also cause difficulties when expectations about the availability of external funding change (see Box 1.1).[4] Adverse events affecting emerging markets become more likely in the context of higher interest rates and financial market volatility in the advanced economies, and could be initiated by global shocks that prompt a reduction in risk appetite, a downward shift in emerging market growth prospects, and a weakening of non-oil commodity prices. As illustrated in Box 1.2, a sharp reversal of market sentiment away from emerging markets could put downward pressures on exchange rates that would need to

Figure 1.10. Global Outlook

(Real GDP; percent change from four quarters earlier)

World growth is expected to remain very strong in 2006, with only a modest deceleration in 2007.

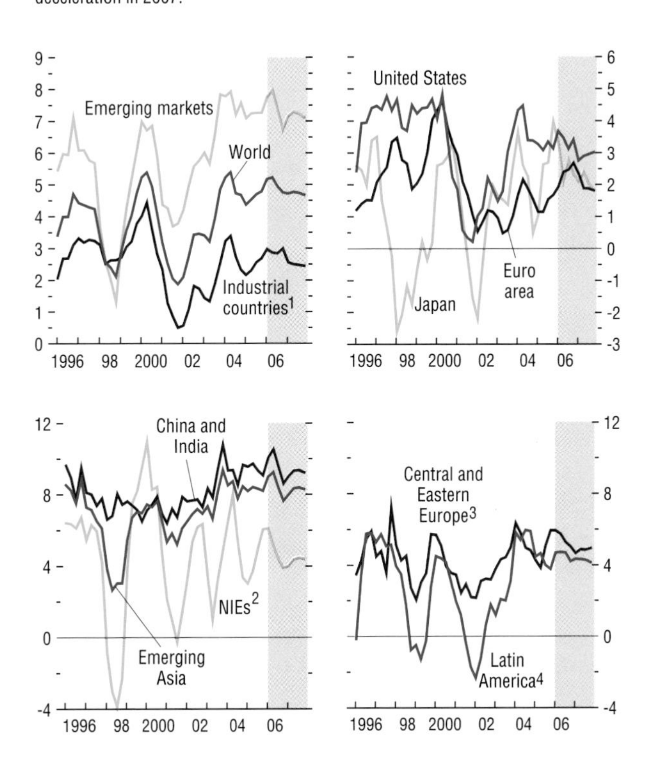

Sources: Haver Analytics; and IMF staff estimates.

[1]Australia, Canada, Denmark, euro area, Japan, New Zealand, Norway, Sweden, Switzerland, the United Kingdom, and the United States.

[2]Newly industrialized economies (NIEs) include Hong Kong SAR, Korea, Singapore, and Taiwan Province of China.

[3]Czech Republic, Estonia, Hungary, Latvia, Lithuania, and Poland.

[4]Argentina, Brazil, Chile, Colombia, Mexico, Peru, and Venezuela.

[4]Recent experience with the rapid growth in bank credit to the household sector is examined in detail in Chapter II of the IMF's September 2006 *Global Financial Stability Report*.

Table 1.2. Emerging Market and Developing Countries: Net Capital Flows[1]
(Billions of U.S. dollars)

	1995–97	1998	1999	2000	2001	2002	2003	2004	2005	2006	2007
Total											
Private capital flows, net[2]	199.7	61.2	75.4	58.2	64.6	77.3	165.6	205.9	238.5	211.4	182.2
Private direct investment, net	120.3	159.8	177.3	168.4	179.4	150.6	159.1	176.9	255.9	263.3	246.1
Private portfolio flows, net	61.3	34.1	60.7	12.5	–78.2	–91.7	–10.9	13.9	3.2	–31.1	–4.6
Other private capital flows, net	18.1	–132.7	–162.6	–122.7	–36.6	18.4	17.3	15.1	–20.6	–20.8	–59.2
Official flows, net	3.7	39.1	13.0	–44.2	–3.3	–4.3	–53.1	–64.7	–151.8	–238.7	–174.1
Change in reserves[3]	–104.3	–29.6	–98.4	–132.3	–121.9	–200.6	–362.7	–513.5	–592.5	–666.3	–747.9
Memorandum											
Current account[4]	–88.5	–50.2	31.6	117.3	87.1	133.3	229.6	303.8	514.7	666.8	720.4
Africa											
Private capital flows, net[2]	7.0	9.2	9.9	1.7	8.2	4.1	6.8	16.1	29.4	24.9	21.7
Private direct investment, net	4.3	6.3	8.6	7.6	23.1	13.4	15.3	16.7	28.6	27.6	27.8
Private portfolio flows, net	4.8	4.3	9.1	–1.8	–7.7	–1.3	–0.1	5.5	4.5	5.1	4.2
Other private capital flows, net	–2.0	–1.4	–7.8	–4.1	–7.2	–8.0	–8.4	–6.2	–3.6	–7.9	–10.3
Official flows, net	–2.4	3.9	1.8	0.6	–2.7	3.0	1.6	1.0	–14.4	–17.8	–1.3
Change in reserves[3]	–6.2	3.5	–0.4	–12.8	–9.7	–5.6	–11.5	–32.8	–42.2	–62.0	–75.2
Central and eastern Europe											
Private capital flows, net[2]	27.2	27.1	36.9	39.8	11.8	53.2	51.4	70.4	113.5	88.8	84.8
Private direct investment, net	11.7	19.3	22.8	24.2	24.2	25.5	16.0	34.4	47.7	56.7	44.4
Private portfolio flows, net	4.5	–1.2	5.7	3.2	0.5	1.6	6.2	26.2	20.4	1.5	11.4
Other private capital flows, net	10.9	9.1	8.5	12.4	–12.8	26.0	29.1	9.8	45.4	30.6	29.1
Official flows, net	0.5	1.0	–2.5	1.7	6.1	–7.8	–5.2	–6.7	–8.5	–3.2	–2.2
Change in reserves[3]	–15.7	–9.4	–12.0	–6.5	–4.4	–20.4	–12.5	–14.6	–46.3	–18.8	–17.1
Commonwealth of Independent States[5]											
Private capital flows, net[2]	–1.3	–8.6	–13.3	–27.7	7.2	15.7	17.7	7.5	37.6	18.8	5.4
Private direct investment, net	4.6	5.6	4.7	2.3	5.0	5.2	5.4	12.8	13.3	18.0	17.5
Private portfolio flows, net	1.5	0.4	–0.9	–10.0	–1.2	0.4	–0.5	8.2	–3.2	1.0	–1.8
Other private capital flows, net	–7.4	–14.6	–17.1	–20.0	3.4	10.2	12.8	–13.5	27.5	–0.1	–10.3
Official flows, net	–1.1	1.5	–2.0	–5.7	–5.0	–10.4	–8.8	–7.3	–22.5	–30.2	–4.5
Change in reserves[3]	–1.4	12.6	–6.3	–20.3	–14.5	–15.1	–32.9	–55.0	–76.6	–115.0	–139.2
Emerging Asia[6]											
Private capital flows, net[2,7]	91.2	–53.6	0.2	4.7	20.2	20.6	68.1	130.4	64.0	97.9	69.0
Private direct investment, net	54.0	56.9	70.9	59.8	50.8	50.5	68.2	57.8	99.6	94.0	96.0
Private portfolio flows, net	20.7	9.0	54.1	19.6	–50.0	–60.1	6.4	5.2	–12.7	–13.1	–8.4
Other private capital flows, net[7]	16.5	–119.5	–124.9	–74.7	19.4	30.2	–6.5	67.3	–22.9	17.0	–18.5
Official flows, net	–3.2	18.9	1.6	–13.8	–13.2	3.0	–20.7	–9.1	–11.7	–8.4	–12.0
Change in reserves[3]	–41.8	–52.7	–84.8	–59.5	–85.8	–154.4	–235.8	–340.4	–286.6	–344.8	–331.4

be met by prompt interest rate hikes to contain a pickup in inflation. Growth would be dampened in the short term, but stronger public sector balance sheets should provide a basis for emerging markets to avoid deeper crises provided that they continue to manage policies prudently and respond quickly to emerging stresses.

Lastly, while the probability and potential risks of an avian flu pandemic are impossible to assess with any certainty, a worse-case outbreak scenario could have extremely high human and economic costs, particularly in developing countries in Africa and Asia (see Appendix 1.2 of the April 2006 *World Economic Outlook*).

Unwinding Global Imbalances

Large global imbalances continue to be a concern for the outlook. To be clear, the existence of significant current account deficits and surpluses does not by itself imply the threat of instability. In an increasingly globalized world economy, the free movement of capital across borders permits periods in which countries' savings and investment rates may diverge, imply-

Table 1.2 ***(concluded)***

	1995–97	1998	1999	2000	2001	2002	2003	2004	2005	2006	2007
Middle East[8]											
Private capital flows, net[2]	8.3	14.8	–4.4	–11.6	–7.1	–20.0	4.4	–19.6	–20.0	–31.8	–17.3
Private direct investment, net	5.0	9.5	4.3	4.7	9.9	9.6	17.4	9.1	17.4	20.9	13.8
Private portfolio flows, net	2.6	–4.0	–8.5	–1.2	–12.2	–17.9	–14.1	–17.4	–31.1	–29.9	–20.7
Other private capital flows, net	0.7	9.2	–0.1	–15.1	–4.7	–11.8	1.0	–11.3	–6.4	–22.8	–10.5
Official flows, net	5.7	–0.2	8.1	–20.8	–13.8	–9.6	–24.5	–33.7	–64.6	–166.5	–151.8
Change in reserves[3]	–13.9	8.3	–2.5	–31.6	–11.1	–2.9	–33.9	–47.6	–108.0	–85.7	–135.7
Western Hemisphere											
Private capital flows, net[2]	67.3	72.3	46.1	51.3	24.1	3.8	17.3	1.1	14.0	12.7	18.5
Private direct investment, net	40.6	62.2	66.1	69.8	66.5	46.5	36.8	46.0	49.2	46.1	46.6
Private portfolio flows, net	27.2	25.6	1.3	2.7	–7.6	–14.4	–8.8	–13.9	25.4	4.3	10.7
Other private capital flows, net	–0.5	–15.5	–21.3	–21.1	–34.8	–28.2	–10.7	–31.1	–60.6	–37.7	–38.8
Official flows, net	4.2	14.0	5.9	–6.3	25.3	17.5	4.5	–9.0	–30.1	–12.6	–2.2
Change in reserves[3]	–25.4	8.1	7.6	–1.6	3.5	–2.2	–36.0	–23.1	–32.8	–39.9	–49.3
Memorandum											
Fuel exporting countries											
Private capital flows, net[2]	–2.4	2.8	–27.4	–57.5	–13.2	–11.7	12.0	–22.2	–4.8	–58.0	–58.1
Other countries											
Private capital flows, net[2]	202.1	58.4	102.8	115.7	77.7	89.1	153.6	228.1	243.3	269.4	240.3

[1]Net capital flows comprise net direct investment, net portfolio investment, and other long- and short-term net investment flows, including official and private borrowing. In this table, Hong Kong SAR, Israel, Korea, Singapore, and Taiwan Province of China are included.
[2]Because of data limitations, flows listed under "private capital flows, net" may include some official flows.
[3]A minus sign indicates an increase.
[4]The sum of the current account balance, net private capital flows, net official flows, and the change in reserves equals, with the opposite sign, the sum of the capital account and errors and omissions. For regional current account balances, see Table 25 of the Statistical Appendix.
[5]Historical data have been revised, reflecting cumulative data revisions for Russia and the resolution of a number of data interpretation issues.
[6]Consists of developing Asia and the newly industrialized Asian economies.
[7]Excluding the effects of the recapitalization of two large commercial banks in China with foreign reserves of the Bank of China ($45 billion), net private capital flows to emerging Asia in 2003 were $113.1 billion while other private capital flows net to the region amounted to $38.5 billion.
[8]Includes Israel.

ing substantial current account deficits and surpluses. Such financial flows can be positive for the world economy, representing the shift of resources from parts of the world with abundant savings relative to investment opportunities to areas offering higher rates of return to capital. However, past experience suggests that high current account deficits relative to GDP have typically not been sustained for long periods, either because domestic saving and investment patterns change or because countries run up against financing constraints—for example, because of shifting perceptions about relative rates of return across countries or because international investors resist a continued buildup in country exposure in their portfolios. In this latter situation, savings and investment behavior has had to adjust to bring current account positions back in line with available financing. The key issues then are the sustainability of the current pattern of global imbalances and whether the eventual adjustment will be orderly or disorderly.

To assess the sustainability of the current pattern of global imbalances, one must understand the source of the imbalances and how they have been financed. A variety of factors have been suggested to explain the current situation, including the positive impact of the strong U.S. productivity performance on asset prices, household wealth, and consumption; the emergence of a sizable fiscal deficit in the United States since the turn of the century; the investment slowdown in emerging Asia outside China since the Asian Crisis; the highly liquid conditions in world financial markets, especially since the collapse of the information technology bubble; the willingness of emerging market countries,

Figure 1.11. Prospects for World GDP Growth[1]
(Percent)

Global growth is projected to remain about 5 percent in 2006–07, but the risks are slanted to the downside, especially next year.

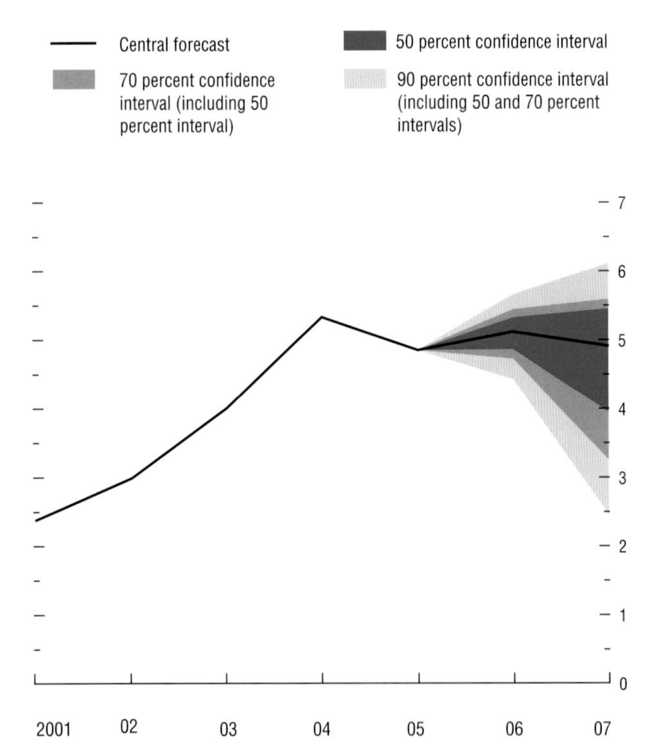

Source: IMF staff estimates.
[1]This so-called fan chart shows the uncertainty around the *World Economic Outlook* central forecast with 50, 70, and 90 percent probability intervals. See Box 1.3 in the April 2006 *World Economic Outlook* for details.

particularly in Asia, to build high levels of international reserves; and the need to recycle oil exporters' surpluses after the recent escalation of petroleum prices.[5]

An element of the story that has received increasing attention recently is the role played by the U.S. financial system in attracting foreign savings in increasingly integrated global capital markets (see, for example, Caballero, Farhi, and Gourinchas, 2006.). The depth and liquidity of U.S. financial markets, together with the rapid pace of innovation and development of new products offering wide and increasing opportunities for effective risk management, have made the United States an attractive destination for global investors' funds. At the same time, financial innovations and new products have increased opportunities for "consumption smoothing," in particular for households to increase spending out of wealth generated from the large increases in U.S. equity and house prices. A notable part has been played by the rapid rise in the asset-backed securities markets, particularly mortgage-backed securities, which now account for over 10 percent of global bond markets, together with borrowing instruments that have facilitated equity extraction and cash-flow management. These market developments have played a part in allowing the continuing decline in the U.S. savings rate since the mid-1990s, while also offering a major conduit for capital inflows to the United States.

Chapter 4 of this report offers some perspective on this phenomenon, aiming to assess the degree to which financial systems in advanced economies have migrated from relationship-based to arm's length financing structures and the implications of this shift for economic cycles. It suggests that while all financial systems have moved in the direction of arm's length systems,

[5]See discussions in previous issues of the *World Economic Outlook*, including "Global Imbalances—A Saving and Investment Perspective" in the September 2005 issue, and "Oil Prices and Global Imbalances" in the April 2006 issue.

the process has gone farthest in the United States, and in some respects the gap between the United States and most others has widened. It also provides some evidence that arm's length structures provide greater potential for consumption smoothing and that the dynamism of the U.S. financial system has played a significant role in attracting financing for the U.S. current account deficit. The chapter cautions, however, that arm's length systems may provide less support for activity in the face of asset price corrections.

It is beyond the scope of this report to allocate the causality precisely among the various factors contributing to global imbalances. To a large extent, different explanations complement rather than compete with each other, and their relative importance has varied over time. However, what is clear is that while the explanations help one to understand why the imbalances have emerged and have been sustained over a period of time, none of them implies that large imbalances can be sustained indefinitely.

To be sure, the United States' high and widening current account deficits in recent years have been financed without undue strain on the global financial system, with real long-term interest rates remaining on the low side. The pattern of such financing has varied over time, with direct investment and portfolio equity inflows playing an important role in the late 1990s, and debt-related flows providing the bulk of financing more recently, including a significant but not dominant role played by official flows corresponding to the accumulation of large international reserves by a number of countries. Moreover, recent months have seen some developments that, over time, will be helpful in reducing the imbalances, including some depreciation of the U.S. dollar, stronger growth in U.S. exports, news that the U.S. fiscal deficit in the present fiscal year will be lower than earlier predictions, rising growth of domestic demand in the euro area and Japan, and some increased exchange rate flexibility in Asian countries. However, the underlying prob-

Figure 1.12. Productivity Developments in Selected Advanced Economies[1]

(Percent change from four quarters earlier)

Productivity performance has remained strong in the United States and Japan, with the euro area lagging. Unit labor costs have generally been contained, but accelerated recently in the United States.

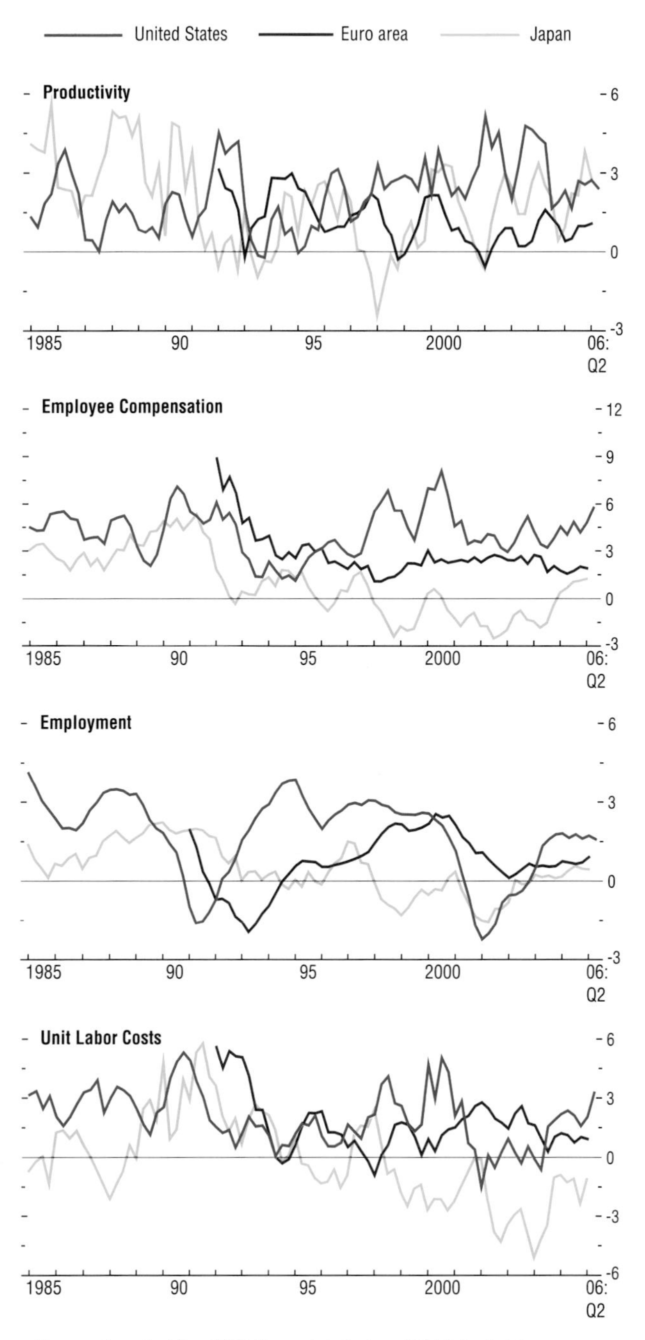

Sources: Haver Analytics; OECD, *Economic Outlook*; and IMF staff calculations.

[1]Estimates are for non-farm business sector for the United States, and the whole economy for the euro area and Japan.

Figure 1.13. Impact of Commodity Price Movements on Trade Balances in Emerging Market and Developing Countries[1]

(Percent of 2005 GDP)

For a number of countries, terms-of-trade gains from nonfuel commodity price increases have defrayed losses from higher oil import bills.

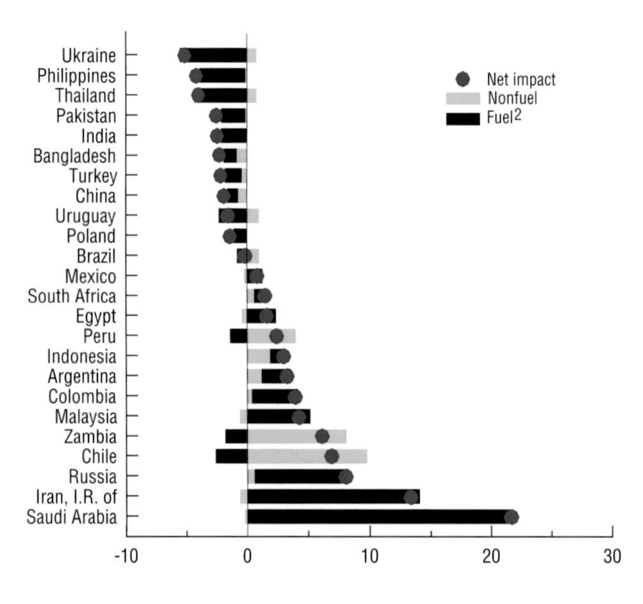

Source: IMF staff calculations.
[1]Impact of change in commodity price movement since 2002 on trade balance in 2005.
[2]Fuel includes oil, natural gas, and coal.

lem remains little diminished. Medium-term projections assuming constant real effective exchange rates show the U.S. current account deficit remaining close to 2 percent of global GDP, with Asia and oil exporters continuing to run substantial surpluses (Figure 1.14). These projections imply that the United States would need to continue absorbing a rising share of world asset portfolios. However, eventually, the buildup of U.S.-based assets in global asset portfolios would approach saturation, and an adjustment of current account imbalances would be required.

The most likely outcome is still a gradual and orderly unwinding of the imbalances over a number of years. With the housing market cooling in the United States, private saving is likely to rise as the asset price boost to wealth accumulation fades away. By contrast, consumption growth would accelerate in emerging Asia (especially China) as precautionary savings motives moderate, and absorption by oil exporters is also expected to rise, particularly in the Middle East where the authorities are advancing ambitious investment plans. This shift in relative growth of domestic demand, accompanied by a sustained depreciation of the U.S. dollar in real terms and real exchange rate appreciation in surplus countries, notably in parts of Asia and oil exporters, would contribute to a more normal pattern of current accounts over a number of years. Such an adjustment could occur as a market-led process, without the need for major shifts in policy frameworks.

However, as discussed in Box 1.3, such a smooth, market-led process is likely to succeed only if investors are prepared to continue increasing the share of their portfolios in U.S. assets for many years. If not, there would be some risk of a disorderly unwinding, involving a more rapid fall of the U.S. dollar, volatile conditions in financial markets, rising protectionist pressures, and a significant hit to global output. The potentially heavy cost of such a disorderly unwinding underlines the importance of joint efforts to reduce the imbalances in a timely fashion, as discussed further below.

Policy Challenges

The heightened uncertainty about economic prospects, the associated increased volatility in financial markets, and the concerns over global imbalances have made it all the more important for policymakers to respond flexibly to events, to act with foresight to head off potential strains, and to take a joint approach to managing global risks.

The environment is particularly challenging for the major central banks that provide the linchpin for global stability. In the United States, monetary policy faces the difficult situation of rising inflation in a slowing economy, and the Federal Reserve will need to continue to monitor incoming data carefully while clearly communicating its assessment to the market. Given the importance of keeping inflation expectations firmly in check, some further policy tightening may still be needed. In Japan, while recent price data have confirmed the end of entrenched deflation and the transition from zero interest rates has been handled smoothly, interest rate increases going forward should be gradual since there is little danger of an inflationary surge, while reemergence of deflation would be costly. In the euro area, further interest rate increases are likely to be needed if the expansion develops as expected, but for now inflation pressures seem broadly contained, and faced by continuing downside risks, policymakers can afford to be cautious in tightening the monetary policy stance.

Policymakers in emerging markets must also adjust to the more testing environment, being careful to respond promptly to any emerging strains. A major challenge in China and some other emerging Asian countries is to manage a transition to more flexible exchange rates that would allow necessary appreciation to take place and provide more room for monetary policy to respond to shifts in the global environment and in domestic conditions. For similar reasons, Russia and some other oil exporters could also benefit from more flexible exchange rates. Emerging market countries that rely heavily on external financing (such as those in Eastern Europe) or that still have high public debt (in

Figure 1.14. Current Account Balances and Net Foreign Assets
(Percent of world GDP)

Under the baseline forecast, which assumes unchanged real effective exchange rates, global current account imbalances remain sizable through the projection period, implying a continued increase in the U.S. net foreign liability position.

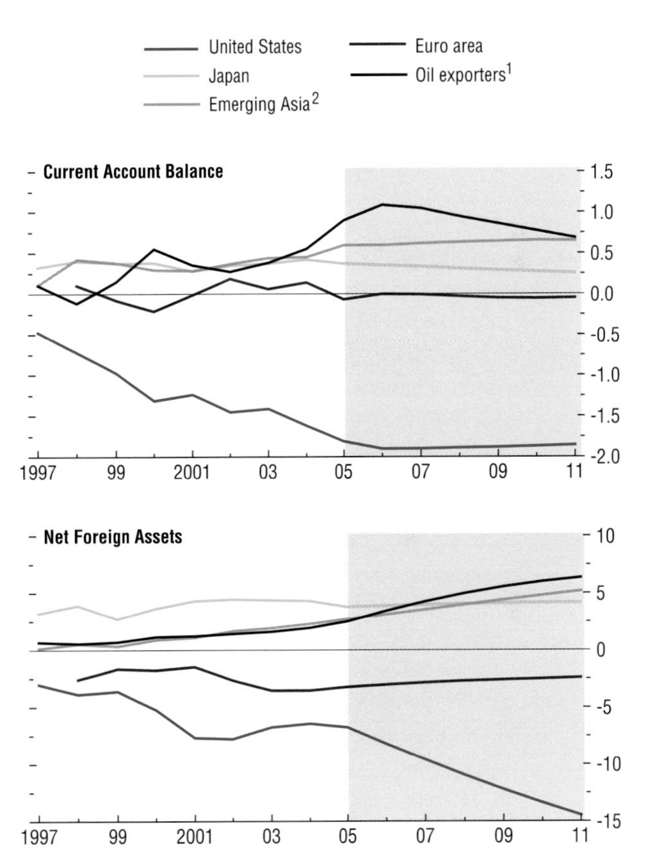

Sources: Lane and Milesi-Ferretti (2006); and IMF staff estimates.
[1]Algeria, Angola, Azerbaijan, Bahrain, Republic of Congo, Ecuador, Equatorial Guinea, Gabon, I.R. of Iran, Kuwait, Libya, Nigeria, Norway, Oman, Qatar, Russia, Saudi Arabia, Syrian Arab Republic, Turkmenistan, United Arab Emirates, Venezuela, and the Republic of Yemen.
[2]China, Hong Kong SAR, Indonesia, Korea, Malaysia, the Philippines, Singapore, Taiwan Province of China, and Thailand.

Box 1.1. Capital Flows to Emerging Market Countries: a Long-Term Perspective

After a period of relative calm, volatility in global financial markets increased sharply in the first half of 2006. The first turbulence occurred in late February–early March when several Middle Eastern stock markets fell sharply. Next, exchange rates in Iceland and New Zealand—two countries that had built up substantial external imbalances in previous years—came under pressure. Finally, in early May a more broad-based correction of emerging markets' currencies and equity valuations set in, taking place in the context of tightening monetary conditions in the main currency areas. The sharpest corrections in asset prices were in those markets where foreign investors had taken large exposures and that had appreciated the most in 2005 and early 2006.[1] Dedicated emerging market equity funds saw outflows of $15.8 billion between mid-May and end-June of this year, after having received inflows of more than $50 billion between the beginning of 2005 and mid-May 2006 (see the first figure). Often the outflows triggered substantial exchange rate depreciations, exceeding 10 percent (from mid-May until end-June) in countries such as Turkey, South Africa, and Colombia.

While this reversal of portfolio equity flows has received considerable attention, such flows constitute only a small share of all capital flows to emerging market countries. Over the past 30 years, they have accounted for less than 6 percent of all net inflows, and even in 2005, their share was only 15 percent. In comparison, net foreign direct investment (FDI) has been more than seven times as large over the past 20 years, and net debt flows—public and private combined—almost nine times as large. Hence, a broader reversal of capital flows beyond portfolio equity investments could be far more disruptive for emerging markets. So far, there have been no indications that other flows have been severely affected by recent developments:

Note: The main authors of this box are Bas B. Bakker and Johannes Wiegand.

[1]These developments are reviewed in more detail in the September 2006 *Global Financial Stability Report.*

Emerging Market Countries: Equity Market Developments

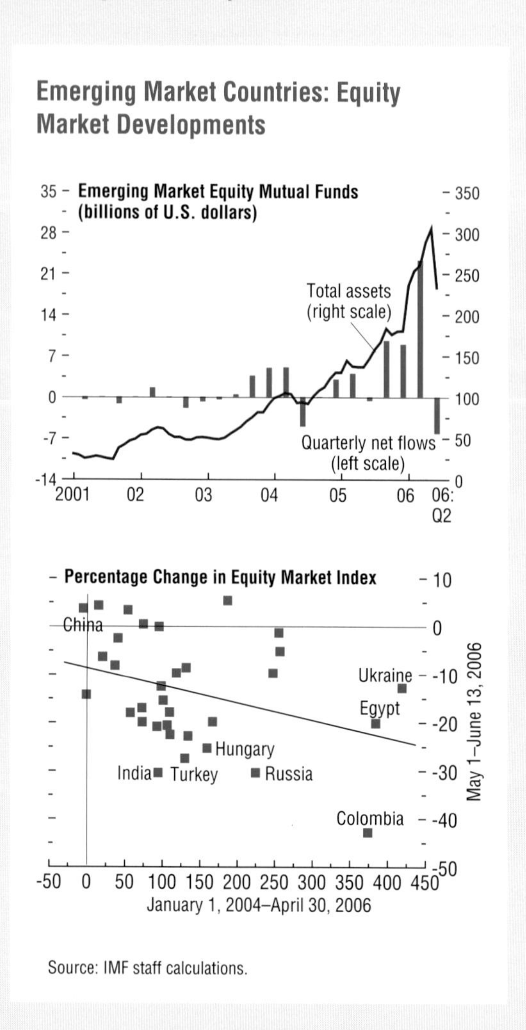

Source: IMF staff calculations.

sovereign bond spreads, for example, have remained close to record lows.

To assess the risks of a wider reversal, it is helpful to analyze the historical experience with capital flows to middle- and low-income countries over the past three decades, focusing on the three main recipient regions: East Asia and the Pacific, emerging Europe and Central Asia, and Latin America and the Caribbean (see the second figure).

- Net FDI inflows have been the most stable category, and also the most important since the early 1990s. FDI flows do vary cyclically around a secular increase—flows to Latin America halved between 1999 and 2002

Net Capital Flows to Middle- and Low-Income Countries, 1975–2005

(Billions of real U.S. dollars, base year = 2000)

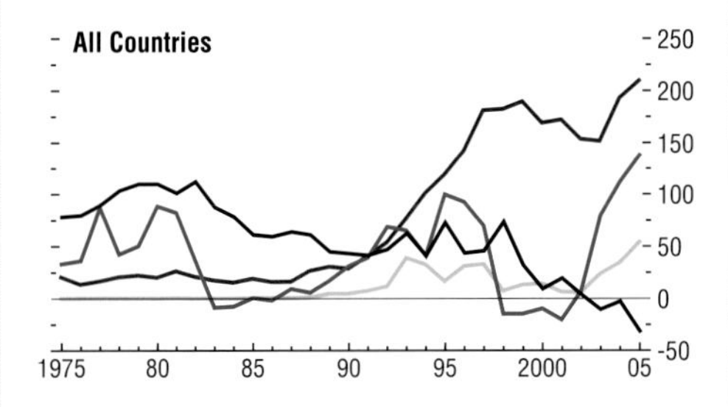

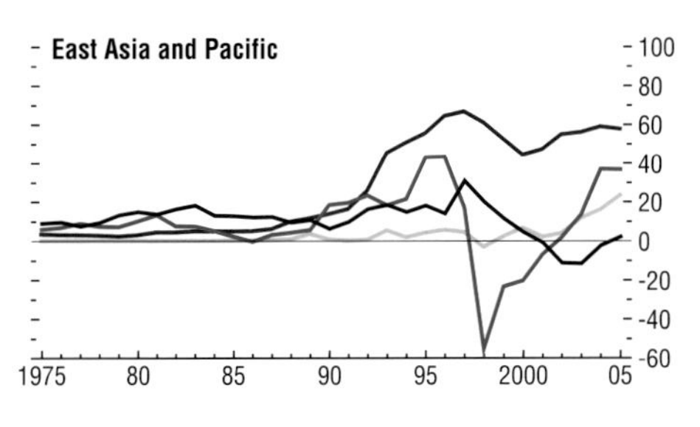

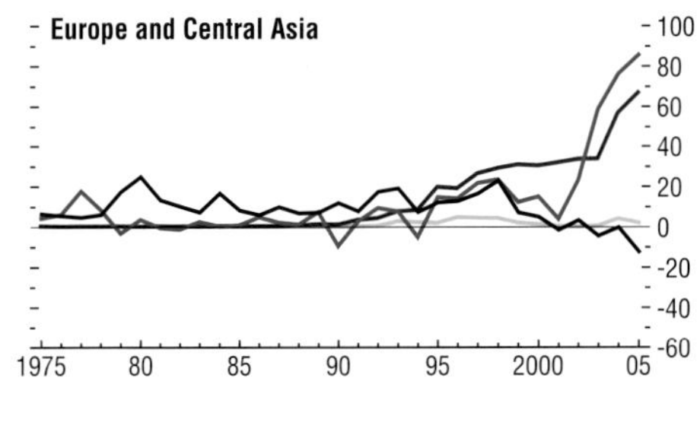

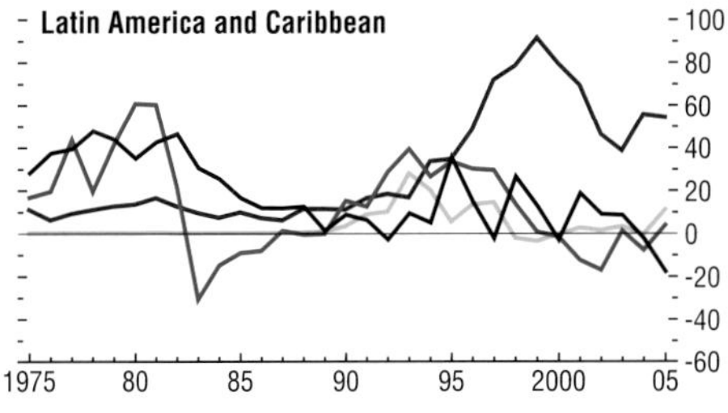

Sources: World Bank, Global Development Finance database; and IMF staff calculations.

before recovering during the current expansion phase[2]—but year-to-year changes have tended to be relatively small.

- Public sector debt flows have also been fairly stable. Moreover, their importance as a source of financing has declined sharply in recent years. Since 2003, public debt flows have even turned negative, as many sovereigns have used their improved fiscal positions to reduce external debt levels. This may help explain why most sovereign bond spreads have remained relatively unaffected by the recent turmoil.
- In contrast, net debt flows to the private sector have been much more volatile.[3] There have been three periods when private debt flows surged rapidly: the late 1970s–early 1980s; the mid-1990s; and, more recently, since about 2003. The first two episodes corresponded to region-specific, boom-bust credit cycles, culminating in the Latin American debt crisis of 1982 and the Asian financial crisis of 1997. In both cases, net debt flows to the private sector turned negative in the crisis and remained so for several years, imposing severe contractions on the affected economies. The more recent surge reflects to a large part lending by banks in advanced economies to emerging Europe and Central Asia,[4] and to a lesser extent a revival of private debt flows to East Asia, notably China. In emerging Europe, private sector debt has replaced foreign direct investment as the primary source of external financing; in 2005, it accounted for 60 percent of net capital inflows.

[2]This drop in part reflected a slowdown in privatizations in the late 1990s and the chilling effect on infrastructure investments of private investors' losses in Argentina after the crisis.

[3]Historically, there has been a strong and positive correlation between portfolio equity flows and private debt flows to emerging market countries (0.78 in the 1990–2005 period). For individual regions, the correlation is not as strong, but is still positive.

[4]In 2005, $46 billion of all net private debt flows to Emerging Europe and Central Asia were medium- and long-term bank loans, $32 billion short-term debt flows, and $19 billion bond financing.

Box 1.1 *(concluded)*

Historical experience would caution that the recent heavy debt flows to Eastern Europe and Asia could again prove unsustainable—even though there are good reasons why the recent surge may be less risky than previous ones. For example, in China and Russia—the two countries that have received the largest private debt inflows in recent years—risks are mitigated by large net foreign assets of the public sector, reflecting high reserve cushions and relatively low external debt levels.[5] In central and southeastern Europe, a mitigating factor is the presence of well-supervised and largely foreign-owned banks. Moreover, in some countries progress toward joining the European Union and the prospect of Economic and Monetary Union (EMU) membership may boost investor confidence sufficiently to render a reversal in capital flows less likely.

In spite of these factors, the risks associated with the recent surge in private debt flows should not be discounted. The debt flow reversals in Latin America in the 1980s and in East Asia in the 1990s were also considered unlikely—until they occurred. Many central and eastern European countries run large current account deficits, which would be difficult to finance if private debt flows dried up (also see the discussion in the Emerging Europe section of Chapter 2). The presence of foreign banks does not eliminate such risks: bank inflows could suddenly stop if the parent bank decides to reduce its exposure to the region. In the event of a reversal, fixed exchange rates—which remain widespread in the region—might be difficult to maintain. Floating the exchange rate would help to restore external balance, but would weaken balance sheets, as a sharp depreciation would increase the burden of the private sector's foreign currency debts (including to the domestic banking system), a process illustrated by earlier experience elsewhere. Of course, vulnerabilities differ across countries, but regional spillovers and common lender contagion could lead to problems for the region at large. Furthermore, even if private debt inflows did not reverse but "only" fell back to historical averages, this would still imply a substantial decline in net external financing, and could force sharp adjustments on many economies.

[5]In both China and Russia, the net foreign asset position of the economy as a whole is positive, see Lane and Milesi-Ferretti (2006). This distinguishes them from most other recipient countries of large private debt inflows in recent years.

Latin America and elsewhere) will need to be adaptable, taking advantage of opportunities to reduce these vulnerabilities further, while being quick to respond to adverse developments to maintain market confidence and preserve hard-won inflation-fighting credentials.

At the same time, reforms needed to sustain longer-term growth should not be put on the back burner. In most of the major advanced economies, fiscal consolidation in the face of aging populations remains a huge challenge. Some welcome progress has been made in reducing high fiscal deficits over the past three years, particularly in France, Japan, and the United States, while Canada's surplus has been maintained (Table 1.3). However, for most countries, trajectories going forward look unambitious, even assuming steady growth. As a result, fiscal deficits and net public debt would still be quite high at the end of the five-year projection period (with the notable exception of Canada), especially considering the rising fiscal costs of an increasingly elderly population. Italy and Japan face particularly large tasks, while fiscal consolidation efforts in the United States take on particular importance in light of the need to raise national savings and contain the current account deficit. Tackling these fiscal concerns effectively will require setting suitably ambitious medium-term budget objectives, as well as addressing deep-seated issues, including putting social security systems on a sound

Table 1.3. Major Advanced Economies: General Government Fiscal Balances and Debt[1]

(Percent of GDP)

	1990–99	2000	2001	2002	2003	2004	2005	2006	2007	2011
Major advanced economies										
Actual balance	–3.3	–0.2	–1.7	–4.0	–4.8	–4.3	–3.6	–3.2	–3.2	–2.4
Output gap[2]	0.6	2.5	1.1	–0.3	–1.1	–0.6	–0.7	–0.3	–0.3	—
Structural balance[2]	–3.4	–1.5	–2.2	–3.9	–4.3	–4.0	–3.4	–3.1	–3.1	–2.4
United States										
Actual balance	–2.8	1.6	–0.4	–3.8	–4.8	–4.6	–3.7	–3.1	–3.2	–2.2
Output gap[2]	1.5	4.4	1.8	—	–0.9	–0.3	–0.2	0.1	–0.1	—
Structural balance[2]	–3.4	0.1	–1.1	–3.8	–4.5	–4.4	–3.6	–3.1	–3.2	–2.2
Net debt	53.7	39.5	38.3	41.0	43.8	45.4	46.1	46.3	47.3	48.3
Gross debt	69.5	57.2	56.6	58.9	61.9	62.6	62.7	62.5	63.4	63.8
Euro area										
Actual balance	. . .	–1.0	–1.9	–2.6	–3.0	–2.7	–2.2	–2.0	–1.9	–1.5
Output gap[2]	. . .	1.8	1.6	0.5	–0.7	–0.7	–1.2	–0.7	–0.6	—
Structural balance[2]	. . .	–1.7	–2.4	–2.6	–2.7	–2.4	–2.0	–1.7	–1.6	–1.6
Net debt	. . .	57.7	57.5	57.5	59.0	60.1	61.0	60.1	59.7	57.8
Gross debt	. . .	69.6	68.3	68.1	69.3	69.8	70.6	69.8	69.2	66.8
Germany[3]										
Actual balance	–2.6	1.3	–2.8	–3.7	–4.0	–3.7	–3.3	–2.9	–2.4	–2.0
Output gap[2]	0.2	1.8	1.7	0.5	–0.9	–0.9	–1.2	–0.5	–0.5	—
Structural balance[2,4]	–2.1	–1.2	–2.8	–3.3	–3.3	–3.3	–3.0	–2.6	–2.1	–2.0
Net debt	40.5	51.5	52.1	54.3	57.8	60.1	62.5	63.5	64.2	65.3
Gross debt	50.7	58.7	57.9	59.6	62.8	64.8	66.4	68.0	68.5	69.2
France										
Actual balance	–3.7	–1.5	–1.6	–3.2	–4.2	–3.7	–2.9	–2.7	–2.6	–1.7
Output gap[2]	–1.3	1.2	1.0	—	–0.9	–0.9	–1.7	–1.4	–1.2	—
Structural balance[2,4]	–2.8	–2.1	–2.2	–3.1	–3.5	–3.0	–2.2	–1.8	–1.8	–1.7
Net debt	39.7	47.0	48.2	48.5	52.6	54.8	57.0	54.8	54.3	51.8
Gross debt	48.9	56.6	56.3	58.2	62.3	64.5	66.7	64.5	64.0	61.5
Italy										
Actual balance	–7.4	–0.7	–3.1	–2.9	–3.4	–3.4	–4.1	–4.0	–4.1	–4.0
Output gap[2]	—	2.0	2.3	0.9	–0.4	–0.6	–1.9	–1.6	–1.5	—
Structural balance[2,4]	–7.3	–3.0	–4.4	–4.1	–3.5	–3.5	–3.4	–3.3	–3.4	–4.0
Net debt	105.9	103.4	103.0	100.4	100.5	102.7	105.4	106.4	107.5	111.9
Gross debt	112.0	109.1	108.7	105.5	104.3	103.9	106.4	107.5	108.6	113.0
Japan										
Actual balance	–2.8	–7.7	–6.4	–8.2	–8.1	–6.3	–5.6	–5.2	–4.9	–4.0
Excluding social security	–4.9	–8.2	–6.5	–7.9	–8.2	–6.6	–5.3	–4.8	–4.6	–4.1
Output gap[2]	—	–1.0	–1.6	–2.9	–2.7	–2.1	–1.2	–0.2	0.1	—
Structural balance[2]	–2.9	–7.2	–5.7	–6.9	–7.0	–5.5	–5.2	–5.1	–5.0	–4.0
Excluding social security	–4.9	–8.0	–6.1	–7.2	–7.6	–6.2	–5.1	–4.8	–4.6	–4.1
Net debt	27.3	60.4	66.1	72.8	77.3	82.2	86.8	89.7	92.4	98.3
Gross debt	93.2	142.5	151.9	161.4	167.6	178.6	181.7	181.8	181.8	177.3
United Kingdom										
Actual balance	–3.7	1.7	1.0	–1.6	–3.3	–3.2	–3.3	–3.2	–2.8	–2.0
Output gap[2]	–0.7	0.9	0.7	–0.1	—	0.7	–0.2	–0.2	—	—
Structural balance[2]	–3.3	1.5	0.5	–1.9	–3.3	–3.4	–3.2	–3.1	–2.8	–2.0
Net debt	32.9	34.2	32.7	32.7	34.5	36.1	38.1	37.8	38.8	40.5
Gross debt	38.3	41.6	38.4	37.9	39.3	40.8	42.7	43.1	44.2	45.6
Canada										
Actual balance	–4.5	2.9	0.7	–0.1	—	0.7	1.7	1.1	1.0	0.6
Output gap[2]	–0.6	1.9	0.4	0.3	–0.7	–0.3	–0.2	—	—	—
Structural balance[2]	–4.0	2.0	0.4	–0.2	0.3	0.9	1.8	1.1	1.0	0.6
Net debt	80.5	65.3	60.2	58.0	51.5	46.7	41.9	38.7	35.8	27.3
Gross debt	112.7	101.5	100.3	97.5	92.1	87.8	84.8	79.6	74.6	59.4

Note: The methodology and specific assumptions for each country are discussed in Box A1 in the Statistical Appendix.

[1]Debt data refer to end of year. Debt data are not always comparable across countries. For example, the Canadian data include the unfunded component of government employee pension liabilities, which amounted to nearly 18 percent of GDP in 2001.

[2]Percent of potential GDP.

[3]Beginning in 1995, the debt and debt-service obligations of the Treuhandanstalt (and of various other agencies) were taken over by general government. This debt is equivalent to 8 percent of GDP, and the associated debt service, to ½ to 1 percent of GDP.

[4]Excludes one-off receipts from the sale of mobile telephone licenses (the equivalent of 2.5 percent of GDP in 2000 for Germany, 0.1 percent of GDP in 2001 and 2002 for France, and 1.2 percent of GDP in 2000 for Italy). Also excludes one-off receipts from sizable asset transactions, in particular 0.5 percent of GDP for France in 2005.

Box 1.2. How Emerging Market Countries May Be Affected by External Shocks

While emerging market countries have strengthened their underlying policy fundamentals during recent years, pressures on emerging market asset prices in May–June have provided a reminder that many of these countries remain vulnerable to shifts in global economic and financial conditions. This box explores these downside risks based on some illustrative simulations for a generic Latin American country that is exposed to these vulnerabilities. The simulations are generated from a small open economy model that has now been calibrated for a number of Latin American countries by IMF staff.[1] The results show the potential costs of delaying policy responses to a changing external environment for economies in Latin America and elsewhere where inflation expectations are not yet firmly anchored and where investor risk perceptions can change quickly.

Underlying the simulations, it is assumed that inflation in the United States rises by about ½ percentage point more than previously expected, prompting the Fed to raise the federal funds rate by an additional 75 basis points (see the figure). This increase dampens growth in the United States in the short run. At the same time, it is also assumed that investor appetite for riskier emerging market assets is reduced in the context of more unsettled global financial conditions, implying a rise in the risk premium, particularly for holding paper issued by subinvestment grade countries.

Such an external shock could put immediate downward pressure on the exchange rate of Latin American countries, and raise inflation expectations. Faced with this situation, a forward-looking central bank operating under an inflation-targeting framework would quickly tighten the stance of monetary policy. In the "no delay" simulation an increase in interest rates of around 200 basis points is sufficient to limit the increase in headline year-on-year inflation to 1 percentage point in the short term, and then subsequently return it to its target rate (see the figure). The tightening in monetary conditions, combined with reduced confidence in the context of more uncertain international conditions would result in a more pronounced slowdown in economic activity than in the United States and a larger negative output gap.

The figure also illustrates the costs of a delayed policy response in the face of such a shock. In this case, there would be a larger upward shift in inflation expectations and a sharper depreciation of the exchange rate, fueling a sustained rise in headline inflation. In the "delayed response" simulation, it is assumed that there is a monetary policy response only after two quarters, and as a result the hike in interest rates would need to be substantially greater to bring inflation back under control. Moreover, the delayed policy response would imply a further deterioration in confidence. Altogether, the economy would undergo a larger and more protracted slowdown in this scenario.

The appropriate timing and strength of monetary policy responses to such external shocks in emerging market countries will obviously vary from country to country, depending, among other things, on the track record of policy management that has been established, the extent of balance sheet and other vulnerabilities, and the scale of external financing needs. In countries where long-term inflation expectations are well-anchored and there is confidence in sustained prudent policy management, pressure on the exchange rate may be limited, and it may not be necessary to hike rates by more than U.S. rates. However, in cases where monetary regimes have a short track record or where balance sheet vulnerabilities and external financing needs remain more of an issue, it may be necessary to raise rates aggressively to prevent a sustained slide in the exchange rate, deteriorating confidence, and significant second-round effects on inflation.

Note: The authors of this box are Ricardo Adrogue and Roberto Garcia-Saltos.

[1]The model includes an inflation equation, a monetary policy reaction function, and a risk-adjusted interest rate arbitrage equation. For a more detailed description, see Berg, Karam, and Laxton (2006).

Impact of an External Financial Shock on Latin America[1]

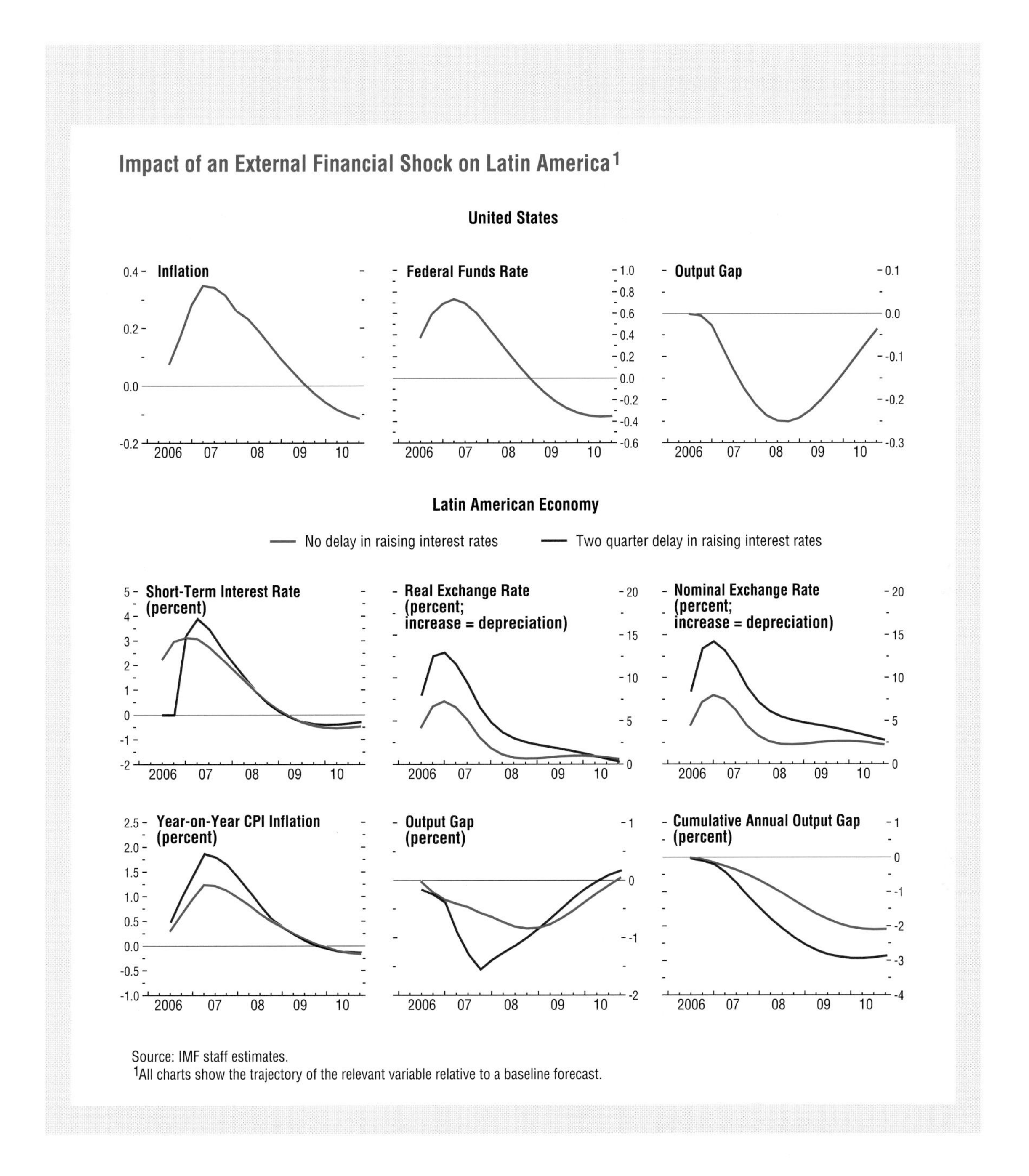

Source: IMF staff estimates.
[1]All charts show the trajectory of the relevant variable relative to a baseline forecast.

footing and finding effective ways to contain the seemingly inexorable rising trend of health care costs.

Structural reforms to improve business environments and global competitiveness remain essential to bolster medium-term prospects. In the euro area, faster progress to advance the Lisbon agenda—particularly more open competition in services and more flexible labor markets—and financial sector reforms remain key to raising productivity prospects and improving job opportunities. In Japan, priorities include public sector reforms, steps to enhance labor market flexibility and financial sector efficiency, and reforms to improve productivity performance in the service sector.

Box 1.3. How Will Global Imbalances Adjust?

The September 2005 and April 2006 issues of the *World Economic Outlook* presented alternative scenarios for the unwinding of global imbalances based on a four-region version of the Global Economy Model (GEM).[1] These illustrative simulations have now been updated with 2006 as the new starting point, using historic data up to 2005. The 2005 data show a further widening in the U.S. current account deficit, while the U.S. net foreign asset position has in fact improved slightly due to favorable valuation effects.

"No Policies" Scenario

The "no policies" scenario assumes that imbalances are unwound through changes in private sector saving behavior and orderly movements in exchange rates (see first figure).[2] The adjustment occurs without substantial policy changes in any of the major economies, but depends critically on the willingness of non-U.S. residents to hold substantial and rising amounts of U.S. assets at relatively low interest rates.

- In the *United States*, the private savings rate rises gradually as households adjust to lower rates of increase in asset prices (and particularly the cooling of the housing market), and U.S. output growth moderates to around 3 percent, in line with potential. Combined with a further 15 percent real effective depreciation of the U.S. dollar, these changes slow the growth of U.S. domestic demand, and produce a steady decline in the current account deficit to about 4 percent of GDP by 2015. U.S. net foreign liabilities rise to 55 percent of GDP by 2015 and would eventually stabilize at around 85 percent of GDP in the long run.[3]
- The main counterpart of the reduction in the U.S. current account deficit would be in *emerging Asia.* In the scenario, productivity growth in emerging Asia is assumed to decline gradually over time to converge toward rates in more advanced economies, while domestic demand is boosted by a progressive decline in the private savings rate from current high levels. This more balanced growth pattern is accompanied by a real effective exchange rate appreciation of about 15 percent.[4] Accordingly, the current account surplus declines from its recent highs of around 5 percent of GDP to about 2 percent of GDP by 2015. Emerging Asia therefore maintains a rising creditor position vis-à-vis the United States, but the trajectory of this position is no longer explosive.
- Adjustments in the *euro area and Japan* and the *rest of the world* are more limited. In the scenario, there are competing influences on the real exchange rate and therefore on the current account: depreciation against emerging Asia dominates in the short run, but is offset in the medium term by appreciation against the U.S. dollar. Productivity growth in the euro area and Japan is assumed to remain sluggish over the medium term, so that output growth remains low. Domestic demand in the rest of the world is boosted by rising absorption, both investment and consumption, in oil exporters.

In summary, real exchange rate and current account adjustments in this scenario are sizable but orderly. However, this benign outcome

Note: The authors of this box are Michael Kumhof and Douglas Laxton.

[1]For a description of the model, see Faruqee and others (2005). Parameters have been set for the model in a way that is intended to provide a plausible and consistent modeling of macroeconomic behavior in the main country groups, but it should be emphasized that judgment plays a part in this exercise, and alternative models will give different results. In particular, the quantitative effects of U.S. fiscal consolidation on the current account balance depend on a number of assumptions, with some models producing smaller effects than others. See, for example, Erceg, Guerrieri, and Gust, 2005; and Kumhof, Laxton and Muir, 2005.

[2]This scenario is different from the WEO baseline scenario, in part because real effective exchange rates are allowed to adjust rather than held constant by assumption.

[3]These calculations do not take into account the possible impact of valuation changes on the net foreign asset position.

[4]In the simulation, the rise in the real effective exchange rate comes about as a result of higher domestic inflation, as sterilization of the reserve buildup is assumed to be only partially effective.

How Will Global Imbalances Adjust?[1]

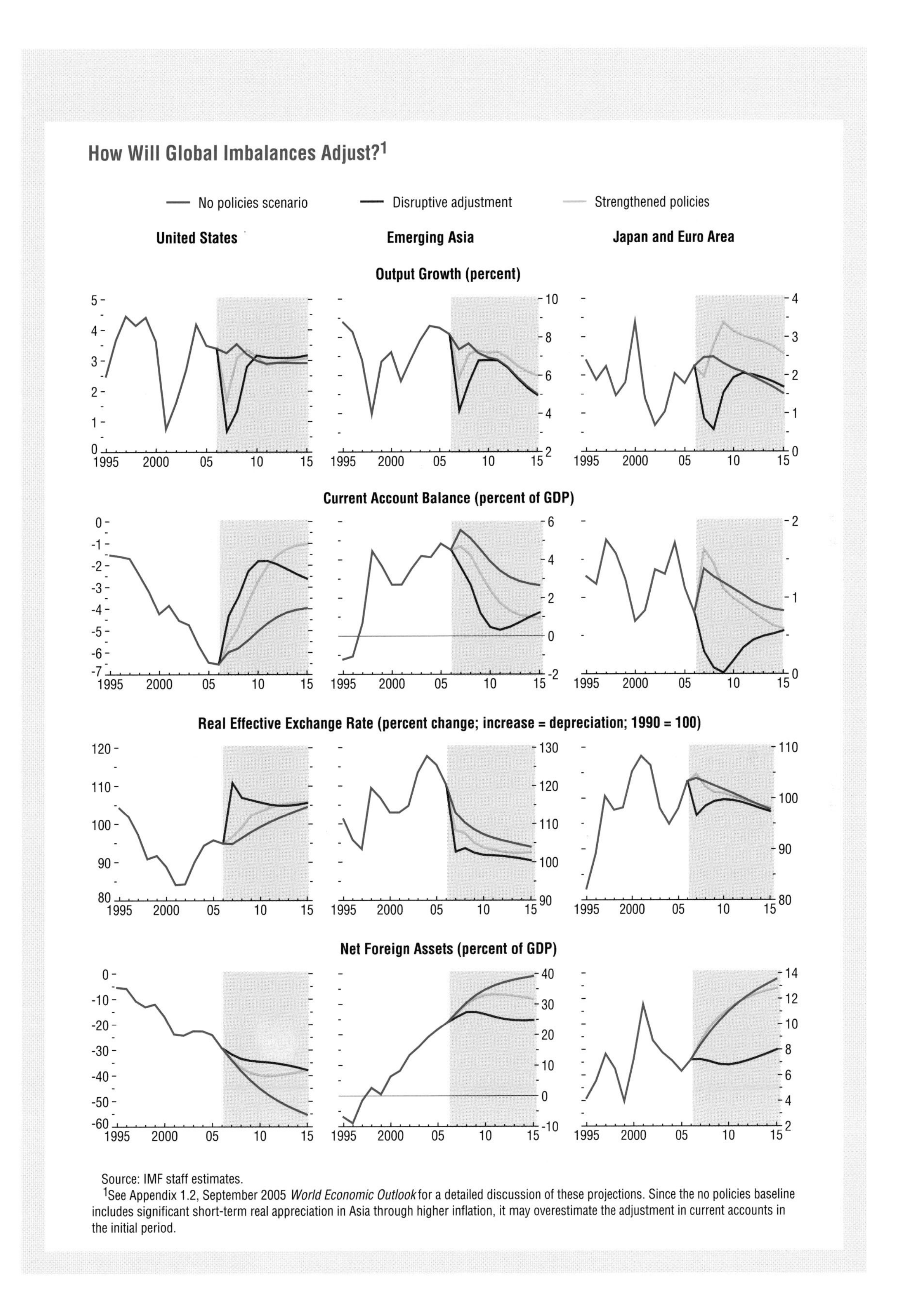

Source: IMF staff estimates.

[1]See Appendix 1.2, September 2005 *World Economic Outlook* for a detailed discussion of these projections. Since the no policies baseline includes significant short-term real appreciation in Asia through higher inflation, it may overestimate the adjustment in current accounts in the initial period.

Box 1.3 *(concluded)*

depends critically on two interrelated assumptions. First, foreigners are assumed to be willing to accommodate a further very substantial buildup in U.S. foreign liabilities, from currently less than 30 percent to ultimately around 85 percent of U.S. GDP. This would represent a very high level of external indebtedness, even for a large industrialized country. Second, foreigners would be willing to allocate an increasing share of their asset portfolios to U.S. assets without demanding a large risk premium, even though they may face continued foreign exchange losses. As emphasized in previous issues of the *World Economic Outlook*, these assumptions may not be realistic, and it is relevant to explore alternative scenarios based on more pessimistic assumptions.

Disruptive Adjustment Scenario

The updated disruptive adjustment scenario shows how a much more abrupt and disorderly adjustment could be triggered by a worldwide reduction in appetite for U.S. assets combined with a significantly increased interest rate risk premium. The decline in the demand for U.S. assets is strongest in emerging Asia, where policymakers are assumed to reduce the rate of reserve accumulation and allow more rapid exchange rate appreciation. The resulting abrupt exchange rate realignments are assumed to temporarily reduce global competitive pressures, implying higher wage and price markups.[5] With inflation rising, central banks around the world would be prompted to raise interest rates.

- In the *United States* the current account deficit contracts rapidly to 2 percent of GDP, accompanied by a drop in the currency and a sharp increase in interest rates to combat inflationary pressures. U.S. growth declines to around 1 percent for two years as a sharp drop in domestic demand from higher interest rates more than offsets rising net exports.
- Among the *remaining three regions*, the sharpest real exchange rate appreciation occurs in emerging Asia, almost eliminating the region's current account surplus by 2010. Growth also declines, although remaining over 4 percent. The euro area and Japan and the remaining countries experience similar effects, but on a smaller scale.
- There are clear risks of even worse outcomes than shown in the disruptive adjustment scenario. A major concern is that a disorderly exchange rate adjustment and global recession would risk a *severe disruption in financial markets*, hurting productive capacity, depressing access to credit and aggregate demand, and leading to asset price deflation.[6] Another concern is that a downturn in activity could trigger a *wave of protectionism*, causing a substantial reduction in living standards across all countries.[7]

The Strengthened Policies Scenario

The strengthened policies scenario is based on a menu of policies implemented across different regions of the world economy that would significantly reduce the risk of a disorderly adjustment (see second figure).[8]

- *Greater exchange rate flexibility in emerging Asia.* This is assumed to be accompanied by gradually reduced foreign exchange purchases by monetary authorities and by an improvement in productivity as an increasing share of wealth is invested in productive physical capital inside the region.

[5]The increase in markups could result either from an unleashing of inflationary pressures that have been contained by low prices of traded goods produced in emerging Asia or from a temporary increase in protectionist actions.

[6]Channels for such disruption would include exchange rate–related valuation losses on corporate and especially bank balance sheets, and the effect of increased interest rate volatility on financial intermediaries through its effects on the solvency of corporate borrowers and on exposures from international arbitrage transactions (the carry trade).

[7]The worldwide output losses caused by such policies could be very high. For a quantitative analysis, see Faruqee and others (forthcoming).

[8]Policy actions other than the ones mentioned here may be feasible, including measures to boost private investment in some parts of Asia, and measures to encourage private saving in the United States.

Effects of Policy Measures on Real Exchange Rates, World Growth, and U.S. Net Foreign Liabilities

- No policies scenario
- Flexible exchange rate for emerging Asia
- Fiscal adjustment for United States
- Structural reform in Europe and Japan
- Additional spending by oil exporters

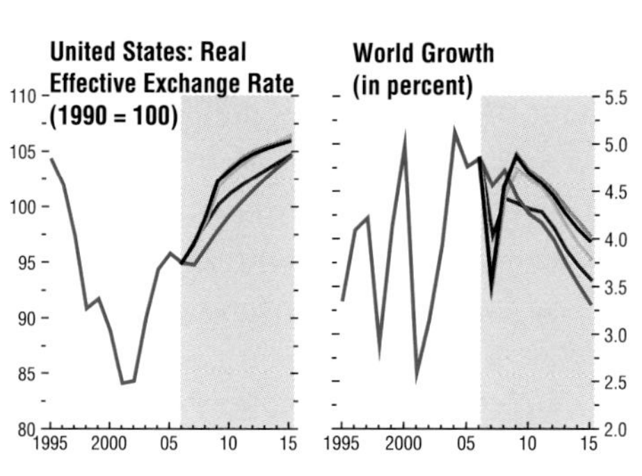

Source: IMF staff estimates.

- *Fiscal consolidation in the United States.* The initial U.S. general government deficit of around 4 percent of GDP is assumed to be eliminated by 2012 by a combination of spending restraint and tax increases. This reinforces the underlying tendency for private savings to rise embedded in the "no policies" scenario, allowing both a reduction in foreign liabilities and a greater increase in the domestic physical capital stock. These shifts lower world real interest rates by 25 basis points after 10 years, contributing to raise growth worldwide.
- *Structural reforms in the euro area and Japan.* More ambitious product and labor market reforms are assumed to lower markups in Europe and Japan over time, eliminating about two-thirds of the gap with U.S. levels over a 10-year period. This shift induces households and firms in this region to invest more in their economies, raising productivity growth.
- *Additional spending by oil exporters.* The large wealth transfer from higher oil prices is assumed to be used by these economies to increase investment and productivity (at a greater pace than built into the baseline scenario).

The strengthened policies scenario illustrates the clear payoffs to joint action both in terms of reducing imbalances and improving growth prospects on a sustainable basis (see first figure for comparisons with the no policies and disruptive adjustment scenarios). The negative effect of policy action on short-run growth is limited—substantially less severe than under the disruptive adjustment scenario—while there would be beneficial effects for medium- and long-run growth everywhere. This is due not only to the direct effect of domestic policies, but also to the spillover effects from successful policies implemented elsewhere. Growth becomes better balanced across regions, with the euro area and Japan catching up and growth in emerging Asia settling at a higher rate than in the alternative scenarios. Growth also becomes better balanced within each economy, with lower but more sustainable consumption growth in the United States and higher consumption growth in the euro area, Japan and emerging Asia.

Under the strengthened policies scenario, the U.S. current account deficit declines to around 1 percent of GDP by 2015. As a result, the buildup in U.S. net foreign liabilities is contained at below 40 percent rather than 85 percent of U.S. GDP, implying a much reduced risk that changes in the preferences of foreign creditors of the United States could lead to an abrupt adjustment that would have a very negative growth impact in all regions.

In emerging market and developing countries too, more needs to be done to move forward market-oriented reforms while also taking steps to ensure that the opportunities and the benefits of growth are broadly shared. Chapter 3 of this report looks at the Asian growth experience in some detail. It concludes that maintaining the successful growth record in Asia and further reducing poverty and income disparities will increasingly depend on reforms that enhance competition and flexibility, while at the same time improving access, especially for low-income groups, to education, health care, and a reasonable social safety net. These lessons are also very relevant outside Asia. Corporate governance and financial sector reforms to increase market discipline would help to ensure an efficient allocation of investment in China, while stronger social safety nets could help support consumption growth. Tighter financial regulation in emerging Europe would reduce vulnerabilities related to rapid credit growth. Labor market reforms and fiscal reforms to improve the targeting of public spending on social and investment priorities would substantially improve prospects for low-income groups across a range of countries.

High and volatile prices in world energy markets remain a major concern that will require sustained efforts from all sides to address. Plans for increased investment by major oil producers in the Middle East are highly welcome. However, recent unilateral efforts to ensure national energy security through self-sufficiency—including keeping foreign companies out of national markets, promotion of national champions, and rushing to secure oil fields abroad at any cost—is a path that could increase global inefficiencies without reducing the risks to the international community. Rather than such "energy protectionism," what is needed is to make sure that markets function well, providing appropriate and predictable incentives to producers to invest (particularly in riskier and higher cost sources of energy), and to ensure adequate spare capacity. Moreover, conservation efforts should be encouraged by ensuring that consumers face prices that reflect the full social costs of energy use. Further efforts to improve energy statistics, including more consistent and reliable measures of petroleum reserves, would encourage more rational and far-sighted decision-making.

Continuing at the global level, multilateral trade liberalization remains essential for enhancing prospects for sustained global growth. The present deadlock in the Doha Round negotiations is deeply disappointing, and raises concerns about a resurgence of protectionism. Renewed efforts are needed to reinvigorate the process of multilateral trade liberalization, guard against protectionist pressures, and avoid over-reliance on bilateral trade agreements as a means to advance trade liberalization. Trade liberalization on a nondiscriminatory (i.e., most favored nation, or MFN) basis remains the best way to open up global growth opportunities.

Continued attention is also needed to maintain the buildup in aid flows to the poorest countries, to supplement their own efforts to reach the Millennium Development Goals. Such efforts would become doubly important if the Doha Round cannot be resuscitated or if there is a softening of the buoyant commodity prices that have helped to underpin robust growth in sub-Saharan Africa.

As emphasized in previous issues of the *World Economic Outlook*, policy actions across the major players in the world economy would help to ensure a smooth resolution of the problem of global imbalances. Box 1.3 discusses how this resolution could be achieved through a combination of steps to boost national saving in the United States, including through a more ambitious commitment to fiscal consolidation over the medium term; greater progress on structural reforms in Europe and Japan; reforms to boost domestic demand in emerging Asia (consumption in China and investment elsewhere), together with greater exchange rate flexibility; and increased expenditures by oil-exporting countries in high return areas, consistent with absorptive capacity constraints, especially in the Middle East, where the large buildup of investment projects already in train is welcome. Each of these policy goals is in the best interest of the countries concerned, but progress in advancing toward these goals has been in some cases slower than desirable, hampered in part by the difficulty of developing national political consensus on policy changes that will have distributional consequences. A joint, multilateral approach may help to advance implementation by stressing cross-border linkages and spillovers; providing additional reassurance that possible risks associated with individual actions would be alleviated by policy initiatives elsewhere; and generating a sense of common commitment by the world community that would provide the best hope to ensure continued rapid global growth and prosperity. The multilateral consultation now being undertaken by the International Monetary Fund with China, the euro area, Japan, Saudi Arabia, and the United States aims to help toward developing such a joint approach.

Appendix 1.1. Recent Developments in Commodity Markets

The main author of this appendix is Valerie Mercer-Blackman, with contributions from To-Nhu Dao and Nese Erbil.

In the first seven months of 2006, the IMF commodities and energy price index increased by over 15 percent in dollar terms, led by surging base metals prices (in particular copper, zinc, and nickel). The increase was underpinned by higher demand for commodities, driven by robust global economic growth. Energy prices continued to rise, albeit at a more moderate pace, with crude oil prices posting new highs in early August in the context of heightened tensions in the Middle East.

Crude Oil and Other Petroleum Products

Oil price increases over the past eight months have reflected buoyant global activity, which has tempered the response of oil demand to higher prices, and supply concerns related to geopolitical uncertainties. Looking forward, with spare capacity expected to remain tight, futures markets suggest that prices for crude oil will remain high for the remainder of 2006 and 2007 (Figure 1.15).

Price Developments

During the first eight months of 2006, the average petroleum spot price rose by 16 percent.[6] The oil price rose sharply above its pre-Katrina peak in early May and again in early August to reach a new record high of $76, amid concerns related to the intensification of the standoff over the Islamic Republic of Iran's nuclear program, the outbreak of fighting in Lebanon and Israel, and the closing of a large Alaskan oil field by British Petroleum. Continued violence in the Nigerian oil-producing region and security threats to Iraqi oil infrastructure have also contributed to market fears about potential supply shortages (the Islamic Republic of Iran, Iraq, and Nigeria together export almost four times as much as the current global spare capacity). Announcements by some governments of policies aimed at greater control of their oil and gas fields (as in Venezuela, Bolivia, and Russia) have also contributed to higher uncertainty and cautious investment behavior (see below). However, despite these uncertainties, price volatility does not appear to have increased (see Figure 1.15).

Gasoline prices in OECD member countries and in Asia have increased by 25–30 percent so far in 2006, and in the United States in August were only 13 percent below their record level following hurricane Katrina. Temporary upward pressure on margins came in part because many U.S. refineries were still shut down or operating at reduced rates due to last year's hurricane damage, while others had deferred planned

[6]The IMF average petroleum spot price (APSP) is an equally weighted average of the West Texas Intermediate, Brent, and Dubai crude oil prices. Unless otherwise noted, all subsequent references to the oil price are to the APSP.

Figure 1.15. Crude Oil Spot and Futures Prices, Price Volatility, and Consumption-Production Changes

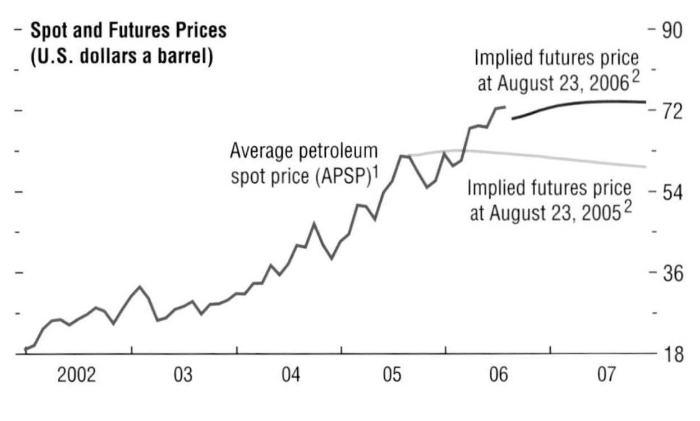

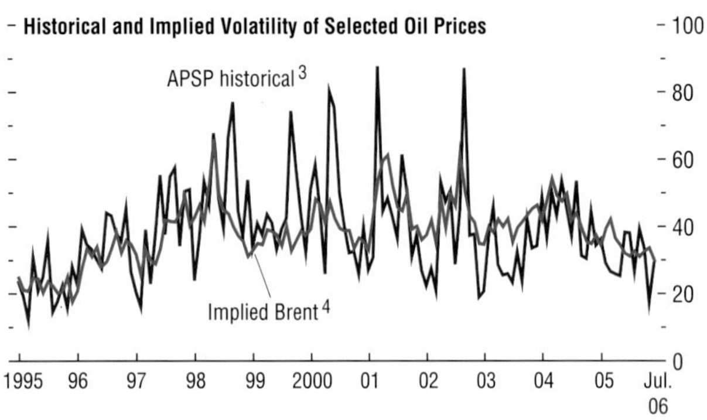

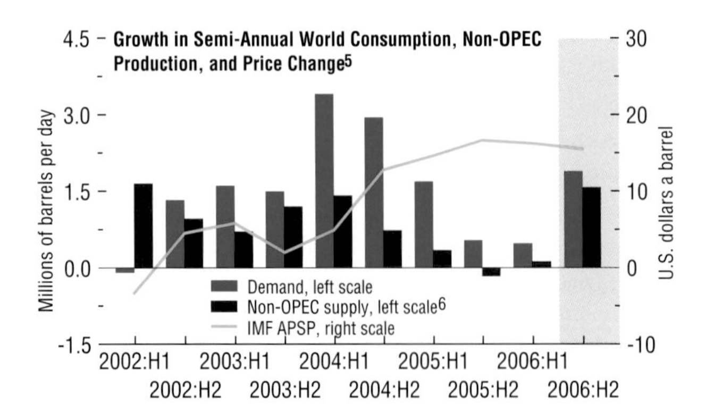

Sources: Bloomberg Financial Markets, LP; International Energy Agency; and IMF staff calculations.

[1]Average unweighted petroleum spot price of West Texas Intermediate, U.K. Brent, and Dubai Fateh crude.

[2]Five-day weighted average of NYMEX Light Sweet Crude, IPE Dated Brent, and implied Dubai Fateh.

[3]The standard deviation of the level of prices over 30-day rolling periods divided by the mean over the same period.

[4]The weighted average of the volatilities of the front month's 3 options closest to the at-the-money strike.

[5]2006:H2 supply and demand projections are from the International Energy Agency.

[6]Includes non-crude production.

routine maintenance to the spring; and in part because of bottlenecks created by the transition to reformulated gasoline blended with ethanol. Natural gas prices in the United States have continued to decline, and at end-August were below European prices.

Oil Consumption

Global oil consumption increased by 0.5 million barrels per day (mbd) (0.6 percent) in the first half of 2006 relative to the same period in 2005 (Table 1.4 and Figure 1.15). Consumption in the United States fell somewhat over this period (in part owing to one-off factors), but still was higher than expected, with gasoline consumption recovering strongly in the second quarter of 2006. Oil consumption growth remained high in China (the second largest consumer of oil) and in the Middle East, while it fell slightly in Europe and Japan. Evidence suggests that in countries such as Indonesia, Malaysia, and Jordan, efforts to increase the pass-through of global oil prices into domestic prices, while politically difficult, have helped dampen demand (Table 1.5). Retail gasoline and diesel prices were also recently raised almost 10 percent in China and India, but in these countries the effect on household consumption in the short term is expected to be limited.[7]

Overall, it appears that price increases since 2003 have had some dampening effect on demand, but the strength of GDP growth in many countries—especially China and the United States—has prevented a fall in overall consumption. This is in contrast with the significant weakening in demand observed following the oil price hikes of 1979–80.[8]

[7]In China, refiners will now have a marginally higher incentive to supply the domestic market than before, so the easing of shortages could lead to higher consumption, which had been suppressed by rationing; while in India, prices of kerosene—a heavily consumed domestic fuel—were not changed.

[8]Most studies show that the short-term price elasticity of demand for oil is very low (on the order of 0.01 to 0.03 percent within a year), and the income effect tends to dominate.

Table 1.4. Global Oil Demand by Region
(Millions of barrels per day)

	Demand			Change	
	2006:H1	2005:H1	2005:H2	2006:H1/2005:H1	2006:H1/2005:H1
	(millions of barrels a day)			*(millions of barrels a day)*	*(percent)*
North America	25.15	25.45	25.45	–0.30	–1.2
Europe	16.05	16.10	16.25	–0.05	–0.3
OECD Pacific	8.55	8.75	8.45	–0.20	–2.3
China	6.95	6.55	6.75	0.40	6.1
India	2.70	2.65	2.55	0.05	1.9
Other Asia	6.25	6.25	6.15	0.00	0.0
Former Soviet Union	3.80	3.75	3.85	0.05	1.3
Middle East	6.40	6.05	6.20	0.35	5.8
Africa	3.00	2.90	2.85	0.10	3.4
Latin America	5.15	5.05	5.15	0.10	2.0
World	84.00	83.50	83.65	0.50	0.6

Source: International Energy Agency, *Oil Market Report,* August 2006.

Oil Production and Inventories

Non-OPEC production in the first half of 2006 rose by 0.14 mbd compared to the same period last year, somewhat lower than expected at the beginning of this year (Figure 1.15). Production increases came from Russia (where production is recovering from a low in 2005), Azerbaijan, Brazil, and non-OPEC Africa. In the OECD region, a recovery in U.S. production following the hurricanes was somewhat offset by production declines in Europe, particularly the North Sea. OPEC production fell marginally during the first half of 2006, with output declines in Saudi Arabia and to a lesser extent the Islamic Republic of Iran. Lower-than-planned OPEC production mostly reflects the situation in Nigeria, where about 0.7 mbd of its 2.5 mbd production has been shut down since the beginning of the year due to violence in the Niger delta. Overall, supplies remain tight: most analysts currently estimate readily available OPEC spare capacity at between 1–2 mbd, and much of it is of the heavy sour crude type, which is difficult to refine (see Figure 1.16).[9]

[9]Readily available capacity excludes capacity from Indonesia, the Islamic Republic of Iran, Nigeria, and Venezuela.

OECD crude oil inventory levels remain at historically high levels, likely reflecting strong precautionary demand (accommodated, in part, by OPEC's willingness to make additional supplies available) amid perceptions that prices will remain high and market tightness will persist. OECD commercial crude and product stocks increased steadily to 2.4 billion barrels in June 2006, equivalent to 54 days of forward cover (Figure 1.16).

Short-Term Prospects and Risks

Despite signs of slowing demand in some regions, the crude oil market is expected to remain tight for the foreseeable future. The International Energy Agency (IEA) has lowered projections for global consumption growth in 2006 from 1.8 mbd early in the year to 1.2 mbd, as increased pass-through in many countries and sustained high prices are expected to impact demand further. However, many analysts are projecting somewhat higher consumption growth above 1.3 mbd, citing continued strength in China and the United States. Projections of non-OPEC supply growth in 2006 range widely from 0.6 to 1.1 mbd (the latter by the IEA), but may prove overly optimistic as they assume a substantial recovery in the second half of 2006. In turn, OPEC estimates its capacity to increase by 1 mbd by end-2006 relative to end-2005.

Table 1.5. Selected Domestic Fuel Price Changes, January 2005–June 2006

Country and Time of Last Change	Price and Policy Change	Nature of Policy
Fuel exporters		
Iran, Islamic Republic of[1]	Fuel prices were frozen in 2003 at subsidized levels.	Rationing of refined imports under consideration. Cost of subsidies is almost 16 percent of GDP.
Iraq (June 2006)	Fuel prices increased between 300 and 1,400 percent since September 2005, depending on product.	Prices are gradually being brought into line with regional average.
Nigeria (August 2005)	25 percent (gasoline).	
Saudi Arabia (April 2006)[1]	–30 percent (gasoline and diesel).	Price reduction aimed at distributing part of the increased oil wealth to the population.
United Kingdom (through 2005–06)	Excise taxes on petroleum products frozen.	
Vietnam (early 2006)	Removed import duties on all petroleum products as of April 2006.	Domestic prices were raised three times in 2005 (in March, July, and August), lowered once (in November), and increased again in April 2006.
Fuel importers		
China (May 2006)[1]	9.6 percent (gasoline). 11.1 percent (diesel).	National Development and Reform Commission (NDRC) ordered to ensure that domestic supplies do not suffer and subsidies are targeted to poor.
India (June 2006)	9.2 percent (gasoline). 6.6 percent (diesel). Cumulative price increases since end-2004 are 26 percent for gasoline, and 24 percent for diesel.	Gasoline and diesel prices were also increased in June and September 2005, however, there has been no change in kerosene prices.
Indonesia (March 2006)	29 percent (gasoline and diesel). This followed a price increase in October 2005 of 88 percent for gasoline, 105 percent for diesel, and 186 percent for kerosene.	Dissemination and cash transfer program to poor families implemented simultaneously. Moreover, since October 2005 industry prices adjust every month to reflect market prices.
Jordan (April 2006)	30 percent (diesel and kerosene). Prices were also raised by 15 percent in September 2005 and by 25 percent in July 2005.	Gradual reduction of subsidies accompanied by measures to protect vulnerable groups.
Malaysia (February 2006)	23 percent (gasoline, kerosene and LPG).	Follows price increases in February, March, and July 2005.
Thailand (July 2005)	Ended diesel subsidy.	

Sources: International Energy Agency; and IMF staff.
[1]Domestic gasoline prices remain significantly below international prices.

Therefore, even under optimistic scenarios for demand and supply, global spare capacity is likely to remain low. Refining capacity is also expected to remain tight in 2006–07, especially in the United States.

Against this background, futures markets suggest that oil prices would remain in the $70–75 range in 2006–07, with short-term fluctuations driven by political developments. A sharp drop in prices (say, to $50 a barrel) would require either a significant fall in demand induced by slower economic growth or (less likely), an easing of ongoing geopolitical tensions.[10] However, adverse developments on the supply side, such as further production outages in Nigeria and Iraq, or potential supply problems in the Islamic Republic of Iran, Venezuela, and the Gulf of Mexico (a strong hurricane season is expected), could push prices up further. Oil options prices suggest that in August 2006 markets put a

[10]OPEC has argued that the market fundamentals support a price no lower than $50. Should oil prices drop close to this level, OPEC would likely reduce quotas.

10 percent chance on Brent oil exceeding $90 a barrel in December 2006.

Medium-Term Prospects: How Will Supply Respond?

Even if the response of demand to higher prices strengthens, rebalancing the oil markets will depend fundamentally on supply adjustments in an industry with very long investment cycles (5–10 years). The key in the years ahead, therefore, is whether sufficient investment will take place. However, both international oil companies (IOCs) and national oil companies (NOCs) appear to be following a cautious approach toward investment. Medium-term forecasts by the IEA and others suggest that current investment rates could be as much as 20 percent below what would be necessary to satisfy future global demand under the assumption that prices weaken somewhat from current high levels. This section discusses possible reasons for this cautious investment behavior and how it could be related to the changing supply structure of the global oil market. Data deficiencies, however, in particular in the case of NOCs, do not permit a conclusive statement on investment behavior.

Investment by International Oil Companies (IOCs)

It is often argued that IOCs are not doing enough to increase investment—and thus capacity—to mitigate upward pressures on oil prices. According to data on companies listed on stock exchanges in the Group of Seven (G-7) countries, oil and gas companies have posted record profits in the past two years—well above the rest of the nonfinancial corporate sector—largely owing to the increase in energy prices. In the United States, the oil and gas corporate sector has almost doubled in valuation since mid-2000, well above the increase in the total S&P index, while oil service companies, which supply equipment and related services, have done even better (Figure 1.17). However, notwithstanding a significant increase in real investment since 2000, investment levels are still below the levels in the early 1990s, when spare

Figure 1.16. OPEC Production, OPEC Spare Capacity, and OECD Inventories

(Millions of barrels a day unless otherwise stated)

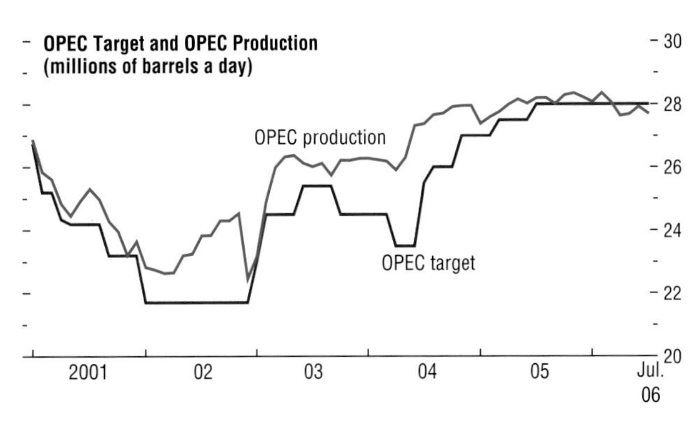

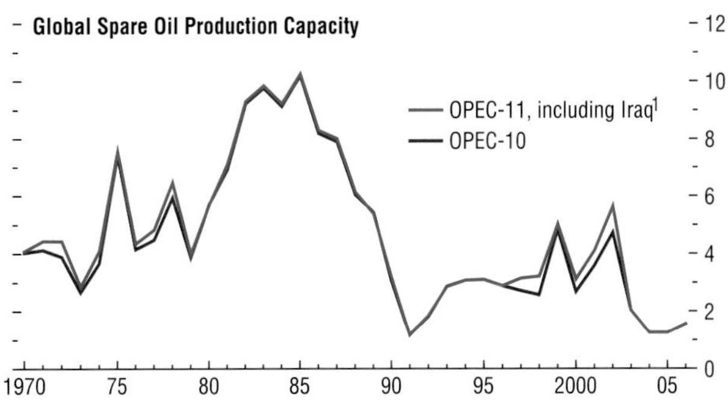

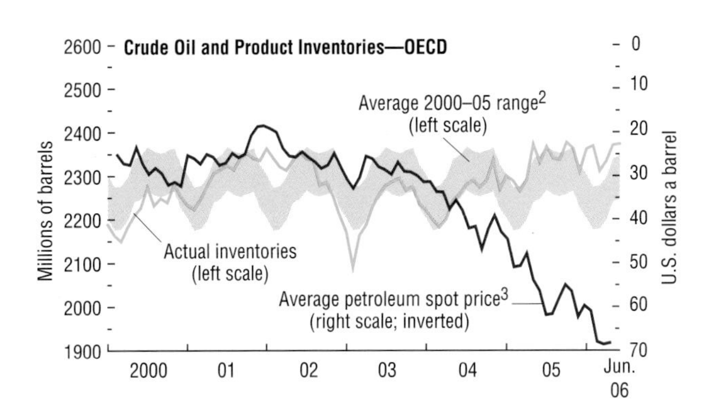

Sources: Bloomberg Financial, LP; International Energy Agency; U.S. Department of Energy; and IMF staff calculations.

[1]OPEC-11 spare capacity refers to production capacity that can be brought online within 30 days and sustained for 90 days.

[2]Average of each calendar month during 2000–05, with a 40 percent confidence interval based on past deviations.

[3]Average unweighted petroleum spot price of West Texas Intermediate, U.K. Brent, and Dubai Fateh crude.

Figure 1.17. Stock Market Valuations and Real Investment in Oil and Non-Oil Sectors

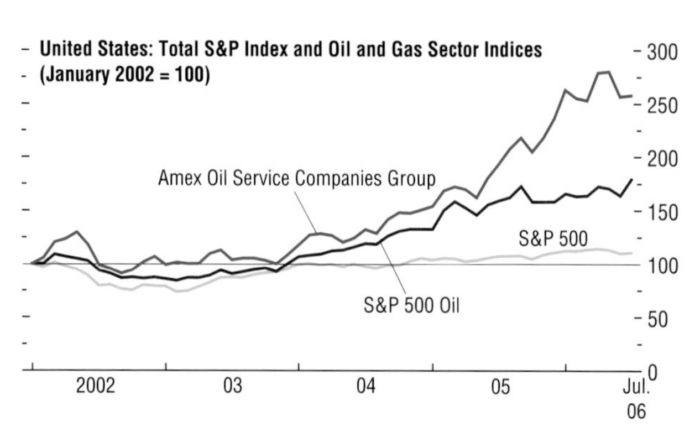

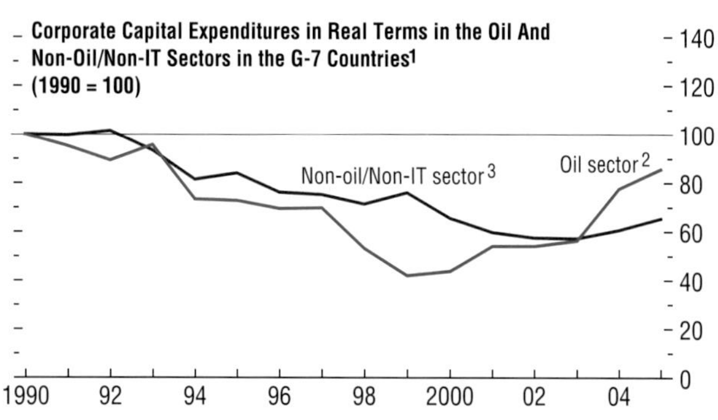

Sources: Bloomberg Financial Markets, LP; Worldscope; U.S. Bureau of Labor Statistics; and IMF staff calculations.

[1]2005 estimates were derived from company listings of a few representative companies in each sector (for oil and gas, the nine major international oil companies); therefore, they are not directly comparable with the 2004 figures.

[2]Adjusted by the average of oil support and oil equipment producer price index (PPI), 1990 = 100.

[3]PPI adjusted, 1990 = 100.

capacity was much higher, and a large share of profits has gone toward paying higher dividends and acquiring new assets.[11]

A number of specific factors have impeded higher investment by IOCs. First, investment opportunities are constrained by limited access to reserves in some oil-rich countries, while changes in regulatory regimes and risks of nationalization in some countries have made returns on new investments more uncertain. Second, in OECD countries and in others where IOCs dominate production, existing conventional fields are going into decline, and it has become more difficult and costly to extend their production life. Third, following the extensive downsizings of the 1990s, the IOCs are constrained by the availability of qualified staff and are facing higher short-term investment costs.[12] As a result, an increasing share of earnings has been used to acquire other oil companies as a less risky alternative to greenfield investments. The median share of oil and gas companies' cash earnings spent on domestic and foreign asset acquisitions increased from 13 percent in the 1990s to 20 percent during 2001–04. Such acquisitions imply an increase in capital expenditures and production capacity for an individual IOC, but not for the global economy as a whole.

Faced by limited opportunities in conventional fields, the IOCs have become active in developing alternative production sources (such as fields in new areas or new technologies). In these areas too, the IOCs face competition from NOCs—including from oil-importing countries—which in recent years have become just as active as IOCs in acquiring foreign assets, as well as in forging

[11]Investment data from international oil companies listed in the G-7 countries' exchanges is derived from balance sheet data from the *Thomson Worldscope* database. Data are not always comparable across companies owing to differences in accounting standards and in the number of companies reporting, which varies over time.

[12]This is also an issue in many NOCs (although less so for very large oil producers where expertise has been maintained). Moreover, there are cost pressures on equipment and other input since their suppliers are working at full capacity.

downstream and upstream ventures abroad, creating new challenges and opportunities for IOCs (see Box 1.4).

Investment by National Oil Companies (NOCs)

NOCs in a number of major oil producers—particularly where financial constraints are less binding or there is flexibility in attracting private capital—have ratcheted up plans for investment in the past year. Large companies—such as Saudi Arabia's Aramco, UAE's ADNOC, and Kuwait's KPC, which can self-finance projects and have maintained their human and productive capital base during the lean years of the 1990s—have developed ambitious capacity expansion plans at all levels of the production chain.[13] Some NOCs in more fiscally strapped countries have recently sought new ways of accessing private sector financing and know-how, while at the same time abiding by the constitutionally mandated prohibition of foreign ownership. NOCs such as Mexico's Pemex, Algeria's Sonatrach, and the Islamic Republic of Iran's INOC set up "build-operate-transfer" projects with IOCs, and have seen investment in these projects take off very rapidly, although overall investment has lagged.

Real investment of most other NOCs does not appear to have recovered from the decline in the 1990s despite a slight pickup since 2000, although data are limited.[14] Investment has been constrained by numerous explicit and implicit restrictions imposed by their own governments. NOCs in many low-income, but oil-rich, countries are often short of financial resources, because cash flow is siphoned off to the budget—for example, through high implicit fuel subsidies (when the domestic fuel price for consumers is kept artificially low) and in some cases as a result of corruption. Even where the intentions of the government are benign, competing objectives can lead to politically difficult trade-offs. For example, if the government needs to undertake fiscal adjustment, it may do so at the cost of reducing resources available to the NOC. Dada (2005) shows that budgetary allocations to NOCs are a significant determinant of NOCs' investment the following year. Consequently, the lack of investment in oil production infrastructure over a number of years can imply that NOCs are not in a position to take full advantage of potential gains from current price levels.

[13]Aramco has already started implementing plans to invest more than $50 billion over three to six years to expand production by almost 20 percent and refining by 50 percent; ADNOC plans to increase production by 30 percent and KPC by 60 percent by 2020.

[14]Based on information on capital and exploratory expenditures from the *Oil and Gas Journal* for 19 NOCs to 2004. The NOCs that publish investment data produced about 53 percent of total NOC oil output. There is no investment information on four major Middle Eastern NOCs—Aramco, ADNOC, INOC and NIOC (Iraq)—and limited data on other NOCs.

Table 1.6. Nonenergy Commodity Prices
(Percent change between January–July 2006)

	U.S. Dollar Terms	Contribution[1]	Special Drawing Right (SDR) Terms
Food	10.7	35.9	8.4
Beverages	–2.2	3.6	–4.2
Agricultural raw materials	4.0	9.2	1.8
Metals	32.0	51.3	29.2
Overall nonenergy	18.5	100.0	16.1

Sources: IMF Primary Commodity Price Database; and IMF staff estimates.
[1]Contributions to change in overall nonenergy price index in U.S. dollar terms, in percent. Contributions to change in SDR terms are similar.

Nonenergy Commodities

The IMF nonfuel commodity index rose by 19 percent in dollar terms between January and July 2006, reaching its highest level in real terms since 1990 (Table 1.6). Metals prices increased by 32 percent between January and July 2006 mostly on the strength of copper, zinc, and nickel: prices of these base metals spiked by 60–70 percent over a six-week period through early May, then dropped by 25 percent by end-June. Metal prices are expected to fall further in the second half of 2006, but are still projected to show a 45 percent increase for 2006 relative to 2005.

Figure 1.18. Nonenergy Commodities

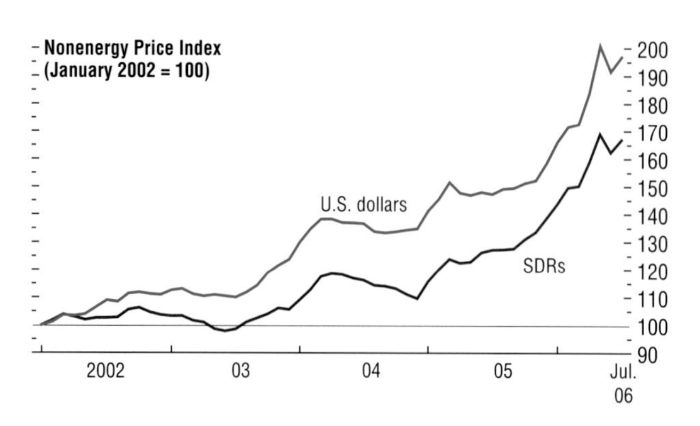

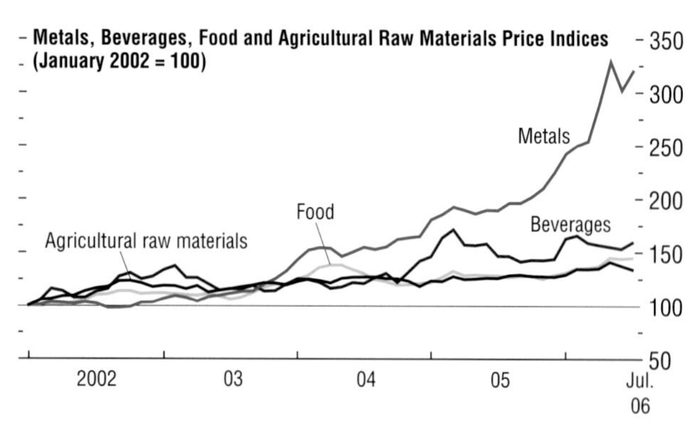

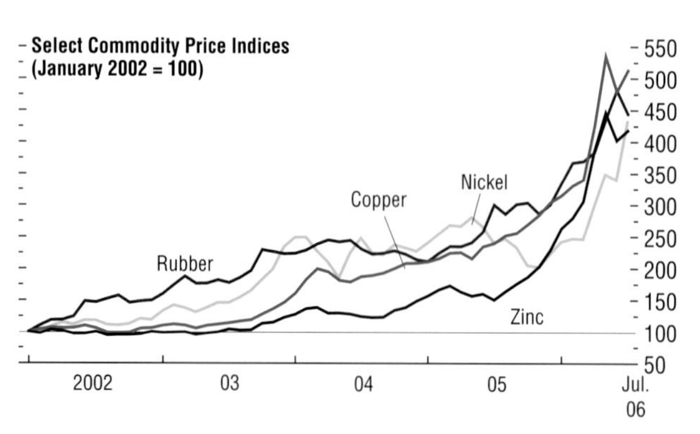

Source: IMF staff calculations.

While demand remains strong, supply concerns have also contributed to high and volatile prices. Many producers, particularly of copper, zinc, and nickel, have been affected by deteriorating ore quality, production disruptions caused by outages and earth slides, and labor disputes. Moreover, global inventories remain at historically low levels, while the introduction of new capacity has been delayed because of high energy and equipment costs and labor shortages. A surge in investor interest in commodities has come hand in hand with the tightening of market conditions, but empirical analysis by IMF staff suggests that speculative activity—measured as the number of net long noncommercial positions—has followed rather than been the cause of the high price levels (see Chapter 5, Box 5.1). Looking forward, despite an expected capacity increase in metals this year, the tight market situation will probably continue into late 2007–early 2008, until sufficient new capacity comes into operation.

The food price index rose 11 percent between January–July 2006 (Figure 1.18). Unfavorable weather conditions early this year reduced grain production significantly, while demand continued at record highs, drawing down already low global stocks. Seafood prices rose sharply during this period, largely on robust demand in European countries. Beverage prices fell by 2 percent in the first seven months, due mostly to increases in coffee supplies. Looking ahead, for 2006 as a whole, food prices are expected to rise by 8 percent, while beverage prices will increase by less than 2 percent.

The agricultural raw material price index rose 4 percent between January and July 2006, led by natural rubber and hardwood prices. Natural rubber shortages in 2005 have been extended into 2006 and pushed prices up by 33 percent, in part because continued high oil prices have boosted prices of synthetic rubber. Hardwood prices continued their gain from 2005, mainly as a result of strong Chinese demand. Raw materials prices are expected to ease in the second half of 2006, but still increase 5 percent overall in 2006.

Semiconductors

In the first half of 2006, semiconductor demand was stronger than anticipated, mainly in the consumer electronic product sectors (Figure 1.19). Total worldwide sales revenues grew by 9 percent year-on-year, particularly in the Americas and the Asia-Pacific regions, on surging volume growth; the number of units sold rose 8 percent, while prices rose slightly. The Semiconductor Industry Association (SIA) has revised up its forecast for growth in worldwide semiconductors sales, to 10 percent in 2006, and expects sales growth to continue at around this pace in 2007 before slowing down in early 2008.

The fastest-growing global major end-market segment is cellular telephones, especially third-generation (3G) phones. This segment is now second only to personal computers in terms of total chip consumption. Other major drivers of demand for semiconductors include digital cameras, digital television, and MP3 players, with increasing demand for products using flash memory.[15] Indeed, the explosive growth in flash memory demand has drained traditional capital from the DRAM market, which has consequently had limited capacity expansion.

Continuing high demand and tight capacity utilization rates have led to surging investment in the semiconductor industry. Capital expenditure, in particular in the Asia-Pacific, is expected to increase 16 percent worldwide in 2006. Despite adequate inventory levels, new construction and upgrades of foundries continue, with more than one-third of all new capacity planned in 2007 for flash memory production. Concerns have thus been raised by industry analysts about too much capacity coming online at the end of 2006, in particular if a slowdown in major consumer markets impacts equipment spending.

[15]Flash memory is a nonvolatile memory device that can be electrically erased and programmed anew and retains its data when power is off. It is durable and operates at low voltages.

Figure 1.19. Semiconductor Market

(Seasonally adjusted; quarterly percent change of three-month moving average unless otherwise noted)

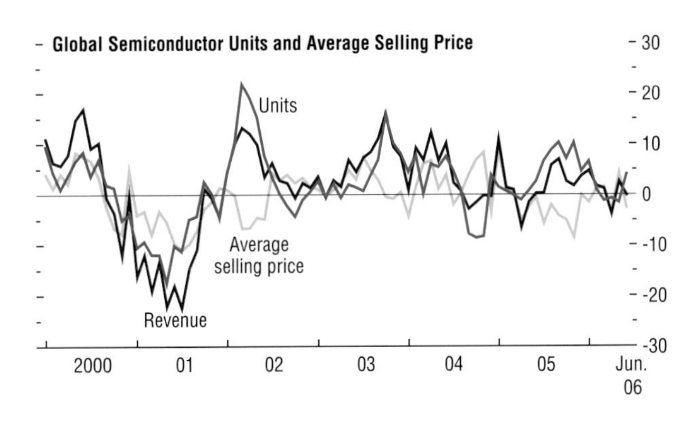

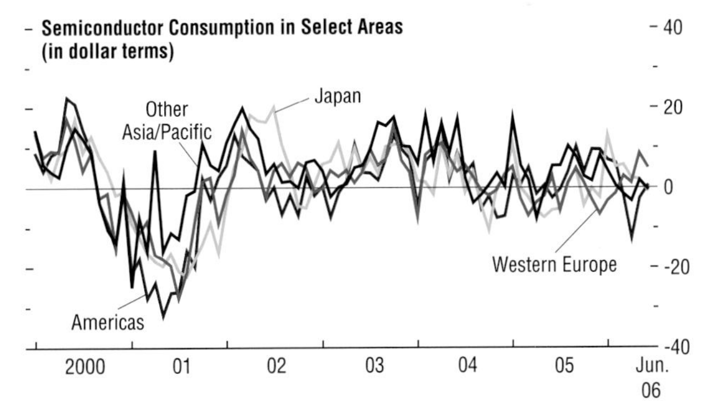

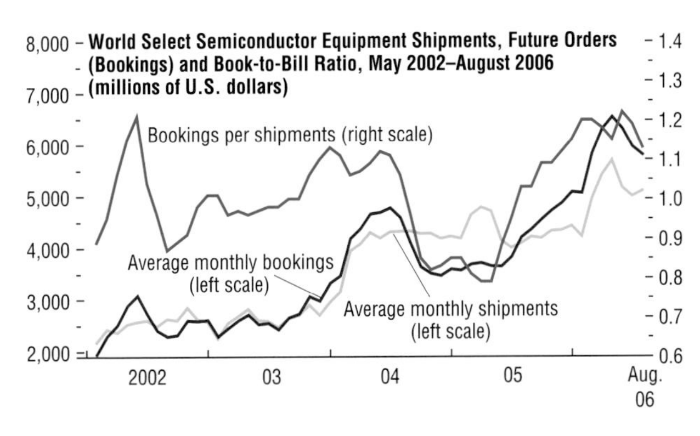

Sources: Semiconductor Industry Association; Semiconductor Equipment and Materials International (SEMI); VLSI Research; and IMF staff calculations.

Box 1.4. International and National Oil Companies in a Changing Oil Sector Environment

The increasing importance of national oil companies (NOCs) has brought new challenges and potential opportunities for international oil companies (IOCs). This box discusses the changing relationship between IOCs and NOCs, and suggests that improved partnership between the two—taking better advantage of each other's strengths and needs—would strengthen prospects for increasing investment in the oil sector as a whole.

The structure of NOCs and their governance and partnership arrangements with IOCs vary considerably. Oil production growth in 2000–05 has generally been higher in countries where IOCs' presence is greater.[1] The bulk of world reserves are in countries with majority NOC control. However, the regulatory quality of the government is lower in this group of countries (this remains true if only developing countries are compared; see table).

Characteristics of the Oil Sector in the Largest Oil-Producing Countries[1] Classified by Production Control of the National Oil Company (NOC)[2]
(In percent unless otherwise indicated)

	No State Ownership or Minority State Control	Majority State Control
Total share of world reserves in 2004	28	72
Average oil production growth, 2000–05	16.7	6.1
Share of country group in 2005 world production	44	50
Average 'Regulatory Quality' (percentile rank)[3]	46	33
Average 2005 government net debt as a share of GDP	44	17
Memorandum		
Number of countries in group	19	15

Source: BP Statistics; WEO; World Bank Governance Indicators, 2004; and IMF staff estimates.

[1]Includes the largest 34 countries in terms of proven oil reserves in 2004. Together they own 98 percent of world reserves and produce 94 percent of world oil.

[2]Most NOCs are 100 percent government-owned, but their participation in production varies by type and amount. A few countries do not have NOCs.

[3]*Regulatory Quality* refers to the ability of the government to formulate and implement sound policies and regulations enabling private sector development, based on a survey of 204 countries. A higher percentile rank indicates better quality.

The global oil industry continues to have an oligopolistic structure, but the importance of NOCs in the control of production has risen dramatically. Twenty national and international oil companies own almost 80 percent of the world's proven reserves. Significantly, the top four—which own 60 percent of the world's reserves—are NOCs from Saudi Arabia, the Islamic Republic of Iran, Iraq, and Kuwait with full ownership and control of their oil wells. Moreover, some NOCs are quickly expanding outside their borders. Companies like PetroChina, Petronas, and Petrobras, formerly exclusively involved in domestic production, have won lucrative international contracts. NOCs from oil-importing countries such as China, Japan, and India have been very active in forging foreign upstream ventures and acquiring foreign assets, a behavior akin to traditional major IOCs. The difference is that these strategies are often driven by their countries' energy security policies. The distinction between types of companies is also becoming blurred. It is not uncommon to have a project run as a joint venture where the partners are a subsidiary of the host NOC, an IOC, and a foreign NOC.

Partnerships among different types of companies should, in theory, allow each side to contribute its strengths, but in practice differences between major IOCs and large NOCs make such unions rare. Part of the explanation may have to do with fundamentally different and clashing objectives between the two, as suggested in Marcel (2006). IOCs want access to equity, acceptable rates of return, and incentives for enhanced recovery. NOCs, for their part, want access to the managerial, technical, and financial expertise of IOCs without having to give up ownership and control of their

[1]Most NOCs are fully publicly owned, although some NOCs (such as Brazil's Petrobras, China's Sinopec, and Oman's PDO) have some private ownership. When oil companies forge joint ventures, typically a new company or subsidiary is created with equal ownership rights of each partner.

national reserves.[2] NOC managers sometimes express concern that IOCs have a tendency to over produce fields in a quest to satisfy the short-term expectations of their shareholders, and that in the past they have not received the full benefits of production-sharing agreements. A number of governments have recently altered contracting laws and production-sharing rules with foreign investors so as to increase control over their resources to varying degrees (as in Bolivia, Ecuador, Venezuela, and Russia). For their part, IOCs have expressed frustration about changing "rules of the game," project delays, and dealing with the bureaucratic structures of NOCs. They believe the host governments do not always adequately factor in the risks associated with unpredictable political and tax environments.

Well-designed partnerships could lead to increasing investment levels in the oil industry as a whole, especially if the risks and returns from the production venture are appropriately distributed. Given that NOCs today own the majority of the world's reserves, IOCs are coming to terms with the reality that their future activity may have to increasingly take place in partnerships in which profits and control must be shared. In turn, governments of NOCs will have to work to provide a more stable and transparent investment environment and stronger governance of NOCs. Once these frictions are worked out, global investment in the sector would be better placed to respond to price incentives.

[2]Indeed, this may partly explain why profitability of international oil service companies has been even higher than oil and gas exploration and production companies since 2002 (see Figure 1.17); their services are in high demand by NOCs because they provide the know-how without generating competition for the NOC assets.

References

Berg, Andrew, Phillipe Karam, and Douglas Laxton, 2006, "A Practical Model-Based Approach to Monetary Policy Analysis—An Overview," IMF Working Paper 06/80 (Washington: International Monetary Fund).

Caballero, Ricardo J., Emmanuel Farhi, and Pierre-Olivier Gourinchas, 2006, "An Equilibrium Model of 'Global Imbalances' and Low Interest Rates," NBER Working Paper No. 11996 (Cambridge, Massachusetts: National Bureau of Economic Research).

Dada, Wagner, 2005, "Modeling Investment Decisions for Oil Exploration Companies: Do International Oil Companies Differ from National Oil Companies?" (unpublished; Washington: International Monetary Fund, Research Department).

Erceg, Christopher J., Luca Guerrieri, and Christopher Gust, 2005, "Expansionary Fiscal Shocks And The Trade Deficit," International Finance Discussion Paper No. 825 (Washington: Board of Governors of the Federal Reserve System, International Finance Division).

Faruqee, Hamid, Doug Laxton, Dirk Muir, and Paolo Pesenti, 2005, "Smooth Landing or Crash? Model-Based Scenarios of Global Current Account Rebalancing," NBER Working Paper No. 11583 (Cambridge, Massachusetts: National Bureau of Economic Research).

———, forthcoming, "Would Protectionism Defuse Global Imbalances and Spur Economic Activity? A Scenario Analysis," NBER Working Paper (Cambridge, Massachusetts: National Bureau of Economic Research).

Kumhof, Michael, Douglas Laxton, and Dirk Muir, 2005, "Consequences of U.S. Fiscal Consolidation for the U.S. Current Account" in *United States: Selected Issues,* IMF Country Report No. 05/258 (July 2005), available at http://www.imf.org.

Lane, Philip R., and Gian Maria Milesi-Ferretti, 2006, "The External Wealth of Nations Mark II: Revised and Extended Estimates of Foreign Assets and Liabilities, 1970–2004," IMF Working Paper 06/69 (Washington, International Monetary Fund).

Marcel, Valérie, 2006, *Oil Titans: National Oil Companies in the Middle East* (London and Washington: Brookings Institution Press and Chatham House).

CHAPTER 2

COUNTRY AND REGIONAL PERSPECTIVES

Against the backdrop of the global outlook discussed in Chapter 1, this chapter analyzes prospects and policy issues in the major industrial countries and in the main regional groupings of emerging market and developing countries. More extensive discussion of country and regional issues may be found in the IMF's *Regional Economic Outlooks* to be issued in parallel with this report, and in individual country reports available from the IMF website.

United States and Canada: Inflationary Pressures Are Beginning to Rise

Following exceptionally strong growth in early 2006, the pace of expansion in the United States has subsequently moderated. The advance GDP estimate for the second quarter suggests that growth slowed to 2.9 percent, from 5.6 percent in the first quarter. Private consumption growth weakened against the background of higher interest rates, a cooling housing market, high gasoline prices, and lackluster employment gains. Business investment in equipment and software was also surprisingly weak, but net exports contributed positively to growth as imports slowed. For the year as a whole, growth is projected at 3.4 percent, before slowing to 2.9 percent in 2007 (0.4 percentage points below that expected at the time of the April 2006 *World Economic Outlook;* see Table 2.1). Underlying this forecast is the expectation that consumption and residential investment growth will slow further as the housing market weakens, but that business investment should rebound against the background of strong profits and limited spare capacity. Risks, however, are slanted to the downside.

The most likely source of headwinds in the short term is the housing market. Rising house prices have provided a significant boost to consumption, residential investment, and employment in recent years, but the market now looks overvalued and, as mortgage rates have risen, activity has slowed. Mortgage applications have declined sharply from their peak, the supply of homes on the market is rising, homebuilder confidence has fallen to a 15-year low, and house price appreciation has slowed.[1] A further cooling of the market would dampen residential investment and consumption, including through a decline in confidence, a drop in home equity withdrawal, and lower employment in the real estate and related sectors.[2] The impact of slowing house price appreciation on consumption would be reinforced by a further decline in equity prices or an increase in gasoline prices.

Despite the recent slowing in growth, inflationary pressures have begun to edge up as excess capacity in product and labor markets has diminished (and actually been eliminated on some measures), energy prices have risen and begun to feed through into some other prices (particularly transportation), and the restraining effect that globalization has had on inflation in recent years has faded (Figure 2.1).[3]

[1]The year-on-year increase in the price of a new single family home slowed from over 11 percent in September 2005 to 1½ percent in July 2006. The sales price of existing homes, as measured by the Office of Federal Housing Enterprises Oversight (OHFEO), has so far decelerated less dramatically, from a peak of 14 percent in June 2005 to 10 percent in the second quarter of 2006, but other more frequent measures of existing home prices have slowed sharply.

[2]See Box 1.2 of the April 2006 *World Economic Outlook* for an analysis of house prices in industrial countries and the possible impact of a sharp slowing in house price appreciation in the United States on growth. Specifically, the analysis suggested that a slowing in the rate of real house price appreciation from 10 percent to zero could reduce growth in the United States by up to 2 percentage points after one year.

[3]See Chapter III of the April 2006 *World Economic Outlook* for an analysis of the impact of globalization on inflation.

Table 2.1. Advanced Economies: Real GDP, Consumer Prices, and Unemployment
(Annual percent change and percent of labor force)

	Real GDP				Consumer Prices				Unemployment			
	2004	2005	2006	2007	2004	2005	2006	2007	2004	2005	2006	2007
Advanced economies	**3.2**	**2.6**	**3.1**	**2.7**	**2.0**	**2.3**	**2.6**	**2.3**	**6.3**	**6.0**	**5.6**	**5.5**
United States	3.9	3.2	3.4	2.9	2.7	3.4	3.6	2.9	5.5	5.1	4.8	4.9
Euro area[1]	2.1	1.3	2.4	2.0	2.1	2.2	2.3	2.4	8.9	8.6	7.9	7.7
Germany	1.2	0.9	2.0	1.3	1.7	2.0	2.0	2.6	9.2	9.1	8.0	7.8
France	2.0	1.2	2.4	2.3	2.3	1.9	2.0	1.9	9.6	9.5	9.0	8.5
Italy	1.1	—	1.5	1.3	2.3	2.3	2.4	2.1	8.1	7.7	7.6	7.5
Spain	3.1	3.4	3.4	3.0	3.1	3.4	3.8	3.4	11.0	9.2	8.6	8.3
Netherlands	2.0	1.5	2.9	2.9	1.4	1.5	1.7	1.8	4.6	4.9	4.5	3.9
Belgium	2.4	1.5	2.7	2.1	1.9	2.5	2.4	1.9	8.4	8.4	8.2	8.2
Austria	2.4	2.0	2.8	2.3	2.0	2.1	1.8	1.7	4.8	5.2	4.8	4.6
Finland	3.5	2.9	3.5	2.5	0.1	0.8	1.5	1.5	8.8	8.4	7.9	7.8
Greece	4.7	3.7	3.7	3.5	3.0	3.5	3.6	3.5	10.5	9.9	9.7	9.5
Portugal	1.2	0.4	1.2	1.5	2.5	2.1	2.6	2.2	6.7	7.6	7.7	7.6
Ireland	4.3	5.5	5.8	5.6	2.3	2.2	2.8	2.5	4.5	4.3	4.3	4.2
Luxembourg	4.2	4.0	4.0	3.8	2.2	2.5	2.8	2.3	3.9	4.2	4.5	4.7
Japan	2.3	2.6	2.7	2.1	—	–0.6	0.3	0.7	4.7	4.4	4.1	4.0
United Kingdom[1]	3.3	1.9	2.7	2.7	1.3	2.0	2.3	2.4	4.8	4.8	5.3	5.1
Canada	3.3	2.9	3.1	3.0	1.8	2.2	2.2	1.9	7.2	6.8	6.3	6.3
Korea	4.7	4.0	5.0	4.3	3.6	2.7	2.5	2.7	3.7	3.7	3.5	3.3
Australia	3.5	2.5	3.1	3.5	2.3	2.7	3.5	2.9	5.5	5.1	5.0	5.0
Taiwan Province of China	6.1	4.1	4.0	4.2	1.6	2.3	1.7	1.5	4.4	4.1	3.9	3.7
Sweden	3.7	2.7	4.0	2.2	1.0	0.8	1.6	1.8	5.5	5.8	4.5	4.3
Switzerland	2.1	1.9	3.0	1.9	0.8	1.2	0.9	1.2	3.5	3.4	2.6	2.5
Hong Kong SAR	8.6	7.3	6.0	5.5	–0.4	0.9	2.3	2.5	6.9	5.7	4.6	4.0
Denmark	1.9	3.2	2.7	2.3	1.2	1.8	1.8	2.0	6.4	5.7	4.8	4.9
Norway	3.1	2.3	2.4	2.8	0.4	1.6	2.3	2.0	4.5	4.6	3.9	3.9
Israel	4.8	5.2	4.1	4.4	–0.4	1.3	2.8	2.0	10.3	9.0	8.7	8.5
Singapore	8.7	6.4	6.9	4.5	1.7	0.5	1.8	1.7	3.4	3.1	2.7	2.7
New Zealand[2]	4.4	2.3	1.3	1.7	2.3	3.0	3.8	3.4	3.9	3.7	3.9	4.5
Cyprus	3.9	3.7	3.5	3.8	2.3	2.6	3.0	2.3	3.6	5.2	3.0	3.0
Iceland	8.2	5.5	4.0	1.0	3.2	4.0	6.1	4.5	3.1	2.1	1.5	1.9
Memorandum												
Major advanced economies	3.0	2.4	2.9	2.5	2.0	2.3	2.6	2.3	6.3	6.0	5.7	5.6
Newly industrialized Asian economies	5.9	4.5	4.9	4.4	2.4	2.2	2.2	2.2	4.2	4.0	3.7	3.4

[1]Based on Eurostat's harmonized index of consumer prices.
[2]Consumer prices excluding interest rate components.

Headline and core (excluding food and energy) CPI inflation rates have moved higher—indeed the core CPI increased by 3.5 percent (annualized rate) during May–July 2006, the fastest pace since mid-1995—and inflation expectations have risen, albeit modestly. Wage gains has also accelerated, and with productivity growth slowing, unit labor cost growth has picked up.

Against this background, the Federal Reserve increased the Federal funds rate by 25 basis points to 5.25 percent at its June policy meeting but left rates unchanged at its August meeting, while cautioning that inflation risks remain. The future path of the monetary policy stance is now dependent on what incoming data suggest about the balance of the competing risks to growth and inflation. Nevertheless, given the importance of keeping inflation expectations firmly in check, some further policy tightening may still be needed. There will also be a premium on the Federal Reserve clearly communicating its policy intentions, and a more explicit statement of its medium-term inflation objective may be helpful in this regard.

With the U.S. current account deficit expected to reach nearly 7 percent of GDP next year, boosting national saving in the United States—through fiscal consolidation

Table 2.2. Advanced Economies: Current Account Positions
(Percent of GDP)

	2004	2005	2006	2007
Advanced economies	**–0.8**	**–1.4**	**–1.6**	**–1.7**
United States	–5.7	–6.4	–6.6	–6.9
Euro area[1]	0.9	—	–0.1	–0.2
Germany	3.7	4.1	4.2	4.0
France	–0.3	–1.6	–1.7	–1.7
Italy	–0.9	–1.6	–1.4	–1.0
Spain	–5.3	–7.4	–8.3	–8.7
Netherlands	8.9	6.3	7.6	7.9
Belgium	3.4	2.7	2.8	2.7
Austria	0.2	1.2	1.5	1.7
Finland	7.8	5.1	5.1	4.6
Greece	–6.2	–7.8	–8.1	–8.0
Portugal	–7.3	–9.3	–9.8	–9.6
Ireland	–0.6	–2.6	–3.0	–3.2
Luxembourg	10.5	9.7	8.2	8.2
Japan	3.8	3.6	3.7	3.5
United Kingdom	–1.6	–2.2	–2.4	–2.3
Canada	2.1	2.3	2.0	1.9
Korea	4.1	2.1	0.4	0.3
Australia	–6.3	–6.0	–5.6	–5.3
Taiwan Province of China	5.7	4.7	5.8	5.9
Sweden	6.8	6.0	5.8	5.6
Switzerland	14.1	13.8	13.3	13.3
Hong Kong SAR	9.5	11.4	8.7	7.8
Denmark	2.3	3.0	2.2	2.3
Norway	13.6	16.8	19.9	22.2
Israel	2.6	2.9	1.2	1.0
Singapore	24.5	28.5	28.5	27.3
New Zealand	–6.7	–8.9	–9.6	–9.1
Cyprus	–5.7	–5.8	–4.6	–3.5
Iceland	–10.1	–16.5	–12.5	–4.4
Memorandum				
Major advanced economies	–1.6	–2.2	–2.4	–2.6
Euro area[2]	0.6	–0.3	–0.1	–0.1
Newly industrialized Asian economies	7.0	6.0	5.0	4.9

[1]Calculated as the sum of the balances of individual euro area countries.
[2]Corrected for reporting discrepancies in intra-area transactions.

and increased private saving—is a key component of the multilateral strategy to reduce global imbalances (Table 2.2). Encouragingly, recent fiscal performance has been better than expected, largely because of unexpected revenue buoyancy, the permanency of which remains to be seen. The U.S. administration now expects to achieve its goal of halving the federal deficit by FY2008, a year ahead of schedule. Nevertheless, much remains to be done, given that a number of factors not fully reflected in the administration's forecast could boost the deficit (including pressures to curtail the rising impact of the

Figure 2.1. United States: Are Inflationary Pressures Building?

As excess capacity in product and labor markets has diminished, inflation in the United States has begun to edge up.

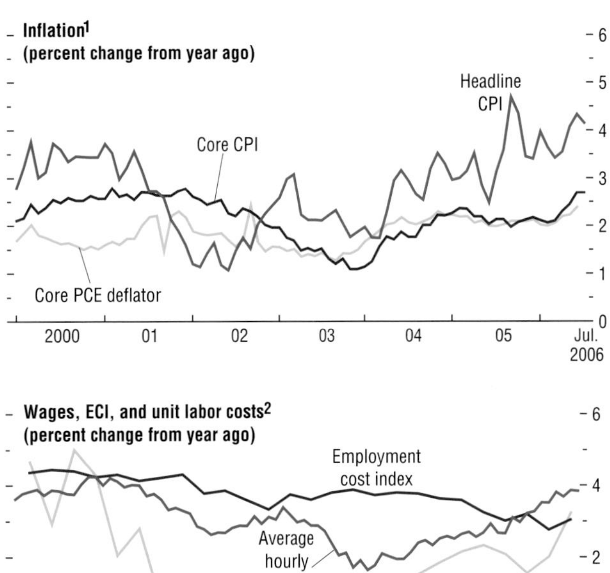

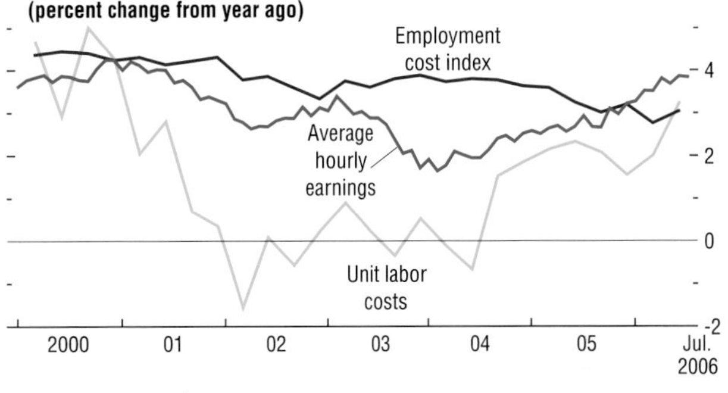

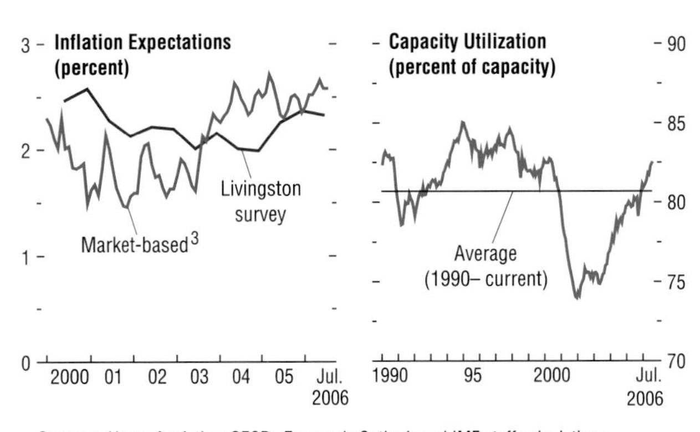

Sources: Haver Analytics; OECD, *Economic Outlook;* and IMF staff calculations.
[1]Core CPI excludes food and energy. PCE refers to personal consumption expenditure.
[2]Wages as average hourly earnings of total private industries, employment cost index of civilian workers, and unit labor costs of non-farm business sector.
[3]Differential between 10-year nominal treasury note yield and treasury inflation-protected securities (TIPS).

Alternative Minimum Tax, or AMT, and the costs of the ongoing military operations in Iraq and Afghanistan). Setting a more ambitious deficit reduction path—for example, a goal of achieving budget balance (excluding social security) over the next five years, requiring fiscal consolidation of some ¾ percent of GDP a year—would help provide a firmer basis for the United States to face future demographic pressures, put the budget in a stronger position to respond to future economic downturns, and help reduce global imbalances. The likely impact that this accelerated fiscal consolidation would have on growth—both domestically and overseas—in the short term could be partly mitigated if it were part of joint policy action to tackle global imbalances and if it provided scope for an easier monetary policy stance (see Chapter 1, Box 1.3).

The focus of fiscal consolidation appropriately remains on the expenditure side, although the unprecedented and back-loaded compression of discretionary non-defense spending already assumed in the budget will make further savings difficult. Revenue measures therefore should not be ruled out, particularly initiatives that broaden the revenue base—including a reduction in tax preferences, such as for mortgage interest and other proposals by the President's Commission on Tax Reform—or help achieve other objectives, such as higher taxes on energy that would lower oil consumption. Fiscal consolidation needs to be supported by entitlement reform to put the Social Security and Medicare systems on a sustainable long-term footing in the face of population aging and rising health care costs.

Regarding private saving, some increase is already built into the projections as the housing market slows. In terms of policies, the administration has introduced health saving accounts that should raise incentives for household saving. Recently passed pension legislation will also help in this regard, both by making it easier for employers to offer defined-contribution (401(k)) plans that require employees to "opt-out" rather than "opt-in," which should lead to higher enrollment in such plans, and by requiring companies to reduce funding gaps in their defined-benefit pension plans. Moving to a tax system with a greater reliance on a consumption tax rather than taxes on income would also increase incentives to save, while greater transparency about likely future shortfalls in the social security system and in private pension plans may increase awareness of the need for higher saving to ensure adequate retirement income.

The Canadian economy continues to perform robustly, benefiting from its strong macroeconomic policy framework and the boom in global commodity prices. The main risks to the outlook are external, including the possibility of a sharper-than-expected slowing in the U.S. economy and a disorderly adjustment of global imbalances that could result in a substantial further appreciation of the Canadian dollar. With wage growth decelerating and CPI inflation well contained, the Bank of Canada recently halted the process of monetary tightening that had begun in September 2005. A strong fiscal position remains at the center of the new government's economic policies, with the FY2006/07 budget including welcome commitments to lower public debt (to 25 percent of GDP by FY2013/14), contain expenditure growth, and reduce the tax burden on the corporate sector.

Western Europe: Structural Reforms Remain the Key to Stronger Growth

Economic activity in Western Europe is strengthening. In the euro area, the recovery has gained further traction, with real GDP growth accelerating to 3.6 percent (annualized rate) in the second quarter of 2006. Growth is increasingly being driven by domestic demand, particularly investment. Second quarter growth accelerated in Germany—helped by a boost from the World Cup—and France, and remained robust in Spain. In the United Kingdom, where the economic cycle is more advanced, growth was around 3 percent in the first half of 2006. Robust employment creation and the stabilization of the housing market underpinned consumption spending, while investment remained strong.

Looking forward, recent indicators suggest that the pace of expansion in the euro area should be sustained during the second half of 2006, and real GDP growth is now projected at 2.4 percent for the year as a whole, up from 1.3 percent in 2005, before slowing to 2 percent in 2007. Corporate investment is expected to remain buoyant—among the three largest economies, this pickup should be strongest in Germany, where profitability has recovered and corporate restructuring is well advanced, and weakest in Italy where corporate debt is still rising and profitability is weaker. Consumption growth is expected to be more moderate given modest employment and wage growth (the announced 3 percentage point increase in the VAT rate in Germany is expected to boost consumption in late 2006 and reduce it in early 2007). In the United Kingdom, growth is expected at 2.7 percent this year and next, broadly in line with potential.

There are a number of uncertainties to the outlook. On the upside, robust business confidence in the euro area could generate stronger-than-expected investment and employment growth. On the downside, against the background of large global imbalances, Europe remains exposed to the possibility of sharp currency appreciation that could undercut exports and investment in the traded goods sector and impose capital losses on holders of U.S. dollar assets. Further increases in energy prices would reduce disposable incomes and slow consumption, while recent falls in equity markets, if sustained, could also weigh on business and consumer confidence going forward. Lastly, house prices in Spain, Ireland, and the United Kingdom still look elevated, and could come under pressure in a rising interest rate environment.

A critical challenge for Europe is to ensure that the current cyclical upswing translates into a sustained and long-lasting expansion so that it can deal effectively with the domestic problems it faces—particularly the need to strengthen fiscal positions ahead of the onset of population aging—and contribute to an orderly unwinding of global imbalances. Over the past decade, growth in Europe has fallen short of that in the United States (although some individual countries have outperformed the United States). Although increases in labor utilization have been similar—with a stronger rise in the employment ratio in Europe offset by a larger decline in hours worked—productivity growth has declined in Europe while it has increased in the United States (Figure 2.2). The decline in productivity growth in Europe is widespread across sectors, reflecting extensive product and labor market regulations that limit competition and impede the movement of resources between industries in response to technological change and globalization. Indeed, in the United Kingdom where labor and product market reforms are relatively advanced, productivity growth has been stronger. The productivity growth differential with the United States, however, has been particularly large in three sectors—manufacturing, financial services (and more so if the insurance subsector is excluded), and retail/wholesale—where substantial gains have been achieved in the United States as a result of industry consolidation and the greater use of information technology.[4]

Under the Lisbon Strategy, EU countries have agreed to address existing impediments to stronger productivity growth, but implementation needs to be accelerated, particularly in sectors where productivity growth in Europe is lagging.[5] For example, under the European Commission's

[4]See Inklaar, O'Mahony, and Timmer (2005) and Timmer and van Ark (2005), for detailed analyses of how differences in producing and using information technology have affected productivity differentials between the United States and Europe. On the other hand, Gordon and Dew-Becker (2005), argue that the productivity slowdown in Europe is too widespread to be solely due to IT.

[5]Chapter IV In the April 2003 *World Economic Outlook* ("Unemployment and Labor Market Institutions: Why Reforms Pay Off") found that labor and product market reforms could increase real GDP in the euro area by 10 percent in the long run. A report by the European Commission (2005) found that the implementation of reforms in the Lisbon strategy could increase potential growth in the European Union by around ¾ percentage point a year.

Figure 2.2. Western Europe: Boosting Productivity Is the Key to Stronger Growth
(Percent change)

Labor productivity growth in Europe has been disappointing over the past decade. Europe has underperformed in the manufacturing, financial services, and retail sectors compared to the United States.

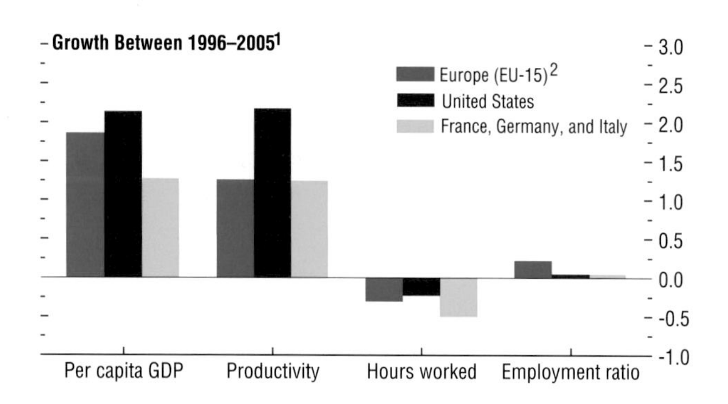

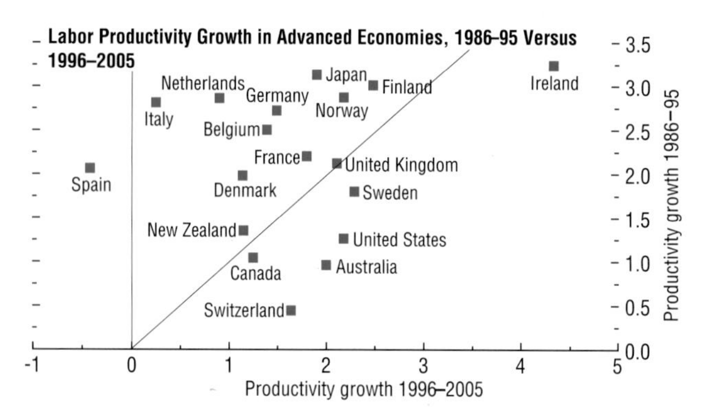

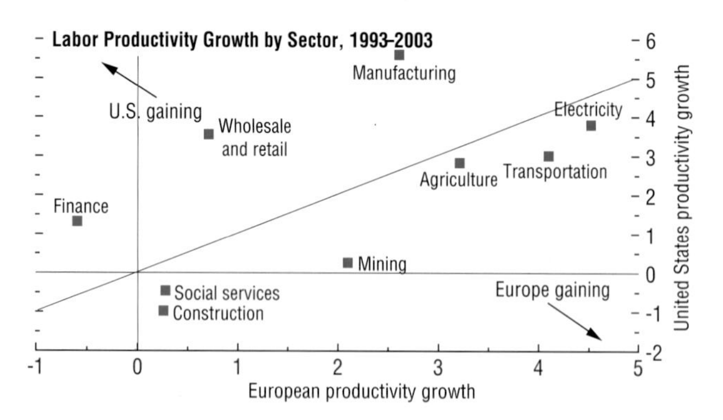

Sources: OECD, *Economic Outlook;* and IMF staff calculations.
[1]Employment ratio defined as employed persons as a percent of working age population.
[2]Austria, Belgium, Denmark, Finland, France, Germany, Greece, Ireland, Italy, Luxembourg, the Netherlands, Portugal, Spain, Sweden, and the United Kingdom.

Financial Services Action Plan considerable progress has been made in the integration and harmonization of the financial sector, but further steps are needed to reduce barriers to competition across Europe. These include speeding up the integration of payments, clearing, and settlement systems, reducing obstacles to cross-border mergers—including by reducing differences in legal, regulatory, and supervisory frameworks across countries—reducing state involvement in the financial system, and integrating mortgage markets. In the retail sector, the easing of regulations that limit the establishment of new stores and impede cross-border competition would boost efficiency.

Fiscal outcomes in the euro area were generally better than expected in 2005, with the aggregate deficit declining by ½ percent of GDP. A more modest fiscal adjustment is expected this year based on published budgets, and two countries (Italy and Portugal) are expected to have fiscal deficits in excess of 3 percent of GDP. In Italy, the fiscal situation is particularly difficult, with the general government deficit projected at 4 percent of GDP this year, although strong revenue growth provides scope to achieve a better outcome if expenditure is firmly controlled. Turning to 2007, on current policies little change is projected in the deficit, and achieving the targeted reduction to 2.8 percent of GDP will depend on the implementation of structural fiscal reforms covering key expenditure areas.

The current upswing provides an important opportunity for policymakers to make progress in further reducing fiscal deficits. Under the reformed Stability and Growth Pact (SGP), most countries in the euro area are aiming for budget balance or even a small surplus over the medium term. Yet how such consolidation will be achieved remains largely unspecified, and firm plans still need to be put in place to give credibility to these commitments. Welfare reforms and reductions in the government wage bill are key, not only to lower deficits, but also to provide room to cut taxes on labor and thereby boost employment. In Spain, while the budget is in surplus, a tighter short-term fiscal policy stance would help contain existing demand pressures.

Population aging will put heavy pressure on pension and healthcare spending over the medium term, with European Commission estimates suggesting that age-related spending will rise by close to 4 percent of GDP by 2050. Reforms to pension systems are under way in France, Germany, and Italy—yet more will be needed. An important dynamic of pension reforms is that demographic change—by increasing the political weight of older persons who may have the most to lose—could make the implementation of such reforms more difficult in the future.

Turning to monetary policy, with inflation running above its "below but close to" 2 percent objective, credit growth remaining strong, and the economic recovery solidifying, the European Central Bank has appropriately withdrawn monetary stimulus, raising interest rates by a cumulative 100 basis points since December. Looking forward, further interest rate increases will likely be needed to maintain price stability over the medium term if the expansion develops as expected. But, with underlying inflationary pressures still well contained—unit labor costs are subdued, core inflation (excluding food and energy) is around 1½ percent, and inflation expectations are well-anchored—policymakers can afford to be cautious in tightening the monetary policy stance, all the more so given the risk of euro appreciation and weaker growth in the United States.

In the United Kingdom, after holding its policy rate constant for a year, the Bank of England raised its rate in early August by 25 basis points to 4.75 percent. Future monetary policy decisions are delicately balanced. While risks to aggregate demand are skewed to the downside, particularly in 2007, there is also a possibility that energy price increases may yet give rise to second-round effects on inflation. On fiscal policy, the budget deficit is expected to narrow slightly, reflecting strong revenues from higher energy prices and the booming financial sector. Over the medium term, fiscal consolidation will depend critically on restraint of current spending, the plans for which are being developed as part of the 2007 Comprehensive Spending Review. The fiscal position in the United Kingdom is less sensitive to population aging than elsewhere in the European Union, but with the public pension being considerably less generous than in other European countries, concerns have centered on whether individuals are saving enough to provide an adequate retirement income. As suggested by the Pensions Commission, the introduction of a national defined contribution scheme with automatic enrollment and low operating costs may be useful to boost private savings.

Japan: Monetary Policy Adjusts to the End of Deflation

In Japan, after a solid first quarter, real GDP growth eased in the second quarter of 2006, owing primarily to inventory decumulation, a sharp contraction in public investment, and drag from net exports. Nevertheless, the expansion remains well-founded as private final domestic demand, the main driving force since 2005, has grown at a solid pace. Private fixed investment in particular continues to be buoyant, underpinned by robust profits and a turnaround in bank credit, while private consumption is increasing at a more moderate rate, as labor income gains have been modest. Growth is projected at 2.7 percent for 2006 as a whole, moderating to just above 2 percent in 2007. The near-term risks to the outlook are broadly balanced. On the upside, growth could be boosted by stronger-than-expected domestic demand, as confidence remains high and the pace of household income growth may pick up with the continued expansion. On the downside, the economy is vulnerable to adverse external developments, including a further rise in oil prices, a cooling U.S. economy, or a sharp appreciation of the yen against the backdrop of a disorderly unwinding of global imbalances.

Indications are growing that after seven years of falling prices, Japan has finally escaped from

Figure 2.3. Japan: Balancing Inflation and Deflation Risks

(Percent change from a year ago unless otherwise stated)

The future path of policy interest rates in Japan needs to balance risks of deflation against those of rising inflation. Measures of expected future inflation suggest that inflation remains well anchored at low levels. At the same time, some deflation risks remain.

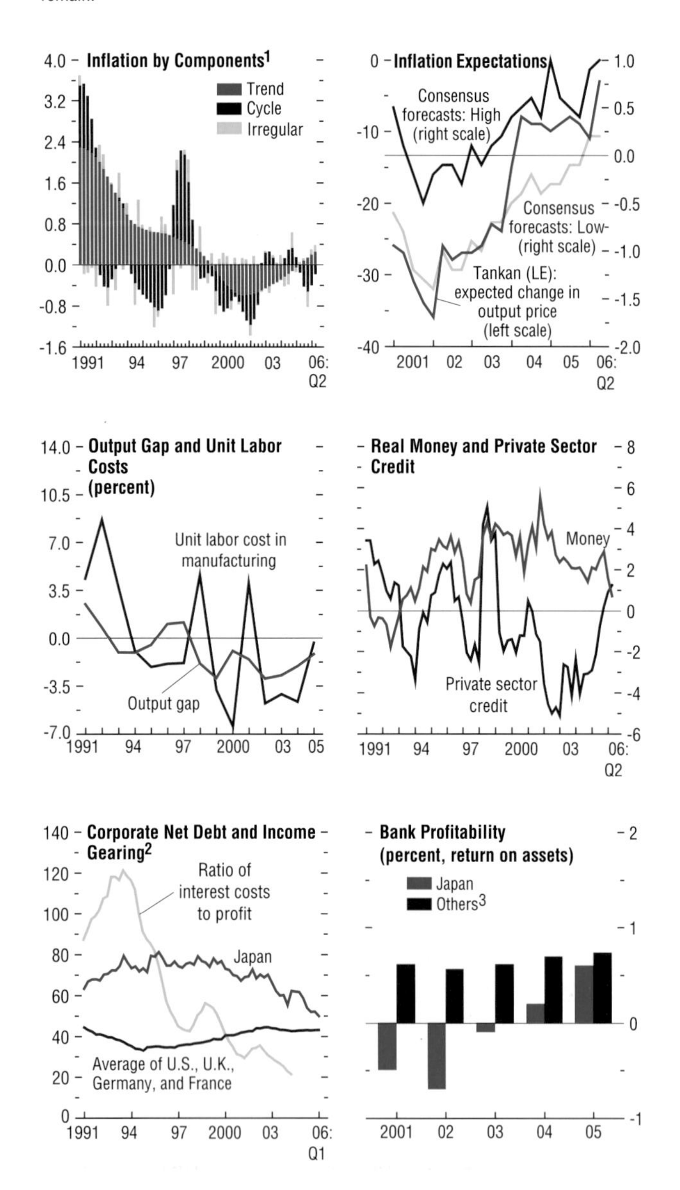

Sources: Bank of Japan; Consensus Economics, Inc.; Haver Analytics; IMF, *International Financial Statistics;* and IMF staff calculations.

[1]Derived with a bandpass filter.

[2]Corporate net debt, expressed as percent of GDP, defined as financial liabilities less financial assets of the nonfinancial corporate sector. Ratio of interest costs to profit, expressed in percent, measured as four-quarter moving average.

[3]Averages of return on assets for Canada, France, Germany, Italy, Spain, the United Kingdom, and the United States.

entrenched deflation. Year-on-year changes in the headline and core CPI have been positive in recent months, with core inflation at about ¼ percent. Producer prices have led the CPI transition by about one and a half years because of global price increases for raw materials and industrial supplies. While the GDP deflator continues to decline on a year-on-year basis (although primarily reflecting higher prices of commodity imports), changes in the final domestic demand deflator have begun to enter positive territory.

With the expansion now well established and favorable prospects for low, but steady, inflation in 2006–07, the normalization of monetary policy has become the key near-term macroeconomic policy challenge. Since March 2006, the Bank of Japan has largely reversed the extra-injection of bank liquidity under its former policy of quantitative easing. The nominal policy rate, which was raised to 25 basis points in mid-July after having been pegged at zero since early 2001, will eventually have to be raised further to more normal levels. However, with actual inflation barely positive and estimates of trend inflation—a measure of expected average inflation—just above zero, risks of a relapse into deflation in response to an adverse shock, such as a substantial slowing in global growth, cannot be ignored (Figure 2.3). The future path of the policy interest rate, therefore, needs to carefully balance the risks of a return to deflation against those of the possibility of accelerating inflation. The risks of the latter at this stage appear limited given that inflation expectations are anchored at very low levels, unit labor cost growth is subdued, and the very rapid expansion of base money until recently has not translated into strong broad liquidity and/or credit growth.

Against this background, the Bank of Japan appropriately plans to err on the side of caution and raise policy rates gradually. In support of such an approach, it would be helpful for the Bank of Japan to define its medium-term inflation goals clearly so as to avoid any uncertainty about its intentions. Recently, the central bank has reported that the "understanding of price stability among members of the Policy Board" is annual CPI inflation of 0 to 2 percent. This range, however, is not a target to be achieved over a pre-set time horizon, and it will be reviewed annually. As inflation becomes established, it would be desirable for the range (or its floor) to rise over time since a lower bound of zero for the range would leave open a risk that adverse disturbances could push the economy back into deflation. In addition, more explicit communication on the risks and policies at the lower end of the current range for inflation would guide market expectations and further clarify the Bank of Japan's policy intentions.

Restoring fiscal sustainability is the key medium-term macroeconomic policy challenge. Despite fiscal adjustment during 2003–05—the deficit (excluding social security) was reduced by about 3 percentage points to 5.3 percent of GDP in 2005—gross and net public debt continue to rise and, at around 180 and 90 percent of GDP, respectively, are among the highest in industrial countries. Current fiscal policy plans aim to achieve a primary surplus for the central and local government by FY2011. This adjustment, however, would not be sufficient to stabilize net government debt over the six-year period, given current estimates of potential output growth, which are depressed by the low rate of labor force growth (see Chapter 3, Box 3.1). IMF staff estimates suggest that an additional adjustment of about 2 percent of GDP over this period would be necessary to stabilize net debt, an important objective given the high public debt ratios and prospects of growing pressures on expenditure from the rapidly aging population. While adjustment measures so far have been concentrated on the expenditure side, future efforts likely would need to include some revenue measures. Raising the consumption tax rate, which is currently low by international standards, and broadening the income tax base would help to generate revenues with the least adverse effects on underlying growth.

Structural fiscal reforms should be complemented by broader reform efforts aimed at raising productivity growth. If appropriately designed, such a package would have a mutually reinforcing impact on fiscal sustainability. The priorities are reforms of government financial institutions—the impending privatization of Japan Post is a welcome step forward; steps to strengthen competition in the services sector (e.g., by facilitating market access in the retail sector); and enhanced labor market flexibility (including through higher female labor force participation, and increased pension portability to bolster mobility across firms and sectors). It will also be important to fully complete the financial and corporate sector reform agenda. Leverage in the nonfinancial corporate sector has declined substantially, but it remains high by international standards—especially in small and medium-size enterprises outside the manufacturing sector—and higher corporate profitability partly reflects very low nominal interest costs. Similarly, while balance sheets of large banks have improved with declines in nonperforming loans, progress by regional banks has been more limited, and bank profitability, while improved, remains below average in international comparison.

Emerging Asia: China's Growth Spurt Benefits the Region but Carries Risks

Growth continues to run above 8 percent in emerging Asia, with much of the momentum due to vibrant expansions in China and India (Table 2.3). In China, real GDP grew by 11.3 percent (year-on-year) in the second quarter of 2006, with a renewed acceleration in investment growth and surging net exports. In the newly industrialized economies (NIEs), growth has strengthened since mid-2005 with a pickup in exports, especially of electronic goods due to rapid growth in China and the strong global economy. In contrast, growth has started to slow in most of the ASEAN-4 countries, owing mainly to the effects of higher oil prices and monetary policy tightening in response to rising inflation.

The outlook is for continued strong growth of 8¼ percent in 2006–07—about ½ percentage point higher than projected at the time

Table 2.3. Selected Asian Countries: Real GDP, Consumer Prices, and Current Account Balance
(Annual percent change unless noted otherwise)

	Real GDP				Consumer Prices[1]				Current Account Balance[2]			
	2004	2005	2006	2007	2004	2005	2006	2007	2004	2005	2006	2007
Emerging Asia[3]	**8.5**	**8.5**	**8.3**	**8.2**	**3.9**	**3.4**	**3.6**	**3.5**	**3.9**	**4.7**	**4.3**	**4.2**
China	10.1	10.2	10.0	10.0	3.9	1.8	1.5	2.2	3.6	7.2	7.2	7.2
South Asia[4]	**7.8**	**8.2**	**7.9**	**7.2**	**4.2**	**4.8**	**6.0**	**5.6**	**0.3**	**–1.5**	**–2.2**	**–2.8**
India	8.0	8.5	8.3	7.3	3.9	4.0	5.6	5.3	0.2	–1.5	–2.1	–2.7
Pakistan	7.4	8.0	6.2	7.0	4.6	9.3	7.9	7.3	1.8	–1.4	–3.9	–4.6
Bangladesh	6.1	6.2	6.2	6.2	6.1	7.0	6.8	6.1	–0.3	–0.5	–0.3	–0.7
ASEAN-4	**5.8**	**5.1**	**5.0**	**5.6**	**4.6**	**7.5**	**8.6**	**4.5**	**4.0**	**2.8**	**3.1**	**3.0**
Indonesia	5.1	5.6	5.2	6.0	6.1	10.5	13.0	5.9	0.6	0.3	0.2	0.6
Thailand	6.2	4.5	4.5	5.0	2.8	4.5	4.9	2.6	4.2	–2.1	–0.8	–1.3
Philippines	6.2	5.0	5.0	5.4	6.0	7.6	6.7	5.0	1.9	2.4	2.4	1.7
Malaysia	7.2	5.2	5.5	5.8	1.4	3.0	3.8	2.7	12.6	15.2	15.6	15.7
Newly industrialized Asian economies	**5.9**	**4.5**	**4.9**	**4.4**	**2.4**	**2.2**	**2.2**	**2.2**	**7.0**	**6.0**	**5.0**	**4.9**
Korea	4.7	4.0	5.0	4.3	3.6	2.7	2.5	2.7	4.1	2.1	0.4	0.3
Taiwan Province of China	6.1	4.1	4.0	4.2	1.6	2.3	1.7	1.5	5.7	4.7	5.8	5.9
Hong Kong SAR	8.6	7.3	6.0	5.5	–0.4	0.9	2.3	2.5	9.5	11.4	8.7	7.8
Singapore	8.7	6.4	6.9	4.5	1.7	0.5	1.8	1.7	24.5	28.5	28.5	27.3

[1]In accordance with standard practice in the *World Economic Outlook*, movements in consumer prices are indicated as annual averages rather than as December/December changes, as is the practice in some countries.
[2]Percent of GDP.
[3]Consists of developing Asia, the newly industrialized Asian economies, and Mongolia.
[4]The country composition of this regional group is set out in Table F in the Statistical Appendix.

of the last *World Economic Outlook*—reflecting more favorable global economic conditions, continued high growth in China, and moderate deceleration in India after the strong momentum in 2005 and early 2006. Growth in the NIEs is set to slow, especially in 2007, when growth in the import demand of advanced economies is projected to decelerate. In contrast, a modest rebound in activity is expected in the ASEAN-4 countries as the factors behind the recent slowing recede.

The near-term risks to the outlook are broadly balanced for the region, albeit with some differences across countries, depending on external and financial vulnerabilities on the one hand and on the exposure to growth in the advanced economies on the other. On the upside, there is the possibility of even faster-than-projected growth in China—if the recent pace is maintained—and in India. A higher growth rate in China would elevate growth elsewhere in the region—but especially in Hong Kong SAR, Indonesia, Korea, the Philippines, Singapore, and Thailand—given the strengthening intra-regional trade linkages (Figure 2.4). On the downside, risks include the possibility of an investment boom-bust cycle in China and its regional impact, higher oil prices, the heightened threat of protectionist action in advanced economies following the deadlock of the Doha Round, an outbreak of an avian flu pandemic, and slower growth in the advanced economies, especially Japan and the United States. The latter remain the final destinations for a substantial share of the region's final goods exports, and business cycle fluctuations in the United States and Japan still affect the region to a considerable degree, especially in the NIEs. In addition, tighter monetary policy to head off inflationary pressures may lower growth prospects in the region. The region would also be vulnerable to a deterioration in international financial market conditions, although, compared to other market regions and their own past, most economies in emerging Asia generally now seem better positioned to weather such a deterioration. External vulnerabilities in particular have been substantially reduced throughout the region, given persistent current account surpluses and substantial reserve accumulation in recent years.

Headline inflation has increased with higher oil prices, but most countries have succeeded so far in restraining core inflation with quite small increases in nominal policy rates, helped by real currency appreciation that reflects strong external positions, although price controls and energy subsidies have also contributed in some countries. Together with declining currency risk premiums, this has provided for narrowing real interest differentials against the major currencies, and the generally low real interest rates throughout the region have supported domestic demand. However, to head off risks of rising inflation, policymakers in the region may need to respond to increasing interest rates in the major currencies areas—especially Japan—and to more testing international financial market conditions, with some likely adverse effects on growth. In India, inflation has picked up with rising oil prices and strong domestic demand. While the Reserve Bank of India has raised interest rates in recent months, further tightening may be needed to resist inflationary pressures.

With robust domestic demand growth in many countries and high oil prices, the regional current account surplus is expected to moderate by about ½ of a percentage point to around 4¼ percent of GDP in 2006–07. Within the region, current account performance varies considerably. In Korea and, more recently, Indonesia, current account surpluses have declined, while Thailand and India have experienced a turnaround to a deficit. In all of these countries, exchange rate flexibility has increased in the past two years, often in the context of inflation-targeting monetary policy frameworks, while domestic demand has begun to play a more prominent role in output growth. Nevertheless, private investment remains relatively weak in many countries, and reforms aimed at enhancing the business environment are particularly important at this juncture. Priorities include measures to deepen and integrate capital markets across the region and steps to lower regulatory burdens.

Figure 2.4. Emerging Asia: The Regional Impact of China's Rapid Growth

The strong growth momentum in emerging Asia owes much to vibrant growth in China, given its increasingly prominent role in intraregional trade, and India. Nevertheless, growth fluctuations in the advanced economies still have a considerable impact on fluctuations in the region, since markets in the advanced economies remain important destinations for the region's exports of final goods.

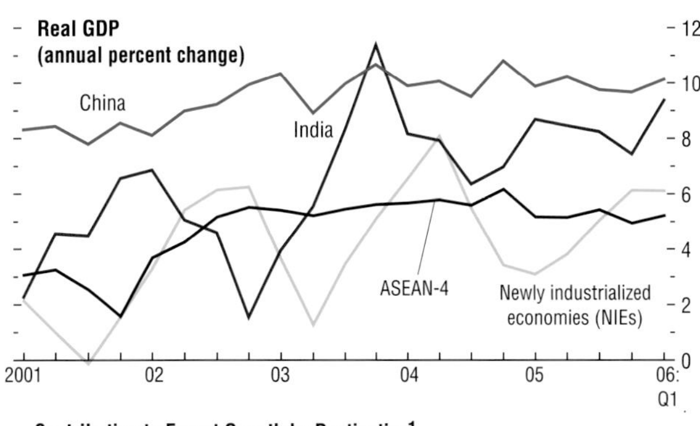

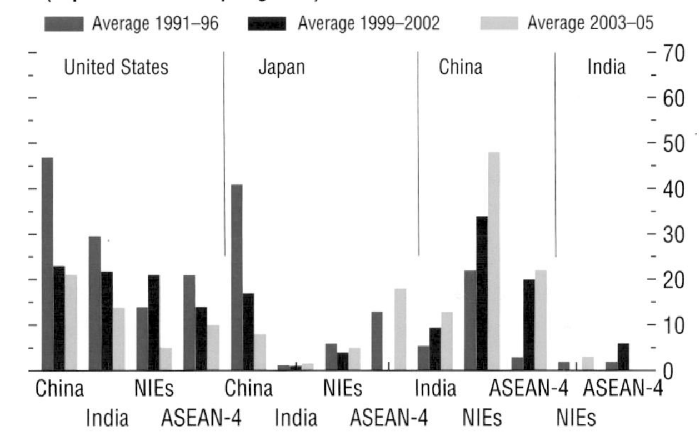

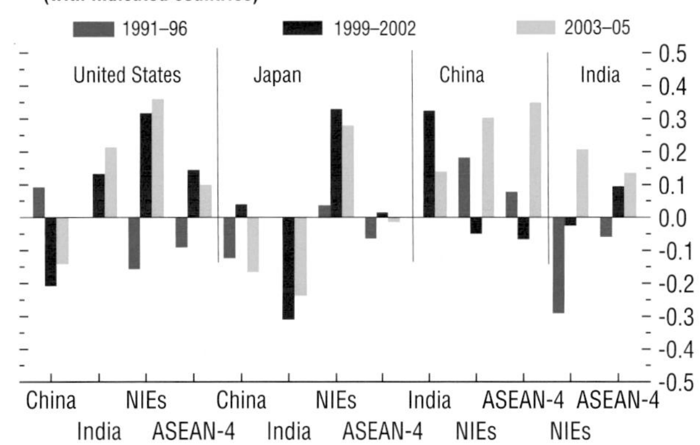

Source: IMF staff calculations.

[1]Excluding intragroup trade for the NIEs and ASEAN-4 group countries.

[2]In the case of the NIEs and ASEAN-4, the values represent the medians of the correlations coefficients of all countries in the group.

In contrast, China's current account surplus continued to rise in 2005 and the first half of 2006 and now accounts for some 70 percent of the regional surplus of about $260 billion (annual basis). Structural factors, including capacity expansion in sectors producing import substitutes, account for some of the rise in China's surplus, but continued exceptionally strong export growth has also contributed. While there has been some limited flexibility in the renminbi exchange rate in recent months, in current circumstances—with the large current account surplus continuing to rise and capital inflows remaining strong—more substantial appreciation of the currency would help to reduce the current account surplus and give the central bank greater control of domestic monetary conditions. The central bank's current focus on limiting renminbi fluctuations against the dollar makes effective liquidity control difficult, and direct measures of monetary control and limited interest rate increases have not been sufficient to restrain strong credit growth. The latter has contributed to concerns about the possibility of an investment boom-bust cycle, as the current exceptionally rapid investment growth could lead to overcapacity, falling profits, and balance sheet problems in the corporate and financial sectors. The move toward greater exchange rate flexibility would have to be supported by a continuation of the complementary financial sector reform currently under way, which would strengthen the economy's capacity to cope with greater interest rate and exchange rate movements. Exchange rate appreciation would also bolster households' purchasing power, which, together with reforms to the pension, health, and education systems and to the financial sector, would boost consumption.[6]

Policymakers across the region should take advantage of the broadly favorable growth outlook to implement structural reforms aimed at promoting fiscal sustainability and reducing vulnerabilities. In countries with high public debt and/or budget deficits (particularly India, Pakistan, and the Philippines), fiscal positions need to be put on a sustainable medium-term footing. In the Philippines and, to a lesser extent, Indonesia, the structure of public debt is associated with foreign currency risks, and continued fiscal consolidation and improvements in the composition of this debt would contribute to reducing the vulnerability to swings in global investor sentiment and enhance monetary policy credibility. In India, strong spending pressures have emerged, limiting fiscal adjustment in FY2006/07 after more substantial consolidation in recent years. With the general government deficit and debt still high, further consolidation is clearly warranted at both the central and state government levels, including through measures aimed at broadening the tax base and reducing subsidies.

Asia has benefited from impressive high growth over an extended period. Chapter 3, "Asia Rising: Patterns of Economic Development and Growth," analyzes this experience and looks at the policy implications. Drawing on the experience of fast-growing Asian countries at various stages of the catch-up process, it argues that policymakers need to meet a number of challenges to ensure that rapid growth in the region is sustained. First, steps to promote trade openness, widespread access to education, and financial sector development and to encourage entrepreneurship (such as reducing the costs of starting a business) will be important to facilitate the continued shift of resources out of agriculture to industry and services. Second, productivity growth in the services sector would be boosted by policies to strengthen market access and competition. Third, Asian countries that are the least advanced in the catch-up process can learn from the experience of other countries in the region, including the important role that institutional quality, financial development, business climate, and trade openness play in creating a favorable environment conducive to capital accumulation and productivity growth.

[6]See Chapter 5 of the IMF's September 2006 *Regional Outlook* for the Asia and Pacific region for evidence of lower-than-expected consumption in China against a benchmark estimate based on standard determinants.

Table 2.4. Selected Western Hemisphere Countries: Real GDP, Consumer Prices, and Current Account Balance
(Annual percent change unless noted otherwise)

	Real GDP				Consumer Prices[1]				Current Account Balance[2]			
	2004	2005	2006	2007	2004	2005	2006	2007	2004	2005	2006	2007
Western Hemisphere	**5.7**	**4.3**	**4.8**	**4.2**	**6.5**	**6.3**	**5.6**	**5.2**	**0.9**	**1.4**	**1.2**	**1.0**
Mercosur[3]	**6.0**	**4.2**	**4.8**	**4.5**	**5.7**	**7.1**	**6.2**	**5.6**	**1.9**	**1.7**	**0.7**	**0.5**
Argentina	9.0	9.2	8.0	6.0	4.4	9.6	12.3	11.4	2.2	1.9	1.0	0.6
Brazil	4.9	2.3	3.6	4.0	6.6	6.9	4.5	4.1	1.9	1.8	0.6	0.4
Chile	6.2	6.3	5.2	5.5	1.1	3.1	3.5	3.1	1.7	0.6	1.8	0.9
Uruguay	11.8	6.6	4.6	4.2	9.2	4.7	5.9	4.3	0.3	–0.5	–4.3	–3.2
Andean region	**8.0**	**6.3**	**5.7**	**4.1**	**8.4**	**6.4**	**5.7**	**6.1**	**4.0**	**6.6**	**7.0**	**6.7**
Colombia	4.8	5.1	4.8	4.0	5.9	5.0	4.7	4.2	–1.0	–1.6	–1.2	–1.7
Ecuador	7.9	4.7	4.4	3.2	2.7	2.1	3.2	3.0	–0.9	–0.3	4.4	3.7
Peru	5.2	6.4	6.0	5.0	3.7	1.6	2.4	2.5	—	1.3	0.7	0.2
Venezuela	17.9	9.3	7.5	3.7	21.7	15.9	12.1	15.4	12.5	19.1	17.5	17.6
Mexico, Central America, and Caribbean	**4.0**	**3.5**	**4.3**	**3.8**	**7.0**	**4.9**	**4.5**	**4.0**	**–1.4**	**–1.0**	**–0.5**	**–0.8**
Mexico	4.2	3.0	4.0	3.5	4.7	4.0	3.5	3.3	–1.0	–0.6	–0.1	–0.2
Central America[3]	3.9	4.3	4.8	4.4	7.4	8.4	7.4	6.3	–6.3	–5.5	–5.2	–5.1
The Caribbean[3]	2.6	6.1	5.6	4.8	26.5	6.7	8.3	5.8	1.2	0.8	0.9	–1.8

[1]In accordance with standard practice in the *World Economic Outlook*, movements in consumer prices are indicated as annual averages rather than as December/December changes, as is the practice in some countries. The December/December changes in CPI for 2004, 2005, 2006, and 2007 are, respectively, for Brazil (7.6, 5.7, 3.8, and 4.5); Mexico (5.2, 3.3, 3.3, and 3.0); Peru (3.5, 1.5, 2.5, and 2.5) and Uruguay (7.6, 4.9, 5.5, and 4.9).
[2]Percent of GDP.
[3]The country composition of this regional group is set out in Table F in the Statistical Appendix.

Latin America: Continuing to Build Resilience

The economic expansion in Latin America gathered momentum in the first half of this year, with regional GDP on track to rise by 4¾ percent in 2006 as a whole and by 4¼ percent in 2007 (Table 2.4). Moreover, inflation largely remained subdued, anchored by credible monetary policy regimes in most of the larger countries. While external performance has continued to be supported by high prices for key commodity exports, domestic demand has become the main engine of growth. Convergence of inflation to targets has provided room to unwind previous monetary tightening in Brazil and Mexico, supporting a pickup in growth in both countries. In rapidly growing Argentina, the monetary policy stance has been gradually tightened in response to double-digit inflation but remains accommodative. At the same time, public spending has picked up across the region, on the back of continued revenue buoyancy, especially in Venezuela. There have also been signs of a resurgence of private investment, helped by increasing confidence, declining interest rates, and quite rapid increases in bank credit, although investment rates remain far lower than in emerging Asia. Political uncertainty remains a concern, however, reflecting in part questions about the ability of governments in a number of countries to resist populist measures.

Unsettled conditions in global financial markets in May–June 2006 initially dampened Latin American equity prices and exchange rates, particularly in the most liquid markets (e.g., Brazil) or in markets that had previously seen strong price run-ups (e.g., Colombian equities). However, markets have since recovered much of the lost ground, and Latin America's expansionary momentum seems to have been little affected. This resilience seems to reflect in part reduced vulnerabilities, including a shift to current account surpluses, more flexible exchange rate regimes, higher reserve cushions, and strengthened fiscal positions across the region. Nevertheless, recent market pressures have provided a timely reminder that the global context is likely over time to become less friendly to emerging markets, with rising interest rates, less buoyant non-oil commodity prices, and reduced appetite for the riskier assets. This prospect poses the question of what further steps countries in Latin America could take to prepare for more testing conditions ahead.

Disciplined fiscal policy should be at the core of an effective policy framework for dealing with this challenge. Taking advantage of cyclically strong revenues to raise the primary surplus in good times helps to lower public sector debt and provide a more robust basis to weather periods of weakness. Fiscal restraint also provides greater room for monetary easing, thus reducing incentives for potentially destabilizing capital inflows and encouraging private investment. Chile has shown what can be achieved: its fiscal surplus is likely to rise to 6 percent of GDP in 2006 in line with its rule-based framework, reducing public debt to low levels and directing a significant proportion of copper-based revenues into an offshore stabilization fund. Moreover, the effective fiscal sterilization of the impact of rapid export growth has helped to contain appreciation of the Chilean peso, without recourse to foreign exchange market intervention in the context of rapid increases in copper-related revenues.

Looking across Latin America more broadly, primary surpluses have increased significantly during the present cyclical upswing, on the back of strong revenue growth, but there have been signs of an acceleration in government spending over the past two years, in contrast to the more restrained policies followed in 2003–04 (Figure 2.5 and Box 2.1). While greater spending on infrastructure and social priorities could bring long-term dividends, there is a concern that not all of the increased expenditure is well-targeted—in oil exporters and importers alike—and may prove difficult to unwind if and when global economic conditions become more testing. Moreover, public debt levels, while coming down, still remain high (over 50 percent of GDP in many of the Latin American countries shown in Figure 2.5), limiting scope for a counter-cyclical response to any future weakening of growth.

Faced with heavy foreign exchange inflows over the past two years, many Latin American countries have allowed exchange rates to strengthen, with some intervention to lean against upward pressures on the exchange rate, using the proceeds to build up international reserves and finance debt operations. Exchange rates have appreciated substantially from the lows of 2002 in a number of countries, but measures of real effective exchange rates are still broadly in line with long-term averages. Brazil and Colombia have been particularly active in retiring external debt and shifting the structure of public sector liabilities away from dollar-denominated debt, and in net terms Brazil has now eliminated dollar exposure from its public sector balance sheet. As a result, public sector balance sheet vulnerabilities have been substantially reduced across the region, although the transition toward long-term, fixed-rate, domestic-currency-denominated debt remains incomplete.

Looking ahead, recent more difficult market conditions have provided a reminder of the importance of allowing adequate exchange rate flexibility in both directions. In the context of more stable global financial market conditions, strong foreign exchange inflows may return. Sustained sterilized intervention would impose heavy quasi-fiscal costs—more so than in Asia where interest rates are generally lower. Moreover, excessively reducing exchange rate variations in the face of foreign exchange inflows may discourage appropriate risk management by market participants and could lead to easy monetary conditions—a concern in Argentina, for example, where the use of regulatory countermeasures will need to be supported by a further tightening of macroeconomic policies to contain inflation. Some further appreciation of the real exchange rate may be hard to avoid in such circumstances, although the impact on competitiveness may be mitigated by broader structural reforms to reduce domestic costs and improve the business climate. In the face of more turbulent conditions—as exemplified by the sell-off in May–June 2006—countries would need to allow rates to depreciate in line with market conditions, generally limiting intervention to what may be helpful to stabilize disorderly market conditions, while tightening monetary policy if needed to safeguard inflation objectives.

The long-term challenge for Latin America remains to unlock the region's clear growth potential. Despite recently improved performance, Latin America has remained consistently the slowest-growing region among the emerging market and developing countries in recent years. These growth outcomes, and the slow progress in reducing poverty, have fueled popular frustrations. Continued progress toward strengthening macroeconomic policies and reducing balance sheet vulnerabilities should help to provide the basis for more sustained growth than in the past, but stepping up the pace of growth and more tangible progress toward social goals is likely to depend on extending market-based reforms, while also taking steps to ensure that benefits of growth are broadly shared.[7] Most Latin American countries made considerable progress in advancing reforms through the 1990s, but the pace of reforms slowed toward the end of the decade, against the background of financial crisis. More recently there have been renewed advances in some countries, but there have also been setbacks, including steps that partially unwind privatization and pension reforms in a number of countries. Looking forward, reform priorities include tackling budget rigidities to improve the targeting of public spending (including especially infrastructure and pro-poor social programs); reforms to encourage deepening financial intermediation; measures to raise economic openness (where Latin America still lags well behind other regions); labor market reforms to increase the flexibility of response to new opportunities and encourage job growth in the formal sector; and reforms to strengthen governance and the business environment.

The policy framework for production of oil and gas is an important issue in the region. Latin America possesses the world's second larg-

[7]Zettelmeyer (forthcoming) provides a good recent overview of this issue.

Figure 2.5. Latin America: Progress Toward Fiscal Sustainability

(Unweighted averages; change in percent of GDP)

Latin American countries have significantly improved primary balances in recent years, helped by strong revenue growth. However, primary spending has risen sharply over the past two years, after a period of restraint. Public-debt-to-GDP ratios have declined, but remain high for a number of countries.

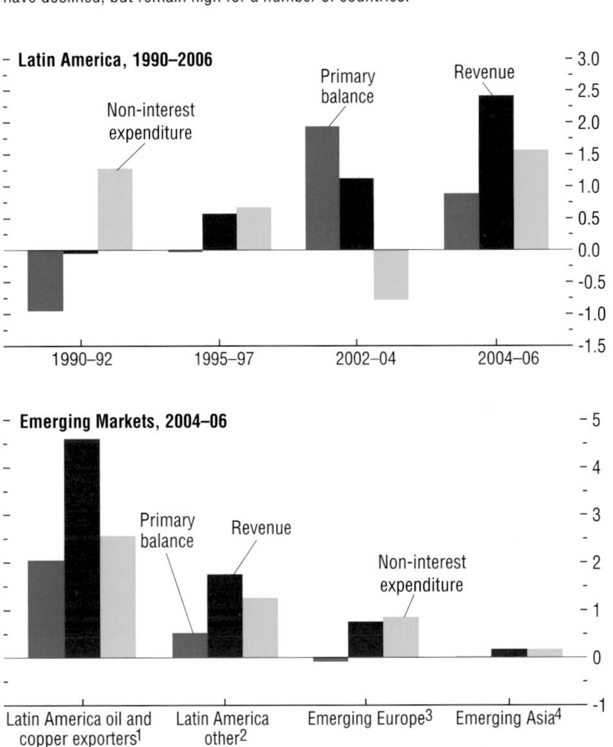

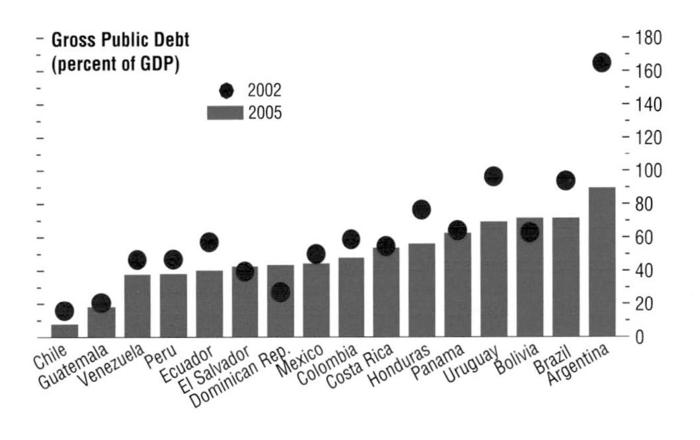

Source: IMF staff calculations.

[1]Chile, Ecuador, Mexico, and Venezuela.

[2]Argentina, Bolivia, Brazil, Colombia, Costa Rica, El Salvador, Guatemala, Honduras, Nicaragua, Panama, Paraguay, Peru, and Uruguay.

[3]Bulgaria, Czech Republic, Estonia, Hungary, Latvia, Lithuania, Poland, Romania, Slovak Republic, Slovenia, and Turkey.

[4]China, Hong Kong SAR, India, Indonesia, Korea, Malaysia, Pakistan, the Philippines, Singapore, Taiwan Province of China, and Thailand.

Box 2.1. Improved Emerging Market Fiscal Performance: Cyclical or Structural?

Fiscal performance in many emerging market countries has improved substantially in recent years. The average overall fiscal balance of the largest 37 emerging market countries improved by nearly 3 percent of GDP from 2002 to 2005 (see first figure), and public debt dropped substantially, although it still remains above 50 percent of GDP in nearly half of those countries. These averages conceal an even better record for some regions and countries (although of course a less stellar performance in others). Nonetheless, this improvement potentially has significant economic and financial market implications, depending on whether it signifies a sustainable trend, or whether it is a transitory phenomenon that will be reversed when these economies encounter more difficult times. In other words, the key question is: to what extent has the improvement been driven by structural or by cyclical factors?

There is no doubt that there has been some underlying structural improvement in fiscal positions in emerging market economies. Helped by improvements in the underlying fiscal institutions, strengthened expenditure management, increased transparency, and sounder fiscal responsibility frameworks, many governments have been able to restrain expenditures in the face of buoyant revenues and easy access to capital markets—a departure from procyclical behavior in previous upturns. This is reflected in the drop in the average primary expenditure-to-GDP ratio in Latin America and Asia, although in emerging Europe revenues and primary spending rose in tandem.[1] For the average of emerging market countries, the primary expenditure ratio was no higher in 2005 than in 2002 before revenues started to boom (see first figure), although in some countries there has been a tendency to ease spending restraint in 2005 and 2006.

Emerging Market Fiscal Performance

(Percent of GDP; general government; unweighted average of 37 emerging market countries)

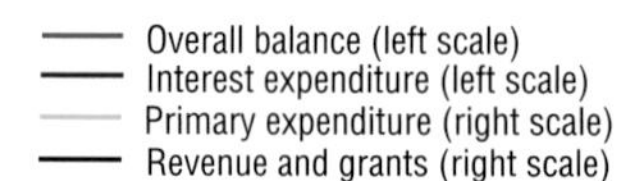

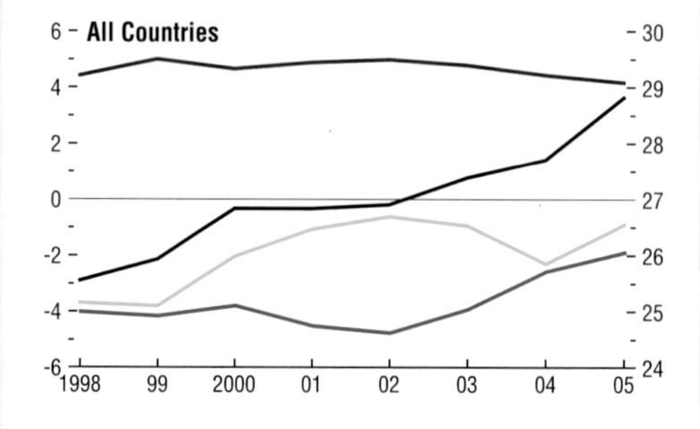

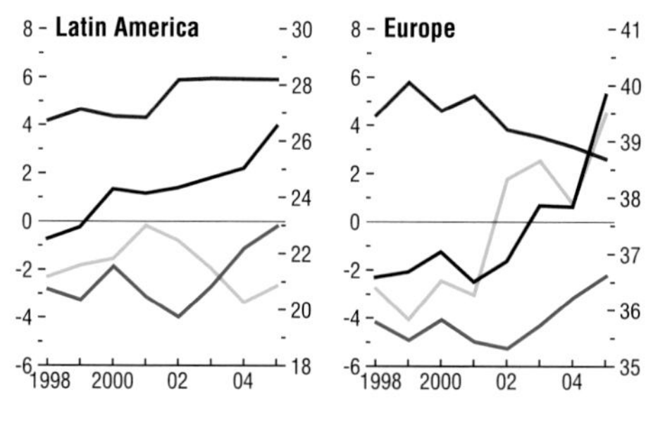

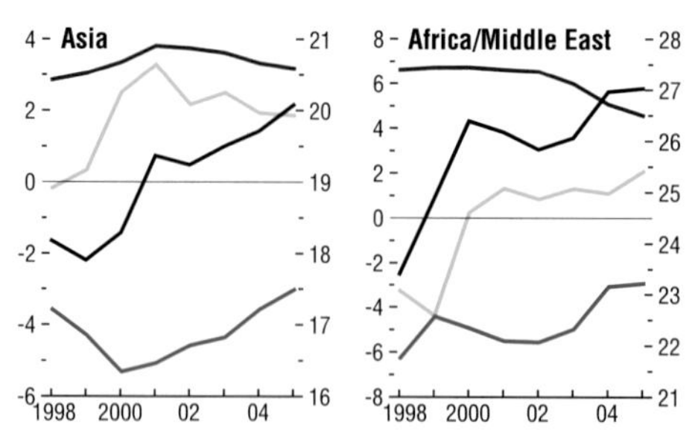

Sources: IMF, World Economic Outlook database; and IMF staff estimates.

Note: The authors of this box are David Hauner and Manmohan S. Kumar.

[1]Government revenues in emerging Europe include grants from the European Union.

Second, several emerging market countries have reduced their financing costs through debt restructuring and generally sound economic policies. Stronger policies have helped to accelerate integration in global financial markets, further lowering borrowing costs. For instance, the fact that, with credit ratings improving, institutional investors in the major industrial countries—particularly pension funds—have begun to invest systematically in emerging market financial instruments has led to an expectation of more stable capital flows. This in turn has further reduced the risk premiums demanded on emerging market assets, and lowered interest costs.

Nevertheless, part of the improvement in emerging market countries' government finances appears to have reflected favorable cyclical factors. Buoyant GDP growth and soaring commodity prices have boosted government revenues in many countries (by an average of 2 percentage points of GDP from 2002 to 2005). Given a stable expenditure-to-GDP ratio, the improvement in the average primary balance is essentially due to rising revenues. Such revenue buoyancy, however, has an important cyclical component that, although not readily quantifiable, is likely to account for a significant part of the rapid increase in revenues. For example, revenues rose by a full 6 percent of GDP on average in the five of the 37 sample countries that are mainly exporting commodities.[2] The public debt ratio has also benefited from strong GDP growth. Growth subtracted on average about 7 percent of GDP from this ratio over the past four years, while primary balances subtracted only about 1 percent of GDP (second figure).

Benign global financial conditions in recent years have also helped fiscal performance. Global interest rates have been very low, and high liquidity and search for yield have contributed to declining yield spreads (see, for example, IMF, 2004). Moreover, many emerging market countries' currencies have strengthened substantially relative to the dollar and other currencies in which much of their debt is denominated, particularly in 2005. Both interest rate and exchange rate factors contributed to

Change in Emerging Market Public Debt[1]

(Percent of GDP; change from end-2001 to end-2005)

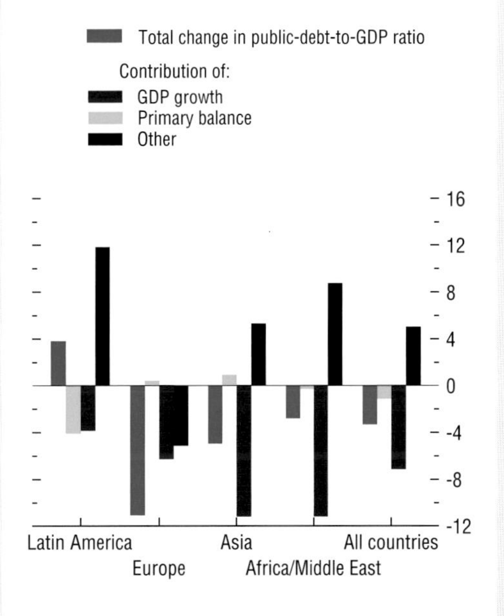

Sources: IMF, World Economic Outlook database; and IMF staff estimates.

[1]Public debt includes debt in domestic and foreign currency. The category "Other" includes exchange rate and interest rate effects, the stock-flow adjustment, as well as the statistical discrepancy.

the decline in interest expenditure over 2002–05 and to the improvement in the overall fiscal balance (Hauner and Kumar, 2005). This is particularly evident for the emerging European countries, which have benefited not only from the global environment, but also from interest rate convergence in the context of EU accession.

There is a risk that a reversal in cyclical conditions and the external financial environment could induce a deterioration in budgetary positions. And the most vulnerable countries could be hit hardest, because they tend to have benefited most from higher risk appetite. It is thus important for emerging market countries—especially those with larger underlying vulnerabilities—to maintain disciplined fiscal policies to take maximum advantage of continued favorable global conditions.

[2]Excluding countries that are mainly exporting commodities does not materially change these results: the average primary balance would be about 0.7 percent of GDP worse for 2004 and 2005.

Figure 2.6. Latin America: Mixed Performance in the Hydrocarbons Sector
(Percent change in output over 2000–05 relative to total output in 2000)

Latin American countries have had mixed success in raising output of oil and gas in response to higher prices.

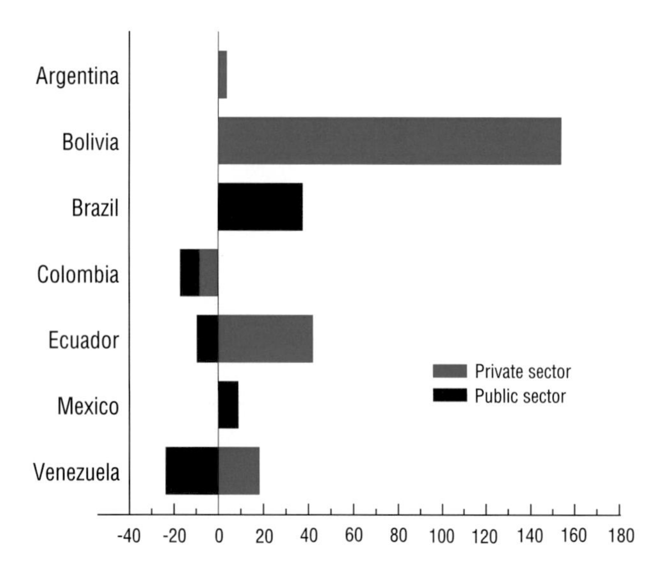

Source: IMF staff calculations.

est hydrocarbons reserves, but for the most part has not responded to the rise in international prices since 2004 with increased production and investment. On the positive side, long-term investment by partially state-owned Petrobras has allowed Brazil—the region's third largest producer—to achieve self-sufficiency in 2006. However, production has grown slowly or contracted elsewhere, including such major oil producers as Mexico and Venezuela, reflecting low rates of investment in the past and governance issues that are only now beginning to be addressed (Figure 2.6). In Mexico, investment has been boosted recently to counter the decline of the country's largest oil field. Bolivia was able to achieve a rapid increase in gas exports after opening up its hydrocarbons sector to private companies, but the recent decision to nationalize production and raise royalties has raised uncertainty and may have jeopardized prospects for new investment. Similarly in Ecuador, private oil production rose rapidly in 2005 after completion of a major pipeline, but public production has declined, and prospects now depend on the government's ability to improve the investment climate to attract new private investors and to strengthen public sector governance. The key issue here is less whether production and investment rights are allocated to the private or public sector, but whether the government is able to establish a stable and predictable set of production and investment incentives and governance structures to provide a firm basis for the huge financing and the long-term planning horizons required for major hydrocarbons projects.

Emerging Europe: Managing Risks from Heavy Reliance on Foreign Savings

The economic expansion has remained robust in emerging Europe, with regional growth running at about 5½ percent in 2005 (Table 2.5). Buoyant domestic demand generally has been the main driving force—fueled by increasing net capital inflows and credit growth. The growth momentum varies across the region, depending in part on the strength of the forces underpin-

Table 2.5. Emerging Europe: Real GDP, Consumer Prices, and Current Account Balance
(Annual percent change unless noted otherwise)

	Real GDP				Consumer Prices[1]				Current Account Balance[2]			
	2004	2005	2006	2007	2004	2005	2006	2007	2004	2005	2006	2007
Emerging Europe	**6.6**	**5.5**	**5.4**	**5.0**	**6.3**	**4.9**	**5.4**	**4.7**	**–5.7**	**–5.2**	**–5.7**	**–5.4**
Turkey	8.9	7.4	5.0	5.0	8.6	8.2	10.2	7.2	–5.2	–6.4	–6.7	–5.8
Excluding Turkey	5.7	4.6	5.5	5.0	5.3	3.6	3.4	3.7	–6.0	–4.6	–5.2	–5.2
Baltics	**7.6**	**8.8**	**8.6**	**7.6**	**3.0**	**4.2**	**4.7**	**4.3**	**–10.4**	**–9.5**	**–10.5**	**–10.4**
Estonia	7.8	9.8	9.5	8.0	3.0	4.1	4.6	3.8	–13.0	–11.0	–12.0	–11.7
Latvia	8.6	10.2	11.0	9.0	6.2	6.8	6.6	6.3	–12.9	–12.4	–14.0	–13.7
Lithuania	7.0	7.5	6.8	6.5	1.2	2.7	3.6	3.3	–7.7	–6.9	–7.5	–7.4
Central Europe	**5.0**	**4.3**	**5.2**	**4.6**	**4.3**	**2.4**	**2.2**	**3.2**	**–5.2**	**–3.1**	**–3.4**	**–3.1**
Czech Republic	4.2	6.1	6.0	4.7	2.8	1.8	2.9	3.3	–6.0	–2.1	–1.9	–1.6
Hungary	5.2	4.1	4.5	3.5	6.8	3.6	3.5	5.8	–8.6	–7.4	–9.1	–8.0
Poland	5.3	3.4	5.0	4.5	3.5	2.1	0.9	2.3	–4.2	–1.4	–1.7	–1.9
Slovak Republic	5.4	6.1	6.5	7.0	7.5	2.7	4.7	3.6	–3.6	–8.6	–7.7	–5.9
Slovenia	4.2	3.9	4.2	4.0	3.6	2.5	2.5	2.3	–2.1	–1.1	–2.0	–2.3
Southern and south-eastern Europe	**6.8**	**4.4**	**5.3**	**5.4**	**8.7**	**7.0**	**6.9**	**4.7**	**–7.3**	**–8.8**	**–10.3**	**–10.4**
Bulgaria	5.7	5.5	5.6	6.0	6.1	5.0	7.4	3.8	–5.8	–11.8	–12.4	–12.2
Croatia	3.8	4.3	4.6	4.7	2.1	3.3	3.5	2.8	–5.4	–6.3	–6.8	–6.8
Malta	–1.5	2.5	1.6	1.8	2.7	2.5	2.9	2.8	–9.6	–13.1	–12.5	–12.0
Romania	8.4	4.1	5.5	5.5	11.9	9.0	7.8	5.7	–8.5	–8.7	–10.9	–11.1

[1]In accordance with standard practice in the *World Economic Outlook*, movements in consumer prices are indicated as annual averages rather than as December/December changes, as is the practice in some countries.
[2]Percent of GDP.

ning domestic demand, exchange rate developments, and progress in addressing structural rigidities. Growth has been particularly vibrant in the Baltic countries and Turkey, and it has accelerated in the Czech Republic and the Slovak Republic. The pace has been weaker in Hungary, Poland, and Slovenia, although more recently growth in Poland has picked up, supported by higher export market growth, improving investor sentiment, and firming labor market conditions.

The outlook is for continued solid regional growth in the range of 5–5½ percent in 2006–07, as robust domestic demand growth is expected to continue, and with the strengthening expansion in the euro area adding an external impetus. Compared to the last *World Economic Outlook*, however, growth is expected to slow more noticeably in Turkey—policy interest rates have been raised by 425 basis points since June to head off a weakening currency and intensifying inflation pressures—and in Hungary, in 2007, in view of the substantial fiscal consolidation that is targeted in that year. The adverse impact on regional growth is roughly offset by Poland's improved near-term growth prospects. The region's characteristic large current account deficits—only in the Czech Republic, Poland, and Slovenia are deficits relatively modest—are projected to widen in 2006, reaching 5.7 percent of GDP for the region as a whole, before declining slightly in 2007. The risks to the growth outlook are slanted to the downside, with the region's heavy reliance on foreign savings a particular vulnerability if international financial market conditions become even more testing.

When assessing such risks, one needs to consider that the region's generally large current account deficits have reflected in part favorable investment opportunities, given scarce capital and low labor costs, in the context of EU accession and integration. That said, to varying degrees within the region, these deficits have also been associated with rapid credit and consumption growth, asset price increases, and, in some cases, substantial real exchange rate appreciations—often in the context of limited

Figure 2.7. Emerging Europe: Rapid Growth and Its Risks

Strong domestic demand has buoyed growth in emerging Europe, underpinned by sizable and increasing net capital inflows and rapid credit growth. However, with its heavy reliance on foreign savings, the region is vulnerable to changes in international financial market conditions. Weak fiscal positions in some countries exacerbate the situation.

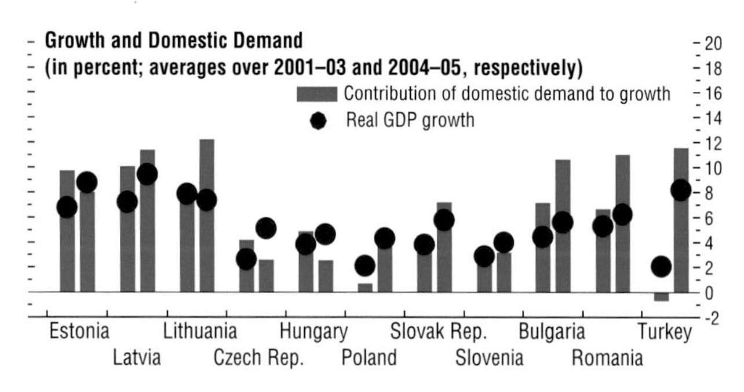

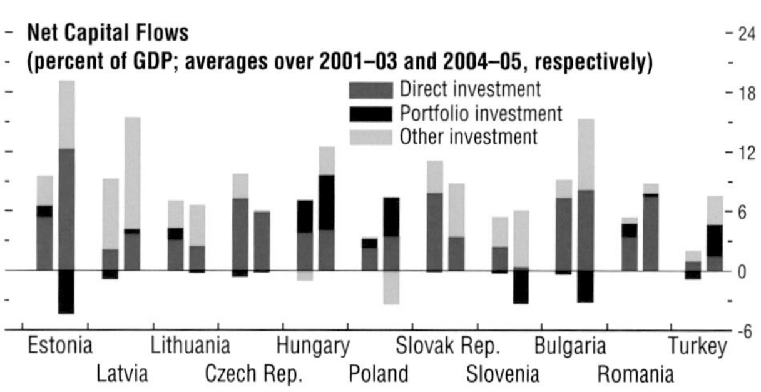

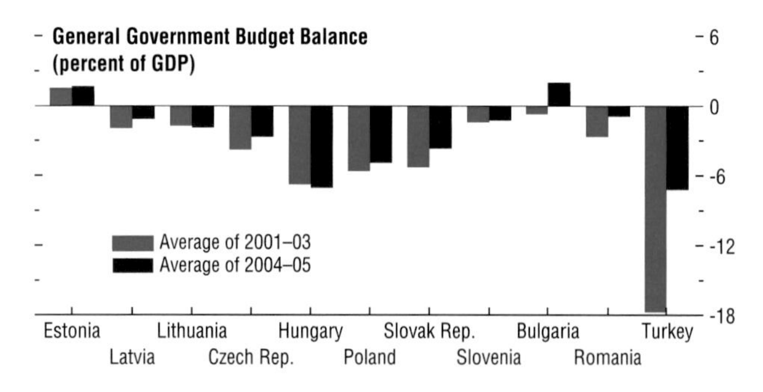

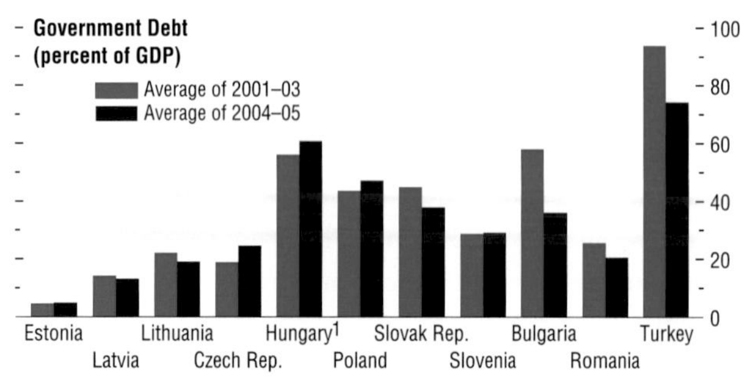

Source: IMF staff calculations.
[1]General government net debt.

nominal exchange rate flexibility—a constellation prone to create external vulnerabilities. In some countries, the inflows have been associated not just with private sector financial imbalances, but also with substantial fiscal imbalances, notably in Hungary but, to a lesser extent, also in Poland and the Slovak Republic. On the supply side, a key concern is that the large net capital inflows are increasingly in the form of more volatile portfolio and so-called "other flows," including short-term debt, rather than foreign direct investment (FDI). Indeed, as noted in Box 1.1, the region became the largest recipient of net non-FDI flows among all emerging market regions in 2005 (Figure 2.7). The important share of lending from advanced-economy banks to their subsidiaries in "other flows" may mitigate the risks to some extent, although any reduction in net financing would still require substantial external adjustment.

Against this background, policymakers must carefully balance the growth opportunities provided by foreign savings against the risks. While the extent of risks varies considerably across countries, given large differences in factors such as the size of short-term external debt and reserve coverage, reducing vulnerabilities is a policy priority, not the least in view of possible regional spillovers, given that the countries share similar vulnerabilities and common creditors. The policy mix to achieve this depends on country circumstances, but generally includes the following:

- *Fiscal consolidation.* In countries with fiscal sustainability problems, determined fiscal adjustment is needed to maintain investor confidence and avoid unfavorable public debt dynamics. This is most urgent in Hungary, where the deficit is likely to reach 10 percent of GDP this year. While the authorities plan to reduce the deficit by some 4 percentage points of GDP in 2007, the proposed measures may be challenging to implement, given legal and administrative complexities, and since they are mostly tax-based, the consolidation package may adversely affect potential growth, not just aggregate demand in the near term. In other countries, some fiscal tightening may be helpful to moderate domestic demand pressures and their impact on external balances and inflation. This is particularly relevant when a fixed nominal exchange rate constrains monetary policy options, as in the Baltic countries, or when public debt ratios are still high, as is the case in Turkey.

- *Adequate prudential supervision and regulatory frameworks.* The often rapid credit growth in the region partly reflects normal financial deepening from a low base. However, as noted in previous issues of the *World Economic Outlook*, there has been a notable increase in riskier forms of credit, especially a substantial fraction of bank lending in foreign currency, and the share of credit financed by short-term borrowing from foreign banks has risen. Regulators need to ensure that financial systems are in a position to manage exchange and interest rate risks, including by tightening regulatory standards when appropriate.
- *Monetary policy tightening.* Higher interest rates need to be the first line of defense when inflation risks increase either because of strong domestic demand or acute downward pressures on the exchange rate. This policy challenge is well illustrated by the Turkish central bank's strong response to the sharp depreciation of the Turkish lira (19 percent in nominal effective terms between January and June this year). The bank will need to stand ready to tighten further if incoming data point to an unfavorable medium-term inflation outlook. Inflationary pressures have been more moderate in Central European countries, especially in the Czech Republic and Poland, but they have begun to pick up more recently, and some central banks raised policy rates in response (Czech Republic, Hungary, and Slovak Republic). Policymakers will need to stand ready to tighten further if continued rapid growth, depreciating exchange rates, or rising global inflationary pressures add to current pressures on prices.

In some of the new member states of the European Union that have already begun to keep fluctuations in the external value of their currencies within the required limits before euro adoption, strengthening external positions through domestic demand moderation would also reduce the vulnerabilities of exchange rates to swings in investor confidence and capital flow reversals.[8] The most relevant problem is that despite successful disinflation, inflation convergence—to less than 1.5 percentage points above the average level in the three European Union countries with the lowest rates—has been hampered by the combination of limited nominal exchange rate flexibility and pressures for real appreciation, which has tended to push inflation above the average in key trading partners. While some of the pressures for real appreciation are difficult to avoid as they result from so-called "Balassa-Samuelson" effects stemming from rapid productivity growth in the tradables sectors, they also reflect buoyant domestic demand and large capital inflows which, in the absence of monetary policy tools, should be offset primarily by fiscal tightening, although measures aimed at restraining credit growth may also be needed.

More broadly, with most countries in the region aiming for euro adoption in the medium term, policymakers need to ensure adequate preparation for the loss of monetary policy autonomy and the capacity to achieve external adjustment through nominal exchange rate changes in the face of country-specific events. Otherwise, if countries give up nominal exchange rate flexibility too early, such adjustment could require relative price changes

[8]The recently acceded members of the European Union in emerging Europe are committed to adopting the euro and, thereby, to the associated process of macroeconomic policy convergence. This process is most advanced in the five countries that have entered the so-called European Exchange Rate Mechanism (ERM II) and have begun to limit fluctuations in the external value of their currencies against the euro—Slovenia, Lithuania, Estonia, Latvia, and Slovak Republic. Slovenia was recently accepted into the euro area from January 2007, while Lithuania's entry was delayed because its 12-month average inflation rate over the period April 2005 to March 2006 was slightly above the relevant criterion and was expected to rise further during 2006.

Table 2.6. Commonwealth of Independent States: Real GDP, Consumer Prices, and Current Account Balance

(Annual percent change unless noted otherwise)

	Real GDP				Consumer Prices[1]				Current Account Balance[2]			
	2004	2005	2006	2007	2004	2005	2006	2007	2004	2005	2006	2007
Commonwealth of Independent States	**8.4**	**6.5**	**6.8**	**6.5**	**10.3**	**12.3**	**9.6**	**9.3**	**8.1**	**8.8**	**10.1**	**9.4**
Russia	7.2	6.4	6.5	6.5	10.9	12.6	9.7	8.5	9.9	10.9	12.3	10.7
Ukraine	12.1	2.6	5.0	2.8	9.0	13.5	9.3	13.5	10.6	3.1	–2.2	–3.8
Kazakhstan	9.6	9.4	8.3	7.7	6.9	7.6	8.5	7.9	1.1	–0.9	2.3	2.1
Belarus	11.4	9.3	7.0	4.5	18.1	10.3	7.9	9.0	–5.2	1.6	0.2	–1.1
Turkmenistan	14.7	9.6	9.0	9.0	5.9	10.7	9.0	8.0	0.6	5.1	7.6	8.0
Low-income CIS countries	**8.5**	**11.9**	**12.5**	**13.2**	**7.5**	**11.9**	**11.4**	**9.8**	**–7.0**	**1.7**	**10.2**	**21.1**
Armenia	10.1	13.9	7.5	6.0	7.0	0.6	3.0	3.0	–4.6	–3.3	–4.4	–4.6
Azerbaijan	10.2	24.3	25.6	26.4	6.7	9.7	8.7	10.5	–29.8	1.3	26.0	44.8
Georgia	5.9	9.3	7.5	6.5	5.7	8.3	9.6	6.0	–8.4	–5.4	–9.9	–11.5
Kyrgyz Republic	7.0	–0.6	5.0	5.5	4.1	4.3	5.7	4.5	–3.4	–8.1	–7.9	–7.7
Moldova	7.4	7.1	3.0	3.0	12.5	11.9	11.5	10.5	–2.0	–8.3	–10.5	–6.8
Tajikistan	10.6	6.7	8.0	6.0	7.1	7.1	7.8	5.0	–4.0	–3.4	–4.2	–4.8
Uzbekistan	7.7	7.0	7.2	7.0	8.8	21.0	19.3	14.5	10.0	13.1	12.0	11.9
Memorandum												
Net energy exporters[3]	7.6	7.1	7.2	7.3	10.4	12.4	9.8	8.6	8.7	10.0	11.8	11.0
Net energy importers[4]	11.5	4.3	5.5	3.4	10.2	12.0	8.8	11.8	4.8	1.5	–2.4	–3.7

[1]In accordance with standard practice in the *World Economic Outlook*, movements in consumer prices are indicated as annual averages rather than as December/December changes, as is the practice in some countries.

[2]Percent of GDP.

[3]Includes Azerbaijan, Kazakhstan, Russia, Turkmenistan, and Uzbekistan.

[4]Includes Armenia, Belarus, Georgia, Kyrgyz Republic, Moldova, Tajikistan, and Ukraine.

through deflation, which is of particular concern in those countries with already large current account deficits that will eventually have to unwind. On the fiscal front, meeting the relevant Maastricht criteria will require sustained policy discipline in a number of countries, especially in Hungary, but also in Poland and the Slovak Republic. Structural reforms are also key to strengthen economic flexibility, as well as to boost prospects for the closing of the productivity gap with EU15 countries, both for new and prospective new members in the region (see Schadler and others, 2006). Policy priorities again vary across countries, given wide differences in structural regimes, but generally include:

- *Reducing labor market rigidities.* Employment rates in the region remain low compared to other emerging market countries. While partly reflecting transition-specific factors, such as an unusually rapid rate of job destruction that will gradually dissipate, low employment rates also owe to labor market rigidities, such as cumbersome restrictions on dismissals and temporary employment, fiscal disincentives to both labor supply and demand, and rigidities hampering regional mobility (e.g., in the housing market).
- *Institutional reform.* Reforms in this domain would aim at reducing costs of doing business, increasing product market competition, fostering further financial deepening, and increasing efficiency in government operations.

Commonwealth of Independent States: Managing Large Foreign Currency Inflows

Real GDP growth in the Commonwealth of Independent States (CIS) is on course to reach close to 7 percent in 2006, before easing to about 6½ percent in 2007 (Table 2.6). The region continues to benefit from high commodity prices and correspondingly strong export earnings (Figure 2.8). In several countries, domestic demand has received an additional boost from substantial private capital inflows (Russia, Kazakhstan), official financing (Georgia), and/or remittances (Armenia, Georgia, Kyrgyz Republic, Moldova, Tajikistan). Investment is recovering, including in Russia, where the impact of factors responsible for the slowdown in 2004–05—including banking sector turbulences and a tax-induced decline in oil sector profitability—is waning. Short-term growth prospects are generally positive, although they remain heavily dependent on commodity price developments. In the Ukraine, growth picked up quite strongly in the first half of 2006, but the outlook remains clouded by a projected deterioration in the terms of trade—due to the repricing of gas imports from Russia and a possible reversal in the export price of steel—and lingering policy uncertainties.[9]

The favorable external environment has created important challenges for macroeconomic management, however, that need to be addressed with some urgency to boost longer-term growth prospects. High commodity prices have relaxed short-term fiscal policy constraints, both directly—by increasing export tax revenues and the profits of state-owned enterprises—and indirectly by boosting aggregate demand, and thereby receipts from consumption and income taxes. Often policymakers have used these extra funds prudently, including to pay down public debt and/or to build up foreign currency reserve cushions. More recently, however, some governments have granted large pension and wage increases (Azerbaijan, Belarus, Kyrgyz Republic, Tajikistan), which have further boosted consumption, undermined competitiveness, and would be hard to reverse should the commodity price cycle turn. Policymakers

[9]At present, the Russian energy company Gazprom charges between $47 (Belarus) and $160 (Moldova) for 1000 cubic meters of natural gas. This compares to a price of $230 per 1000 cubic meters for customers in western Europe. Gazprom increased export prices to some CIS customers earlier this year, and has announced its intention to bring prices even more closely in line with "market valuations."

Figure 2.8. Commonwealth of Independent States: Strong Foreign Currency Inflows Create Macroeconomic Challenges

Strong commodity export earnings and capital inflows have boosted growth, but they have also contributed to inflationary pressures. In some countries, private external debt is rising rapidly.

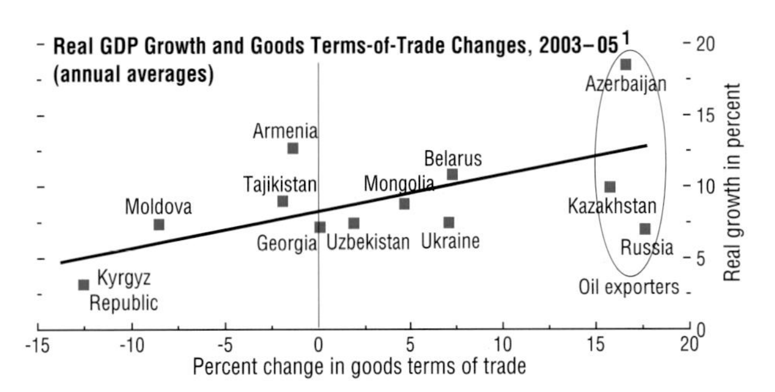

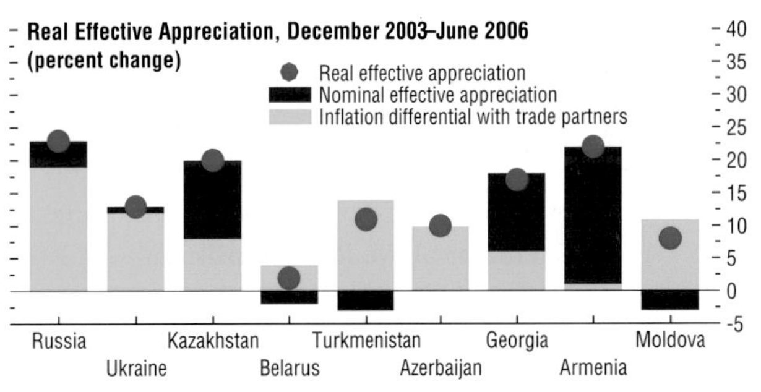

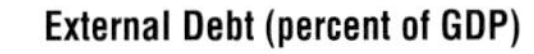

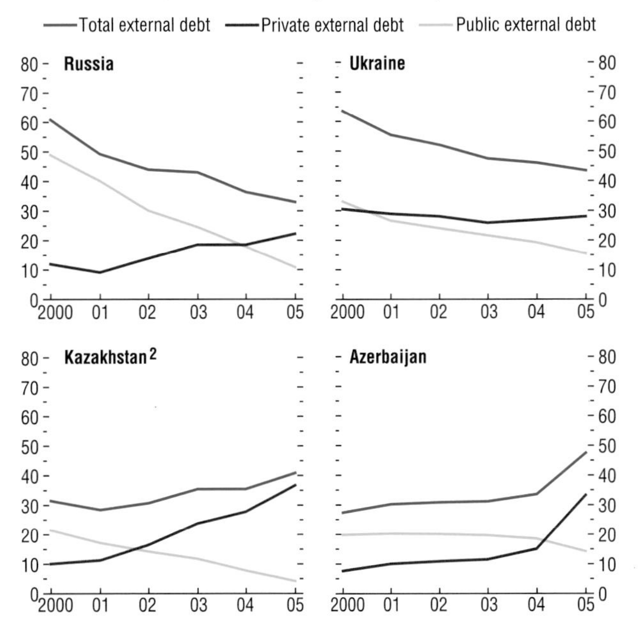

Source: IMF staff calculations.
[1]Merchandise trade.
[2]Excluding intracompany obligations without fixed repayment schedule and pre-specified rate of return.

should not assume that recent revenue gains will all be permanent (see Chapter 5). In countries where scope for fiscal easing exists—such as in Russia, where there is room for some increase in public spending without sacrificing sustainability, and in Kazakhstan—a more expansionary stance should be accompanied by a reinvigoration of stalled reforms to ensure that higher spending boosts investment and potential GDP growth.

Monetary policy also faces important challenges. While inflation has declined in recent months, it remains at or close to double-digit levels in many countries, especially oil exporters. Further progress is needed, but addressing disinflation is complicated by the focus of many central banks on stabilizing the nominal exchange rate against the U.S. dollar in the face of large current account surpluses and capital inflows. With the scope for sterilization of foreign exchange purchases limited by underdeveloped domestic debt markets, base money growth remains above levels consistent with low, single-digit inflation rates. The danger is that inflationary pressures may become entrenched, in which case costly measures may be required in the future to reverse the inflation buildup. While early repayment of external public debt or transfers into offshore oil funds (Azerbaijan, Kazakhstan) can help to reduce base money growth, the most effective way to lower inflation would be to allow for further nominal exchange rate appreciation, thus enhancing the scope for monetary control aimed at disinflation. In some energy-importing countries, inflationary pressures could also emerge from the prospective repricing of fuel and gas imports, in which case monetary policymakers will need to ensure that the necessary pass-through of higher costs does not feed into core inflation, wages, and inflation expectations.

The commodity price boom has also complicated efforts to diversify production and exports away from primary materials to goods with a higher value-added component. Attracted by high expected export earnings, recent investments—both domestic and foreign financed—have often focused on extractive industries (Azerbaijan, Turkmenistan) or on commodity transport infrastructure (oil and gas pipeline projects in Armenia, Azerbaijan, Georgia, Kazakhstan). Moreover, the overall level of investment in the region remains too low at 21 percent of GDP—the recent recovery notwithstanding—which casts doubt on the sustainability of current growth rates over the medium term. Structural reforms to improve the investment climate are crucial to avoid the emergence or aggravation of supply bottlenecks. In countries with large current account surpluses—notably Russia—higher investment would also contribute to reducing global macroeconomic imbalances.

External positions are strong in many countries in the region, especially fuel exporters. For the region as a whole, a current account surplus of over 10 percent of GDP is projected for 2006. Large surpluses have permitted a rapid reduction in the overall level of external debt in oil exporters, especially by the public sector. In several countries (including Azerbaijan, Kazakhstan, and Russia), however, the private sector has accumulated substantial foreign currency liabilities in recent years (Figure 2.8), often intermediated by the banking system. As a consequence, the private sector's vulnerability to a tightening in external financing conditions has increased. Financial system soundness indicators have remained broadly stable, but this is partly on account of the favorable macroeconomic environment. A strengthening of prudential regulations and risk-based supervision would help to reduce risks of financial instability in the face of a downturn, as would measures to restrict regulatory forbearance and—in some cases—policies to assure that the risks associated with the buildup of foreign currency liabilities remain contained.

Africa: Strong Growth Continues Despite High Oil Prices

Sub-Saharan Africa is currently enjoying its strongest period of sustained economic expansion since the early 1970s. Regional growth is

Table 2.7. Selected African Countries: Real GDP, Consumer Prices and Current Account Balance
(Annual percent change unless noted otherwise)

	Real GDP				Consumer Prices[1]				Current Account Balance[2]			
	2004	2005	2006	2007	2004	2005	2006	2007	2004	2005	2006	2007
Africa	**5.5**	**5.4**	**5.4**	**5.9**	**8.0**	**8.5**	**9.9**	**10.6**	**–0.1**	**2.3**	**3.6**	**4.2**
Maghreb	**5.1**	**4.0**	**5.8**	**4.7**	**2.9**	**1.5**	**4.1**	**3.8**	**7.1**	**12.2**	**14.5**	**11.1**
Algeria	5.2	5.3	4.9	5.0	3.6	1.6	5.0	5.5	13.1	21.3	24.8	19.1
Morocco	4.2	1.7	7.3	3.3	1.5	1.0	2.5	2.0	1.9	1.8	0.5	–0.1
Tunisia	6.0	4.2	5.8	6.0	3.6	2.0	3.9	2.0	–2.0	–1.3	–1.6	–1.4
Sub-Sahara	**5.6**	**5.8**	**5.2**	**6.3**	**9.6**	**10.7**	**11.7**	**12.6**	**–2.3**	**–0.6**	**0.4**	**2.3**
Horn of Africa[3]	**8.1**	**8.2**	**9.4**	**9.0**	**8.4**	**7.8**	**9.0**	**7.7**	**–5.8**	**–10.0**	**–7.0**	**–4.0**
Ethiopia	12.3	8.7	5.4	5.5	8.6	6.8	12.3	12.2	–5.1	–9.1	–10.1	–7.1
Sudan	5.2	7.9	12.1	11.3	8.4	8.5	7.0	5.0	–6.3	–10.6	–5.9	–2.8
Great Lakes[3]	**5.6**	**6.0**	**5.7**	**6.2**	**6.9**	**11.6**	**9.1**	**5.7**	**–3.3**	**–3.4**	**–5.6**	**–6.4**
Congo, Dem. Rep. of	6.6	6.5	6.5	7.2	4.0	21.4	10.0	8.9	–5.7	–4.9	–4.2	–0.2
Kenya	4.6	5.7	5.4	5.2	11.6	10.3	13.0	1.6	–2.7	–2.2	–3.8	–5.8
Tanzania	6.7	6.8	5.9	7.3	4.1	4.4	7.5	6.5	–3.9	–5.2	–8.3	–9.8
Uganda	5.7	6.0	5.5	6.0	5.0	8.0	6.7	7.0	–1.0	–1.6	–5.0	–7.1
Southern Africa[3]	**5.0**	**6.5**	**6.1**	**11.4**	**46.5**	**33.9**	**53.3**	**68.2**	**–0.6**	**3.8**	**4.8**	**6.9**
Angola	11.2	20.6	14.3	31.4	43.6	23.0	12.9	8.3	3.5	12.8	12.2	17.4
Zimbabwe	–3.8	–6.5	–5.1	–4.7	350.0	237.8	1,216.0	4,278.8	–8.3	–11.1	0.5	–0.5
West and Central Africa[3]	**6.5**	**5.6**	**4.6**	**5.7**	**8.0**	**11.6**	**7.1**	**5.6**	**–0.5**	**4.1**	**7.4**	**10.1**
Ghana	5.8	5.8	6.0	6.0	12.6	15.1	8.8	7.1	–2.7	–7.7	–7.6	–7.9
Nigeria	6.0	6.9	5.2	6.4	15.0	17.9	9.4	8.0	4.6	12.4	15.7	18.9
CFA franc zone[3]	**7.6**	**4.7**	**3.2**	**4.7**	**0.2**	**4.3**	**3.1**	**2.7**	**–3.6**	**–1.7**	**0.4**	**2.1**
Cameroon	3.7	2.6	4.2	4.3	0.3	2.0	2.9	3.0	–3.4	–1.5	—	0.3
Côte d'Ivoire	1.8	1.9	1.9	3.0	1.5	3.9	2.6	2.8	1.6	–0.1	1.8	3.1
South Africa	**4.5**	**4.9**	**4.2**	**4.0**	**1.4**	**3.4**	**4.6**	**5.7**	**–3.4**	**–4.2**	**–5.5**	**–4.7**
Memorandum												
Oil importers	4.8	4.5	4.8	4.5	7.3	8.3	11.1	12.5	–2.8	–3.3	–4.1	–3.8
Oil exporters[4]	7.3	7.4	6.7	9.1	9.7	9.0	7.2	6.2	5.8	12.2	15.4	15.8

[1]In accordance with standard practice in the *World Economic Outlook*, movements in consumer prices are indicated as annual averages rather than as December/December changes, as is the practice in some countries.
[2]Percent of GDP.
[3]The country composition of this regional group is set out in Table F in the Statistical Appendix.
[4]Includes Chad and Mauritania in this table.

expected at 5.2 percent this year—the third successive year it has exceeded 5 percent—before increasing to 6.3 percent in 2007 as oil output recovers in Nigeria and new oil fields in Angola and Equatorial Guinea come on stream (Table 2.7). Oil-exporting countries have contributed significantly to this strong performance. Increased oil production in a number of countries and the large terms-of-trade gains from the significant rise in oil prices have boosted domestic incomes and spending. Growth in oil-importing countries—although lagging that in oil exporters by a substantial margin—has also been surprisingly robust, despite higher oil prices and the removal of international textile trade quotas, which has adversely affected a number of countries, most particularly Lesotho and Swaziland. This resilience contrasts with earlier periods of high international oil prices, when growth in these countries was hit hard (the exception being 1972–74, when the regional terms of trade actually increased because of the concurrent boom in nonfuel commodity prices; see Figure 2.9; and Dudine and others, 2006).

Why has growth in oil-importing countries held up so well in the face of high oil prices?

- The rise in nonfuel commodity prices has certainly helped to cushion the impact of higher oil prices in some countries, but this has not been universal (Box 2.2). For example, Mozambique, Zambia, and South Africa have benefited from higher metals prices, and

Figure 2.9. Sub-Saharan Africa: Oil-Importing Countries Record Strong Growth Despite High Oil Prices

(Sample medians)

Growth in oil-importing countries in sub-Saharan Africa has been resilient despite rising oil prices. Higher nonfuel commodity prices—which have cushioned the deterioration in the terms of trade—strong global growth, and better domestic policies have all helped.

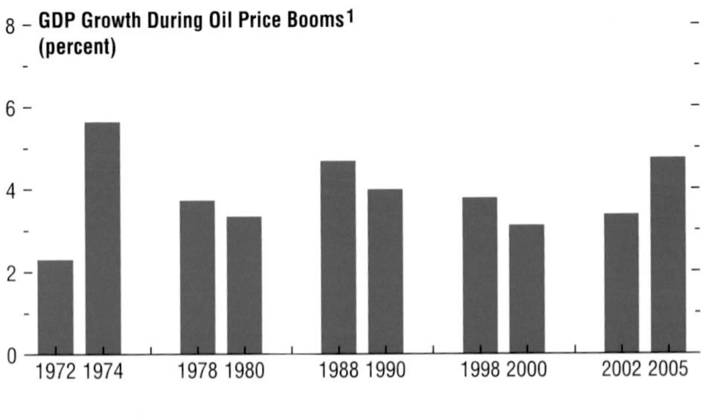

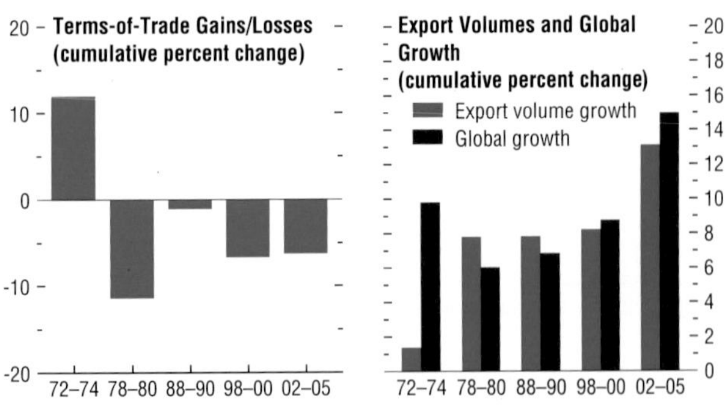

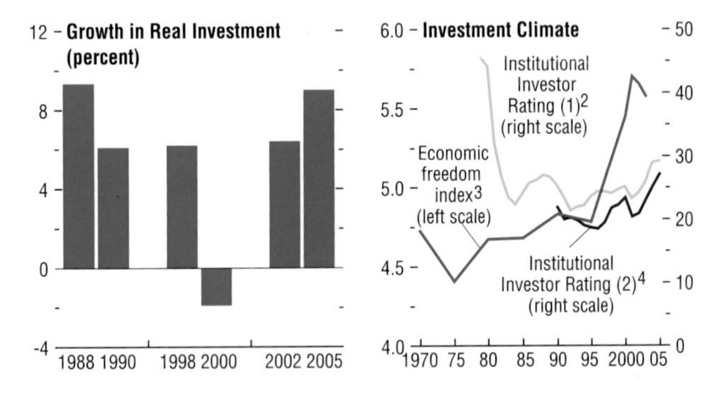

Source: IMF staff calculations.

[1]Five oil price booms are identified as: 1972–74; 1978–80; 1988–90; 1998–2000; 2002–05. For this panel and the real investment growth panel, the first and last year of each boom are shown. For the terms of trade and export volume panels, the cumulative growth during the boom are shown.

[2]Comprises Côte d'Ivoire, Kenya, Mauritius, Senegal, South Africa, and Tanzania.

[3]Cato Institute.

[4]Comprises Benin, Botswana, Burkina Faso, Cameroon, Côte d'Ivoire, Ethiopia, Ghana, Kenya, Mali, Mauritius, Senegal, South Africa, Swaziland, Tanzania, and Togo.

Burundi, Ethiopia, Sierra Leone, Rwanda, and Uganda from stronger coffee prices. By contrast, exporters of cotton (Benin, Burkina Faso, Mali, and Togo) and cocoa (Côte d'Ivoire, Ghana, São Tomé and Príncipe) have seen a substantial deterioration in their terms of trade.

- The global economic environment has been supportive and regional export growth has generally been strong.
- Countries that have experienced a deterioration in their terms of trade in recent years have seen an increase in aid and stronger capital inflows that have helped cushion the income loss (see Box 2.2).
- Stronger domestic policy frameworks have helped support economic activity, particularly investment. Despite the impact of higher oil prices, inflation generally remains well contained and fiscal positions have deteriorated only modestly. Together with the institutional transitions that have taken place in a number of countries in recent years—see the September 2005 *World Economic Outlook*—this has created a better business climate, although the costs of doing business in Africa remain high.[10]

Nevertheless, while strong growth is expected to continue, there are a number of risks to the outlook. First, if oil prices remain elevated, they may have a more detrimental impact on growth going forward than they have done in the recent past, particularly if combined with a sharper-than-expected decline in non-oil commodity prices (see the analysis of the outlook for nonfuel commodity prices in Chapter 5). Second, export performance would suffer if global growth slowed or—against the background of large global imbalances—the euro appreciated

[10]An institutional transition is defined as a sustained improvement in the quality of economic institutions in a country. The quality of institutions is assessed using an overall index composed of indicators encompassing the legal structure and property rights, the freedom to trade internationally, and regulation of credit, labor, and business (see Chapter III of the September 2005 *World Economic Outlook* for details). The importance of sound institutions for growth was taken up in Chapter III of the April 2003 *World Economic Outlook*.

Box 2.2. Commodity Price Shocks, Growth, and Financing in Sub-Saharan Africa

The recent sharp increase in oil prices has been a burden on oil-importing countries around the world, especially low-income countries that can ill afford higher oil bills. However, unlike earlier episodes of oil price hikes (1979–80; 1998–2000), there have been simultaneous increases in prices of a number of other commodities, including metals and some agricultural products, that are exported by low-income countries, in the context of buoyant world demand. This box looks at the overall impact of commodity price changes on low-income countries in sub-Saharan Africa. In particular, it asks which countries have benefited from the commodity price changes; which have suffered, and by how much; and what has been the impact on growth?

Gainers and Losers

Oil prices increased by about 25 percent per year in real terms over the period 2002–05, but major price gains were also recorded by a number of other commodities, including uranium (38 percent per year), copper (30 percent), coffee (19 percent), gold (10 percent), and aluminum and diamonds (about 9 percent). Prices of other important commodity exports, such as tea, coffee, beef, and cotton, rose in the range of 3 to 5 percent a year.

In net terms, countries in sub-Saharan Africa have gained from these commodity price changes (column 1 of the table).[1] But this aggregate masks quite disparate developments at the country level. Out of the 33 countries for which disaggregated trade data are available through *World Integrated Trade Solution* (WITS), 13 countries experienced a terms-of-trade gain, averaging 4.3 percent of GDP per year, while 20 countries suffered terms-of-trade losses, averaging 1.7 percent of GDP per year. The net gainers were predominantly oil exporters (Cameroon, Gabon, Nigeria, and the Sudan), but also included exporters of diamonds (Botswana), uranium (Niger), copper (Zambia), aluminum (Mozambique) and tobacco (Zimbabwe). The largest losers were all net oil importers (Ghana, Madagascar, and Senegal).

Note: The authors of this box are Arvind Subramanian and Thierry Tressel.

[1]Disaggregated commodity trade data (available from the United Nations WITS Trade database) for countries in sub-Saharan Africa. In calculating the terms-of-trade impact, the counterfactual assumption is that prices would have otherwise remained at their 2002 levels; and to isolate the pure price effect, the changes were computed in terms of base period import and export volumes.

Commodity Terms-of-Trade Shocks and Financing
(Percent of GDP unless noted otherwise)

	Terms-of-Trade Shock (1)	Real GDP Growth (percent) (2)	Change in Net ODA (3)	Change in Net Private Capital Flows (4)	Total of: Terms of Trade Effect, Change in Net ODA and Private Capital Flows (5)
Average (33 countries)[1]	0.8	4.1	0.9	0.2	1.9
Average positive shock (13 countries)	4.3	3.2	0.2	–0.3	4.2
Average negative shock (20 countries)[1]	–1.7	4.2	1.7	0.6	0.6
Positive shocks (top third) (11 countries)	5.1	3.2	0.2	–0.9	4.4
Intermediate shocks (11 countries)[1]	–0.4	3.8	1.2	1.1	1.8
Negative shocks (bottom third) (11 countries)	–2.5	4.6	1.8	0.7	0.1

Source: OECD-DAC; and IMF, *World Economic Outlook*.
Note: Change in aid and net private capital flows are computed as changes between 2003–05 averages and 2002. Net private capital flows include net FDI, net private portfolio investments and net other private investment. Net ODA includes debt relief.
[1]Excluding Burundi and Mozambique.

Box 2.2 *(concluded)*

Impact on Growth

The remarkable feature of this commodity price cycle has been the fact that virtually all countries, even those that have suffered a terms-of-trade loss, have maintained robust growth.[2] Real GDP growth averaged 4.1 percent over 2003–05 in the 33 countries in the sample, with net terms-of-trade gainers and losers registering broadly similar growth (3.2 percent and 4.2 percent, respectively) (column 2).[3] This is surprising since, other things equal, countries that experience real income gains would usually be expected to experience higher aggregate demand growth, and hence higher overall growth. To look at this in more detail, the correlation between this income effect of terms-of-trade and growth across countries is depicted in the figure. The presumption is that this correlation would be positive, but in fact the figure shows a surprisingly weak correlation. The disaggregated picture is even more puzzling. The correlation is actually strongly negative for cases where there has been a positive terms-of-trade change and mildly negative for terms-of-trade losers.

One possible explanation for why growth in terms-of-trade losers has held up well is that world growth has remained robust, which has supported export volumes of all countries, especially in countries that suffered terms-of-trade losses. For the period 2003–05, the annual average growth in export volumes for the terms-of-trade losers was about 6.8 percent compared with about 2.5 percent for the gainers. In other words, volume effects have offset price effects, helping to maintain overall growth rates.[4]

Consumption and hence growth in the terms-of-trade losers could have been buttressed by aid and private capital flows, offsetting the dampening income effects of adverse

Commodity Prices, Aid, and Growth in Africa

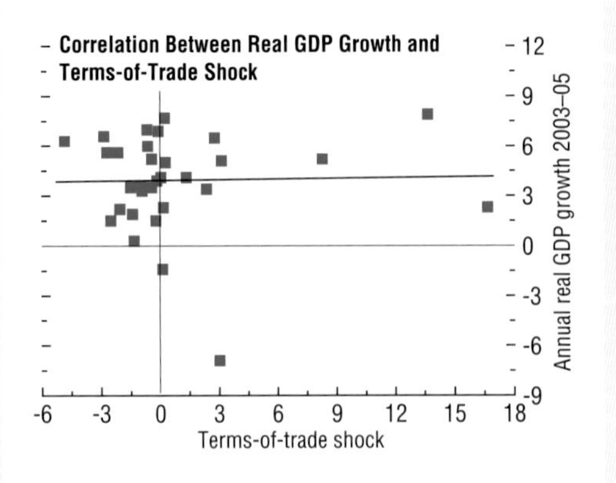

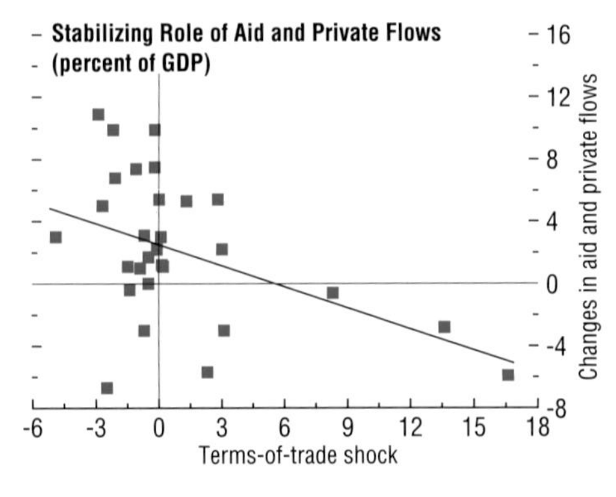

Source: IMF staff calculations.

[2]Dudine and others (2006); and the IMF's September 2006 *Regional Outlook* for Sub-Saharan Africa.

[3]These growth figures differ from the data on sub-Saharan Africa aggregates shown in Table 1.10 because they include only the 33 countries for which the WITS data are available. Calculations based on WEO data for terms-of-trade (goods), rather than the disaggregated WITS data, yield a slightly different listing of terms-of-trade gainers and losers, especially since WITS does not include data on some major oil exporters, including Angola, Chad, and the Republic of Congo. Nonetheless, based on WEO data too, the growth performance of terms-of-trade losers is broadly similar to that of the gainers.

[4]Another possible channel shoring up demand would be movements in real exchange rates. But the data suggest that terms-of-trade losers also saw a real exchange rate appreciation (of about 6 percent on average), even though the magnitudes were lower on average for this group than for the terms-of-trade gainers.

terms-of-trade developments. For countries in sub-Saharan Africa, the predominant source of financing has been aid. Have aid flows helped countries facing terms-of-trade losses? In aggregate, aid flows to sub-Saharan Africa have increased since 2002, on average by about 1 percent of GDP per year (column 3 in the table). Moreover, the pattern of aid flows has helped to cushion countries facing net terms-of-trade losses: terms-of-trade gainers saw a small increase in aid flows while losers saw a much larger increase, averaging nearly 2 percentage points of GDP. Private capital flows have also contributed to consumption smoothing, rising by ½ percentage point of GDP per year for net terms-of-trade losers, contributing further to cushioning the impact of the shocks (column 4).[5]

Overall, adding up changes in aid flows, private capital flows and earnings from commodities, terms-of-trade gainers saw an increase in external flows of about 4.2 percent of GDP (column 5), but terms-of-trade losers also saw an increase of 0.6 percent of GDP on average.[6] The negative correlation between aid and private flows, on the one hand, and the terms-of-trade changes on the other, illustrates the stabilizing role performed by the former (lower panel of the figure). This may have been an important factor in explaining the resilience of growth even in countries that experienced terms-of-trade losses.

[5]Private capital flows includes foreign direct investment (FDI), portfolio investments and other private capital flows (including trade credit and bank borrowing), but not private transfers such as remittances.

[6]Nine countries, however, did experience a decline in their overall flows (Burkina-Faso, Cameroon, Côte d'Ivoire, Lesotho, Mauritius, Mozambique, Senegal, Togo, and Uganda).

There is also a possible supply side explanation for the observed pattern of growth: differences in governance. The average score for a measure of governance compiled by the World Bank that measures the rule of law is on average lower for terms-of-trade gainers than for losers, and this difference is statistically significant.[7] This is not surprising because, worldwide, commodity exporters typically tend to fare less well on measures of institutional quality. The most telling illustration is Zimbabwe, which experienced one of the largest terms-of-trade gains and yet registered the worst growth performance (–6.9 percent on average) over the period in question. The low correlation between the income effect from commodity price changes and growth is consistent with the view that the impact on overall growth depends to a great deal on the broader institutional context.

In conclusion, the welcome surprise of this commodity price cycle is that the net terms-of-trade losers in sub-Saharan Africa have maintained robust growth on average, cushioned in part by aid and private capital flows. However, the resilience of these economies could be tested if nonfuel commodity prices moderate (as suggested in Chapter 5), while oil prices stay high. Another open question is whether the large terms-of-trade gainers (mainly the oil exporters) will use their commodity earnings prudently to improve economic management and governance on a durable basis (for example, Nigeria and some other oil producers are saving a high and increasing proportion of their oil revenues) or whether they will once again be victims of the oil curse.

[7]Similar results are obtained using other measures of institutional quality.

substantially (undermining the competitiveness of the CFA franc-zone countries). Third, countries that have widening current account deficits and are more reliant on private capital flows—such as South Africa—would be hurt if global financial market conditions deteriorate. Fourth, an avian flu pandemic could have major implications for Africa given relatively undeveloped health care systems. Lastly, political uncertainties and armed conflicts could adversely affect the outlook in a number of countries (e.g., ongoing unrest in the Niger delta presents a downside risk to growth in Nigeria).

The improved growth performance in sub-Saharan Africa in recent years is very welcome, but it still falls well short of the 7 percent annual growth needed to meet the Millennium Development Goal (MDG) of halving poverty by 2015 (and sub-Saharan Africa is not on target to meet the other MDGs either). It is important that governments in the region continue to press ahead with reforms to promote private sector investment—including foreign investment, which remains low and largely concentrated in Nigeria and South Africa—and employment. Such reforms will need to encompass further trade liberalization, reduced government involvement in the economy, improvements to the business environment through the streamlining of regulations and improved governance, the development of infrastructure, and the further strengthening of economic institutions. Efforts to strengthen domestic policies should continue to be supported by the international community, including through debt relief,[11] making good on recent commitments to further boost aid, and bold market opening initiatives by advanced and developing countries to improve access for regional exports.

In addition to these broad policy requirements, oil-exporting and -importing countries in the region face specific challenges. In oil exporters, policymakers will need to strike an appropriate balance between spending and saving the additional oil revenues. The higher revenues certainly provide scope for some additional government spending to foster growth, generate employment, and reduce poverty, but they should be managed in a way that is consistent with achieving overall macroeconomic policy objectives (notably containing inflation, which in many oil exporters is running above the regional average). In Nigeria, for example, a key challenge is to reduce inflation decisively to single-digit levels, which will require a tight fiscal stance in the near term. Improved transparency in the use of oil revenues is also important to ensure that the benefits of this sector are spread widely among the population. In this regard, implementation of the Extractive Industries Transparency Initiative (EITI) in oil-producing countries in the region should be a priority.

In oil-importing countries, the challenge is to continue to adjust to high oil prices, while pursuing reforms that strengthen medium-term growth prospects. Most countries have so far appropriately allowed the increase in international oil prices to pass through to domestic energy prices so that demand adjusts. This will need to continue, with countries with weaker fiscal and external positions having little scope to avoid passing through higher prices without delay. Exchange rates will have to adjust to the deterioration in the terms of trade (through nominal depreciation in countries with flexible exchange rates, or wage and price adjustment in countries with fixed exchange rate regimes), and if higher oil prices feed into wages and inflation, a tightening of monetary conditions would be called for. In South Africa, for example, the inflation outlook has deteriorated against the backdrop of rising oil prices, rapid credit growth, and the recent depreciation of the rand, and the central bank has appropriately tightened monetary policy to counter these pressures. Adjustment to high oil prices will need to go hand-in-hand with efforts to strengthen the social safety net to assist the poor who are disproportionately affected by higher energy prices. In countries where a social safety net does not exist, other pro-poor programs could be introduced or strengthened—for example, in Ghana, the government eliminated school fees and increased spending on health care and rural electrification at the same time that it increased fuel prices.

[11]Fifteen countries in sub-Saharan Africa have received $2.8 billion in debt relief from the IMF under the Multilateral Debt Relief Initiative (MDRI).

Table 2.8. Selected Middle Eastern Countries: Real GDP, Consumer Prices, and Current Account Balance
(Annual percent change unless noted otherwise)

	Real GDP				Consumer Prices[1]				Current Account Balance[2]			
	2004	2005	2006	2007	2004	2005	2006	2007	2004	2005	2006	2007
Middle East	**5.5**	**5.7**	**5.8**	**5.4**	**7.6**	**7.7**	**7.1**	**7.9**	**11.9**	**18.5**	**23.2**	**22.5**
Oil exporters[3]	**5.8**	**6.0**	**6.0**	**5.3**	**7.3**	**7.0**	**7.9**	**8.4**	**13.8**	**21.3**	**26.6**	**25.8**
Iran, I.R. of	5.6	5.4	5.4	4.9	15.2	12.1	14.0	15.0	0.9	7.3	10.0	8.9
Saudi Arabia	5.3	6.6	5.8	6.5	0.4	0.7	1.0	1.0	20.7	29.3	32.9	31.9
Kuwait	6.2	8.5	6.2	4.7	1.3	3.9	3.5	3.0	31.1	43.3	52.5	51.9
Mashreq	**4.3**	**4.5**	**4.7**	**5.2**	**8.1**	**9.5**	**4.5**	**7.3**	**–0.4**	**–1.7**	**–2.5**	**–3.4**
Egypt	4.1	4.9	5.6	5.6	10.3	11.4	4.1	6.2	4.3	3.3	2.0	1.2
Syrian Arab Republic	3.1	2.9	3.2	3.7	4.4	7.2	5.6	14.4	—	–2.2	–1.8	–1.8
Jordan	8.4	7.2	6.0	5.0	3.4	3.5	6.3	5.7	–0.2	–18.2	–20.7	–19.7
Lebanon	6.0	1.0	–3.2	5.0	–1.3	0.3	4.5	3.0	–18.2	–11.9	–12.8	–16.2
Memorandum												
Israel	4.8	5.2	4.1	4.4	–0.4	1.3	2.8	2.0	2.6	2.9	1.2	1.0

[1]In accordance with standard practice in the *World Economic Outlook*, movements in consumer prices are indicated as annual averages rather than as December/December changes during the year, as is the practice in some countries.
[2]Percent of GDP.
[3]Includes Bahrain, I.R. of Iran, Kuwait, Libya, Oman, Qatar, Saudi Arabia, Syrian Arab Republic, United Arab Emirates, and the Republic of Yemen.

Middle East: Living with Booming Oil Exports

Oil revenues in the Middle East region have risen further in the first half of 2006, because of both higher prices and some expansion in production (notably in Kuwait, Libya, Saudi Arabia and the United Arab Emirates). Reflecting the income gains, oil-exporting countries have continued to enjoy robust growth, particularly in the non-oil sectors, while external current account and fiscal balances have improved further. With non-oil sector growth running at 8 percent, inflation has begun to pick up, although it remains generally well contained (except in the Islamic Republic of Iran) by the combination of pegged exchange rates, open product and labor markets, and low global inflation. Equity markets in the region faced major corrections in early 2006—prices fell by some 25 to 35 percent from their peaks—but so far, financial stability has been preserved and the macroeconomic impact is likely to be contained.

Despite large terms-of-trade losses, growth in oil-importing countries in the Mashreq (which account for about 20 percent of regional GDP) generally has held up well. This resilience reflects the supportive global economic environment and rapid credit growth as well as country-specific factors, such as delays in the pass-through of higher oil prices (Jordan) and higher Suez Canal receipts (Egypt).[12] In Lebanon, growth has been hampered by political uncertainty over the last year, and real GDP is expected to decline substantially in 2006 as a result of the recent conflict. Higher oil prices have also led to a pick up in headline inflation, and in weaker external positions (Jordan).

Looking forward, the outlook for the region generally remains favorable, given that oil prices are expected to remain high, and regional GDP growth is projected at close to 6 percent in 2006 (Table 2.8). With continued prudent financial policies and little growth in oil production, GDP growth is expected to moderate slightly to about 5½ percent in 2007. The regional current account surplus is projected to rise further to 23 percent of GDP in

[12]Egypt is not classified as an oil exporter in the *World Economic Outlook* even though the country is a net exporter of crude oil and, increasingly, natural gas because the share of fuel exports in total exports of goods and services is less than 50 percent. Accordingly, the country has directly benefited from higher oil prices, not just indirectly through position regional spillovers.

Figure 2.10. Middle East: Spending Booming Oil Revenue Wisely

Booming oil revenues provide an opportunity to address long-standing structural problems. However, rapid credit growth and asset price increases could signal risks of overheating, and further spending increases should depend on the extent of excess capacity and a country's absorptive capacity.

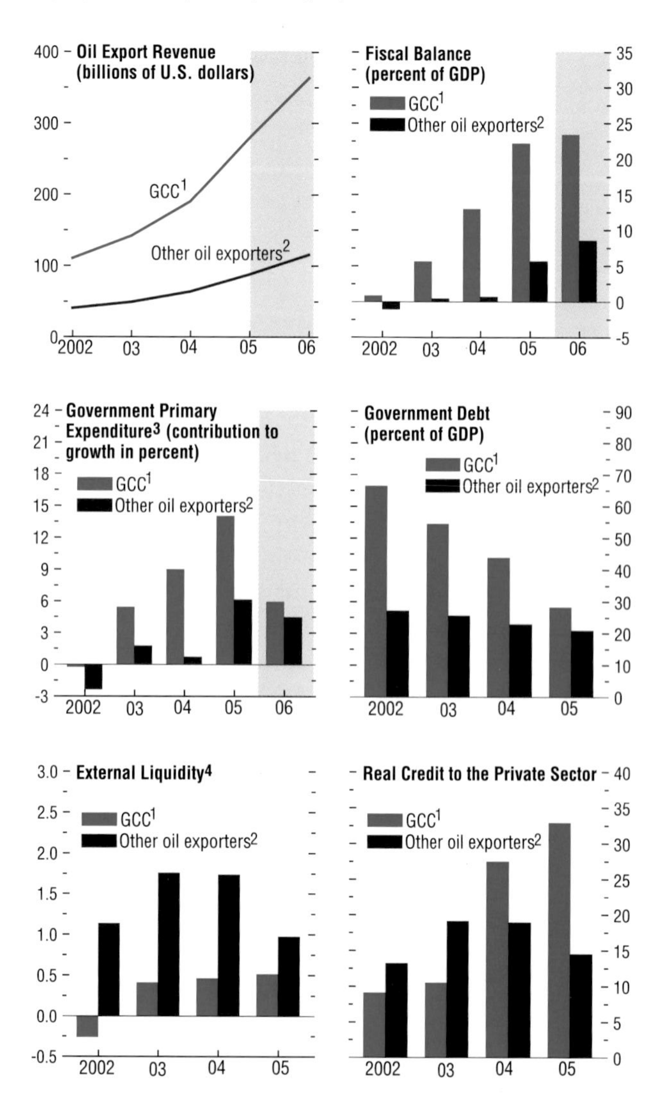

Sources: IMF, *International Financial Statistics;* and IMF staff calculations.

[1]The Cooperation Council of the Arab States of the Gulf (GCC) includes Bahrain, Kuwait, Oman, Qatar, Saudi Arabia, and United Arab Emirates.

[2]Consists of I.R. of Iran, Libya, Syrian Arab Republic, and the Republic of Yemen.

[3]Real growth in primary government expenditure weighted by the share of these expenditures in GDP in the previous period.

[4]Foreign reserve accumulation as a fraction of the current account balance.

2006—to around $280 billion—before starting to decline in 2007. Near-term prospects for oil exporters are generally more propitious than for non-oil exporters in the Mashreq, although the latter will continue to benefit from a supportive environment at both the regional and the global levels. Risks to growth are broadly balanced. On the upside, surging oil revenues could provide for higher government expenditure, while possible further corrections in some still richly valued asset prices are a downside risk. For the non-oil exporters, the external balance implications of the large terms-of-trade losses add an element of vulnerability to the outlook. Finally, geopolitical risks remain a serious concern.

The central policy challenge for the oil-exporting countries remains managing booming oil revenues. Most countries have appropriately begun to use the opportunity provided by higher revenues to increase spending to address long-standing structural problems, in particular the need to generate employment for the rapidly growing working-age population and to boost infrastructure and human capital development (Figure 2.10). In addition, national oil companies in the region have developed plans for ambitious capacity expansion and are ratcheting up investment. At the current juncture, there seems ample scope for this buildup of spending, given high unemployment in many countries and still low inflation, although with continued rapid credit growth, the risks of overheating need to be carefully monitored. It will however, be important for higher expenditure to be accompanied by determined efforts at capacity-enhancing reforms to ensure that the funds are well used and bring lasting supply-side benefits; otherwise, growth will remain dependent on continued high oil prices. Priorities in this regard are reforms that contribute to increasing private sector participation and investment in major sectors that would help to diversify oil-dependent economies.

With many oil exporters in the region pegging their currencies to the U.S. dollar, inflation will inevitably rise somewhat with higher expenditure, as prices of locally produced goods and services will increase compared to those traded internationally. However, if expenditure increases are appropriately aligned with macroeconomic conditions and are accompanied by structural reforms, any pick-up in inflation should remain contained and temporary. In contrast to the generally low inflation in the region, inflation is running at about 12 percent (year-on-year basis) in the Islamic Republic of Iran, reflecting the combination of rising government expenditure and expansionary monetary policy. With monetary control hampered by multiple, internally inconsistent policy objectives and limited operational autonomy of the central bank, some fiscal policy tightening will be required to reduce inflation, with additional support from greater exchange rate flexibility.

In oil-importing countries, the key macroeconomic policy challenge is to facilitate the economic adjustment to the terms-of-trade loss, which is likely to include a substantial permanent component. Allowing for the full pass-through of the higher world oil prices to final users will be key to ensure budget sustainability and adjustment in energy consumption. Recent fuel price increases in Jordan were appropriate steps in this direction. In view of generally large current account deficits, fiscal consolidation is urgently needed to reduce external vulnerabilities related to public debt. In Egypt, the favorable outlook provides an excellent opportunity to reduce the large fiscal deficit and put public debt on a declining path. In some countries, real exchange rate depreciation may be helpful to support the external adjustment. Given limited exchange rate flexibility in the oil-importing countries, this adjustment may require some macroeconomic policy tightening to rein in domestic demand and reduce inflation below partner country levels. Concurrent structural reforms aimed at raising trade openness and productivity would provide important synergies.

Finally, policymakers throughout the region should be mindful of prudential risks in the financial sector. With oil export proceeds partly flowing into the domestic banking system and substantial net capital flows to non-oil exporters, broad money and, even more so, credit growth have accelerated sharply in many countries over the past three years and remain very high. At the same time, the favorable oil market outlook and buoyant investor confidence have underpinned large increases in equity and property prices relative to GDP in 2004–05, even though some of these gains were reversed in the first half of 2006. This combination has raised concerns about increased leverage in private sector balance sheets, including in the household sector, rising financial sector exposure to asset price corrections, and a possible deterioration in credit quality. Supervisors need to monitor such risks carefully and ensure adequate prudential standards. At the same time, reforms aimed at improving market liquidity and transparency will help to reduce asset price volatility that is not related to fundamentals. The recent lifting of restrictions in equity markets for foreign investors in Saudi Arabia was a welcome step in this regard.

References

Dudine, Paolo, James John, Mark Lewis, Luzmaria Monasi, Helaway Tadesse, and Joerg Zeuner, 2006, "Weathering the Storm So Far: The Impact of the 2003–05 Oil Shock on Low-Income Countries," IMF Working Paper 06/171 (Washington: International Monetary Fund).

European Commission, 2005, "The Economic Costs of Non-Lisbon: A Survey of the Literature on the Economic Impact of Lisbon-Type Reforms," European Commission Occasional Paper No. 16 (Brussels, Belgium: European Commission).

Gordon, Robert J., and Ian Dew-Becker, 2005, "Why Did Europe's Productivity Catch-up Sputter Out? A Tale of Tigers and Tortoises," November 15, 2005 version of paper presented at FRBSF/CSIP Conference, *Productivity Growth: Causes and Consequences*, Federal Reserve Bank of San Francisco, November 18, 2005.

Hauner, David, and Manmohan S. Kumar, 2005, "Financial Globalization and Fiscal Performance in Emerging Markets," IMF Working Paper 05/212 (Washington: International Monetary Fund).

Inklaar, Robert, Mary O'Mahony, and Marcel P. Timmer, 2005, "ICT and Europe's Productivity Performance: Industry-Level Growth Account Comparisons with the United States," *Review of Income and Wealth,* Vol. 51 (December), pp. 505–36.

International Monetary Fund, 2004, "Determinants of the Rally in Emerging Market Debt—Liquidity and Fundamentals," in the *Global Financial Stability Report,* April (Washington).

Schadler, Susan, Ashoka Mody, Abdul Abiad, and Daniel Leigh, 2006, "Growth in the Central and Eastern European Countries of the European Union: A Regional Review," IMF Occasional Paper No. 252 (Washington: International Monetary Fund).

Timmer, Marcel P., and Bart van Ark, 2005, "Does Information and Communication Technology Drive EU-US Productivity Growth Differentials?" *Oxford Economic Papers,* Vol. 57 (October), pp. 693–716.

Zettelmeyer, Jeromin, forthcoming, "Growth and Reforms in Latin America: A Survey of Facts and Arguments, IMF Working Paper (Washington: International Monetary Fund).

ASIA RISING: PATTERNS OF ECONOMIC DEVELOPMENT AND GROWTH

Asia's striking growth performance has long attracted the interest of both policymakers and researchers. For several decades, growth has been very strong in the region as a whole—even spectacular in the newly industrialized economies (NIEs)[1] and, more recently, China. Between 1981 and 2001, the number of people living in extreme poverty declined dramatically in East Asia (by over 400 million in China alone). At the same time, given the presence of both early and late developers, Asia continues to display wide disparities in per capita income, ranging from over $33,000 in Singapore to $2,000 in Bangladesh. Average income levels in developing Asia as a whole are still well below those in other regions.

This chapter looks at relative growth performance across Asia, with a focus on the following questions:

- To what extent is the development path blazed by Japan, and later the NIEs, now being followed by the ASEAN-4,[2] China, India, and the newly emerging economies, such as Vietnam? Are there systematic differences between East Asia and the rest of Asia? Or between Asia and other regions of the world?[3]
- What have been the sources of growth differences, both within Asia, and compared with other regions? What has been the role of policies in achieving strong outcomes in Asia?
- How can Asia's exceptionally high growth rates be sustained? What policy measures would help to maintain strong growth? Have the reforms introduced after the Asian financial crises already had a detectable impact on growth and productivity?

Overall, the chapter finds that Asia's remarkable growth performance reflects strong total factor productivity (TFP) growth, as well as rapid accumulation of both physical and human capital. In turn, these accomplishments were driven by a more favorable institutional and policy environment than observed in other developing economies, including in particular greater trade openness, macroeconomic stability, financial development, and in many cases educational attainment. Looking ahead, further improvements in policies and institutional quality would help to sustain high sectoral productivity growth rates and facilitate the continued shift of resources from agriculture to industry and services, hence supporting sustained rapid growth, convergence toward advanced-economy income levels, and the elimination of poverty across the region.

Asia's Economic Success

Asia's real income per capita rose sevenfold between 1950 and 2005 (Figure 3.1), significantly reducing its gap relative to the United States. Asia's success stands in marked contrast with the failure of Latin America and other developing economies to catch up with advanced economies.

Note: The principal authors of this chapter are Florence Jaumotte, Hélène Poirson, Nikola Spatafora, and Khuong Vu, with support from Christian de Guzman and Patrick Hettinger.

[1]Comprising Hong Kong SAR, Korea, Singapore, and Taiwan Province of China.

[2]The group consists of the following four members of the Association of South-East Asian Nations: Indonesia, Malaysia, the Philippines, and Thailand.

[3]The chapter focuses on the following Asian countries and subregions: Japan; the NIEs; the ASEAN-4; China; India; and "Other Asia" (Bangladesh, Cambodia, Lao P.D.R., Myanmar, Pakistan, Sri Lanka, and Vietnam). "Asia" is defined as comprising all the above countries; "developing Asia," all the above countries except Japan and the NIEs; "East Asia," all the above countries except Japan, India, Pakistan, and Sri Lanka. Asia as a whole is contrasted with the following regions: advanced economies excluding Asia; Latin America and the Caribbean; and other developing economies. All regional and subregional averages refer to unweighted means, unless otherwise noted.

Figure 3.1. Output Per Capita

Asia's real income per capita rose sevenfold between 1950 and 2005. As a result, its income gap relative to the United States was significantly reduced.

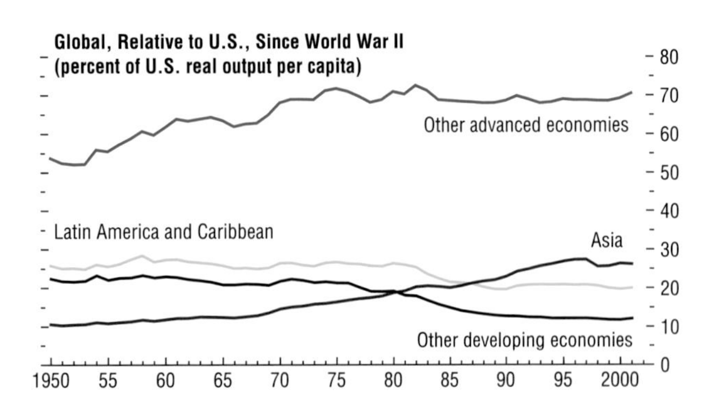

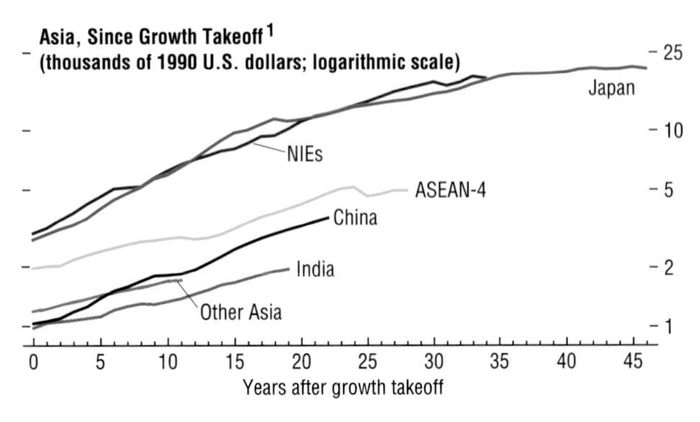

Sources: Maddison (2003); and IMF staff calculations.
[1] The growth takeoff is defined as occurring in 1955 for Japan, 1967 for the newly industrialized economies (NIEs), 1973 for the ASEAN-4 (Indonesia, Malaysia, the Philippines, and Thailand), 1979 for China, 1982 for India, and 1990 for other Asian economies.

Within Asia, there have been significant, well-known differences across countries in the timing of their initial "takeoff" into sustained growth and, more broadly, the start of their "integration" into the world economy.[4] Later developers, including China, appear to have started their takeoff at lower income levels than Japan or the NIEs. At the same time, the overall pace of growth in later developers does not appear significantly different from that experienced by Japan and the NIEs at similar stages of the integration process.

A similar story emerges when looking at broader development indicators. Asia's share of world trade more than doubled during 1970–2005, whereas Latin America's decreased (Figure 3.2). Within Asia, all regions have captured a rising share of world trade, but the rapid expansion in China's trade over the past decade stands out, even though it started from a very low base. Asia has also enjoyed an especially rapid increase over the last half century in levels of educational attainment.

Declining dependency ratios (a measure of the nonworking age population to total population) have certainly been supportive of growth in Asia, but not significantly more so than in other developing regions (Figure 3.2). However, the heterogeneity within Asia is very striking. In the NIEs and China, population aging will likely cause dependency ratios to start rising again within the next five years, whereas in India the demographic transition started only relatively recently.

Strong policy frameworks have been a key element behind Asia's success stories.[5] Over the last several decades, Asian fast developers have been characterized by a broadly stable macro-

[4] This chapter defines the growth takeoff as occurring in 1955 for Japan; 1967 for the NIEs; 1973 for ASEAN-4; 1979 for China; 1982 for India; and 1990 for Other Asia. The first four dates follow Chapter II of the April 2004 *World Economic Outlook*; the dating for India follows Hausmann, Pritchett, and Rodrik (2005); the dating for Other Asia is somewhat arbitrary, but in any case data for much of this group are not available before 1990.

[5] See World Bank (1993) for a fuller discussion of the policy record, including industrial policy.

economic environment. Inflation has been contained within relatively narrow bands, with the exception of the periods following the oil-price shocks and the 1997 Asian Crisis. Related to this, while some high-performing Asian economies ran substantial fiscal deficits, their high savings and rapid growth enabled them to avoid inflationary debt financing. More broadly, Asia has benefited from continued institutional strengthening, financial development, and in many cases more open trade policies.

Nevertheless, while considerable progress has been made, many developing Asian countries still have far to go before their income and development levels approach those in advanced economies. Indeed, almost 700 million Asians, or 20 percent of the total population, still live in extreme poverty, a substantial proportion of them in rural areas (Chen and Ravallion, 2004). To get a sense of whether and to what extent Asia's growth is indeed likely to be sustained over the long run, the chapter undertakes a systematic analysis of this growth performance. It first examines the sources of growth, and then considers the role that policies have played in achieving these outcomes.

Perspiration or Inspiration?

Asia's strong growth performance can be analyzed in terms of demographic developments, the movement of labor and capital from low- to high-productivity sectors, within-sector factor accumulation, and technological progress. To the extent that growth reflects increases in total factor productivity as well as, say, capital accumulation, it is more likely to prove sustainable over the long term. To explore this issue, the respective contributions of the various sources of growth are calculated using different growth accounting exercises, first at the aggregate level and then at the sectoral level. The findings are then related to policy variables to help understand what underlies the observed trends.

As a first step, growth in output per capita is decomposed into changes in (1) labor productivity (output per worker); (2) participation

Figure 3.2. Selected Indicators

Asia's share of world trade more than doubled during 1970–2005. Asia also enjoyed a very rapid increase in levels of educational attainment.

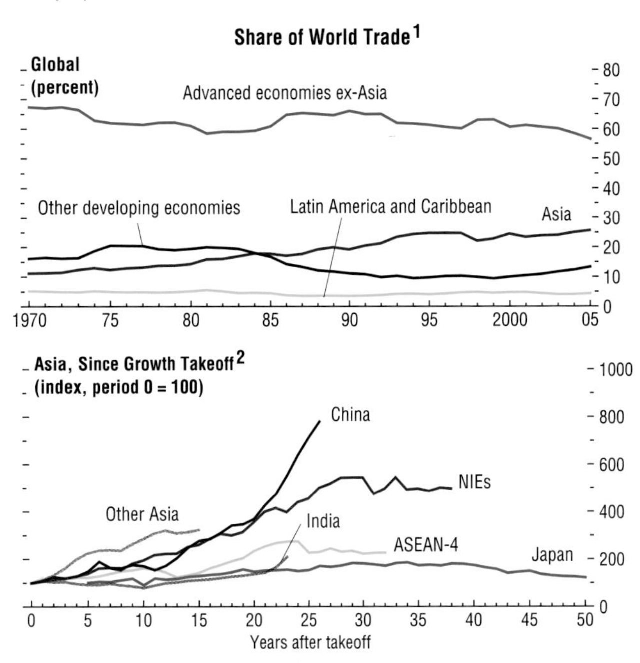

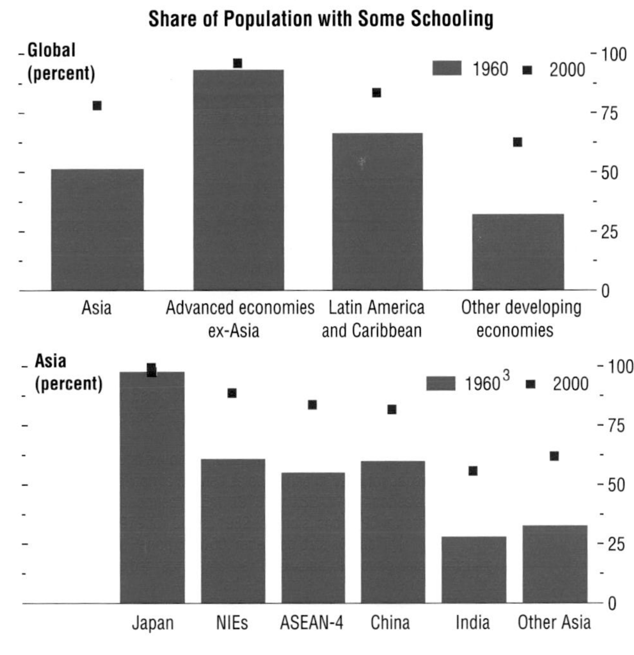

Sources: World Bank, *World Development Indicators* (2006); CEIC; United Nations, *World Population Prospects: The 2002 Revision* (2003); Barro and Lee (2000); and IMF staff calculations.

[1] Defined as (total exports + total imports)/(world exports + world imports).

[2] The growth takeoff is defined as occurring in 1955 for Japan, 1967 for the newly industrialized economies (NIEs), 1973 for ASEAN-4 (Indonesia, Malaysia, the Philippines, and Thailand), 1979 for China, 1982 for India, and 1990 for other Asian economies. For this figure, for Japan, Period 5 = 100, reflecting data availability.

[3] For China, the bar represents the 1975 value, reflecting data availability.

Figure 3.2. Selected Indicators *(concluded)*

Declining dependency ratios have been supportive of growth in Asia (except Japan), but this trend will soon be reversed in the newly industrialized economies (NIEs) and China.

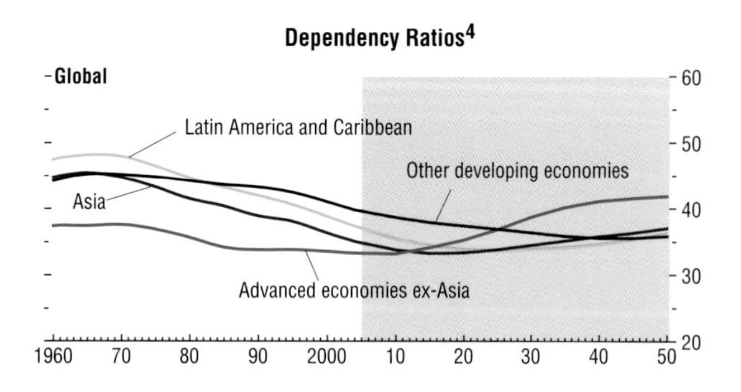

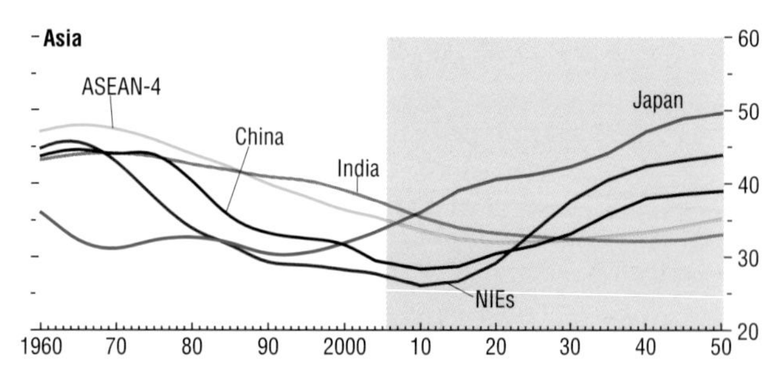

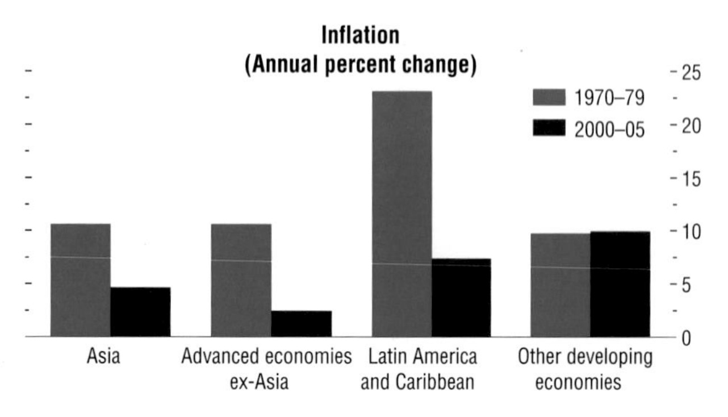

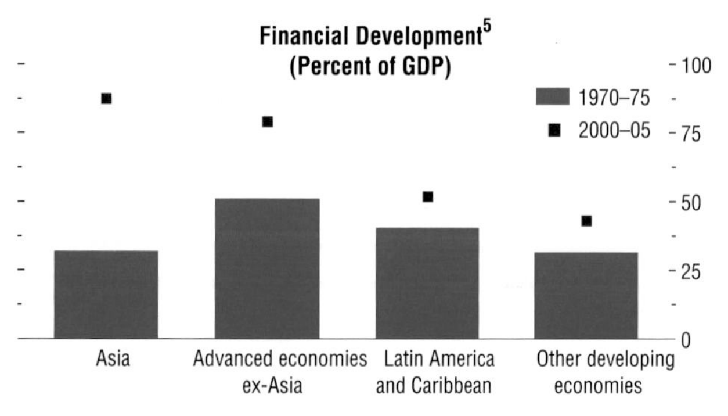

[4]Defined as 100 - (ratio of working-age (15–64) population to total population).
[5]As measured by stock of broad money (M2).

rates;[6] and (3) the age structure of the population.[7] The results show that, during 1970–2005, growth differences—both across regions and within Asia—were driven mainly by labor productivity (Figure 3.3). That said, in both Asia and Latin America, demographic developments provided an important boost to growth. In a few countries, such as Indonesia, Korea, and Taiwan Province of China, the demographic growth impact amounted to more than 1 percentage point per year.

Next, growth in labor productivity can be decomposed into (1) capital deepening (i.e., increases in physical capital per worker); (2) rising labor quality; and (3) growing TFP.[8] The results indicate that, during 1970–2005, Asia enjoyed both faster physical capital accumulation and faster TFP growth than other developing economies; in contrast, Asia's catch-up with advanced economies largely reflected capital accumulation. More specifically, physical capital accumulation contributed 1.75 to 3 percentage points to growth in fast-developing Asian countries, much more than observed in other regions (Figure 3.3). Rising education levels were also important, boosting Asian growth on average by ½ percentage point. TFP contributed 0.75 to 2 percentage points to growth in India, Japan, the NIEs, and Thailand.[9] In Japan,

[6]Defined as the ratio of labor force to working-age population. "Working age" is defined throughout this chapter as ages 15–64 inclusive.

[7]Specifically, the ratio of working-age population to total population, or one minus the total dependency ratio.

[8]See Jorgenson, Ho, and Stiroh (2005) and Jorgenson (forthcoming) for a discussion and summary of the relevant growth-accounting methodology. In line with much of the literature, the capital share in income is assumed equal to 0.35. The main results are robust to estimating its value. Estimates of physical capital are based on Nehru and Dhareshwar (1993) updated as in Fajnzylber and Lederman (1999) using *World Economic Outlook* data on gross fixed capital formation. Estimates of human capital are based on Barro and Lee (2000).

[9]Our results for the NIEs are broadly similar (over comparable periods) to those reported in Young (1995) with the exception that TFP growth for Singapore through 1990 is estimated at over 1 percentage point, rather than 0.2 percentage point. Sarel (1996) discusses the sensitivity of the estimates to alternative assumptions.

Figure 3.3. Growth Decompositions

(Percentage points, per year)

During 1970–2005, growth differences—both across regions and within Asia—were driven mainly by labor productivity. In particular, physical capital accumulation boosted growth in fast-developing Asian countries by 1.75 to 3 percentage points, much more than observed in other regions. Rising education levels were also important. Total factor productivity (TFP) contributed 0.75 to 2 percentage points to growth in Japan, the newly industrialized economies (NIEs), Thailand, and India.

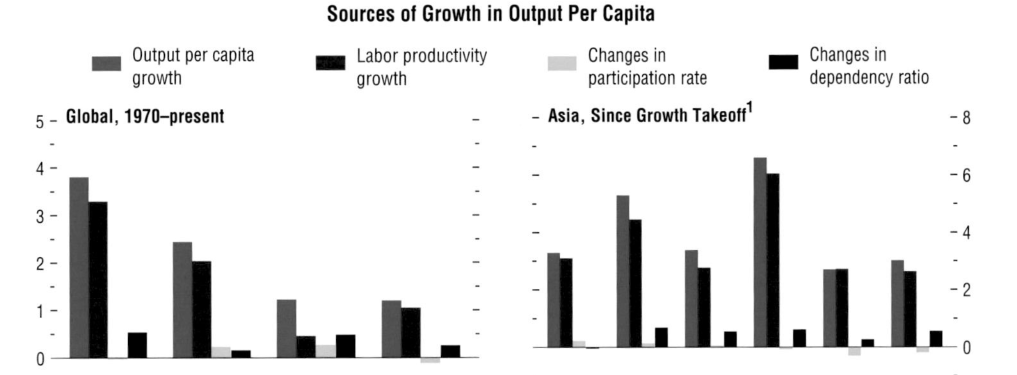

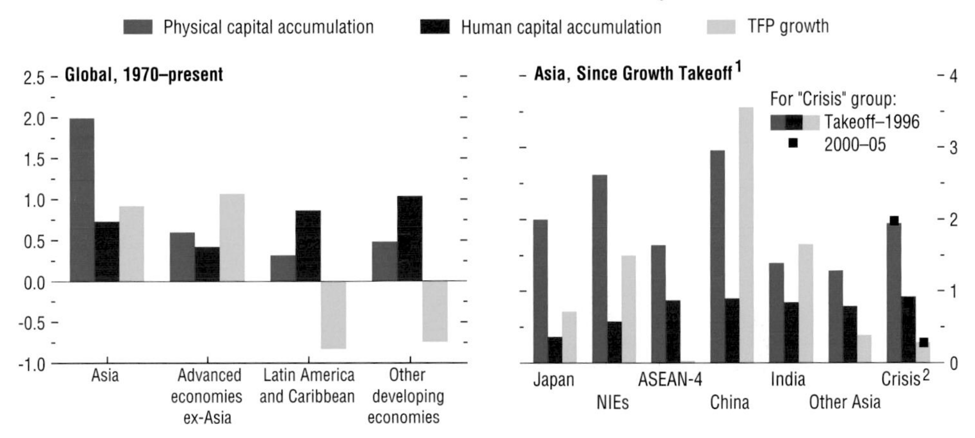

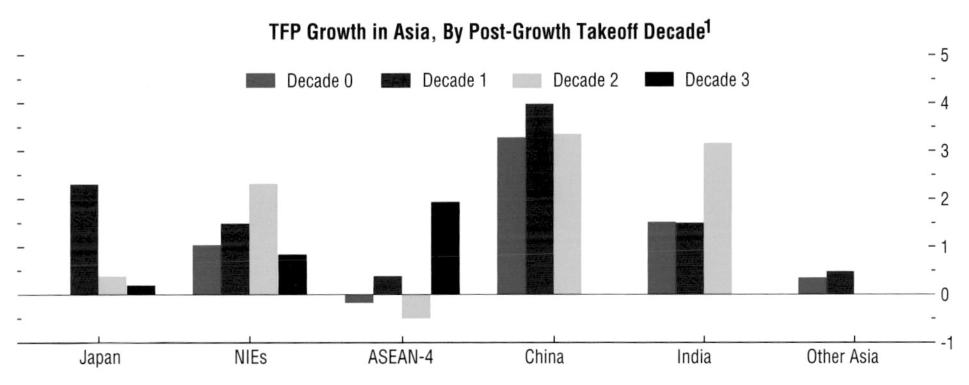

Source: IMF staff calculations.

[1]The growth takeoff is defined as occurring in 1955 for Japan, 1967 for the newly industrialized economies (NIEs), 1973 for the ASEAN-4 (Indonesia, Malaysia, the Philippines, and Thailand), 1979 for China, 1982 for India, and 1990 for other Asian economies. Each decade corresponds to 10-year periods following the takeoff years stated above.

[2]The crisis countries group consists of Indonesia, Korea, Malaysia, the Philippines, and Thailand.

Figure 3.4. Information and Communications Technologies (ICT) Investment and Labor Productivity Growth, 1989–2005
(Percentage points, per year)

Economy-wide investment in ICT capital is having an impact on Asian growth, averaging about ½ percentage point in the newly industrialized economies (NIEs) and China. However, the impact of non-ICT capital accumulation remains much larger.

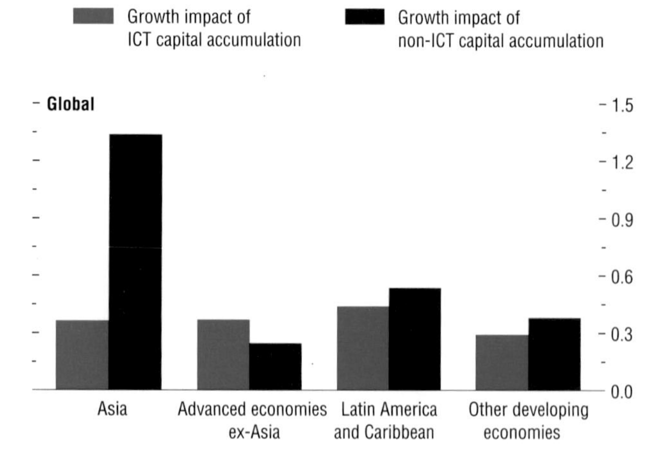

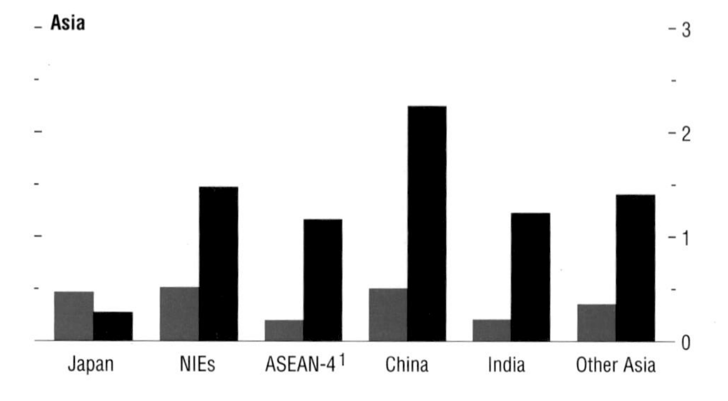

Source: IMF staff calculations.
[1]ASEAN-4 includes Indonesia, Malaysia, the Philippines, and Thailand.

TFP growth declined steadily after the initial takeoff; Box 3.1 analyzes in greater detail the determinants of, and future prospects for, Japanese productivity growth. In the ASEAN-4, low average TFP growth masks significant cross-country heterogeneity, with the Philippines having performed relatively poorly (see also IMF, 2005a, 2006a). In China, strikingly, both capital accumulation and TFP growth were substantially higher than in other Asian fast developers, both when compared over the same period, and at similar stages of their integration process.[10]

The growth literature has recently devoted much attention to the impact of investment in information and communications technology, or ICT (see, for instance, Jorgenson and Vu, 2005). Key questions are whether the accelerated decline in ICT prices that characterized the 1990s led to a surge of investment in ICT equipment and software, and whether this had a significant impact on productivity. These issues are analyzed using a smaller cross-country data set covering the period 1989–2005.[11] The results suggest that economy-wide investment in ICT capital indeed had an impact on growth, averaging about ½ percentage point in the NIEs and China (Figure 3.4). However, Asia does not stand out along this dimension, and the impact of non-ICT capital accumulation is much larger.[12]

Regarding the effects of the Asian Crisis, growth rates have typically recovered to pre-crisis levels.[13] In contrast, investment rates

[10]Estimates for TFP growth in China may be influenced by inaccurate investment price deflators. See also Young (2003) for a discussion of Chinese statistics.

[11]This is an updated version of the dataset in Jorgenson and Vu, 2005.

[12]The ICT revolution can also affect aggregate productivity more directly, through TFP growth in ICT-producing sectors themselves. These sectors account for 10 percent or more of total value added in several Asian countries, including Korea, Malaysia, the Philippines, Singapore, and Taiwan Province of China. However, it did not prove possible to estimate TFP growth within these sectors.

[13]See, for instance, Cerra and Saxena (2003). Studies of a broader sample of financial and currency crises also typically find that such crises do not have long-term effects on growth (Barro, 2001; and Park and Lee, 2001).

Box 3.1. Japan's Potential Output and Productivity Growth

After four decades of rapid growth, Japan's economy stagnated in the 1990s, following the collapse of the asset-price bubble. Japan's economic revival over the past four years raises the question of whether the country's potential output growth has now begun to recover as structural adjustments to the imbalances of the so-called "bubble" years have strengthened fundamentals. At the same time, an aging population weighs against strong growth of potential output. With Japan's birth rate well below the population's replacement rate, the working-age population has been contracting since 2000, and the elderly dependency ratio (the share in the working-age population of people at least 65 years old) is now the highest among industrial countries. With a declining labor force, per capita income growth will depend critically on higher productivity.[1]

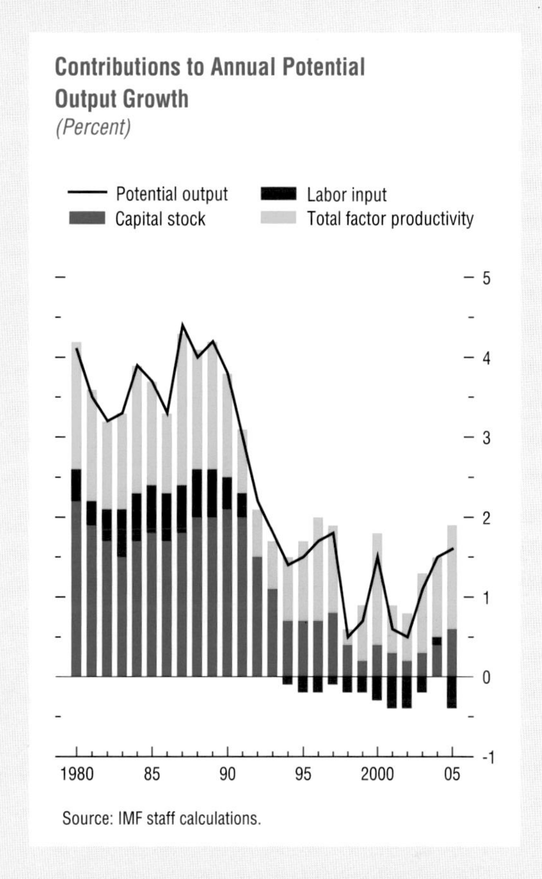

What Is Potential Output Growth in Japan?

There are a plethora of studies on Japan's potential output growth. Depending on the methodology used, results differ markedly in terms of the estimated potential output growth and the contributions of key factors.[2] Estimates of potential output growth prepared by official agencies range between 1½ and 2 percent. A recent IMF staff study (IMF, 2006b) seeks to get a new handle on the determinants of Japan's potential growth, taking into account gains from past structural reforms as well as capital deepening and embodied technical change. The key results are as follows.

- Potential output growth has increased steadily since 2001 to over 1½ percent in 2005, from less than 1 percent a year at the end of the 1990s (first figure). Nonetheless, it remains well below levels attained during the 1980s, when it was close to 4 percent a year.
- The improvement in potential output growth is mainly attributable to a rise in total factor productivity (TFP) growth—the outcome of an improved use of resources and increased competition. TFP growth has increased to 1¼ percent a year in 2005, from less than ¼ percent in 1998.
- The contribution of the capital stock, on the other hand, has declined since the collapse of investment in the early 1990s: growth in the capital stock now accounts for just over ½ percentage point of potential output growth, down from more than 2 percentage points in the early 1990s. This decline partly reflects adjustments in the corporate sector that have delayed new investment and disposed of old capital stock.

Note: The principal authors of this box are Papa N'Diaye and Dan Citrin.

[1]A recent government-sponsored report, "Japan's 21st Century Vision," sets out the importance of raising productivity and reaping the benefits of globalization to avoid deteriorating living standards.

[2]See, for example, Hayashi and Prescott (2002); and Fukao and others (2003).

Box 3.1 *(concluded)*

- Finally, labor inputs continue to contribute negatively to potential output growth, reflecting a shrinking working-age population as well as a plateau in the labor force participation rate and a secular rise in structural unemployment. The negative contribution of employment has, however, been partly offset by a positive contribution of the number of hours worked, as a result of the recent pickup in full-time job growth.

How Broad-Based Was the Recovery in TFP Growth?

The recent pickup in TFP growth reflects improvements across most sectors of the Japanese economy, particularly manufacturing (see second figure).

- TFP growth in the manufacturing sector averaged 3¾ percent a year between 2000 and 2004, up from virtually zero on average between 1995 and 1999. Within the manufacturing sector, there have been large improvements in TFP growth in information technology (IT)-related sectors such as "electrical machinery, equipment and supplies," "precision instruments," and "machinery." These developments are consistent with the findings by Jorgenson and Motohashi (2005) that the IT sector's contribution to aggregate productivity growth has increased since the mid-1990s.
- Both the real estate sector and the finance and insurance industry also contributed significantly to the rise in productivity growth. For example, TFP growth in the real estate industry rose to an average of ½ percent a year during 2000–04, compared with –3¾ percent during 1995–99. However, gains in aggregate TFP growth have been somewhat limited by developments in the wholesale and retail construction, and "other services" sectors, which now account for just over a third of total output and about 50 percent of total employment (broadly speaking, these sectors have suffered from over-regulation or excess capacity).

Contribution of TFP Growth to Sectoral Real GDP Growth
(Percentage points)

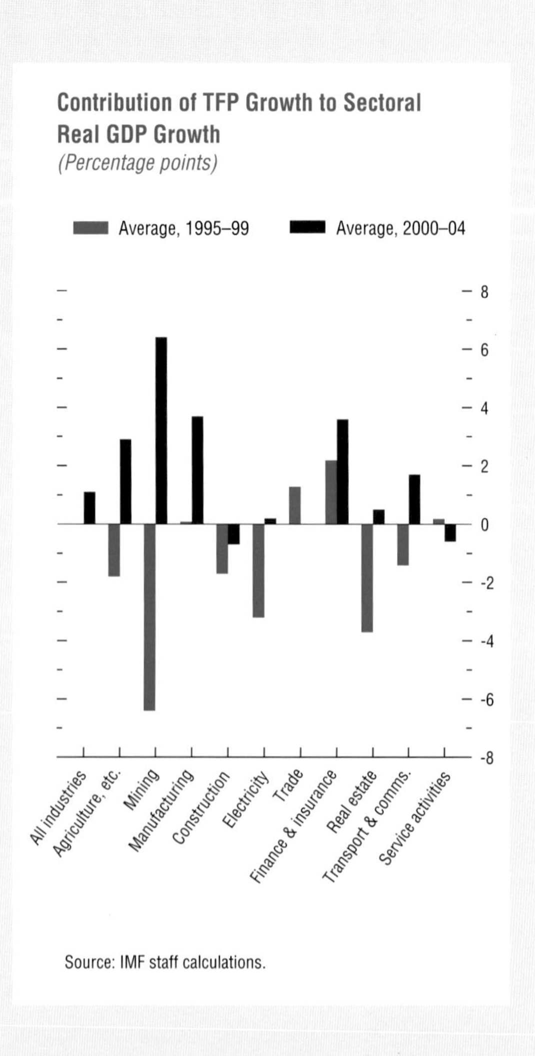

Source: IMF staff calculations.

What Is the Likely Impact of Reforms Undertaken in Recent Years?

The empirical evidence suggests that the recent improvement in TFP stems at least in part from greater product market competition (notably in tradables), higher openness, and increased research and development (R&D) intensity (see table). Econometric estimates imply that reducing markups by 1 percentage point stimulates TFP growth by about the same amount; raising import penetration by 10 percentage points increases TFP growth by about ¼ percentage point; and increasing R&D intensity by 1 percentage point raises TFP growth by broadly the same amount.

Determinants of Potential Output and Non-Accelerating Inflation Rate of Unemployment (NAIRU)

Explanatory Variables	Dependent Variable	
	TFP	NAIRU
Total factor productivity (TFP) at ($t-1$)	1.00 (. . .)	. . .
Change in R&D intensity	1.08 (2.0)*	. . .
Competition[1]	–1.12 (–4.8)*	. . .
Import penetration[2]	0.02 (2.8)*	. . .
NAIRU at ($t-1$)	. . .	1.00 (. . .)
Change in replacement ratio	. . .	0.03 (2.5)*
Share of old in labor force	. . .	0.10 (3.0)*

Source: IMF staff estimates.

Note: Reported coefficients refer to selected coefficients of a simultaneous system of equations estimated over the period 1964:Q1–2005:Q4; figures in parenthesis are *T*-statistics; * denotes statistical significance at the 5 percent level.

[1]Markup as measured by operating profits over sales net of cost of sales.

[2]Ratio of imports to domestic demand.

These results suggest that going forward, the removal of lingering product market distortions—for example, cutting excessive domestic regulation (especially in the retail sector), strengthening the anti-trust framework, and further liberalizing trade (specifically, agricultural)—together with R&D investment could significantly boost TFP, and hence potential output growth. Further efforts to liberalize the labor market to reduce structural unemployment could also provide substantial gains to potential output growth. Structural unemployment appears to be in part related to the generosity of the unemployment insurance system (the level of out-of-work benefits relative to in-work wages and salaries) and the aging of the labor force, which worsens skills mismatches, increases rigidities through seniority-based pay scales and lower reallocation of workers, and reduces participation.

Combining product and labor market reforms with a moderate increase in women's participation rate over five years could raise potential growth over the same period by ½ percent a year.[1] Of this ½ percentage point increase in potential output growth, a ¼ percentage point would stem from higher TFP growth, and the remainder from rising labor inputs.

[1]Women's participation rate is assumed to increase by 2¾ percentage points, to 64 percent. The average for the United States and the United Kingdom is 69 percent.

in those countries most severely impacted by the crisis are still below pre-crisis levels (IMF, 2005b), suggesting that increases in TFP may now be playing a more important role. That said, the empirical results in this chapter indicate that it is still too early to detect any statistically significant post-crisis shift in trend TFP growth.[14]

[14]It bears emphasizing that the available data are plagued by severe measurement problems, especially with respect to capital stocks. For instance, it remains unclear to what extent the effective write-off of capital after the financial crises of the mid-1990s is reflected in the national accounts, an issue that may be especially relevant for the ASEAN-4.

Sectoral Effects: Cross-Sector Shifts or Within-Sector Growth?

This section gauges to what extent strong Asian productivity growth reflects sectoral shift and composition effects, as opposed to pure within-sector productivity growth. The sectoral shift effect refers to the increase in average labor productivity that results as labor and capital move over time from lower- toward higher-productivity sectors, in response to economic incentives and policies. The sectoral composition effect captures the higher aggregate productivity growth that follows from having a higher share of sectors with intrinsically high productivity growth. Importantly, sectoral shifts are not mechanical processes: their speed and

Figure 3.5. Sectoral Shares of Value Added and Employment for Asia
(Percent, latest available year)

The share of industry in value added is higher than predicted in developing Asia, especially in ASEAN-4 (Indonesia, Malaysia, the Philippines, and Thailand) and China, reflecting strong productivity in this sector. On the other hand, the share of employment in agriculture is very high across developing Asia and much more so than predicted by fundamentals, suggesting low productivity in this sector. India stands out with a relatively high productivity in services.

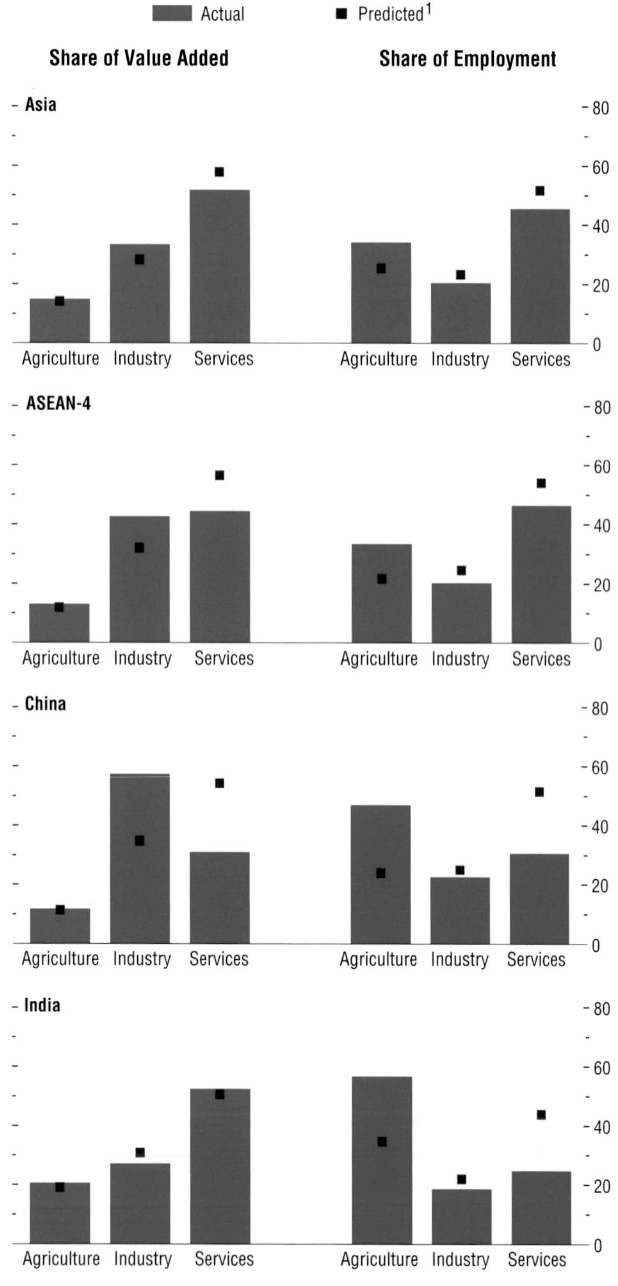

Sources: World Bank, *World Development Indicators* (2006); and IMF staff calculations.
[1]Based on a regression including initial income per capita, country size, and population. The predicted value is calculated as the difference between the actual share and the value of the dummy variable for the region/country.

extent reflect the willingness and ability of labor and capital to move toward higher-productivity uses, all of which are strongly affected by the policy environment.

The analysis is performed at two levels of aggregation. First, a distinction is made between agriculture, industry, and services, using data from the *World Development Indicators* (World Bank, 2006). The second decomposition focuses on sectoral effects within manufacturing (the main component of industry), and draws a distinction between high-skill and low-skill subsectors (here, the UNIDO Industrial Database is the main source of data). Throughout, the focus is on labor productivity, rather than TFP, owing to the limited data available on sectoral capital stocks.

Across Agriculture, Industry, and Services

Asia currently stands out as having a relatively high share of value added in industry, and a low share in services (Figure 3.5 and Appendix 3.1).[15] This holds true whether Asia is compared to the United States, to Latin America, or to the levels predicted on the basis of its fundamental characteristics.[16] However, there is significant variation within Asia. Japan and the NIEs are advanced economies and they share the sectoral composition of similarly placed economies in other regions. In contrast, China and to a lesser extent the ASEAN-4 are characterized by an exceptionally high share of value added in industry and an exceptionally low share in services, compared to both other countries and predicted levels; the opposite holds true for India.

In addition, developing Asia in general, and China and India in particular, have a much higher employment share in agriculture (and a correspondingly lower share in services) than

[15]Services include wholesale and retail trade; hotels and restaurants; transport; telecommunications; financial and insurance services; other business services; and community, social, and personal services.

[16]Including income per capita, country size, and population. See Appendix 3.1 for details.

predicted based on fundamental characteristics. Combining the information on value added and employment suggests relatively low agricultural productivity throughout developing Asia. In contrast, productivity levels are relatively high in industry for China and the ASEAN-4 and in services for India.

Although still large, the relative importance of agriculture has in fact declined sharply in Asia over the last three decades (Figure 3.6).[17] The shift was larger than observed in other regions, and proved especially strong in China, the ASEAN-4, Korea, and Taiwan Province of China. For instance, agriculture accounted for about a third of Korea's and Taiwan Province of China's economies in the 1960s, but less than one-tenth by the 1980s. Throughout developing Asia, the movement of labor into the services sector was at least as large as that toward industry. Also, while in most of Asia the share of industry in total employment is still growing, in Japan and the NIEs a movement from industry to services is well under way.

The effect of sectoral shifts on aggregate productivity depends on the intersectoral differences in productivity levels. For the world as a whole, labor productivity in nonagricultural sectors is about three times higher than in agriculture; in Asia, the differential is even larger, consistent with the finding that agricultural productivity is lower than predicted (Figure 3.6).[18] As a result, the shift from agriculture to industry and services has had a significant positive effect on Asian productivity levels (see below). Intersectoral productivity differentials remained high at the end of the period; indeed, they have widened over time in both China and India, reflecting strong productivity growth in, respectively, industry and services. This suggests further potential growth benefits from future intersectoral resource movements.

[17]The employment share of agriculture declined by an average 0.6 percentage point per year.

[18]While the measurement of productivity, especially in services, is subject to many caveats, these intersectoral gaps appear sufficiently large to reflect real productivity differences.

Figure 3.6. Employment and Labor Productivity in the Agricultural Sector Over Time

(Percent of total employment unless otherwise noted)

The agricultural sector's share of total employment has generally decreased over time in all regions, but the decline has been faster in Asia, which started from a higher level. Despite some convergence, productivity in non-agricultural sectors remains well above that of agriculture, particularly in Asia.

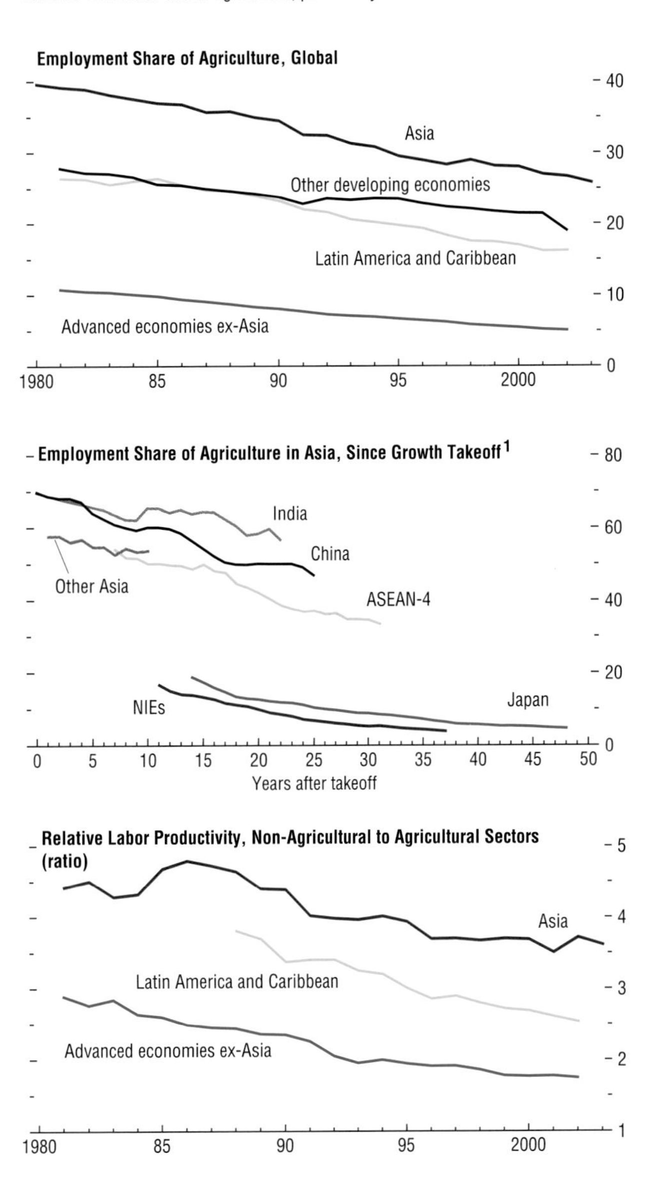

Sources: World Bank, *World Development Indicators* (2006); and IMF staff calculations.
[1]The growth takeoff is defined as occurring in 1955 for Japan, 1967 for the newly industrialized economies (NIEs), 1973 for the ASEAN-4 (Indonesia, Malaysia, the Philippines, and Thailand), 1979 for China, 1982 for India, and 1990 for other Asian economies.

Figure 3.7. Productivity Growth by Sector

(Annual percent change unless otherwise noted)

Across all regions, productivity growth in both industry and agriculture exceeded that in services. Asian productivity growth in industry and (until recently) in services far exceeded that in other regions of the world, implying a catch-up in sectoral productivity toward U.S. levels.

Agriculture Industry Services

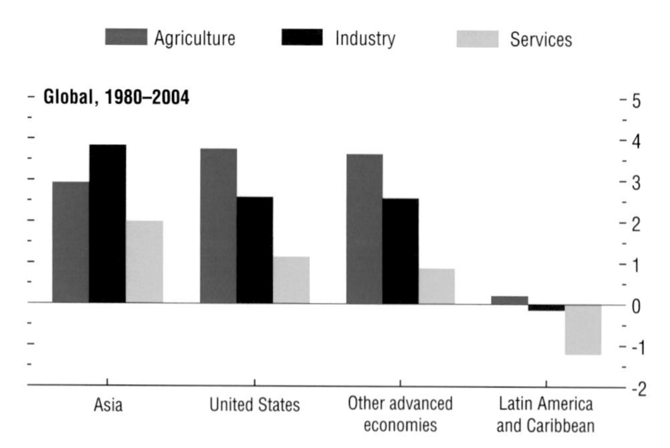

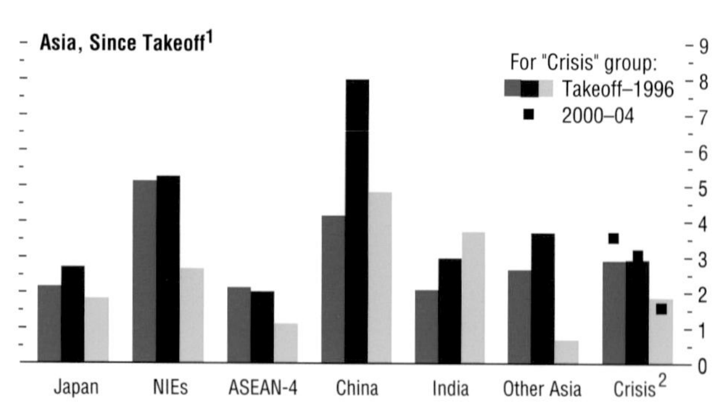

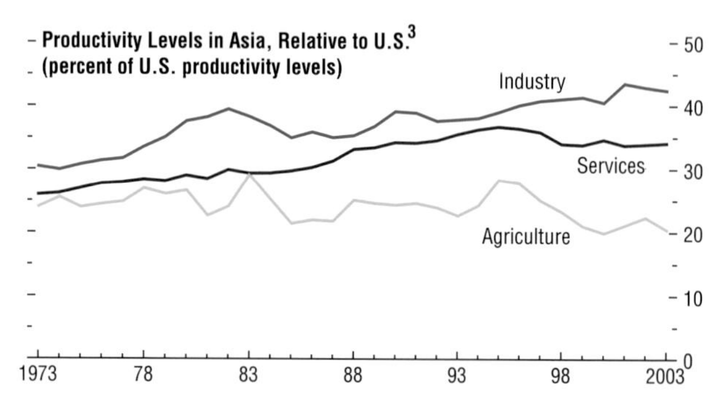

Sources: World Bank, *World Development Indicators* (2006); and IMF staff calculations.

[1]Not all years since takeoff have available data. The takeoff is defined as occurring in 1955 for Japan, 1967 for the newly industrialized economies (NIEs), 1973 for the ASEAN-4 (Indonesia, Malaysia, the Philippines, and Thailand), 1979 for China, 1982 for India, and 1990 for other Asian economies.

[2]Crisis countries consist of Indonesia, Korea, Malaysia, the Philippines, and Thailand.

[3]Sample includes China, India, Japan, Korea, Pakistan, the Philippines, Singapore (except for agriculture, which has a marginal role in this country), and Thailand. Productivity levels are adjusted based on economy-wide PPP factors; this may overstate productivity in industry, while understating productivity in services.

Turning to sectoral composition, its effect on aggregate productivity depends on the sector-specific rates of productivity growth (Figure 3.7). A general pattern, observed across all regions of the world during 1980–2004, is that productivity growth in both industry and agriculture exceeded that in services. For Asia, three other facts stand out.

First, productivity growth was highest in industry—with the exception of India, where productivity grew most rapidly in services. A number of reasons have been put forward for India's performance, including advances in communications technology, which have allowed India to exploit its comparative advantage in services (especially its plentiful supply of trained English-speaking personnel); the successful deregulation of services sectors such as communications;[19] privatization and opening up to foreign direct investment (FDI); and financial sector reforms (Gupta, 2005; and Kochhar and others, 2006).

Second, productivity growth in Asia in both industry and (until recently) services far exceeded that in other regions of the world, consistent with Asia's faster aggregate productivity growth, and implying a catch-up in sectoral productivity toward U.S. levels. Within Asia too, countries with higher productivity growth in one sector tended to have higher productivity growth in other sectors. This suggests that growth is importantly influenced by country-specific factors, which affect similarly the performance of all sectors of an economy.

Third, after the initial takeoff, productivity growth eventually decelerated, especially in services—although this process has not yet begun in China nor India (Figure 3.8). Indeed, while Asian countries on average continue catching up to advanced-economy industrial productivity levels, in services this process may be coming to a

[19]Productivity levels in the less protected software and telecommunications sectors are about 40–50 percent of U.S. levels. In contrast, productivity levels in the more sheltered retail and retail banking sectors are only, respectively, 6 and 12 percent of U.S. levels. See McKinsey Global Institute (2001 and 2006).

halt before full convergence has been achieved, and in agriculture little catch-up has been observed since the end of the Green Revolution. To offset this, as discussed later in this chapter, determined policy action is needed to tackle barriers to productivity growth.

The gap in average labor productivity growth between any given country and, say, the United States can be decomposed into three components, reflecting differences in sectoral shifts; sectoral composition; and within-sector productivity growth (see Appendix 3.1). Such a decomposition suggests that sectoral shifts have in general helped Asia catch up to U.S. productivity levels, both because labor moved out of agriculture at a faster rate in Asia, and because the initial intersectoral productivity differentials were higher in Asia (Figure 3.9).[20] Specifically, sectoral shifts boosted productivity growth in Asia relative to the United States by ½ percentage point per year, out of a total observed differential of 2 percentage points. Regression analysis confirms the potentially large productivity-enhancing effect of employment moving from agriculture to other sectors,[21] in line with existing estimates for developing countries.[22] All Asian subregions except Japan benefited substantially over the last three decades from sectoral shifts, especially China. By contrast, in Latin America, sectoral shifts were too weak to help promote convergence toward the United States.

Turning to the sectoral composition effect, this is positive, though relatively modest, for both Asia and Latin America, reflecting the smaller share of services (where productivity has

Figure 3.8. Sectoral Productivity Growth Since Takeoff[1]

(Annual percent change)

After the initial takeoff, productivity growth eventually decelerated, especially in services, bringing the catch-up process in this sector to a halt before full convergence has been achieved.

Sources: World Bank, *World Development Indicators* (2006); and IMF staff calculations.

[1]Not all years since takeoff have available data. The takeoff is defined as occurring in 1955 for Japan, 1967 for the newly industrialized economies (NIEs), 1973 for the ASEAN-4 (Indonesia, Malaysia, the Philippines, and Thailand), 1979 for China, and 1982 for India.

[2]Taiwan Province of China and Hong Kong SAR are excluded because data are only available from Decade 2 onwards. The broad patterns are robust to including these two latter economies in the group. Singapore is also excluded from the panel on agriculture, owing to the sector's marginal role in that country.

[20]In the United States, most of the reallocation occurred from industry to services.

[21]Over a broad panel, a 1 percentage point reduction in the average annual change in the agricultural employment share is associated with a 1.5 percentage points increase in average annual labor productivity growth (after controlling for initial productivity and the initial agricultural share in employment).

[22]See, for instance, Poirson (2000 and 2001), and Bloom, Canning, and Malaney (1999). Dekle and Vandenbroucke (2006) find also that labor reallocation from the public to the private nonagricultural sector has played an important role in China's growth in recent years.

Figure 3.9. Contributions to Average Labor Productivity Growth Differential with the United States

(Percentage points, per year)

Asia's gradual convergence toward U.S. productivity levels reflects mainly strong productivity growth within both industry and services, with a significant contribution also from sectoral shift and composition effects.

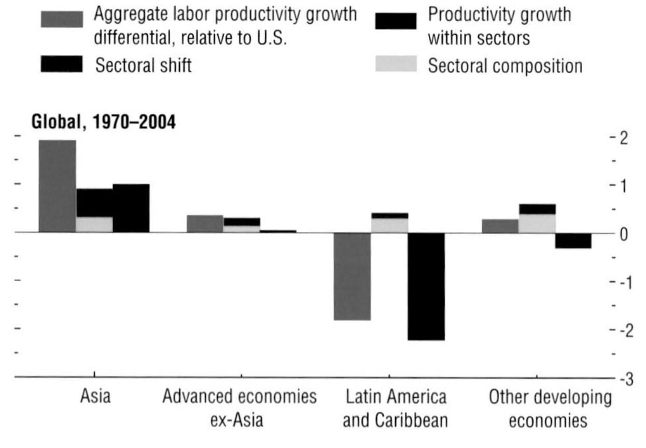

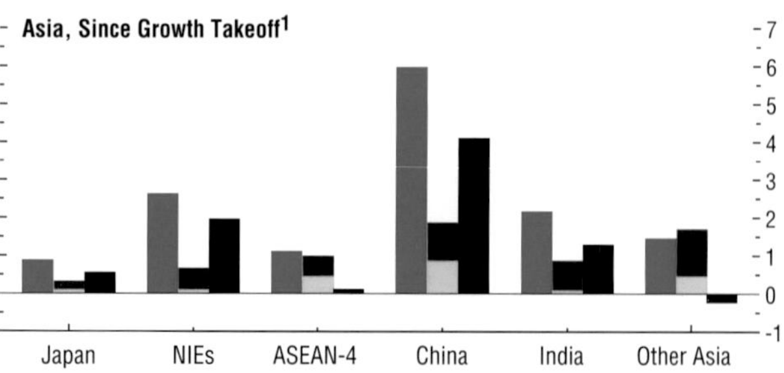

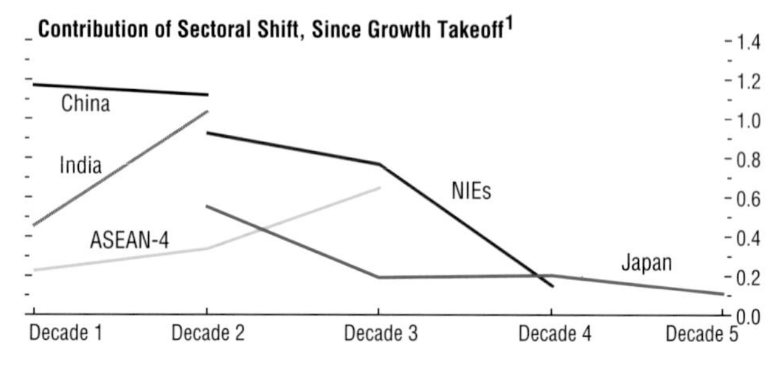

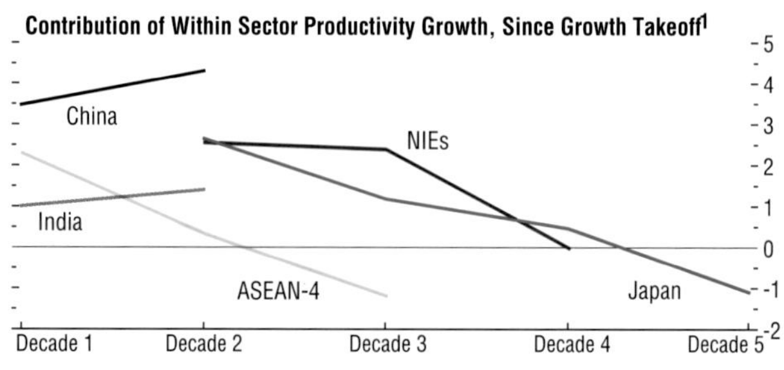

Sources: World Bank, *World Development Indicators* (2006); and IMF staff calculations.
[1]The growth takeoff is defined as occurring in 1955 for Japan, 1967 for the newly industrialized economies (NIEs), 1973 for the ASEAN-4 (Indonesia, Malaysia, the Philippines, and Thailand), 1979 for China, 1982 for India, and 1990 for other Asian economies.

grown relatively slowly) in these countries than in the United States. Within Asia, the composition effect was especially large in China and the ASEAN-4, reflecting the very high share of industry in their value added.

Altogether, sectoral shift and composition effects account for about 40 percent of Asia's productivity catch-up toward U.S. levels. Thus, the greater part of Asia's catch-up reflects strong productivity growth within both industry and services. Conversely, Latin America's relative stagnation and divergence from the United States largely reflect lagging productivity growth within both industry and services. The key question, to which we return, is what are the deeper fundamentals, including policy variables, that explain these differences in outcomes.

Within Manufacturing

A similar analysis was performed to determine to what extent shift and composition effects affected productivity within the manufacturing sector. For this purpose, manufacturing was divided into skill-intensive and nonskill-intensive sectors.[23] Asia, and in particular the NIEs, China, and India, stand out as having a relatively large share of manufacturing value added and employment in skill-intensive sectors. This holds compared to both Latin America and (in most cases) the levels that would be predicted based on fundamentals such as income per capita, country size, and population (Figure 3.10).[24] Since the

[23]Specifically, the 28 manufacturing subsectors in the UNIDO database were aggregated into skill-intensive versus nonskill-intensive sectors. Each aggregate contained 14 subsectors. The definition of skill intensity was based on the income share of skilled labor, calculated using the input-output matrix for South Africa (Kochhar and others, 2006).

[24]Hausmann, Hwang, and Rodrik (2005) and Rodrik (2006) also find that China and India export an abnormally high share of products that are typically produced by higher-income countries. Note also that when population is not included as a control, the difference between Asia's actual and predicted skill-intensive employment share rises to 10 percentage points.

mid-1960s,[25] the rate at which labor has moved from nonskill to skill-intensive sectors has been about the same as in the United States and other advanced economies, and much higher than in Latin America (although the magnitudes involved are much smaller than is the case for the shift out of agriculture). The data confirm that both productivity levels and productivity growth are higher in skill-intensive than in nonskill-intensive sectors.[26]

Aggregate manufacturing productivity grew faster in Asia than in the United States. However, the differential was smaller than in the case of overall productivity; indeed, manufacturing productivity in the ASEAN-4 and India actually grew more slowly than in the United States (Figure 3.11). Most of Asia's catch-up in manufacturing productivity was attributable to high productivity growth within skill-intensive sectors. The contribution of sectoral shifts was generally small.[27] Driving this, both the magnitude of labor shifts across manufacturing subsectors and the productivity differentials between these subsectors were smaller than between agriculture and the nonagricultural sector. The contribution from sectoral composition was actually negative and quite significant for Asia, at close to ½ percentage point per year. This result was driven mostly by Indonesia and Other Asia, where the share of skill-intensive, high productivity-growth sectors is substantially smaller than in the United States. Unlike Asia, Latin America experienced a decline over time in manufacturing productivity relative to the United States, above all because of slower productivity growth within nonskill-intensive sectors, combined with a relatively large share of such sectors in overall manufacturing.

[25]For China, reliable data are only available since 1990.

[26]The average gap over the period amounts to, respectively, 35 percent and 0.6 percentage points per year.

[27]This holds even when the analysis is carried out on the full 28 subsector dataset, rather than on just the two broad aggregate sectors.

Figure 3.10. Skill-Intensive Manufacturing Sectors: Employment and Value-Added Shares

(Percent, latest available year)

Asia stands out as having a large share of manufacturing value-added and employment in skill-intensive sectors. This holds compared both to Latin America and, in some instances, to the levels that would be predicted based on fundamentals.

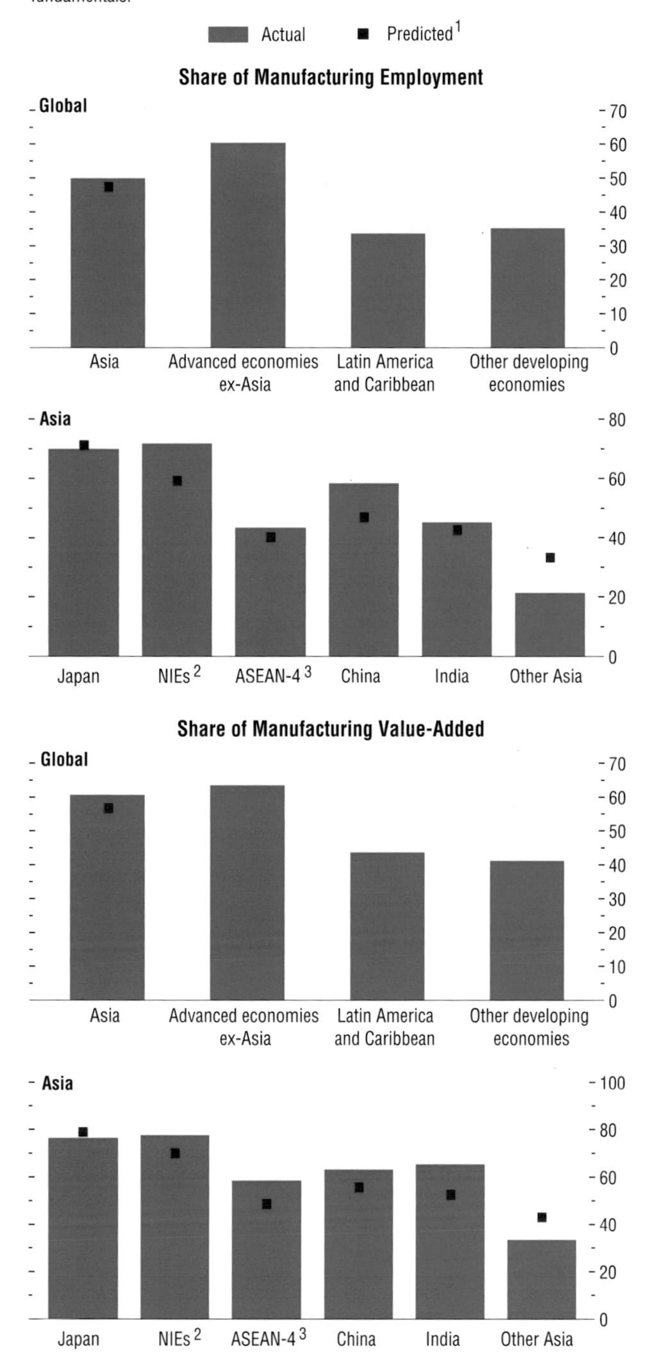

Sources: World Bank, *World Development Indicators* (2006); and IMF staff calculations.
[1]Based on a regression including initial income per capita, country size, and population.
[2]Newly industrialized economies.
[3]ASEAN-4 includes Indonesia, Malaysia, the Philippines, and Thailand.

Figure 3.11. Contributions to Average Manufacturing Productivity Growth Differential with the United States
(Percentage points, per year)

Most of Asia's catch-up in manufacturing productivity was attributable to high productivity growth within skill-intensive sectors. The contribution from sectoral composition was actually negative, driven by the lower share of value added in skill-intensive sectors vis-à-vis the United States.

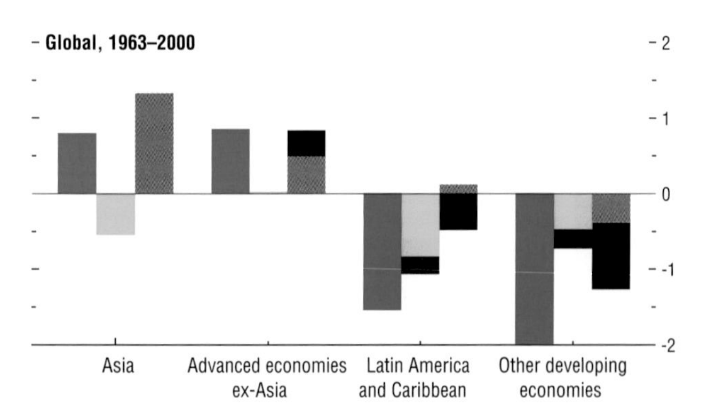

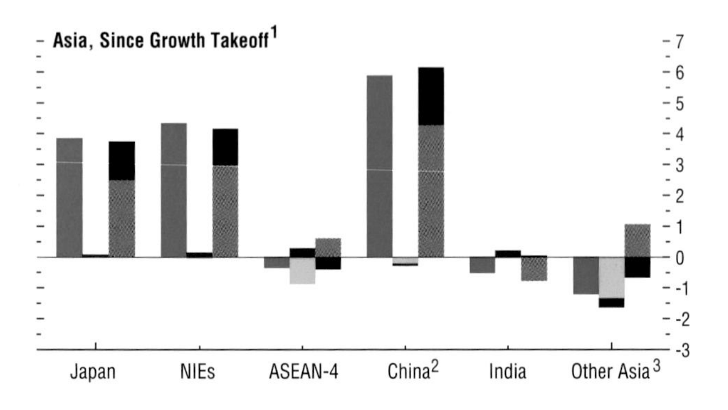

Sources: World Bank, *World Development Indicators* (2006); UNIDO, Industrial Statistics database; and IMF staff calculations.
[1]The growth takeoff is defined as occurring in 1955 for Japan, 1967 for the newly industrialized economies (NIEs), 1973 for the ASEAN-4 (Indonesia, Malaysia, the Philippines, and Thailand), 1979 for China, 1982 for India, and 1990 for other Asian economies.
[2]Data for China start in 1990.
[3]Other Asia includes only Bangladesh, Pakistan, and Sri Lanka.

Policy Determinants of Productivity Growth

The analysis so far suggests that Asia's strong productivity performance has in good part reflected differences in within-sector productivity growth rates. Further, those countries that have performed well across countries in a sector also have tended to perform well in other sectors, and this is not purely related to catch-up effects. All this is consistent with a significant role for country-specific factors, such as strong institutions and favorable macroeconomic policies—an issue now examined in greater detail. Intersectoral resource movements have also contributed significantly to Asia's growth, and this section goes on to examine how the policy environment has facilitated such shifts of resources.

In recent years, the large empirical literature on cross-country differences in output growth (see, for instance, *World Economic Outlook*, April 2003, Chapter III; and Bosworth and Collins, 2003) has emphasized the key role of institutional quality and human capital. The empirical literature on determinants of TFP growth across broad samples of countries is more limited,[28] and has generally emphasized the importance of trade openness.[29]

The data set used in this chapter is consistent with these conclusions. Over the period 1965–2005, cross-country differences in productivity growth, as proxied by either labor productivity or TFP growth, were closely related to variables that capture key aspects of the policy environment (see Figure 3.12). In particular, countries with higher productivity growth also

[28]There is, however, a substantial literature on the determinants of productivity differences across industrial countries, as well as national studies on the sources of inter-industry productivity differences.

[29]For instance, Edwards (1998) uses alternative openness indicators to demonstrate that more open countries experience faster TFP growth; Coe, Helpman, and Hoffmaister (1997) show that developing countries that trade with R&D intensive industrial countries have higher productivity growth; and Miller and Upadhyay (2000) find that human capital boosts TFP in low-income countries only when these countries achieve certain levels of openness.

tended to have relatively strong institutions, a better-developed financial system, a generally more favorable business climate (as indicated by lower costs of starting a business), better infrastructure, less restrictive trade policies, higher education levels, and a lower initial share of agricultural employment.[30]

Figure 3.12 also shows that Asia performs better than Latin America and other developing countries on most of these indicators, especially with regard to institutional quality, trade openness, and financial sector development, suggesting they have been important factors behind its strong productivity growth. That said, the quality of Asia's institutions, business climate, infrastructure, and policies do not yet match those of advanced economies. In addition, regional aggregates mask significant intraregional variations: for instance, the quality of infrastructure is much higher in Japan and the NIEs than elsewhere in Asia. In this context, it is worth underscoring that the quality of a country's institutions are not a given, and can be strengthened by reforms, even within relatively short periods.[31]

A more formal econometric analysis of the determinants of aggregate productivity growth confirms these broad correlations (see Appendix 3.1). Interestingly, the significance of the

[30]Throughout, institutional quality is measured by the Kaufmann-Kraay-Mastruzzi index of government effectiveness. The entrepreneurial climate is proxied by the cost of starting a business (as a share of per capita income) from the World Bank's Doing Business database. Education levels are measured by average educational attainment, from Barro and Lee (2000). Trade openness is measured by the Welch-Wacziarg index (countries are considered closed if any of the following hold: an export-marketing board exists; the economy is considered socialist; the period-average tariff rate exceeds 40 percent; the share of goods subject to nontariff barriers exceeds 40 percent; or the local-currency black market premium exceeds 20 percent).

[31]For instance, the Korean civil service was radically transformed during the 1960s, through, among other moves, the introduction of merit-based systems in recruitment and promotion, eventually becoming a well-regarded bureaucracy by the 1970s (World Bank, 1993, Box 4.4). See Chapter III, "Building Institutions," of the September 2005 *World Economic Outlook,* for a broader discussion of institutional change.

Figure 3.12. Determinants of Productivity Growth, 1965–2005

(Level expressed as multiple of sample standard deviations)

Countries with higher productivity growth tend to have relatively strong institutions, a more favorable business climate, better infrastructure, less restrictive trade policies, higher education levels, and a lower initial share of agricultural employment.

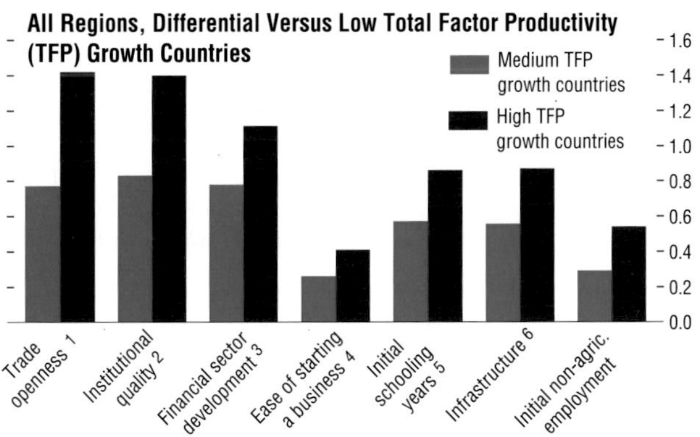

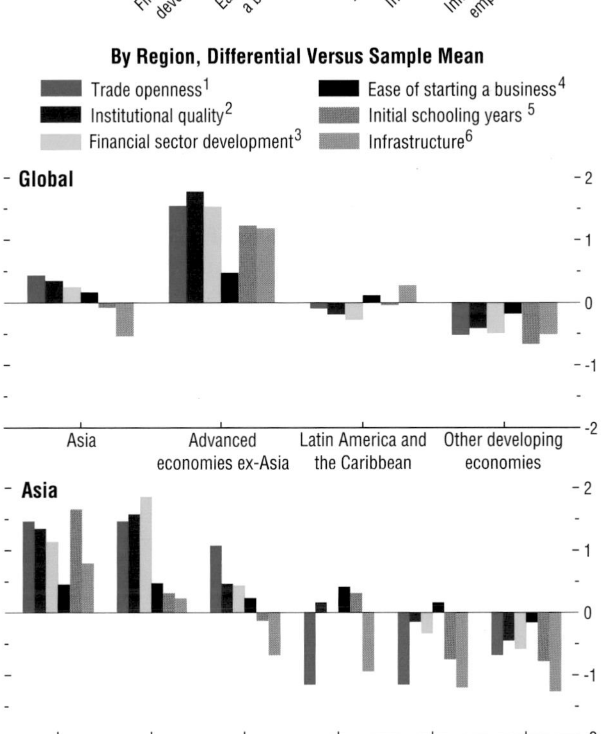

Sources: Barro and Lee (2000); Wacziarg and Welch (2003); Kaufmann, Kraay, and Mastruzzi (2005); World Bank, Doing Business Database; Calderón and Servén (2004); Beck, Demirgüç-Kunt, and Levine (2000); and IMF staff calculations.

1 Fraction of the sample period in which a country is considered as open according to the Wacziarg and Welch indicator.

2 Kaufmann and Kraay government effectiveness measure for 1996.

3 Private credit extended by deposit money banks and other financial institutions as a percent of GDP for 2004. No data for China or Taiwan Province of China.

4 Defined as the negative of the cost of starting a business, from the World Bank, Doing Business Database.

5 Initial average schooling years in 1960 (for China, 1975).

6 Infrastructure defined as main telephone lines per 1,000 workers (in logs) for 1960.

7 Newly industrialized economies.

8 Indonesia, Malaysia, the Philippines, and Thailand.

openness and initial schooling variables weakens after controlling for institutions, confirming earlier results from the literature. As argued in Chapter III of the September 2005 *World Economic Outlook,* openness and educational quality may affect growth outcomes in part precisely through their impact on institutional quality. Turning to within-sector productivity growth, similar determinants emerge for industry as at the aggregate level, while in services the cost of starting a business appears especially important, suggesting that fixed costs act more as a barrier to entry in this sector given the typically smaller scale of operations.

Some of these same factors are also important in facilitating shifts of labor from agriculture toward nonagricultural sectors, another source of aggregate productivity growth. Most prominently, trade liberalization has a statistically and economically significant impact on the magnitude of shifts in employment toward nonagricultural sectors, especially among Asian countries, and this effect is quite robust to the introduction of other determinants (see Figure 3.13, as well as Appendix 3.1). For instance, trade openness played an important role in encouraging the movement of labor out of the agriculture sector in Japan, the NIEs, and the ASEAN-4, whereas relatively low openness to trade in China and India significantly slowed this process. This suggests that trade openness may boost productivity to a large extent through its impact on sectoral reallocation.

Greater financial development has also promoted the movement of labor toward industry and services, especially by alleviating liquidity constraints facing current and potential entrepreneurs (see Rajan and Zingales, 1998). This factor helped support the structural transformation process in Japan and the NIEs, but less so elsewhere. Investments in human as well as physical capital also played a role (albeit more limited) in supporting migration out of agriculture (see Poirson, 2000 and 2001). Physical capital accumulation is associated with increases in the relative labor productivity of industry; similarly, higher education levels increase an individual's capacity to make the transition to the modern economy. Finally, and not surprisingly, the greater the initial share of employment in agriculture, the larger the scope for labor to shift.

As discussed, productivity growth in Asia has been relatively slow in service sectors. Indeed, productivity in services relative to the United States has stagnated in recent years. Empirical studies suggest that deregulation and further opening to foreign competition would be particularly beneficial in unlocking these sectors' growth potential (see Nicoletti and Scarpetta, 2003; Conway and others, forthcoming; as well as Box 3.1 for Japan; and the previous discussion of India). Priorities include steps to promote greater competition in infrastructure-related services, such as telecommunications; further opening the retail and financial sectors to foreign competition (McKinsey Global Institute, 2001 and 2006); and lifting restrictions on entry into social services, including health and education. Increasing the transparency and consistency of regulation and streamlining administrative procedures would also prove advantageous. For instance, in India, where regulation of some sectors is decentralized, harmonizing regulations across states would facilitate greater private sector participation.

Much effort has recently been devoted to improving the quality of Asian corporate governance. As emphasized in Box 3.2, better governance may be expected to yield significant benefits in terms of growth and productivity, particularly for those industries that rely most heavily on external finance (see Khatri, Leruth, and Piesse, 2002). Yet, while reforms in the past few years have led to important improvements, the region still lags significantly behind advanced-economy standards.

Cross-country data sets can, admittedly, only provide crude indications of the factors behind individual countries' performance.[32] For exam-

[32]Among other issues, cross-country panel data for most institutional measures are not widely available, making it difficult to relate productivity growth to the change in (as opposed to level of) institutional quality.

ple, while the cross-country analysis above does not explain well China's remarkable productivity growth, more detailed, country-specific studies confirm a strong link to its post-1979 reforms. These involved, among other moves, the substantial development of property rights, whose impact was most dramatically felt in agriculture; the opening of markets; the removal of barriers to capital and labor mobility; and the setting up of Special Economic Zones (see Tseng and Rodlauer, 2003, in particular Chapter II; and the April 2005 *World Economic Outlook*). In contrast, slow TFP growth in the ASEAN-4, and especially in the Philippines, may have reflected, among other things, weaknesses in the quality of institutions and of infrastructure (IMF, 2005a and 2006a). As for Japan, Box 3.1 suggests that the reduction of lingering product market distortions (e.g., cutting excessive domestic regulation of the retail sector and further liberalizing agricultural trade), together with efforts to liberalize labor markets and boost R&D investment, could significantly boost TFP growth.

Looking ahead, late developers (such as the ASEAN-4, China, and India) will continue to enjoy favorable catch-up effects for the foreseeable future. Nevertheless, this analysis suggests that continued convergence toward advanced-economy income and productivity levels will require further structural reforms to maintain and indeed improve the favorable business climate. In particular, this will require improved corporate governance, as well as further upgrading of education levels and continued trade liberalization, so as to both underpin strong within-sector productivity growth and create incentives for further labor reallocation toward higher-productivity sectors.

Conclusions

Asia has enjoyed a remarkable growth performance since the end of World War II. Both income per capita and labor productivity in most sectors have rapidly increased toward advanced-economy levels. An analysis of this striking record highlights several key lessons,

Figure 3.13. Determinants of Labor Shifts from Agriculture[1]

(Difference from Asia average; annual average; percentage points)

The magnitude of labor shifts out of agriculture is to a large extent determined by the initial employment share of the sector and trade openness. Financial development and capital accumulation also play a role in the structural transformation process.

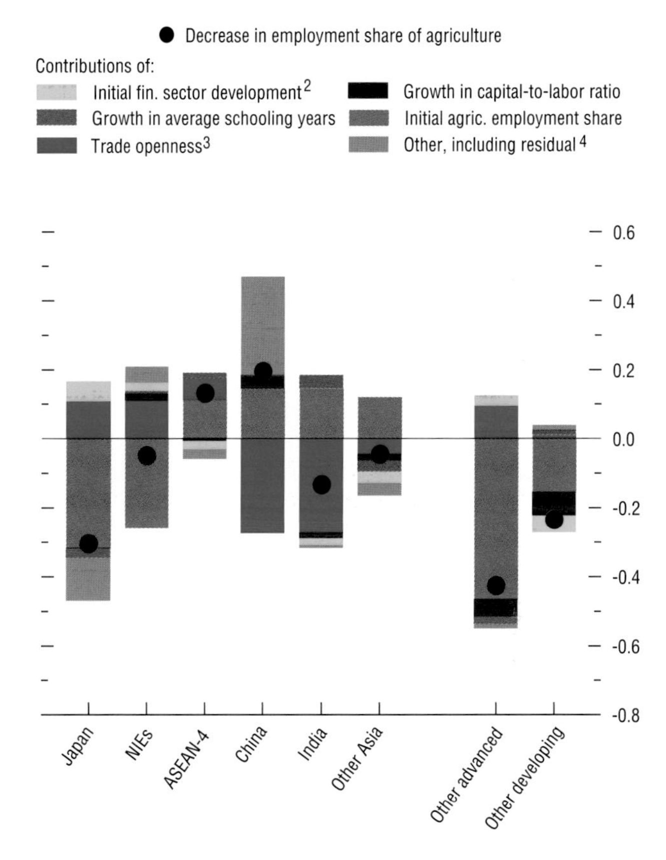

Source: IMF staff calculations.

[1]Contributions are calculated based on regression analysis (see Appendix Table 3.2). For Asian subgroups, the labor shift is examined for the period following the growth takeoff. The takeoff is defined as occurring in 1955 for Japan, 1967 for the newly industrialized economies (NIEs), 1973 for the ASEAN-4 (Indonesia, Malaysia, the Philippines, and Thailand), 1979 for China, 1982 for India, and 1990 for other Asian economies. For other advanced economies and other developing economies, the labor shift is examined over the full sample period, 1970–2004.

[2]Private credit extended by deposit money banks and other financial institutions as a percent of GDP in initial year (not available for China).

[3]Fraction of the sample period in which a country is considered as open according to the Wacziarg and Welch indicator.

[4]The residual for China includes any effect of financial sector development.

Box 3.2. The Evolution and Impact of Corporate Governance Quality in Asia

In the aftermath of the East Asian financial crisis of 1997–98, many Asian countries implemented new laws and regulations aimed at strengthening corporate governance.[1] However, assessing the evolution of corporate governance quality using measures of *de jure* changes is difficult for two reasons. First, actual improvements may not necessarily immediately follow the enactment of new rules because of lags in implementation and/or enforcement. Second, firms can choose to implement measures strengthening their corporate governance *prior to* or *independently of* the enactment of new rules whenever the benefits of good corporate governance, especially in terms of easier and less costly access to finance, are critical for their growth prospects.[2] The relevant question, then, is whether corporate governance quality in Asia has *actually* improved. And, do improvements in corporate governance contribute to growth?

A study by De Nicolò, Laeven, and Ueda (2006) addresses these questions by constructing a time series of a composite Corporate Governance Quality (CGQ) index for Asian countries and other major emerging markets and advanced economies for the period 1994–2003. The CGQ index is a simple average of three indicators, called *Accounting Standards, Earning Smoothing,* and *Stock Price Synchronicity.* These indicators are constructed from accounting and market data for samples of nonfinancial companies listed in domestic stock markets and are standardized so that they vary between zero and unity. Larger values denote better corporate governance quality.

The *Accounting Standards* indicator is a simple measure of the amount of accounting information disclosed by each country's 10 largest firms (by asset size). Specifically, it measures the fraction of variables reported out of 40 key accounting items, selected based on data availability among those identified by the Center for International Financial Analysis and Research (CIFAR, 1993). The *Earning Smoothing* indicator is a measure of "earnings opacity" proposed by Leuz, Nanda, and Wysocki (2003) and Bhattacharya, Daouk, and Welker (2003) and tracks the extent to which managers may conceal the true performance of firms. Specifically, it equals the rank correlation between cash flows (before any accounting adjustments) and profits (after accounting adjustments) across a set of firms in each year. The *Stock Price Synchronicity* indicator is a measure proposed by Morck, Yeung, and Yu (2000), who find that stock price movements are more correlated in countries where corporate governance is poor and financial systems are less developed. The latter two measures can be viewed as indicators capturing different, albeit complementary, dimensions of firm transparency.[3]

As shown in the first figure, the aggregate CGQ index has improved in most Asian countries since the 1997–98 crisis, although in some countries the changes are small or indeed negligible.[4] As shown in the second figure, a similar pattern characterizes the evolution of each component of the index: some countries exhibit notable improvements in all dimensions, while others record negligible improvements (or even a worsening) in some dimensions. Overall, the most notable improvements appear to be in the *Earnings Smoothing* and *Stock Price Synchronicity* indicators, rather than in the *Accounting Standards* dimension.

Note: The main authors of this box are Gianni De Nicolò, Luc Laeven, and Kenichi Ueda.

[1]See OECD (2003). For reviews of the literature on corporate governance, see Becht, Bolton, and Roell (2003); and Berglöf and Claessens (2006).

[2]Corporate governance quality may be viewed partly as an "endogenous" firm-level choice, as pointed out by Himmelberg, Hubbard, and Palia (1999); and Coles, Lemmon, and Meschke (forthcoming).

[3]The correlation between the three measures is low, ranging between 0.15 and 0.35.

[4]As the CGQ index measures corporate governance quality at the country level, it records not only improvements taking place in existing firms, but also those due to the exit of poorly governed firms, which may have occurred during episodes of severe financial stress, such as the Asian Crisis.

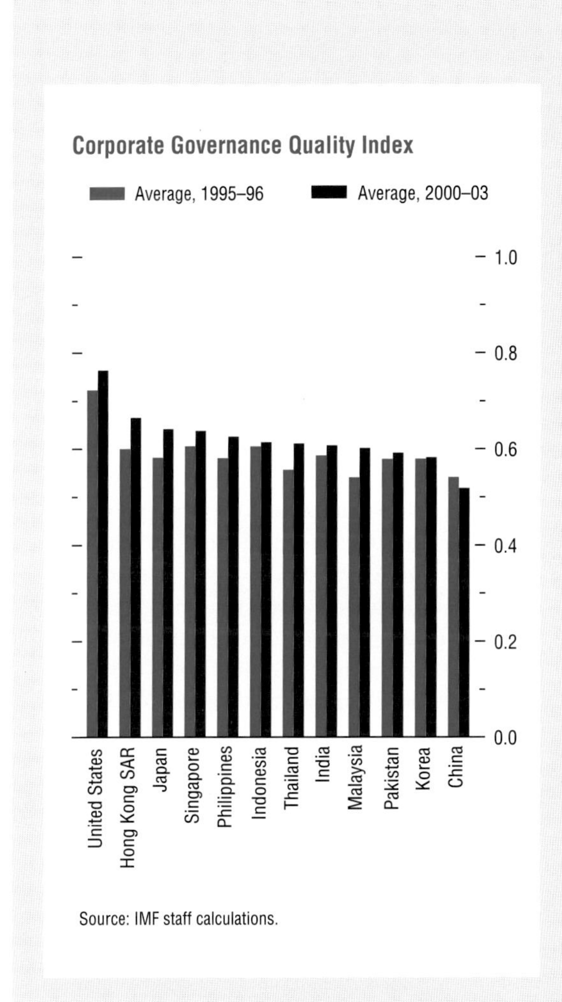

Source: IMF staff calculations.

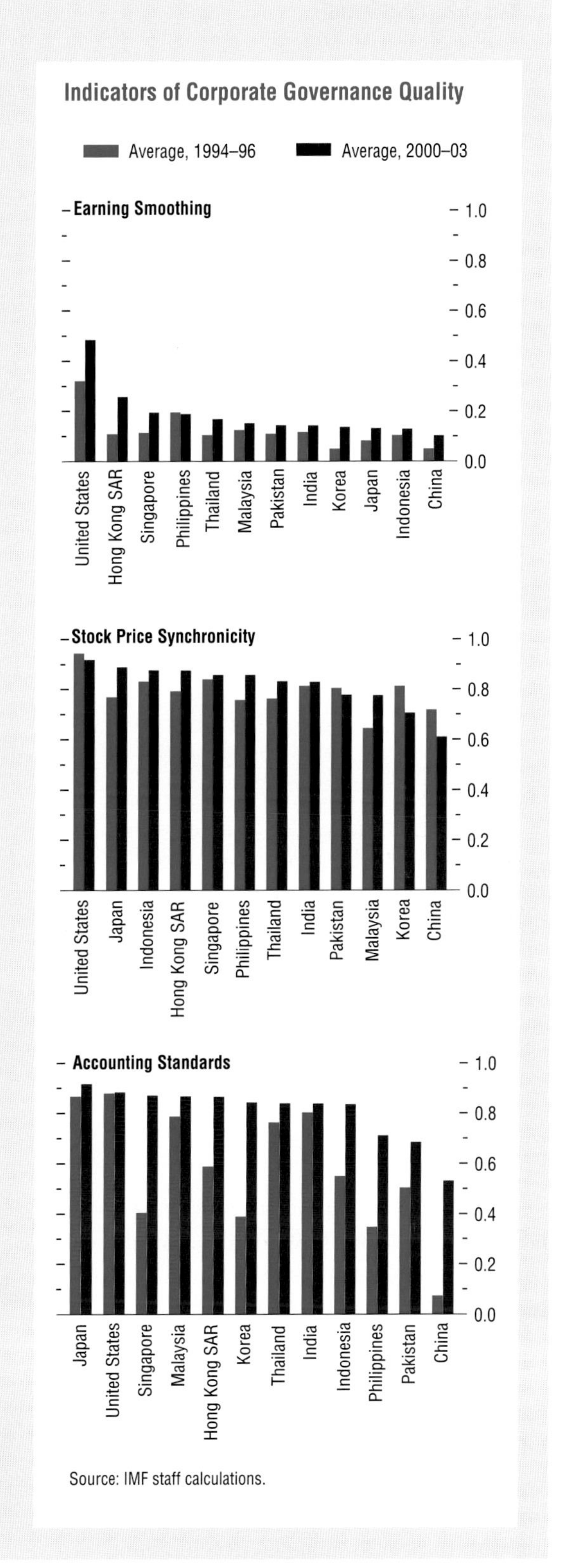

Source: IMF staff calculations.

A critical question is whether improvements in corporate governance quality have "real" effects. Aggregate economic activity and industry growth may be affected through several channels. For example, improvements in the quality of corporate governance may affect growth by lowering firms' cost of funds and increasing the supply of credit, thereby encouraging investment. Industries that rely more on outside finance are likely to benefit most from this channel. Better governed firms may align managers' and stakeholders' interests more closely, providing stronger incentives for managers to attain improvements in firms' productivity.

De Nicolò, Laeven, and Ueda (2006) assess the relevance of these effects indirectly through

Box 3.2 *(concluded)*

Aggregate Economic Activity, Industry Growth, and Corporate Governance Quality
(Dependent variable)

	Change in GDP Growth in Year *t* (1)	Change in TFP Growth in Year *t* (2)	Industry Sales Growth (3)
Change in the Corporate Governance Index in year $t-1$	0.209**	0.154**	. . .
	(0.079)	(0.061)	. . .
Share in industry sales	. . .	. . .	–0.786**
			(0.311)
Change in CGQ Index	. . .	. . .	0.770
* Financial Dependence	. . .	. . .	(1.175)
Number of countries	40	40	36
Number of observations	311	311	610
Number of industries			36
R-squared (overall)	0.0431	0.0243	0.55
R-squared (within)	0.0048	0.0001	. . .
R-squared (between)	0.0421	0.0235	. . .

Source: De Nicolò, Laeven and Ueda (2006).
Notes: Regressions (1) and (2) are country fixed effects panel regressions over 1996–2004. Regression (3) is a cross-country regression with country and industry fixed effects of the type introduced by Rajan and Zingales, (1998), with data averaged over 1994–2003. White's heteroskedasticity-consistent standard errors are reported between brackets. *, **, and *** denote significance at, respectively, the 10 percent, 5 percent, and 1 percent level.

cross-country panel regressions, covering both advanced economies and emerging markets, that relate the CGQ index to measures of output growth, total factor productivity (TFP) growth, and industry growth. As shown in the table, their results indicate that improvements in corporate governance quality indeed have a positive and significant effect on GDP and TFP growth, as well as on the relative growth of those industries dependent on external finance, consistent with the notion that well-governed firms are better able to attract outside financing. For instance, a one standard deviation increase in the CGQ index boosts subsequent GDP growth by 0.9 percentage point (or half the sample standard deviation of GDP growth). The impact on TFP growth is of a similar magnitude. Further, industry-level sales growth depends positively on the interaction between the CGQ index and a measure of the industry's dependence on external finance,[5] showing that "financially dependent" industries benefit relatively more from improvements in corporate governance.[6]

In sum, improvements in corporate governance quality appear to yield tangible benefits in terms of growth and productivity, particularly for those industries that rely most on external finance. Thus, effective implementation of corporate governance reform appears to be an important contributing factor to economic growth. Those Asian countries that effectively improved their corporate governance appear to have reaped these benefits. There remains, however, considerable scope to strengthen corporate governance in Asia further.

[5]Defined as the share of investment not financed by operating cash flow (see Rajan and Zingales, 1998).

[6]The relevant coefficient is not measured with precision, that is, it is not statistically significant. However, a similar regression where each component of the CGQ index enters separately yields an economically and statistically significant effect of the *Stock Price Synchronicity* indicator on the growth of those industries most dependent on external finance (see De Nicolò, Laeven, and Ueda, 2006)

both for Asian countries aiming to continue converging toward advanced-economy income levels, and for other developing economies seeking to emulate their success.

First, in most of Asia growth has benefited from rapid increases in TFP, as well as fast accumulation of both physical and human capital. In turn, these developments reflected a stronger institutional and policy environment (including with respect to financial development, the business climate, and in many cases trade openness) than observed in other developing economies. Looking ahead, late developers in Asia, and indeed other parts of the world, can draw important lessons from these aspects of the experience of fast-growing Asian economies. In particular, the findings in this chapter underline the importance of fostering higher standards of education, so as to support skill- and innovation-based industries and move up the value-added chain, as well as of continuing to strengthen the quality of corporate and financial-sector governance. Related to this, financial development also plays a critical part in the growth process. Within Asia, financial systems, still heavily centered on banks, will need to be broadened and deepened, for instance, through efforts to develop the corporate bond market; among other things, this will facilitate the financing of required infrastructural improvements.

Second, Asia's long-run macroeconomic achievements have also depended importantly on policies that encouraged resource shifts from low- to high-productivity sectors. This applied both to the overall shift from agriculture toward industry and services and to the continuing move within manufacturing toward higher value-added products. Looking ahead, a continuing shift of labor away from the still-large agricultural sector will, especially in lower-income countries, provide an important channel to boost growth and reduce rural poverty. Further efforts to increase trade openness, ensure widespread access to education and health care, and encourage entrepreneurship will help these countries sustain this vital transition. More generally, ensuring significant structural flexibility, including in labor markets, while establishing effective social safety nets will prove increasingly important as Asia strives to maintain its competitive edge, provide growing employment in industry and services, and make significant inroads into poverty eradication.

Third, in Asia (as in many advanced economies) there remains a persistent gap in productivity growth rates between industry and services, partly reflecting the sheltered nature of many service sectors. Further, over time Asian service-sector productivity growth has decelerated markedly, in many cases stalling convergence toward advanced-economy productivity levels; this can be viewed as an indication of missed opportunities. As economies grow wealthier and become ever more focused on services, it will prove increasingly important to encourage competition and productivity growth in this sector, including by removing barriers to entry, streamlining regulations, and strengthening human capital.

Appendix 3.1. Methods and Additional Results

The main authors of this appendix are Florence Jaumotte and Hélène Poirson.

This appendix presents the methodology underlying the results presented in this chapter, as well as some additional results for the effects of institutions and policies on productivity growth.

Sectoral Structure: Actual Versus Predicted

This section presents the methodology used to evaluate the structure of Asian economies and, in particular, to determine whether the relative importance of agriculture, industry, and services is in line with what would be predicted based on fundamentals, such as GDP per capita and the size of the economy. Following Kochhar and others (2006) the actual share of each sector in value added (or, alternatively, employment) is regressed on a set of fundamental determinants and a dummy variable for Asia or the Asian subregions. Fundamentals included are the logs of output per capita (in PPP U.S. dollars), geographic size, and population. The cross-country regressions are estimated by ordinary least squares (OLS)[33] using the latest available data for the sectoral shares and a broad sample of advanced and developing economies. The predicted value for the sectoral share of value added is then calculated as the difference between the actual share and the value of the dummy variable for that region. Table 3.1 shows for each region, both globally and within Asia, the actual shares of agriculture, industry, and services in value added and in employment in the latest available year, as well as the difference between the actual and the predicted values. A similar analysis is performed for the respective

[33]Using a generalized linear model, and imposing that the share be between 0 and 100, yields similar results.

Table 3.1. Sectoral Shares in Value Added and Employment[1]
(Level in latest available year, percentage points)

	Actual			Actual Minus Predicted		
Region/Country	Agriculture	Industry	Services	Agriculture	Industry	Services
			Value added share			
Asia	15	33	52	1	**5****	**–6*****
Advanced economies ex-Asia	3	28	69	. . .	. . .	. . .
Latin America and the Caribbean	11	30	59	. . .	. . .	. . .
Other developing economies	18	29	53	. . .	. . .	. . .
Japan	1	32	67	0	2	–2
Newly industrialized economies (NIEs)	1	29	69	0	2	–2
ASEAN-4[2]	13	43	44	1	**11*****	**–12*****
China	12	57	31	0	**23*****	**–23*****
India	21	27	52	2	–4	2
Other Asian economies	27	27	46	1	2	–3
			Employment share			
Asia	34	20	45	**9****	–3	**–6***
Advanced economies ex-Asia	5	25	70	. . .	. . .	. . .
Latin America and the Caribbean	15	22	63	. . .	. . .	. . .
Other developing economies	28	24	47	. . .	. . .	. . .
Japan	5	29	66	–3	2	1
NIEs	4	25	71	–4	–3	7
ASEAN-4[2]	33	20	46	**12****	–4	**–8***
China	47	23	31	**23*****	–2	**–21*****
India	57	19	25	**22*****	–3	**–19*****
Other Asian economies	54	16	30	**14****	–2	**–12*****

Source: World Bank, *World Development Indicators.*
[1]Unweighted country average. *** denotes significance at the 1 percent level, ** at the 5 percent level, and * at the 10 percent level. Predicted value is based on a regression of the actual share on fundamentals and a dummy variable for the region. It is calculated as the difference between the actual value and the value of the dummy variable. Predicted shares need not sum to unity since equations for each sector are estimated independently.
[2]Comprising Indonesia, Malaysia, the Philippines, and Thailand.

shares of skill- and nonskill-intensive sectors in manufacturing, as presented in the chapter.

Sectoral Decomposition: Methodology

This section describes the methodology used to isolate the contributions of sectoral effects and within-sector productivity growth to aggregate labor productivity growth. The analysis focuses on two types of sectoral effects:

- *The sectoral reallocation effect.* When a country reallocates labor from a low-productivity to a high-productivity sector, this contributes to raising its aggregate labor productivity (and hence temporarily boosts labor productivity growth).
- *The sectoral composition effect.* When a country has a higher value added share of high-productivity growth sectors, this will also raise its aggregate labor productivity growth.

Denoting labor productivity by y, the employment shares by s, the value added shares by s^Y, sectors by j, and first difference by d, aggregate labor productivity growth for any given country and year can first be decomposed as follows:

$$\frac{dy_t}{y_{t-1}} = \sum_j ds_{j,t} \frac{y_{j,t}}{y_{t-1}} + \sum_j \frac{dy_{j,t}}{y_{j,t-1}} s^Y_{j,t-1}.$$

The first term on the right is the sectoral reallocation effect, where the change in the employment share of a sector is weighted by its productivity (scaled by initial aggregate productivity), while the second term is the contribution of within-sector productivity growth, as measured by the sector's productivity growth weighted by the initial value added share of the sector. Other studies that have used similar decompositions include Denison (1962 and 1967) and, more recently, Bloom, Canning, and Malaney (1999), and Dekle and Vandenbroucke (2006).

In order to isolate a sectoral composition effect, the chapter further introduces a cross-country dimension, by focusing on the differential in aggregate labor productivity growth between the examined country and a comparator country, say the United States. In this case, the second term, the contribution of within-sector productivity growth, can be further decomposed into a sectoral composition effect and a new cross-country measure of the contribution of within-sector productivity growth:

$$\frac{dy_t}{y_{t-1}} - \frac{dy_{US,t}}{y_{US,t-1}} = \left[\sum_j ds_{j,t}\frac{y_{j,t}}{y_{t-1}} - \sum_j ds_{US,j,t}\frac{y_{US,j,t}}{y_{US,t-1}}\right] + \left[\sum_j \left(s^Y_{j,t-1} - s^Y_{US,j,t-1}\right)\left(\frac{1}{2}\right)\left(\frac{dy_{j,t}}{y_{j,t-1}} + \frac{dy_{US,j,t}}{y_{US,j,t-1}}\right)\right] + \left[\sum_j \left(\frac{dy_{j,t}}{y_{j,t-1}} - \frac{dy_{US,j,t}}{y_{US,j,t-1}}\right)\left(\frac{s^Y_{j,t-1} + s^Y_{US,j,t-1}}{2}\right)\right].$$

The first term is now simply the difference between the sectoral reallocation effects of the country and the United States; this is called the "sectoral reallocation" effect in the chapter. The second term is the sectoral composition effect, measured by the difference between the sector's value added shares in the examined country and the United States, weighted by the average productivity growth of the sector in the two countries. Finally, the last term measures the contribution from within-sector productivity growth, as the difference between the sector's productivity growth in the examined country and the United States, weighted by the average sector's share in value added in the two countries.

This decomposition is carried out for each year of the sample period[34] and then a geometric average of the contributions is calculated for the whole period. The average annual contributions are rescaled to add up to the average aggregate labor productivity growth. It should be noted that the use of average labor productivity (instead of marginal productivity) to evaluate the effect of the reallocation of employment from one sector to the other (the first term) rests on the simplifying assumption that the ratio of marginal labor productivity to average labor productivity is the same in all sectors. Some other studies have used alternative (regression-based) approaches to circumvent the absence of data on marginal labor productivity when estimating the sectoral reallocation effect (e.g., Poirson, 2000 and 2001). Although samples and data sources are different, the order of magnitude obtained in these studies for the sectoral reallocation effect is broadly comparable to the one obtained in this chapter.

[34]This implicitly rebases the sectoral structure in each year, allowing a more precise decomposition of the respective contributions of sectoral effects and productivity than if only the initial and end points of the sample were used.

Econometric Analysis of the Determinants of Productivity Growth

The analysis uses a standard growth model to capture the effects of institutions and policies on cross-country variation in labor productivity and TFP growth. It also examines the determinants of within-sector productivity growth (in industry and services) and of labor shifts from agriculture to nonagricultural sectors, since these are the main sources of labor productivity growth. Throughout, institutions are measured by the Kaufmann-Kraay-Mastruzzi index of government effectiveness. The cost of starting a business, as a share of per capita income, is taken from the World Bank's Doing Business database. The measure of trade openness is the fraction of years where the country was considered as open according to the Welch-Wacziarg index, and reflects the policy stance. Financial sector development is proxied by the ratio of private sector credit to GDP, and education by the Barro-Lee measure of average schooling years. The initial level of the productivity gap (relative to the United States) is included to capture possible convergence effects (see Barro, 1997). The initial share of employment in agriculture is also introduced to control for sectoral composition effects. Other fundamentals (such as the quality of macroeconomic policies and foreign direct investment) were not significant

Table 3.2. Determinants of Productivity Growth[1]

Variable	Aggregate Labor Productivity Growth	TFP Growth	Industry Labor Productivity Growth	Services Labor Productivity Growth	Labor Shifts from Agriculture[2]
			Policy variables and initial conditions		
Initial productivity gap (ln)	**–1.9*** **	**–0.8*** **	**–1.9*** **	**–1.2*** **	. . .
Initial employment share in agriculture (in percent)	**–1.0*** **	**–0.4** **	. . .	. . .	**0.28*** **
Initial average years of education	0.2	0.1	**1.1*** **	**0.7*** **	. . .
Trade openness	**0.8*** **	**0.9*** **	**0.7** **	**0.5* **	**0.12*** **
Initial financial sector development (ln)	**0.5*** **	0.2	**0.5* **	0.3	**0.06** **
Growth in average schooling years	. . .	. . .	. . .	. . .	0.04
Growth in capital-to-labor ratio	. . .	. . .	. . .	. . .	**0.04* **
R-squared	0.67	0.62	0.55	0.36	0.79
Observations/countries	77	67	58	58	55
			Adding institutional quality and the cost of starting a business		
Initial productivity gap (ln)	**–1.8*** **	**–0.7*** **	**–2.0*** **	**–1.5*** **	. . .
Initial employment share in agriculture (in percent)	**–0.8*** **	–0.2	. . .	. . .	**0.30*** **
Initial average years of education	–0.1	–0.2	0.4	–0.1	
Trade openness	**0.5** **	**0.6** **	0.5	0.2	**0.15*** **
Initial financial sector development (ln)	0.2	0.0	0.0	–0.1	**0.07** **
Cost of starting new business (in percent of GDP per capita)	**–0.4* **	–0.2	**–0.7* **	**–0.7*** **	–0.04
Institutional quality	**0.6* **	**0.6* **	**1.0** **	**1.1*** **	–0.04
Growth in average schooling years	. . .	. . .	. . .	. . .	0.05
Growth in capital-to-labor ratio	. . .	. . .	. . .	. . .	0.03
R-squared	0.73	0.66	0.68	0.65	0.80
Observations/countries	74	65	57	57	53

Source: IMF staff estimates.

[1]The coefficients denote the impact on the dependent variable (in percentage points) of a one standard deviation increase in its determinants. The estimates are based on weighted least squares regressions (with robust errors) using as dependent variable the average annual value over 1965—2005 of the variable in the given column. *** denotes coefficients significant at the 1 percent level, ** at the 5 percent level , and * at the 10 percent level.

[2]Labor shifts from agriculture are defined as minus the change in agriculture's employment share. The specification includes both the initial employment share and its square, and the coefficient shown is the sum of the coefficients on the variable and on its square.

once these main determinants were controlled for, and were thus omitted from the regressions. The specification for intersectoral labor shifts is broadly similar, but includes the rates of accumulation of physical and human capital, in line with previous studies (see Poirson, 2000 and 2001).[35] The dataset covers the period 1965–2005 and the model is estimated by weighted least squares (with robust standard errors), with each country's variance assumed to be inversely proportional to the number of years for which the country's data are available. Initial levels of financial sector development and education are used to minimize endogeneity problems, while for institutions and the cost of starting a business, values are only available for the end of the sample period.

The results broadly indicate that initial income, openness, education, financial sector development, and institutions have a strong and significant impact on productivity growth consistent with the empirical literature on TFP and growth per capita differences across countries (Table 3.2 and Figure 3.14). The first panel of the table shows results for a basic model that omits institutions and the cost of starting a

[35]It also includes the square of the initial employment share in agriculture (to capture possible nonlinearities), but excludes the initial aggregate productivity gap (relative to the United States) and initial education (which was not significant).

business. These suggest that strong productivity growth relies importantly on:

- *A convergence effect* (proxied by low initial labor productivity relative to the United States). The catch-up effect is indicated by a negative and significant coefficient on the initial productivity gap in all regressions. The negative coefficient on initial agricultural employment in the regression for labor productivity growth suggests that countries with a larger initial share of agricultural employment tend to experience slower aggregate productivity growth. Unsurprisingly, the initial employment share in agriculture is also a major determinant of the magnitude of labor shifts.
- *Trade openness and financial sector development.* Both variables are strongly significant determinants of aggregate productivity growth. Their effects work mostly through stimulating labor shifts out of agriculture and boosting industry productivity growth. The effects of these variables are not estimated precisely in the services productivity growth equation: in the case of trade openness, this might reflect the fact that the indicator used in the regressions is not a good proxy of the degree of openness in the services sector.
- *Education.* Initial education levels are most significant, both economically and statistically, in the regressions for within-sector productivity growth. For labor shifts from agriculture, the small and only weakly significant effects from human and physical capital accumulation may reflect that these variables are themselves endogenous to other determinants of labor shifts, and have little separate effect.

In the second panel of Table 3.2, the model is augmented with the measures of institutions and business climate. The results underscore the importance of these variables. Institutional quality has an economically and statistically significant effect on productivity growth at the aggregate and sectoral levels.[36] However,

[36]No significant effect of institutional quality on intersectoral labor shifts was found and the coefficient has the wrong sign.

Figure 3.14. Partial Correlations Between Labor Shift from Agriculture and Its Determinants [1]

(Unexplained sectoral shift on y-axis) [2]

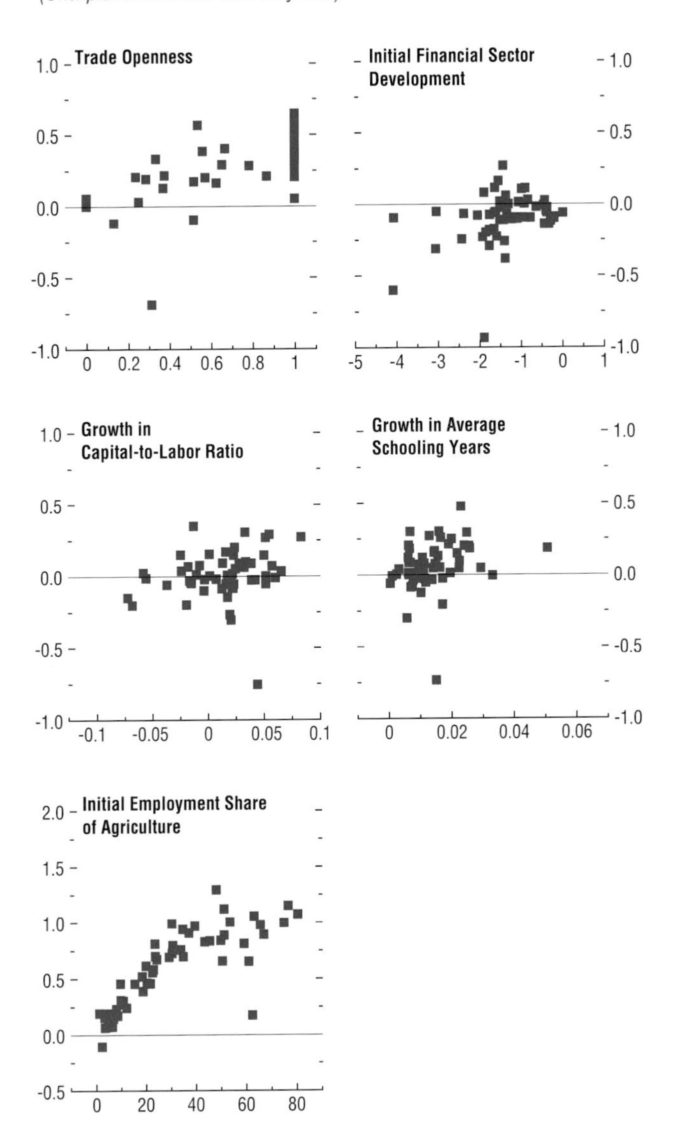

Source: IMF staff calculations.

[1]Based on the specification in column 5 of Table 3.2 (top panel). Labor shifts from agriculture are defined as minus the change in agriculture's employment share.

[2]The unexplained sectoral shift is the part of the change in the employment share of agriculture not explained by other regressors.

controlling for institutions weakens the significance of the openness and initial schooling variables (in line with earlier results from the literature and subject to the earlier caveat about possible endogeneity of the institutional variable).

The cost of starting a business exerts a negative effect on productivity growth, especially in services. Controlling for the cost of starting a business tends to lower the significance of financial sector development in the productivity growth regressions. In the equation for labor shifts, no significant effect of start-up costs is found. However, a more general specification allowing for an interaction term between the cost of starting a business and financial sector development suggests that the latter matters to the extent that it reduces the negative effects of start-up costs.

References

Barro, Robert J. 1997, *Determinants of Economic Growth: A Cross-Country Empirical Study* (Cambridge, Massachusetts: MIT Press).

———, 2001, "Economic Growth in East Asia Before and After the Financial Crisis," NBER Working Paper No. 8330 (Cambridge, Massachusetts: National Bureau of Economic Research).

———, and Jong-Wha Lee, 2000, "International Data on Educational Attainment: Updates and Implications," CID Working Paper No. 42 (Cambridge, Massachusetts: Center for International Development at Harvard University).

Becht, Marco, Patrick Bolton, and Ailsa Roell, 2003, "Corporate Governance and Control," in *Handbook of the Economics of Finance*, ed. by George M. Constantinides, Milton Harris, and Rene M. Stulz, Vol. 1, pp. 1–109 (Amsterdam, Boston: Elsevier/North-Holland).

Beck, Thorsten, Asli Demirgüç-Kunt, and Ross Levine, 2000, "A New Database on Financial Development and Structure," *The World Bank Economic Review*, Vol. 14, pp. 597–605 (Washington: World Bank).

Berglöf, Erik, and Stijn Claessens, 2006, "Enforcement and Good Corporate Governance in Developing Countries and Transition Economies," *The World Bank Research Observer*, Vol. 21, No.1 (Spring), pp. 121–50.

Bhattacharya, Utpal, Hazem Daouk, and Michael Welker, 2003, "The World Price of Earnings Opacity," *Accounting Review*, Vol. 78 (July), pp. 641–78.

Bloom, David E., David Canning, and Pia N. Malaney, 1999, "Demographic Change and Economic Growth in Asia," CID Working Paper No. 15 (Cambridge, Massachusetts: Center for International Development at Harvard University).

Bosworth, Barry, and Susan M. Collins, 2003, "The Empirics of Growth: an Update," *Brookings Papers on Economic Activity: 2*, Brookings Institution.

Calderón, César, and Luis Servén, 2004, "The Effects of Infrastructure Development on Growth and Income Distribution," World Bank Policy Research Working Paper No. 3400 (Washington: World Bank).

Cerra, Valerie, and Sweta C. Saxena, 2003, "Did Output Recover from the Asian Crisis," IMF Working Paper 03/48 (Washington: International Monetary Fund).

Chen, Shaohua, and Martin Ravallion, 2004, "How Have the World's Poorest Fared Since the Early 1980s?" *The World Bank Research Observer*, Vol. 9, No.2 (Fall), pp. 141–69.

CIFAR, 1993, *International Accounting and Auditing Trends*, third edition (Princeton: Center for International Financial Analysis and Research, Inc.).

Coe, David T., Elhanan Helpman, and Alexander W. Hoffmaister, 1997, "North-South R&D Spillovers," *Economic Journal*, Vol. 107 (January), pp. 134–49.

Coles, Jeffrey, Michael Lemmon, and Felix Meschke, forthcoming, "Structural Models and Endogeneity in Corporate Finance: The Link Between Managerial Ownership and Performance," *Journal of Financial Economics*.

Conway, Paul, Donato De Rosa, Giuseppe Nicoletti, and Faye Steiner, forthcoming, "Regulation, Competition and Productivity Convergence," OECD Economics Department Working Paper (Paris: Organization for Economic Cooperation and Development)

De Nicolò, Gianni, Luc Laeven, and Kenichi Ueda, 2006, "Corporate Governance Quality in Asia: Comparative Trends and Impact," (unpublished; Washington: International Monetary Fund, Research Department).

Dekle, Robert, and Guillaume Vandenbroucke, 2006, "A Quantitative Analysis of China's Structural Transformation" (unpublished; University of Southern California). Available via the Internet at http://ssrn.com/abstract=902497.

Denison, Edward F., 1962, "The Sources of Economic Growth in the United States and the Alternatives Before Us," Supplementary Paper of the Committee for Economic Development, No. 13 (New York).

———, 1967, "Why Growth Rates Differ; Postwar Experience in Nine Western Countries" (Washington: Brookings Institution).

Edwards, Sebastian, 1998, "Openness, Productivity, and Growth: What Do We Really Know?" *Economic Journal*, Vol. 108 (March), pp. 383–98.

Fajnzylber, Pablo, and Daniel Lederman, 1999, "Economic Reforms and Total Factor Productivity Growth in Latin America and the Caribbean (1950–95). An Empirical Note," Policy Research Working Paper No. 2114 (Washington: World Bank)

Fukao, Kyoji, Tomohiko Inui, Hiroki Kawai, and Tsutomu Miyagawa, 2003, "Sectoral Productivity and Economic Growth in Japan: 1970–98: An Empirical Analysis Based on the JIP Database," ESRI Cabinet Office, Discussion Paper Series No. 67 (Tokyo: Economic and Social Research Institute).

Gupta, Poonam, 2005, "Understanding the Growth Momentum in India's Services," Chapter II in *India: Selected Issues*, IMF Country Report No. 05/87 (Washington: International Monetary Fund).

Hausmann, Ricardo, Jason Hwang, and Dani Rodrik, 2005, "What You Export Matters," NBER Working Paper No. 11905 (Cambridge, Massachusetts: National Bureau of Economic Research).

Hausmann, Ricardo, Lant Pritchett, and Dani Rodrik, 2005, "Growth Accelerations," *Journal of Economic Growth*, Vol. 10, No. 4 (December), pp. 303–29.

Hayashi, Fumio, and Edward Prescott, 2002, "The 1990s in Japan: A Lost Decade" *Review of Economic Dynamics*, Vol. 5 (January), pp. 206–35.

Himmelberg, Charles, Glenn Hubbard, and Darius Palia, 1999, "Understanding the Determinants of Managerial Ownership and the Link Between Ownership and Performance," *Journal of Financial Economics*, Vol. 53 (September), pp. 353–84.

IMF, 2005a, *Indonesia: Selected Issues*, IMF Country Report No. 05/327 (Washington: International Monetary Fund).

———, 2005b, *Regional Outlook*, September 2005, Asia and Pacific Department (Washington: International Monetary Fund).

———, 2006a, *Philippines: Selected Issues*, IMF Country Report No. 06/181 (Washington: International Monetary Fund).

———, 2006b, *Japan: Selected Issues*, IMF Country Report No. 06/276 (Washington: International Monetary Fund).

Jorgenson, Dale W., forthcoming, "Accounting for Growth in the Information Age," in *Handbook of Economic Growth*, ed. by Philippe Aghion and Steven Durlauf (Amsterdam: North-Holland).

———, Mun S. Ho, and Kevin J. Stiroh, 2005, *Productivity: Information Technology and the American Growth Resurgence*, Vol. 3 (Cambridge, Massachusetts: MIT Press).

Jorgenson, Dale W., and Kazuyuki Motohashi, 2005, "Information Technology and the Japanese Economy," *Journal of the Japanese and International Economies*, Vol. 19 (December), pp. 460–481.

Jorgenson, Dale W., and Khuong Vu, 2005, "Information Technology and the World Economy," *Scandinavian Journal of Economics*, Vol. 107 (December), pp. 631–50.

Kaufmann, Daniel, Aart Kraay, and Massimo Mastruzzi, 2005, "Governance Matters IV: Governance Indicators for 1996–2004," World Bank Policy Research Working Paper No. 3630 (Washington: World Bank).

Khatri, Yougesh, Luc Leruth, and Jenifer Piesse, 2002, "Corporate Performance and Governance in Malaysia," IMF Working Paper 02/152 (Washington: International Monetary Fund). Available via the Internet at http://www.imf.org/external/pubs/ft/wp/2002/wp02152.pdf.

Kochhar, Kalpana, Utsav Kumar, Raghuram Rajan, and Arvind Subramanian, 2006, "India's Patterns of Development: What Happened, What Follows," NBER Working Paper No. 12023 (Cambridge, Massachusetts: National Bureau of Economic Research).

Leuz, Christian, Dhananjay Nanda, and Peter Wysocki, 2003, "Earnings Management and Investor Protection: An International Comparison," *Journal of Financial Economics*, Vol. 69 (September), pp. 505–27.

Maddison, Angus, 2003, *The World Economy: Historical Statistics*, Development Centre Studies (Paris: Organization for Economic Cooperation and Development).

McKinsey Global Institute, 2001, "India: The Growth Imperative" (Washington: McKinsey and Company).

———, 2006, *Accelerating India's Growth Through Financial System Reform* (Washington: McKinsey and Company).

Miller, Stephen M., and Mukti P. Upadhyay, 2000, "The Effects of Openness, Trade Orientation, and Human Capital on Total Factor Productivity," *Journal of Development Economics*, Vol. 63 (December), pp. 399–423.

Morck, Randall, Bernard Yeung, and Wayne Yu, 2000, "The Information Content of Stock Markets: Why Do Emerging Markets Have Synchronous Price Movements?" *Journal of Financial Economics*, Vol. 58, Issues 1–2, pp. 215–60.

Nehru, Vikram, and Ashok Dhareshwar, 1993, "A New Database on Physical Capital Stock: Sources, Methodology and Results," *Revista de Análisis Económico*, Vol. 8, No. 1 (June), pp. 37–59.

Nicoletti, Giuseppe, and Stefano Scarpetta, 2003, "Regulation, Productivity, and Growth: OECD Evidence," *Economic Policy*, Vol. 18, No. 36 (April), pp. 9–51.

OECD, 2003, *White Paper on Corporate Governance in Asia* (Paris: Organization for Economic Cooperation and Development).

Park, Yung Chul, and Jong-Wha Lee, 2001, "Recovery and Sustainability in East Asia," NBER Working Paper No. 8373 (Cambridge, Massachusetts: National Bureau of Economic Research).

Poirson, Hélène, 2000, "Factor Reallocation and Growth in Developing Countries," IMF Working Paper 00/94 (Washington: International Monetary Fund).

———, 2001, "The Impact of Intersectoral Labour Reallocation on Economic Growth," *Journal of African Economies*, Vol. 10 (March), pp. 37–63.

———, 2006, "The Tax System in India: Could Reform Spur Growth?" IMF Working Paper 06/93 (Washington: International Monetary Fund).

Rajan, Raghuram, and Luigi Zingales, 1998, "Financial Dependence and Growth," *American Economic Review*, Vol. 88 (June), pp. 559–86.

Rodrik, Dani, 2006, "What's So Special About China's Exports?" NBER Working Paper No. 11947 (Cambridge, Massachusetts: National Bureau of Economic Research).

Sarel, Michael, 1996, "Growth in East Asia: What We Can and What We Cannot Infer," Economic Issues No. 1 (Washington: World Bank). Available via the Internet at http://www.imf.org/external/pubs/ft/issues1/index.htm.

Tseng, Wanda, and Markus Rodlauer, eds. 2003, *China: Competing in the Global Economy* (Washington: International Monetary Fund).

United Nations, 2003, *World Population Prospects: The 2002 Revision*, Population Division, Department of Economic and Social Affairs, United Nations (New York).

Wacziarg, Romain, and Karen Horn Welch, 2003, "Trade Liberalization and Growth: New Evidence," NBER Working Paper No. 10152 (Cambridge, Massachusetts: National Bureau of Economic Research).

World Bank, 1993, *The East Asian Miracle: Economic Growth and Public Policy* (Washington: World Bank).

———, 2006, *World Development Indicators* (Washington: World Bank).

Young, Alwyn, 1995, "The Tyranny of Numbers: Confronting the Statistical Realities of the East Asian Growth Experience," *Quarterly Journal of Economics*, Vol. 110 (August), pp. 641–80.

———, 2003, "Gold into Base Metals: Productivity Growth in the People's Republic of China During the Reform Period," *Journal of Political Economy*, Vol. 111, No. 6 (December), pp. 1220–61.

CHAPTER 4

HOW DO FINANCIAL SYSTEMS AFFECT ECONOMIC CYCLES?

Financial systems in advanced economies have undergone remarkable changes in recent years, driven primarily by deregulation and improvements in technology. The pace of these changes has varied across countries, and important differences remain in the structure of financial systems across these economies. This chapter explores how these differences in financial systems may affect the response of households and firms to changes in the economic environment, and thus influence the cyclical behavior of national economies.

The changes that have occurred in financial systems have transformed the opportunities for borrowing and saving facing households and firms. Households now have access to a broader range of borrowing options (e.g., through the widespread use of credit cards and home equity loans) and can easily invest in a wide range of financial instruments, such as stocks, bonds, mutual funds, and derivatives. Firms have been able to increasingly diversify their financing away from banks through the issuance of bonds in capital markets, while banks themselves have increasingly moved away from their traditional deposit-taking and lending role into fee-generating activities, such as the securitization of loans and the sale of risk management products. The increase in securitization—through instruments such as collateralized debt obligations (CDOs)—has allowed the unbundling of financial risks, which can be repackaged into portfolios of financial instruments and transferred to investors willing to assume such risks. The cross-border component of financial intermediation has also grown rapidly, particularly at the wholesale level (i.e., between financial institutions). For example, although household mortgages are still typically originated by domestic financial institutions, markets for mortgage-backed securities attract a significant presence of foreign investors in a number of countries.

Note: The main authors of this chapter are Subir Lall, Roberto Cardarelli, and Irina Tytell. Ross Levine, George Kapetanios, and Christopher Otrok provided consultancy support, and Ben Sutton and Stephanie Denis provided research assistance.

Despite these overall trends, however, there are still wide differences across national financial systems. Variations persist in the size of financial markets and in the importance of bank and nonbank financial intermediaries (such as mutual funds, private pension funds, and insurance companies; see Figure 4.1). Average stock market capitalization as a ratio to GDP during 1995–2004, for example, ranged from 140 percent in the United Kingdom to 40 percent in Italy. Over the same period, nearly half of the financial liabilities of the German nonfinancial sector (including households, nonfinancial corporates, and the government) were with the banking sector, while in the United States this ratio was only around 15 percent.

Given the close link between the financial sector and household and firm balance sheets, a key question is how these differences in financial systems affect macroeconomic behavior. Although the amplitude of business cycle fluctuations has been on a declining trend across advanced economies, differences remain in the resilience of individual countries to business cycle downturns, asset price fluctuations, and technological changes (see, for example, Cotis and Coppel, 2005). Yet few empirical studies to date have analyzed the effect of different financial structures on business cycle behavior—attention has mostly focused on the role of overall financial development for growth performance (see, for example, Levine, 1997; and Wurgler, 2000).

Against this background, this chapter constructs an index that captures the key differences between financial systems across advanced economies. This index is then used to examine the relationship between the structure of

Figure 4.1. Stock and Bond Market Capitalization and Nonfinancial Sector Liabilities, 1995–2004

Substantial differences exist across advanced economies in terms of the size of their financial markets and the volume of funds intermediated by banks and nonbank financial institutions.

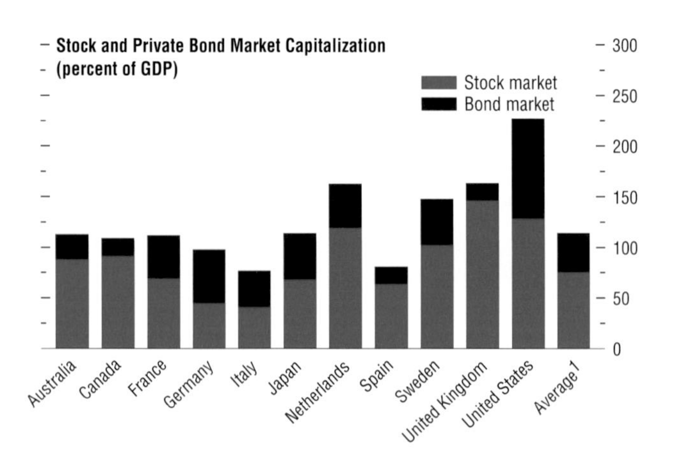

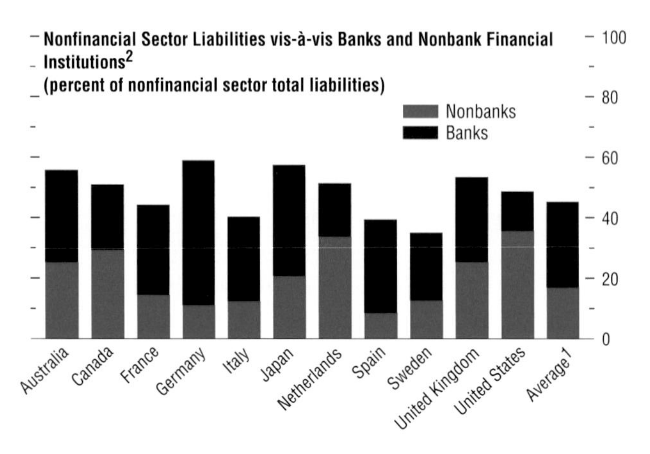

Sources: National financial accounts from Eurostat and OECD; World Bank, Financial Structure Database; and IMF staff calculations.
[1]Average includes Austria, Belgium, Denmark, Finland, Greece, Norway, and Portugal in addition to other coutries already listed.
[2]The remaining nonfinancial sector liabilities are primarily securities held directly by households.

national financial systems and economic cycles. In particular, the chapter addresses the following questions:

- How have financial systems evolved in the advanced economies? Have they converged across countries, or have changes in financial structure proceeded at a differing pace, leading to greater divergence? Have these trends influenced the relative attractiveness of different countries as a destination for cross-border capital flows?
- Does the responsiveness of household consumption and residential investment to changes in income and wealth differ across countries depending on the financial system?
- Does the character of the financial system influence how firms respond to short-term changes in demand and longer-term changes in investment opportunities?

The chapter finds that while there has been a general trend toward bank disintermediation and a greater role for financial markets in many countries, the pace has differed and there are still important differences across financial systems. The results support the view that these differences in financial structures do affect how households and firms behave over the economic cycle. In financial systems characterized by a greater degree of arm's length transactions,[1] households seem to be able to smooth consumption more effectively in the face of unanticipated changes in their income, although they may be more sensitive to changes in asset prices. In financial systems that rely less on arm's length transactions, firms appear to be better able to smooth investment during business cycle downturns, as they are better positioned to access external financing based on their long-term relationships with financial intermediaries. However, when faced with more fundamental changes in the environment that require a reallocation of resources across sectors, financial

[1]An arm's length transaction is typically defined as one between two unaffiliated parties or between two related parties acting as if they were unaffiliated parties with no relationship with each other.

systems with a greater degree of arm's length transactions appear to be better placed to shift resources to take advantage of new growth opportunities. There is also evidence that cross-border portfolio investors appear to allocate a greater proportion of their holdings in countries where the arm's length content of the financial system is higher, which may contribute to the financing of current account deficits.

How Have Financial Systems Changed?

A first step in exploring the links between financial systems and macroeconomic responses is to characterize the key differences among financial systems in the advanced economies.[2] While there are various ways of classifying financial systems, the approach taken in this chapter focuses on the degree to which financial transactions are conducted on the basis of a direct (and generally longer-term) relationship between two entities, usually a bank and a customer, or are conducted at arm's length—where entities typically do not have any special knowledge about each other that is not available publicly.

A financial system featuring a high volume of arm's length transactions (hereafter referred to as a "more arm's length financial system") is highly dependent on publicly available information and on the enforcement of contracts through formal and standard legal mechanisms and procedures applicable to unrelated parties. There is a strong role for price signals and open competition among lenders. On the other hand, in a more relationship-based system, transactions between two parties—such as a bank and a corporate borrower—primarily rely on information the lender has about the borrower that is not available publicly. Mechanisms for enforcement of contracts rely more heavily on the lender's direct influence on the borrower and/or the lender's monopolistic power in the market. In practice, no system is purely relationship-based or purely arm's length, and even systems that are more reliant on arm's length transactions do not preclude the use of relationships. Indeed, recent years have seen the rise of certain types of financial intermediation that do have relationship-based elements—such as venture capital and private equity—within arm's length structures.[3] Nevertheless, it is useful to assess where financial systems are placed along a spectrum—with a country's position depending on the degree to which arm's length contracts dominate its financial transactions.

For this purpose, a new Financial Index is constructed to summarize the extent of the arm's length content of a financial system.[4] The index ranges between 0 and 1 for each country, with a higher value representing a greater arm's length content in the financial system. The overall Financial Index is derived from three subindices (which are weighted equally in the overall index) that seek to capture key elements of a financial system:[5]

[2]Data availability limited the sample to the following 18 countries: Australia, Austria, Belgium, Canada, Denmark, Finland, France, Germany, Greece, Italy, Japan, the Netherlands, Norway, Portugal, Spain, Sweden, the United Kingdom, and the United States.

[3]It is important to recognize that the distinction between more or less arm's length–based financial systems is different from the more conventional distinction drawn in the literature between bank-based and market-based financial systems (see, for example, Levine, 2002). The analysis in this chapter attempts to take into account, for example, the higher or lower degree of arm's length content within national banking systems.

[4]While a summary indicator of course cannot capture all the aspects in which financial systems differ across countries, it provides a broad measure that is helpful for analyzing the link between financial systems and economic cycles.

[5]Each subindex was constructed as an average of three (third-level) indicators capturing key aspects relevant to arm's length content, building on a range of underlying indicators. For each of these indicators, a country is assigned a value equal to the ratio of the variable for this country and the maximum value across all countries. While an ideal index in the context of this chapter would include only fundamental determinants of how a financial system influences economic agents' decisions, data limitations have led to the inclusion of a mix of indicators capturing both fundamentals (such as the degree of investor protection) and outcomes (such as the existing financial structure). See Appendix 4.1 for further details on the index construction methodology and data sources.

Figure 4.2. Traditional Banking: Index for Selected Advanced Economies

Banks still intermediate a larger volume of funds in European countries and Japan, despite faster bank disintermediation in these countries over the last decade. However, the inclusion of indicators of competition in the banking sector and of financial information disclosure narrows cross-country differences in traditional banking, as several European countries score high on these measures.

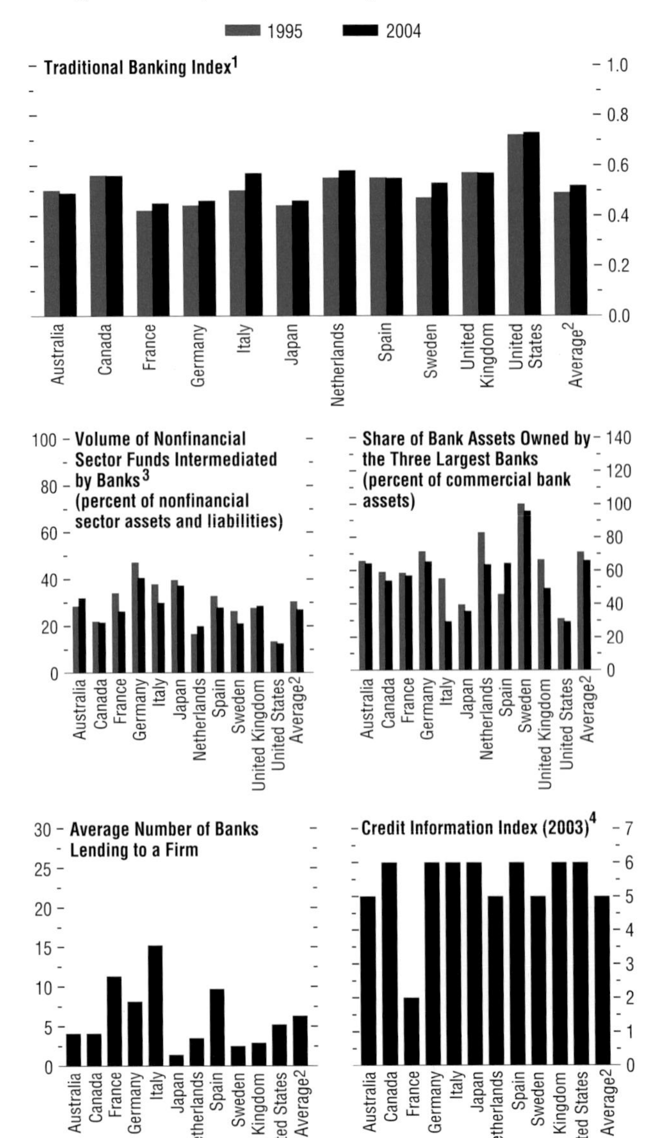

Sources: National financial accounts from Eurostat and OECD; Ongena and Smith (2000); World Bank, Doing Business Database; World Bank, Financial Structure Database; and IMF staff calculations.

[1]A higher value on the index denotes a lower degree of traditional banking.

[2]Average includes Austria, Belgium, Denmark, Finland, Greece, Norway, and Portugal in addition to other coutries already listed.

[3]Average of assets with banks and liabilities vis-à-vis banks of the nonfinancial sector (household, nonfinancial corporate, government, and rest of the world), as a percent of the nonfinancial sector average of assets and liabilities. IMF staff calculations based on national financial accounts.

[4]The index ranges from 0 to 6, with higher values indicating that more credit information is available from either a public registry or a private bureau.

- The degree of *traditional bank intermediation*, which is the most obvious manifestation of a high degree of relationship-based financial transactions.[6] This measure of the extent to which deposit-taking institutions dominate the process of intermediating savings takes into account factors that may weaken the role of relationships in lending decisions, most notably the degree of competition between banks and the availability of public financial information.[7]
- The degree to which *new financial intermediation* has developed to provide an alternative non-bank channel for financing and/or to facilitate the transformation of traditional relationships between intermediaries and final customers. New financial intermediation includes the activities of a range of nondeposit taking institutions, such as pension and insurance companies; nontraditional activities undertaken by banks, including the securitization of loans; and the extent of financial innovation through the use of new financial instruments, including derivatives. The measures of financial innovation used in this subindex are intended to gauge the transformation of aspects of traditional relationship-based lending not captured elsewhere. For example, the market for credit derivatives and collateralized debt obligations (CDOs) may allow banks to develop lending relationships less influenced by long-term credit risk considerations.[8] Similarly, the use of interest rate swaps allows lenders to meet the demand for specific loan structures by

[6]This is because historically banks have been the main intermediaries in a financial system, and have based lending decisions on insider knowledge about their clients. Traditional banking in this chapter also includes the activities of other deposit-taking institutions, such as credit unions and building societies.

[7]The role of relationships is likely to be weaker in a system where banks pose greater competitive challenges to each other and where inside information about borrowers is much more limited.

[8]Securitization through CDOs allows credit risk to be distributed in various tranches tailored to the different risk tolerances of investors, with the sponsoring organizations (such as banks) able to remove the credit risk from their own balance sheets.

their customers, while transferring interest rate risk to investors more willing to assume such exposures.

- The role played by *financial markets,* which have a symbiotic relationship with nonbank financial intermediation and the expansion of banks into nontraditional activities described above (see, for example, Allen and Santomero, 2001). Deep and liquid financial markets are essential, for example, for the efficient functioning of a mutual fund industry. The ease of market access, efficiency of contract enforcement, and the degree of investor protection are important determinants of how well financial markets can perform their functions.

One conclusion to emerge from the first of these subindices is that the importance of traditional banking activities has declined in most countries, with differences between countries narrowing, and several countries moving closer to the United States, the country where the role of traditional banking is the smallest (Figure 4.2).[9] Nevertheless, there are still large differences in the volume of funds intermediated by banks across countries. For example, over the last decade, the share of nonfinancial sector assets and liabilities intermediated by banks has declined an average of 5 percentage points in the euro area countries, but at about 30 percent in 2004 this share was still twice as high as in the United States. These differences, however, are partly offset by the fact that the degree of competition and availability of information is generally high in most countries where the banking system still has a prominent role. This suggests that there is a greater degree of arm's length content in banking activity in Europe than suggested only by the higher volumes of funds intermediated by banks.

Differences across countries are more striking in the area of new financial intermediation (Figure 4.3). Countries with a greater proportion of household savings allocated outside the

[9]A *higher* score on the index implies a *lower* degree of traditional bank intermediation.

Figure 4.3. New Financial Intermediation: Index for Selected Advanced Economies

Differences persist and have increased in the extent to which financial intermediation is conducted through new financial intermediaries. The United States, United Kingdom, Australia, and the Netherlands are characterized by a relatively larger role of nonbank financial institutions, a greater diffusion of new financial products, and a greater shift of banks away from traditional intermediation services.

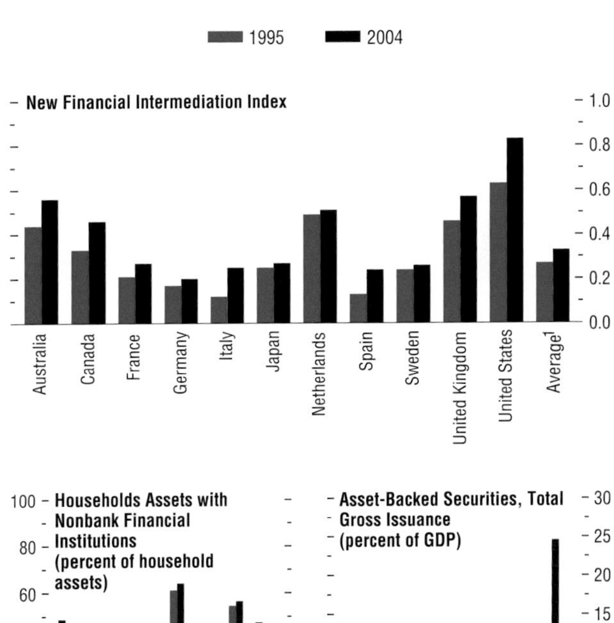

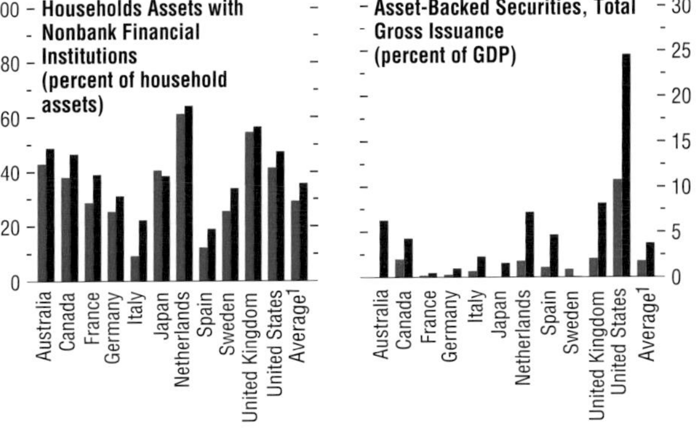

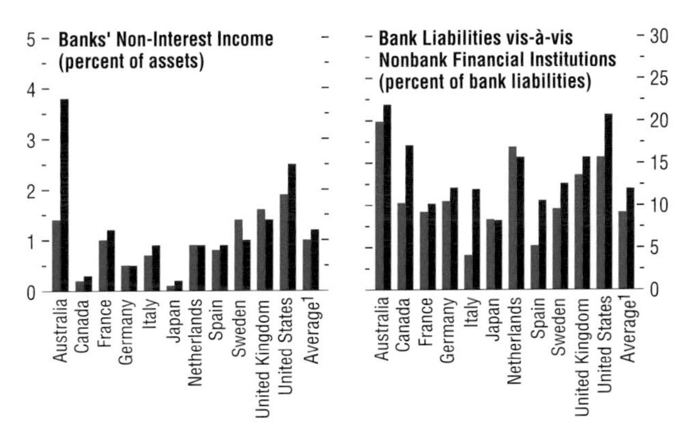

Sources: National financial accounts from Eurostat and OECD; European Securitization Forum and other sources, see Appendix 4.1; OECD, Bank Profitability database; and IMF staff calculations.

[1]Average includes Austria, Belgium, Denmark, Finland, Greece, Norway, and Portugal in addition to other coutries already listed.

Figure 4.4. Financial Markets: Index for Selected Advanced Economies

Over the past decade, all countries have shown a trend toward larger, more liquid, and more accessible financial markets.

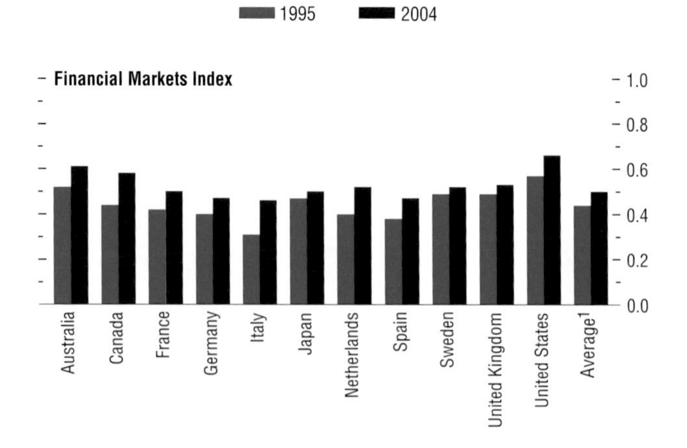

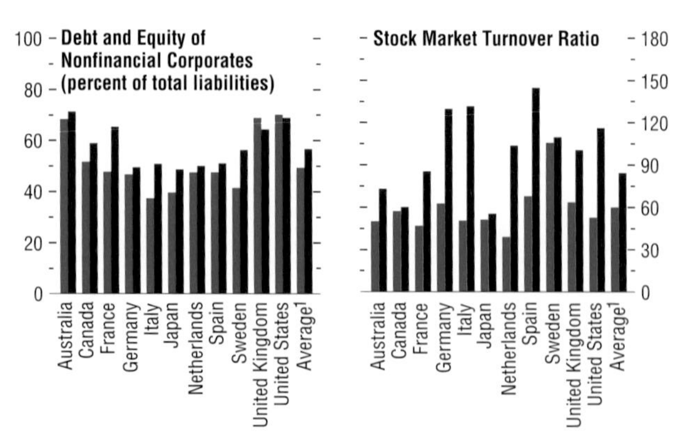

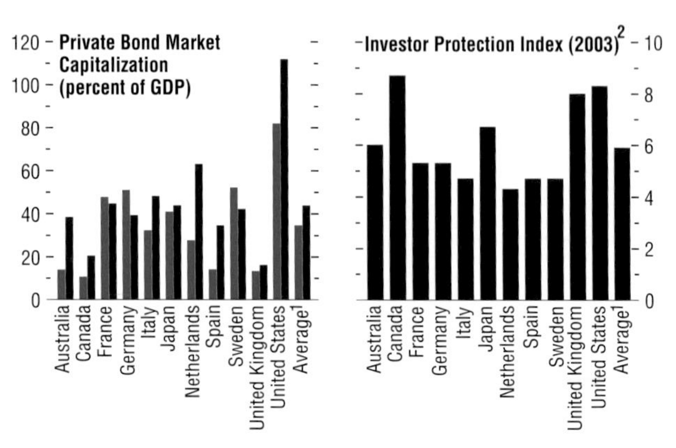

Sources: National financial accounts from Eurostat and OECD; World Bank, Financial Structure Database; World Bank, Doing Business Database; and IMF staff calculations.

[1]Average includes Austria, Belgium, Denmark, Finland, Greece, Norway, and Portugal in addition to other coutries already listed.

[2]The index ranges from 0 to 10, with higher values indicating better investor protection.

banking system include Australia, Canada, the Netherlands, the United Kingdom, and the United States. In response to competitive pressures from the nonbank financial sector, banks in these countries have also expanded more into nontraditional fee-generating areas of intermediation such as loan securitization.[10] In general, they also appear to make greater use of financial innovations such as asset-backed securities and alternative investment vehicles such as venture capital. While venture capital relies importantly on relationships with firms (including managerial influence, informational advantages, and a longer investment horizon), its rapid growth over the past two decades has been facilitated by the evolution in its financing structure and by the associated increase in the importance of institutional investors as suppliers of venture capital financing (see Gompers and Lerner, 1998).[11]

Cross-country differences in the financial market development subindex are generally smaller across countries than for the banking and new financial intermediation indices (Figure 4.4). This is in part due to the rapid convergence of market infrastructure and securities regulation across advanced economies. In particular, many countries have either improved market access

[10]Clearly, differences in these indicators also reflect heterogeneous regulatory and legislative environments. For example, the large degree of nonbank financial intermediation in countries like the Netherlands and the United Kingdom reflects in part the relative importance of private pension funds in these two countries. See Allen and Gale (2000) for a study of the historical factors underlying observed differences across financial systems.

[11]Venture capital (VC) is now predominantly set up as a pooled fund with a VC firm as a general partner and other investors—institutional investors, in particular—as limited partners. As a result, the growth of institutional investors has supported the expansion of venture capital financing. The VC firm provides the management expertise and charges the other partners a management fee (similar to other investment managers, such as mutual and hedge funds). As a result, both the size and the arm's length content of venture capital have risen rapidly over the past two decades. Reflecting in part these factors, venture capital financing as a percent of GDP in the United States was three times as large as in European countries during 1998–2004 (see OECD, 2006).

(as in France and Italy, where the share of nonfinancial corporate liabilities financed by markets through bonds and equities has increased sharply over the last decade) or increased the liquidity and depth of their stock and bond markets (as in Italy, the Netherlands, and Spain).

The aggregate picture, as measured by the overall Financial Index, suggests that despite an increase in the arm's length content of financial systems across advanced economies, important differences remain (Figure 4.5). Indeed, the increase in the index has generally been larger for those countries with relatively high values already in 1995. Thus, there is little evidence of convergence, a conclusion confirmed by more formal statistical tests (see Appendix 4.1). The differences across countries are mainly related to persistent dissimilarities in the area of new financial intermediation, the wider use of financial innovation, and banks' expansion into nontraditional banking activities.

This variation across countries in the Financial Index is indicative of important differences in the way financial systems perform their intermediation function. In countries with more arm's length content, a larger share of household and firm financing takes place through capital markets. At the same time, banks have moved away from traditional relationship-based lending, and their decisions are guided less by the imperatives of their relationship with borrowers and more by their ability to sell financial claims on to capital markets. Since their credit exposures are lower—as fewer loans now remain on balance sheets for the life of the loan contract—banks can increasingly choose from a larger pool of potential borrowers, and themselves have become one of a greater number of potential lenders. Finally, in systems with higher arm's length content, investors who move away from holding traditional bank deposits provide the necessary depth and liquidity to capital markets and take on associated risks, either directly, or more commonly through nonbank financial intermediaries such as hedge funds, mutual funds, and investment and pension companies.

Figure 4.5. Financial Index Scores for Advanced Economies

Despite a general trend toward arm's length financial systems, cross-country differences persist and have even increased as countries with the highest scores in 1995 are also at the top in 2004.

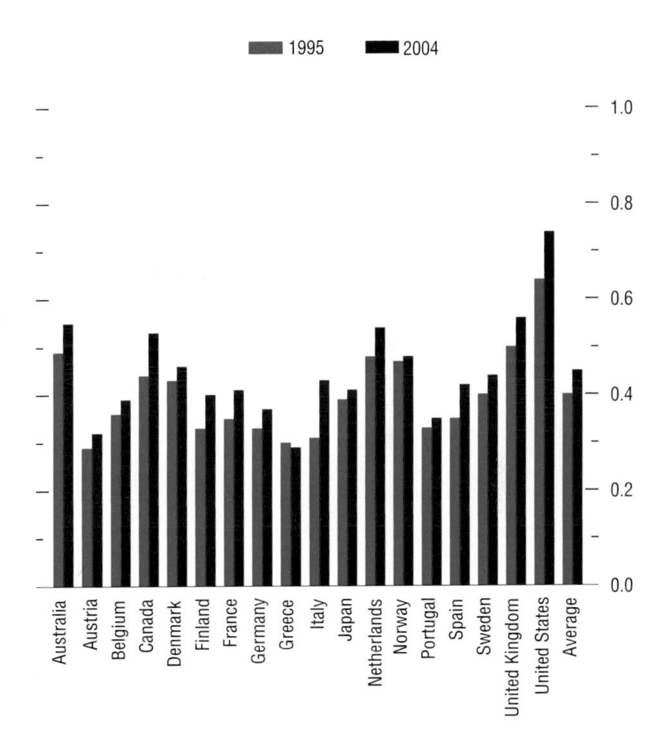

Sources: See Appendix 4.1 for sources used in the Financial Index.

These differences in the way financial systems function are well illustrated in the structure of mortgage markets in different countries (Figure 4.6). Despite important differences between mortgage markets, even among countries with broadly similar financial systems, countries with more arm's length systems typically offer a higher degree of leverage, longer repayment horizons, and greater access to mortgage equity, with the latter representing a vehicle for extracting liquidity from housing assets to finance consumption. Additionally, certain economies with more arm's length systems (notably Denmark and the United States) provide better risk sharing for households through greater use of fixed-rate mortgages with long repayment schedules and fee-free refinancing; refinancing is typically subject to early repayment fees in countries where financial systems are less arm's length–based (see Green and Wachter, 2005). The ability of more arm's length systems to offer greater flexibility in housing finance is underpinned by supporting institutions that allow effective enforcement of collateral, and by securitization of mortgage loans that helps pool and diversify risks from individual borrowers.[12] The extent of mortgage securitization varies greatly across countries, with the United States securitizing over 60 percent of new mortgages with mortgage-backed securities, while France and Germany securitize less than 5 percent of new mortgages this way.[13]

Figure 4.6. Features of Mortgage Markets
(Percent of countries)

Mortgage markets in more arm's length financial systems typically offer borrowers more advantageous loan attributes.

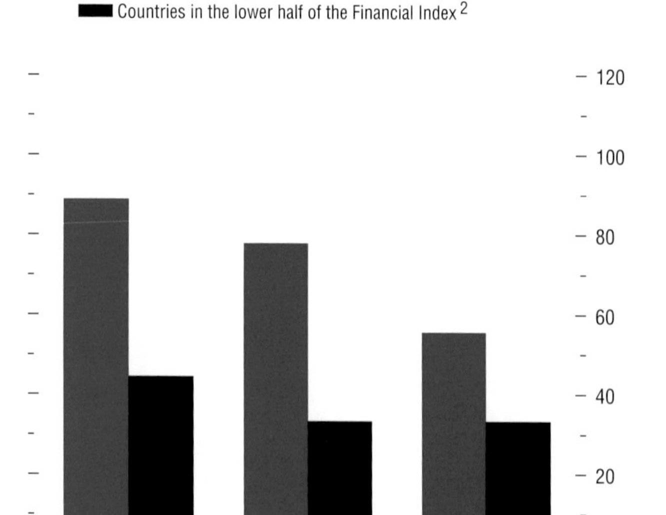

Sources: Tsatsaronis and Zhu (2004); Catte and others (2004); and IMF staff calculations.
[1]Countries included are Australia, Canada, Denmark, Italy, the Netherlands, Norway, Sweden, the United Kingdom, and the United States.
[2]Countries included are Austria, Belgium, Finland, France, Germany, Greece, Japan, Portugal, and Spain.

[12]For example, the usual time required for mortgage enforcement procedures, from the writ of execution to the distribution of the proceeds to creditors, is 60 to 84 months in Italy, 15 to 25 months in France, 8 months in the United Kingdom and the United States, and 6 months in Denmark and the Netherlands. See Catte and others (2004).

[13]A number of European countries, notably Denmark and Germany, fund mortgage loans in the capital markets using bonds (such as German Pfandbriefe) that allow for better risk sharing than the traditional funding by depository institutions. However, these bonds differ from mortgage-backed securities as they remain on the balance sheet of the issuer, therefore limiting the extent of risk transfer by originating banks. In contrast, mortgage-backed securities can be traded away from the balance sheets of mortgage originators.

How Do Differences in Financial Systems Affect the Behavior of Households, Firms, and Cross-Border Capital Flows?

This section presents evidence that suggests that the substantial differences across financial systems do affect the behavior of households and firms over the economic cycle and influence financial flows across countries.[14] It should be emphasized at the outset, however, that analyzing the links between financial systems and macroeconomic behavior is a challenging task, especially when trying to establish a causal link from one to the other, and it is important to keep in mind the possibility that third factors may also play a role in affecting both financial systems and economic outcomes.

The Household Sector

The degree of arm's length transactions in a financial system may affect household behavior through two channels:

- In a more arm's length financial system, households may be better able to smooth consumption in the face of income shocks. In such systems, investors can price collateral more effectively in a liquid market and acquire financial claims on a diversified pool of borrowers. This reduces the exposure of investors to risks emanating from individual households, such as the increased credit risk from a loss of income or employment, and makes available, on average, a larger amount of financial resources to households.[15] Indeed, as systems have moved toward more arm's length transactions, household borrowing has grown across advanced economies, with the increase more dramatic and the level of household debt higher in countries with a higher level of arm's length content in their financial systems (Figure 4.7).
- The flip side is that in such systems households themselves may be more exposed to asset price changes as they hold a greater proportion of market securities as assets on their balance sheets. Further, since more effective collateralization allows a greater degree of leverage, a sufficiently large change in the value of the collateral (such as a decline in housing prices) may require households to adjust their consumption sharply (see Box 4.1).

The Sensitivity of Households to Changes in Income

A large body of empirical evidence shows that private consumption is sensitive to changes in current income, contrary to the implications of the permanent income hypothesis, which proposes that consumption is determined by permanent income, typically defined as average or expected income or the annuity value of lifetime resources (see Deaton, 1992). This finding of "excess sensitivity" of consumption to current income has most often been attributed to borrowing constraints faced by households, implying that as borrowing constraints ease, consumption can be expected to become less sensitive to current income. Empirical studies suggest that the excess sensitivity of consumption is relatively low in Canada and the United States, somewhat higher in the United Kingdom, and higher yet in France, Italy, and Spain.[16]

To investigate whether the degree of arm's length financing affects the ability of households to cope with variations in income, two exercises were conducted. Both suggest that a higher degree of arm's length financing can reduce the

[14]The analysis in this section is based on the Financial Index measured in 2004 because a larger amount of information is available for that year. However, using 1995 values yields broadly similar conclusions.

[15]Evidence on the link between home equity withdrawal and consumption in advanced economies is examined in Catte and others (2004) and Klyuev and Mills (2006). For a discussion of the growth of household credit in emerging markets, see Chapter II of the IMF's *Global Financial Stability Report* (September 2006).

[16]See Campbell and Mankiw (1991); and Jappelli and Pagano (1989). Several studies, including Bacchetta and Gerlach (1997) and Dynan, Elmendorf, and Sichel (2006), have documented the decline in the excess sensitivity of consumption in the United States, attributing this to financial deregulation.

Figure 4.7. Total Household Liabilities
(Ratio to disposable income; group average)

Household indebtedness is higher and has risen more sharply in arm's length financial systems than in relationship-based systems.

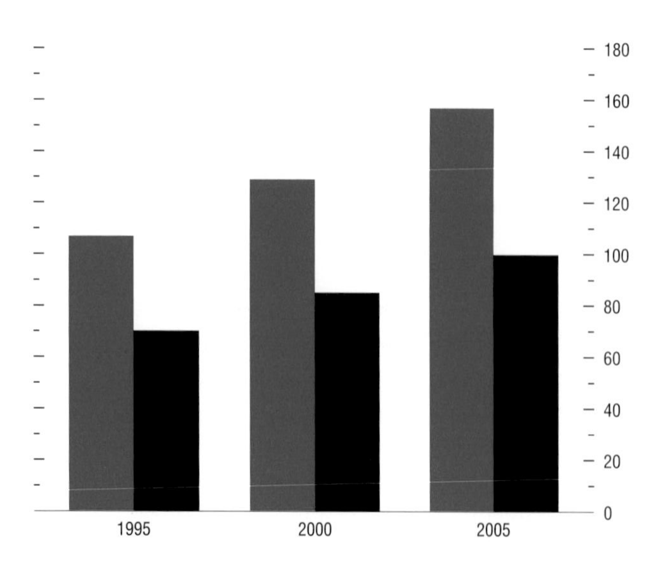

Sources: National financial accounts from Eurostat and OECD; OECD Analytic Database; and IMF staff calculations.
[1]Countries included are Australia, Canada, Denmark, Italy, the Netherlands, Norway, Sweden, the United Kingdom, and the United States.
[2]Countries included are Austria, Belgium, Finland, France, Germany, Greece, Japan, Portugal, and Spain.

impact of changes in current income on household behavior (see Appendix 4.2 for details):

- First, a simple panel regression was estimated relating consumption growth to the growth of disposable income and an interaction term with the Financial Index (controlling also for the impact of real short-term interest rates). In general, countries with more arm's length systems tend to exhibit a lower correlation between consumption and current income growth, suggesting a greater degree of consumption smoothing. The marginal propensity to consume out of current income is smaller for countries with higher values of the Financial Index, as captured by the negative interaction term in the estimation.[17] This result can also be seen from the mapping between the Financial Index and the correlation of consumption and current income growth (Figure 4.8).[18] These findings are consistent with the notion that consumers in these countries are better able to smooth consumption in the face of changes in their income.[19]
- Second, country-by-country estimations using rolling regressions were analyzed to see if residential investment is less sensitive to mortgage rates and income when financial systems are more arm's length. The results suggest that these sensitivities have diminished over time in the United States, but generally not elsewhere.[20] These findings may be explained

[17]When interpreting the results, the issue of simultaneous determination of consumption and income needs to be kept in mind. The estimated marginal propensity to consume captures the correlation between private consumption and disposable income, and does not necessarily reflect causality.

[18]Appendix 4.2 reports the results of the formal empirical estimation.

[19]There may be a potential nonlinearity in the consumption response that is difficult to capture empirically. Households that are highly leveraged at the time of a downturn may be unwilling to increase their indebtedness further in order to smooth consumption.

[20]Recent studies for the United States have attributed the observed decline in the sensitivity of residential investment to income and mortgage rates to the development of mortgage markets. See, for example, Peek and Wilcox (2006); and Dynan, Elmendorf, and Sichel (2006).

by the fact that the mortgage market in the United States has attained a high degree of sophistication and flexibility through the use of securitization (see Green and Wachter, 2005, for a detailed discussion).

Impact of Changes in Asset Prices on Household Spending

While more arm's length systems may be conducive to consumption smoothing in the face of income shocks, this section presents evidence that they may also be more sensitive to changes in asset prices—through so-called "financial accelerator" effects—although both equity and housing price busts appear to have been shallower in such systems over the past two decades (see Bernanke, Gertler, and Gilchrist, 1996, for elaboration on the financial accelerator mechanism).

In a more arm's length financial system, the increased dependence of credit on housing values could exacerbate the impact of adverse house price developments, creating a ripple effect that depresses consumption. A severe downturn in the housing market could cause a drop in the value of the collateral, reducing households' ability to borrow, curbing their spending, and exacerbating the initial downturn. This mechanism is more likely to be set in motion in response to a substantial house price decline if households' ability to borrow is more closely linked to real estate values. Regarding financial assets, the higher proportion of marketable securities in a household's portfolio, and the lower share of bank deposits in a more arm's length system also could expose households to greater wealth shocks from equity market fluctuations.

An event analysis was conducted to compare responses of private consumption and residential investment to equity and housing downturns in different financial systems. Equity and housing busts were defined as episodes in which the associated price declines were in the top half of all such episodes in the sample, corresponding to real price declines of at least 26 percent for equity downturns and at least 6

Figure 4.8. Consumption-Income Correlations and the Financial Index, 1985–2005

(Correlations between quarter-on-quarter growth rates)

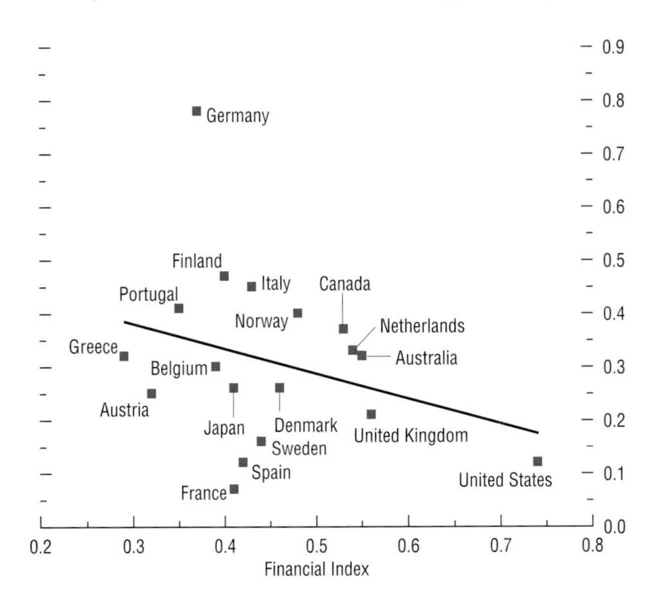

Sources: OECD Analytic Database; and IMF staff calculations.

Figure 4.9. Private Consumption: Response to Equity Busts, 1985–2005

(Percent change year-on-year; constant prices; x-axis in quarters)[1]

The consumption response to equity busts has been larger in more arm's length financial systems.

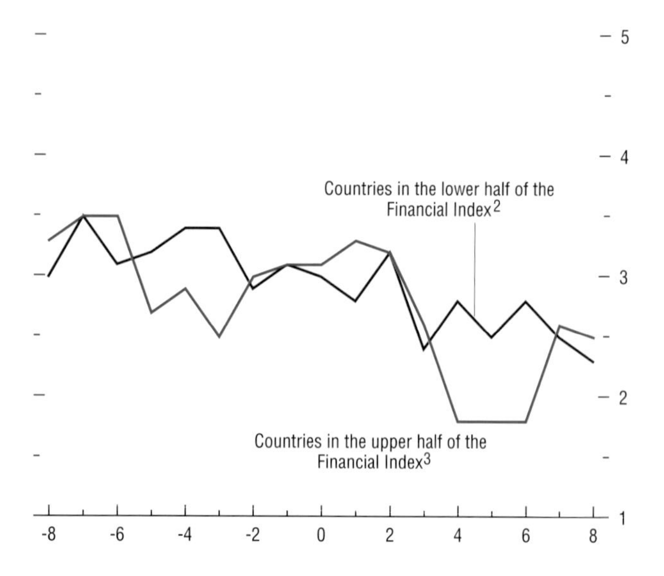

Sources: OECD Analytic Database; and IMF staff calculations.
[1]Zero denotes the quarter after which a bust begins.
[2]Countries included are Austria, Belgium, Finland, France, Germany, Greece, Japan, Portugal, and Spain.
[3]Countries included are Australia, Canada, Denmark, Italy, the Netherlands, Norway, Sweden, the United Kingdom, and the United States.

percent for housing declines (Figures 4.9 and 4.10).[21]

Looking at equity market downturns, differences in the response of private consumption across countries in the upper and lower halves of the Financial Index were analyzed over the past two decades. The results of this event analysis suggest that countries with more arm's length financial systems do exhibit a larger median response of private consumption to equity market downturns, consistent with what would be expected given that households are more exposed to changes in stock market valuations.[22]

For housing downturns, the responses of consumption and residential investment have become stronger since 1985 (the period during which mortgage markets have been liberalized in many advanced economies). This finding is consistent with the proposition that the increased role of housing as collateral has made household spending more dependent on housing prices. Because of data limitations, the analysis of responses of households was restricted to more arm's length systems.[23]

While these results suggest that asset price declines can have a larger impact on household behavior in more arm's length systems, there is also evidence suggesting that asset price busts have been shallower in such systems, consistent with more continuous adjustments of asset valuations (Figure 4.11). Evidence from the United States, for example, suggests that the volatility of real housing activity and errors in the pricing of housing have been reduced through the expansion of the mortgage finance market (see Schnure, 2005). Empirical analysis of equity markets also suggests that more arm's length systems incorporate firm-specific information

[21]See Chapter II of the April 2003 *World Economic Outlook* and Appendix 4.2 for a more detailed explanation of the event analysis.

[22]This is in line with Ludwig and Sløk (2002), who found that the wealth effect on consumption from stock prices is larger in market-based systems than in bank-based systems.

[23]Complete data on house prices were available only for a limited number of countries in the upper half of the Financial Index.

more efficiently, indicating that stock prices adjust to underlying fundamentals more quickly and prevent systematic mispricing.

The Corporate Sector

Does a financial system with a greater degree of arm's length transactions dampen or amplify investment volatility during business cycles? And how does such a system perform in the face of longer-term changes in growth opportunities?

During normal business cycle downturns, financial systems with a lower degree of arm's length transactions (and a higher degree of relationship-based lending) could be expected to give greater weight to the longer-term gains from maintaining an existing relationship with a borrower by providing short-term assurance that financing will be available in the event of a temporary disruption in cash flow, particularly as the lender's own balance sheet is on average more exposed to the borrower. Providing financing to ride out such temporary downturns may then not only be in the interest of the borrower, but also of the lender.[24] A more arm's length financial system, on the other hand, may help smooth firm financing by diversifying the sources of financing—making them less vulnerable to credit crunches.

Empirical evidence supports the view that countries with a higher degree of relationship-based lending may experience shallower contraction in nonresidential business fixed investment during cyclical downturns (Figure 4.12, upper panel).[25] Evidence from the investment cycle in the aftermath of the bursting of the equity bubble in 2000 is also consistent with this view (Figure 4.12, middle and lower panels). In the United States, firms reduced investment

Figure 4.10. Private Consumption and Residential Investment: Response to Housing Busts, 1970–2005[1]
(Percent change year-on-year; constant prices; x-axis in quarters)[2]

Responses of consumption and residential investment to housing busts have become stronger.

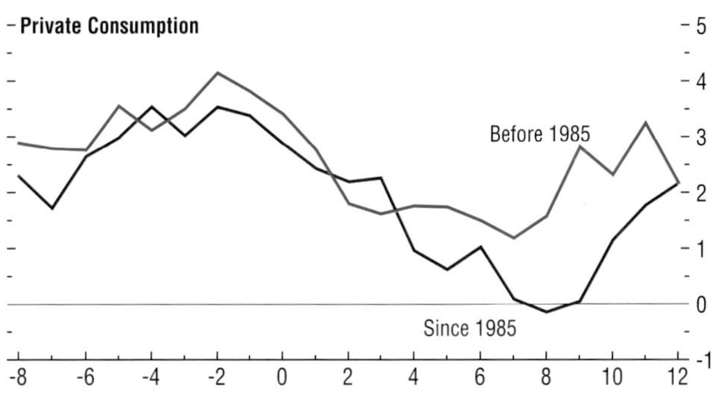

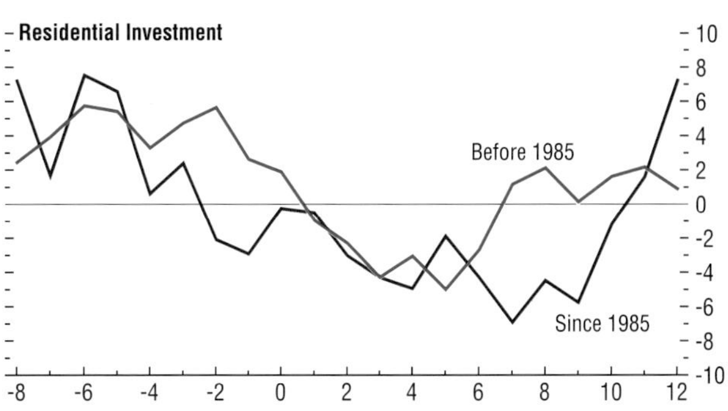

Sources: OECD Analytic Database; and IMF staff calculations.
[1]Countries included are Australia, Canada, Denmark, Italy, the Netherlands, Norway, Sweden, the United Kingdom, and the United States.
[2]Zero denotes the quarter after which a bust begins.

[24]At the extreme, of course, this can lead to the perverse incentive to "evergreen" loans that are effectively in default in order to disguise the poor underlying asset quality on a bank's balance sheet.

[25]See also Issing (2003). Kaufmann and Valderrama (2004) provide empirical evidence on the smoothing of business cycles in more relationship-based financial systems.

Figure 4.11. Depth of Equity and Housing Busts and the Financial Index, 1985–2005

Equity and housing busts have been shallower in more arm's length financial systems.

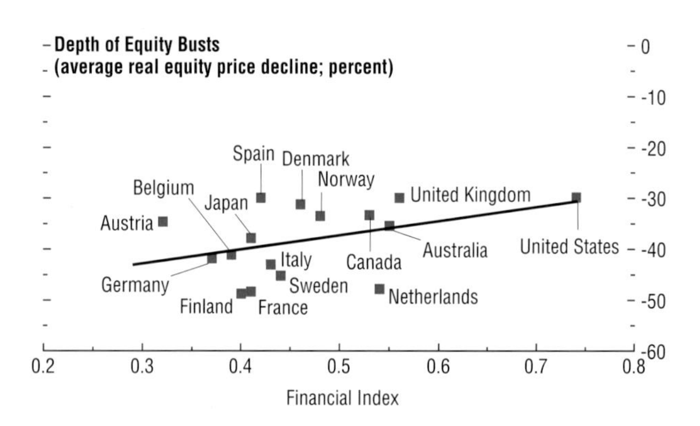

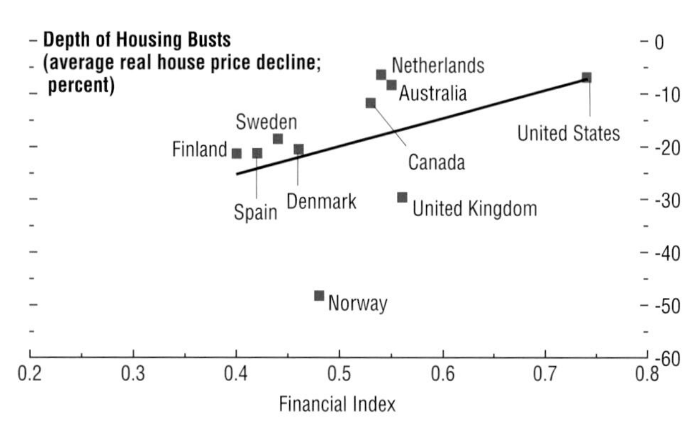

Sources: OECD Analytic Database; and IMF staff calculations.

sharply and relied to a greater degree on internal financing compared with their European counterparts.[26]

From a longer-term perspective, an important question is whether a more arm's length financial system is better equipped to reallocate resources relatively quickly in response to developments that necessitate investment in new areas and by new firms, as such systems are relatively unfettered by the constraints imposed by longer-term relationships with a borrower. One approach to this question is to examine the differences in the growth of industrial subsectors in response to global growth opportunities. A more arm's length system could be expected to take greater advantage of growth opportunities that lie away from the basic specialization of existing industry in a country. A more relationship-based system may conversely be expected to be more successful at taking advantage of organic growth opportunities—those within the area of expertise of existing industry, and thus likely requiring minor modifications of prevailing technologies (Rajan and Zingales, 2003).

To examine the difference in corporate sector responses to growth opportunities, this section looks at two separate measures:

- The correlation between real output growth in an industry within a country and world output growth of the same industry.[27] This gives a measure of the ability of an economy to grasp investment opportunities that emerge globally (and thus to achieve allocative efficiency).[28] A high correlation would indicate

[26]One important caveat regarding the smoother response of European corporates during the most recent cycle is that, while relying less than their U.S. counterparts on internal financing, they have been able to tap into the rapidly growing corporate bond market. It remains to be seen, however, whether corporates in Europe will be more successful than in other countries in accessing bond financing during a downturn once the market has matured (ECB, 2001).

[27]World output growth for an industry is calculated based on data for the sample of 181 countries covered by the United Nations Industrial Development database (see Appendix 4.2).

[28]A detailed description of the methodology and data used in the analysis is contained in Appendix 4.2.

that this country is better able to take advantage of global growth opportunities. To the extent that more arm's length systems are in general more flexible in financing innovations that require a substantial change in production technology, this correlation should be positively linked to a country's score on the Financial Index.

- The ability of a country to take advantage of global growth opportunities in an industry can generally be expected to be higher if that country already has a high degree of specialization in that industry. One measure of the distance between a country's initial specialization and the one that would maximize growth based on global growth opportunities is the correlation between the contribution of an industry to world growth and the share of that industry in a country's value added at the outset of the period under consideration, with a higher correlation indicating a smaller distance. At the same time, a greater degree of arms' length financing should be able to mitigate the disadvantages of being initially specialized in other industries—that is, at a greater distance from the optimal industry mix. Hence, one could expect that the higher the score in the Financial Index, the lower the impediment to growth coming from the distance between the initial industry mix of a country and the mix that would maximize its growth potential.

A formal econometric analysis testing the above propositions for the manufacturing sector supports the view that more arm's length systems allowed domestic industry to adapt better to a changing global environment.[29]

- During 1980–2001, countries that scored higher on the Financial Index were also those that were better able to seize growth opportunities available worldwide.
- Those countries that in 1980 had already specialized in the (globally) fast-growing sectors

[29]See Appendix 4.2 for regression results. These results are robust to the exclusion of the United States from the sample.

Figure 4.12. Investment and Financing by the Corporate Sector

Business investment tends to move sharply during cyclical downturns in more arm's length financial systems. Following the burst of the equity bubble in 2000 (1990 for Japan), U.S. nonfinancial corporates reduced investment and increased their reliance on internal funding faster than Japanese and Euro 3 firms.

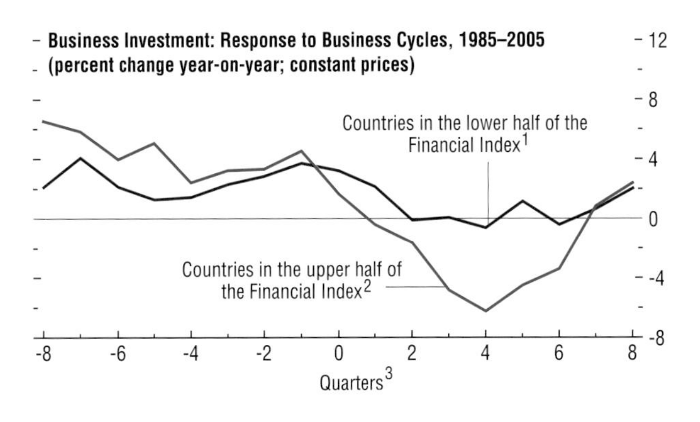

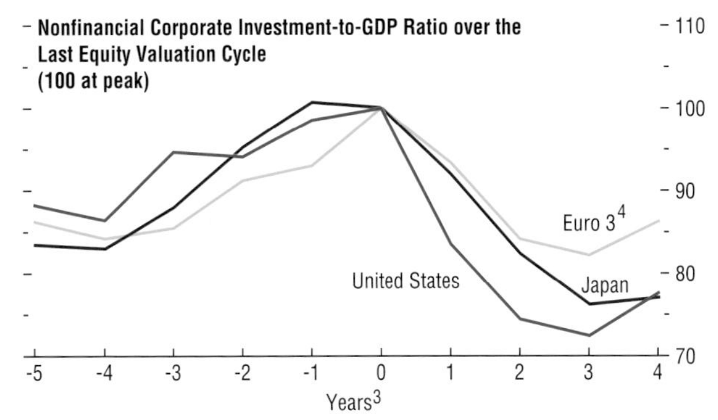

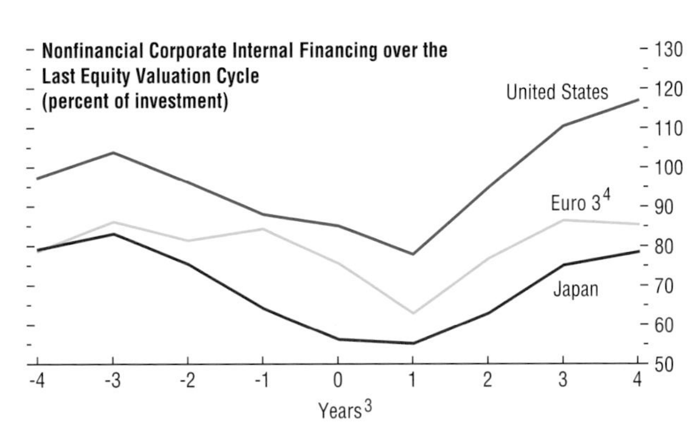

Sources: National financial accounts from Eurostat and OECD; OECD Analytic Database; and IMF staff calculations.
[1]Countries included are Austria, Belgium, Finland, France, Germany, Greece, Japan, Portugal, and Spain.
[2]Countries included are Australia, Canada, Denmark, Italy, the Netherlands, Norway, Sweden, the United Kingdom, and the United States.
[3]Zero denotes the peak quarter or year of the business cycle.
[4]GDP-weighted average of France, Germany, and Italy (GDP at market exchange rates).

Box 4.1. Financial Leverage and Debt Deflation

Despite their increasing sophistication, modern financial systems still operate under informational and institutional constraints, such as the limited enforceability of credit contracts and imperfect information on the creditworthiness of borrowers. "Financial frictions," such as constraints on borrowing against collateral and margin calls when the value of collateral falls, have provided mechanisms to protect financial systems from excessive credit risks related to such constraints. As discussed in the chapter, however, in more arm's length financial systems new risk and information-sharing mechanisms have been used to extend the effective use of collateralization, thus allowing borrowers to acquire higher levels of debt relative to their assets or income, which are reflected in higher leverage ratios (see Figure 4.8 in the main text).

Under what circumstances does the move to more arm's length financial systems, by permitting higher leverage ratios, generate increased systemic risks or raise macroeconomic vulnerabilities to asset price collapses? This box examines how asset price declines can damage the real economy and cause financial distress in financial systems characterized by different levels of leverage and collateralization.

One explanation for the intensity of financial crises is that asset price declines interact with increasing restrictions on access to credit to generate a downward spiral driven by financial frictions. Thus, a relatively "small" negative shock hitting a highly leveraged economy induces a decline in asset and/or goods prices, which causes financial institutions to cut back on credit creation as collateral constraints and other forms of credit limits become increasingly binding. As a result, borrowers are forced to engage in fire sales of assets and goods, inducing further declines in prices, which tighten borrowing constraints further (effectively increasing the real values of debts as borrowers rush to pay them). Irving Fisher labeled this process the "debt-deflation" mechanism in his classic analysis of the Great Depression (Fisher, 1933).[1] As will become clear below, this mechanism provides a vehicle for the degree of financial leverage to amplify the effects of shocks on the real economy.

The likelihood that countries may run into collateral constraints and suffer debt-deflation crises is difficult to gauge because leverage ratios and effective limits on leverage vary widely across countries, across industries within countries, and over time. Recent episodes in which this phenomenon, however, played a role include the Asian Crisis of 1997–98 and the bursting of the bubble in technology stocks of the late 1990s.

To analyze the impact of asset prices on an economy through financial leverage, it is useful first to establish a benchmark case using the familiar example of a small open economy with perfect credit markets. This economy can be viewed as a country that is a small player in world capital markets, or as a region or industry within a country that takes domestic interest rates as given. In this small open economy with perfect credit markets, real shocks (e.g., to total factor productivity, the terms of trade, or government expenditures) have no impact on the economy as long as they are wealth-neutral—that is, if they induce a reduction in income at some initial date followed by an exactly offsetting increase in future income so that the present value of income is unchanged. Output, investment, the price of capital (Tobin's q) and consumption would be unchanged, as there is

Note: The author of this box is Enrique Mendoza.

[1]More recent studies that develop similar mechanisms include Kiyotaki and Moore (1997); Aiyagari and Gertler (1999); Bernanke, Gertler, and Gilchrist (1999); Mendoza (2005); and Mendoza and Smith (forthcoming).

As is common in models of the financial accelerator, Fisher's debt-deflation theory works through balance sheet effects. The debt-deflation framework differs in that the spiral of collapsing asset prices and increasingly tight credit access amplifies the impact of balance sheet effects. Mendoza (2005) provides an example showing that the additional amplification due to the debt-deflation process dwarfs standard balance sheet effects.

no credit constraint to prevent households and firms from borrowing as needed to implement their pre-shock consumption and investment plans.[2]

The results are strikingly different when credit market imperfections are introduced. Suppose that agents are allowed to borrow only up to a fraction of the value of their assets. This can be the case because, for example, legal institutions or monitoring costs allow lenders to recover only a fraction of a borrower's assets in case of default, or because borrowers are only able to "securitize" a fraction of their assets as collateral. What happens if this economy is hit by the same wealth-neutral shock? As long as the collateral constraint does not bind, the results do not change: consumption, output, investment, and Tobin's q are unchanged because economic agents can borrow to smooth the temporary shock to income. For a "sufficiently large" shock, however, the collateral constraint becomes binding, and when this happens the debt-deflation mechanism is set in motion, triggering declines in consumption, investment, and output. Moreover, the real effects are persistent because the initial decline in investment lowers the economy's future productive capacity.

To explore the potential quantitative significance of this debt-deflation mechanism, an example was constructed using plausible parameter values that yields a predicted initial leverage ratio for the economy of 11 percent (see Mendoza, 2005).[3] Now, suppose there is a wealth-neutral shock that initially reduces income by 2 percent of GDP (similar to the standard deviation of real GDP over the business cycle in many industrial countries). Agents in the economy would want to borrow because of the negative shock (to smooth consumption) and because the capital stock is low relative to its long-run level. If credit markets were perfect, the leverage ratio would rise to almost 15 percent in this example. Hence, the economy requires sufficiently high access to leverage (of at least 15 percent of the value of assets) for consumption and investment to remain unaffected by the shock. However, if the degree of financial development is such that it supports leverage ratios at least as large as 11 percent, but not larger than 15 percent, the shock would trigger the debt-deflation mechanism. This does not imply, however, that arm's length financial systems necessarily make countries more vulnerable to a debt-deflation crisis just because they allow leverage to increase. Indeed, since the potential for leverage (i.e., the leverage limit) increases when these systems develop and work efficiently to provide better risk and information sharing, a higher degree of financial development that increases the scope for borrowing in response to a shock *reduces* the effects of a debt-deflation crisis for a real shock of a given size.

The table shows the real effects of the debt-deflation mechanism in response to the 2 percent of GDP wealth-neutral shock for a range of values of the limit on leverage from 11 to 15 percent. Within this range, the effects are stronger the lower the limit on leverage.

The effects decline to zero when the leverage ratio can rise as high as 15 percent because at that point the ability to leverage is sufficient so that the wealth-neutral shock does not trigger the collateral constraint. At the other extreme, when the limit on leverage is set at 11 percent, the shock would have a maximum effect on the

[2]Tobin's q is defined as the ratio of the market value of a firm's assets to the replacement cost of these assets.

[3]The real interest rate is set at 6 percent, the capital share in GDP is 34 percent, the intertemporal elasticity of substitution in consumption is 0.5, and the coefficient of capital adjustment costs is set at 1. The initial stock of debt is 60 percent of GDP and the initial stock of physical capital is 50 percent of its long-run value.

The leverage limits in the model pertain to the aggregate of all net liabilities of households and corporates as a share of the market value of all the capital stock (equipment and structures, including housing and business buildings). Actual measures of these ratios vary widely across industrial countries. For example, the ratio of mortgage liabilities (a proxy for collateralized debt) to nonfinancial wealth of the household sector ranges from about 10 percent in Japan to about 30 percent in the United States (see Mendoza, Quadrini, and Rios-Rull, 2006).

Box 4.1. *(concluded)*

Macroeconomic Effects of the Debt-Deflation Mechanism in Response to a 2 Percent Wealth-Neutral Shock to Total Factor Productivity

Leverage Limit	Output	Consumption	Investment	Tobin's q	Credit Flow as a Share of GDP
0.11	–1.32	–3.75	–3.72	–3.72	–18.02
0.12	–0.95	–3.13	–2.69	–2.69	–13.50
0.13	–0.57	–2.47	–1.62	–1.62	–8.78
0.14	–0.18	–1.79	–0.52	–0.52	–3.85
0.15	0.00	0.00	0.00	0.00	0.00

Note: Macroeconomic effects are defined as differences between economies with and without credit frictions in percent of the value of each variable in the economy with perfect credit markets. All the effects are for the initial date on which the shock hits, except for the output effect, which is for the following period.

economy with a decline in output of about 1.3 percent and a drop in consumption and investment of nearly 4 percent (see the table). Net exports, on the other hand, rise sharply because of the large decline in imports that accompanies the contraction of domestic demand induced by the loss of access to credit, which can be as large as 18 percentage points of GDP.[4]

[4]Chapter II of the April 2003 and Chapter IV of the April 2004 issues of the *World Economic Outlook* provide empirical evidence on the sharp swings in leverage of publicly listed corporations of emerging economies and discuss further their significance for explaining emerging markets crises.

The above results suggest that for a shock of a given magnitude, countries that are close to their financial leverage limits are the most vulnerable. Hence, economies with higher potential for leverage can be more resilient to small shocks than economies with relatively lower credit access, but they remain vulnerable if a sufficiently large shock triggers the debt-deflation mechanism. In contrast, the lower use of collateral as a basis for lending may make relationship-based financial systems less vulnerable to large swings in asset prices and to the related risk of a debt-deflation spiral, but at the same time they leave unexploited the benefits that can result from financial development.

during 1980–2001 were better able to take advantage of worldwide growth opportunities.

- However, the strength of this relationship between existing specialization and subsequent fast growth is weakened by a high score in the Financial Index—that is, the greater the degree of arm's length financing, the lower the impediment to growth from the "wrong" initial industry specialization.

These results provide support to the view that more arm's length systems are better equipped to deal with the reallocation process required at times of significant innovation and change in the industrial structure of the global economy. In other words, they may be better at reallocating resources from declining to growing industries.[30] On the other hand, more relationship-based financial systems appear to be better at helping smooth temporary business cycle downturns.

Financial Systems and Cross-Border Flows

With the rising importance of cross-border financial flows, an issue that has recently received considerable attention is how differences in financial systems may affect a country's

[30]Of course, financial systems that enable greater flexibility in industry also need to be complemented by other factors—such as flexible labor markets—in order to successfully allow industries to restructure.

ability to attract portfolio inflows, and hence finance its current account deficit. For example, Caballero, Farhi, and Gourinchas (2006) argue that it is the ability of a country to generate financial assets from real investments that is important, while Chinn and Ito (2005) find that overall financial development seems to matter, but only in advanced economies. Differences in the degree of arm's length transactions may also be important in influencing cross-border flows. Foreign investors typically do not have existing relationships with potential borrowers in a country, making a more arm's length system particularly well suited for intermediating foreign inflows. Moreover, a more arm's length system may typically offer a broader array of financial instruments for savers to meet investment and risk management goals, as well as greater liquidity and transparency. These factors can increase the pool of savings to which domestic households and firms have access, potentially supporting a higher level of consumption and investment. This suggests that aggregate domestic demand can on average be higher in countries that have higher scores in the Financial Index, supporting larger current account deficits in the short run.[31]

In the United States, for example, the high degree of securitization of mortgages has played an important role in attracting foreign investors. More than 10 percent of the $8 trillion in outstanding U.S. residential mortgages is now estimated to be financed by foreign investors through their investment in mortgage-related securities (see Knight, 2006; and IMF, 2006a). Financial systems in the United States and the United Kingdom, in particular, also provide investors with a diverse pool of liquid instruments that can be tailored—by a highly developed financial services industry—to the risk-return preferences of individual investors, increasing their attractiveness to foreign investors (see IMF, 2006b). Of course, other well-documented factors—including expected returns on investment, currency, and tax and regulatory frameworks—remain important additional driving forces in explaining the global pattern of cross-border flows.

More systematic empirical evidence on the relationship between the extent of arm's length financial transactions and cross-border flows across the broader group of advanced economies is, however, mixed. There is some evidence of a positive correlation between the extent of arm's length transactions and portfolio inflows, with the United States and the United Kingdom scoring high on both dimensions, when portfolio inflows are measured as a proportion of that country's exports and imports (Figure 4.13, upper panel). The correlation is less evident when portfolio inflows or the level of foreign holdings are measured as a proportion of total outstanding portfolio securities, with the proportion of domestic securities held by foreigners in the euro area relatively high despite the area's generally less arm's length financial systems (Figure 4.13, lower panel). However, this high share may reflect the influence of a common currency as well as harmonization of regulations. Taken as a whole, the euro area has a lower share of foreign-held securities than the United States or the United Kingdom.

In an effort to identify more clearly the relationship between the arm's length content of financial systems and private cross-border portfolio holdings, a gravity model was estimated using data from the IMF's Coordinated Portfolio Investment Survey (CPIS). This exercise took into account the impact of country size and geographic proximity (as in standard gravity models) and also the effect of a common currency among euro area economies. The results, reported in Appendix 4.2, suggest that bilateral portfolio holdings are positively associated with the extent of arm's length financing in the destination countries.[32] Overall, foreign inves-

[31]See the April 2005 *World Economic Outlook* for more on the links between globalization and external imbalances.

[32]Among advanced economies, the evidence suggests that cross-border holdings of portfolio securities are positively related to the Financial Index scores of both the source and destination countries.

Figure 4.13. The Financial Index and Foreign Portfolio Investment

There is evidence of a positive correlation between foreign portfolio inflows and the Financial Index.

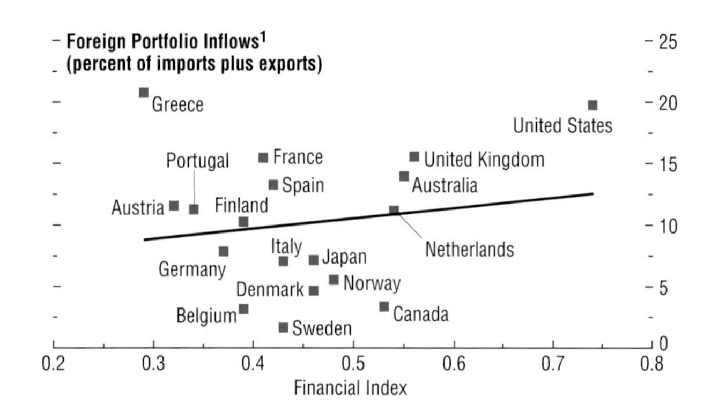

Foreign and Domestic Holdings of Debt and Equity Securities[2] (percent of GDP)

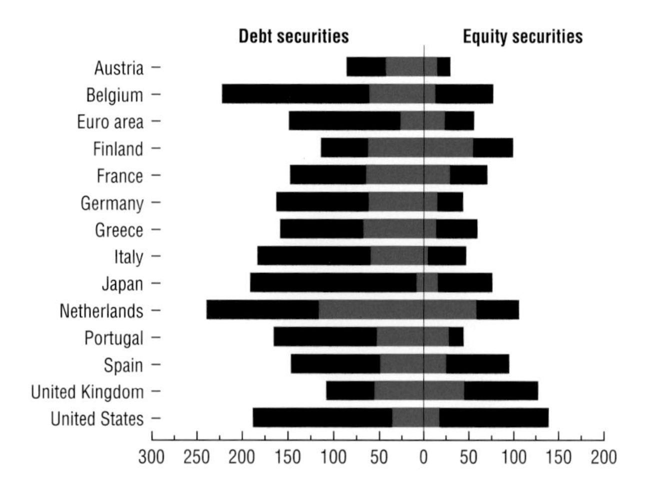

Sources: Bank for International Settlements; Lane and Milesi-Ferretti (2006); OECD; and IMF staff calculations.
[1]Data are for 2000–2004 averages.
[2]Data are for 2004.

tors seem to hold a greater amount of portfolio securities in countries with a higher degree of arm's length transactions. The degree of arm's length transactions in the destination country, however, appears to matter less for cross-border investments within continental Europe.

Conclusions

Financial systems in advanced economies have changed significantly in recent years as technology has improved and financial deregulation has proceeded apace. Nevertheless, this chapter suggests that significant differences persist across countries in how funds are intermediated across household and firm balance sheets. The variations reflect underlying differences in the degree to which financial transactions are conducted at arm's length and the importance of longer-term relationships between borrowers and lenders. The financial systems of Australia, the Netherlands, the United States, and the United Kingdom are increasingly characterized by a relatively high degree of arm's length transactions; those in France, Germany, Italy, and Japan have moved in the same direction, but remain relatively more reliant on borrower/lender relationships.

The empirical results in this chapter suggest that these differences in financial system structure may affect household and corporate behavior over economic cycles. More arm's length and more relationship-based systems each seem to have particular strengths and weaknesses depending on the specific challenges facing the economy. For example, under a more arm's length system, households are able to access a larger amount of financing and seem better able to smooth consumption in the face of temporary changes in their income. This may have contributed to the reduction in consumption volatility over the business cycle. In more arm's length systems, however, households appear to be more vulnerable to swings in asset prices, implying larger effects on demand from major asset price booms and busts. This effect, however, may be countered to some degree by the fact that the amplitude of swings in asset prices may be lower in more arm's length systems.

Turning to the corporate sector, cyclical changes in investment seem to be shallower in more relationship-based systems, perhaps because such systems provide greater cash flow support to firms in the face of temporary changes in demand. Thus, the more closely aligned incentives of firms and lenders under these systems may allow for greater smoothing during economic downturns and less pressure for drastic balance sheet restructuring. However, when resources need to be reallocated away from declining to relatively new sectors and firms—such as those arising from the emergence of new technology—more arm's length systems seem better able to capitalize on these opportunities, with benefits for productivity growth and profitability.

The degree of arm's length content of financial systems also appears to be a factor affecting the portfolio allocation decisions of international investors. In addition to well-known factors such as the size of financial markets, international portfolio investors appear to place more assets in the financial systems of advanced economies with a higher degree of arm's length content. Among the advanced economies, investors in countries with more arm's length financial systems also seem to invest more in the portfolio securities of other countries.

The results in this chapter support the view that financial system structure does affect economic behavior and cyclical patterns. It is worth reiterating, however, that this is a new area of research, and the results are suggestive rather than definitive. This is in part due to the limited time span for observing cyclical behavior in economies with a high degree of arm's length financial transactions, and the need to characterize highly complicated financial systems using a single index. Further research in this area could, for example, look at how subcomponents of the Financial Index interact with cyclical behavior.

Looking forward, the move toward more arm's length financial systems is likely to continue as deregulation fosters greater competition in financial markets, globalization of financial markets and services continues, information and communications technology advances, and corporate governance, accounting, and legal standards are enhanced. In such an environment, competition across financial institutions can be expected to continue increasing the role of arm's length transactions intermediated through markets and reducing—but certainly not eliminating—the scope for profitable long-term financial relationships based on informational advantages. The move toward private pension plans is also likely to further boost the arm's length content of many financial systems by increasing the role of nonbank financial intermediaries and adding depth and liquidity to financial markets. There will still, however, be niches in financial systems for relationship-based transactions—such as private equity partnerships—that seek to exploit specialized knowledge of sectors and technologies. More generally, the move toward more arm's length systems facilitates the transformation of the nature of relationships themselves.

The key question for policymakers is how to maximize the benefits of this continuing move toward financial systems that are more reliant on arm's length transactions, while minimizing the downside risks. Financial and regulatory policies have to adapt to changing financial systems in order to maintain stability. The greater speed and flexibility with which transactions can be executed and the higher degree of leverage in the household sector in more arm's length systems could become sources of financial instability with macroeconomic consequences, if not adequately monitored (see Geithner, 2006). Supervisors and regulators will therefore need to continually assess and upgrade their policy tools to match financial systems' increased sophistication. The effect of interest rate changes on asset prices will also likely become an increasingly relevant channel of monetary policy transmission through the impact on consumption and residential investment. In this environment, wealth effects could be larger than expected on the basis of historical data, and monetary policymakers will need to remain flexible, adapting their assessments of developments to reflect possible changes in the impact of asset prices on economic behavior.

Greater demands will also be placed on firms to restructure their operations in the face of business cycle downturns as the temporary insurance provided by relationship-based lenders diminishes. Complementary reforms would help to ensure that firms are able to smoothly adjust all aspects of their operations to business cycle downturns and to facilitate the reorientation toward newer growth opportunities. Labor markets, the portability of employee pension plans, and bankruptcy laws are three key areas where reforms can support the corporate sector's ability to respond to the changing environment. Finally, strong, but well defined, social safety nets would ensure adequate support for individuals and help in retraining for new employment opportunities.

Appendix 4.1. Building the Financial Index

The main author of this appendix is Roberto Cardarelli.

This appendix describes in detail the methodology and data used to build the Financial Index discussed in the chapter. The overall Financial Index is computed as the simple average of three indices that capture the position of each of the 18 advanced economies considered in the chapter along three dimensions: the relevance of traditional (relationship-based) banking intermediation; the development of new types of financial intermediation conducted largely at arm's length; and, finally, the role played by financial markets. Each of these subindices is described below (see also Figure 4.14).

Figure 4.14. The Financial Index

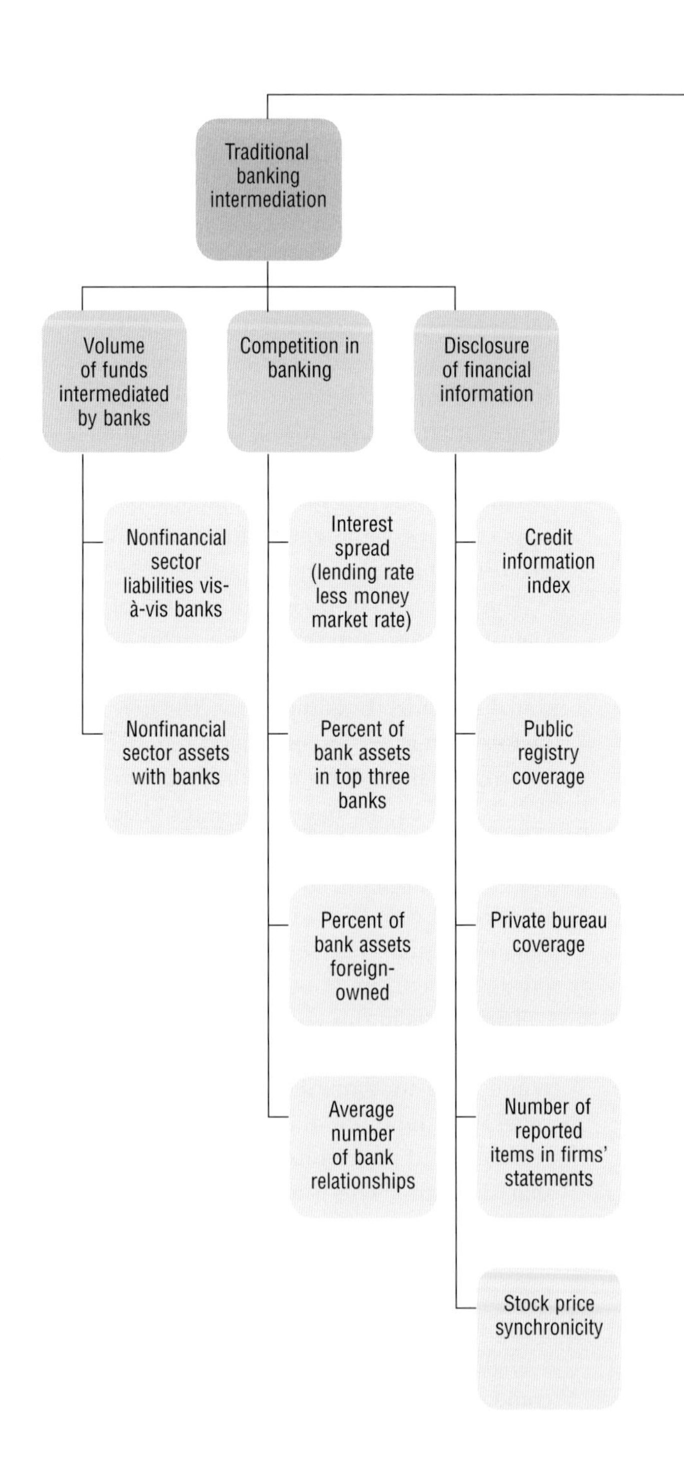

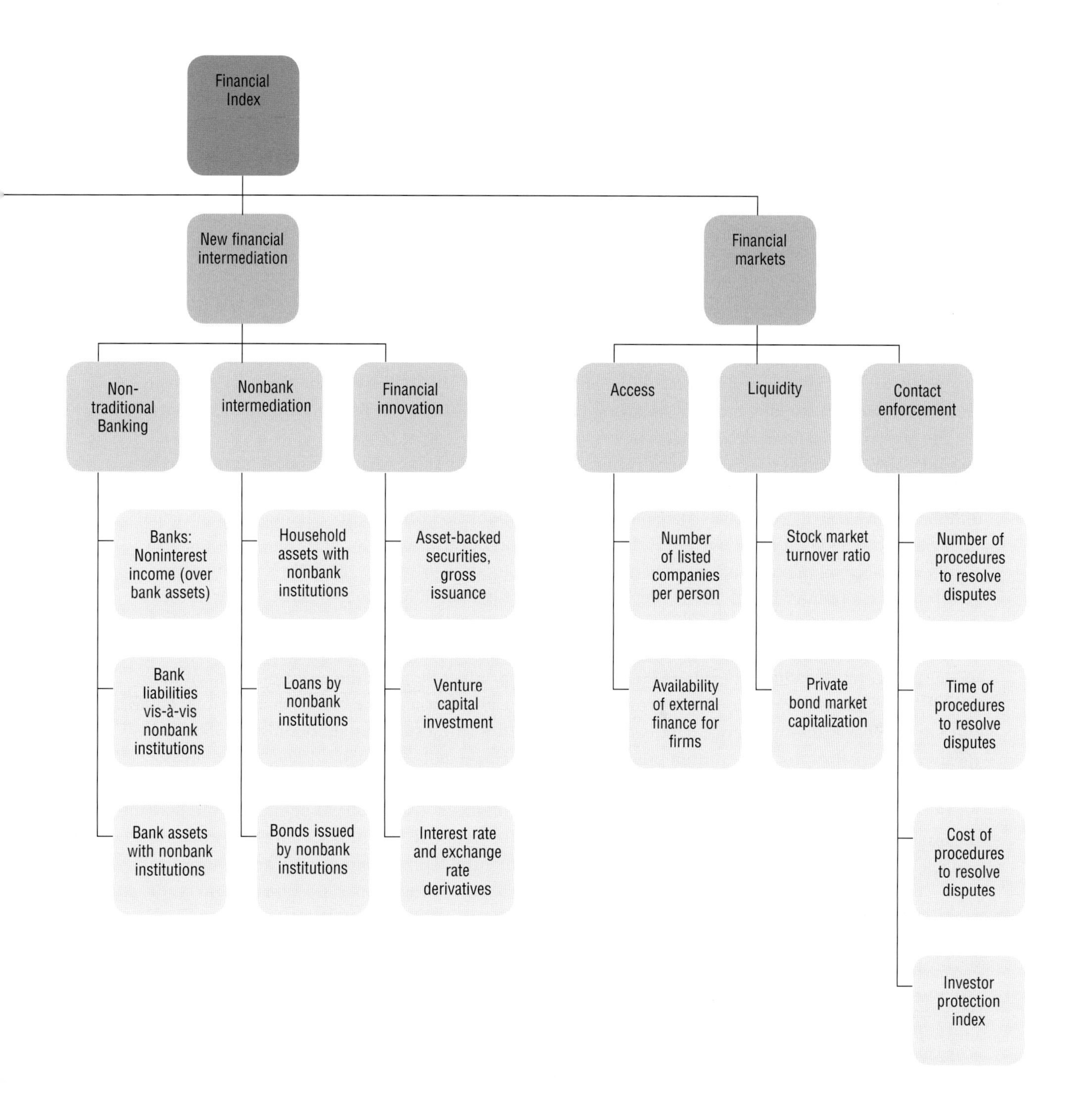
Financial Index
New financial intermediation
Financial markets
Non-traditional Banking
Nonbank intermediation
Financial innovation
Access
Liquidity
Contact enforcement
Banks: Noninterest income (over bank assets)
Bank liabilities vis-à-vis nonbank institutions
Bank assets with nonbank institutions
Household assets with nonbank institutions
Loans by nonbank institutions
Bonds issued by nonbank institutions
Asset-backed securities, gross issuance
Venture capital investment
Interest rate and exchange rate derivatives
Number of listed companies per person
Availability of external finance for firms
Stock market turnover ratio
Private bond market capitalization
Number of procedures to resolve disputes
Time of procedures to resolve disputes
Cost of procedures to resolve disputes
Investor protection index

Traditional Banking Intermediation Index

This index is constructed as the simple average of three subindices (shown in Figure 4.15).[33] The first subindex captures the traditional role of banks in taking deposits and making loans to firms and consumers. The other two capture the degree of competition in the banking sector and the extent to which financial information is publicly available in the economy. While the latter two variables may be grouped under more than one index (for example, as part of the new financial intermediation index, and/or of the financial market index), this grouping reflects the view that two key factors characterizing the traditional (relationship-based) banking mode of financing are the presence of some form of market power by banks over the borrowers they finance (which is lower in a more competitive banking system) and the relative scarcity of publicly available financial information on these borrowers. Hence, despite the large volume of funds intermediated by banks, a country would score lower on this index if there was considerable competition among banks—making a long-term borrower/lender relationship less likely—or there was widespread availability of information on borrowers' capacity to repay loans and service debt (which means the bank does not benefit from private information gleaned from its relationship with a borrower). Each of the three subindices is in turn obtained as the simple average of a number of variables, which are described below.[34]

[33]In principle, other aggregation methodologies could have been used, such as principal components. Djankov and others (2005), however, show that using principal components is likely to lead to similar conclusions as those obtained using simple averages. The methodology used in the chapter has the advantage of simplicity and transparency, and avoids imposing implicit weights on the different components of the indexes.

[34]Each country was given a score equal to the ratio of the variable for that country to its maximum value across the 18 countries. This means that all indices considered in this chapter are between 0 and 1. An alternative methodology was also utilized, based on a quadratic distance approach that gives a zero value to the country with the minimum value, and gave very similar results. It should also be noted that, in constructing the overall index, the traditional banking index was included with a "negative" sign—that is, the lower the traditional banking content of the system (the lower the score on this index) the higher the score on the overall financial index.

Volume of Funds Intermediated by the Banking Sector

- *Nonfinancial sector assets with banks (percent of total nonfinancial sector assets)*—a measure of the role of banks in attracting savings. Clearly, deposits on the asset side of the balance sheet of the nonfinancial sector (household, nonfinancial corporates, government, and rest of the world) correspond to a liability of the banking sector, and are included in this variable. For other instruments (such as "securities other than shares" and "shares and other equity"), it is difficult to identify the sector that has issued the claim, as national accounts do not break down financial assets by the sector of the issuer (e.g., it is impossible to know what fraction of bonds held by households has been issued by firms or the public sector). Hence, financial claims (such as bonds) are "allocated" to the various sectors according to the sector's shares of the total liabilities (bonds) outstanding in that particular year. The share of nonfinancial sector assets with banks is thus estimated as the product between the assets of the nonfinancial sector and the banks' share of total liabilities (for a similar methodology see Schmidt, Hackethal, and Tyrell, 1999; and Samolyk, 2004). The banking sector includes monetary financial institutions as defined by the System of National Accounts (SNA) 93 (it comprises central banks, commercial banks, "universal" banks, savings banks, post banks, and credit unions).[35] Source: IMF staff estimates using data from Eurostat and national statistical offices.
- *Nonfinancial sector liabilities vis-à-vis banks (percent of nonfinancial sector liabilities)*—a measure of the role of banks in lending to consumers, firms, and the public sector. As for assets,

[35]For Japan, the Trust Fund Bureau (a public, nondepository, financial institution) was included in the banking sector, given the strong linkages between this institution and postal savings.

several instruments on the liability side of the nonfinancial sector balance sheet cannot be allocated to a particular sector (it is impossible to know the extent to which bond financing for firms has been provided by banks or nonbank financial institutions). The rule for assets is also applied to liabilities, namely, they are allocated to each sector based on that sector's share of total assets outstanding in that particular year. Hence, nonfinancial sector liabilities vis-à-vis banks are estimated from national financial accounts as the product of the liabilities of the nonfinancial sector and the banks' share of total assets. Source: IMF staff estimates using data from Eurostat and national statistical offices.

Competition in the Banking Sector

- *Interest spread.* The difference between the bank lending rate and the money market rate. The interest spread is a measure of the degree of market power of banks. Source: *International Financial Statistics* (IMF).
- *Share of bank assets owned by the three largest banks*—a measure of concentration in the banking sector. Source: Beck, Demirgüç-Kunt, and Levine (1999; A New Database on Financial Development and Structure).
- *Percent of bank assets that are foreign owned.* A larger presence of foreign banks is likely to signal a more open and competitive banking sector. Source: Barth, Caprio, and Nolle (2004).
- *Average number of firms' relationships with banks.* If firms in a country maintain relationships with several banks, this is taken to indicate a more competitive banking system. Source: Ongena and Smith (2000).

Disclosure of Financial Information

- *Credit Information Index.* The index ranges from 0 to 6, with higher values indicating that more credit information is available from either a public registry or a private bureau to facilitate lending decisions. Source: Doing Business database (World Bank).
- *Public credit registry coverage (percent of adults).* The number of individuals and firms listed in the public credit registry with current information on repayment history, unpaid debts, or credit outstanding. Source: Doing Business database (World Bank).
- *Private credit bureau coverage (percent of adults).* The coverage indicator reports the number of individuals or firms listed by the private credit bureau with current information on repayment history, unpaid debts or credit outstanding. Source: Doing Business database (World Bank).
- *Number of reported items in firms' statements.* The number of selected items that are reported in the annual balance sheet, income, and cash-flow statements for the top 20 companies in terms of market capitalization for each country. It is a measure of the amount of information communicated by firms to the general public. Source: De Nicoló, Laeven, and Ueda (2006).
- *Stock price synchronicity.* The fraction of stocks that move in the same direction in a country (as in Morck, Yeung, and Yu, 2000). It measures the ability of a national stock market to communicate firm-specific information to investors (the larger this fraction, the lower the firm-level information contained in the stock market). Source: De Nicoló, Laeven, and Ueda (2006).

New Financial Intermediation Index

This index measures the extent to which financial intermediation is conducted at arm's length in financial systems—by banks as well as other financial intermediaries. It is constructed as the simple average of three subindices (shown in Figure 4.15), which capture (1) the evolution of banks into new area of financial intermediation (by moving to fee-generating activities and establishing financial links with other financial institutions); (2) the relevance of nonbank financial intermediaries; and (3) the extent to which a country has embraced financial innovation by developing new types of financial

Figure 4.15. The Financial Index: Subindices for Selected Advanced Economies

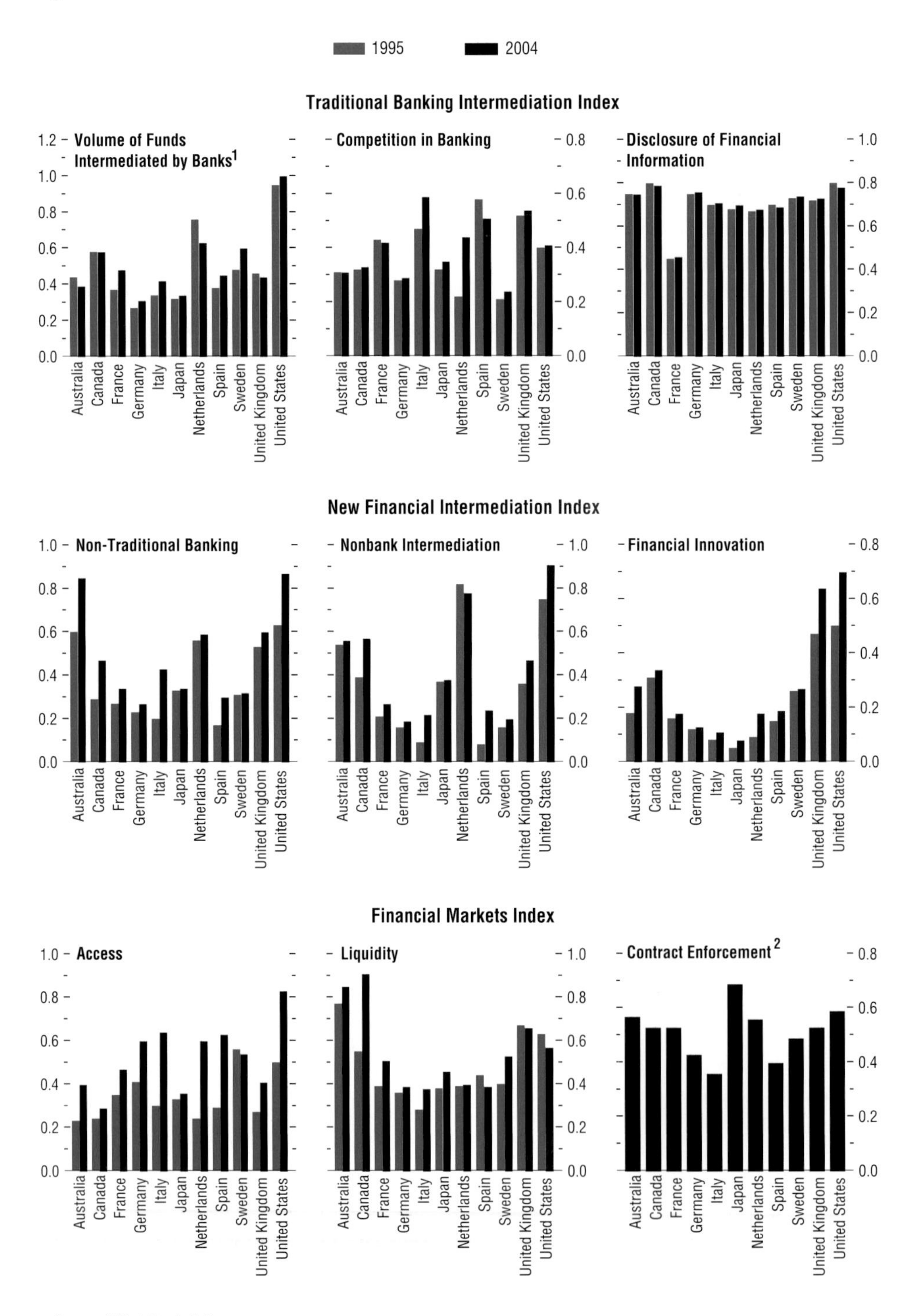

Source: IMF staff calculations.
[1]A higher value on the index denotes a lower volume of funds intermediated by banks.
[2]Data available only for 2003.

products, such as asset-backed securities, venture capital, and derivatives. Each of these subindices is obtained as a simple average of a number of variables, described below.

Nontraditional Banking Intermediation

- *Bank noninterest income (ratio to total assets)*—a measure of banks' ability to diversify their activity away from traditional credit risk intermediation and toward new (fee-generating) activities. Source: OECD, Bank Profitability database.
- *Bank liabilities vis-à-vis nonbank financial institutions (share of bank liabilities)*—a measure of the degree to which banks borrow from nonbank financial institutions. It is estimated from national financial accounts as the product of bank liabilities and nonbank financial institutions' share of total assets. Together with banks' assets with nonbank financial institutions (see below), this measure captures the financial linkages between banks and nonbank financial institutions. Source: IMF staff estimates using data from Eurostat and national statistical offices.
- *Bank assets with nonbank financial institutions (share of bank assets)*—a measure of the extent to which banks have extended credit to nonbank financial institutions. It is estimated from national financial accounts as the product of bank assets and the nonbank financial institutions' share of total liabilities. Source: IMF staff estimates using data from Eurostat and national statistical offices.

Nonbank Financial Intermediation

- *Household assets with nonbank financial institutions (share of household assets)*—a measure of the ability of nonbank financial institutions to attract household savings. Estimated as the product of household assets and the nonbank financial institutions' share of total liabilities. Source: IMF staff estimates using data from Eurostat and national statistical offices.
- *Loans by nonbank financial institutions (share of total loans)*—a measure of the extent to which loans are funded by nonbank financial institutions (e.g., after they have been securitized). Estimated as the ratio of loan assets of nonbank financial institutions to total loan assets. Source: IMF staff estimates using data from Eurostat and national statistical offices.
- *Bonds issued by nonbank financial institutions (share of total bonds)*—a measure of the relevance of nonbank financial institutions that use bond issuance as a major form of financing. Estimated as the ratio of "securities other than shares" liabilities of nonbank financial institutions to total "securities other than shares" liabilities. Source: IMF staff estimates using data from Eurostat and national statistical offices.

Financial Innovation

- *Asset-backed securities, gross issuance (ratio to GDP)*. Sources: IMF staff estimates based on data from the European Securitization Forum for European countries; the Bond Market Association for the United States; Dominion Bond Rating Service for Canada; Australian Securitization Forum for Australia; and FinanceAsia.Com for Japan.
- *Venture capital investment (ratio to GDP)* (average 1998–2004). Source: OECD (2006).
- *Average daily turnover in foreign exchange and interest rate derivatives (ratio to GDP)*. Source: BIS, "Survey of Foreign Exchange and Derivatives Market Activity," several issues.

Financial Markets Index

This index captures key factors determining the efficiency and depth of financial markets. It is constructed as the simple average of three subindices capturing (1) the existence of well-functioning mechanisms to enforce contracts and thus reduce the frictions that may impede the development of arms' length relations; (2) the ability of firms to access markets to finance their activities; and (3) the liquidity and depth of stock and bond markets. Each of these subindices is in turn obtained as the average of a number of variables, which are described below.

Contract Enforcement

- *Number of procedures.* The number of procedures from when the plaintiff files a lawsuit in court until when payment is received. Source: Doing Business database (World Bank).
- *Time of procedures.* Time (in calendar days) to resolve the dispute. Source: Doing Business database (World Bank).
- *Cost of procedures (as a percentage of the debt value).* Cost of going through court procedures, including court costs and attorney fees where the use of attorneys is mandatory or common, or the costs of an administrative debt recovery procedure. Source: Doing Business database (World Bank).
- *Investor Protection Index.* The index ranges from 0 to 10, with higher values indicating better investor protection. It is an average of subindices on (1) the transparency of transactions; (2) the extent to which directors are liable for damages to the company; and (3) shareholders' ability to sue officers and directors for misconduct. Source: Doing Business database (World Bank).

Access to Markets

- *Number of listed companies per person.* Source: IMF staff estimates based on data from the World Federation of Exchanges, and national statistical sources.
- *Availability of external finance for firms.* Estimated as the ratio of the sum of "securities other than shares" (bonds) and "shares and other equity" liabilities over total liabilities of nonfinancial corporates. Source: IMF staff estimates using data from Eurostat and national statistical offices.

Liquidity of Markets

- *Stock market turnover.* The ratio of the value of total shares traded and average real market capitalization. Source: Beck, Demirgüç-Kunt, and Levine (1999; A New Database on Financial Development and Structure).
- *Private bond market capitalization (ratio to GDP).* Source: Beck, Demirgüç-Kunt, and Levine (1999; A New Database on Financial Development and Structure).

Clustering Analysis

Evidence on whether the financial systems of advanced economies have converged over the last decade can be gauged through a clustering exercise, which statistically groups countries based on similarities in their financial indicators. The objective of the cluster analysis is to group countries together based on their "distance" from each other in terms of their scores on all financial indicators in 1995 and 2004. Agglomerative hierarchical methods have been used, based on a series of successive mergers of the clusters of countries (see Johnson and Wichern, 2002). Starting with each country as a separate entity, successive iterations added the closest country to a cluster until finally all countries are grouped as a single cluster. When large differences persist between countries, a greater number of iterations are required to join a cluster. Based on this exercise, European countries tend to be grouped together in both years (Figure 4.16), even if some of them (France, Italy, and Spain) have increasingly differentiated themselves as they moved away from a relationship-based system in 2004 (when they are grouped to other European countries at a later stage of the clustering algorithm). In both 1995 and 2004, the United States was the last country to join the cluster, suggesting its financial system remains quite different from that of all the other advanced economies.

Appendix 4.2. Econometric Methodology

The main authors of this appendix are Roberto Cardarelli and Irina Tytell.

This appendix describes more fully the empirical evidence presented in the chapter, and in particular the econometric methodology and data used in linking the Financial Index to household consumption, residential investment, the response of national economies to global growth opportunities, and foreign portfolio inflows.

Household Sector and the Financial Index

To study how the extent of arm's length finance affects the marginal propensity to consume out of current income, the following model was estimated using annual data for 18 countries over 1996–2004:

$$\Delta c_{it} = \alpha_i + \beta \Delta y_{it} + \gamma[\Delta y_{it} \times FI_i] + \delta r_{it} + \eta_t + \varepsilon_{it},$$

where i indexes countries, t indexes years, c stands for (log) consumption, y stands for (log) income, r denotes the real interest rate, and FI is the Financial Index (α and η are country and year fixed effects, respectively). Private consumption and disposable income were measured in real per capita terms. All the data are from the OECD.

This formulation is grounded in the literature on the "excess sensitivity" of consumption (see Campbell and Mankiw, 1991), but is implemented in a panel setup. To maintain comparability across countries, total consumption expenditure was used, which includes durables, in addition to nondurables and services. The model was estimated without using instrumental variables, hence the coefficients should be interpreted as correlations only. The negative coefficient on the interaction term suggests that the marginal propensity to consume out of current income is smaller for countries with more arm's length financial systems (Table 4.1).

To study how the move toward more arm's length finance affects the behavior of residential investment, a model in which the first difference of residential investment depends on current and lagged first differences in residential investment, disposable income, mortgage rate, and inflation rate was estimated using quarterly data (three lags of each variable were included). Residential investment and disposable income were measured in logs in real per capita terms. The model was estimated using 40-quarter rolling regressions.[36] The results for the United States suggest that the sensitivities of residential invest-

[36]A similar model was estimated for the United States by Dynan, Elmendorf, and Sichel (2006).

Figure 4.16. Clustering Results[1]

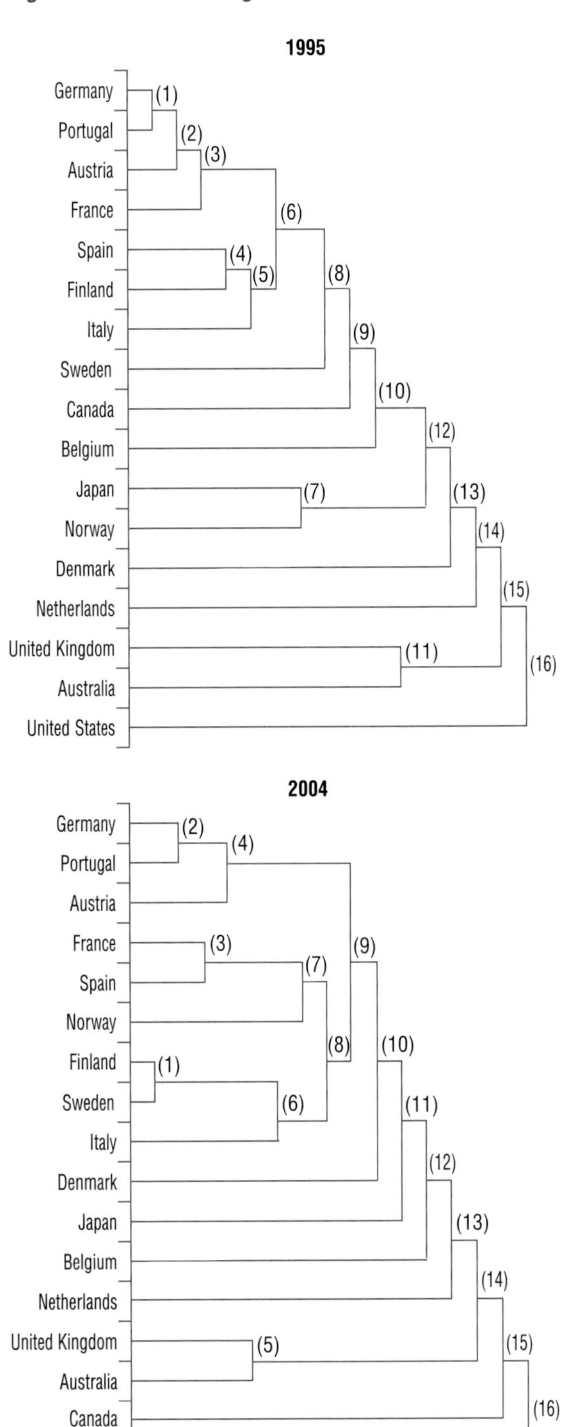

Source: IMF staff calculations.
[1]At each stage of clustering, one country is clustered to another country or an existing cluster. Numbers in parentheses indicate the stage at which two countries or existing clusters are put together.

Table 4.1. Dependent Variable: Private Consumption[1]
(Log difference)

Disposable income[1] (log difference)	0.599***
Interaction with Financial Index	–0.810**
Real short-term interest rate	0.001
Fixed country and year effects	Yes
Observations	161
R-squared	0.45

Source: IMF staff estimates.
Note: Heteroskedasticity and autocorrelation robust standard errors; ** significant at 5 percent; *** significant at 1 percent.
[1]Private consumption and disposable income in real per capita terms.

ment to income and to mortgage rates have declined over the past two decades.[37] Analogous estimations for other countries did not indicate robust declines in these sensitivities. While some evidence of declining sensitivities was detected in Australia, it was not sufficiently clear. It is worth noting that in several European countries the estimations were complicated by short data series on mortgage rates.

Event Analyses Around Equity and Housing Busts

For this analysis, equity and housing price cycles were identified using the methodologies for the identification of business cycle turning points described in April 2003 *World Economic Outlook*. Busts were defined as those episodes where peak-trough asset price declines were large enough to fall into the top half of all declines in the sample, which included 19 countries since 1959 for equity busts and 14 countries since 1970 for housing busts. This methodology yielded 49 equity busts since 1985 and 34 housing busts throughout the period.[38] Responses of macroeconomic variables to asset price busts (as defined above) were assessed using median four-quarter growth rates across several subsamples. Countries were assigned to one of two groups based on whether they were in the top or bottom half of the sample ranked by Financial Index scores. For equity busts, the analysis focused on the recent period of financial liberalization beginning in 1985. During this period, 26 equity busts occurred in countries in the top half of the sample while 23 occurred in the other group. For housing busts, the analyses focused on countries in the top half of the Financial Index, due to data limitations. The analysis separated the pre-1985 period (prior to widespread financial liberalization) from the subsequent period. Among the countries in the top half of the Financial Index, 18 housing busts occurred prior to 1985 and 12 have occurred since then.

Resource Allocation and the Financial Index

The sectoral data used were from the United Nations Industrial Development Organization (UNIDO) database. Based on the three-digit ISIC standards, the database provides data on 29 industries in the manufacturing sector for 181 countries.

The econometric methodology consisted of estimating the following specification:

$$\rho_{1,i,t} = \alpha FI_i + \beta\rho_{2,i,t} + \gamma(\rho_{2,i,t} \times FI_i),$$

where:

- $\rho_{1,i,t}$ is the correlation—at time t and for country i—between real output growth of industry j (j = 1...29) in country i and the world output growth of industry j. It is meant to capture the ability of an economy to grasp growth opportunities available worldwide.
- FI_i is the Financial Index for country i (at year 2004). A positive value of the coefficient α would suggest that countries with more arm's length financial systems are better able to grasp worldwide growth opportunities (as they tend to have higher correlations $\rho_{1,i,t}$)
- $\rho_{2,i,t}$ is the correlation—at time t and for country i—between the contribution of industry j (j = 1...29) to world real output growth and the share of industry j in country i total

[37]The rates on conventional 30-year mortgages were taken from the Federal Reserve Board.

[38]Due to insufficient data, housing busts could not be identified in Austria, France, Germany, Greece, Italy, Japan, and Portugal. Equity busts could not be identified in Greece and Portugal.

output in the first year of the sample. It is meant to capture the initial distance between the industry specialization of country i and the industry specialization that, over the years, would maximize the country's growth rate (a higher value of $\rho_{2,i,t}$ indicates that the country specializes in the fast-growing sectors). One would expect the coefficient of $\rho_{2,i,t}(\beta)$ to be positive if countries that specialize initially in the fast-growing sectors are better positioned to benefit from world growth opportunities over the years. However, the coefficient of the interaction term of this variable with the Financial Index (γ) should be negative if having an arm's length financial system makes it easier for a country with an initial specialization in low-growth industries to reallocate resources toward fast-growing sectors.

The world growth of real output in industry j was estimated as the GDP-weighted average of the real output growth of industry j in the 181 countries covered by the database. Every year the GDP weights were recalculated so as to exclude the countries for which output was missing or where a change in industrial classification was detected. Real output growth was estimated as the log-difference of nominal output in U.S. dollars deflated by the U.S. industrial producer price indices for each sector (base year 1982). Yearly log-output changes in the top 5 percent and bottom 5 percent of the distribution were excluded to reduce the influence of outliers. The contribution of industry j to world real output growth at time t was estimated as follows:

$$\sum_{i=1}^{181} \frac{\Delta y_{i,j}\left(\frac{y_{i,j}}{y_{w,j}}\right)}{\Delta y_{w,j}},$$

where $y_{i,j}$ is (log) real output of industry j in country I and $y_{w,j}$ is (log) real world output of industry j.

Table 4.2 shows the results of the estimation for the panel of 18 advanced economies considered in the chapter over the 1980–2001 period. All the coefficients have the expected sign, and are significant at the 1 percent level. Including year dummies and estimating cross-sections on the averages of the correlations across different time periods gave broadly consistent results, but yielded less precise estimates of the coefficient of the interaction term.

Table 4.2. Dependent Variable: $\rho_{1,i,t}$

Financial Index	1.30***
$\rho_{2,i,t}$	0.45***
Interaction of $\rho_{2,i,t}$ with Financial Index	–1.29***
Observations	345
R-squared	0.68

Source: IMF staff estimates.
Note: Heteroskedasticity and autocorrelation robust standard errors; *** significant at 1 percent.

Cross-Border Flows and the Financial Index

To examine whether the nature of the financial system affects cross-border capital flows among advanced economies, the following gravity model was estimated using 2004 data on bilateral portfolio holdings from the Coordinated Portfolio Investment Survey (CPIS):

$$\ln P_{ij} = \alpha + \beta_1 \ln Y_i + \beta_2 \ln Y_j + \beta_3 \ln D_{ij} + \beta_4 Euro + \beta_5 FI_i + \beta_6 FI_j + \varepsilon_{ij},$$

where i denotes the source country and j stands for the destination country. P is total bilateral portfolio investment of country i in country j (in millions of U.S. dollars), Y measures market size of, respectively, country i and country j (in millions of U.S. dollars), D stands for the great circle distance between countries i and j (based on the CIA World Factbook), *Euro* is a dummy variable for country pairs in the euro area, and, finally, FI_i and FI_j refer to the Financial Index of countries i and j, respectively. The market size is measured by GDP (using total equity and bond market capitalization produced similar results).

The regression was estimated on three different samples. The first included all source countries for which portfolio data are reported in the CPIS, while destination countries were limited to those for which the Financial Index has been computed. In order to assess the effect of the financial system of the source country on portfolio holdings, the second sample included only those industrial

Table 4.3. Dependent Variable: Log Bilateral Portfolio Investment

	All Countries	Industrial Countries	Continental Europe
Log source GDP	0.876***	0.967***	0.824***
Log destination GDP	0.759***	0.868***	0.880***
Log distance	–1.182***	–0.755***	–0.713***
Euro area	1.789***	0.970***	0.994***
Source Financial Index	. . .	4.284***	7.280***
Destination Financial Index	5.700***	3.240***	1.276
Observations	943	305	156
R-squared	0.46	0.78	0.77

Source: IMF staff estimates.
Note: Heteroskedasticity robust standard errors; *** significant at 1 percent.

countries for which the Financial Index is available. Finally, the third sample focused on cross-border flows within continental Europe.

The regressions explain a large share of the variation in bilateral portfolio holdings (Table 4.3). The results show that countries with larger domestic markets both invest more abroad and receive more foreign investment and that cross-border portfolio holdings are negatively correlated with distance.[39] The results also reflect the fact that cross-border portfolio holdings are higher within the euro area. The findings suggest that the extent of arm's length finance matters for cross-border portfolio holdings. Bilateral investment depends positively on the extent of arm's length finance in the destination country, as well as in the source country in the sample of advanced economies, as reflected by the coefficient on the Financial Index. In other words, more arm's length economies tend to both invest more in foreign stock and bond markets and receive more portfolio investments from abroad. The extent of arm's length finance in the destination economy does not seem to matter, however, for cross-border portfolio holdings within continental Europe, which appear to be dominated by other factors.

[39]Similar findings are reported and discussed in Faruqee, Li, and Yan (2004); and Portes and Rey (2005).

References

Aiyagari, S. Rao, and Mark Gertler, 1999, "'Overreaction' of Asset Prices in General Equilibrium," *Review of Economic Dynamics*, Vol. 2 (January), pp. 3–35.

Allen, Franklin, and Douglas Gale, 2000, *Comparing Financial Systems* (Cambridge, Massachusetts: MIT Press).

Allen, Franklin, and Anthony Santomero, 2001, "What Do Financial Intermediaries Do?" *Journal of Banking and Finance*, Vol. 25 (February), pp. 271–94.

Bacchetta, Philippe, and Stefan Gerlach, 1997, "Consumption and Credit Constraints: International Evidence," *Journal of Monetary Economics*, Vol. 40 (October), pp. 207–38.

Bank for International Settlement (BIS), "Survey of Foreign Exchange and Derivatives Market Activity," various editions.

Barth, James, Gerard Caprio Jr., and Daniel Nolle, 2004, "Comparative International Characteristics of Banking," Economics Working Paper No. WP2004-1 (Washington: U.S. Office of the Comptroller of the Currency).

Beck, Thorsten, Asli Demirgüç-Kunt, and Ross Levine, 1999, "A New Database on Financial Development and Structure," Policy Research Working Paper No. WPS2146, revised January 10, 2006 (Washington: World Bank). Also available via the Internet at http://econ.worldbank.org.

Bernanke, Ben, Mark Gertler, and Simon Gilchrist, 1996, "The Financial Accelerator and the Flight to Quality," *The Review of Economics and Statistics*, Vol. 78 (February), pp. 1–15.

———, 1999, "The Financial Accelerator in a Quantitative Business Cycle Framework," in J. Taylor and M. Woodford, eds., *Handbook of Macroeconomics*, Volume 1C, (Amsterdam: North-Holland).

Caballero, Ricardo, Emmanuel Farhi, and Pierre-Oliver Gourinchas, 2006, "An Equilibrium Model of 'Global Imbalances' and Low Interest Rates," CEPR Discussion Paper No. 5573 (London: Centre for Economic Policy Research).

Caballero, Ricardo, Takeo Hoshi, and Anil Kashyap, 2006, "Zombie Lending and Depressed Restructuring in Japan," MIT Department of Economics Working Paper No. 06-06. Available via the Internet at http://econ-ww.mit.edu/faculty/download-pdf.php.

Campbell, John Y., and N. Gregory Mankiw, 1991, "The Response of Consumption to Income: A Cross-Country Investigation," *European Economic Review*, Vol. 35 (May), pp. 723–56.

Catte, Pietro, Nathalie Girouard, Robert Price, and Christophe André, 2004, "Housing Markets, Wealth and the Business Cycle," OECD Economic Department Working Paper No. 394. (Paris: Organization for Economic Cooperation and Development).

Chinn, Menzie D., and Hiro Ito, 2005, "Current Account Balances, Financial Development and Institutions: Assaying the World 'Savings Glut,'" NBER Working Paper No. 11761 (Cambridge, Massachusetts: National Bureau of Economic Research).

Cotis, Jean-Philippe, and Jonathan Coppel, 2005, "Business Cycle Dynamics in OECD Countries: Evidence, Causes and Policy Implications," in *The Changing Nature of the Business Cycle*, Reserve Bank of Australia 2005 Conference Volume, ed. by Christopher Kent and David Norman (Sydney).

De Nicoló, Luc Laeven, and Kenichi Ueda, 2006, "Corporate Governance Quality in Asia: Comparative Trends and Impact" (unpublished).

Deaton, Angus, 1992, *Understanding Consumption* (New York: Oxford University Press).

Djankov, Simeon, Darshini Manraj, Caralee McLiesh, and Rita Ramalho, 2005, "Doing Business Indicators: Why Aggregate, and How to Do It" (Washington: World Bank). Available via the Internet at http://www.doingbusiness.org/documents/how_to_aggregate.pdf.

Dynan, Karen E., Douglas W. Elmendorf, and Daniel E. Sichel, 2006, "Can Financial Innovation Help to Explain the Reduced Volatility of Economic Activity?" *Journal of Monetary Economics*, Vol. 53 (January) pp. 123–50.

European Central Bank (ECB), 2001, "Characteristics of Corporate Finance in the Euro Area," *Monthly Bulletin*, February, pp. 37–50.

Faruqee, Hamid, Shujing Li, and Isabel K. Yan, 2004, "The Determinants of International Portfolio Holdings and Home Bias," IMF Working Paper 04/34 (Washington: International Monetary Fund).

Fisher, Irving, 1933, "The Debt-Deflation Theory of Great Depressions," *Econometrica 1*, pp. 337–57.

Geithner, Timothy F., 2006, "Risk Management Challenges in the U.S. Financial System," remarks at the Global Association of Risk Professionals (GARP) 7th Annual Risk Management Convention and Exhibition in New York City, March 1.

Gompers, Paul, and Josh Lerner, 1998, "The Determinants of Corporate Venture Capital Successes: Organizational Structure, Incentives, and Complementarities," NBER Working Paper No. 6725 (Cambridge, Massachusetts: National Bureau of Economic Research).

Green, Richard K., and Susan M. Wachter, 2005, "The American Mortgage in Historical and International Context," *Journal of Economic Perspectives*, Vol. 19, No. 4, pp. 93–114.

IMF, 2006a, "The Attractiveness of U.S. Financial Markets: the Example of Mortgage Securitization," in *United States: Selected Issues*, IMF Country Report No. 06/278 (Washington: International Monetary Fund).

———, 2006b, *Global Financial Stability Report*, September (Washington: International Monetary Fund).

Issing, Otmar, 2003, "Relationship Lending in the Euro Area," in *The Transformation of the European Financial System*, ed. by Vitor Gaspar, Philipp Hartmann, and Olaf Sleijpen (Frankfurt: European Central Bank).

Jappelli, Tullio, and Marco Pagano, 1989, "Consumption and Capital Market Imperfections: An International Comparison," *American Economic Review*, Vol. 79 (December), pp. 1088–1105.

Johnson, Richard, and Dean Wichern, 2002, *Applied Multivariate Statistical Analysis* (Upper Saddle River, N.J.: Prentice-Hall).

Kaufmann, Sylvia, and Maria Teresa Valderrama, 2004, "Modeling Credit Aggregates," Working Paper No. 90 (Vienna: Oesterreichische Nationalbank).

Kiyotaki, Nobuhiro, and John Moore, 1997, "Credit Cycles," *Journal of Political Economy*, Vol. 105 (April), pp. 211–48.

Klyuev, Vladimir, and Paul Mills, 2006, "Is Housing Wealth an 'ATM'? The Relationship Between Household Wealth, Home Equity Withdrawal, and Saving Rates," IMF Working Paper 06/162 (Washington: International Monetary Fund).

Knight, Malcolm, 2006, "Globalisation and Financial Markets," speech at the 34th Economic Conference of the Austrian National Bank, Vienna, May 22.

Lane, Philip R., and Gian Maria Milesi-Ferretti, 2006, "The External Wealth of Nations Mark II: Revised and Extended Estimates of Foreign Assets and Liabilities, 1970–2004," IMF Working Paper 06/69 (Washington: International Monetary Fund).

Levine, Ross, 1997, "Financial Development and Economic Growth: Views and Agenda," *Journal of Economic Literature*, Vol. 35, No. 2 (June), pp. 688–726.

———, 2002, "Bank-Based or Marked-Based Financial Systems: Which Is Better?" NBER Working Paper

No. 9138 (Cambridge, Massachusetts: National Bureau of Economic Research).

Ludwig, Alexander, and Torsten Sløk, 2002, "The Impact of Changes in Stock Prices and House Prices on Consumption in OECD Countries," IMF Working Paper 02/1 (Washington: International Monetary Fund).

Mendoza, Enrique G., 2005, "Real Exchange Rate Volatility and the Price of Nontradables in Sudden-Stop-Prone Economies," *Economía*, Vol. 6, No. 1 (Fall), pp.103–48.

———, and Katherine A. Smith, forthcoming, "Quantitative Implications of a Debt-Deflation Theory of Sudden Stops and Asset Prices," *Journal of International Economy*.

Mendoza, Enrique G., Vincenzo Quadrini, and Victor Rios-Rull, 2006, "Capital Markets Liberalization, Savings, and Global Imbalances," (unpublished: Marshall School of Business, University of Southern California).

Morck, Randall, Bernard Yeung, and Wayne Yu, 2000, "The Information Content of Stock Markets: Why Do Emerging Markets Have Synchronous Stock Price Movements?" *Journal of Financial Economics*, Vol. 58, Issues 1–2, pp. 215–60.

OECD, 2006, "Risk Capital in OECD Countries: Past Experience, Current Situation and Policies for Promoting Entrepreneurial Finance," in *Financial Market Trends*, No. 90, April (Paris: Organization for Economic Cooperation and Development).

Ongena, Steven, and David C. Smith, 2000, "What Determines the Number of Bank Relationships? Cross-Country Evidence," *Journal of Financial Intermediation*, Volume 9 (January) pp. 26–56.

Peek, Joe, and James A. Wilcox, 2006, "Housing, Credit Constraints, and Macro Stability: the Secondary Mortgage Market and Reduced Cyclicality of Residential Investment," Fisher Center Working Paper No. 298 (Fisher Center for Real Estate and Urban Economics, University of California, Berkeley).

Portes, Richard, and Helene Rey, 2005, "The Determinants of Cross-Border Equity Flows," *Journal of International Economics*, Vol. 65 (March), pp. 269–96.

Rajan, Raghuram G., and Luigi Zingales, 2003, "Banks and Markets: The Changing Character of European Finance," NBER Working Paper No. 9595 (Cambridge, Massachusetts: National Bureau of Economic Research).

Samolyk, Katherine, 2004, "The Future of Banking in America. The Evolving Role of Commercial Banks in U.S. Credit Markets," *FDIC Banking Review*, Vol. 16, No. 1–2, pp. 29–65.

Schmidt, Reinhard, Andreas Hackethal, and Marcel Tyrell, 1999, "Disintermediation and the Role of Banks in Europe: An International Comparison," *Journal of Financial Intermediation*, Vol. 8 (January–April), pp. 36–67.

Schnure, Calvin, 2005, "Boom-Bust Cycles in Housing: The Changing Role of Financial Structure," IMF Working Paper 05/200 (Washington: International Monetary Fund).

Tsatsaronis, Kostas, and Haibin Zhu, 2004, "What Drives Housing Price Dynamics: Cross-Country Evidence," *BIS Quarterly Review*, Bank for International Settlements, (March).

Wurgler, Jeffrey, 2000, "Financial Markets and the Allocation of Capital," *Journal of Financial Economics*, Vol. 58 (October–November), pp. 187–214.

THE BOOM IN NONFUEL COMMODITY PRICES: CAN IT LAST?

Over the past four years, fuel and nonfuel commodity prices have risen significantly. Developments in fuel markets (especially oil) have dominated the attention of policymakers so far, although the increase in nonfuel commodity prices has also had considerable consequences for trade balances and growth in many countries.

Nonfuel commodities have a higher share in world trade (about 14 percent during 2000–04) than fuel commodities (7 percent). As in the case of oil, many developing countries are highly dependent on nonfuel commodities as a source of export earnings—36 countries have a ratio of nonfuel commodity exports to GDP of over 10 percent, and in 92 countries the ratio is over 5 percent (Figure 5.1). Indeed, in many low-income countries, a large share of export receipts are generated by just a few commodities (see Table 5.1 for selected examples). Moreover, prices of some nonfuel commodities have increased more than oil prices—for example, the IMF metals index has risen by 180 percent in real terms since 2002, while oil prices increased by 157 percent.

Given the significant exposure of many countries to fluctuations in nonfuel commodity prices, the future dynamics of commodity markets have important policy implications. Some observers have suggested that the rise of China and other large emerging markets may have led to a fundamental change in long-term price trends, and that the world has now entered a period of sustained high prices, particularly of metals (see Barclays Capital, 2006a). In contrast, others believe that speculative forces have largely decoupled metals prices from market fundamentals (Societe Generale, 2006), and that prices will inevitably fall back and continue to decline gradually in real terms, as during most of the past century.

This chapter examines these issues by:

- identifying the underlying causes of the recent increases in nonfuel commodity prices and putting them in historical perspective;
- assessing the roles of rising commodity demand from large emerging market countries (especially China) and of financial investors in pushing up prices; and
- evaluating whether the current high price levels are likely to be temporary or lasting.

Long-Term Trends in Commodity Prices and Volatility

Despite recent increases, the prices of most nonfuel commodities remain below their historical peaks in real terms. Over the past five decades, commodity prices have fallen relative to consumer prices at the rate of about 1.6 percent a year (Figure 5.2).[1] This downward trend is usually attributed to large productivity gains in the agricultural and metals sectors relative to other parts of the economy.[2] Compared with the prices of manufactures, however, commodity prices stopped falling in the 1990s as the growing globalization of the manufacturing sector slowed producer price inflation.[3]

The main author of this chapter is Martin Sommer with consultancy support from Christopher Gilbert. Angela Espiritu provided research assistance.

[1]This long-term trend has been apparent for most of the past century and was highlighted by Prebisch (1950) and others in the 1950s. See Cashin and McDermott (2002); Deaton and Laroque (2003); Grilli and Yang (1988); and Borensztein and others (1994) for a detailed discussion. Due to data deficiencies and inherent volatility in commodity prices, the academic literature does not uniformly share the view that real commodity prices are falling—see Cuddington (1992) for an alternative account.

[2]See Tilton (2003) for a review of the recent literature and Barnett and Morse (1963) for a historical assessment of productivity gains.

[3]See Chapter III, "Globalization and Inflation," in the April 2006 *World Economic Outlook.*

Figure 5.1. Dependence on Exports of Nonfuel Commodities and Geographical Concentration of Production

Many developing countries and emerging markets continue to be highly dependent on exports of nonfuel commodities (these countries are marked in red). Production of some commodities is highly geographically concentrated, potentially making world prices sensitive to country-specific events.

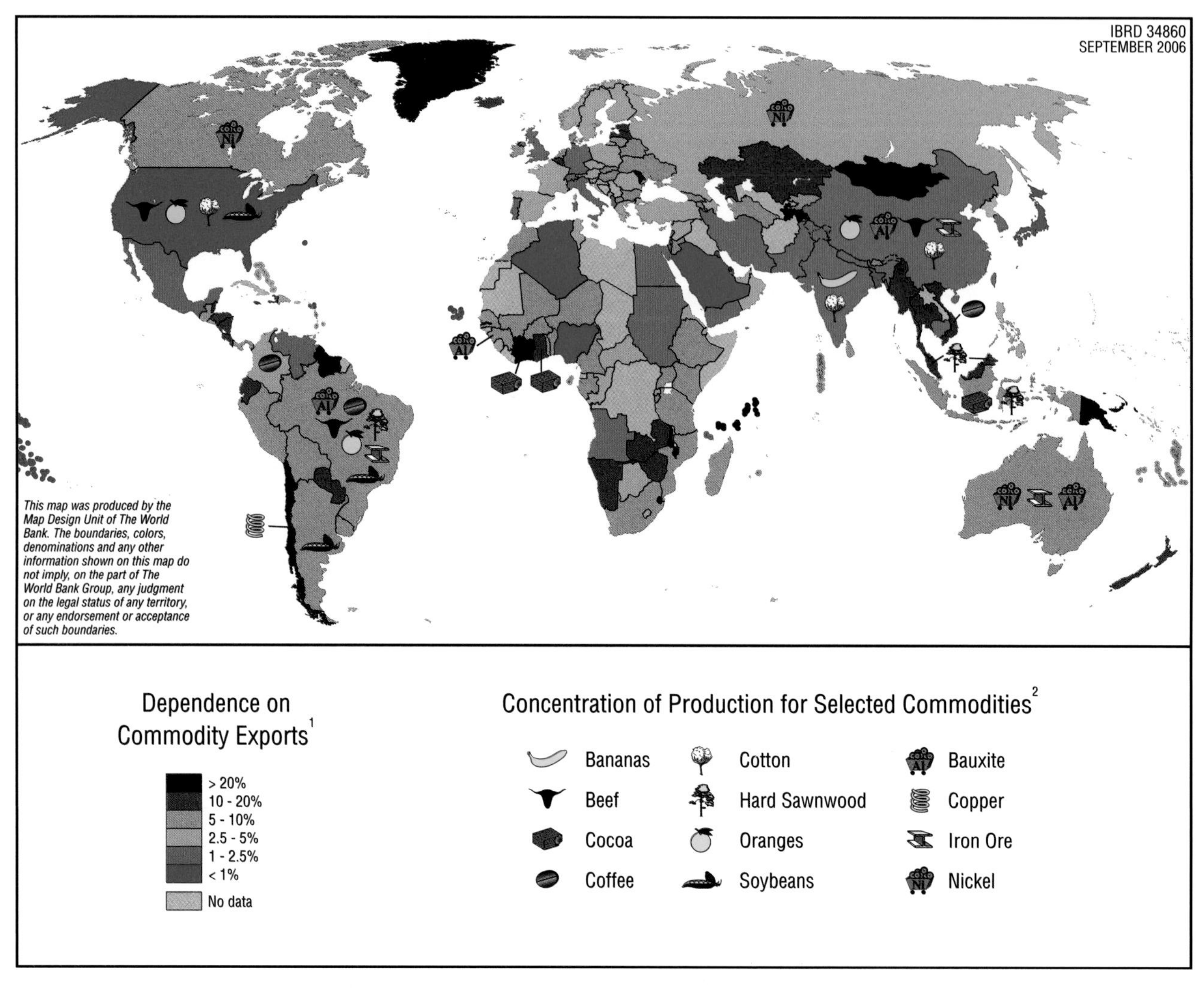

Sources: British Geological Survey, *World Mineral Statistics 1998/2002* (2004); FAOSTAT data (2006); Foreign Agricultural Service, Official USDA estimates (2006); World Bank, World Integrated Trade Solution Database; World Bureau of Metal Statistics, *World Metal Statistics Yearbook 2006* (2006); and IMF staff calculations.

[1] Share of nonfuel commodity exports in gross domestic product. See Appendix 5.1 for details.

[2] Symbols are assigned to the countries whose share of world production is over 10 percent. For metals, the production shares refer to mining output. Bauxite is the raw material most widely used in the production of aluminum.

Table 5.1. Dependence on Exports of Selected Nonfuel Commodities

(2000–04; in percent)

	Country	Share in Total Exports
Aluminum	Suriname	47
	Tajikistan	46
	Guinea	36
	Mozambique	26
Cocoa	Côte d'Ivoire	34
Coffee	Burundi	43
Copper	Zambia	41
	Chile	31
	Mongolia	20
Cotton	Burkina Faso	42
	Benin	28
Fish	Iceland	30
	Seychelles	30

Sources: World Bank, World Integrated Trade Solution database; and IMF staff calculations.

On a year-to-year basis, commodity prices can significantly deviate from the long-term downward trend, as price volatility is much higher than the average real price decline (one standard deviation of annual price changes is about 11.5 percent, compared with the long-term price decline of 1.6 percent a year; see Figure 5.3). The current volatility in nonfuel commodity markets is not unusual by historical standards. In fact, the volatility of food and raw agricultural material prices seems to have fallen on average over the past couple of decades, as growing geographical diversification of production and technological advances have reduced the sensitivity of prices to supply shocks, such as bad weather or natural disasters (FAO, 2004b).[4]

[4]For example, the emergence of major new exporters of coffee such as Vietnam has helped to reduce the dependence of coffee prices on weather in Brazil. The aggregate volatility figures, however, mask significant variability in the price behavior of individual food commodities. The median correlation between annual price changes of two randomly selected food commodities is 15 percent, compared with 33 percent for metals. See Cashin, McDermott, and Scott (2002) and Gilbert (2006) for analysis of volatility in commodity prices. Dehn, Gilbert, and Varangis (2005) discuss the policies to manage the negative consequences of volatile commodity markets.

Figure 5.2. Long-Term Price Trends[1]

Prices of many nonfuel commodities have been falling in real terms relative to the consumer price index (CPI) for at least the last 50 years. Globalization has slowed price increases in the manufacturing sector and as a result commodity prices stopped declining relative to the prices of manufactures in the early 1990s. However, commodity prices exhibit significant volatility and prices can deviate from trend for long periods.

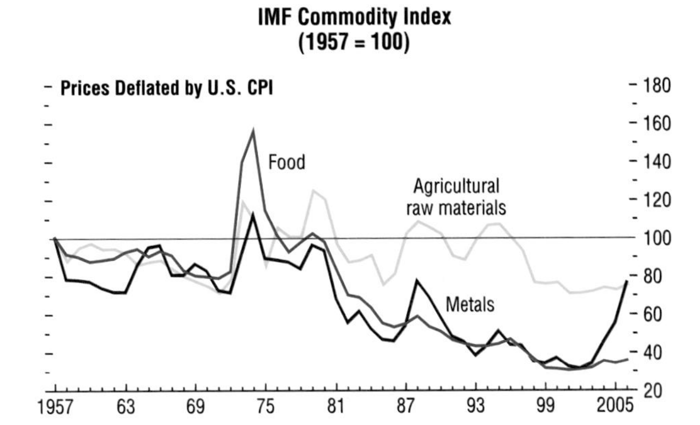

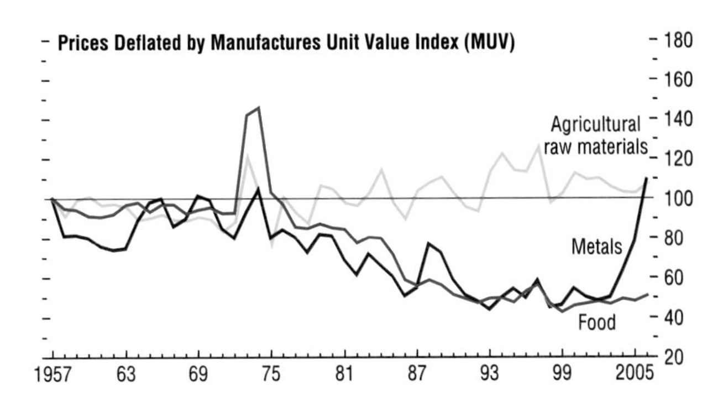

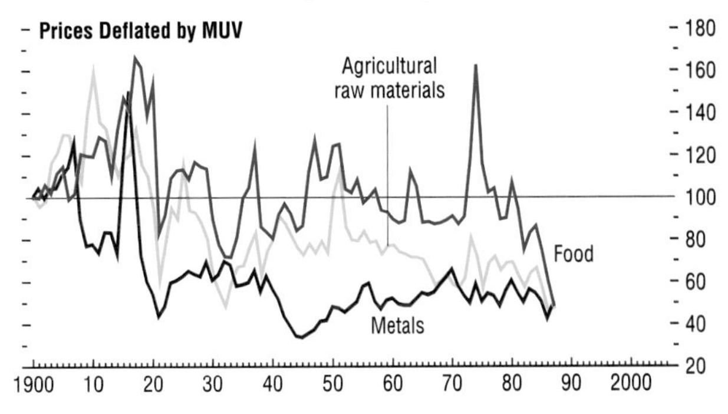

Sources: Cashin, Liang, and McDermott (2000); Grilli and Yang (1988); IMF, Commodity Price System database; UNCTAD, Handbook of Statistics database; and IMF staff calculations.

[1]Price data for 2006 are based on the average of January–June.

[2]Grilli and Yang indexes are only available for the period 1900–87. See Appendix 5.1 for details.

Figure 5.3. Volatility in Nonfuel Commodities Prices
(Percent)

Recent volatility in the nonfuel commodity markets is not unusual by historical standards. In fact, the volatility of food and agricultural raw materials prices has fallen over the past couple of decades as a result of technological advances and geographical diversification of production.

Average annual change in real price
One standard deviation bands[1]

Nonfuel Commodities

40
30
20
10
0
-10
-20
-30

1957–70 1971–80 1981–90 1991–2000 2001–05 1957–2005

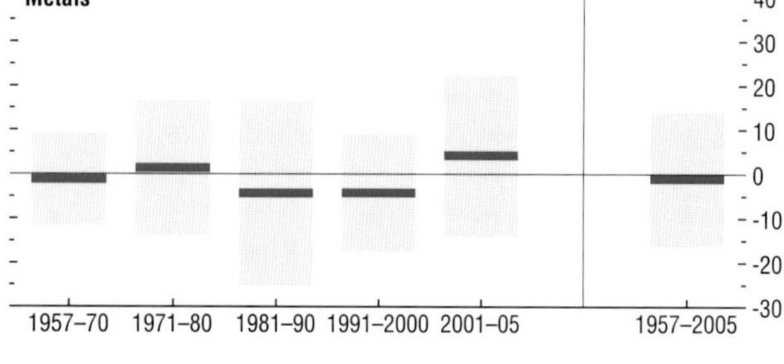

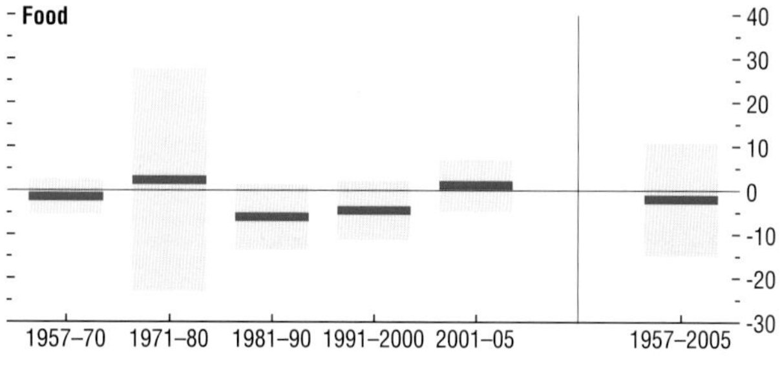

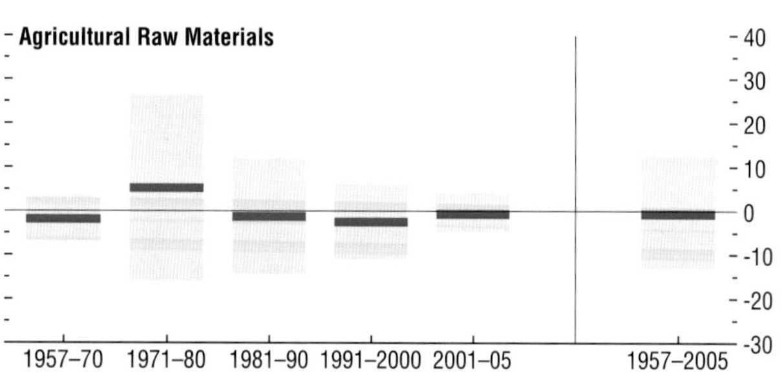

Sources: IMF, Commodity Price System database; and IMF staff calculations.
[1]Standard deviation of annual real price changes.

Nonfuel commodity prices—especially metals—have a strong business-cycle component (Figure 5.4). The correlation between world growth and annual changes in real metals prices is about 50 percent. Moreover, almost all periods of large upward movements in metals prices have been associated with strong world growth. Prices of agricultural commodities also tend to rise during cyclical upturns, but their response is much more muted than in the case of metals because of more flexible supply and the low income elasticity of demand.

Assessment of Recent Developments

Over the past four years, commodity prices have evolved very differently across various subgroups of the nonfuel index (Figure 5.5). Metals prices have risen sharply since 2002 to the present (by 180 percent in real terms), while food and agricultural raw materials prices have increased much less (by 20 and 4 percent, respectively). As a result, metals contributed almost 90 percent to the cumulative 60 percent real increase in the IMF nonfuel commodity index since 2002 (Table 5.2).

The current price dynamics of food and agricultural raw material prices are similar to earlier cyclical episodes (Figure 5.6). In fact, some of the increase in food prices accumulated since 2001 can be attributed to the depreciation of U.S. dollar—real food prices expressed in the IMF's special drawing rights (SDRs) are now only 9 percent higher than four years ago, and the SDR prices of agricultural raw materials are lower than their 2002 level.

Until recently, metals prices have also tracked historical patterns[5]—but the continued run-up in metals prices this year has made the cumulative price increase significantly larger than usual. A part of the unusually strong run-up in metals prices can be attributed to low invest-

[5]Metals prices have increased by over 75 percent during previous cyclical upturns, reflecting long gestation lags for increasing capacity in the industry and the low price elasticity of demand.

Table 5.2. Decomposition of IMF Nonfuel Commodities Price Index, 2002–06[1]

(Prices expressed as real changes; contributions to growth in percent)

	Prices in U.S. Dollars[2]		Prices in Special Drawing Rights (SDRs)[3]	
	Increase	Contributions to increase	Increase	Contributions to increase
All nonfuel commodities	60.1	100.0	45.3	100.0
Metals	179.7	87.5	153.5	99.3
Food	19.9	7.7	8.9	4.6
Beverages	21.5	1.8	10.4	1.1
Agricultural raw materials	4.3	3.1	–5.3	–5.0

Sources: IMF, Commodity Price System database; and IMF staff calculations.

[1]Data for 2006 refer to July 2006.

[2]Prices deflated using U.S. consumer prices.

[3]Prices deflated using the weighted average of consumer prices in SDR basket countries.

ment in the metals sector in the late 1990s and the early 2000s that followed a period of earlier price declines. Some analysts have also suggested that the intensity of the price upswing in this cycle has been amplified by new factors—the increasing weight of rapidly growing emerging markets (especially China) in the world economy and investment activity of financial investors in commodity markets.[6] All these potential explanations are further examined below.

Role of Emerging Markets

China has become a key driver of price dynamics in the metals markets. During 2002–05, China contributed almost all of the increase in the world consumption of nickel and tin (Table 5.3). In the cases of lead and zinc, China's contribution even exceeded net world consumption growth. For the two most widely traded base metals (aluminum and copper) and for steel, the contribution of China to world consumption growth was about 50 percent.[7] These

[6]The September 2006 edition of the IMF's *Global Financial Stability Report* discusses the growing allocation of investors' portfolios in commodities markets.

[7]Interestingly, Chinese demand made up a higher proportion of world demand growth for metals than for oil.

Figure 5.4. Commodity Prices over the Business Cycle[1]

(Annual percent change; prices deflated by U.S. CPI)

Nonfuel commodity prices are correlated with global growth. However, the response of food and agricultural raw materials prices to cyclical conditions is much more muted than in the case of metals.

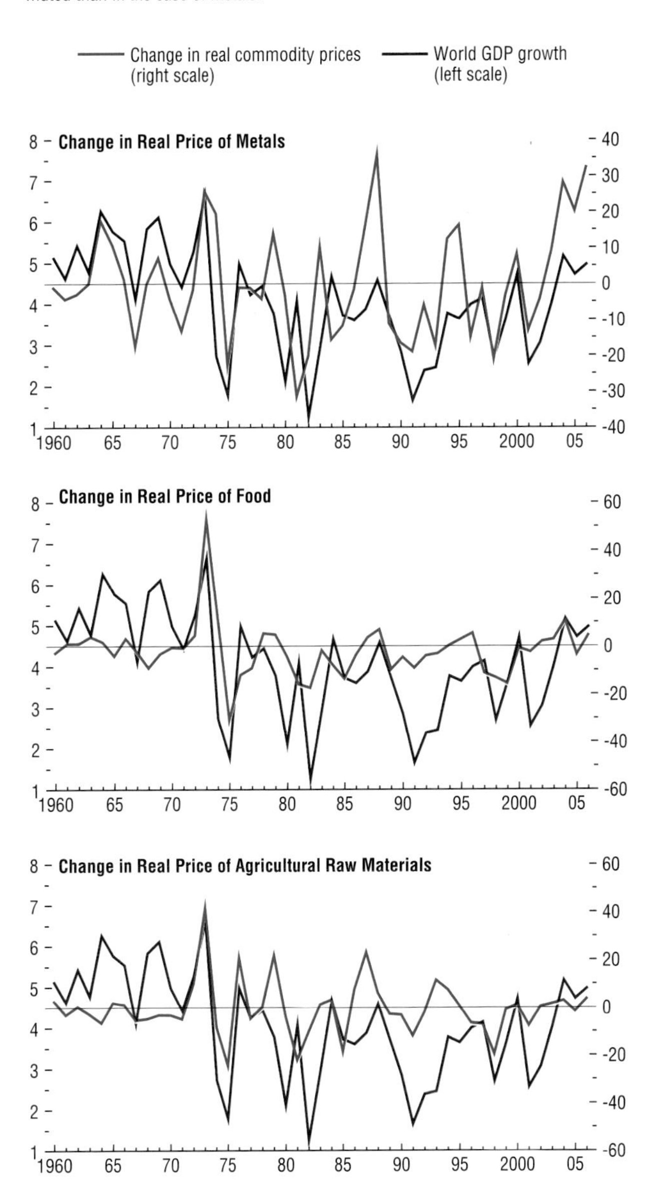

Sources: IMF, Commodity Price System database; and IMF staff calculations

[1]Price data for 2006 are based on the average of January–June.

figures exceed China's 29 percent contribution to world PPP-adjusted GDP growth and are much higher than the current 15 percent share of China in world output. Compared with the last decade, the relative contribution of China to global demand for commodities has increased considerably, as a result of both its rising weight in the world economy and its particularly rapid industrial production growth—including industrial exports—which is closely linked to the demand for metals.[8] Other emerging market countries have also contributed significantly to demand in specific metals markets but, overall, their contribution was not as broad-based as China's (Table 5.3).[9]

Figure 5.5. Recent Developments in Commodity Prices
(2002 = 100; monthly data; prices deflated by U.S. CPI)

During the past four years, metals prices have increased more than oil prices and have contributed heavily to the overall rise in the index of nonfuel commodity prices.

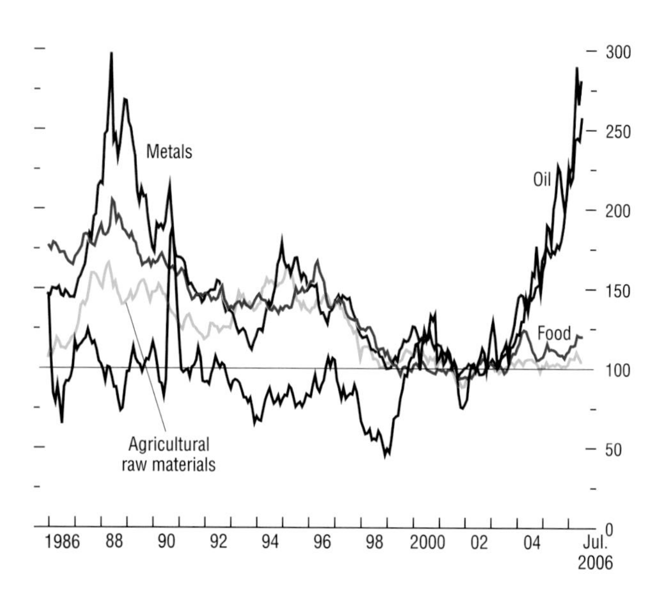

Sources: Haver Analytics; IMF, Commodity Price System database; and IMF staff calculations.

Is the strength of Chinese demand for metals temporary or permanent? Historical patterns suggest that consumption of metals typically grows together with income until about $15,000–$20,000 per capita (in purchasing power parity, or PPP, adjusted dollars) as countries go through a period of industrialization and infrastructure building (Figure 5.7). At higher incomes, growth typically becomes more services-driven and, therefore, the use of metals per capita starts to stagnate.[10] So far, China (with its current PPP-adjusted real income of about $6,400 per capita) has generally tracked the patterns of Japan and Korea during their initial development phase. For some metals, China's per capita consumption at a given income level is higher than in the other emerging markets, partly because it has a much greater share of industry in its gross domestic product than is

[8]China has become the largest consumer of several key metals, generating about one-quarter of the total world demand for aluminum, copper, and steel. For comparison, China contributes 8–25 percent of the world industrial value added, depending on whether current or PPP-adjusted exchange rates are used for currency conversion.

[9]For example, Russia accounted for 25 percent of the increase in world copper demand during 2002–05, but only 0.5 percent of the rise in aluminum consumption.

[10]Demand for metals can continue to rise even at higher income levels if metal-intensive industrial sectors continue to grow strongly (such as, for example, in Korea).

typical for other countries at a similar stage of development (Figure 5.8; see also Chapter 3). This outcome reflects historical antecedents[11] as well as the strong competitiveness of the Chinese economy and relocation of manufacturing production from advanced economies and other emerging markets to China.

Looking ahead, rapid industrial output growth, construction activity, and infrastructure needs could sustain the growth of demand of emerging markets for metals at high rates in the medium term. That said, some of the current demand strength could be temporary—especially as the Chinese government is aiming at a rebalancing of growth from investment to consumption over the medium term. Moreover, China's size and heavy concentration in industry make it somewhat a special case. India's industrial sector, for example, has a considerably lower share in the economy, and India's continued rapid growth would in the medium term have a less pronounced impact on metals markets than growth in China.

The impact of emerging markets on agricultural prices is less clear-cut. China and other fast-developing countries have often contributed significantly to world demand growth (e.g., in the cases of cotton and beef; see Table 5.4).[12] However, this has not necessarily led to rising prices—the price of cotton, for example, fell by almost 20 percent during 2004–05. Generally, food consumption in developing countries shifts gradually toward high-protein commodities such as meats, dairy products, and oils (FAO, 2004b). But this type of substitution has started at a much lower level of income in China and other countries—for example, meat consumption growth was particularly fast in China when its per capita income was below $3,000 in PPP

[11]A high degree of industrialization was common in many former centrally planned economies.

[12]The contribution of China to food consumption growth tends to be lower than in the cases of metals and other intermediate commodities, such as cotton. As discussed above, the more prominent role of China in the intermediate commodity markets reflects the very strong growth of industrial production in China.

Figure 5.6. Perspective on the Recent Price Developments, 1957–2006[1]

(Bottom of the cycle at time t = 100)

The current dynamics of real food and agricultural raw materials prices expressed in U.S. dollars are similar to earlier cyclical episodes. After accounting for exchange rate changes, both food and raw materials prices are very close to their levels from four years ago. Until recently, metals prices have also tracked historical patterns, but the continued run-up in metals prices this year has made the cumulative price increase significantly larger than usual.

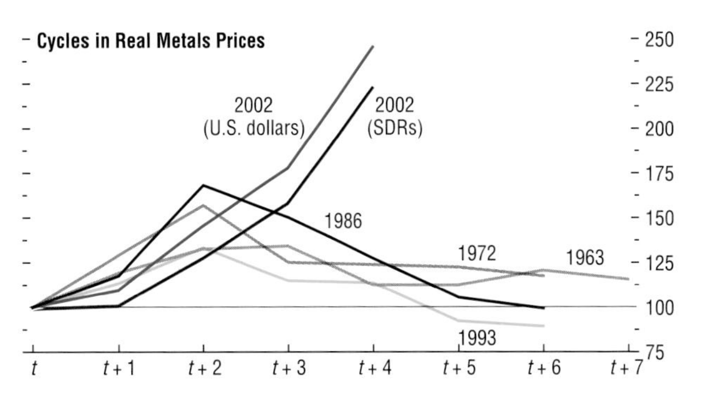

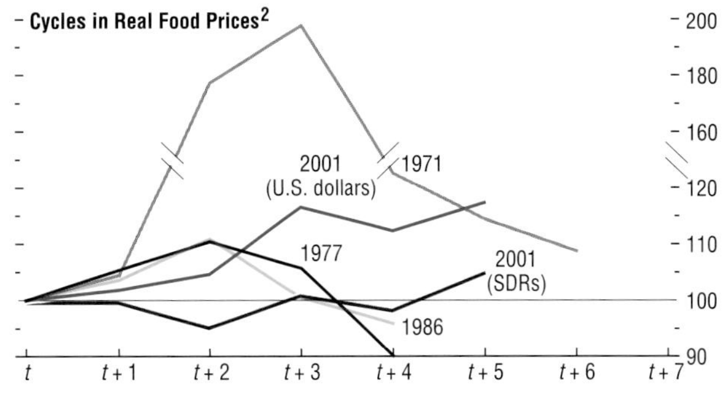

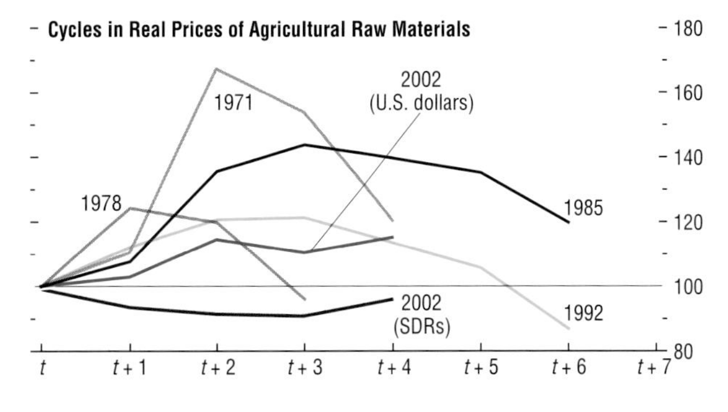

Sources: IMF, Commodity Price System database; and IMF staff calculations.

[1]Commodity prices are expressed in constant U.S. dollars and are indexed such that cyclical troughs have a value of 100. The most recent episode of rising commodity prices is also expressed in constant special drawing rights (SDRs). Price data for 2006 are based on the average of January–June.

[2]Double slash denotes a break in the scale of the vertical axis.

Table 5.3. Consumption of Industrial Metals and Oil
(Consumption expressed as real annual percent change; contributions to growth in percent)

	1993–2002			2002–05[1]		
	World consumption growth	Contribution to growth of: China	Contribution to growth of: Other major emerging markets[2]	World consumption growth	Contribution to growth of: China	Contribution to growth of: Other major emerging markets[2]
Metal						
Aluminum	3.8	38	9	7.6	48	9
Copper	3.5	43	15	3.8	51	41
Lead	3.0	42	15	4.3	110	–7
Nickel	4.4	12	–11	3.6	87	–11
Steel	3.4	38	11	9.2	54	8
Tin	1.3	34	16	8.1	86	2
Zinc	3.4	42	10	3.8	113	7
Oil	1.5	21	18	2.2	30	7
		1993–2000	*(In percent)*	2002–05		
Memorandum items:						
World GDP growth		3.5		4.8		
China's share in world GDP		10		13		
China's industrial production growth		10.5		16.2		

Sources: International Energy Agency; International Iron and Steel Institute, *Steel Statistical Yearbook* (various issues); World Bureau of Metal Statistics, *World Metal Statistics Yearbook* (various issues); and IMF staff calculations.
[1]The sample is selected to match the recent period of rising real metal prices. Due to limited data availability, figures for steel are over the period 2002–04.
[2]Brazil, India, Mexico, and Russia. Due to missing data for 2005, Russia is not included in the group for oil.

terms. The contribution of China to consumption growth in some key commodity markets such as bananas, beef, corn, and cotton was higher than its population share during much of the past decade without any noticeable break in the trend of falling real prices (Table 5.4 and Figure 5.5). A similar point can also be made about India and other major emerging market countries.

Will the Recent Run-Up in Metals Prices Be Sustained?

A central question, especially for metal-exporting countries, is whether the recent run-up in prices will prove lasting, or whether the longer-term downward price trend discussed earlier will eventually reassert itself.

Commodities futures markets suggest that the current high prices may not be sustained in the medium term.[13] Over the next five years, the futures prices of metals retain only about one-half of the increase accumulated since 2002 (in real terms, metals prices fall by 45 percent from current levels; see Figure 5.9). This decline contrasts with oil futures prices, which remain very close to the current spot price. There are differences within the group of metals—for example, aluminum futures prices decline less over time (by 31 percent) than copper futures prices (49 percent in real terms). Against this background, Box 5.1 examines the role of financial investors in determining commodity prices. The analysis suggests that while the investors may have played a role in providing liquidity to the markets, there is little evidence that speculative investments have been a significant driver of nonfuel commodity price movements.

[13]While futures prices are not accurate predictors of future spot prices, they nevertheless reflect current beliefs of market participants about forthcoming price developments. Bowman and Husain (2004) find that futures-prices-based models produce more accurate forecasts than the models based on historical data or judgment, especially at long horizons.

The market price of base metals is typically close to the production costs of marginal (i.e., relatively less-efficient) producers—especially at the bottom of the cycle (Deutsche Bank, 2006; see Table 5.5). During booms, the market price can rise to a multiple of the production cost, although over the past couple of decades, the market price has tended to return to a little above costs within a few years. For aluminum, copper, and nickel, the current ratios of market price-to-cost in the range of 1½–2¾ are similar to, or somewhat higher than, those experienced during the cyclical peak in the late 1980s. Back then, it took approximately two years for the market price to come down from the peak to near the cost level. For aluminum, the market-to-cost price ratio is currently less elevated than for the other base metals, supporting the indications from the futures markets that price declines are likely to be less pronounced for this metal.

Production costs vary considerably over time, mainly reflecting energy prices, exchange rate changes, and cyclical factors, such as availability of skilled personnel and hardware. During 2002–05, production costs escalated for all metals reported in the table—by about 20–50 percent for the marginal producers—with rising energy costs playing a significant part.[14] It is clear, however, that the doubling to tripling of market prices over the past four years cannot be fully explained by the cost structure of the industry.

Since demand for metals seems to be rising due to higher global growth and rapidly increasing income and industrial production in large countries such as China, the speed and costs of supply additions will determine whether metals prices retreat from the current high levels in the medium term. To bring the demand and supply factors affecting the metals market together in a more complete framework, two parallel models were built for aluminum and copper

[14]According to Alcan (2006) and Alcoa (2004), energy costs account for about 30 percent of the cost structure of refined aluminum.

Figure 5.7. Consumption of Base Metals and Steel, 1960–2005

Per capita consumption of base metals and steel generally rises with income. Some countries reach saturation in their per capita consumption at income levels between 15,000–20,000 purchasing-power-parity (PPP) adjusted U.S. dollars. Demand for metals, however, can continue to grow even at higher income levels if industrial production and construction contribute significantly to growth.

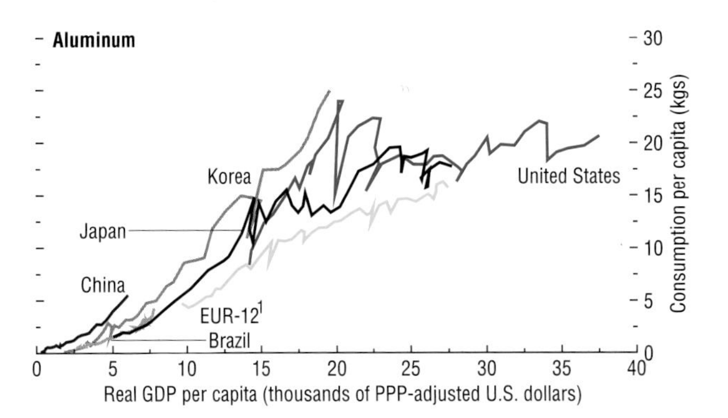

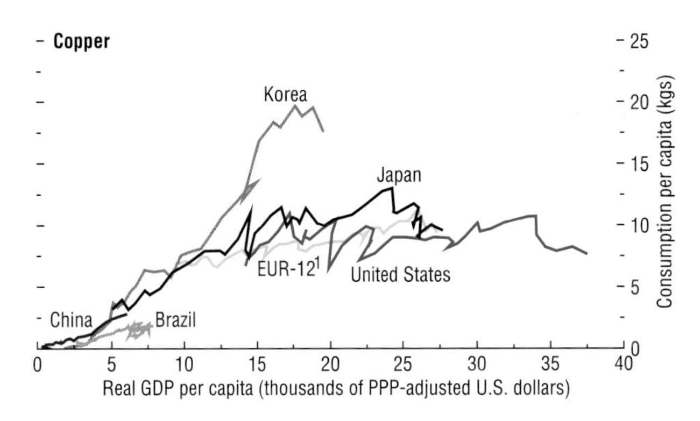

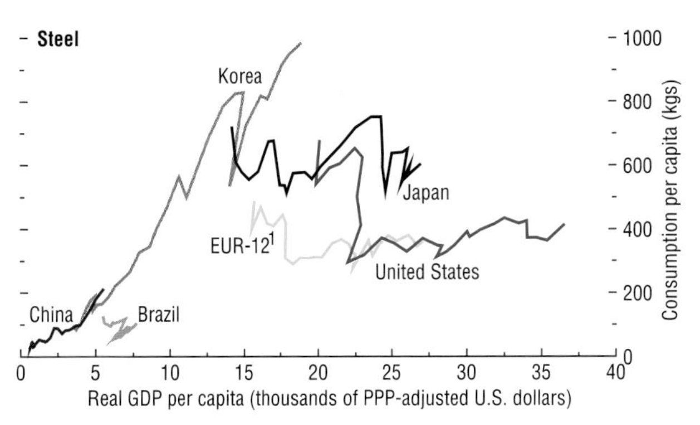

Sources: International Iron and Steel Institute, *Steel Statistical Yearbook* (various issues); World Bank, *World Development Indicators* (2006); World Bureau of Metal Statistics, *World Metal Statistics Yearbook* (various issues); and IMF staff calculations

[1]Austria, Belgium, Denmark, Finland, France, Germany, Italy, the Netherlands, Norway, Sweden, Switzerland, and the United Kingdom.

Figure 5.8. The Importance of Industry at Various Stages of Economic Development, 1965–2004[1]

At low income levels, countries tend to go through a period of industrialization and infrastructure building. At incomes of about 15,000 purchasing-power-parity (PPP) adjusted U.S. dollars per capita, growth becomes more services-driven and the share of industry in GDP starts to fall. China has an unusually large share of industry in its economy relative to its peers from the same income group.

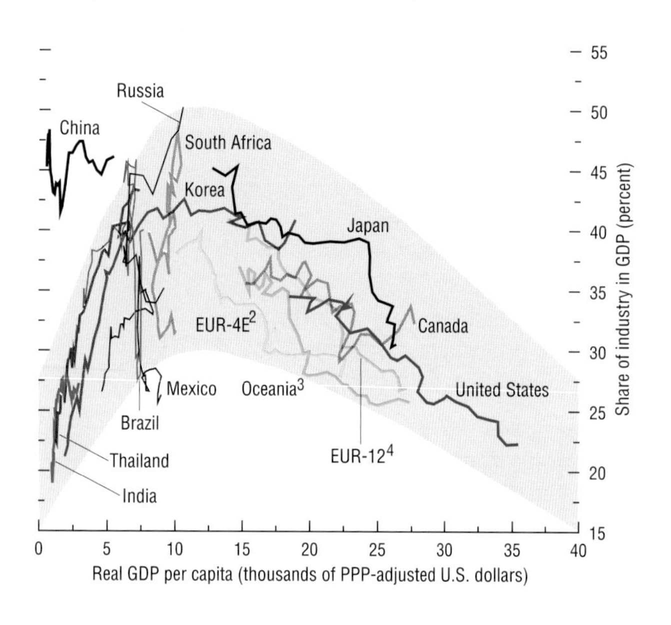

Sources: World Bank, *World Development Indicators* (2006); and IMF staff calculations.
[1]Industry share for country groups were aggregated using 2004 PPP-adjusted real GDP values as weights.
[2]Greece, Ireland, Portugal, and Spain.
[3]Australia and New Zealand.
[4]Austria, Belgium, Denmark, Finland, France, Germany, Italy, the Netherlands, Norway, Sweden, Switzerland, and the United Kingdom.

that together account for over two-thirds of the IMF metals price index. Each model consists of four parts (the full model is described in Appendix 5.1).

- First, demand for each metal is estimated as a function of industrial production and the real price (relative to consumer prices) for 17 country groups that together make up about 90 percent of world metal consumption. The sample period is 1960–2005 and the estimated equations include a lagged endogenous variable.[15] By disaggregating consumption data into many country groups and using industrial production as an explanatory variable, the model broadly captures the nonlinearity between metals consumption and income illustrated in Figure 5.7. The estimated elasticity of demand with respect to industrial production is somewhat higher for emerging market and developing countries than for the advanced economies (for aluminum, 1.2 compared with 1.0; see Table 5.6). This reflects differences in the industrial structure and the lower efficiency of production in developing countries. The long-term price elasticity of demand is estimated at low levels, which is consistent with earlier studies (see, for example, Ghosh, Gilbert, and Hughes Hallett, 1987).[16]
- The second element of the model is a production function that incorporates information about planned increases in capacity as well as a price-elasticity term. Given the gestation lags of several years for building new capacity in the industry, information about the existing green field and brown field projects is critical for the assessment of medium-term supply prospects. The supply projection draws on the expert assessment of the Australian Bureau of Agricultural and Resource Economics (ABARE, 2006). In the model, the

[15]The sample is shorter for some countries due to limited availability of industrial production data.

[16]Substitution across metals is modest even in the medium term and, therefore, is not modeled explicitly. See Appendix 5.1 for details.

Table 5.4. Consumption of Selected Agricultural Commodities
(Consumption expressed as real annual percent change; contributions to growth in percent)

	1993–2001			2001–05[1]		
	World consumption growth	Contribution to growth of: China	Contribution to growth of: Other major emerging markets[2]	World consumption growth	Contribution to growth of: China	Contribution to growth of: Other major emerging markets[2]
Agricultural commodity						
Bananas	2.6	26	45	3.5	15	73
Beef	0.9	102	17	0.8	103	40
Corn	2.6	26	4	2.6	14	19
Cotton	1.1	52	54	5.4	90	12
Sugar	1.6	5	45	2.1	26	27
		1993–2001		2001–05		
			(In percent)			
Memorandum items:						
World GDP growth		3.7		4.4		
China's share in world population		22		21		

Sources: FAOSTAT data (2006); Foreign Agriculture Service official USDA estimates (2006); and IMF staff calculations.
[1]The sample is selected to match the recent period of rising real prices. Owing to limited data availability, figures for bananas are for the period 2001–03.
[2]Brazil, India, Mexico, and Russia.

supply of refined aluminum and copper is allowed to deviate from the ABARE forecast whenever the price projection is different from that assumed by ABARE (see Appendix 5.1 for details).

- Third, a price equation relates the current real price of metals to the market balance (the gap between demand and supply), the exchange rate of the U.S. dollar to SDR (as the metals prices are denominated in U.S. dollars), and other variables.
- Finally, for each of the 17 country groups, equations are estimated to build a link between industrial production and GDP growth rates. These equations are needed since the *World Economic Outlook* projects real GDP growth but not industrial production. The equations are estimated over a shorter sample, 1990–2005, because the relationship between industrial production and GDP changes over time (Figure 5.8).

The estimated model is used to prepare a forecast of demand, supply, and prices in aluminum and copper markets during 2006–10. The main inputs into the model are *World Economic Outlook* GDP forecasts (in turn, determining future demand for metals) and ABARE supply projections (which contain information about forthcoming supply).[17] The results suggest that:

- Consumption of aluminum and copper will continue to grow fast—averaging 5.6 and 4.8 percent a year, respectively—given expected rapid expansion of industrial production in emerging markets, with China contributing about 50 percent to average future demand growth (Appendix 5.1 provides additional details on expected market developments).
- The real annual average price of aluminum and copper will decline from current levels by 35 and 57 percent, respectively, by 2010. In other words, rising supply will be able to meet robust demand growth at falling prices. The price decline is generated by a combination of factors: (1) recent accumulated price increases will have some dampening impact on demand; (2) considerable supply expansion is projected by ABARE in the next five years; and (3) some additional supply is expected to come on stream as the current

[17]The medium-term scenario presented in Chapter 1 of this *World Economic Outlook* expects continued robust world economic growth in the range of 4¾ to 5 percent a year. This represents an increase of ¾–1 percentage point over the average annual growth during 1995–2005.

Figure 5.9. Base Metal Prices on Futures Markets
(2002 = 100; monthly data in nominal terms)

At present, futures markets expect the price of metals to fall gradually to the middle of the range between the current prices and the trough of 2002 (in nominal terms). The expected price decline is smaller in the aluminum industry where the gap between market prices and production costs has been narrower than for the other metals.

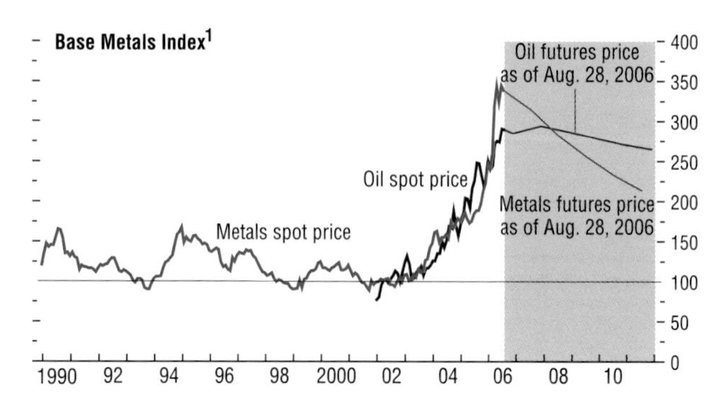

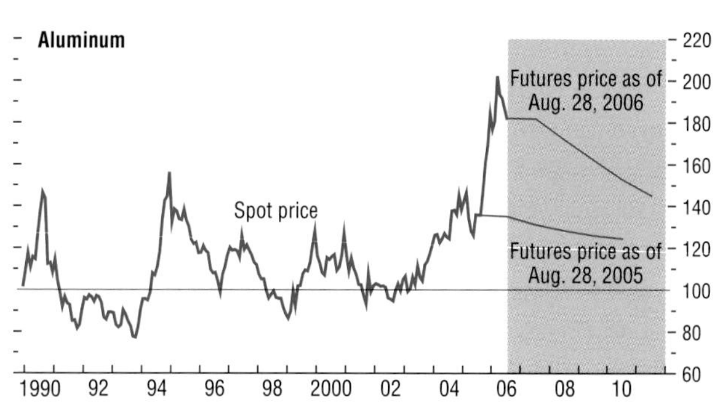

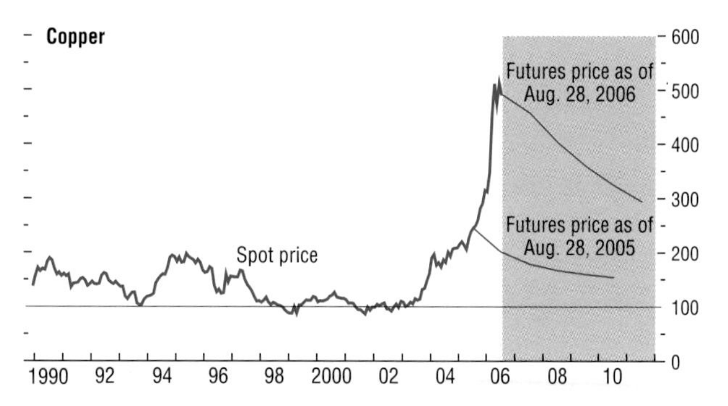

Sources: Barclays Capital (2006b); Bloomberg Financial Markets, LP; IMF, Commodity Price System database; and IMF staff calculations.
[1]Weighted average of aluminum, copper, lead, nickel, tin, and zinc prices.

metals prices are higher than in the ABARE projections. In addition, the price forecast reflects the unwinding of the models' error terms, since the recent run-up in prices has been greater than the models would have predicted based on their explanatory variables.[18] Naturally, there is significant uncertainty around these central price projections, reflecting uncertainties about global growth, the speed of supply additions, and the econometric models (Figure 5.10).

- The price of copper is forecast to fall relatively more than the price of aluminum. This is consistent with prices in the futures markets and the fact that the market-price-to-cost ratio is currently much higher for copper than for aluminum (Table 5.5).

Considering price developments beyond 2010, the key issue is whether metals supply would be able to meet rising demand in an environment of continued strong growth. In this regard, several features of the metals markets are important:

- In contrast to hydrocarbons, overall reserves of base metals are practically unlimited (Tilton, 2003).[19]
- While output concentration is high (the top three producing countries account for about 46 percent of refined aluminum production and 41 percent of refined copper production), market structures are competitive and there is currently no formal attempt by producers to control prices. This stands in contrast with the oil industry, where the majority of reserves

[18]The model on average explains 80–90 percent of variability in real prices of aluminum and copper. However, it does not fully capture the price behavior during cyclical peaks. See Appendix 5.1 for details.

[19]Base metals are abundant—for example, aluminum and iron account for over 8 and 5 percent, respectively, of the earth's crust. The resource base for many metals could therefore last hundreds of years, although only a fraction of these supplies can be extracted profitably using the current technology (Tilton, 2003). Moreover, the metals are not destroyed when processed and used, and can be recycled, which would further increase the estimates of reserves life expectancy. For comparison, the International Energy Agency (2004) estimates that the remaining oil resources could cover 70 years of annual average consumption between 2003 and 2030.

Table 5.5. Cash Costs of Production for Selected Base Metals
(U.S. dollars per ton)

	Year	Phase of Cycle	Marginal Cost[1] Typical producer[2]	Marginal Cost[1] Least-efficient producer[3]	Market Price	Ratio of Price to Marginal Cost[4]
Aluminum	1985	Trough	1,000	1,200	1,000	0.8
	1988	Peak	1,200	1,400	2,500	1.8
	2002	Trough	1,000	1,200	1,400	1.2
	2005	Upturn	1,500	1,800	1,900	1.1
	2006	Current	. . .	. . .	2,500[5]	1.4[6]
Copper	1985	Trough	1,000	1,400	1,400	1.0
	1989	Peak	1,300	1,800	2,800	1.6
	2002	Trough	1,000	1,500	1,600	1.1
	2005	Upturn	1,200	2,200	3,700	1.7
	2006	Current	. . .	. . .	6,100[5]	2.8[6]
Nickel	1985	Trough	3,400	5,300	4,900	0.9
	1988	Peak	4,000	7,400	13,800	1.9
	2002	Trough	3,700	6,100	6,800	1.1
	2005	Upturn	4,700	7,300	14,800	2.0
	2006	Current	. . .	. . .	17,400[5]	2.4[6]

Sources: Brook Hunt Metal Consultants; Deutsche Bank (2006); and IMF staff calculations.
[1]Operating cash cost of production rounded to the nearest hundred.
[2]50th percentile of the industry cost curve.
[3]90th percentile of the cost curve.
[4]Cost of the least-efficient producers.
[5]Average January–June.
[6]Relative to the 2005 marginal cost.

Table 5.6. Estimated Elasticities of Demand for Selected Base Metals

	Industrial Production	Price Deflated by CPI
Aluminum	1.1	–0.01
Advanced economies	1.0	–0.03
Emerging markets	1.2	0.00
Copper	1.1	–0.04
Advanced economies	0.7	–0.04
Emerging markets	1.6	–0.04

Source: IMF staff calculations.
Note: Elasticities are weighted using 2005 metal consumption shares. See Appendix 5.1 for the description of country groups.

are controlled by OPEC countries and there is a long tradition of attempted price management.[20]

- While investment gestation lags can reach three to five years in the sector (or more in case of green field investments), they are generally shorter than in the oil industry.

These supply-side factors tilt the long-term price risks for metals to the downside and clearly differentiate the metals sector from the oil market where prices are expected to remain high in the foreseeable future.[21]

Outlook for Food and Other Agricultural Commodities

As noted above, rapid growth in emerging market economies has not had a noticeable

[20]Gilbert (1996) discusses several past attempts to control prices in nonfuel commodity markets. These have failed for a variety of reasons, including emergence of alternative supplies, coordination problems, and disagreement over the division of benefits.

[21]Oil prices are currently being kept high by robust oil demand, geopolitical developments, and limited spare production capacity (Appendix 1.1). Chapter IV, "Will the Oil Market Continue to Be Tight?," in the April 2005 *World Economic Outlook* documents frictions on the supply side of the oil industry that may prevent long-term oil prices from returning to the average levels of the 1990s. These include, among other factors, the limited potential for production growth in the non-OPEC region and the lack of incentives for OPEC countries to increase long-term output sufficiently to help lower oil prices to the levels typical during the previous decade.

Figure 5.10. Model-Based Forecasts of Aluminum and Copper Prices[1]
(U.S. dollars per ton)

The demand and supply analysis suggests that aluminum and copper prices should moderate by the end of this decade. However, the estimated price range is very wide, reflecting uncertainties about global growth, capacity expansion in the metal industry, and the econometric model.

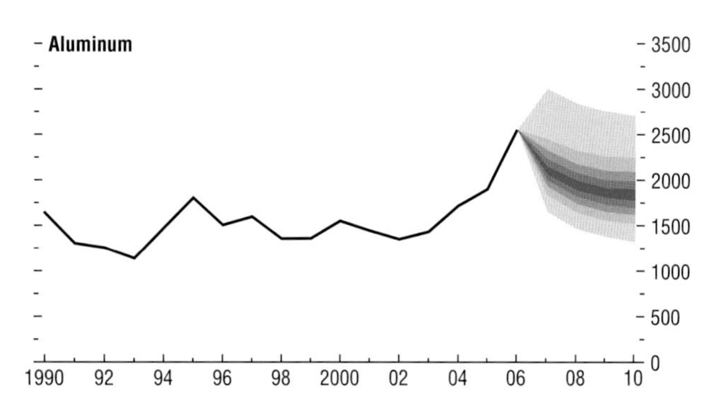

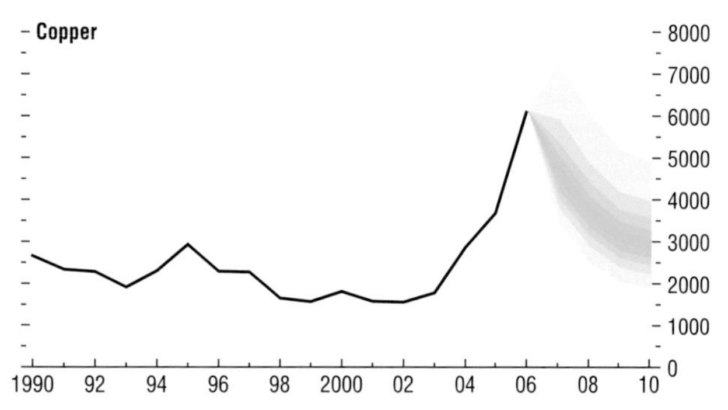

Sources: IMF, Commodity Price System database; and IMF staff estimates.
[1]The fan chart corresponds to a 95 percent probability band for future metal prices. Each shade represents a 10 percent likelihood with the exception of the central band (represented by the darkest shade in the fan), which represents a 15 percent likelihood. See Appendix 5.1 for details.

impact on price trends for agricultural commodities. Prices of food and raw materials are also much less sensitive to cyclical conditions than metals. Clearly, the speed of supply response is significantly faster in the agricultural sector than in metals—for example, crops can be switched from harvest to harvest relatively quickly in response to price signals. Moreover, the demand for agricultural commodities is less cyclical and therefore more predictable.

Given these factors, long-term agricultural prices will mostly be determined by productivity gains, which are expected to continue in the future due to technological progress (FAO, 2004b). Prices of some agricultural commodities will be influenced—like metals—by rising input costs, especially fertilizers whose price is linked to oil. Baffes (2006) estimates that the average pass-through from higher oil prices to agricultural prices is about 0.18. This factor (together with exchange rate changes) can explain why the current food price cycle—while very benign—has exhibited some persistence (Figure 5.6). However, as the example of cotton illustrates, weather-related supply shocks are the main source of price volatility in the agricultural sector and year-to-year fluctuations in the harvest size can dominate the impact of higher input costs for specific commodities.

For a narrow group of commodities, the price pressures from higher energy costs may be more substantial. These are the commodities that have a particularly large exposure to the oil market—such as sugar (through ethanol production for flex-fuel cars in Brazil), natural rubber (substitute for synthetic rubber produced from oil), and possibly also corn (fuel for flex-fuel cars in the United States).

In the future, agricultural prices could also be affected by shifts in the agricultural support system in the advanced economies. Production subsidies and import tariffs in advanced economies have served to systematically lower world prices for agricultural products, and successful completion of a multilateral agreement to reduce this support system would be expected to raise prices of certain key commodi-

Box 5.1. Has Speculation Contributed to Higher Commodity Prices?

Investor interest in commodity futures as assets has increased significantly in recent years. For example, participation in the NYMEX oil futures market—as measured by the number of contracts reported by the U.S. Commodity Futures Trading Commission (CFTC)—has risen almost fourfold since 1995 (first figure). Furthermore, the share of noncommercial contracts (long plus short—or total open positions) has steadily increased over this period—from 9 percent to 16 percent of the total. A similar trend can be observed in other commodity markets. The value of noncommercial contracts, however, is not large relative to total transactions in the physical market over a comparable period.[1]

The increased investor interest has led some private analysts to suggest that speculative activity has been a major contributor to the recent surge in crude oil and metals prices and may have even caused a bubble (see, for example, Societe Generale, 2006). They argue that speculation has magnified the impact of changes in the fundamental determinants of supply and demand (which have been supportive of higher prices) to an extent that in some cases prices have risen far in excess of levels justified by fundamentals.[2] The Organization of the Petroleum Exporting Countries (OPEC) has also suggested that while geopolitical uncertainties have been a major force behind higher prices, speculation has also been a significant factor, given the organization's accommodative supply policies and the historically high level of inventories in OECD countries.[3] Despite

Number of Positions in Commodity Markets
(Long plus short; in millions of contracts)

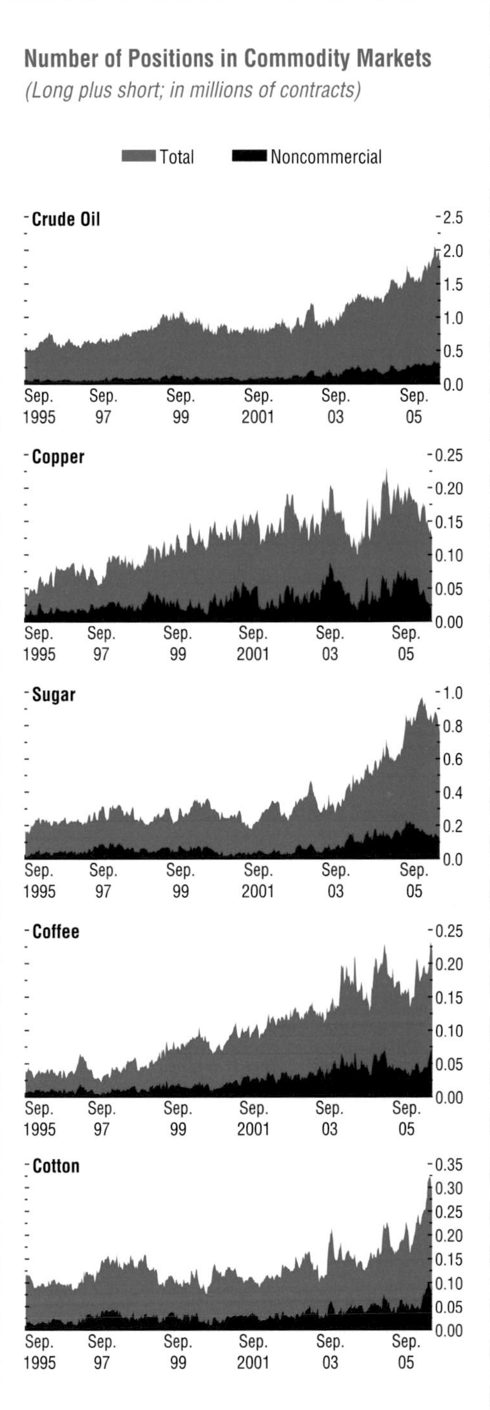

Source: Commodity Futures Trading Commission.

Note: The authors of this box are Sergei Antoshin and Hossein Samiei.

[1]For example, the value of total crude oil non-commercial positions of all maturities (up to six years) in the NYMEX is currently only about 3 percent of the value of U.S. oil consumption over six years at current prices. Contracts up to one-year maturity are equivalent to about 10 percent of U.S. consumption over one year.

[2]Note that speculators may also appear to affect prices if they have additional information that helps them make better forecasts than the average trader.

[3]See, for example, OPEC's press release "OPEC reassures market of continuing commitment to stability," July 14, 2006 at http://www.opec.org.

Box 5.1 *(continued)*

the attractiveness of some of these arguments, however, the supporting evidence has often focused on correlations rather than tests of causality, and has tended to be anecdotal or circumstantial—based on, for example, the increased hedge fund activity accompanying the rise in prices or the deviation of prices from long-run marginal costs. The lack of solid evidence in part reflects data and definitional problems associated with defining and measuring speculation.

A price bubble is certainly a theoretical possibility and a periodic occurrence in financial and housing markets. Excessive speculation in the commodity futures market could, in principle, push up futures prices and (through arbitrage opportunities) spot prices above levels justified by fundamentals. However, an alternative view is that increased investor activity, by providing the necessary liquidity, is simply a vehicle to translate changing views about fundamentals into changing prices. In this case, higher prices would be the cause (rather than the effect) of increased investor participation. In the intermediate case, there could be a two-way causality between prices and speculation, so that higher prices induce an increase in speculation, which in turn pushes prices up further until a new equilibrium is achieved.

Note also that the supposed impact of speculation is sometimes confused with the so-called "security premium," which essentially reflects concerns about future fundamentals (e.g., potential shortages because of geopolitical developments). The security premium, in contrast to speculation, results from a genuine desire by consumers to hedge against risks. Such a precautionary desire could push up prices—for example, by raising demand for inventories—as has happened in the oil market where global inventories are at record levels, likely because of concerns about future supply (leading to higher precautionary demand) rather than (as argued by some commentators) genuine excess supply in the spot market.

To assess the empirical validity of the speculation hypothesis, this box provides an econometric assessment of the direction of causality between movements in spot and futures prices,[4] and changes in speculative positions in a sample of major commodities, comprising crude oil, copper, sugar, coffee, and cotton (Appendix 5.2 provides details of the approach taken). The objective is to test for the presence of a set of relationships between these three variables that goes beyond anecdotal evidence or one-off events.

A related issue of interest is whether speculation stabilizes or destabilizes prices—that is, whether speculation reduces or increases the amplitude of price fluctuations around equilibrium. While this issue is not the focus of this box, the causality tests carried out in the box can throw some light on the matter. Specifically, to the extent that the presence of stabilizing or destabilizing effects requires speculators to systematically influence price changes (as opposed to broader measures of volatility), the absence of causality from speculation to price levels could be taken to suggest that speculators are neutral as far as price fluctuations are concerned.

Two caveats/clarifications are in order before describing the results. First, a thorough analysis of price formation in the commodity markets would require a more complete model incorporating the role of current fundamentals (supply and demand factors) and perceptions about future fundamentals (including the fear factor). Such an exercise, however, is constrained by the lack of high-frequency data on most fundamental factors and given that the relationship between speculation and prices is most important in the short term.

Second, empirical analysis is hampered by definitional problems related to information on types of trader. The CFTC reports on a weekly basis the number of contracts for two categories of traders: commercial and noncommercial. Commercial traders are defined as those who use futures contracts for the purpose of hedging (e.g., oil producers, merchants, and major consumers, such as airlines). Other participants

[4]One-year ahead futures prices are used since activity is the largest in this market. The results were broadly similar for longer-dated maturities.

are treated as noncommercial traders. Noncommercial traders are clearly speculators, as they take positions in the market to bet on price changes. However, some of the traders classified as commercial may also be engaged in speculative activity. For example, commodity index traders, who are classified as commercial, may take market positions that are driven by speculative motives from the clients' perspective. Since the CFTC only reports the data in an aggregated form, one cannot distinguish amongst trader types within the commercial category and isolate those that may potentially qualify as speculators. Nevertheless, a recent CFTC study using disaggregated unpublished data collected by the Commission suggests that, among commercial traders, the main groups that may potentially be involved in speculation (namely, managed money traders, including hedge funds) do not appear to impact price volatility and act largely as providers of liquidity (see Haigh, Hranaiova, and Overdahl, 2005). Note also that since data is weekly (measuring the activity on the Tuesday of each week), it is not possible to capture the impact of within-the-week activity, which could be significant.[5] Finally, CFTC data do not distinguish the contracts by maturity. Therefore, it is not possible to study the relationship between speculation and futures prices of different maturities. Subject to the above limitations and considerations, this box uses the number of net long noncommercial positions as a proxy for speculation.[6]

The second figure shows the behavior of spot prices and the number of speculative positions

[5]Note that in the following analysis, average weekly prices (Tuesday to Monday) are used to partly overcome this problem. Using prices for each Tuesday produced qualitatively similar results.

[6]Note that since each contract comprises a fixed volume, using the number of positions is equivalent to using volumes. Note also that the alternative of total open noncommercial positions (i.e., the sum of short and long positions) would not be a suitable measure because a rise in this variable could result from a rise in short or long positions, which have potentially opposite impacts on prices.

Commodity Prices and Speculative Positions

(Spot prices in log scale; net long noncommercial positions in millions of contracts)

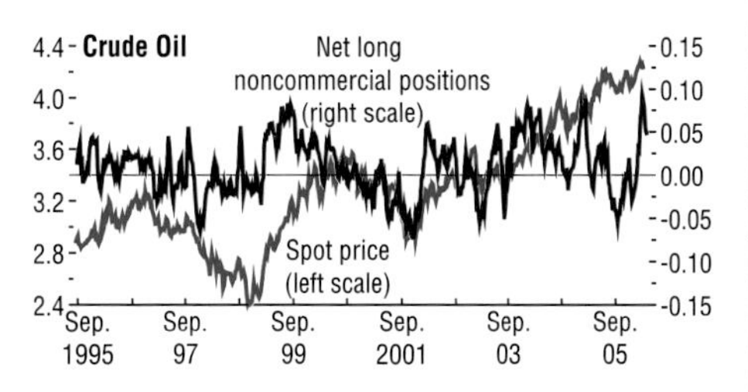

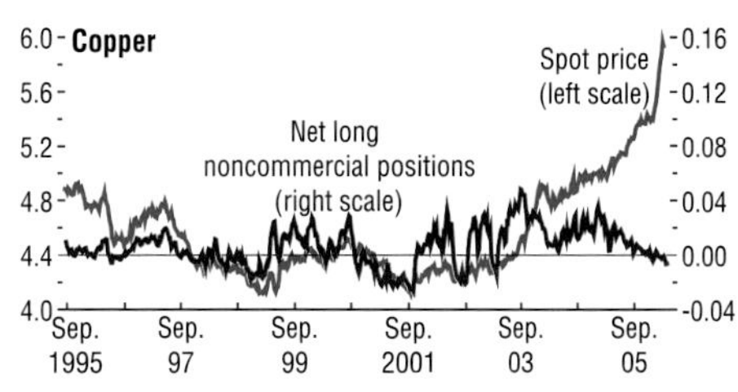

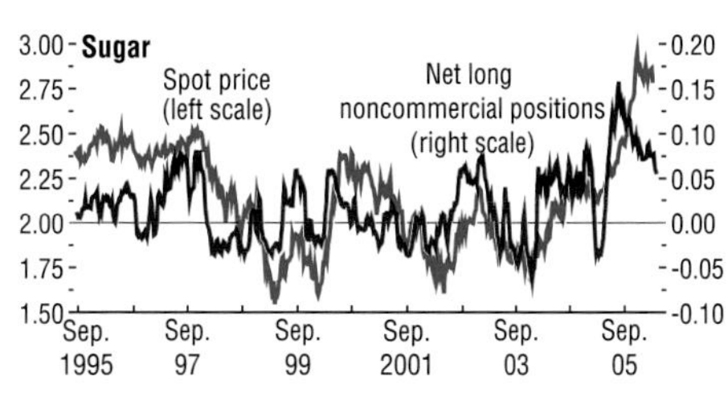

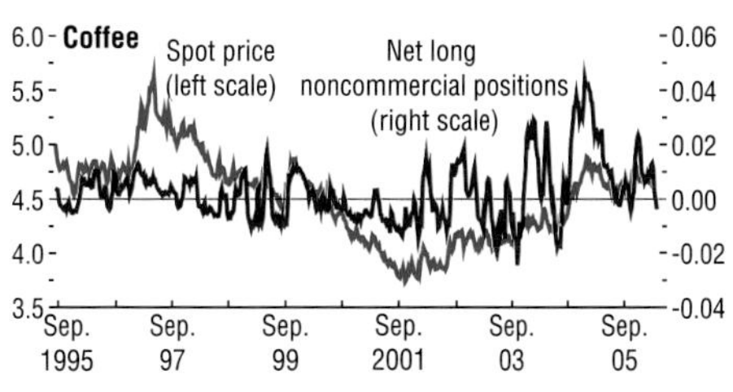

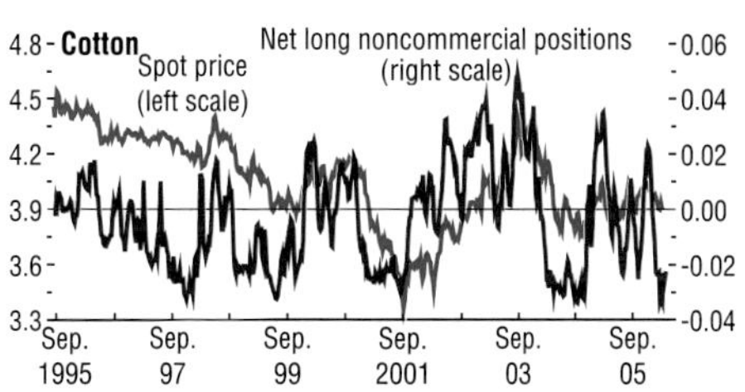

Sources: Bloomberg Financial, LP; and Commodity Futures Trading Commission.

Box 5.1 *(concluded)*

for various commodities. This figure suggests two generalizations. First, prices appear less volatile than speculative positions across commodities, with no discernible common trend between prices and speculation. For example, in the crude oil market there has been no persistent pickup in net long noncommercial positions in recent years when oil prices have had a strong upward trend. More strikingly, in the copper market, net positions have actually fallen steadily over the past year, during which prices have reached record highs, suggesting that contrary to common perceptions, speculation may not have played a major role in the recent price run-up. Second, while the series do not appear to be correlated over the long run, for most commodities some correlation appears to be present over subperiods, as peaks and turning points seem to occur around the same time across the two series.[7] The key question then concerns the direction of causality.

The visual analysis suggests the relevance of distinguishing short- and long-run causality. To this end, and to account for the nonstationarity of the price and speculative positions series, a Vector Error Correction Model (VECM) is employed (see Appendix 5.2 for details). Furthermore, given that the relationships have varied over time, and to enhance the reliability of the results, the parameters are estimated using rolling regressions. This approach will, in particular, allow us to assess whether speculation has played a major role in the recent episode of rising prices.

The results from the regressions for the five commodities—summarized in Table 5.11 in Appendix 5.2—indicate that the short-run causality generally runs from spot and futures prices to speculation, and not vice versa.[8] This is true even when the long-run (error-correction) term is removed from the estimation.[9] This finding is rather consistent across commodities. For crude oil, speculation appears to have had a significant but very small effect on futures prices. However, this has not been translated into a causal impact on spot prices. This finding is consistent with previous work by IMF staff on the oil market (which tested for causality in the frequency rather than time domain and used longer-dated futures prices).[10]

Turning to the long run, while the estimated parameters vary considerably over time, the three series are mostly cointegrated, permitting an analysis of causality. The results suggest that whenever there is cointegration, causality is from prices to speculative activity, and not vice versa. In the case of cotton, there is some evidence of two-way causality—although the absence of short-run causality from speculation to prices weakens the importance of this result. Finally, based on measured correlation coefficients, the model explains a much larger part of variations in speculation than variations in spot or futures prices.

All in all—and subject to the data limitations stressed at the outset—the results for the five commodities in the sample provide little support for the hypothesis that speculative activity (as measured by net long noncommercial positions) affects either price levels over the long run or price swings in the short run. In contrast, there is evidence (both across commodities and over time) that speculative positions follow price movements. These findings are consistent with the hypothesis that speculators play a role in providing liquidity to the markets and may benefit from price movements, but do not have a systematic causal influence on prices.

[7]For clarity, futures prices are omitted from the figure, but these generalizations apply equally well to the relationship between speculative positions and futures prices.

[8]Similar results are reported—using a different approach and sample—for energy futures markets by Sanders, Boris, and Manfredo (2004).

[9]The reason for this additional robustness check is that in the absence of cointegration, the short-run causality tests in the VECM may not be valid since the error-correction terms would be I(1).

[10]See Appendix 1.1 in the September 2005 *World Economic Outlook*.

ties. As discussed in Box 5.2, such agricultural reforms would have important implications for income in many developing countries, although the impact on world food prices is likely to be smaller than the year-to-year volatility from weather-related shocks.

Conclusion

Most of the recent increase in nonfuel commodity indices is due to metals. The current upturn in their prices has been amplified by rapid growth in emerging market economies, particularly in China. Over the medium term, however, metals prices are expected to retreat from recent highs as new capacity comes on stream, although probably not falling back to earlier levels—in part because higher energy prices have increased production costs. That said, the timing and the speed of the price reversal is uncertain, because with current high capacity utilization rates and low inventories, markets are very sensitive to even small changes in supply and demand.

This assessment has a number of implications for exporters of metals. Policymakers in exporting countries will need to ensure that the current income windfall is either largely saved—such as in the case of Chile—or used in a way that supports future growth in noncommodity sectors, for example, through investment in education, health, and infrastructure. Fiscal transparency should help to ensure that the most is made from any additional budget revenues. Governments, however, must be prepared for a decline in prices in the future and ensure that spending does not increase above sustainable levels in hard-to-reverse areas such as public sector wages.

The prices of agricultural commodities have increased much less than metals prices and for exporters of these commodities, the main policy question remains how to manage year-to-year volatility. Generally, governments of both exporting and importing countries should approach the volatility in commodity prices—including metals prices—from a "risk management" perspective and incorporate market information about prices and volatility into their fiscal planning and budgetary process. More broadly, governments in commodity-exporting countries should continue to aim at diversifying their economies to help reduce vulnerabilities to commodity price shocks. The IMF also stands ready to provide assistance in cases of extremely large and negative impacts of market volatility on external balances.[22]

Appendix 5.1. Model of Aluminum and Copper Markets

The main author of this appendix is Martin Sommer with consultancy support from Christopher Gilbert and contributions from Angela Espiritu.

The analysis of future price trends in this chapter is based on four integrated models of the demand, supply, and price of metals, and of industrial production. This appendix provides a description of each model.

Demand for Metals

The estimated model takes the following form:

$$\log C_{i,t} = c_i + \alpha_i \log C_{i,t-1} + (\beta_i + \omega_i Dummy_{2000}) \log IP_{i,t} + \gamma_i \log \frac{P_{t-1}}{CPI_{t-1}} + \varepsilon_{i,t},$$

where $C_{i,t}$ denotes metal consumption in country i at time t; c_i is a country-specific constant; $IP_{i,t}$ stands for industrial output in country i at time t; P/CPI is the real price of a metal (United

[22]The Exogenous Shocks Facility (ESF) is available to low-income countries that have defined (or are in the process of defining) their poverty reduction strategy. The assistance takes the form of short-term quick-disbursing concessional loans to meet immediate balance of payments needs. Alternatively, loans can also be provided under the Compensatory Financing Facility (CFF), which assists countries experiencing either a sudden shortfall in export earnings or an increase in the cost of cereal imports due to fluctuating world commodity prices.

Box 5.2. Agricultural Trade Liberalization and Commodity Prices

Rich countries provide hefty support to their agricultural producers in a variety of forms, which tends to raise domestic prices for these products and depress international prices. Such support—including import tariffs, production, and export subsidies, and direct payments to farmers—averages about 30 percent of farm receipts in OECD countries, and is particularly high for rice, sugar, milk, and grains (first table). Low- and middle-income countries also provide support to agricultural producers, mainly through import barriers.

A number of researchers have sought to estimate the magnitude of the increases in world prices of agricultural commodities that would result from cuts in rich-country agricultural support (second table). The estimates vary widely, reflecting differences in modeling approaches, the time frame considered, and the degree of liberalization (e.g., full versus partial reform). As shown, the magnitude of the price increases could be as large as 35 percent for some commodities, although the average percentage price increases are more modest: wheat (5.1), maize (4.6), beef (5.1), sugar (5.8), and rice (5.5). The world price of cotton, a key export of some poor countries in West Africa, is estimated to increase by between 2.3 and 35 percent, with an average estimate of about 13.5 percent. It is worth noting that the average size of the estimated price increases is less than the average year-to-year variation in prices.

These estimated price increases can be thought of as the short-run impact of liberalization. In the long run, the distribution of production and exports would shift across countries. In many OECD countries, liberalization would make it less attractive for farmers to undertake investment and expand production capacity, while agricultural land would be diverted to other uses. In contrast, producers in countries with a comparative advantage in agriculture (e.g., Australia, New Zealand, and Brazil) would expand production following the rise in world prices. It is even possible that the increases in commodity prices could cause some countries that are now importers of agricultural commodities to become exporters. Research has shown that the elimination of agricultural

Note: The main author of this box is Stephen Tokarick.

Support Provided to Various Agricultural Commodities in OECD Countries, 2004

	United States	European Union	Japan	All OECD
	Producer support estimate[1]			
Rice	18	39	82	75
Sugar	56	65	65	58
Wheat	32	39	85	33
Maize	27	43	. . .	31
Beef and veal	4	68	31	34
All commodities	18	33	56	30
	Nominal protection coefficient[1]			
Rice	1.08	1.00	5.46	3.76
Sugar	2.13	3.03	2.79	2.36
Wheat	1.01	1.06	5.50	1.08
Maize	1.15	1.38	. . .	1.20
Beef and veal	1.00	1.99	1.43	1.26
All commodities	1.11	1.29	2.20	1.28

Source: *Agricultural Policies in OECD Countries: Monitoring and Evaluation*, Organization for Economic Cooperation and Development, 2005.

[1]Producer support estimate is defined as the dollar amount of support provided to producers as a percent of the total value of production. The nominal protection coefficient measures the ratio of the prices received by producers of agricultural products to international prices.

Price Changes Resulting from Cuts in Agricultural Support in OECD Countries
(In percent)

	Range of Estimated Price Changes	Average of Estimated Price Changes	Coefficient of Variation of Prices 1990–2004	Average Year-to-Year Percentage Change of Prices[1]
Wheat	0.1–18.1	5.1	16.9	11.8
Maize	0.1–15.2	4.6	17.2	10.1
Beef	0.8–22.3	5.1	15.4	8.6
Sugar	1.1–16.4	5.8	23.9	14.1
Rice	0.1–10.6	5.5	19.6	11.8
Cotton	2.3–35.0	13.5	21.7	17.3

Sources: Mitchell and Hoppe (2006); Food and Agriculture Organization (FAO, 2004a); and staff estimates.

[1]Average of the absolute values of price changes.

Box 5.2 *(concluded)*

support policies could also reduce the variability of international food prices. For example, Tyers and Anderson (1992) showed that the coefficient of variation in world food prices could be reduced by two-thirds if all countries ceased to insulate their domestic markets. This is because agricultural policies in rich countries are designed to prevent domestic prices from changing rapidly. Domestic supply shocks, such as droughts, are therefore offset through changes in trade volumes in order to keep domestic prices fairly stable. These changes in trade volumes tend to cause international prices to fluctuate to a much greater degree than they would in the absence of agricultural support policies.

Since liberalization of agricultural trade would raise world prices, the import bills of net food-importing countries would likely increase. The estimated price changes suggest that as a group, import bills would rise from between $300 million to $1¼ billion, depending on the degree of liberalization. While these magnitudes are small in aggregate—they represent less than 1 percent of total imports for these countries—a number of low-income countries could experience substantial increases in their import bills, and could require additional assistance to adjust to the higher international prices. For this purpose, in 2004, the International Monetary Fund (IMF) introduced the trade integration mechanism (TIM) to support countries that experience an adverse shift in their terms of trade as a consequence of multilateral trade liberalization, by making resources more predictably available under existing IMF arrangements. Of course, countries could also mitigate at least some of the impact of higher world food prices by reducing their import tariffs.

States CPI is used as a deflator); and $\varepsilon_{i,t}$ is a residual. This model is similar to the specification used by Gilbert (1995).

The model is estimated with ordinary least squares (OLS) using annual data for 17 country groups over 1960–2005. The demand equations do not impose any restrictions on the country-specific coefficients c, α, β, ω, and γ to allow for cross-country heterogeneity (Robertson and Symons, 1992). Consumption of metals is tightly linked to industrial production and the relationship is approximately linear (Figure 5.11). Given evidence provided by Chow tests on a time change in the elasticity of consumption with respect to industrial production for a few countries (such a parameter break may occur due to changes in the industrial structure), the model also contains a slope dummy that takes a value of one during 2000–05, and zero otherwise. The estimated coefficient on the slope dummy is small on average, but statistically significant for some countries—the dummy is therefore included in the model. The average estimated coefficients are reported in Table 5.7.[23]

The consumption data used in the model are for primary refined consumption—secondary consumption of recycled metals is therefore not modeled explicitly. This approach is taken due to the lack of country-level data on secondary consumption. However, accounting for the secondary consumption and production would not materially change the price forecasts in Figure 5.10 (Ghosh, Gilbert, and Hughes Hallett, 1987).

The estimated parameter values are relatively robust with respect to a change in the sample period and alternative specifications of the real price term. The estimated price elasticity is similar when producer prices are used instead of consumer prices, or when the price term also

[23]Tests confirmed existence of a cointegrating relationship between consumption of metals and industrial production for most countries, which helps achieve consistency of estimates.

contains a country-specific real exchange rate. In the reported specification, only United States CPI is used to deflate metals prices to simplify forecasting. The impact of this simplifying assumption on the forecast of global metal consumption is very small given the low estimated price elasticity and—in the case of the missing exchange rate term—the tendency for the errors to offset each other across countries. In line with the literature, the equations for metal demand do not include prices of other metals, as substitution across metals is almost negligible in the short term and only modest in the medium term.[24]

Production Function

The supply of metals is based on the expert assessment of the Australian Bureau of Agricultural and Resource Economics (ABARE, 2006) and a price elasticity term. For each metal, ABARE reports its supply projection taking into account the pipeline of existing supply expansion projects. This supply path is adjusted as follows whenever the simulated price differs from that used by ABARE:

$$S_t = S_t^{ABARE}\left(\frac{S_{t-1}}{S_{t-1}^{ABARE}}\right)^{1-\delta}\left(\frac{P_t}{P_t^{ABARE}}\right)^{\delta}.$$

In this equation, S_t stands for the metal supply at time t, and P_t is the metal price. Variables with a superscript *ABARE* denote projections of the Australian Bureau. This specification was initially used by Gately (2004) and a similar approach was also used in the IMF's study of the oil market in Chapter IV of the April 2005 *World Economic Outlook*. Given the considerable uncertainty about the price elasticity of metal supply,

Figure 5.11. Consumption of Base Metals and Industrial Production, 1960–2005
(1996 = 100)

Consumption of base metals is tightly linked to industrial output.

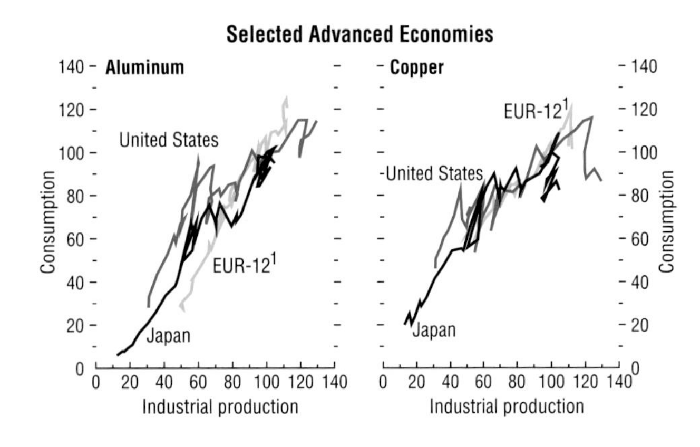

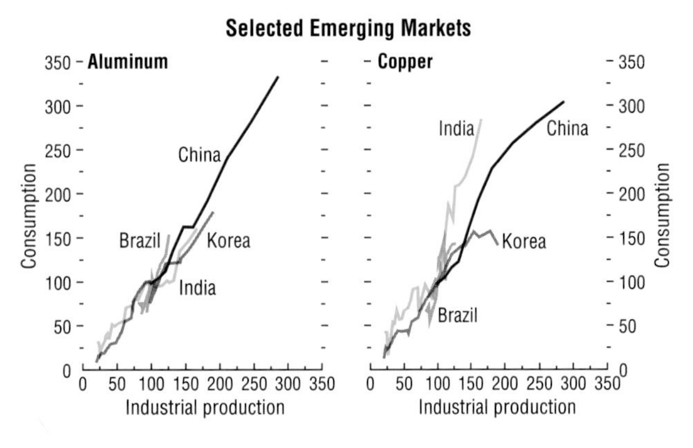

Sources: World Bureau of Metal Statistics, *World Metal Statistics Yearbook* (various issues); and IMF staff calculations.
[1]Austria, Belgium, Denmark, Finland, France, Germany, Italy, the Netherlands, Norway, Sweden, Switzerland, and the United Kingdom. Industrial production for the group was aggregated using 2005 purchasing-power-parity adjusted real GDP values as weights.

[24]Product specifications are embedded into production techniques and metals cannot be changed in most uses except at significant cost. In the long term, substitution may be considerable as relative price changes lead to purchases of new tools, retooling, and research and development activity (Ghosh, Gilbert, and Hughes Hallett, 1987). However, the fit and statistical properties of the estimated equations are very satisfactory, and any substitution across metals resulting from the recent price developments is not likely to be important over the forecast horizon considered in this study.

Table 5.7. Estimates of Metal Demand

$\log C_{i,t} = c_i + \alpha_i \log C_{i,t-1} + (\beta_i + \omega_i Dummy_{2000}) \log IP_{i,t} + \gamma_i \log \frac{P_{t-1}}{CPI_{t-1}} + \varepsilon_{i,t}$

	Aluminum	Copper
c	−0.113	−0.736
α	0.174	0.389
β	1.128	0.921
ω	0.008	0.000
γ	−0.050	−0.037
Adjusted R^2	0.85	0.87
LM serial correlation (p-value)	0.39	0.40
White heteroskedasticity (p-value)	0.52	0.51
Sample	1960–2005	1960–2005
Number of observations	464	464
Memorandum:		
Long-term elasticity of demand with respect to industrial production		
Advanced economies[1]	1.0	0.7
Emerging markets[2]	1.2	1.6
Long-term elasticity of demand with respect to price		
Advanced economies[1]	−0.03	−0.04
Emerging markets[2]	0.00	−0.04

Source: IMF staff estimates.

Note: Reported ordinary least squares (OLS) coefficient estimates and regression statistics (with the exception of the number of observations) are simple averages across all 17 estimated equations. Estimates have a non-normal distribution and standard errors are therefore not reported. The elasticities of demand are weighted by 2005 metal consumption shares.

[1]Canada, EUR-12 (Austria, Belgium, Denmark, Finland, France, Germany, Italy, the Netherlands, Norway, Sweden, Switzerland, and the United Kingdom), EUR-4E (Greece, Ireland, Portugal, and Spain), Japan, Oceania (Australia, New Zealand), and the United States.

[2]Argentina, Brazil, China, Indonesia, India, Korea, Mexico, Russia, Thailand, Turkey, South Africa.

the parameter δ is assumed to be uniformly distributed between 0.03–0.05. Over a five-year period, this translates into the price elasticity of supply of about 0.16–0.26 for permanent price shocks,[25] and elasticity of about 0.02–0.04 for price changes that only last one year.

Price Equation

The price equation relates the current real price of metals to the following explanatory variables:

$$(\log P_t - \log CPI_t) = c_0 + \phi(\log P_{t-1} - \log CPI_{t-1}) + \chi \log(USD/SDR)_t + \mu t + \kappa(\log C_{t-1} - \log S_{t-1}) + \nu_t,$$

where c_0 is a constant, *USD/SDR* is the exchange rate of U.S. dollar to SDR,[26] t is the time trend, and $\log C_t - \log S_t$ reflects the market balance (i.e., the difference between world consumption and production). The model is estimated with OLS using annual data over 1960–2005. The fit of the estimated equations for aluminum and copper is high (Table 5.8). That said, the model does not fully capture the price behavior during cyclical peaks, which suggests that at low inventory levels, prices respond to fundamentals in a nonlinear fashion.[27] In 2005, the price of aluminum and copper were above their values fitted by the model by 7 and 14 percent, respectively, and in 2006, the deviations were 32 and 58 percent. While large, these deviations are comparable with those experienced during earlier cycles (Box 5.1 finds little evidence that speculative investments have been a significant driver of nonfuel commodity price movements). This uncertainty about the link between actual price movements and the model's explanatory variables is explicitly taken into account when generating the price forecast in Figure 5.10 in the main text.

Industrial Production Growth

Finally, for each of the 17 country groups, equations were estimated to build a link between industrial production (denoted *IP* below) and GDP growth rates. The equations were estimated over a shorter sample, 1990–2005, because the relationship between

[25]The responsiveness of metal supply to prices is therefore assumed to be the same or greater than in the April 2005 *World Economic Outlook* oil study.

[26]The exchange rate term is included because metal prices are denominated in U.S. dollars. As a simplifying assumption, the nominal exchange rate is used instead of the real exchange rate—U.S. consumer prices and SDR-based consumer prices have a very similar dynamics.

[27]The available time series for inventories are short and are subject to large measurement error—their inclusion in the price equation was not successful.

Table 5.8. Estimates of Price Equations

$(\log P_t - \log CPI_t) = c_0 + \phi(\log P_{t-1} - \log CPI_{t-1}) + \chi\log(USD/SDR)_t + \mu t + \kappa(\log C_{t-1} - \log S_{t-1}) + \nu_t$

	Aluminum	Copper
c_0	30.523***	24.282*
	(8.397)	(12.349)
ϕ	0.500***	0.682***
	(0.116)	(0.116)
χ	0.809**	0.594
	(0.311)	(0.466)
μ	−0.015***	−0.012**
	(0.004)	(0.006)
κ	1.457***	2.168**
	(0.533)	(0.883)
Adjusted R^2	0.91	0.77
LM serial correlation (p-value)	0.20	0.47
White heteroskedasticity (p-value)	0.38	0.61
Sample	1960–2006	1960–2006
Number of observations	46	46

Source: IMF staff estimates.

Note: Equations were estimated by ordinary least squares (OLS). Data for 2006 refer to the average for January–June. *** denotes statistical significance at the 1 percent level, ** denotes statistical significance at the 5 percent level, and * denotes significance at the 10 percent level.

Table 5.9. Equation for Industrial Production

$\Delta\log IP_{i,t} = k_i + \lambda_i\Delta\log GDP_{i,t} + \upsilon_{i,t}$

	Advanced Economies[1]	Emerging Markets[2]
k	−0.018***	−0.017*
	(0.006)	(0.009)
λ	1.526***	1.434***
	(0.207)	(0.122)
Adjusted R^2	0.76	
LM serial correlation (p-value)	0.58	
White heteroskedasticity (p-value)	0.57	
Sample	1990–2005	
Number of observations	252	

Source: IMF staff estimates.

Note: Reported ordinary least squares (OLS) coefficient estimates and regression statistics (with the exception of the number of observations) are simple averages across estimated equations. Standard errors are in parentheses. *** denotes statistical significance at the 1 percent level and * denotes significance at the 10 percent level.

[1]Canada; EUR-12 (Austria, Belgium, Denmark, Finland, France, Germany, Italy, the Netherlands, Norway, Sweden, Switzerland, and the United Kingdom); EUR-4E (Greece, Ireland, Portugal, and Spain); Japan; Oceania (Australia, New Zealand); and the United States.

[2]Argentina, Brazil, China, Indonesia, India, Korea, Mexico, Russia, Thailand, and South Africa.

industrial production and GDP changes over time (Figure 5.8 in the main text).

$$\Delta\log IP_{i,t} = k_i + \lambda_i\Delta\log GDP_{i,t} + \upsilon_{i,t}.$$

In the equation, k_i and λ_i are country-specific parameters and $\upsilon_{i,t}$ is a residual. OLS coefficient estimates for the main country groups are reported in Table 5.9.

Price Forecast

The estimated equations were used to prepare a forecast for aluminum and copper prices during 2006–10. The main inputs into the model are GDP forecasts for each country group from the *World Economic Outlook* (in turn, helping to determine future demand for metals) and ABARE supply projections (which contain information about forthcoming supply).

Given the GDP forecast, industrial production is calculated for each country group. Together with the previous period's price, industrial production determines the current demand for metals.[28] Supply is predetermined using the ABARE forecast and the deviation between the actual price and the price assumed by ABARE. The current market balance (the difference between world consumption and production) then helps to determine the next period's price, together with the exchange rate and CPI index. Table 5.10 reports the baseline consumption growth for aluminum and copper over the forecast period.

The fan chart (Figure 5.10 in the main text) is generated by a stochastic simulation as follows. Residuals are drawn randomly from the three estimated equations for metal demand, price, and industrial production, and are added to the

[28]Consumption in the rest of the world (about 10 percent of the total) is assumed to rise at the rate of previous year's world consumption growth. In the case of copper, elasticities of consumption with respect to industrial production were estimated for a few countries at unsustainably high levels of 2.5–5 (Argentina, Indonesia, Mexico, and Russia)—in part because the sample period for these countries is short. The countries are included in the rest-of-the-world group for the purpose of forecasting copper prices.

Table 5.10. Consumption of Metals
(Annual percent change)

	1993–2002	2002–05	2005–10 (forecast)
Aluminum	3.8	7.6	5.6
Copper	3.5	3.8	4.8
Memorandum:			
World GDP	3.5	4.8	4.9

Source: IMF staff estimates.

forecasted values of industrial production, metal demand, and price in each year. In the equations for metal demand and industrial production, the residuals are drawn jointly across all 17 country groups to preserve the contemporaneous cross-country correlation structure. In general, the uncertainty about the future price path also reflects the uncertainty about future global growth and the speed of supply additions. Additional randomization is therefore performed as follows: (1) the world GDP growth rates are assumed to be two-piece uniformly distributed around the WEO baseline, with the maximum global growth rate exceeding the baseline by ½ percentage point and the minimum growth rate underperforming the baseline by 1 percentage point; (2) the actual metal supply growth (net of price changes) is assumed to deviate from projected ABARE supply growth by up to 1 percent every year; and (3) the medium-term elasticity of metal supply with respect to prices is assumed to be uniformly distributed between 0.16 and 0.26.

Data Definitions and Sources

The main author of this section is Angela Espiritu.

- *Nonfuel commodities* are defined as industrial metals, food, beverages, and agricultural raw materials. In terms of the SITC (Revision 3) classification,[29] nonfuel commodities are the commodity groups with codes 0, 1, 2, 4, 67, and 68. Precious metals and stones are excluded from the analysis.
- *Country coverage.* The econometric analysis is based on data for 14 countries and 3 country groups. The individual countries are Argentina, Brazil, Canada, China, India, Indonesia, Japan, Korea, Mexico, Russia, South Africa, Thailand, Turkey, and the United States. The country groups are EUR-12 (Austria, Belgium, Denmark, Finland, France, Germany, Italy, the Netherlands, Norway, Sweden, Switzerland, and the United Kingdom); EUR-4E (Greece, Ireland, Portugal, and Spain); and Oceania (Australia and New Zealand).
- *Commodity prices.* Price data are primarily from the IMF's Commodity Price System database (CPS).[30] In general, the CPS commodity data are available since 1957. Data from Cashin, Liang, and McDermott (2000) were used to extend the coverage of CPS as necessary.[31] The data for 2006 are generally an average of January–June prices. Figure 5.2 presents the Grilli and Yang (1988) measures of long-term commodity prices over 1900–87. Due to definitional changes, the Grilli and Yang indices are not directly comparable with the data from CPS and Cashin, Liang, and McDermott (2000), and are therefore presented without any transformations or updates. Prices of metal futures were obtained from Bloomberg Financial Markets, LP (London Metal Exchange data as of August 28, 2006) and the July 19 and August 23 and 29, 2006 *Commodity Daily Briefings* from Barclays Capital.
- *General price indexes.* The historical data (since 1900) on the United States consumer price index are available from the Federal Reserve Bank of Minneapolis.[32] The United Nations'

[29]For the structure and definitions of SITC (Rev. 3), see the United Nations' website http://unstats.un.org/unsd/cr/registry/regcst.asp?Cl=14.

[30]For more information on the data, see http://www.imf.org/external/np/res/commod/index.asp.

[31]The average correlation coefficient between the aggregate indices of metals, food, and agricultural raw materials from CPS and Cashin, Liang, and McDermott (2000) is 0.94.

[32]See http://woodrow.mpls.frb.fed.us/Research/data/us/calc/hist1800.cfm for the data.

Manufactures Unit Value index measures the unit values of manufactured goods exports (SITC groups 5 to 8) by 24 developed market economies. Data prior to 1960 are from Cashin and McDermott (2002); data from 1960 onwards are from UNCTAD's *Handbook of Statistics* database.[33]

- *Commodity exports.* The data on commodity exports are from the World Bank's World Integrated Trade Solution database.[34] In Figure 5.1, the total exports of nonfuel primary commodities are expressed in percent of gross domestic product (GDP). Dependence on commodity exports is assessed using the average export-to-GDP ratio during the most recent five years of available data. A total of 171 countries are classified, of which 12 countries have the ratio of nonfuel commodity exports to GDP greater than 20 percent; 24 countries have the ratio between 10–20 percent; 56 countries between 5–10 percent; 39 countries between 2½–5 percent; 25 countries between 1–2½ percent; and 15 countries have the ratio below 1 percent.
- *Consumption and production of metals.* Data on metal consumption and production are from the World Bureau of Metal Statistics' *World Metal Statistics Yearbook* (1991, 1995, 2000, and 2005) and *Metal Statistics* (1970, 1975, 1980, 1985, and 1995). The data sets from the various editions were compiled together to create a time series for metal consumption and production for period 1960–2005. In the case of steel, the data were compiled using the same method using The International Iron and Steel Institute's *Steel Statistical Yearbook* (1983, 1985, 1990, 1995, 2000, and 2004). Finally, data on iron ore mining are from the British Geological Survey's *World Mineral Statistics 1998/2002* (2004) and *World Mineral Production 2000–04* (2006).
- *Consumption of agricultural commodities.* Data on consumption of agricultural commodities are, generally, from the United States Department of Agriculture (USDA).[35] Data for bananas, cocoa, shrimp, and wool are from the Food and Agriculture Organization's FAOSTAT database.[36] Data are typically available for period 1960–2005.
- *Output measures.* Data on purchasing power parity (PPP)-adjusted real GDP are from the World Bank's 2006 *World Development Indicators* (WDI) for the period 1970–2004.[37] These data are expressed in constant 2000 purchasing power-adjusted dollars. Two databases were used to extend the coverage of WDI data: where available, data from the Organization for Economic Cooperation and Development's databases,[38] and otherwise, *World Economic Outlook* database. The industrial production data were gathered from Haver Analytics, Global Insight, and national statistical agencies. The share of industrial value added in GDP is from WDI.
- *Other variables.* Population data are from following three sources: WDI, *World Economic Outlook* database, and the United Nations' Population Information Network database.[39] The United States dollar to SDR exchange rate is from the IMF's *International Financial Statistics.*

Appendix 5.2. Modeling the Relationship Between Speculation and Commodity Prices

The authors of this appendix are Sergei Antoshin and Hossein Samiei.

This appendix describes the estimation procedure for the analysis in Box 5.1 and presents a detailed discussion of the results.

[33]See http://www.unctad.org/Templates/Page.asp?intItemID=1890&lang=1 for more information.

[34]See http://wits.worldbank.org for more information.

[35]See http://www.fas.usda.gov/psd for the data.

[36]See http://faostat.fao.org for the data.

[37]See http://www.worldbank.org/data, and follow the link for World Development Indicators for more information.

[38]See http://www.oecd.org/statistics for more information.

[39]See http://www.un.org/popin/ for the data.

Methodology

A Vector Error Correction Model (VECM) is used to test for causality, given that both spot and futures prices, and speculative positions contain unit roots. The VECM allows the examination of both short- and long-run causality: the former is determined by the significance of the coefficients on the first difference terms and the latter by the significance of the coefficient on the error-correction term when a long-run cointegrating relation in levels exists.[40] The following model is estimated:

$$\Delta y_t = \alpha(\beta' y_{t-1} + \mu + \rho t) + \sum_{i=1}^{L-1} \Gamma_i \Delta y_{t-i} + \gamma + \varepsilon_t ,$$

where $y_t = (s_t, f_t, n_t)'$; and s_t, f_t, and n_t are, respectively, the logarithms of spot and one-year ahead futures prices, and the level of net long noncommercial positions; cointegration rank is 1; the number of VAR lags L is 3; α is a 3×1 vector of adjustment coefficients; β is a 3×1 cointegrating vector; $\{\Gamma_i\}_{i=1}^{L-1}$ are 3×3 matrices of VAR coefficients; and t is a linear time trend.

We test the null hypothesis of speculative positions causing spot and futures prices.[41] Average weekly data (Tuesday to Monday) are used for commodity prices (from Bloomberg) and weekly data for speculative positions for every Tuesday (proxied by net noncommercial positions from the CFTC—defined as positions taken by investors who do not use futures contracts for the purpose of hedging). The estimation period is September 1995 to June 2006. The model is estimated using rolling regressions, using the window length of 4.5 years (234 weeks), as a reasonable duration for a business cycle and to cover the time length of the recent run-up in prices. Shorter windows were also tried and the results were qualitatively similar. The results were also quite robust to changes in the number of lags (from 3 to 12), the trend specification, and the assumed number of cointegrating equations (from 0 to 2). Finally, given that in the absence of cointegration the short-run causality tests may not be valid, we also estimated the models by focusing only on the relationship between first differences. The results on short-run causality did not change.

Estimation Results

We first discuss the results for crude oil, using charts of the rolling estimates of parameters and confidence bands—to illustrate what the raw results of the exercise may look like—and then present all the results in a simple and summary fashion.

Crude Oil

Figure 5.12 depicts the evolution of the long-run coefficients (left panels) and adjustment coefficients (right panels), and their confidence bands. The relationship is clearly unstable over time. However, the rolling values of the cointegration rank suggest that cointegration mostly exists, thus permitting the broad examination of long-run causality based on the significance of the adjustment coefficients. The results interestingly suggest that while the estimated adjustment coefficient in the speculative position equation is significantly different from zero for most of the period (zero lies mostly outside the 90 percent confidence band), the opposite is true for the spot and futures price equations. This means that when a long-run relationship holds, causality is from spot and futures prices to speculative positions.

The three panels in Figure 5.13 show the evolution of the short-run coefficients. Specifically, each figure shows the confidence bands around the estimates of the first or the second lag of the first difference of a variable in the equation for another. The results are surprisingly conclusive.

[40] More specifically, for any two variables x and y, y is said to cause x in the short run if Δy Granger-causes Δx—that is, given the past values of Δx, past values of Δy are useful in predicting Δx. Furthermore, if the adjustment coefficient in the equation for x is significant, then y is said to cause x in the long run.

[41] We do not carry out a joint test of significance for the first and second lags. Instead, we look at the p-values of individual coefficients and the explanatory power the equations (R^2). Note, however, that if one of the two lags is significant then they are likely significant jointly too.

Figure 5.12. Crude Oil: Rolling Estimates of the Model's Long-Run Parameters[1]

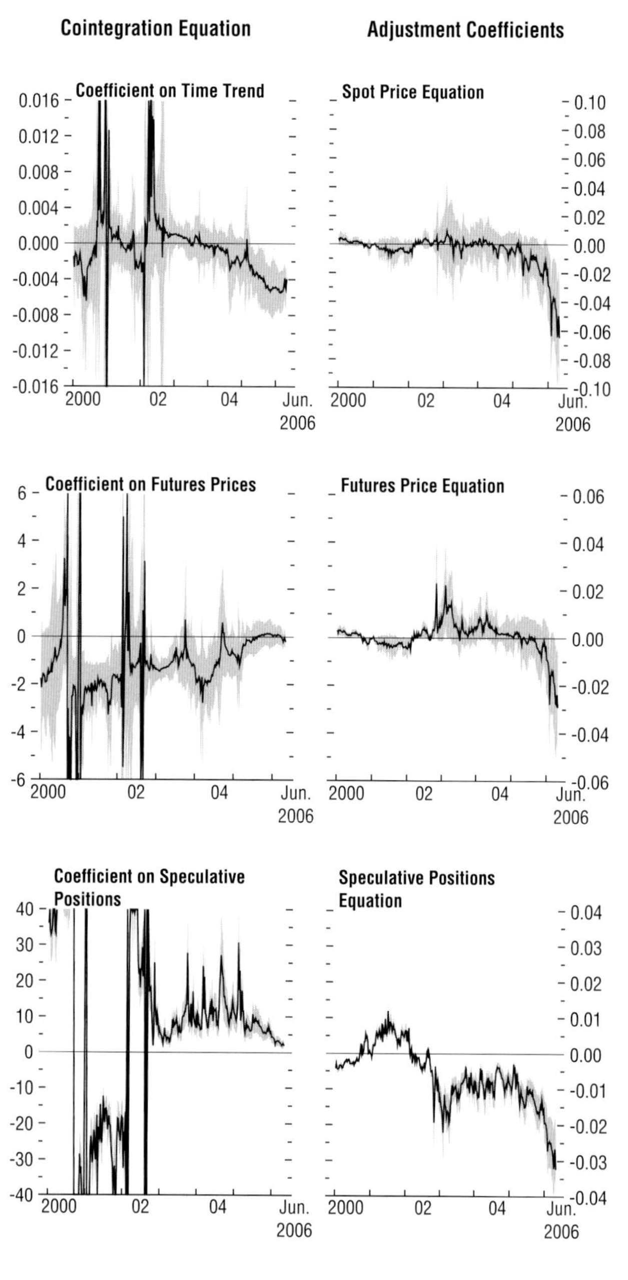

Source: IMF staff estimates.

[1]Blue areas are 90 percent confidence bands. The Vector Error Correction Model is estimated with cointegration rank = 1, number of lags = 3, and a restricted trend. The cointegrating vector is estimated with the coefficient on the spot price set equal to 1. Rolling window length is 234 weeks. Dates on the x-axis correspond to period ending dates.

Figure 5.13. Crude Oil: Rolling Estimates of the Model's Short-Run Parameters[1]

(Coefficients)

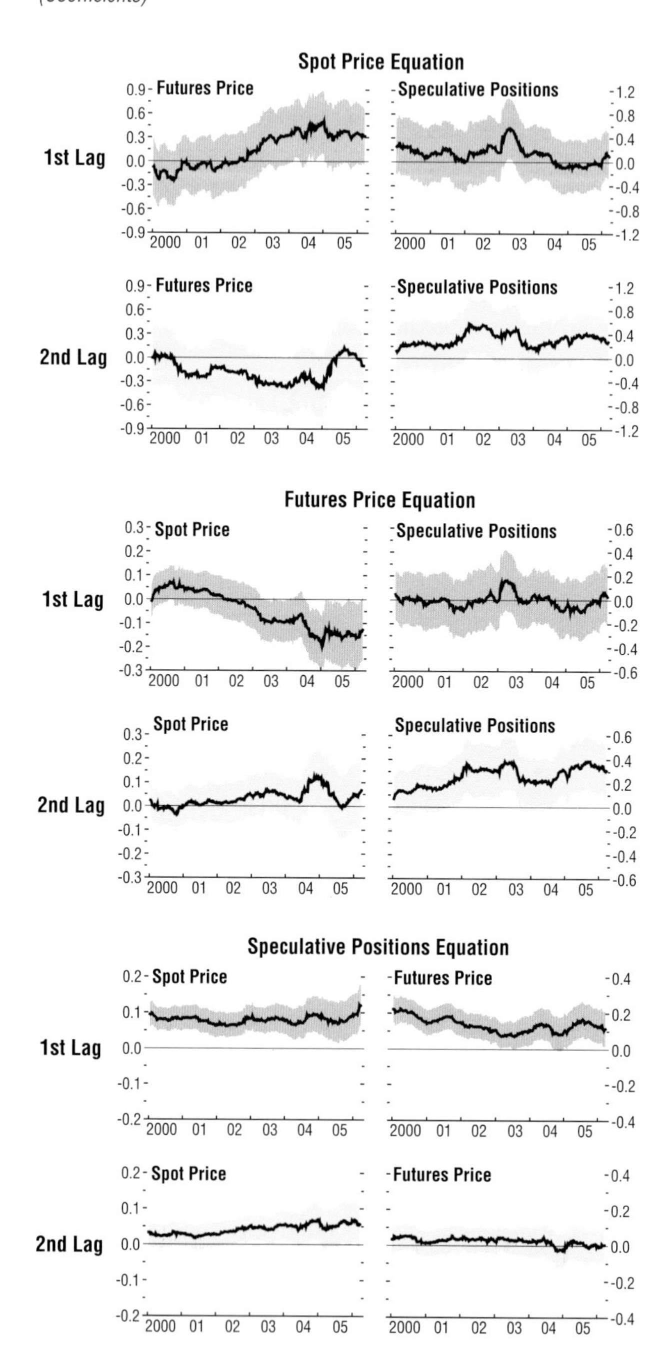

Source: IMF staff estimates.

[1]Shaded areas are 90 percent confidence bands. The Vector Error Correction Model is estimated with cointegration rank = 1, number of lags = 3, and a restricted trend. The cointegrating vector is estimated with the coefficient on the spot price set equal to 1. Rolling window length is 234 weeks. Dates on the x-axis correspond to period ending dates.

Table 5.11. Summary of the Results from Rolling Regressions

	Spot Price Equation	Futures Price Equation	Speculative Positions Equation
Crude Oil			
Short-run coefficients			
Spot price	. . .	Rarely significant	Always significant
Futures price	Rarely significant	. . .	Always significant
Speculative positions	Rarely significant	Mostly significant	. . .
Long-run coefficients			
Cointegrating relation		Mostly present; rarely stable	
Adjustment coefficients	Never significant	Rarely significant	Always significant
R-squared average	0.06	0.08	0.36
Copper			
Short-run coefficients			
Spot price	. . .	Never significant	Always significant
Futures price	Rarely significant	. . .	Mostly significant
Speculative positions	Rarely significant	Rarely significant	. . .
Long-run coefficients			
Cointegrating relation		Mostly present; rarely stable	
Adjustment coefficients	Never significant	Never significant	Always significant
R-squared average	0.11	0.10	0.66
Sugar			
Short-run coefficients			
Spot price	. . .	Rarely significant	Always significant
Futures price	Sometimes significant	. . .	Always significant
Speculative positions	Rarely significant	Rarely significant	. . .
Long-run coefficients			
Cointegrating relation		Mostly present; mostly stable	
Adjustment coefficients	Rarely significant	Never significant	Always significant
R-squared average	0.06	0.05	0.48
Coffee			
Short-run coefficients			
Spot price	. . .	Never significant	Always significant
Futures price	Rarely significant	. . .	Mostly significant
Speculative positions	Rarely significant	Rarely significant	. . .
Long-run coefficients			
Cointegrating relation		Mostly present; rarely stable	
Adjustment coefficients	Sometimes significant	Sometimes significant	Mostly significant
R-squared average	0.06	0.05	0.56
Cotton			
Short-run coefficients			
Spot price	. . .	Rarely significant	Always significant
Futures price	Never significant	. . .	Always significant
Speculative positions	Never significant	Never significant	. . .
Long-run coefficients			
Cointegrating relation		Mostly present; mostly stable	
Adjustment coefficients	Mostly significant	Rarely significant	Always significant
R-squared average	0.13	0.11	0.55

Source: IMF staff calculations.

In the equation for the spot price (top panel), neither lags of futures prices and speculative positions are significantly different from zero for any reasonable length of time (i.e., confidence bands almost always include zero). In the equation for futures prices (middle panel) the second lag of speculation is often significant, but other variables are not. The magnitude of the impact of speculation on futures prices, however, is very small. Finally, in the equation for speculative positions (bottom panel) the first lags of spot and futures prices are almost always significant. Furthermore, the R^2 for this relationship is 36 percent, compared with 6–8 percent for the other two equations.

Other Commodities

Having examined the results for crude oil in detail, this section summarizes and compares the results for all commodities (Table 5.11).

We call a variable significant in the short-run relationship for another if at least one of its lags is significant at 5 percent. We then describe in the table the frequency of observing significance using the following terms (with the degree of significance in percent terms in parentheses): always significant (above 90 percent), mostly significant (60–90 percent), sometimes significant (40–60 percent), rarely significant (10–40 percent), and never significant (below 10 percent). As for the long-run relationship, we report the frequency of cointegration, the stability of the relationship, and the significance of the adjustment coefficient (using the rule in the previous paragraph), as well as the average value of the R^2s of the regressions. The results are discussed in Box 5.1.

References

Australian Bureau of Agricultural and Resource Economics (ABARE), 2006, *Australian Commodities*, March, Vol. 13, No. 1 (Canberra).

Alcan, 2006, Presentation at the Alcan Bauxite & Alumina Group Investor Meetings, Tampa, Florida, February 27.

Alcoa, 2004, Presentation at the Alcoa's North American Primary Businesses Meeting, Rockdale, Texas, November 2.

Baffes, John, 2006, "Oil Spills Over to Other Commodities" (unpublished; Washington: World Bank).

Barclays Capital, 2006a, *The Commodity Refiner*, Q1 (New York).

———, 2006b, *Commodity Daily Briefings*, July 19, and August 23 and 29 (New York).

Barnett, Howard, and Chandler Morse, 1963, *Scarcity and Growth* (Baltimore: Johns Hopkins University Press for Resources for the Future).

Borensztein, Eduardo, Mohsin Khan, Carmen Reinhart, and Peter Wickham, 1994, *The Behavior of Non-Oil Commodity Prices*, IMF Occasional Paper No. 112 (Washington: International Monetary Fund).

Bowman, Chakriya, and Aasim Husain, 2004, "Forecasting Commodity Prices: Futures Versus Judgment," IMF Working Paper 04/41 (Washington: International Monetary Fund).

British Geological Survey, 2006, *World Mineral Production 2000–04* (London).

———, 2004, *World Mineral Statistics 1998/2002* (London).

Cashin, Paul, Hong Liang, and John McDermott, 2000, "How Persistent Are Shocks to World Commodity Prices?" *IMF Staff Papers*, International Monetary Fund, Vol. 47 (December), pp. 177–217.

Cashin, Paul, and John McDermott, 2002, "The Long-Run Behavior of Commodity Prices: Small Trends and Big Variability," *IMF Staff Papers*, International Monetary Fund, Vol. 49 (July), pp. 175–97.

———, and Alasdair Scott, 2002, "Booms and Slumps in World Commodity Prices," *Journal of Development Economics*, Vol. 69 (October), pp. 277–96.

Cuddington, John, 1992, "Long-Run Trends in 26 Primary Commodity Prices: A Disaggregated Look at the Prebisch-Singer Hypothesis," *Journal of Development Economics*, Vol. 39 (October), pp. 207–27.

Deaton, Angus, and Guy Laroque, 2003, "A Model of Commodity Prices After Sir Arthur Lewis," *Journal of Development Economics*, Vol. 71 (August), pp. 289–310.

Dehn, Jan, Christopher Gilbert, and Panos Varangis, 2005, "Agricultural Commodity Price Volatility," in *Managing Economic Volatility and Crises*, ed. by Joshua Aizenman and Brian Pinto (Cambridge: Cambridge University Press).

Deutsche Bank, 2006, *Commodities Weekly*, May 5 (New York).

Food and Agriculture Organization (FAO), 2004a, *Cotton: Impact of Support Policies on Developing Countries*, Trade Policy Brief (Rome: Food and Agriculture Organization).

———, 2004b, *The State of Agricultural Commodity Markets* (Rome: Food and Agriculture Organization).

Gately, Dermot, 2004, "OPEC's Incentives for Faster Output Growth," *Energy Journal*, Vol. 25, No. 2, pp. 75–96.

Ghosh, S., Christopher L. Gilbert, and Andrew J. Hughes Hallett, 1987, *Stabilizing Speculative Commodity Markets* (New York: Oxford University Press).

Gilbert, Christopher, 2006, "Trends and Volatility in Agricultural Commodity Markets," in *Agricultural Commodity Markets and Trade: New Approaches to Analyzing Market Structure and Instability*, ed. by Alexander Sarris and David Hallam (Cheltenham: Food and Agriculture Organization and Edward Elgar), pp. 31–60.

———, 1996, "International Commodity Agreements: An Obituary Notice," *World Development*, Vol. 24 (January), pp. l–19.

———, 1995, "Modelling Market Fundamentals: A Model of the Aluminium Market," *Journal of Applied Econometrics*, Vol. 10, No. 4, pp. 385–410.

Grilli, Enzo, and Maw Cheng Yang, 1988, "Primary Commodity Prices, Manufactured Goods Prices, and the Terms of Trade of Developing Countries: What the Long Run Shows," *The World Bank Economic Review*, Vol. 2, No. 1, pp. 1–47.

Haigh, Michael S., Jana Hranaiova, and James Overdahl, 2005, "Price Volatility, Liquidity Provision, and the Role of Managed Money Traders in Energy Futures Markets" (unpublished; Washington: Commodity Futures Trading Comission).

International Energy Agency, 2004, *World Energy Outlook* (Paris).

International Iron and Steel Institute, *Steel Statistical Yearbook*, various issues (Brussels: The Committee on Statistics).

International Monetary Fund, 2006, *International Financial Statistics*, various issues (Washington).

Mitchell, Donald, and Mombert Hoppe, 2006, "From Marrakesh to Doha: Effects of Removing Food Subsidies on the Poor," in *Trade, Doha, and Development: A Window Into the Issues*, ed. by Richard Newfarmer (Washington: World Bank).

Organization for Economic Cooperation and Development, 2005, *Agricultural Policies in OECD Countries: Monitoring and Evaluation* (Paris).

Prebisch, Raúl, 1950, *The Economic Development of Latin America and Its Principal Problems* (New York: United Nations).

Robertson, D., and J. Symons, 1992, "Some Strange Properties of Panel Data Estimators," *Journal of Applied Econometrics*, Vol. 7 (April–June), pp. 175–89.

Sanders, Dwight R., Keith Boris, and Mark Manfredo, 2004, "Hedgers, Funds, and Small Speculators in the Energy Futures Markets: an Analysis of the CFTC's Commitments of Traders Reports," *Energy Economics*, Vol. 26, (May), pp. 425–45.

Societe Generale, 2006, "Bubble About to Burst," June 8 (Paris).

Tilton, John, 2003, *On Borrowed Time? Assessing the Threat of Mineral Depletion* (Washington: Resources for the Future).

Tyers, Rodney, and Kym Anderson, 1992, *Disarray in World Food Markets* (Cambridge: Cambridge University Press).

UNCTAD, 2005, *Handbook of Statistics 2005* (New York: United Nations).

World Bank, 2006, *World Development Indicators* (Washington).

World Bureau of Metal Statistics, *World Metal Statistics Yearbook*, various issues (London).

———, *Metal Statistics*, various issues (London).

ANNEX IMF EXECUTIVE BOARD DISCUSSION OF THE OUTLOOK, AUGUST 2006

The following remarks by the Acting Chair were made at the conclusion of the Executive Board's discussion of the World Economic Outlook *on August 23, 2006.*

Executive Directors welcomed the continued strong, broad-based global expansion. They noted that during the first half of 2006, activity in most regions met or exceeded expectations. Among the advanced economies, growth was particularly strong in the United States in the first quarter, activity in the euro area gathered momentum, and the expansion in Japan remained on track. Directors were pleased that growth performance in emerging market and other developing countries remained robust despite more testing conditions in global financial markets.

Looking forward, Directors considered that the strong global expansion is likely to continue in 2007, with a better balanced composition of demand across the major advanced economies. Directors saw some upside potential to the outlook from even more rapid growth in emerging market economies, notably China, and the possibility of stronger-than-expected investment in a number of advanced economies. Overall, however, Directors felt that the risks to the forecast are clearly tilted to the downside, with the weight of such risks having risen compared to the *World Economic Outlook* in April 2006.

Directors identified a number of downside risks facing the global economy going forward. These include the possibility that a continued buildup of inflationary pressures in advanced economies might require a more aggressive monetary policy response; the continued potential for supply-side shocks in the oil and nonfuel commodity markets; the risk of a more abrupt slowdown in housing markets in advanced economies, notably the United States; and the possibility of weaker-than-expected growth in private consumption in Europe and Japan, due to slow productivity growth and labor market rigidities. Directors believed that a smooth, market-led unwinding of the large global imbalances remains the most likely outcome, but that the risk of a more disorderly resolution of these imbalances cannot be ruled out.

Advanced Economies

Directors noted that the pace of expansion in the United States has moderated after exceptionally strong growth in the first quarter of 2006. Risks to the outlook appear to be slanted to the downside, with a more abrupt cooling of the housing market being a particular concern. Directors observed that the Federal Reserve is faced by the difficult situation of rising core inflation and inflation expectations in the context of a slowing economy. In light of this, the policy stance going forward should depend on the evolving balance between the competing risks to growth and inflation; given the importance of keeping inflation expectations in check, further interest rate increases should not be ruled out. The better-than-expected fiscal performance in FY2006 is encouraging, although the permanence of the recent unexpected revenue buoyancy is not yet established. Directors welcomed the authorities' intention to halve the Federal deficit a year ahead of schedule, by FY2008, while observing that a more ambitious deficit reduction path would provide a firmer basis for the United States to face future demographic pressures, put the budget in a stronger position to respond to future economic downturns, and help reduce global imbalances.

Action to ensure fiscal sustainability should include measures to contain growth in entitlement spending, notably Social Security and Medicare/Medicaid.

Directors welcomed the acceleration in real GDP growth in the euro area in the first half of the year, and noted that prospects for a sustained, more robust, expansion have consolidated. They considered the risks to the outlook to be broadly balanced, with the upside potential arising from strong corporate positions offsetting the downside risks related to higher energy prices, elevated house prices in a number of countries, and the possibility of a sharp appreciation of the euro against the background of the large global imbalances. Directors anticipated a need for some further monetary policy tightening in the euro area if the expansion develops as expected but felt that—with inflation pressures broadly contained for now—interest rate increases could be gradual, especially in view of the downside risks. Directors emphasized that, given the importance of ensuring that the current cyclical upswing is translated into a sustained and long-lasting expansion, priority should be given to further reforms to promote greater competition in goods and service markets, more flexible labor markets, and increased cross-border financial sector integration. The need for further reductions in fiscal deficits was also underscored. Directors stressed that the credibility of medium-term budget targets would be strengthened by welfare, pension, and healthcare reforms, as well as reductions in the government wage bill that would provide much needed room to cut taxes on labor.

Directors welcomed the ongoing expansion in Japan, noting that final domestic demand is being supported by buoyant investment underpinned by robust profits and a turnaround in bank credit. They viewed the normalization of monetary policy as the key near-term macroeconomic policy challenge. They considered that—with the risk of accelerating inflation low and the costs of a reemergence of deflation high—further interest rate increases should be gradual. Directors underscored that further substantial fiscal adjustment is needed to ensure sustainable public finances and meet pressures from an aging population. Given this, while current budget plans aim to eliminate the primary deficit by 2011, some additional adjustment would be warranted to stabilize net government debt by the end of this period.

Directors welcomed staff's analysis of how differences across financial systems might affect economic cycles in advanced countries, while emphasizing that the findings should be seen as tentative. Directors broadly agreed that the recent trend away from bank- and relationship-based systems toward more arm's length financial systems, where securities markets play a greater role, is likely to continue given technological innovations and the removal of regulatory barriers. At the same time, they noted that important differences in financial systems across countries remain. They concurred that in more arm's length systems, households may be able to better smooth consumption in response to changes in income, but that their spending may be more sensitive to changes in asset prices. Corporate investment appears to react more smoothly to cyclical downturns in relationship-based systems, but arm's length systems seem better at reallocating resources in response to structural changes. They emphasized that supervisory and regulatory policies will need to keep up with the changes, while macroeconomic policy management will need to adapt to variations in cyclical behavior.

Emerging Market and Other Developing Countries

Directors agreed that the most immediate policy priority for emerging market and developing economies is the continued implementation of policies to reduce vulnerabilities and sustain the current strong growth momentum. They noted that emerging market economies remain susceptible to rising interest rates and reduced liquidity in global financial markets. Countries at risk include those with weak public sector balance sheets, large current account deficits, and less well anchored inflation expectations. In this regard, Directors viewed the increasing reliance by a number of emerging European countries on private debt flows to finance large current account deficits as a source of concern. They also emphasized that emerging market and developing economies should continue to advance market-oriented reforms, particularly by reducing barriers to competition, in order to create the climate for vigorous private sector-led growth.

Directors observed that sharply rising prices of nonfuel commodities, particularly metals, had underpinned strong growth in many emerging market and other developing countries. Most Directors noted staff findings that speculative activity had not been a significant driver leading commodity price movements. Looking forward, Directors advised that current revenue windfalls should be saved or invested to support future growth in noncommodity sectors, rather than be used to increase spending in areas that would be difficult to reverse later.

Directors welcomed the strong growth performance of the economies in emerging Asia, noting that much of the momentum is due to vibrant expansions in China and India. Nevertheless, some Directors expressed concern that the exceptionally rapid growth in fixed investment in China could lead to overheating of the economy and a boom-bust cycle. While most countries have succeeded in restraining core inflation with quite small increases in nominal policy rates, Directors noted the need to stand ready to increase policy rates further, if needed. Directors observed that, while increased exchange rate flexibility in some countries had helped to achieve a better balance between domestically and externally led growth, China's current account surplus continued to rise in 2005 and the first half of 2006. Most Directors called for greater flexibility of the renminbi, which would help to relieve overheating concerns and encourage a more balanced composition of demand. The move toward greater exchange rate flexibility should be supported by a continuation of complementary financial sector reforms, which, together with reforms to the pension, health, and education systems, would also help to foster a shift toward consumption.

Directors broadly agreed that the remarkable growth performance of many countries in Asia holds important lessons for less advanced developing countries. They welcomed staff's analysis of growth in Asia, and concurred with the finding that the favorable policy environment in the region has been the key to strong total factor productivity growth and rapid accumulation of physical and human capital. Directors considered that prospects for sustaining strong growth in Asia in the future will be strengthened by continued progress in trade liberalization, improving access to education, and steps to promote financial development and encourage entrepreneurship. These would facilitate the ongoing shift of resources out of agriculture and into industry and services. Efforts to boost productivity growth and increase competition in industry, and particularly the relatively more sheltered services sector, will also pay important dividends.

The economic expansion in Latin America gathered momentum in the first half of this year, underpinned by high prices for key commodities, declining interest rates, and a pick up in public spending, while inflation largely remained subdued. Directors expressed satisfaction that the region's expansionary momentum was largely unaffected by the increased financial market volatility during the spring of 2006, as higher reserve cushions, more flexible exchange rate management, and improved fiscal indicators reduced vulnerabilities. Nevertheless, they advised countries in the region to continue preparing for the possibility of more testing financial market conditions, with disciplined fiscal policy at the core of such efforts. Directors noted that the region remains the slowest growing among the emerging market and developing countries, and emphasized the importance of unlocking Latin America's growth potential. This will depend on extending market-based reforms, while taking steps to ensure that benefits of growth are broadly shared.

The economic expansion remains robust in emerging Europe, mainly driven by buoyant domestic demand, underpinned by increasing net capital inflows and credit growth. Directors expected continued solid growth in the region but were concerned by the heavy reliance on foreign savings and the substantial fraction of bank lending that is in foreign currency, while recognizing that generally large current account deficits reflect, in part, favorable investment opportunities in the context of EU accession and integration. Against this background, they agreed that growth opportunities provided by foreign savings must be carefully balanced against risks, and that reducing vulnerabilities is a broad priority in the region. With most countries in the region aiming for euro adoption in the medium term, adequate preparation is needed for the loss of monetary policy autonomy and to establish the capacity to achieve external adjustment in the absence of nominal exchange rate flexibility.

Directors observed that activity in the Commonwealth of Independent States has been buoyant, given high commodity prices and support from capital inflows, and that growth prospects are generally positive. Directors noted that care should be taken to avoid undue further increases in consumption and to preserve competitiveness. Inflationary pressures might become entrenched, particularly in countries with limited possibilities for sterilization. Directors suggested that the real effective appreciation would better be achieved by allowing the nominal exchange rate to appreciate. They also stressed the importance of structural reforms to improve the investment climate and avoid the emergence or aggravation of supply bottlenecks.

Directors welcomed sub-Saharan Africa's strongest economic expansion since the early 1970s. While growth is expected to remain high, the persistence of elevated oil prices could have a detrimental impact on growth in oil-importing countries, particularly if combined with a sharp decline in non-oil commodity prices. Against such risks, the challenge is to continue adjusting to high oil prices, including by passing on increases in international oil prices to domestic energy prices. Directors emphasized that sub-Saharan Africa's growth performance, while improved, still falls short of the 7 percent annual growth needed to meet the Millennium Development Goal of halving poverty by 2015. Continued support from the international community, including through debt relief, making good on recent commitments to further boost aid, and bold market opening initiatives, will accordingly be crucial to promoting private sector investment and employment.

Oil revenues in the Middle East rose further in the first half of 2006, and oil-exporting countries continued to enjoy robust growth, combined with rising external current account and fiscal surpluses. Looking forward, Directors expected the outlook for the region to remain favorable, given prospects for high oil prices, although geopolitical risks remain a concern. Directors observed that most oil exporting countries have appropriately begun to use the opportunity provided by higher revenues to increase spending to address long-standing structural problems. They felt that, at the current juncture, there is scope for this buildup of spending, given high unemployment in many countries and still low inflation. Nevertheless, they cautioned that with credit growing rapidly, the risks of overheating need to be carefully monitored, and underscored that higher expenditures should be accompanied by determined efforts at capacity-enhancing reforms to ensure the proper use of funds and lasting supply-side benefits. Directors emphasized that policymakers throughout the region should be mindful of prudential risks in the financial sector, given rapid credit growth, rising financial sector exposure to asset price corrections, and a possible deterioration in credit quality.

Multilateral Issues

Against the background of important downside risks to the global outlook, Directors underscored that policymakers across the world share a responsibility for maintaining the foundations for strong global growth. In this regard, they emphasized that the risks of a disorderly adjustment of the existing large global imbalances will be considerably reduced by sustained policy actions across the major economies, particularly steps to boost national saving in the United States, including through fiscal consolidation; greater progress on structural reforms in Europe and Japan; reforms to boost domestic demand in emerging Asia (consumption in China, investment elsewhere) together with greater exchange rate flexibility; and increased spending in oil-producing countries, particularly in the Middle East where a large buildup is already in train, consistent with absorptive capacity constraints and cyclical considerations. Directors noted that a multilateral approach will enhance the prospect that possible risks associated with individual actions will be alleviated by simultaneous policy initiatives elsewhere. In this respect, Directors considered that the present multilateral consultation by the Fund could contribute to this process.

Directors expressed disappointment about the apparent deadlock in the Doha Round, and emphasized that trade liberalization on a nondiscriminatory basis remains the best way to open up new global growth opportunities. The threat of protectionist pressures will need to be firmly resisted, with all member countries stepping up efforts to reinvigorate the process of multilateral trade liberalization. Directors considered that high and volatile prices in world energy markets remain a major concern that will require sustained efforts from all sides to address. Increased investment is needed to build up adequate production and refining capacity, while appropriate incentives for consumers would encourage improved energy conservation.

STATISTICAL APPENDIX

The statistical appendix presents historical data, as well as projections. It comprises five sections: Assumptions, What's New, Data and Conventions, Classification of Countries, and Statistical Tables.

The assumptions underlying the estimates and projections for 2006–07 and the medium-term scenario for 2008–11 are summarized in the first section. The second section presents a brief description of changes to the database and statistical tables. The third section provides a general description of the data, and of the conventions used for calculating country group composites. The classification of countries in the various groups presented in the *World Economic Outlook* is summarized in the fourth section.

The last, and main, section comprises the statistical tables. Data in these tables have been compiled on the basis of information available through end-August 2006. The figures for 2006 and beyond are shown with the same degree of precision as the historical figures solely for convenience; since they are projections, the same degree of accuracy is not to be inferred.

Assumptions

Real effective *exchange rates* for the advanced economies are assumed to remain constant at their average levels during the period July 5 to August 2, 2006. For 2006 and 2007, these assumptions imply average U.S. dollar/SDR conversion rates of 1.468 and 1.485, U.S. dollar/euro conversion rate of 1.25 and 1.28, and yen/U.S. dollar conversion rates of 115.6 and 115.1, respectively.

It is assumed that the *price of oil* will average $69.20 a barrel in 2006 and $75.50 a barrel in 2007.

Established *policies* of national authorities are assumed to be maintained. The more specific policy assumptions underlying the projections for selected advanced economies are described in Box A1.

With regard to *interest rates,* it is assumed that the London interbank offered rate (LIBOR) on six-month U.S. dollar deposits will average 5.4 percent in 2006 and 5.5 percent in 2007, that three-month euro deposits will average 3.1 percent in 2006 and 3.7 percent in 2007, and that six-month Japanese yen deposits will average 0.5 percent in 2006 and 1.1 percent in 2007.

With respect to *introduction of the euro,* on December 31, 1998, the Council of the European Union decided that, effective January 1, 1999, the irrevocably fixed conversion rates between the euro and currencies of the member states adopting the euro are as follows.

1 euro	=	13.7603	Austrian schillings
	=	40.3399	Belgian francs
	=	1.95583	Deutsche mark
	=	5.94573	Finnish markkaa
	=	6.55957	French francs
	=	340.750	Greek drachma[1]
	=	0.787564	Irish pound
	=	1,936.27	Italian lire
	=	40.3399	Luxembourg francs
	=	2.20371	Netherlands guilders
	=	200.482	Portuguese escudos
	=	166.386	Spanish pesetas

See Box 5.4 in the October 1998 *World Economic Outlook* for details on how the conversion rates were established.

What's New

Following the declaration of independence from Serbia by Montenegro, it has been determined that Serbia is the continuing state of the former state union of "Serbia and Montenegro"

[1]The conversion rate for Greece was established prior to inclusion in the euro area on January 1, 2001.

Box A1. Economic Policy Assumptions Underlying the Projections for Selected Advanced Economies

The short-term ***fiscal policy assumptions*** used in the *World Economic Outlook* are based on officially announced budgets, adjusted for differences between the national authorities and the IMF staff regarding macroeconomic assumptions and projected fiscal outturns. The medium-term fiscal projections incorporate policy measures that are judged likely to be implemented. In cases where the IMF staff has insufficient information to assess the authorities' budget intentions and prospects for policy implementation, an unchanged structural primary balance is assumed, unless otherwise indicated. Specific assumptions used in some of the advanced economies follow (see also Tables 12–14 in the Statistical Appendix for data on fiscal and structural balances).[1]

United States. The fiscal projections are based on the Administration's FY2007 mid-session review (July 11, 2006), adjusted to take into account differences in macroeconomic projections as well as staff assumptions about (1) additional defense spending based on analysis by the Congressional Budget Office; (2) slower compression in the growth rate of discretionary spending; and (3) continued AMT relief beyond FY2007. The projections also assume that personal retirement accounts are not introduced.

Japan. The medium-term fiscal projections assume that expenditure and revenue of the general government (excluding social security) are adjusted in line with the current government target to achieve primary fiscal balance by the early 2010s.

Germany. For 2006–2011, the projections reflect the measures announced in the new government's coalition agreement. These aim to reduce the overall fiscal balance to below 3 percent of GDP in 2007. Projections do not include health care financing or corporate tax reforms because of the lack of specific information about their content.

France. The projections for 2006 are based on the initial budget adjusted for the IMF staff's macroeconomic assumptions. For 2007–09, the projections are based on the 2007–09 Stability Program Update, adjusted for the IMF staff's macroeconomic assumptions and different assumptions about nontax revenue and spending growth (less deceleration). For 2010–11, the IMF staff assumes unchanged tax policies and real expenditure growth as in the 2009 projection.

Italy. Fiscal projections from 2007 assume a constant primary structural balance net of one-off measures. They include the estimated structural impact of the correction package announced on June 30, 2006.

United Kingdom. The fiscal projections are based on information provided in the 2006 Budget Report. Additionally, the projections incorporate the most recent statistical releases from the Office for National Statistics, including provisional budgetary outturns through 2006:Q1.

Canada. Projections are based on the 2006 Budget and IMF staff estimates, and incorporate the most recent data releases from the Statistics Canada, including provincial and territorial budgetary outturns through 2006Q1.

Australia. The fiscal projections through the fiscal year 2010/11 are based on the 2006–07 budget published in May 2006. For the remainder of the projection period, the IMF staff assumes unchanged policies.

Austria. Fiscal figures for 2005 are based on the authorities' estimated outturn. Projections for 2006 are based on this year's budget. Projections for 2007–08 are based on the Austrian Stability Program. For 2009–11, projections assume the same overall and structural balances as in 2008.

[1]The output gap is actual less potential output, as a percent of potential output. Structural balances are expressed as a percent of potential output. The structural budget balance is the budgetary position that would be observed if the level of actual output coincided with potential output. Changes in the structural budget balance consequently include effects of temporary fiscal measures, the impact of fluctuations in interest rates and debt-service costs, and other noncyclical fluctuations in the budget balance. The computations of structural budget balances are based on IMF staff estimates of potential GDP and revenue and expenditure elasticities (see the October 1993 *World Economic Outlook*, Annex I). Net debt is defined as gross debt less financial assets of the general government, which include assets held by the social security insurance system. Estimates of the output gap and of the structural balance are subject to significant margins of uncertainty.

Belgium. The projections for 2006 are based on the 2006 budget, adjusted for the IMF staff's macroeconomic assumptions and an assumed lower yield of some specific revenues. For 2007–11, the projections assume unchanged tax policies and real primary expenditure growth as in the recent past.

Denmark. Projections for 2006 are aligned with the latest official projections and budget, adjusted for the IMF staff's macroeconomic assumptions. For 2007–11, the projections incorporate the June 2006 welfare agreement as well as key features of the prior medium-term fiscal plan. The projections imply continued budget surpluses in line with the authorities' objectives of long-term fiscal sustainability and debt reduction.

Greece. Projections are based on the 2006 budget, adjusted for IMF staff's assumptions for economic growth. For 2007 and beyond, tax revenues as a percent of GDP are assumed to be constant, while social insurance contributions are assumed to continue their trend increase and EU transfers are assumed to decline. Total expenditure is assumed to remain broadly constant as a percent of GDP.

Hong Kong SAR. The fiscal projections are based on the authorities' medium-term fiscal consolidation strategy that was announced in October 2003.

Korea. Projections for 2006 are based on the authorities' budget, with some adjustment for IMF staff assumptions. For 2007–11, projections are in line with the authorities' budget plans.

Netherlands. The fiscal projections build on the 2006 budget, the latest Stability Program, and other forecasts provided by the authorities, adjusted for the IMF staff's macroeconomic assumptions.

New Zealand. The fiscal projections through the fiscal year 2009/10 are based on the 2006/07 budget of May 2006. For the remainder of the projection period, the IMF staff assumes unchanged policies.

Portugal. Fiscal projections for 2006 build on the authorities' budget. Projections for 2007 and beyond are based on the current Stability and Growth Program of the authorities.

Singapore. For the 2006/07 fiscal year, budget projections on the expenditure side are mostly based on the authorities' budget and fiscal projections, while revenues grow in line with economic activity. Thereafter, the projections assume a constant budget balance (in percent of GDP).

Spain. Fiscal projections through 2008 are based on the policies outlined in the authorities' updated Stability Program of June 2006, adjusted for the IMF staff's macroeconomic assumptions, information from recent statistical releases, and official announcements. In subsequent years, the fiscal projections assume unchanged policies.

Sweden. The fiscal projections are based on information provided in the budget presented on April 18, 2006. Additionally, the projections incorporate the most recent statistical releases from Statistics Sweden, including provisional budgetary outturns through December 2005.

Switzerland. Estimates for 2005 and projections for 2006–11 are based on IMF staff calculations, which incorporate measures to restore balance in the Federal accounts and strengthen social security finances.

Monetary policy assumptions are based on the established policy framework in each country. In most cases, this implies a nonaccommodative stance over the business cycle: official interest rates will therefore increase when economic indicators suggest that prospective inflation will rise above its acceptable rate or range, and they will decrease when indicators suggest that prospective inflation will not exceed the acceptable rate or range, that prospective output growth is below its potential rate, and that the margin of slack in the economy is significant. On this basis, the LIBOR on six-month U.S. dollar deposits is assumed to average 5.4 percent in 2006 and 5.5 percent in 2007. The projected path for U.S. dollar short-term interest rates reflects the assumption implicit in prevailing forward rates. The rate on three-month euro deposits is assumed to average 3.1 percent in 2006 and 3.7 percent in 2007. The interest rate on six-month Japanese yen deposits is assumed to average 0.5 percent in 2006 and 1.1 percent in 2007. Changes in interest rate assumptions compared with the April 2006 *World Economic Outlook* are summarized in Table 1.1

and that Montenegro has seceded as a new independent state; and data for Liberia are now included in the appendix tables for real GDP, consumer prices, and payments balances on current account.

Data and Conventions

Data and projections for 183 countries form the statistical basis for the *World Economic Outlook* (the World Economic Outlook database). The data are maintained jointly by the IMF's Research Department and area departments, with the latter regularly updating country projections based on consistent global assumptions.

Although national statistical agencies are the ultimate providers of historical data and definitions, international organizations are also involved in statistical issues, with the objective of harmonizing methodologies for the national compilation of statistics, including the analytical frameworks, concepts, definitions, classifications, and valuation procedures used in the production of economic statistics. The World Economic Outlook database reflects information from both national source agencies and international organizations.

The comprehensive revision of the standardized *System of National Accounts 1993 (SNA),* the IMF's *Balance of Payments Manual, Fifth Edition (BPM5), the Monetary and Financial Statistics Manual (MFSM),* and the *Government Finance Statistics Manual 2001 (GFSM 2001)* represented important improvements in the standards of economic statistics and analysis.[2] The IMF was actively involved in all these projects, particularly the *Balance of Payments, Monetary and Financial Statistics,* and *Government Finance Statistics* manuals, which reflects the IMF's special interest in countries' external positions, financial sector stability, and public sector fiscal positions. The process of adapting country data to the new definitions began in earnest when the manuals were released. However, full concordance with the manuals is ultimately dependent on the provision by national statistical compilers of revised country data, and hence the *World Economic Outlook* estimates are still only partially adapted to these manuals.

In line with recent improvements in standards of reporting economic statistics, several countries have phased out their traditional *fixed-base-year* method of calculating real macroeconomic variables levels and growth by switching to a *chain-weighted* method of computing aggregate growth. Recent dramatic changes in the structure of these economies have obliged these countries to revise the way in which they measure real GDP levels and growth. Switching to the chain-weighted method of computing aggregate growth, which uses current price information, allows countries to measure GDP growth more accurately by eliminating upward biases in new data.[3] Currently, real macroeconomic data for Albania, Australia, Austria, Azerbaijan, Canada, Czech Republic, Denmark, euro area, Finland, Georgia, Germany, Greece, Iceland, Ireland, Italy, Japan, Kazakhstan, Lithuania, Luxembourg, the Netherlands, New Zealand, Norway, Portugal, Russia, Slovenia, Spain, Sweden, Switzerland, the United Kingdom, and the United States are based on chain-weighted methodology. However, data before 1996 (Albania), 1995 (Czech Republic), 1990 (Denmark), 1995 (euro area), 1991 (Germany), 1995 (Greece), 1990 (Iceland), 1994 (Japan), 1995 (Luxembourg), 1995 (Russia), 1995 (Slovenia), and 1995 (Spain) are based on unrevised national accounts and subject to revision in the future.

The members of the European Union have adopted a harmonized system for the compila-

[2]Commission of the European Communities, International Monetary Fund, Organization for Economic Cooperation and Development, United Nations, and World Bank, *System of National Accounts 1993* (Brussels/Luxembourg, New York, Paris, and Washington, 1993); International Monetary Fund, *Balance of Payments Manual,* Fifth Edition (Washington, 1993); International Monetary Fund, *Monetary and Financial Statistics Manual* (Washington, 2000); and International Monetary Fund, *Government Finance Statistics Manual* (Washington, 2001).

[3]Charles Steindel, 1995, "Chain-Weighting: The New Approach to Measuring GDP," Current Issues in Economics and Finance (Federal Reserve Bank of New York), Vol. 1 (December).

tion of the national accounts, referred to as ESA 1995. All national accounts data from 1995 onward are presented on the basis of the new system. Revision by national authorities of data prior to 1995 to conform to the new system has progressed, but has in some cases not been completed. In such cases, historical *World Economic Outlook* data have been carefully adjusted to avoid breaks in the series. Users of EU national accounts data prior to 1995 should nevertheless exercise caution until such time as the revision of historical data by national statistical agencies has been fully completed. See Box 1.2, "Revisions in National Accounts Methodologies," in the May 2000 *World Economic Outlook*.

Composite data for country groups in the *World Economic Outlook* are either sums or weighted averages of data for individual countries. Unless otherwise indicated, multiyear averages of growth rates are expressed as compound annual rates of change.[4] Arithmetically weighted averages are used for all data except inflation and money growth for the other emerging market and developing country group, for which geometric averages are used. The following conventions apply.

- Country group composites for exchange rates, interest rates, and the growth rates of monetary aggregates are weighted by GDP converted to U.S. dollars at market exchange rates (averaged over the preceding three years) as a share of group GDP.
- Composites for other data relating to the domestic economy, whether growth rates or ratios, are weighted by GDP valued at purchasing power parities (PPPs) as a share of total world or group GDP.[5]
- Composites for data relating to the domestic economy for the euro area (12 member countries throughout the entire period unless otherwise noted) are aggregates of national source data using weights based on 1995 ECU exchange rates.
- Composite unemployment rates and employment growth are weighted by labor force as a share of group labor force.
- Composites relating to the external economy are sums of individual country data after conversion to U.S. dollars at the average market exchange rates in the years indicated for balance of payments data and at end-of-year market exchange rates for debt denominated in currencies other than U.S. dollars. Composites of changes in foreign trade volumes and prices, however, are arithmetic averages of percentage changes for individual countries weighted by the U.S. dollar value of exports or imports as a share of total world or group exports or imports (in the preceding year).

For central and eastern European countries, external transactions in nonconvertible currencies (through 1990) are converted to U.S. dollars at the implicit U.S. dollar/ruble conversion rates obtained from each country's national currency exchange rate for the U.S. dollar and for the ruble.

All data refer to calendar years, except for the following countries, which refer to fiscal years: Australia (July/June); Bangladesh (July/June); Egypt (July/June); Iran, I.R. of (March/February); Mauritius (July/June); Myanmar (April/March); Nepal (July/June); Netherlands Antilles (February/January); New Zealand (July/June); Pakistan (July/June); Samoa (July/June); and Tonga (July/June).

Classification of Countries

Summary of the Country Classification

The country classification in the *World Economic Outlook* divides the world into two major groups: advanced economies, and other

[4]Averages for real GDP and its components, employment, per capita GDP, inflation, factor productivity, trades, and commodity prices are calculated based on compound annual rate of change except for the unemployment rate, which is based on simple arithmetic average.

[5]See Box A2 of the April 2004 *World Economic Outlook* for a summary of the revised PPP-based weights and Annex IV of the May 1993 *World Economic Outlook*. See also Anne-Marie Gulde and Marianne Schulze-Ghattas, "Purchasing Power Parity Based Weights for the *World Economic Outlook*," in *Staff Studies for the World Economic Outlook* (International Monetary Fund, December 1993), pp. 106–23.

Table A. Classification by World Economic Outlook Groups and Their Shares in Aggregate GDP, Exports of Goods and Services, and Population, 2005[1]

(Percent of total for group or world)

	Number of Countries	GDP		Exports of Goods and Services		Population	
		Advanced economies	World	Advanced economies	World	Advanced economies	World
Advanced economies	**29**	**100.0**	**52.3**	**100.0**	**69.1**	**100.0**	**15.3**
United States		38.4	20.1	14.5	10.1	30.6	4.7
Euro area	12	28.3	14.8	42.9	29.7	32.1	4.9
Germany		7.9	4.1	12.9	8.9	8.5	1.3
France		5.7	3.0	6.3	4.4	6.5	1.0
Italy		5.2	2.7	5.3	3.7	6.0	0.9
Spain		3.4	1.8	3.3	2.3	4.3	0.7
Japan		12.2	6.4	7.7	5.3	13.2	2.0
United Kingdom		5.7	3.0	6.7	4.6	6.2	0.9
Canada		3.5	1.8	4.9	3.4	3.3	0.5
Other advanced economies	13	11.9	6.2	23.3	16.1	14.6	2.2
Memorandum							
Major advanced economies	7	78.7	41.2	58.4	40.4	74.3	11.4
Newly industrialized Asian economies	4	6.2	3.2	13.6	9.4	8.5	1.3
		Other emerging market and developing countries	World	Other emerging market and developing countries	World	Other emerging market and developing countries	World
Other emerging market and developing countries	**145**	**100.0**	**47.7**	**100.0**	**30.8**	**100.0**	**84.7**
Regional groups							
Africa	48	7.0	3.3	8.0	2.5	15.1	12.8
Sub-Sahara	45	5.4	2.6	5.9	1.8	13.7	11.6
Excluding Nigeria and South Africa	43	2.8	1.3	2.9	0.9	10.1	8.6
Central and eastern Europe	15	6.9	3.3	14.0	4.3	3.4	2.9
Commonwealth of Independent States[2]	13	7.9	3.8	9.9	3.1	5.2	4.4
Russia		5.4	2.6	6.8	2.1	2.7	2.3
Developing Asia	23	56.8	27.1	38.7	12.0	61.8	52.3
China		32.4	15.4	21.4	6.6	24.4	20.7
India		12.5	6.0	4.0	1.2	20.4	17.3
Excluding China and India	21	12.0	5.7	13.4	4.1	17.0	14.4
Middle East	13	5.8	2.8	14.7	4.5	4.4	3.7
Western Hemisphere	33	15.6	7.4	14.6	4.5	10.1	8.5
Brazil		5.4	2.6	3.4	1.1	3.4	2.9
Mexico		3.7	1.8	3.9	1.2	2.0	1.7
Analytical groups							
By source of export earnings							
Fuel	23	13.0	6.2	26.5	8.2	10.9	9.3
Nonfuel	122	87.0	41.4	73.5	22.7	89.1	75.4
of which, primary products	23	2.1	1.0	2.4	0.7	5.3	4.5
By external financing source							
Net debtor countries	125	53.8	25.6	49.6	15.3	67.6	57.2
of which, official financing	50	12.7	6.0	8.8	2.7	22.5	19.0
Net debtor countries by debt-servicing experience							
Countries with arrears and/or rescheduling during 1999–2003	55	12.0	5.7	10.5	3.2	23.4	19.8
Other net debtor countries	70	41.8	19.9	39.1	12.1	44.2	37.4
Other groups							
Heavily indebted poor countries	29	1.9	0.9	1.2	0.4	8.0	6.8
Middle East and North Africa	19	7.7	3.7	16.9	5.2	6.4	5.5

[1]The GDP shares are based on the purchasing-power-parity (PPP) valuation of country GDPs. The number of countries comprising each group reflects those for which data are included in the group aggregates.

[2]Mongolia, which is not a member of the Commonwealth of Independent States, is included in this group for reasons of geography and similarities in economic structure.

Table B. Advanced Economies by Subgroup

	Other Subgroups					
Major Currency Areas	Euro area		Newly industrialized Asian economies	Major advanced economies	Other advanced economies	
United States	Austria	Ireland	Hong Kong SAR[1]	Canada	Australia	Korea
Euro area	Belgium	Italy	Korea	France	Cyprus	New Zealand
Japan	Finland	Luxembourg	Singapore	Germany	Denmark	Norway
	France	Netherlands	Taiwan Province of China	Italy	Hong Kong SAR[1]	Singapore
	Germany	Portugal		Japan	Iceland	Sweden
	Greece	Spain		United Kingdom	Israel	Switzerland
				United States		Taiwan Province of China

[1]On July 1, 1997, Hong Kong was returned to the People's Republic of China and became a Special Administrative Region of China.

emerging market and developing countries.[6] Rather than being based on strict criteria, economic or otherwise, this classification has evolved over time with the objective of facilitating analysis by providing a reasonably meaningful organization of data. Table A provides an overview of these standard groups in the *World Economic Outlook,* showing the number of countries in each group and the average 2005 shares of groups in aggregate PPP-valued GDP, total exports of goods and services, and population.

A few countries are presently not included in these groups, either because they are not IMF members and their economies are not monitored by the IMF, or because databases have not yet been fully developed. Because of data limitations, group composites do not reflect the following countries: The Islamic Republic of Afghanistan, Bosnia and Herzegovina, Brunei Darussalam, Eritrea, Iraq, Liberia, Serbia, Somalia, and Timor-Leste. Cuba, the Democratic People's Republic of Korea, and Montenegro are examples of countries that are not IMF members, whereas San Marino, among the advanced economies, and Aruba, Marshall Islands, Federated States of Micronesia, and Palau among the developing countries, are examples of economies for which databases have not been completed.

[6]As used here, the term "country" does not in all cases refer to a territorial entity that is a state as understood by international law and practice. It also covers some territorial entities that are not states, but for which statistical data are maintained on a separate and independent basis.

General Features and Composition of Groups in the *World Economic Outlook* Classification

Advanced Economies

The 29 advanced economies are listed in Table B. The seven largest in terms of GDP—the United States, Japan, Germany, France, Italy, the United Kingdom, and Canada—constitute the subgroup of *major advanced economies,* often referred to as the Group of Seven (G-7) countries. The 12 members of the euro area and the four *newly industrialized Asian economies* are also distinguished as subgroups. Composite data shown in the tables for the euro area cover the current members for all years, even though the membership has increased over time.

In 1991 and subsequent years, data for *Germany* refer to west Germany *and* the eastern Länder (i.e., the former German Democratic Republic). Before 1991, economic data are not available on a unified basis or in a consistent manner. Hence, in tables featuring data expressed as annual percent change, these apply to west Germany in years up to and including 1991, but to unified Germany from 1992 onward. In general, data on national

Table C. European Union

Austria	France	Latvia	Portugal
Belgium	Germany	Lithuania	Slovak Republic
Cyprus	Greece	Luxembourg	Slovenia
Czech Republic	Hungary	Malta	Spain
Denmark	Ireland	Netherlands	Sweden
Estonia	Italy	Poland	United Kingdom
Finland			

accounts and domestic economic and financial activity through 1990 cover west Germany only, whereas data for the central government and balance of payments apply to west Germany through June 1990 and to unified Germany thereafter.

Table C lists the member countries of the European Union, not all of which are classified as advanced economies in the *World Economic Outlook.*

Other Emerging Market and Developing Countries

The group of other emerging market and developing countries (145 countries) includes all countries that are not classified as advanced economies.

The *regional breakdowns* of other emerging market and developing countries—*Africa, central and eastern Europe, Commonwealth of Independent States, developing Asia, Middle East, and Western Hemisphere*—largely conform to the regional breakdowns in the IMF's *International Financial Statistics.* In both classifications, Egypt and the Libyan Arab Jamahiriya are included in the *Middle East* region rather than in Africa. In addition, the *World Economic Outlook* sometimes refers to the regional group of Middle East and North Africa countries, also referred to as the MENA countries, whose composition straddles the Africa and Middle East regions. This group is defined as the Arab League countries plus the Islamic Republic of Iran (see Table D).

Other emerging market and developing countries are also classified according to *analytical criteria.* The analytical criteria reflect countries' composition of export earnings and other income from abroad, exchange rate arrangements, a distinction between net creditor and net debtor countries, and, for the

Table D. Middle East and North Africa Countries

Algeria	Jordan	Morocco	Syrian Arab Republic
Bahrain	Kuwait	Oman	Tunisia
Djibouti	Lebanon	Qatar	United Arab Emirates
Egypt	Libya	Saudi Arabia	Yemen
Iran, I.R. of	Mauritania	Sudan	

Table E. Other Emerging Market and Developing Countries by Region and Main Source of Export Earnings

	Fuel	Nonfuel, of Which Primary Products
Africa	Algeria Angola Congo, Rep. of Equatorial Guinea Gabon Nigeria Sudan	Botswana Burkina Faso Burundi Chad Congo, Dem. Rep. of Côte d'Ivoire Ghana Guinea Guinea-Bissau Malawi Mauritania Namibia Niger Sierra Leone Uganda Zambia Zimbabwe
Commonwealth of Independent States	Azerbaijan Russia Turkmenistan	Tajikistan Uzbekistan
Developing Asia		Papua New Guinea Solomon Islands
Middle East	Bahrain Iran, I.R. of Kuwait Libya Oman Qatar Saudi Arabia Syrian Arab Republic United Arab Emirates Yemen	
Western Hemisphere	Ecuador Trinidad and Tobago Venezuela	Chile Suriname

Table F. Other Emerging Market and Developing Countries by Region, Net External Position, and Heavily Indebted Poor Countries

	Net External Position		Heavily Indebted Poor Countries
	Net creditor	Net debtor[1]	
Africa			
Maghreb			
Algeria	*		
Morocco		*	
Tunisia		*	
Sub-Sahara			
South Africa		*	
Horn of Africa			
Djibouti		•	
Ethiopia		•	*
Sudan		*	
Great Lakes			
Burundi		•	*
Congo, Dem. Rep. of		•	*
Kenya		•	
Rwanda		•	*
Tanzania		•	*
Uganda		*	*
Southern Africa			
Angola		*	
Botswana	*		
Comoros		•	
Lesotho		*	
Madagascar		•	*
Malawi		•	*
Mauritius		*	
Mozambique, Rep. of		*	*
Namibia	*		
Seychelles		*	
Swaziland		*	
Zambia		•	*
Zimbabwe		*	
West and Central Africa			
Cape Verde		*	
Gambia, The		*	*
Ghana		•	*
Guinea		•	*
Mauritania		*	*
Nigeria		*	
São Tomé and Príncipe		*	*
Sierra Leone		•	*
CFA franc zone			
Benin		•	*
Burkina Faso		•	*
Cameroon		*	*
Central African Republic		•	
Chad		•	*
Congo, Rep. of		•	*
Côte d'Ivoire		•	
Equatorial Guinea		*	
Gabon		•	
Guinea-Bissau		•	*
Mali		•	*
Niger		•	*
Senegal		*	*
Togo		•	
Central and eastern Europe			
Albania		*	
Bulgaria	*		
Croatia		*	
Czech Republic		*	
Estonia		*	
Hungary		*	
Latvia		*	
Lithuania		*	
Macedonia, FYR		*	
Malta		*	
Poland		*	
Romania		*	
Slovak Republic		*	
Slovenia	*		
Turkey		*	
Commonwealth of Independent States[2]			
Armenia		*	
Azerbaijan		*	
Belarus		*	
Georgia		*	
Kazakhstan		*	
Kyrgyz Republic		•	
Moldova		*	
Mongolia		•	
Russia	*		
Tajikistan		*	
Turkmenistan	*		
Ukraine	*		
Uzbekistan		*	
Developing Asia			
Bhutan		•	
Cambodia		•	
China	*		
Fiji		*	
Indonesia		•	
Kiribati	*		
Lao PDR		*	
Malaysia	*		
Myanmar		*	
Papua New Guinea		•	
Philippines		*	
Samoa		*	
Solomon Islands		•	
Thailand		*	
Tonga		*	
Vanuatu		•	
Vietnam		•	
South Asia			
Bangladesh		•	
India		*	
Maldives		*	
Nepal		•	
Pakistan		•	
Sri Lanka		•	

Table F *(concluded)*

	Net External Position		Heavily Indebted Poor Countries
	Net creditor	Net debtor[1]	
Middle East			
Bahrain		*	
Iran, I.R. of	*		
Kuwait	*		
Libya	*		
Oman	*		
Qatar	*		
Saudi Arabia	*		
United Arab Emirates	*		
Yemen	*		
Mashreq			
Egypt		*	
Jordan		*	
Lebanon		•	
Syrian Arab Republic		*	
Western Hemisphere			
Mercosur			
Argentina		•	
Bolivia (associate member)		•	*
Brazil		*	
Chile (associate member)		*	
Paraguay		•	
Uruguay		•	
Andean region			
Colombia		•	
Ecuador		*	
Peru		*	
Venezuela	*		

	Net External Position		Heavily Indebted Poor Countries
	Net creditor	Net debtor[1]	
Mexico, Central America, and Caribbean			
Mexico		*	
Central America			
Costa Rica		*	
El Salvador		•	
Guatemala		*	
Honduras		•	*
Nicaragua		*	*
Panama		*	
Caribbean			
Antigua and Barbuda		*	
Bahamas, The		*	
Barbados		*	
Belize		*	
Dominica		*	
Dominican Republic		•	
Grenada		•	
Guyana		*	*
Haiti		•	
Jamaica		*	
Netherlands Antilles		*	
St. Kitts and Nevis		*	
St. Lucia		•	
St. Vincent and the Grenadines		*	
Suriname		*	
Trinidad and Tobago		*	

[1]Dot instead of star indicates that the net debtor's main external finance source is official financing.

[2]Mongolia, which is not a member of the Commonwealth of Independent States, is included in this group for reasons of geography and similarities in economic structure.

net debtor countries, financial criteria based on external financing source and experience with external debt servicing. The detailed composition of other emerging market and developing countries in the regional and analytical groups is shown in Tables E and F.

The analytical criterion, by *source of export earnings*, distinguishes between categories: *fuel* (Standard International Trade Classification—SITC 3) and *nonfuel* and then focuses on *nonfuel primary products* (SITC 0, 1, 2, 4, and 68).

The financial criteria focus on *net creditor, net debtor countries, and heavily indebted poor countries (HIPCs)*. Net debtor countries are further differentiated on the basis of two additional financial criteria: by *official external financing* and by *experience with debt servicing*.[7] The HIPC group comprises the countries considered by the IMF and the World Bank for their debt initiative, known as the HIPC Initiative, with the aim of reducing the external debt burdens of all the eligible HIPCs to a "sustainable" level in a reasonably short period of time.[8]

[7]During 1999–2003, 56 countries incurred external payments arrears or entered into official or commercial bank debt-rescheduling agreements. This group of countries is referred to as *countries with arrears and/or rescheduling during 1999–2003*.

[8]See David Andrews, Anthony R. Boote, Syed S. Rizavi, and Sukwinder Singh, *Debt Relief for Low-Income Countries: The Enhanced HIPC Initiative*, IMF Pamphlet Series, No. 51 (Washington: International Monetary Fund, November 1999).

List of Tables

Output

Inflation

Financial Policies

Foreign Trade

Current Account Transactions

Balance of Payments and External Financing

External Debt and Debt Service

Flow of Funds

Medium-Term Baseline Scenario

Table 1. Summary of World Output[1]
(Annual percent change)

	Ten-Year Averages											
	1988–97	1998–2007	1998	1999	2000	2001	2002	2003	2004	2005	2006	2007
World	**3.4**	**4.1**	**2.8**	**3.7**	**4.9**	**2.6**	**3.1**	**4.1**	**5.3**	**4.9**	**5.1**	**4.9**
Advanced economies	**2.9**	**2.6**	**2.6**	**3.5**	**3.9**	**1.2**	**1.5**	**1.9**	**3.2**	**2.6**	**3.1**	**2.7**
United States	3.0	3.1	4.2	4.4	3.7	0.8	1.6	2.5	3.9	3.2	3.4	2.9
Euro area	. . .	2.1	2.8	3.0	3.9	1.9	0.9	0.8	2.1	1.3	2.4	2.0
Japan	2.9	1.3	–1.8	–0.2	2.9	0.4	0.1	1.8	2.3	2.6	2.7	2.1
Other advanced economies[2]	3.6	3.3	2.0	4.8	5.2	1.7	3.2	2.5	4.0	3.1	3.6	3.3
Other emerging market and developing countries	**4.1**	**5.9**	**3.0**	**4.1**	**6.1**	**4.4**	**5.1**	**6.7**	**7.7**	**7.4**	**7.3**	**7.2**
Regional groups												
Africa	2.3	4.3	2.8	2.7	3.1	4.2	3.6	4.6	5.5	5.4	5.4	5.9
Central and eastern Europe	0.9	4.0	2.9	0.7	5.1	0.3	4.5	4.7	6.5	5.4	5.3	5.0
Commonwealth of Independent States[3]	. . .	5.8	–3.4	5.2	9.0	6.3	5.3	7.9	8.4	6.5	6.8	6.5
Developing Asia	7.9	7.4	4.2	6.2	7.0	6.1	7.0	8.4	8.8	9.0	8.7	8.6
Middle East	4.0	4.7	3.7	1.8	5.3	3.0	4.1	6.4	5.5	5.7	5.8	5.4
Western Hemisphere	2.9	2.8	2.3	0.5	3.9	0.5	0.1	2.2	5.7	4.3	4.8	4.2
Memorandum												
European Union	2.2	2.4	3.0	3.0	3.9	2.0	1.3	1.4	2.4	1.8	2.8	2.4
Analytical groups												
By source of export earnings												
Fuel	—	5.2	–0.3	3.0	7.1	4.3	4.1	6.9	7.2	6.7	6.7	6.7
Nonfuel	4.9	6.0	3.6	4.2	5.9	4.4	5.2	6.7	7.8	7.5	7.4	7.3
of which, primary products	3.1	3.6	3.2	1.1	1.6	2.9	3.0	3.5	5.7	5.3	5.0	5.2
By external financing source												
Net debtor countries	3.6	4.4	2.0	2.9	4.7	2.5	3.2	4.8	6.4	6.0	6.0	5.8
of which, official financing	4.5	3.7	–0.8	1.0	3.4	2.2	1.7	5.2	6.2	6.6	5.8	5.9
Net debtor countries by debt-servicing experience												
Countries with arrears and/or rescheduling during 1999–2003	4.2	4.1	–1.1	1.5	3.7	2.9	2.2	5.6	6.8	7.1	6.1	6.5
Memorandum												
Median growth rate												
Advanced economies	3.1	2.9	3.6	4.0	4.0	1.8	1.6	1.8	3.5	2.9	3.1	2.8
Other emerging market and developing countries	3.3	4.4	3.7	3.4	4.2	3.7	3.7	4.4	5.3	5.3	5.2	5.0
Output per capita												
Advanced economies	2.2	2.0	1.9	2.9	3.3	0.6	0.9	1.3	2.6	2.0	2.5	2.2
Other emerging market and developing countries	2.4	4.6	1.6	2.7	4.7	3.0	3.8	5.4	6.4	6.1	6.1	5.9
World growth based on market exchange rates	**2.7**	**3.0**	**2.1**	**3.1**	**4.1**	**1.5**	**1.8**	**2.7**	**3.9**	**3.4**	**3.8**	**3.5**
Value of world output in billions of U.S. dollars												
At market exchange rates	25,125	37,757	29,682	30,786	31,650	31,456	32,714	36,751	41,258	44,455	47,767	51,057
At purchasing power parities	30,617	53,009	40,173	42,230	45,189	47,434	49,713	52,758	56,965	61,028	65,117	69,489

[1]Real GDP.
[2]In this table, "other advanced economies" means advanced economies excluding the United States, euro area countries, and Japan.
[3]Mongolia, which is not a member of the Commonwealth of Independent States, is included in this group for reasons of geography and similarities in economic structure.

Table 2. Advanced Economies: Real GDP and Total Domestic Demand

(Annual percent change)

	Ten-Year Averages												Fourth Quarter[1]		
	1988–97	1998–2007	1998	1999	2000	2001	2002	2003	2004	2005	2006	2007	2005	2006	2007
Real GDP															
Advanced economies	**2.9**	**2.6**	**2.6**	**3.5**	**3.9**	**1.2**	**1.5**	**1.9**	**3.2**	**2.6**	**3.1**	**2.7**	. . .	. . .	. . .
United States	3.0	3.1	4.2	4.4	3.7	0.8	1.6	2.5	3.9	3.2	3.4	2.9	3.1	3.4	3.0
Euro area	. . .	2.1	2.8	3.0	3.9	1.9	0.9	0.8	2.1	1.3	2.4	2.0	1.8	2.7	1.8
Germany	2.7	1.3	2.0	1.9	3.1	1.2	—	–0.2	1.2	0.9	2.0	1.3	1.7	2.4	1.6
France	1.9	2.2	3.3	3.0	4.0	1.8	1.1	1.1	2.0	1.2	2.4	2.3	1.0	3.0	2.0
Italy	1.9	1.3	1.4	1.9	3.6	1.8	0.3	—	1.1	—	1.5	1.3	0.5	1.6	1.4
Spain	2.9	3.6	4.5	4.7	5.0	3.5	2.7	3.0	3.1	3.4	3.4	3.0	3.5	3.2	3.0
Netherlands	2.9	2.3	4.3	4.0	3.5	1.4	0.1	0.3	2.0	1.5	2.9	2.9	2.2	3.5	2.0
Belgium	2.6	2.1	1.9	3.1	3.7	1.2	1.5	0.9	2.4	1.5	2.7	2.1	1.5	2.8	1.9
Austria	2.5	2.3	3.6	3.3	3.4	0.8	0.9	1.1	2.4	2.0	2.8	2.3	2.2	2.7	2.2
Finland	1.6	3.2	5.2	3.9	5.0	2.6	1.6	1.8	3.5	2.9	3.5	2.5	3.3	3.2	3.4
Greece	2.0	4.0	3.4	3.4	4.5	5.1	3.8	4.8	4.7	3.7	3.7	3.5	3.7	3.1	3.4
Portugal	3.7	1.8	4.8	3.9	3.9	2.0	0.8	–1.1	1.2	0.4	1.2	1.5	0.8	1.5	1.5
Ireland	5.9	6.6	8.5	10.7	9.2	5.7	6.0	4.3	4.3	5.5	5.8	5.6	6.5	5.2	5.3
Luxembourg	5.1	4.7	6.5	8.4	8.4	2.5	3.6	2.0	4.2	4.0	4.0	3.8	. . .	. . .	. . .
Japan	2.9	1.3	–1.8	–0.2	2.9	0.4	0.1	1.8	2.3	2.6	2.7	2.1	3.7	2.4	1.9
United Kingdom	2.2	2.8	3.3	3.0	3.8	2.4	2.1	2.7	3.3	1.9	2.7	2.7	1.8	3.1	2.5
Canada	2.2	3.4	4.1	5.5	5.2	1.8	2.9	1.8	3.3	2.9	3.1	3.0	2.8	3.1	2.9
Korea	7.7	4.2	–6.9	9.5	8.5	3.8	7.0	3.1	4.7	4.0	5.0	4.3	5.3	4.1	4.3
Australia	3.3	3.5	5.0	4.4	3.3	2.2	4.1	3.1	3.5	2.5	3.1	3.5	2.9	3.4	3.6
Taiwan Province of China	7.1	4.0	4.5	5.7	5.8	–2.2	4.2	3.4	6.1	4.1	4.0	4.2	6.4	3.0	4.3
Sweden	1.5	3.0	3.7	4.5	4.3	1.1	2.0	1.7	3.7	2.7	4.0	2.2	3.0	3.6	2.6
Switzerland	1.4	1.8	2.8	1.3	3.6	1.0	0.3	–0.3	2.1	1.9	3.0	1.9	2.8	2.7	1.7
Hong Kong SAR	5.2	4.1	–5.5	4.0	10.0	0.6	1.8	3.2	8.6	7.3	6.0	5.5	7.4	6.4	4.6
Denmark	2.0	2.0	2.2	2.6	3.5	0.7	0.5	0.7	1.9	3.2	2.7	2.3	3.3	4.1	0.4
Norway	3.3	2.3	2.6	2.1	2.8	2.7	1.1	1.1	3.1	2.3	2.4	2.8	2.4	2.4	3.3
Israel	5.2	3.4	4.2	2.9	8.7	–0.6	–0.9	1.5	4.8	5.2	4.1	4.4	6.2	4.4	5.0
Singapore	9.1	4.6	–1.4	7.2	10.0	–2.3	4.0	2.9	8.7	6.4	6.9	4.5	8.7	3.2	6.2
New Zealand	2.1	2.8	–0.1	4.4	3.4	3.0	4.8	3.4	4.4	2.3	1.3	1.7	1.8	1.3	2.4
Cyprus	5.1	3.8	5.0	4.8	5.0	4.1	2.1	1.9	3.9	3.7	3.5	3.8	. . .	. . .	. . .
Iceland	1.2	3.9	5.8	4.3	4.1	3.8	–1.0	3.0	8.2	5.5	4.0	1.0	. . .	. . .	. . .
Memorandum															
Major advanced economies	2.7	2.4	2.6	3.1	3.6	1.1	1.2	1.8	3.0	2.4	2.9	2.5	2.7	3.0	2.5
Newly industrialized Asian economies	7.3	4.2	–2.4	7.4	7.9	1.1	5.3	3.2	5.9	4.5	4.9	4.4	6.1	4.0	4.5
Real total domestic demand															
Advanced economies	**2.9**	**2.7**	**3.0**	**4.0**	**4.0**	**1.1**	**1.6**	**2.1**	**3.2**	**2.7**	**3.0**	**2.7**	. . .	. . .	. . .
United States	2.9	3.5	5.3	5.3	4.4	0.9	2.2	2.8	4.4	3.3	3.4	2.9	3.1	3.2	3.0
Euro area	. . .	2.1	3.6	3.6	3.4	1.2	0.4	1.4	2.0	1.5	2.2	2.1	1.7	2.4	1.8
Germany	2.5	0.8	2.3	2.7	2.2	–0.5	–2.0	0.6	—	0.5	1.5	1.3	1.0	2.4	0.8
France	1.5	2.6	3.9	3.5	4.5	1.7	1.2	1.9	2.8	2.1	2.4	2.3	2.1	2.6	2.0
Italy	1.5	1.7	3.3	3.2	2.8	1.6	1.3	0.9	1.0	0.3	1.2	1.3	1.0	2.0	1.2
Spain	2.9	4.7	6.2	6.5	5.4	3.6	3.3	3.8	5.0	5.3	4.4	3.6	5.0	3.6	3.6
Japan	3.0	1.0	–2.2	–0.1	2.5	1.2	–0.6	1.2	1.5	2.4	2.3	2.3	2.9	2.6	1.9
United Kingdom	2.2	3.3	5.0	4.2	3.9	2.9	3.2	2.7	3.8	1.8	2.9	2.9	1.2	3.3	2.8
Canada	2.0	3.7	2.5	4.2	4.7	1.2	3.3	4.7	4.3	4.8	3.9	3.3	3.6	3.7	3.1
Other advanced economies	5.1	2.9	–1.3	5.4	5.3	0.4	3.5	1.3	4.3	3.1	3.6	3.3	. . .	. . .	. . .
Memorandum															
Major advanced economies	2.6	2.6	3.3	3.8	3.7	1.1	1.3	2.2	3.1	2.6	2.8	2.5	2.6	3.0	2.4
Newly industrialized Asian economies	8.2	2.5	–7.7	7.8	7.6	–0.1	4.1	—	4.4	2.3	3.8	3.9	1.6	3.9	5.0

[1]From fourth quarter of preceding year.

Table 3. Advanced Economies: Components of Real GDP
(Annual percent change)

	Ten-Year Averages											
	1988–97	1998–2007	1998	1999	2000	2001	2002	2003	2004	2005	2006	2007
Private consumer expenditure												
Advanced economies	**2.9**	**2.8**	**2.9**	**4.1**	**3.8**	**2.2**	**2.2**	**1.9**	**2.9**	**2.6**	**2.6**	**2.4**
United States	2.9	3.6	5.0	5.1	4.7	2.5	2.7	2.8	3.9	3.5	3.0	2.6
Euro area	. . .	2.0	3.1	3.4	3.1	2.0	0.9	1.2	1.6	1.4	1.8	1.7
Germany	2.6	0.9	1.5	3.0	2.4	1.9	–0.8	–0.1	0.1	0.1	0.7	0.3
France	1.4	2.7	3.6	3.3	3.5	2.5	2.4	2.2	2.5	2.1	2.7	2.5
Italy	1.8	1.4	3.5	2.5	2.4	0.7	0.2	1.0	0.5	0.1	1.3	1.5
Spain	2.5	3.9	4.8	5.3	4.9	3.2	2.9	2.6	4.4	4.4	3.6	3.4
Japan	2.9	1.2	–0.8	1.1	1.1	1.4	1.1	0.6	1.9	2.1	1.9	2.0
United Kingdom	2.6	3.2	4.0	4.5	4.6	3.0	3.5	2.9	3.4	1.4	2.4	2.8
Canada	2.3	3.4	2.8	3.8	4.0	2.3	3.6	3.0	3.3	3.9	3.9	3.1
Other advanced economies	5.0	3.1	–0.7	5.8	5.5	2.6	3.7	1.1	3.2	3.1	3.4	3.2
Memorandum												
Major advanced economies	2.6	2.7	3.3	3.8	3.6	2.2	2.0	2.0	2.8	2.5	2.5	2.3
Newly industrialized Asian economies	7.8	3.0	–5.2	8.2	7.3	3.2	4.9	–0.4	2.3	3.1	3.8	3.7
Public consumption												
Advanced economies	**1.9**	**2.3**	**1.7**	**2.8**	**2.5**	**2.8**	**3.3**	**2.3**	**1.9**	**1.5**	**1.8**	**1.9**
United States	1.1	2.3	1.6	3.1	1.7	3.1	4.3	2.5	2.1	0.9	1.6	2.2
Euro area	. . .	1.7	1.2	1.9	2.3	2.0	2.3	1.6	1.0	1.2	2.1	1.5
Germany	1.8	0.9	1.8	1.2	1.4	0.5	1.5	0.4	–1.3	0.6	1.5	1.1
France	2.1	1.4	–0.6	1.4	2.0	1.1	1.9	2.0	2.2	1.1	1.7	1.7
Italy	0.4	1.4	0.4	1.3	2.3	3.6	2.1	2.0	0.5	1.2	0.7	0.4
Spain	3.8	4.4	3.5	4.0	5.3	3.9	4.5	4.8	6.0	4.5	3.8	3.6
Japan	3.0	2.3	1.8	4.1	4.3	3.0	2.4	2.3	2.0	1.7	0.4	0.9
United Kingdom	0.9	2.8	1.1	3.7	3.1	2.4	3.5	3.5	3.2	2.6	2.1	2.6
Canada	1.1	2.9	3.2	2.1	3.1	3.9	2.5	3.5	3.0	2.7	2.5	2.0
Other advanced economies	4.4	2.5	2.7	1.9	2.1	3.3	3.6	2.0	1.9	2.3	2.9	2.6
Memorandum												
Major advanced economies	1.5	2.1	1.4	2.8	2.3	2.7	3.2	2.3	1.8	1.2	1.5	1.8
Newly industrialized Asian economies	6.4	2.7	3.0	0.7	2.4	3.7	4.3	2.3	1.7	2.4	3.6	2.7
Gross fixed capital formation												
Advanced economies	**3.6**	**3.2**	**5.0**	**5.5**	**5.1**	**–0.8**	**–1.7**	**2.1**	**4.5**	**4.5**	**4.6**	**3.7**
United States	3.9	4.1	9.1	8.2	6.1	–1.7	–3.5	3.2	6.1	6.4	4.5	3.6
Euro area	. . .	2.9	6.0	6.2	5.0	0.5	–1.5	0.8	2.4	2.3	4.2	3.6
Germany	2.9	1.0	4.0	4.7	3.0	–3.7	–6.1	–0.8	–0.4	0.8	4.9	4.3
France	1.4	3.8	6.9	7.9	7.5	2.3	–1.7	2.3	2.6	3.7	3.6	3.0
Italy	1.4	2.5	4.3	3.6	6.4	2.5	4.0	–1.7	2.2	–0.6	2.3	2.0
Spain	3.4	6.3	11.1	10.3	6.5	4.6	3.4	5.8	4.9	7.3	5.3	4.1
Japan	3.0	0.2	–6.5	–0.7	1.2	–0.9	–5.0	0.3	1.1	3.3	5.5	3.9
United Kingdom	2.6	4.4	14.0	2.8	2.7	2.5	3.7	0.4	6.0	3.0	5.3	4.1
Canada	2.4	5.2	2.4	7.3	4.7	4.0	1.6	6.5	8.0	7.1	6.6	4.2
Other advanced economies	6.7	2.9	–1.0	2.8	6.9	–4.4	3.4	2.5	7.0	4.3	4.3	4.1
Memorandum												
Major advanced economies	3.2	3.1	5.5	5.6	4.8	–0.7	–2.6	1.9	4.2	4.5	4.6	3.6
Newly industrialized Asian economies	10.6	1.8	–9.0	2.8	10.8	–6.5	1.9	1.6	7.6	1.7	2.9	5.2

Table 3 *(concluded)*

	Ten-Year Averages											
	1988–97	1998–2007	1998	1999	2000	2001	2002	2003	2004	2005	2006	2007
Final domestic demand												
Advanced economies	**2.8**	**2.7**	**3.0**	**4.1**	**3.9**	**1.6**	**1.5**	**2.1**	**3.0**	**2.8**	**2.9**	**2.6**
United States	2.8	3.5	5.3	5.4	4.5	1.8	1.8	2.8	4.0	3.6	3.1	2.8
Euro area	. . .	2.0	3.2	3.7	3.1	1.7	0.6	1.2	1.4	1.5	2.0	2.0
Germany	2.4	0.9	2.4	2.7	2.2	−0.5	−2.0	0.6	—	0.5	1.7	1.2
France	1.5	2.6	3.1	3.7	3.9	2.1	1.5	2.2	2.4	2.2	2.7	2.4
Italy	1.4	1.6	3.0	2.5	3.2	1.6	1.4	0.6	0.9	0.1	1.4	1.4
Spain	3.0	4.6	6.0	6.3	5.4	3.7	3.3	3.8	4.8	5.2	4.1	3.6
Japan	2.9	1.1	−2.0	1.1	1.6	1.1	−0.2	0.8	1.8	2.3	2.5	2.3
United Kingdom	2.2	3.3	4.9	4.1	4.0	2.8	3.5	2.6	3.7	1.9	2.8	3.0
Canada	2.0	3.6	2.8	4.2	4.0	2.9	3.0	3.8	4.2	4.3	4.2	3.1
Other advanced economies	5.3	2.8	−0.7	4.2	5.3	0.9	3.6	1.6	3.8	3.2	3.5	3.3
Memorandum												
Major advanced economies	2.5	2.6	3.3	3.9	3.6	1.6	1.2	2.1	2.9	2.7	2.7	2.5
Newly industrialized Asian economies	8.4	2.5	−5.7	5.3	7.6	0.7	4.0	0.6	3.4	2.7	3.5	4.0
Stock building[1]												
Advanced economies	**—**	**—**	**—**	**—**	**0.1**	**−0.5**	**—**	**0.1**	**0.2**	**−0.1**	**0.1**	**—**
United States	0.1	—	—	—	−0.1	−0.9	0.4	—	0.4	−0.3	0.3	0.1
Euro area	. . .	0.1	0.4	−0.1	0.3	−0.5	−0.2	0.2	0.6	—	0.2	0.1
Germany	—	—	0.4	−0.2	−0.1	−0.9	−0.6	0.8	0.3	0.2	−0.3	—
France	—	—	0.7	−0.2	0.6	−0.4	−0.3	−0.3	0.3	—	−0.2	−0.1
Italy	—	—	−0.1	0.1	−0.2	0.1	—	0.1	−0.1	0.1	0.7	−0.3
Spain	—	0.1	0.2	0.3	—	−0.1	—	—	0.2	0.2	0.4	—
Japan	0.1	−0.1	−0.2	−1.1	0.8	0.2	−0.4	0.3	−0.2	0.1	−0.1	—
United Kingdom	—	—	0.1	0.2	−0.1	0.1	−0.3	0.2	0.1	−0.1	—	—
Canada	0.1	—	−0.3	0.1	0.8	−1.7	0.3	0.8	0.1	0.4	−0.2	0.1
Other advanced economies	—	—	−0.7	1.1	—	−0.6	—	−0.2	0.5	−0.1	—	—
Memorandum												
Major advanced economies	—	—	0.1	−0.2	0.1	−0.6	—	0.2	0.2	−0.1	0.1	—
Newly industrialized Asian economies	—	—	−1.9	2.1	−0.1	−0.7	0.1	−0.5	0.9	−0.3	0.2	−0.1
Foreign balance[1]												
Advanced economies	**0.1**	**−0.1**	**−0.4**	**−0.6**	−0.1	0.1	**−0.1**	**−0.2**	**−0.1**	**−0.1**	**0.1**	**—**
United States	0.1	−0.6	−1.2	−1.0	−0.9	−0.2	−0.7	−0.4	−0.7	−0.3	−0.1	−0.1
Euro area	. . .	—	−0.7	−0.5	0.6	0.7	0.6	−0.5	0.2	−0.1	0.2	—
Germany	0.2	0.5	−0.4	−0.8	1.0	1.7	2.0	−0.9	1.2	0.4	0.6	0.1
France	0.4	−0.4	−0.5	−0.4	−0.4	0.2	−0.1	−0.7	−0.7	−1.0	−0.1	−0.1
Italy	0.3	−0.3	−1.7	−1.2	0.8	0.2	−1.0	−0.8	0.1	−0.3	0.4	0.3
Spain	−0.3	−1.3	−1.7	−1.9	−0.5	−0.2	−0.7	−0.9	−2.2	−2.2	−1.4	−1.0
Japan	—	0.3	0.4	−0.2	0.5	−0.8	0.7	0.6	0.8	0.2	0.4	−0.1
United Kingdom	—	−0.5	−1.4	−1.0	−0.1	−0.5	−1.1	−0.1	−0.6	—	−0.2	−0.2
Canada	0.1	−0.2	1.7	1.4	0.6	0.7	−0.1	−2.6	−0.8	−1.6	−0.7	−0.2
Other advanced economies	−0.3	1.0	2.5	0.4	0.7	1.0	0.3	1.5	0.8	0.9	0.9	0.7
Memorandum												
Major advanced economies	0.1	−0.3	−0.7	−0.7	−0.2	—	−0.2	−0.4	−0.2	−0.2	—	−0.1
Newly industrialized Asian economies	−0.9	1.9	5.6	0.4	0.5	1.1	1.2	3.2	2.1	2.5	1.7	1.0

[1]Changes expressed as percent of GDP in the preceding period.

Table 4. Advanced Economies: Unemployment, Employment, and Real Per Capita GDP
(Percent)

	Ten-Year Averages[1]											
	1988–97	1998–2007	1998	1999	2000	2001	2002	2003	2004	2005	2006	2007
Unemployment rate												
Advanced economies	**6.7**	**6.1**	**6.7**	**6.3**	**5.7**	**5.8**	**6.3**	**6.6**	**6.3**	**6.0**	**5.6**	**5.5**
United States[2]	6.0	4.9	4.5	4.2	4.0	4.7	5.8	6.0	5.5	5.1	4.8	4.9
Euro area	. . .	8.5	10.0	9.2	8.2	7.8	8.3	8.7	8.9	8.6	7.9	7.7
Germany	7.0	8.0	8.1	7.5	6.9	6.9	7.7	8.8	9.2	9.1	8.0	7.8
France	10.5	9.4	11.1	10.5	9.1	8.4	8.9	9.5	9.6	9.5	9.0	8.5
Italy	9.9	8.9	11.3	11.0	10.2	9.1	8.6	8.5	8.1	7.7	7.6	7.5
Spain	20.0	11.9	18.6	15.6	13.9	10.6	11.5	11.5	11.0	9.2	8.6	8.3
Netherlands	6.2	3.6	3.8	3.2	2.8	2.2	2.8	3.7	4.6	4.9	4.5	3.9
Belgium	8.3	8.0	9.3	8.6	6.9	6.6	7.5	8.2	8.4	8.4	8.2	8.2
Austria	3.5	4.4	4.5	3.9	3.6	3.6	4.2	4.3	4.8	5.2	4.8	4.6
Finland	10.5	9.2	11.4	10.2	9.8	9.1	9.1	9.0	8.8	8.4	7.9	7.8
Greece	8.6	10.5	11.4	12.3	11.3	10.8	10.3	9.7	10.5	9.9	9.7	9.5
Portugal	5.8	5.8	5.0	4.4	3.9	4.0	5.0	6.3	6.7	7.6	7.7	7.6
Ireland	13.9	4.8	7.6	5.6	4.3	3.9	4.4	4.7	4.5	4.3	4.3	4.2
Luxembourg	2.2	3.4	3.0	2.9	2.5	2.3	2.6	3.5	3.9	4.2	4.5	4.7
Japan	2.6	4.6	4.1	4.7	4.7	5.0	5.4	5.3	4.7	4.4	4.1	4.0
United Kingdom	8.6	5.3	6.3	6.0	5.5	5.1	5.2	5.0	4.8	4.8	5.3	5.1
Canada	9.5	7.2	8.3	7.6	6.8	7.2	7.6	7.6	7.2	6.8	6.3	6.3
Korea	2.5	4.3	7.0	6.6	4.4	4.0	3.3	3.6	3.7	3.7	3.5	3.3
Australia	8.5	6.1	7.7	6.9	6.3	6.8	6.4	6.1	5.5	5.1	5.0	5.0
Taiwan Province of China	1.8	4.0	2.7	2.9	3.0	4.6	5.2	5.0	4.4	4.1	3.9	3.7
Sweden	5.3	5.0	6.5	5.6	4.7	4.0	4.0	4.9	5.5	5.8	4.5	4.3
Switzerland	2.5	2.7	3.4	2.4	1.7	1.6	2.3	3.4	3.5	3.4	2.6	2.5
Hong Kong SAR	2.0	5.7	4.4	6.3	5.1	4.9	7.2	7.9	6.9	5.7	4.6	4.0
Denmark	10.2	5.6	6.6	5.7	5.4	5.2	5.2	6.2	6.4	5.7	4.8	4.9
Norway	5.1	3.9	3.2	3.2	3.4	3.5	3.9	4.5	4.5	4.6	3.9	3.9
Israel	8.6	9.3	8.5	8.8	8.7	9.3	10.3	10.8	10.3	9.0	8.7	8.5
Singapore	1.8	3.0	2.5	2.8	2.7	2.7	3.6	4.0	3.4	3.1	2.7	2.7
New Zealand	7.8	5.1	7.4	6.8	6.0	5.3	5.2	4.6	3.9	3.7	3.9	4.5
Cyprus	2.6	3.5	3.4	3.6	3.4	2.9	3.2	3.5	3.6	5.2	3.0	3.0
Iceland	3.1	2.2	2.8	1.9	1.3	1.4	2.5	3.4	3.1	2.1	1.5	1.9
Memorandum												
Major advanced economies	6.4	6.0	6.2	5.9	5.5	5.8	6.4	6.6	6.3	6.0	5.7	5.6
Newly industrialized Asian economies	2.2	4.3	5.4	5.4	4.0	4.2	4.2	4.4	4.2	4.0	3.7	3.4
Growth in employment												
Advanced economies	**1.1**	**1.0**	**1.1**	**1.3**	**2.1**	**0.6**	**0.3**	**0.6**	**1.1**	**1.2**	**1.3**	**1.0**
United States	1.4	1.2	1.5	1.5	2.5	—	–0.3	0.9	1.1	1.8	1.7	1.2
Euro area	. . .	1.2	1.9	2.0	2.4	1.6	0.7	0.4	0.6	0.7	1.1	1.0
Germany	0.4	0.4	1.2	1.4	1.9	0.4	–0.6	–1.0	0.4	–0.2	0.5	0.2
France	0.3	1.0	1.5	2.0	2.7	1.8	0.6	0.1	—	0.3	0.6	0.6
Italy	–0.2	1.1	1.0	0.7	1.3	1.5	0.9	0.8	3.2	0.7	0.5	0.5
Spain	2.3	3.6	4.5	4.6	5.1	3.2	2.4	2.6	2.6	3.6	3.9	3.2
Japan	1.0	–0.3	–0.7	–0.8	–0.2	–0.5	–1.3	–0.3	0.2	0.4	0.4	–0.1
United Kingdom	0.5	1.0	1.0	1.4	1.2	0.8	0.8	1.0	1.0	1.0	0.8	0.8
Canada	1.1	1.9	2.5	2.6	2.5	1.2	2.4	2.4	1.8	1.4	1.7	0.8
Other advanced economies	1.7	1.3	–1.0	1.6	2.9	1.1	1.6	0.5	1.7	1.5	1.8	1.4
Memorandum												
Major advanced economies	0.9	0.8	1.0	1.1	1.7	0.3	–0.2	0.5	0.9	1.0	1.1	0.7
Newly industrialized Asian economies	2.3	1.2	–3.0	1.5	3.6	0.8	2.0	0.3	1.9	1.2	1.9	1.7

Table 4 *(concluded)*

	Ten-Year Averages[1]											
	1988–97	1998–2007	1998	1999	2000	2001	2002	2003	2004	2005	2006	2007
Growth in real per capita GDP												
Advanced economies	**2.2**	**2.0**	**1.9**	**2.9**	**3.3**	**0.6**	**0.9**	**1.3**	**2.6**	**2.0**	**2.5**	**2.2**
United States	1.8	2.0	3.0	3.3	2.5	–0.3	0.6	1.5	2.9	2.3	2.5	1.9
Euro area	. . .	1.8	2.0	2.7	3.5	1.5	0.4	0.2	1.4	0.8	2.1	1.6
Germany	1.9	1.3	2.0	1.9	2.9	1.0	–0.1	–0.2	1.3	0.9	2.0	1.2
France	1.5	1.6	2.9	2.5	3.4	1.1	0.4	0.5	1.4	0.6	1.8	1.8
Italy	1.8	0.9	1.4	1.9	3.6	1.7	0.3	–0.5	0.1	–1.0	1.1	1.0
Spain	2.7	3.0	4.2	4.3	3.8	2.9	2.0	2.4	2.5	2.8	3.0	2.5
Japan	2.2	1.2	–2.0	–0.4	2.7	0.1	–0.1	1.6	2.2	2.6	2.7	2.1
United Kingdom	1.9	2.4	3.1	2.7	3.5	2.0	1.7	2.3	2.8	1.2	2.2	2.2
Canada	1.0	2.4	3.2	4.7	4.3	0.7	1.8	0.8	2.3	2.0	2.2	2.0
Other advanced economies	3.7	2.8	–0.3	4.5	5.1	0.6	3.0	1.8	4.0	3.0	3.4	3.1
Memorandum												
Major advanced economies	2.0	1.9	2.0	2.5	3.0	0.5	0.6	1.3	2.4	1.9	2.4	2.0
Newly industrialized Asian economies	6.2	3.5	–3.4	6.5	7.0	0.4	4.7	2.6	5.3	4.0	4.4	3.9

[1]Compound annual rate of change for employment and per capita GDP; arithmetic average for unemployment rate.
[2]The projections for unemployment have been adjusted to reflect the survey techniques adopted by the U.S. Bureau of Labor Statistics in January 1994.

Table 5. Other Emerging Market and Developing Countries: Real GDP

(Annual percent change)

	Ten-Year Averages											
	1988–97	1998–2007	1998	1999	2000	2001	2002	2003	2004	2005	2006	2007
Other emerging market and developing countries	**4.1**	**5.9**	**3.0**	**4.1**	**6.1**	**4.4**	**5.1**	**6.7**	**7.7**	**7.4**	**7.3**	**7.2**
Regional groups												
Africa	2.3	4.3	2.8	2.7	3.1	4.2	3.6	4.6	5.5	5.4	5.4	5.9
Sub-Sahara	2.3	4.3	1.9	2.6	3.4	4.2	3.6	4.1	5.6	5.8	5.2	6.3
Excluding Nigeria and South Africa	2.3	4.8	3.3	3.1	2.4	5.5	4.0	3.5	6.4	6.1	6.0	7.7
Central and eastern Europe	0.9	4.0	2.9	0.7	5.1	0.3	4.5	4.7	6.5	5.4	5.3	5.0
Commonwealth of Independent States[1]	. . .	5.8	–3.4	5.2	9.0	6.3	5.3	7.9	8.4	6.5	6.8	6.5
Russia	. . .	5.4	–5.3	6.4	10.0	5.1	4.7	7.3	7.2	6.4	6.5	6.5
Excluding Russia	. . .	6.6	0.8	2.4	6.7	9.1	6.7	9.3	11.0	6.7	7.6	6.4
Developing Asia	7.9	7.4	4.2	6.2	7.0	6.1	7.0	8.4	8.8	9.0	8.7	8.6
China	9.9	9.1	7.8	7.1	8.4	8.3	9.1	10.0	10.1	10.2	10.0	10.0
India	6.0	6.6	5.9	6.9	5.3	4.1	4.3	7.2	8.0	8.5	8.3	7.3
Excluding China and India	6.3	4.2	–4.7	3.6	5.8	3.1	4.8	5.8	6.4	6.1	5.5	6.0
Middle East	4.0	4.7	3.7	1.8	5.3	3.0	4.1	6.4	5.5	5.7	5.8	5.4
Western Hemisphere	2.9	2.8	2.3	0.5	3.9	0.5	0.1	2.2	5.7	4.3	4.8	4.2
Brazil	2.0	2.4	0.1	0.8	4.4	1.3	1.9	0.5	4.9	2.3	3.6	4.0
Mexico	3.0	3.2	5.0	3.8	6.6	—	0.8	1.4	4.2	3.0	4.0	3.5
Analytical groups												
By source of export earnings												
Fuel	—	5.2	–0.3	3.0	7.1	4.3	4.1	6.9	7.2	6.7	6.7	6.7
Nonfuel	4.9	6.0	3.6	4.2	5.9	4.4	5.2	6.7	7.8	7.5	7.4	7.3
of which, primary products	3.1	3.6	3.2	1.1	1.6	2.9	3.0	3.5	5.7	5.3	5.0	5.2
By external financing source												
Net debtor countries	3.6	4.4	2.0	2.9	4.7	2.5	3.2	4.8	6.4	6.0	6.0	5.8
of which, official financing	4.5	3.7	–0.8	1.0	3.4	2.2	1.7	5.2	6.2	6.6	5.8	5.9
Net debtor countries by debt-servicing experience												
Countries with arrears and/or rescheduling during 1999–2003	4.2	4.1	–1.1	1.5	3.7	2.9	2.2	5.6	6.8	7.1	6.1	6.5
Other groups												
Heavily indebted poor countries	1.6	4.5	3.3	3.5	2.7	5.0	3.6	4.2	6.4	5.8	5.3	5.6
Middle East and north Africa	3.6	4.7	4.1	2.0	4.8	3.3	4.1	6.3	5.4	5.5	6.1	5.5
Memorandum												
Real per capita GDP												
Other emerging market and developing countries	2.4	4.6	1.6	2.7	4.7	3.0	3.8	5.4	6.4	6.1	6.1	5.9
Africa	–0.4	2.1	0.4	0.3	0.8	1.9	1.4	2.4	3.3	3.2	3.2	3.8
Central and eastern Europe	0.3	3.6	2.4	0.2	4.6	–0.2	4.0	4.3	6.1	5.0	4.9	4.6
Commonwealth of Independent States[1]	. . .	6.0	–3.3	5.4	9.3	6.6	5.6	8.2	8.7	6.7	7.0	6.7
Developing Asia	6.3	6.2	2.8	4.9	5.7	4.8	5.8	7.2	7.7	7.8	7.6	7.5
Middle East	1.5	2.7	1.6	–0.3	3.3	1.0	2.1	4.5	3.6	3.8	3.9	3.4
Western Hemisphere	1.1	1.4	0.7	–1.1	2.4	–1.0	–1.4	0.7	4.3	2.9	3.4	2.9

[1]Mongolia, which is not a member of the Commonwealth of Independent States, is included in this group for reasons of geography and similarities in economic structure.

Table 6. Other Emerging Market and Developing Countries—by Country: Real GDP[1]
(Annual percent change)

	Average 1988–97	1998	1999	2000	2001	2002	2003	2004	2005	2006	2007
Africa	**2.3**	**2.8**	**2.7**	**3.1**	**4.2**	**3.6**	**4.6**	**5.5**	**5.4**	**5.4**	**5.9**
Algeria	1.0	5.1	3.2	2.2	2.6	4.7	6.9	5.2	5.3	4.9	5.0
Angola	0.9	—	3.2	3.0	3.1	14.5	3.3	11.2	20.6	14.3	31.4
Benin	4.0	4.0	5.3	4.9	6.2	4.5	3.9	3.1	2.9	4.5	5.1
Botswana	7.4	10.8	7.2	8.3	4.9	5.6	6.3	6.0	6.2	4.2	4.3
Burkina Faso	5.7	8.4	4.1	3.3	6.7	5.2	7.9	4.0	7.1	5.6	5.8
Burundi	–1.0	4.8	–1.0	–0.9	2.1	4.4	–1.2	4.8	0.9	6.1	6.6
Cameroon[2]	–1.6	5.0	4.4	4.2	4.5	4.0	4.0	3.7	2.6	4.2	4.3
Cape Verde	5.3	8.4	11.9	7.3	6.1	5.3	4.7	4.4	5.8	5.5	6.0
Central African Republic	—	3.9	3.6	1.8	0.3	–0.6	–7.6	1.3	2.2	3.2	3.8
Chad	3.5	7.0	–0.7	–0.9	11.7	8.5	14.7	31.3	12.2	0.1	2.5
Comoros	1.1	1.2	1.9	1.4	3.3	4.1	2.5	–0.2	4.2	1.2	3.0
Congo, Dem. Rep. of	–5.1	–1.7	–4.3	–6.9	–2.1	3.5	5.8	6.6	6.5	6.5	7.2
Congo, Rep. of	4.7	3.7	–2.6	7.6	3.8	4.6	0.8	3.6	7.9	7.4	2.1
Côte d'Ivoire	3.4	4.7	1.5	–3.3	—	–1.4	–1.5	1.8	1.9	1.9	3.0
Djibouti	–1.6	0.1	3.0	0.5	2.0	2.6	3.2	3.0	3.2	4.2	5.0
Equatorial Guinea	23.5	25.7	24.3	14.1	78.3	21.3	14.1	32.4	6.0	–1.0	9.4
Eritrea	. . .	1.8	—	–13.1	9.2	0.7	3.0	3.5	4.8	2.0	4.0
Ethiopia	2.3	–4.3	6.6	5.4	7.9	—	–3.1	12.3	8.7	5.4	5.5
Gabon	4.8	3.5	–8.9	–1.9	2.1	–0.3	2.4	1.4	2.9	2.2	2.5
Gambia, The	3.6	6.5	6.4	6.4	5.8	–3.2	6.9	5.1	5.0	4.5	5.0
Ghana	4.6	4.7	4.4	3.7	4.2	4.5	5.2	5.8	5.8	6.0	6.0
Guinea	4.4	4.8	4.7	1.9	4.0	4.2	1.2	2.7	3.3	5.0	5.4
Guinea-Bissau	3.6	–27.2	7.6	7.5	0.2	–7.1	–0.6	2.2	3.2	4.6	5.2
Kenya	2.6	3.3	2.4	0.6	4.7	0.3	2.8	4.6	5.7	5.4	5.2
Lesotho	6.0	–3.5	–0.6	1.6	3.3	3.6	3.2	2.7	1.3	1.6	1.4
Liberia	. . .	. . .	34.6	24.0	22.0	31.8	–33.9	–5.2	9.5	7.0	8.1
Madagascar	1.5	3.9	4.7	4.7	6.0	–12.7	9.8	5.3	4.6	4.7	5.6
Malawi	3.9	1.1	3.5	0.8	–4.1	2.1	3.9	5.1	2.1	8.4	5.6
Mali	5.1	8.4	3.0	–3.2	12.1	4.3	7.2	2.4	6.1	5.1	5.4
Mauritania	2.2	2.8	6.7	1.9	2.9	1.1	5.6	5.2	5.4	14.1	10.6
Mauritius	6.2	6.0	4.4	7.1	3.9	2.0	3.6	4.5	3.4	3.4	3.4
Morocco	3.1	7.7	–0.1	1.0	6.3	3.2	5.5	4.2	1.7	7.3	3.3
Mozambique, Rep. of	4.6	12.6	7.5	1.9	13.1	8.2	7.9	7.5	7.7	7.9	7.0
Namibia	3.4	3.3	3.4	3.5	2.4	6.7	3.5	5.9	3.5	4.5	4.5
Niger	1.6	10.4	–0.6	–1.4	7.1	3.0	5.3	–0.6	7.0	3.5	4.2
Nigeria	4.3	0.3	1.5	5.4	3.1	1.5	10.7	6.0	6.9	5.2	6.4
Rwanda	–2.6	8.9	7.6	6.0	6.7	9.4	0.9	4.0	6.0	3.0	4.3
São Tomé and Príncipe	1.3	2.5	2.5	3.0	4.0	4.1	4.0	3.8	3.8	5.5	5.5
Senegal	1.8	5.9	6.3	3.2	4.6	0.7	6.7	5.6	5.5	4.0	5.3
Seychelles	6.0	2.5	1.9	4.3	–2.2	1.3	–6.3	–2.0	–2.2	–1.4	–1.6
Sierra Leone	–6.3	–0.8	–8.1	3.8	18.2	27.5	9.3	7.4	7.2	7.4	6.5
South Africa	1.7	0.5	2.4	4.2	2.7	3.7	3.0	4.5	4.9	4.2	4.0
Sudan	2.6	4.3	3.1	8.4	6.2	6.4	4.9	5.2	7.9	12.1	11.3
Swaziland	4.6	2.8	3.5	2.6	1.6	2.9	2.4	2.1	1.9	1.2	1.0
Tanzania	3.4	3.7	3.5	5.1	6.2	7.2	5.7	6.7	6.8	5.9	7.3
Togo	2.7	–2.3	2.4	1.0	0.2	4.1	1.9	3.0	0.8	4.2	4.5
Tunisia	4.1	4.8	6.1	4.7	4.9	1.7	5.6	6.0	4.2	5.8	6.0
Uganda	6.6	3.6	8.3	5.3	4.8	6.9	4.4	5.7	6.0	5.5	6.0
Zambia	–0.1	–1.9	2.2	3.6	4.9	3.3	5.1	5.4	5.1	6.0	6.0
Zimbabwe	3.6	0.1	–3.6	–7.3	–2.7	–4.4	–10.4	–3.8	–6.5	–5.1	–4.7

Table 6 *(continued)*

	Average 1988–97	1998	1999	2000	2001	2002	2003	2004	2005	2006	2007
Central and eastern Europe[3]	**0.9**	**2.9**	**0.7**	**5.1**	**0.3**	**4.5**	**4.7**	**6.5**	**5.4**	**5.3**	**5.0**
Albania	–1.8	12.7	10.1	7.3	7.0	2.9	5.7	5.9	5.5	5.0	6.0
Bosnia and Herzegovina	. . .	17.6	9.5	5.4	4.3	5.3	4.4	6.2	5.0	5.5	6.0
Bulgaria	–5.8	4.0	2.3	5.4	4.1	4.9	4.5	5.7	5.5	5.6	6.0
Croatia	. . .	2.5	–0.9	2.9	4.4	5.6	5.3	3.8	4.3	4.6	4.7
Czech Republic	0.3	–0.8	1.3	3.6	2.5	1.9	3.6	4.2	6.1	6.0	4.8
Estonia	. . .	4.4	0.3	7.9	6.5	7.2	6.7	7.8	9.8	9.5	8.0
Hungary	–1.0	4.9	4.2	6.0	4.3	3.8	3.4	5.2	4.1	4.5	3.5
Latvia	. . .	4.7	4.7	6.9	8.0	6.5	7.2	8.6	10.2	11.0	9.0
Lithuania	. . .	7.3	–1.7	4.7	6.4	6.8	10.5	7.0	7.5	6.8	6.5
Macedonia, FYR	. . .	3.4	4.3	4.5	–4.5	0.9	2.8	4.1	4.0	4.0	4.0
Malta	5.7	3.4	4.1	9.9	–1.7	1.5	–2.5	–1.5	2.5	1.6	1.8
Serbia	. . .	. . .	–18.0	5.2	5.1	4.5	2.4	9.3	6.3	5.5	5.0
Poland	2.3	5.0	4.5	4.2	1.1	1.4	3.8	5.3	3.4	5.0	4.5
Romania	–2.5	–4.8	–1.2	2.1	5.7	5.1	5.2	8.4	4.1	5.5	5.5
Slovak Republic	. . .	4.2	1.5	2.0	3.2	4.1	4.2	5.4	6.1	6.5	7.0
Slovenia	. . .	3.9	5.4	4.1	2.7	3.5	2.7	4.2	3.9	4.2	4.0
Turkey	4.2	3.1	–4.7	7.4	–7.5	7.9	5.8	8.9	7.4	5.0	5.0
Commonwealth of Independent States[3,4]	**. . .**	**–3.4**	**5.2**	**9.0**	**6.3**	**5.3**	**7.9**	**8.4**	**6.5**	**6.8**	**6.5**
Russia	. . .	–5.3	6.4	10.0	5.1	4.7	7.3	7.2	6.4	6.5	6.5
Excluding Russia	. . .	0.8	2.4	6.7	9.1	6.7	9.3	11.0	6.7	7.6	6.4
Armenia	. . .	7.3	3.3	6.0	9.6	13.2	13.9	10.1	13.9	7.5	6.0
Azerbaijan	. . .	6.0	11.4	6.2	6.5	8.1	10.4	10.2	24.3	25.6	26.4
Belarus	. . .	8.4	3.4	5.8	4.7	5.0	7.0	11.4	9.3	7.0	4.5
Georgia	. . .	2.9	3.0	1.9	4.7	5.5	11.1	5.9	9.3	7.5	6.5
Kazakhstan	. . .	–1.9	2.7	9.8	13.5	9.8	9.3	9.6	9.4	8.3	7.7
Kyrgyz Republic	. . .	2.1	3.7	5.4	5.3	–0.0	7.0	7.0	–0.6	5.0	5.5
Moldova	. . .	–6.5	–3.4	2.1	6.1	7.8	6.6	7.4	7.1	3.0	3.0
Mongolia	–0.1	3.5	3.2	1.1	1.0	4.0	5.6	10.7	6.2	6.5	5.5
Tajikistan	. . .	5.2	3.7	8.3	10.2	9.1	10.2	10.6	6.7	8.0	6.0
Turkmenistan	. . .	6.7	16.5	18.6	20.4	15.8	17.1	14.7	9.6	9.0	9.0
Ukraine	. . .	–1.9	–0.2	5.9	9.2	5.2	9.6	12.1	2.6	5.0	2.8
Uzbekistan	. . .	4.3	4.3	3.8	4.2	4.0	4.2	7.7	7.0	7.2	7.0

Table 6 *(continued)*

	Average 1988–97	1998	1999	2000	2001	2002	2003	2004	2005	2006	2007
Developing Asia	**7.9**	**4.2**	**6.2**	**7.0**	**6.1**	**7.0**	**8.4**	**8.8**	**9.0**	**8.7**	**8.6**
Afghanistan, Rep. of	. . .	. . .	. . .	. . .	. . .	28.6	15.7	8.0	14.0	12.0	11.1
Bangladesh	4.4	5.0	5.4	5.6	4.8	4.8	5.8	6.1	6.2	6.2	6.2
Bhutan	4.3	5.8	7.7	9.5	8.6	7.1	7.1	7.5	7.4	12.7	14.3
Brunei Darussalam	. . .	–0.6	3.1	2.9	2.7	3.9	2.9	0.5	0.4	3.7	2.6
Cambodia	. . .	5.0	12.6	8.4	7.7	6.2	8.6	10.0	13.4	5.0	6.5
China	9.9	7.8	7.1	8.4	8.3	9.1	10.0	10.1	10.2	10.0	10.0
Fiji	4.1	1.2	9.2	–2.8	2.7	4.3	3.0	4.1	2.1	2.6	1.8
India	6.0	5.9	6.9	5.3	4.1	4.3	7.2	8.0	8.5	8.3	7.3
Indonesia	6.9	–13.1	0.8	5.4	3.6	4.5	4.8	5.1	5.6	5.2	6.0
Kiribati	3.6	12.6	9.5	6.9	5.0	2.2	–1.4	–3.7	0.3	0.8	0.8
Lao PDR	6.0	4.0	7.3	5.8	5.7	5.9	6.1	6.4	7.0	7.3	6.6
Malaysia	9.3	–7.4	6.1	8.9	0.3	4.4	5.5	7.2	5.2	5.5	5.8
Maldives	6.6	9.8	7.2	4.8	3.5	6.5	8.5	9.5	–5.5	13.0	4.0
Myanmar	3.5	5.8	10.9	13.7	11.3	12.0	13.8	13.6	13.2	7.0	5.5
Nepal	5.3	2.9	4.5	6.1	5.6	–0.6	3.3	3.8	2.7	1.9	4.2
Pakistan	4.6	2.6	3.7	4.3	2.0	3.2	4.9	7.4	8.0	6.2	7.0
Papua New Guinea	4.0	4.7	1.9	–2.5	–0.1	–0.2	2.0	2.9	3.1	3.7	4.0
Philippines	3.8	–0.6	3.4	6.0	1.8	4.4	4.9	6.2	5.0	5.0	5.4
Samoa	2.6	1.1	2.1	3.7	7.1	4.4	1.8	2.8	5.6	4.0	4.5
Solomon Islands	4.7	1.8	–0.5	–14.3	–9.0	–1.6	6.4	8.0	5.0	5.3	4.3
Sri Lanka	4.8	4.7	4.3	6.0	–1.5	4.0	6.0	5.4	6.0	5.6	6.0
Thailand	8.4	–10.5	4.4	4.8	2.2	5.3	7.0	6.2	4.5	4.5	5.0
Timor-Leste, Dem. Rep. of	. . .	. . .	. . .	15.4	16.6	–6.7	–6.2	0.3	2.3	0.9	4.6
Tonga	0.7	3.5	2.3	5.4	2.6	3.0	3.2	1.4	2.3	1.9	0.6
Vanuatu	4.3	4.5	–3.2	2.7	–2.7	–4.6	2.4	4.0	3.0	3.0	2.8
Vietnam	7.6	5.8	4.8	6.8	6.9	7.1	7.3	7.8	8.4	7.8	7.6
Middle East	**4.0**	**3.7**	**1.8**	**5.3**	**3.0**	**4.1**	**6.4**	**5.5**	**5.7**	**5.8**	**5.4**
Bahrain	4.9	4.8	4.3	5.2	4.6	5.2	7.2	5.4	6.9	7.1	6.3
Egypt	3.4	7.5	6.1	5.4	3.5	3.2	3.1	4.1	4.9	5.6	5.6
Iran, I.R. of	3.6	2.7	1.9	5.1	3.7	7.5	6.7	5.6	5.4	5.4	4.9
Iraq	. . .	. . .	. . .	. . .	. . .	. . .	. . .	. . .	. . .	. . .	. . .
Jordan	2.6	3.0	3.4	4.3	5.3	5.8	4.2	8.4	7.2	6.0	5.0
Kuwait	1.2	3.7	–1.8	4.7	0.7	5.1	13.4	6.2	8.5	6.2	4.7
Lebanon	–3.6	2.3	–1.2	1.2	4.2	2.9	5.0	6.0	1.0	–3.2	5.0
Libya	0.3	–0.4	0.3	1.1	4.5	3.3	9.1	4.6	3.5	5.0	4.6
Oman	5.5	2.7	–0.2	5.5	7.5	2.6	2.0	5.6	6.7	7.1	5.7
Qatar	4.0	11.7	4.5	9.1	4.5	7.3	5.9	11.2	6.5	6.7	4.7
Saudi Arabia	3.7	2.8	–0.7	4.9	0.5	0.1	7.7	5.3	6.6	5.8	6.5
Syrian Arab Republic	6.0	5.6	–3.1	2.3	3.7	3.7	1.0	3.1	2.9	3.2	3.7
United Arab Emirates	6.3	0.1	3.1	12.4	1.7	2.6	11.9	9.7	8.5	11.5	5.8
Yemen	. . .	5.3	3.5	4.4	4.6	3.9	3.1	2.6	3.8	3.9	2.5

Table 6 ***(concluded)***

	Average 1988–97	1998	1999	2000	2001	2002	2003	2004	2005	2006	2007
Western Hemisphere	**2.9**	**2.3**	**0.5**	**3.9**	**0.5**	**0.1**	**2.2**	**5.7**	**4.3**	**4.8**	**4.2**
Antigua and Barbuda	3.6	4.9	4.9	3.3	1.5	2.0	4.3	5.2	5.0	7.1	3.9
Argentina	3.2	3.9	–3.4	–0.8	–4.4	–10.9	8.8	9.0	9.2	8.0	6.0
Bahamas, The	1.1	6.8	4.0	1.9	0.8	2.3	1.4	1.8	2.7	4.0	4.5
Barbados	0.7	6.2	0.5	2.3	–2.6	0.5	1.9	4.8	3.9	4.2	4.9
Belize	7.2	3.7	8.7	13.0	4.9	5.1	9.3	4.6	3.5	5.3	2.6
Bolivia	4.1	5.0	0.4	2.5	1.7	2.5	2.9	3.9	4.1	4.1	3.9
Brazil	2.0	0.1	0.8	4.4	1.3	1.9	0.5	4.9	2.3	3.6	4.0
Chile	7.9	3.2	–0.8	4.5	3.4	2.2	3.9	6.2	6.3	5.2	5.5
Colombia	4.0	0.6	–4.2	2.9	1.5	1.9	3.9	4.8	5.1	4.8	4.0
Costa Rica	4.6	8.4	8.2	1.8	1.1	2.9	6.4	4.1	5.9	6.5	4.5
Dominica	2.6	2.8	1.6	1.4	–4.2	–5.1	0.1	3.0	3.4	3.0	3.0
Dominican Republic	3.7	7.3	8.1	7.8	4.0	4.5	–1.9	2.0	9.3	5.5	5.0
Ecuador	3.7	2.1	–6.3	2.8	5.3	4.2	3.6	7.9	4.7	4.4	3.2
El Salvador	4.4	3.7	3.4	2.2	1.7	2.3	2.3	1.8	2.8	3.5	3.5
Grenada	3.0	7.9	7.3	7.0	–4.4	0.8	5.8	–3.0	5.0	6.5	5.0
Guatemala	4.0	5.0	3.8	3.6	2.3	2.2	2.1	2.7	3.2	4.1	4.0
Guyana	3.8	–1.7	3.0	–1.3	2.3	1.1	–0.7	1.6	–3.0	3.5	4.1
Haiti	–0.7	2.3	2.6	1.3	–0.6	–0.5	0.2	–2.6	0.4	2.3	3.6
Honduras	3.5	2.9	–1.9	5.7	2.6	2.7	3.5	4.6	4.2	4.5	4.5
Jamaica	1.0	–1.2	1.0	0.7	1.5	1.1	2.3	0.9	1.4	2.8	3.0
Mexico	3.0	5.0	3.8	6.6	—	0.8	1.4	4.2	3.0	4.0	3.5
Netherlands Antilles	3.0	–3.1	–1.8	–2.0	1.4	0.4	1.4	1.0	0.7	1.8	2.7
Nicaragua	0.5	3.7	7.0	4.1	3.0	0.8	2.3	5.1	4.0	3.7	4.3
Panama	3.6	7.3	3.9	2.7	0.6	2.2	4.2	7.6	6.4	6.5	6.1
Paraguay	3.7	0.6	–1.5	–3.3	2.1	—	3.8	4.1	2.9	3.5	4.0
Peru	0.6	–0.7	0.9	3.0	0.2	5.2	3.9	5.2	6.4	6.0	5.0
St. Kitts and Nevis	5.2	1.1	3.7	4.4	2.6	1.6	0.6	7.1	6.7	5.2	4.1
St. Lucia	4.5	3.3	3.9	–0.3	–4.1	0.5	3.1	4.0	5.4	6.0	4.0
St. Vincent and the Grenadines	4.2	5.7	3.6	2.0	–0.1	3.2	2.8	6.8	2.2	3.4	3.7
Suriname	1.7	1.6	–0.9	–0.1	4.5	3.0	5.3	7.8	5.1	4.5	4.4
Trinidad and Tobago	1.8	8.1	8.0	6.9	4.2	7.9	13.9	9.1	7.9	12.5	6.9
Uruguay	3.3	4.5	–2.8	–1.4	–3.4	–11.0	2.2	11.8	6.6	4.6	4.2
Venezuela	2.6	0.3	–6.0	3.7	3.4	–8.9	–7.7	17.9	9.3	7.5	3.7

[1]For many countries, figures for recent years are IMF staff estimates. Data for some countries are for fiscal years.

[2]The percent changes in 2002 are calculated over a period of 18 months, reflecting a change in the fiscal year cycle (from July–June to January–December).

[3]Data for some countries refer to real net material product (NMP) or are estimates based on NMP. For many countries, figures for recent years are IMF staff estimates. The figures should be interpreted only as indicative of broad orders of magnitude because reliable, comparable data are not generally available. In particular, the growth of output of new private enterprises of the informal economy is not fully reflected in the recent figures.

[4]Mongolia, which is not a member of the Commonwealth of Independent States, is included in this group for reasons of geography and similarities in economic structure.

Table 7. Summary of Inflation

(Percent)

	Ten-Year Averages											
	1988–97	1998–2007	1998	1999	2000	2001	2002	2003	2004	2005	2006	2007
GDP deflators												
Advanced economies	**3.2**	**1.7**	**1.3**	**0.9**	**1.5**	**1.9**	**1.6**	**1.6**	**1.9**	**2.0**	**2.1**	**1.9**
United States	2.7	2.2	1.1	1.4	2.2	2.4	1.7	2.1	2.8	3.0	2.9	2.0
Euro area	. . .	1.9	1.6	1.0	1.5	2.7	2.6	2.1	1.9	1.9	2.0	2.0
Japan	1.0	–0.9	–0.1	–1.3	–1.7	–1.2	–1.6	–1.6	–1.2	–1.3	—	0.5
Other advanced economies[1]	4.3	1.8	1.9	1.0	2.0	2.0	1.7	2.0	2.1	1.9	1.7	2.1
Consumer prices												
Advanced economies	**3.4**	**2.0**	**1.5**	**1.4**	**2.2**	**2.1**	**1.5**	**1.8**	**2.0**	**2.3**	**2.6**	**2.3**
United States	3.5	2.6	1.5	2.2	3.4	2.8	1.6	2.3	2.7	3.4	3.6	2.9
Euro area[2]	. . .	2.0	1.1	1.1	2.1	2.3	2.2	2.1	2.1	2.2	2.3	2.4
Japan	1.5	–0.2	0.7	–0.3	–0.4	–0.8	–0.9	–0.3	—	–0.6	0.3	0.7
Other advanced economies	4.2	1.9	2.2	1.1	1.8	2.1	1.7	1.8	1.7	2.1	2.3	2.2
Other emerging market and developing countries	**53.5**	**6.7**	**11.0**	**10.0**	**7.0**	**6.5**	**5.7**	**5.8**	**5.6**	**5.3**	**5.2**	**5.0**
Regional groups												
Africa	29.1	10.5	9.3	11.9	13.6	12.8	9.9	10.7	8.0	8.5	9.9	10.6
Central and eastern Europe	65.4	13.9	32.8	23.0	22.8	19.4	14.7	9.2	6.1	4.8	5.3	4.6
Commonwealth of Independent States[3]	. . .	19.5	23.9	69.6	24.6	20.3	13.8	12.0	10.3	12.3	9.6	9.2
Developing Asia	10.5	3.4	7.8	2.5	1.7	2.7	2.0	2.5	4.1	3.5	3.8	3.6
Middle East	12.4	6.3	6.8	6.7	4.1	3.9	5.4	6.3	7.6	7.7	7.1	7.9
Western Hemisphere	162.8	7.4	9.0	8.3	7.6	6.1	8.8	10.5	6.5	6.3	5.6	5.2
Memorandum												
European Union	9.3	2.2	2.2	1.6	2.5	2.6	2.2	2.0	2.1	2.2	2.3	2.4
Analytical groups												
By source of export earnings												
Fuel	73.1	13.9	17.7	36.5	14.0	13.6	11.7	11.3	9.7	10.0	8.6	8.3
Nonfuel	50.6	5.6	10.0	6.5	5.9	5.5	4.8	5.0	5.0	4.6	4.7	4.6
of which, primary products	65.9	20.6	12.9	25.3	31.4	28.5	15.8	18.9	13.9	16.0	20.6	23.9
By external financing source												
Net debtor countries	61.1	8.4	15.3	10.5	8.8	8.3	8.3	7.5	5.8	6.4	6.8	6.1
of which, official financing	37.5	9.1	19.1	10.4	6.2	7.7	9.4	7.7	6.5	8.8	9.4	6.8
Net debtor countries by debt-servicing experience												
Countries with arrears and/or rescheduling during 1999–2003	45.7	12.0	21.0	13.1	9.2	10.9	13.1	10.8	8.7	10.8	12.6	10.7
Memorandum												
Median inflation rate												
Advanced economies	3.3	2.1	1.6	1.3	2.6	2.5	2.1	2.1	1.9	2.1	2.3	2.1
Other emerging market and developing countries	10.3	4.7	6.6	3.8	4.0	4.7	3.3	4.2	4.4	5.6	5.5	4.8

[1]In this table, "other advanced economies" means advanced economies excluding the United States, euro area countries, and Japan.

[2]Based on Eurostat's harmonized index of consumer prices.

[3]Mongolia, which is not a member of the Commonwealth of Independent States, is included in this group for reasons of geography and similarities in economic structure.

Table 8. Advanced Economies: GDP Deflators and Consumer Prices
(Annual percent change)

	Ten-Year Averages												Fourth Quarter[1]		
	1988–97	1998–2007	1998	1999	2000	2001	2002	2003	2004	2005	2006	2007	2005	2006	2007
GDP deflators															
Advanced economies	**3.2**	**1.7**	**1.3**	**0.9**	**1.5**	**1.9**	**1.6**	**1.6**	**1.9**	**2.0**	**2.1**	**1.9**	. . .	. . .	. . .
United States	2.7	2.2	1.1	1.4	2.2	2.4	1.7	2.1	2.8	3.0	2.9	2.0	3.1	2.6	2.0
Euro area	. . .	1.9	1.6	1.0	1.5	2.7	2.6	2.1	1.9	1.9	2.0	2.0	2.1	2.1	1.9
Germany	3.5	0.8	0.6	0.4	–0.6	1.2	1.4	1.1	0.9	0.7	1.1	1.4	0.7	1.7	0.8
France	2.1	1.6	1.2	—	1.5	2.0	2.4	1.8	1.7	1.8	1.9	1.8	1.9	1.8	1.8
Italy	5.3	2.5	2.6	1.3	2.0	3.0	3.4	3.1	2.9	2.1	2.3	2.2	2.9	2.4	1.9
Spain	5.2	3.7	2.5	2.6	3.5	4.2	4.4	4.0	4.1	4.4	4.0	3.5	4.4	3.7	3.4
Netherlands	1.9	2.9	1.7	1.6	3.9	9.7	3.8	2.2	0.7	1.7	1.9	1.9	1.9	1.4	2.4
Belgium	2.6	1.6	1.8	0.7	1.7	1.8	1.8	1.7	2.3	2.2	1.0	1.4	2.8	–0.4	2.8
Austria	2.7	1.4	0.3	0.6	1.8	1.8	1.4	1.3	1.7	1.9	1.7	1.7	1.8	1.8	1.7
Finland	3.2	1.4	3.4	0.9	2.6	3.0	1.3	–0.4	0.6	0.6	1.1	0.9	1.2	0.3	2.6
Greece	13.5	3.7	5.2	3.0	5.7	1.8	3.8	3.5	3.4	3.7	3.7	3.6	3.2	4.9	–0.1
Portugal	7.9	3.1	3.7	3.3	3.0	3.7	3.9	2.7	2.8	2.7	2.6	2.4	2.4	2.5	2.5
Ireland	3.2	3.9	6.5	4.0	5.5	5.6	5.0	2.5	1.8	3.5	2.4	2.3	4.2	0.4	4.4
Luxembourg	2.8	2.5	–0.4	5.3	2.0	0.1	2.7	4.8	1.0	4.2	2.9	2.2	. . .	. . .	. . .
Japan	1.0	–0.9	–0.1	–1.3	–1.7	–1.2	–1.6	–1.6	–1.2	–1.3	—	0.5	–1.6	1.5	–0.6
United Kingdom	4.5	2.5	2.7	2.2	1.3	2.2	3.1	3.1	2.6	2.2	2.9	2.7	2.2	2.5	2.9
Canada	2.4	2.1	–0.4	1.7	4.1	1.1	1.1	3.4	3.0	3.2	1.9	2.2	4.1	0.8	2.3
Korea	7.3	1.8	5.8	–0.1	0.7	3.5	2.8	2.7	2.7	–0.4	–1.6	1.7	–0.6	–2.4	3.7
Australia	3.1	2.9	0.5	0.5	4.1	4.0	2.6	3.2	3.4	4.5	3.8	2.5	5.0	2.3	2.6
Taiwan Province of China	2.7	–0.5	2.6	–1.3	–1.6	0.5	–0.8	–2.1	–1.6	–0.7	–0.5	0.5	—	0.2	0.6
Sweden	4.4	1.4	0.6	0.9	1.4	2.1	1.6	2.0	0.8	1.1	1.6	1.8	1.8	1.6	1.8
Switzerland	2.3	0.8	–0.3	0.7	0.8	0.6	1.6	1.2	0.5	0.6	1.0	1.1	0.1	1.0	1.1
Hong Kong SAR	7.7	–2.6	0.2	–5.7	–5.6	–1.8	–3.5	–6.3	–3.6	–0.2	—	1.3	0.7	–0.4	1.8
Denmark	2.4	2.2	1.2	1.7	3.0	2.5	2.3	1.9	2.2	2.6	2.5	1.7	1.3	4.6	–0.7
Norway	2.8	4.9	–0.7	6.6	15.9	1.1	–1.6	2.6	5.6	8.4	8.5	4.1	9.2	6.2	4.1
Israel	14.2	2.4	6.3	6.0	1.3	1.8	4.8	–0.3	–0.1	0.8	2.1	2.1	2.2	2.2	1.9
Singapore	3.2	0.1	–1.7	–5.3	3.7	–1.8	–0.7	–0.9	3.5	0.6	2.1	2.3	–0.2	4.5	2.3
New Zealand	3.0	2.4	1.8	0.6	2.9	3.9	0.3	2.2	3.7	2.3	3.5	3.0	1.5	3.8	2.4
Cyprus	4.5	2.9	2.4	2.3	3.7	3.2	2.2	5.0	2.4	2.8	3.0	2.3	. . .	. . .	. . .
Iceland	8.3	4.4	5.0	3.2	3.6	8.6	5.6	0.5	2.3	2.9	9.5	3.4	. . .	. . .	. . .
Memorandum															
Major advanced economies	2.8	1.5	1.0	0.8	1.2	1.6	1.4	1.6	1.9	1.9	2.1	1.8	2.0	2.2	1.5
Newly industrialized Asian economies	5.7	0.4	3.6	–1.5	–0.6	1.6	0.7	–0.1	0.6	–0.4	–0.8	1.3	–0.2	–0.9	2.5
Consumer prices															
Advanced economies	**3.4**	**2.0**	**1.5**	**1.4**	**2.2**	**2.1**	**1.5**	**1.8**	**2.0**	**2.3**	**2.6**	**2.3**	. . .	. . .	. . .
United States	3.5	2.6	1.5	2.2	3.4	2.8	1.6	2.3	2.7	3.4	3.6	2.9	3.7	3.3	2.6
Euro area[2]	. . .	2.0	1.1	1.1	2.1	2.3	2.2	2.1	2.1	2.2	2.3	2.4	2.3	2.3	2.2
Germany	2.7	1.6	0.9	0.6	1.5	2.0	1.4	1.0	1.7	2.0	2.0	2.6	2.2	2.0	2.2
France	2.4	1.7	0.7	0.5	1.8	1.8	1.9	2.2	2.3	1.9	2.0	1.9	1.8	1.9	2.1
Italy	4.9	2.3	2.0	1.7	2.6	2.3	2.6	2.8	2.3	2.3	2.4	2.1	2.7	2.2	1.3
Spain	5.1	3.1	1.8	2.2	3.5	2.8	3.6	3.1	3.1	3.4	3.8	3.4	3.5	3.5	3.5
Japan	1.5	–0.2	0.7	–0.3	–0.4	–0.8	–0.9	–0.3	—	–0.6	0.3	0.7	–1.0	0.6	1.1
United Kingdom[2]	4.0	1.6	1.6	1.3	0.9	1.2	1.3	1.4	1.3	2.0	2.3	2.4	2.1	2.7	2.2
Canada	2.8	2.1	1.0	1.7	2.7	2.5	2.3	2.7	1.8	2.2	2.2	1.9	2.3	1.9	2.0
Other advanced economies	4.8	2.0	2.9	0.9	2.0	2.4	1.7	1.8	1.9	2.1	2.3	2.3	. . .	. . .	. . .
Memorandum															
Major advanced economies	3.1	1.9	1.3	1.4	2.2	1.9	1.3	1.7	2.0	2.3	2.6	2.3	2.4	2.5	2.1
Newly industrialized Asian economies	5.3	1.9	4.4	—	1.1	1.9	0.9	1.4	2.4	2.2	2.2	2.2	2.3	2.6	1.9

[1]From fourth quarter of preceding year.
[2]Based on Eurostat's harmonized index of consumer prices.

Table 9. Advanced Economies: Hourly Earnings, Productivity, and Unit Labor Costs in Manufacturing
(Annual percent change)

	Ten-Year Averages											
	1988–97	1998–2007	1998	1999	2000	2001	2002	2003	2004	2005	2006	2007
Hourly earnings												
Advanced economies	**4.7**	**3.7**	**3.3**	**2.9**	**5.3**	**2.9**	**4.4**	**4.6**	**2.4**	**3.5**	**3.4**	**4.0**
United States	3.3	4.9	5.8	3.9	9.0	2.4	7.3	7.0	2.0	4.6	3.6	3.9
Euro area	. . .	3.6	2.8	5.2	5.2	4.3	3.4	2.5	2.7	3.1	3.1	3.5
Germany	5.4	2.3	1.3	2.5	3.6	3.5	2.4	2.5	0.7	1.9	2.1	2.7
France	3.7	2.8	0.6	1.0	3.6	1.5	3.3	3.3	3.4	3.0	3.9	4.5
Italy	6.2	2.1	–1.0	0.9	1.6	2.5	3.2	2.8	4.0	1.5	3.0	2.8
Spain	6.4	3.6	3.3	2.7	2.9	4.1	5.0	4.9	4.0	3.5	3.0	3.0
Japan	3.9	0.6	0.8	–0.7	–0.1	1.0	–1.3	1.0	0.4	1.2	0.9	3.0
United Kingdom	6.4	4.2	4.6	4.0	4.7	4.3	3.5	3.6	3.7	3.6	5.2	5.0
Canada	3.8	3.5	3.4	0.2	1.4	2.1	3.1	3.7	1.6	5.3	6.4	8.6
Other advanced economies	8.2	5.0	2.6	6.5	6.5	5.5	4.5	4.9	5.4	4.6	4.9	5.0
Memorandum												
Major advanced economies	4.1	3.5	3.4	2.4	5.4	2.4	4.4	4.6	2.0	3.4	3.2	3.9
Newly industrialized Asian economies	12.9	6.7	1.7	9.6	7.7	8.3	5.8	7.1	7.6	6.2	6.5	6.3
Productivity[1]												
Advanced economies	**3.2**	**3.4**	**2.6**	**3.9**	**5.0**	**0.8**	**4.2**	**4.5**	**3.5**	**3.1**	**3.2**	**3.0**
United States	3.1	4.1	5.5	4.4	4.2	1.7	7.0	6.2	1.9	4.1	3.6	3.0
Euro area	. . .	3.4	3.8	5.3	6.6	2.5	1.5	2.1	3.9	3.2	2.8	2.6
Germany	3.6	3.4	0.3	2.6	5.4	3.0	1.1	4.3	4.9	5.4	4.0	3.0
France	4.3	4.2	5.5	2.9	6.8	1.0	3.1	4.1	4.6	4.5	4.5	5.0
Italy	1.8	–0.3	–0.8	–0.4	1.7	–0.7	–1.1	–0.7	1.1	–1.9	—	0.1
Spain	3.0	1.5	1.4	1.4	0.5	—	2.0	4.1	3.4	1.0	1.1	0.5
Japan	2.7	2.4	–3.6	3.2	6.8	–3.0	3.7	5.3	5.3	1.6	2.6	2.6
United Kingdom	3.0	3.9	1.3	4.5	6.2	3.5	2.0	4.8	6.4	2.5	3.8	4.6
Canada	2.6	3.2	3.5	2.8	4.3	–1.7	1.9	–0.3	3.8	5.5	4.8	8.0
Other advanced economies	3.7	3.8	0.9	7.9	7.1	—	4.3	3.7	5.1	2.7	3.3	3.1
Memorandum												
Major advanced economies	3.1	3.4	2.6	3.5	4.9	0.8	4.4	4.8	3.3	3.4	3.4	3.2
Newly industrialized Asian economies	5.9	5.7	–0.8	13.0	11.9	–0.5	6.1	5.7	7.7	4.9	5.2	4.7
Unit labor costs												
Advanced economies	**1.6**	**0.3**	**0.9**	**–0.9**	**0.3**	**2.1**	**0.2**	**0.1**	**–1.0**	**0.4**	**0.2**	**0.9**
United States	0.2	0.8	0.3	–0.5	4.6	0.8	0.3	0.8	0.1	0.5	–0.1	0.8
Euro area	. . .	0.2	–0.9	–0.2	–1.3	1.8	1.8	0.3	–1.1	–0.1	0.3	0.9
Germany	1.7	–1.0	1.0	–0.1	–1.7	0.5	1.3	–1.7	–4.0	–3.3	–1.8	–0.3
France	–0.5	–1.3	–4.7	–1.8	–3.1	0.5	0.2	–0.7	–1.1	–1.4	–0.6	–0.5
Italy	4.3	2.4	–0.2	1.3	–0.1	3.3	4.4	3.5	2.8	3.4	3.0	2.7
Spain	3.3	2.1	1.9	1.2	2.3	4.1	2.9	0.9	0.5	2.5	1.9	2.5
Japan	1.1	–1.7	4.6	–3.8	–6.5	4.0	–4.8	–4.1	–4.7	–0.4	–1.7	0.4
United Kingdom[2]	3.4	0.3	3.3	–0.5	–1.4	0.8	1.5	–1.1	–2.5	1.1	1.4	0.4
Canada	1.2	0.3	–0.1	–2.6	–2.8	3.9	1.1	4.0	–2.1	–0.2	1.6	0.5
Other advanced economies	4.5	1.1	2.1	–1.2	–0.7	5.3	0.1	0.8	—	1.5	1.4	1.6
Memorandum												
Major advanced economies	1.1	0.1	0.9	–1.0	0.5	1.5	—	–0.2	–1.2	—	–0.1	0.6
Newly industrialized Asian economies	6.5	0.6	3.2	–2.7	–3.9	8.1	–0.6	0.6	–0.8	0.7	0.9	1.2

[1]Refers to labor productivity, measured as the ratio of hourly compensation to unit labor costs.
[2]Data refer to unit wage cost.

Table 10. Other Emerging Market and Developing Countries: Consumer Prices

(Annual percent change)

	Ten-Year Averages											
	1988–97	1998–2007	1998	1999	2000	2001	2002	2003	2004	2005	2006	2007
Other emerging market and developing countries	**53.5**	**6.7**	**11.0**	**10.0**	**7.0**	**6.5**	**5.7**	**5.8**	**5.6**	**5.3**	**5.2**	**5.0**
Regional groups												
Africa	29.1	10.5	9.3	11.9	13.6	12.8	9.9	10.7	8.0	8.5	9.9	10.6
Sub-Sahara	34.6	12.9	10.9	14.9	17.4	15.9	12.2	13.4	9.6	10.7	11.7	12.6
Excluding Nigeria and South Africa	55.1	18.8	14.1	24.3	29.6	23.3	14.2	19.0	14.5	14.5	17.2	18.4
Central and eastern Europe	65.4	13.9	32.8	23.0	22.8	19.4	14.7	9.2	6.1	4.8	5.3	4.6
Commonwealth of Independent States[1]	. . .	19.5	23.9	69.6	24.6	20.3	13.8	12.0	10.3	12.3	9.6	9.2
Russia	. . .	21.1	27.7	85.7	20.8	21.5	15.8	13.7	10.9	12.6	9.7	8.5
Excluding Russia	. . .	15.9	15.9	37.0	34.3	17.6	9.3	8.3	9.1	11.7	9.4	10.9
Developing Asia	10.5	3.4	7.8	2.5	1.7	2.7	2.0	2.5	4.1	3.5	3.8	3.6
China	11.4	0.9	–0.8	–1.4	0.4	0.7	–0.8	1.2	3.9	1.8	1.5	2.2
India	9.3	5.2	13.2	4.7	3.9	3.7	4.5	3.7	3.9	4.0	5.6	5.3
Excluding China and India	9.9	7.7	21.9	9.0	2.6	6.2	6.4	4.6	5.0	7.8	8.6	6.0
Middle East	12.4	6.3	6.8	6.7	4.1	3.9	5.4	6.3	7.6	7.7	7.1	7.9
Western Hemisphere	162.8	7.4	9.0	8.3	7.6	6.1	8.8	10.5	6.5	6.3	5.6	5.2
Brazil	576.3	6.7	3.2	4.9	7.1	6.8	8.4	14.8	6.6	6.9	4.5	4.1
Mexico	28.0	7.2	15.9	16.6	9.5	6.4	5.0	4.5	4.7	4.0	3.5	3.3
Analytical groups												
By source of export earnings												
Fuel	73.1	13.9	17.7	36.5	14.0	13.6	11.7	11.3	9.7	10.0	8.6	8.3
Nonfuel	50.6	5.6	10.0	6.5	5.9	5.5	4.8	5.0	5.0	4.6	4.7	4.6
of which, primary products	65.9	20.6	12.9	25.3	31.4	28.5	15.8	18.9	13.9	16.0	20.6	23.9
By external financing source												
Net debtor countries	61.1	8.4	15.3	10.5	8.8	8.3	8.3	7.5	5.8	6.4	6.8	6.1
of which, official financing	37.5	9.1	19.1	10.4	6.2	7.7	9.4	7.7	6.5	8.8	9.4	6.8
Net debtor countries by debt-servicing experience												
Countries with arrears and/or rescheduling during 1999–2003	45.7	12.0	21.0	13.1	9.2	10.9	13.1	10.8	8.7	10.8	12.6	10.7
Other groups												
Heavily indebted poor countries	64.6	12.0	10.6	19.4	26.7	20.8	6.0	8.5	6.3	10.0	7.7	6.5
Middle East and north Africa	14.0	5.6	6.5	5.9	3.6	3.7	4.8	5.5	6.7	6.4	6.5	6.9
Memorandum												
Median												
Other emerging market and developing countries	10.3	4.7	6.6	3.8	4.0	4.7	3.3	4.2	4.4	5.6	5.5	4.8
Africa	10.4	5.1	5.9	3.7	5.9	5.2	4.0	5.5	4.1	6.4	5.0	4.9
Central and eastern Europe	51.7	4.2	8.2	3.3	5.8	5.5	3.3	2.3	3.5	2.7	3.5	3.3
Commonwealth of Independent States[1]	. . .	10.8	10.5	23.5	18.7	9.8	5.6	5.6	7.1	10.3	8.7	8.0
Developing Asia	8.6	4.8	8.6	4.0	2.2	3.7	3.8	3.5	4.6	5.8	6.7	5.3
Middle East	5.7	2.6	2.9	2.1	0.7	1.4	0.8	1.7	3.4	3.9	4.5	5.0
Western Hemisphere	12.7	4.4	5.1	3.5	4.6	4.4	4.2	4.5	4.4	4.7	4.7	4.1

[1]Mongolia, which is not a member of the Commonwealth of Independent States, is included in this group for reasons of geography and similarities in economic structure.

Table 11. Other Emerging Market and Developing Countries—by Country: Consumer Prices[1]

(Annual percent change)

	Average 1988–97	1998	1999	2000	2001	2002	2003	2004	2005	2006	2007
Africa	**29.1**	**9.3**	**11.9**	**13.6**	**12.8**	**9.9**	**10.7**	**8.0**	**8.5**	**9.9**	**10.6**
Algeria	18.2	5.0	2.6	0.3	4.2	1.4	2.6	3.6	1.6	5.0	5.5
Angola	363.6	107.4	248.2	325.0	152.6	108.9	98.3	43.6	23.0	12.9	8.3
Benin	6.9	5.8	0.3	4.2	4.0	2.4	1.5	0.9	5.4	3.0	2.5
Botswana	11.5	6.5	7.8	8.5	6.6	8.0	9.3	6.9	8.6	11.3	6.0
Burkina Faso	4.3	5.0	–1.1	–0.3	4.7	2.3	2.0	–0.4	6.4	3.2	2.0
Burundi	13.6	12.5	3.4	24.3	9.3	–1.3	10.7	8.0	13.4	2.5	3.3
Cameroon[2]	4.6	3.9	2.9	0.8	2.8	6.3	0.6	0.3	2.0	2.9	3.0
Cape Verde	7.2	4.4	4.3	–2.4	3.7	1.9	1.2	–1.9	0.4	6.2	0.2
Central African Republic	3.5	–1.9	–1.4	3.2	3.8	2.3	4.4	–2.2	2.9	3.3	1.9
Chad	5.6	4.3	–8.4	3.8	12.4	5.2	–1.8	–5.4	7.9	8.6	3.0
Comoros	2.8	1.2	1.1	5.9	5.6	3.6	3.7	4.5	3.6	3.8	3.0
Congo, Dem. Rep. of	821.6	29.1	284.9	550.0	357.3	25.3	12.8	4.0	21.4	10.0	8.9
Congo, Rep. of	4.2	1.8	3.1	0.4	0.8	3.1	1.5	3.6	2.5	2.5	2.5
Côte d'Ivoire	6.0	4.5	0.7	2.5	4.4	3.1	3.3	1.5	3.9	2.6	2.8
Djibouti	4.9	2.2	0.2	1.6	1.8	0.6	2.0	3.1	3.1	3.0	3.0
Equatorial Guinea	6.2	7.9	0.4	4.8	8.8	7.6	7.9	4.3	6.2	4.8	4.1
Eritrea	. . .	9.5	8.4	19.9	14.6	16.9	22.7	25.1	12.4	16.5	22.0
Ethiopia	7.5	3.6	4.8	6.2	–5.2	–7.2	15.1	8.6	6.8	12.3	12.2
Gabon	4.4	2.3	–0.7	0.5	2.1	0.2	2.1	0.4	—	1.8	1.2
Gambia, The	6.8	1.1	3.8	0.9	4.5	8.6	17.0	14.2	3.2	2.9	3.7
Ghana	29.4	19.2	12.4	25.2	32.9	14.8	26.7	12.6	15.1	8.8	7.1
Guinea	5.2	5.1	4.6	6.8	5.4	3.0	12.9	17.5	31.4	27.0	12.4
Guinea-Bissau	49.9	8.0	–2.1	8.6	3.3	3.3	–3.5	0.8	3.4	2.2	2.2
Kenya	16.0	6.7	5.8	10.0	5.8	2.0	9.8	11.6	10.3	13.0	1.6
Lesotho	12.0	8.2	7.8	6.1	8.0	12.2	6.4	4.4	4.0	4.6	4.8
Liberia	. . .	. . .	. . .	5.3	12.1	14.2	10.3	3.6	6.9	8.0	7.5
Madagascar	18.5	6.2	8.1	10.7	6.9	16.2	–1.1	14.0	18.4	11.2	9.6
Malawi	26.2	29.8	44.8	29.6	27.2	18.1	9.6	11.4	15.5	10.9	8.2
Mali	4.4	4.1	–1.2	–0.7	5.2	5.0	–1.3	–3.1	6.4	1.9	2.5
Mauritania	5.5	6.0	3.6	6.8	7.7	5.4	5.3	10.4	12.1	6.0	5.1
Mauritius	8.1	6.8	6.9	5.5	4.8	4.4	5.1	3.9	5.6	4.9	5.7
Morocco	4.7	2.7	0.7	1.9	0.6	2.8	1.2	1.5	1.0	2.5	2.0
Mozambique, Rep. of	42.4	1.5	2.9	12.7	16.8	13.5	12.6	6.4	10.1	7.4	5.7
Namibia	11.5	6.2	8.6	9.3	9.3	11.3	7.2	4.1	2.4	5.1	5.0
Niger	4.2	4.5	–2.3	2.9	4.0	2.7	–1.8	0.4	7.8	—	2.0
Nigeria	35.7	10.0	6.6	6.9	18.0	13.7	14.0	15.0	17.9	9.4	8.0
Rwanda	16.3	6.8	–2.4	3.9	3.4	2.0	7.4	12.0	9.2	5.5	5.0
São Tomé and Príncipe	43.0	42.1	11.0	11.0	9.5	9.2	9.6	12.8	16.3	19.8	17.2
Senegal	3.7	1.1	0.8	0.7	3.0	2.3	—	0.5	1.7	2.3	2.3
Seychelles	1.5	2.7	6.3	6.3	6.0	0.2	3.2	3.9	1.0	–0.4	1.8
Sierra Leone	45.0	36.0	34.1	–0.9	2.6	–3.7	7.5	14.2	12.1	11.3	8.3
South Africa	11.4	6.9	5.2	5.4	5.7	9.2	5.8	1.4	3.4	4.6	5.7
Sudan	87.6	17.1	16.0	8.0	4.9	8.3	7.7	8.4	8.5	7.0	5.0
Swaziland	10.9	7.5	5.9	7.2	7.5	11.7	7.4	3.4	4.8	5.0	5.9
Tanzania	25.8	13.2	9.0	6.2	5.1	4.6	4.4	4.1	4.4	7.5	6.5
Togo	5.8	1.0	–0.1	1.9	3.9	3.1	–0.9	0.4	6.8	3.0	2.7
Tunisia	5.7	3.1	2.7	2.3	2.0	2.7	2.7	3.6	2.0	3.9	2.0
Uganda	38.6	5.8	0.2	5.8	4.5	–2.0	5.7	5.0	8.0	6.7	7.0
Zambia	82.4	24.5	26.8	26.1	21.7	22.2	21.4	18.0	18.3	9.2	8.6
Zimbabwe	21.4	31.3	58.0	55.6	73.4	133.2	365.0	350.0	237.8	1,216.0	4,278.8

Table 11 ***(continued)***

	Average 1988–97	1998	1999	2000	2001	2002	2003	2004	2005	2006	2007
Central and eastern Europe[3]	**65.4**	**32.8**	**23.0**	**22.8**	**19.4**	**14.7**	**9.2**	**6.1**	**4.8**	**5.3**	**4.6**
Albania	32.1	20.6	0.4	—	3.1	5.2	2.3	2.9	2.4	2.2	3.0
Bosnia and Herzegovina	. . .	–0.4	3.0	5.1	3.2	0.3	0.6	0.3	1.9	6.0	2.5
Bulgaria	108.0	18.8	2.6	10.4	7.5	5.8	2.3	6.1	5.0	7.4	3.8
Croatia	. . .	5.7	4.0	4.6	3.7	1.7	1.8	2.1	3.3	3.5	2.8
Czech Republic	12.7	10.7	2.1	4.0	4.7	1.8	0.1	2.8	1.8	2.9	3.3
Estonia	. . .	8.2	3.3	4.0	5.8	3.6	1.3	3.0	4.1	4.6	3.8
Hungary	22.9	14.2	10.0	9.8	9.2	5.3	4.6	6.8	3.6	3.5	5.8
Latvia	. . .	4.7	2.4	2.6	2.5	1.9	2.9	6.2	6.8	6.6	6.3
Lithuania	. . .	5.4	1.5	1.1	1.6	0.3	–1.1	1.2	2.7	3.6	3.3
Macedonia, FYR	. . .	1.4	–2.7	5.8	4.8	2.2	1.4	0.1	0.5	2.9	2.0
Malta	2.7	3.8	2.2	3.1	2.5	2.6	1.9	2.7	2.5	2.9	2.8
Poland	76.7	11.8	7.3	10.1	5.5	1.9	0.8	3.5	2.1	0.9	2.3
Romania	94.0	59.1	45.8	45.7	34.5	22.5	15.3	11.9	9.0	7.8	5.7
Serbia	. . .	29.8	42.2	71.8	91.8	19.5	11.7	10.1	17.3	14.3	9.7
Slovak Republic	. . .	6.7	10.7	12.0	7.3	3.3	8.5	7.5	2.7	4.7	3.6
Slovenia	. . .	8.0	6.2	8.8	8.4	7.5	5.6	3.6	2.5	2.5	2.3
Turkey	75.8	83.6	63.5	54.3	53.9	44.8	25.2	8.6	8.2	10.2	7.2
Commonwealth of Independent States[3,4]	**. . .**	**23.9**	**69.6**	**24.6**	**20.3**	**13.8**	**12.0**	**10.3**	**12.3**	**9.6**	**9.2**
Russia	. . .	27.7	85.7	20.8	21.5	15.8	13.7	10.9	12.6	9.7	8.5
Excluding Russia	. . .	15.9	37.0	34.3	17.6	9.3	8.3	9.1	11.7	9.4	10.9
Armenia	. . .	8.7	0.6	–0.8	3.1	1.1	4.7	7.0	0.6	3.0	3.0
Azerbaijan	. . .	–0.8	–8.5	1.8	1.5	2.8	2.2	6.7	9.7	8.7	10.5
Belarus	. . .	73.0	293.7	168.6	61.1	42.6	28.4	18.1	10.3	7.9	9.0
Georgia	. . .	3.6	19.1	4.0	4.7	5.6	4.8	5.7	8.3	9.6	6.0
Kazakhstan	. . .	7.3	8.4	13.3	8.4	5.9	6.4	6.9	7.6	8.5	7.9
Kyrgyz Republic	. . .	10.5	35.9	18.7	6.9	2.1	3.1	4.1	4.3	5.7	4.5
Moldova	. . .	7.7	39.3	31.3	9.8	5.3	11.7	12.5	11.9	11.5	10.5
Mongolia	. . .	9.4	7.6	11.6	6.3	0.9	5.1	7.9	12.5	5.0	4.8
Tajikistan	. . .	43.2	27.5	32.9	38.6	12.2	16.4	7.1	7.1	7.8	5.0
Turkmenistan	. . .	16.8	23.5	8.0	11.6	8.8	5.6	5.9	10.7	9.0	8.0
Ukraine	. . .	10.6	22.7	28.2	12.0	0.8	5.2	9.0	13.5	9.3	13.5
Uzbekistan	. . .	16.7	44.7	49.5	47.5	44.3	14.8	8.8	21.0	19.3	14.5

Table 11 *(continued)*

	Average 1988–97	1998	1999	2000	2001	2002	2003	2004	2005	2006	2007
Developing Asia	**10.5**	**7.8**	**2.5**	**1.7**	**2.7**	**2.0**	**2.5**	**4.1**	**3.5**	**3.8**	**3.6**
Afghanistan, Rep. of	. . .	. . .	. . .	. . .	. . .	. . .	5.1	24.1	13.2	12.3	8.2
Bangladesh	6.8	8.6	6.2	2.2	1.5	3.8	5.4	6.1	7.0	6.8	6.1
Bhutan	10.0	10.6	6.8	4.0	3.4	2.5	2.1	4.6	5.5	6.0	6.0
Brunei Darussalam	. . .	–0.4	—	1.2	0.6	–2.3	0.3	0.9	1.1	0.5	1.2
Cambodia	. . .	13.3	–0.5	–0.8	0.2	3.3	1.2	3.9	5.8	5.0	4.0
China	11.4	–0.8	–1.4	0.4	0.7	–0.8	1.2	3.9	1.8	1.5	2.2
Fiji	5.1	5.9	2.0	1.1	4.3	0.8	4.2	2.8	3.7	4.2	3.2
India	9.3	13.2	4.7	3.9	3.7	4.5	3.7	3.9	4.0	5.6	5.3
Indonesia	8.0	58.0	20.7	3.8	11.5	11.8	6.8	6.1	10.5	13.0	5.9
Kiribati	3.7	4.7	0.4	1.0	7.3	1.1	–1.6	–0.6	—	1.6	2.5
Lao PDR	12.5	90.1	128.4	23.2	7.8	10.6	15.5	10.5	7.2	7.7	5.0
Malaysia	3.2	5.1	2.8	1.6	1.4	1.8	1.1	1.4	3.0	3.8	2.7
Maldives	9.7	–1.4	3.0	–1.2	0.7	0.9	–2.8	6.3	3.3	7.0	6.0
Myanmar	25.9	49.1	10.9	–1.7	34.5	58.1	24.9	3.8	10.1	26.3	37.5
Nepal	9.8	11.4	3.4	2.4	2.9	4.7	4.0	4.5	4.5	7.9	7.6
Pakistan	10.0	7.8	5.7	3.6	4.4	2.5	3.1	4.6	9.3	7.9	7.3
Papua New Guinea	6.8	13.6	14.9	15.6	9.3	11.8	14.7	2.1	1.7	3.5	2.9
Philippines	10.4	9.7	6.4	4.0	6.8	2.9	3.5	6.0	7.6	6.7	5.0
Samoa	5.3	5.4	0.8	–0.2	1.9	7.4	4.3	7.9	7.8	3.3	4.0
Solomon Islands	11.8	12.3	8.0	6.9	7.6	9.3	10.0	6.9	7.3	8.2	8.4
Sri Lanka	12.3	9.4	4.0	1.5	12.1	10.2	2.6	7.9	10.6	8.0	7.0
Thailand	5.0	8.1	0.3	1.6	1.7	0.6	1.8	2.8	4.5	4.9	2.6
Timor-Leste, Dem. Rep. of	. . .	. . .	. . .	63.6	3.6	4.8	7.1	3.3	0.9	6.0	2.5
Tonga	5.2	3.0	3.9	5.3	6.9	10.4	11.1	11.7	9.5	7.2	10.3
Vanuatu	4.3	3.3	2.2	2.5	3.7	2.0	3.0	1.4	1.0	2.3	2.4
Vietnam	47.2	7.7	4.2	–1.6	–0.4	4.0	3.2	7.7	8.2	7.6	7.6
Middle East	**12.4**	**6.8**	**6.7**	**4.1**	**3.9**	**5.4**	**6.3**	**7.6**	**7.7**	**7.1**	**7.9**
Bahrain	1.1	–0.4	–1.3	–0.7	–1.2	–0.5	1.7	2.3	2.6	2.6	3.0
Egypt	13.4	5.0	3.7	2.8	2.4	2.4	3.2	10.3	11.4	4.1	6.2
Iran, I.R. of	24.4	18.1	20.1	12.6	11.4	15.8	15.6	15.2	12.1	14.0	15.0
Iraq	. . .	. . .	. . .	. . .	. . .	. . .	. . .	. . .	. . .	. . .	. . .
Jordan	7.7	3.1	0.6	0.7	1.8	1.8	1.6	3.4	3.5	6.3	5.7
Kuwait	3.7	0.6	3.1	1.6	1.4	0.8	1.0	1.3	3.9	3.5	3.0
Lebanon	44.2	4.5	0.2	–0.4	–0.4	1.8	1.3	–1.3	0.3	4.5	3.0
Libya	6.3	3.7	2.6	–2.9	–8.8	–9.9	–2.1	–2.2	2.5	3.0	3.5
Oman	1.8	0.4	0.5	–1.2	–0.8	–0.2	0.2	0.8	3.2	3.0	2.0
Qatar	3.2	2.9	2.2	1.7	1.4	0.2	2.3	6.8	8.8	9.0	8.0
Saudi Arabia	1.5	–0.2	–1.3	–1.1	–1.1	0.2	0.6	0.4	0.7	1.0	1.0
Syrian Arab Republic	12.1	–1.0	–3.7	–3.9	3.4	–0.5	5.8	4.4	7.2	5.6	14.4
United Arab Emirates	3.9	2.0	2.1	1.4	2.8	2.9	3.1	5.0	8.0	7.7	5.0
Yemen	37.2	11.5	8.0	10.9	11.9	12.2	10.8	12.5	11.8	15.5	13.1

Table 11 *(concluded)*

	Average 1988–97	1998	1999	2000	2001	2002	2003	2004	2005	2006	2007
Western Hemisphere	**162.8**	**9.0**	**8.3**	**7.6**	**6.1**	**8.8**	**10.5**	**6.5**	**6.3**	**5.6**	**5.2**
Antigua and Barbuda	4.0	3.8	0.6	–0.6	–0.4	2.4	2.0	2.0	2.1	3.5	2.0
Argentina	159.4	0.9	–1.2	–0.9	–1.1	25.9	13.4	4.4	9.6	12.3	11.4
Bahamas, The	3.5	1.3	1.3	1.6	2.0	2.2	3.0	0.9	2.2	1.7	2.7
Barbados	4.0	–1.3	1.6	2.4	2.8	0.2	1.6	1.4	6.0	6.3	4.9
Belize	2.8	–0.8	–1.3	0.7	1.2	2.2	2.6	3.1	3.7	4.3	3.6
Bolivia	12.5	7.7	2.2	4.6	1.6	0.9	3.3	4.4	5.4	4.1	4.0
Brazil	576.3	3.2	4.9	7.1	6.8	8.4	14.8	6.6	6.9	4.5	4.1
Chile	13.9	5.1	3.3	3.8	3.6	2.5	2.8	1.1	3.1	3.5	3.1
Colombia	24.5	18.7	10.9	9.2	8.0	6.3	7.1	5.9	5.0	4.7	4.2
Costa Rica	18.3	11.7	10.0	11.0	11.3	9.2	9.4	11.7	13.6	13.0	10.9
Dominica	3.1	1.0	1.2	0.9	1.6	0.1	1.6	2.4	1.6	1.5	1.5
Dominican Republic	21.2	4.8	6.5	7.7	8.9	5.2	27.4	51.5	4.2	8.5	5.0
Ecuador	42.7	36.1	52.2	96.1	37.7	12.6	7.9	2.7	2.1	3.2	3.0
El Salvador	13.9	2.6	0.5	2.3	3.8	1.9	2.1	4.5	3.7	4.1	3.5
Grenada	3.0	1.4	0.6	2.1	1.7	1.1	2.2	2.3	3.5	4.3	2.0
Guatemala	15.9	6.6	5.2	6.0	7.3	8.1	5.6	7.6	9.1	6.9	6.6
Guyana	33.2	4.7	7.4	6.1	2.7	5.4	6.0	4.7	6.9	7.5	4.4
Haiti	20.1	10.6	8.7	13.7	14.2	9.9	39.3	21.2	15.8	14.1	9.0
Honduras	18.3	13.7	11.6	11.0	9.7	7.7	7.7	8.1	8.1	5.8	4.4
Jamaica	27.8	8.6	6.0	8.1	7.0	7.1	10.5	13.4	15.3	9.6	9.0
Mexico	28.0	15.9	16.6	9.5	6.4	5.0	4.5	4.7	4.0	3.5	3.3
Netherlands Antilles	2.6	1.4	0.8	4.4	1.6	0.4	1.9	1.6	3.2	2.8	2.5
Nicaragua	269.4	18.5	7.2	9.9	4.7	4.0	6.6	9.3	9.6	8.6	6.8
Panama	1.0	0.6	1.3	1.4	0.3	1.0	0.6	0.5	2.9	2.8	2.3
Paraguay	19.3	11.6	6.8	9.0	7.3	10.5	14.2	4.3	6.8	8.9	4.9
Peru	267.1	7.3	3.5	3.8	2.0	0.2	2.3	3.7	1.6	2.4	2.5
St. Kitts and Nevis	3.3	3.7	3.4	2.1	2.1	2.1	2.3	2.1	3.6	2.0	2.0
St. Lucia	3.1	2.8	3.5	3.7	5.4	–0.3	1.0	1.5	3.9	5.5	4.0
St. Vincent and the Grenadines	3.1	2.1	1.0	0.2	0.8	0.8	0.2	3.0	3.7	1.8	1.7
Suriname	58.0	19.1	98.7	58.6	39.8	15.5	23.0	9.1	9.9	14.8	7.0
Trinidad and Tobago	6.9	5.3	3.4	3.6	5.5	4.2	3.8	3.7	6.9	7.7	7.6
Uruguay	59.0	10.8	5.7	4.8	4.4	14.0	19.4	9.2	4.7	5.9	4.3
Venezuela	51.4	35.8	23.6	16.2	12.5	22.4	31.1	21.7	15.9	12.1	15.4

[1]In accordance with standard practice in the *World Economic Outlook*, movements in consumer prices are indicated as annual averages rather than as December/December changes during the year, as is the practice in some countries. For many countries, figures for recent years are IMF staff estimates. Data for some countries are for fiscal years.

[2]The percent changes in 2002 are calculated over a period of 18 months, reflecting a change in the fiscal year cycle (from July–June to January–December).

[3]For many countries, inflation for the earlier years is measured on the basis of a retail price index. Consumer price indices with a broader and more up-to-date coverage are typically used for more recent years.

[4]Mongolia, which is not a member of the Commonwealth of Independent States, is included in this group for reasons of geography and similarities in economic structure.

Table 12. Summary Financial Indicators
(Percent)

	1998	1999	2000	2001	2002	2003	2004	2005	2006	2007
Advanced economies										
Central government fiscal balance[1]										
Advanced economies	–0.9	–1.0	0.1	–1.0	–2.4	–3.1	–2.8	–2.3	–2.1	–2.1
United States	0.5	1.1	1.9	0.4	–2.6	–3.8	–3.7	–2.9	–2.5	–2.8
Euro area	–2.2	–1.7	–0.4	–1.6	–2.0	–2.3	–2.4	–2.0	–1.8	–1.7
Japan	–3.5	–8.2	–6.7	–6.1	–6.7	–6.8	–5.8	–5.4	–5.2	–5.1
Other advanced economies[2]	0.1	0.6	1.6	0.7	–0.1	–0.6	–0.1	0.2	0.2	0.3
General government fiscal balance[1]										
Advanced economies	–1.4	–1.0	—	–1.5	–3.3	–3.9	–3.3	–2.7	–2.3	–2.3
United States	0.4	0.9	1.6	–0.4	–3.8	–4.8	–4.6	–3.7	–3.1	–3.2
Euro area	–2.3	–1.3	–1.0	–1.9	–2.6	–3.0	–2.7	–2.2	–2.0	–1.9
Japan	–5.6	–7.5	–7.7	–6.4	–8.2	–8.1	–6.3	–5.6	–5.2	–4.9
Other advanced economies[2]	–0.6	0.2	1.7	0.3	–0.5	–0.6	–0.1	0.4	0.4	0.5
General government structural balance[3]										
Advanced economies	–1.5	–1.4	–1.3	–1.9	–3.4	–3.7	–3.4	–2.8	–2.6	–2.5
Growth of broad money[4]										
Advanced economies	6.8	5.9	4.9	8.1	5.6	5.3	5.5	5.6	...	...
United States	8.7	6.0	6.0	10.4	6.3	4.9	5.7	4.0	...	...
Euro area	5.0	5.7	4.1	8.0	6.9	7.1	6.6	7.4	...	...
Japan	4.0	2.7	1.9	3.3	1.8	1.6	1.8	2.0	...	...
Other advanced economies[2]	9.4	9.1	6.7	8.1	6.1	7.1	6.4	9.0	...	...
Short-term interest rates[5]										
United States	4.9	4.8	6.0	3.5	1.6	1.0	1.4	3.2	5.0	5.3
Euro area	3.7	3.0	4.4	4.3	3.3	2.3	2.1	2.2	3.1	3.7
Japan	0.2	0.0	0.2	0.0	0.0	0.0	0.0	0.0	0.2	0.9
LIBOR	5.6	5.5	6.6	3.7	1.9	1.2	1.8	3.8	5.4	5.5
Other emerging market and developing countries										
Central government fiscal balance[1]										
Weighted average	–3.7	–3.8	–2.9	–3.1	–3.5	–2.8	–1.7	–0.9	–0.5	–0.3
Median	–3.0	–3.2	–2.7	–3.7	–3.6	–3.2	–2.7	–2.0	–1.9	–1.7
General government fiscal balance[1]										
Weighted average	–4.6	–4.7	–3.5	–3.9	–4.3	–3.4	–2.1	–1.4	–0.9	–0.8
Median	–3.3	–3.3	–3.2	–3.3	–3.6	–3.0	–2.7	–2.0	–1.7	–1.7
Growth of broad money										
Weighted average	18.5	17.6	16.5	15.4	15.9	16.2	17.1	19.2	18.0	14.4
Median	11.4	13.1	15.1	13.6	13.3	12.4	13.5	14.0	13.0	10.5

[1]Percent of GDP.
[2]In this table, "other advanced economies" means advanced economies excluding the United States, euro area countries, and Japan.
[3]Percent of potential GDP.
[4]M2, defined as M1 plus quasi-money, except for Japan, for which the data are based on M2 plus certificates of deposit (CDs). Quasi-money is essentially private term deposits and other notice deposits. The United States also includes money market mutual fund balances, money market deposit accounts, overnight repurchase agreements, and overnight Eurodollars issued to U.S. residents by foreign branches of U.S. banks. For the euro area, M3 is composed of M2 plus marketable instruments held by euro-area residents, which comprise repurchase agreements, money market fund shares/units, money market paper, and debt securities up to two years.
[5]Annual data are period average. For the United States, three-month treasury bills; for Japan, three-month certificates of deposit; for the euro area, the three-month EURIBOR; and for LIBOR, London interbank offered rate on six-month U.S. dollar deposits.

Table 13. Advanced Economies: General and Central Government Fiscal Balances and Balances Excluding Social Security Transactions[1]
(Percent of GDP)

	1998	1999	2000	2001	2002	2003	2004	2005	2006	2007
General government fiscal balance										
Advanced economies	**–1.4**	**–1.0**	**—**	**–1.5**	**–3.3**	**–3.9**	**–3.3**	**–2.7**	**–2.3**	**–2.3**
United States	0.4	0.9	1.6	–0.4	–3.8	–4.8	–4.6	–3.7	–3.1	–3.2
Euro area	–2.3	–1.3	–1.0	–1.9	–2.6	–3.0	–2.7	–2.2	–2.0	–1.9
Germany	–2.2	–1.5	1.3	–2.8	–3.7	–4.0	–3.7	–3.3	–2.9	–2.4
France[2]	–2.6	–1.7	–1.5	–1.6	–3.2	–4.2	–3.7	–2.9	–2.7	–2.6
Italy	–2.8	–1.7	–0.7	–3.1	–2.9	–3.4	–3.4	–4.1	–4.0	–4.1
Spain	–3.0	–1.1	–0.9	–0.5	–0.3	—	–0.1	1.1	1.3	0.9
Netherlands	–0.8	0.7	2.2	–0.3	–2.0	–3.2	–2.1	–0.1	–0.8	–0.8
Belgium	–0.8	–0.5	0.1	0.6	—	0.1	—	0.1	—	–0.7
Austria[3]	–2.4	–2.3	–1.6	–0.1	–0.7	–1.7	–1.2	–1.6	–1.8	–0.9
Finland	1.7	1.6	6.9	5.0	4.1	2.3	2.1	2.5	2.7	3.3
Greece	–4.3	–3.5	–4.0	–6.0	–4.9	–5.8	–6.9	–4.5	–2.8	–2.7
Portugal	–2.4	–2.7	–2.7	–4.3	–4.2	–5.5	–5.3	–6.0	–4.6	–3.7
Ireland[4]	2.5	2.4	4.4	0.7	–0.4	0.2	1.5	1.0	0.7	–0.4
Luxembourg	3.2	3.3	5.9	5.9	2.0	0.2	–1.1	–1.9	–1.7	–1.9
Japan	–5.6	–7.5	–7.7	–6.4	–8.2	–8.1	–6.3	–5.6	–5.2	–4.9
United Kingdom	0.1	1.2	1.7	1.0	–1.6	–3.3	–3.2	–3.3	–3.2	–2.8
Canada	0.1	1.6	2.9	0.7	–0.1	—	0.7	1.7	1.1	1.0
Korea[5]	–3.9	–2.5	1.1	0.6	2.3	2.7	2.3	2.1	2.4	2.5
Australia[6]	0.8	1.7	1.4	0.1	0.3	1.1	1.7	2.3	2.2	2.0
Taiwan Province of China	–3.2	–5.7	–4.5	–6.4	–4.3	–2.8	–2.9	–2.4	–1.7	–1.7
Sweden	1.9	2.3	5.0	2.6	–0.5	–0.1	1.0	1.4	0.7	1.1
Switzerland	–1.5	–0.6	2.2	—	–1.2	–1.4	–1.2	–0.6	–1.0	–0.8
Hong Kong SAR	–1.8	0.8	–0.6	–4.9	–4.8	–3.3	–0.3	1.0	0.5	0.7
Denmark	—	1.4	2.3	1.2	0.2	–0.1	1.7	3.9	2.6	2.5
Norway	3.6	6.2	15.6	13.6	9.3	7.5	11.4	16.2	17.7	20.4
Israel	–3.7	–4.2	–2.0	–4.0	–4.3	–6.7	–5.1	–2.7	–3.0	–3.0
Singapore	3.6	4.6	7.9	4.8	4.0	5.7	6.0	6.0	4.3	4.5
New Zealand[7]	2.1	1.5	1.2	1.6	1.7	3.4	4.6	4.8	4.4	3.0
Cyprus	–4.2	–4.4	–2.4	–2.3	–4.5	–6.3	–4.1	–2.4	–2.2	–1.6
Iceland	0.5	2.3	2.4	0.2	–0.8	–2.0	0.3	3.2	2.1	–0.8
Memorandum										
Major advanced economies	–1.4	–1.1	–0.2	–1.7	–4.0	–4.8	–4.3	–3.6	–3.2	–3.2
Newly industrialized Asian economies	–2.9	–2.8	–0.5	–2.1	–0.5	0.4	0.5	0.8	1.0	1.1
Fiscal balance excluding social security transactions										
United States	–0.3	–0.2	0.5	–1.3	–4.3	–5.2	–5.0	–4.2	–3.5	–3.7
Japan	–7.0	–8.5	–8.2	–6.5	–7.9	–8.2	–6.6	–5.3	–4.8	–4.6
Germany	–2.3	–1.7	1.3	–2.6	–3.4	–3.6	–3.6	–2.9	–2.2	–1.3
France	–2.5	–2.0	–1.9	–2.0	–2.9	–3.6	–2.7	–2.7	–1.9	–1.4
Italy	1.3	2.6	3.2	0.8	1.2	0.7	0.8	0.1	0.5	0.4
Canada	2.7	3.9	4.8	2.4	1.4	1.4	2.1	3.3	2.6	2.6

Table 13 *(concluded)*

	1998	1999	2000	2001	2002	2003	2004	2005	2006	2007
Central government fiscal balance										
Advanced economies	**–0.9**	**–1.0**	**0.1**	**–1.0**	**–2.4**	**–3.1**	**–2.8**	**–2.3**	**–2.1**	**–2.1**
United States[8]	0.5	1.1	1.9	0.4	–2.6	–3.8	–3.7	–2.9	–2.5	–2.8
Euro area	–2.2	–1.7	–0.4	–1.6	–2.0	–2.3	–2.4	–2.0	–1.8	–1.7
Germany[9]	–1.8	–1.5	1.4	–1.3	–1.7	–1.8	–2.3	–2.5	–1.9	–1.7
France	–2.9	–2.6	–2.5	–2.4	–3.6	–3.9	–3.2	–3.0	–2.5	–2.1
Italy	–2.6	–1.4	–1.0	–2.9	–2.8	–2.6	–3.1	–3.8	–3.7	–3.7
Spain	–2.3	–1.0	–1.0	–0.6	–0.5	–0.3	–1.2	0.4	0.5	0.3
Japan[10]	–3.5	–8.2	–6.7	–6.1	–6.7	–6.8	–5.8	–5.4	–5.2	–5.1
United Kingdom	0.1	1.2	1.8	0.9	–1.8	–3.6	–3.2	–3.1	–3.1	–2.8
Canada	0.8	0.9	1.9	1.1	0.8	0.1	0.6	0.4	0.3	0.2
Other advanced economies	–0.2	0.2	1.5	0.5	0.4	0.6	1.2	1.8	1.7	1.8
Memorandum										
Major advanced economies	–0.9	–1.2	–0.1	–1.2	–3.0	–3.8	–3.5	–3.2	–2.8	–2.9
Newly industrialized Asian economies	–1.1	–0.8	0.2	–0.7	0.3	0.4	0.7	0.9	1.0	1.1

[1]On a national income accounts basis except as indicated in footnotes. See Box A1 for a summary of the policy assumptions underlying the projections.
[2]Adjusted for valuation changes of the foreign exchange stabilization fund.
[3]Based on ESA95 methodology, according to which swap income is not included.
[4]Data include the impact of discharging future pension liabilities of the formerly state-owned telecommunications company at a cost of 1.8 percent of GDP in 1999.
[5]Data cover the consolidated central government including the social security funds but excluding privatization.
[6]Data are on a cash basis.
[7]Government balance is revenue minus expenditure plus balance of state-owned enterprises, excluding privatization receipts.
[8]Data are on a budget basis.
[9]Data are on an administrative basis and exclude social security transactions.
[10]Data are on a national income basis and exclude social security transactions.

Table 14. Advanced Economies: General Government Structural Balances[1]
(Percent of potential GDP)

	1998	1999	2000	2001	2002	2003	2004	2005	2006	2007
Structural balance										
Advanced economies	**–1.5**	**–1.4**	**–1.3**	**–1.9**	**–3.4**	**–3.7**	**–3.4**	**–2.8**	**–2.6**	**–2.5**
United States	–0.7	–0.6	0.1	–1.1	–3.8	–4.5	–4.4	–3.6	–3.1	–3.2
Euro area[2,3]	–1.8	–1.3	–1.7	–2.4	–2.6	–2.7	–2.4	–2.0	–1.7	–1.6
Germany[2]	–1.3	–0.9	–1.2	–2.8	–3.3	–3.3	–3.3	–3.0	–2.6	–2.1
France[2]	–1.8	–1.4	–2.1	–2.2	–3.1	–3.5	–3.0	–2.2	–1.8	–1.8
Italy[2]	–3.1	–1.9	–3.0	–4.4	–4.1	–3.5	–3.5	–3.4	–3.3	–3.4
Spain[2]	–2.8	–1.4	–1.6	–1.2	–0.3	0.1	0.8	1.1	1.3	1.0
Netherlands[2]	–1.4	–0.7	–0.2	–1.2	–2.3	–2.6	–1.5	–0.3	–0.5	–0.9
Belgium[2]	–0.6	–1.0	–1.5	–0.7	–0.4	–1.3	0.3	0.7	0.1	–0.5
Austria[2]	–2.6	–2.7	–3.4	–0.8	–0.5	–0.6	–0.9	–1.4	–1.9	–0.9
Finland	2.0	2.0	6.7	4.8	4.4	3.1	2.5	2.9	2.7	3.3
Greece	–2.5	–2.0	–3.7	–6.4	–5.3	–6.5	–8.1	–5.6	–3.8	–3.8
Portugal[2]	–2.7	–3.5	–4.6	–1.2	–0.4	–2.8	–3.0	–5.4	–3.8	–3.1
Ireland[2]	1.8	0.8	2.5	–0.5	–1.1	0.5	1.9	1.0	0.5	–0.7
Japan	–4.9	–6.3	–7.2	–5.7	–6.9	–7.0	–5.5	–5.2	–5.1	–5.0
United Kingdom	0.1	1.1	1.5	0.5	–1.9	–3.3	–3.4	–3.2	–3.1	–2.8
Canada	0.5	1.3	2.0	0.4	–0.2	0.3	0.9	1.8	1.1	1.0
Other advanced economies	–0.1	0.5	1.2	0.7	—	0.3	0.8	1.3	0.9	0.8
Australia[4]	0.7	1.5	1.3	0.1	0.3	1.1	1.6	2.3	2.2	2.0
Sweden	2.7	2.0	4.6	3.2	0.6	1.2	1.9	2.2	1.0	1.1
Denmark	–1.2	0.1	0.8	1.1	0.4	0.7	0.8	1.7	1.5	1.6
Norway[5]	–4.5	–3.7	–2.4	–1.1	–3.8	–5.8	–4.5	–3.5	–4.3	–4.4
New Zealand[6]	1.8	0.9	1.3	2.1	3.2	4.2	4.8	4.8	4.0	3.3
Memorandum										
Major advanced economies	–1.6	–1.5	–1.5	–2.2	–3.9	–4.3	–4.0	–3.4	–3.1	–3.1

[1]On a national income accounts basis. The structural budget position is defined as the actual budget deficit (or surplus) less the effects of cyclical deviations of output from potential output. Because of the margin of uncertainty that attaches to estimates of cyclical gaps and to tax and expenditure elasticities with respect to national income, indicators of structural budget positions should be interpreted as broad orders of magnitude. Moreover, it is important to note that changes in structural budget balances are not necessarily attributable to policy changes but may reflect the built-in momentum of existing expenditure programs. In the period beyond that for which specific consolidation programs exist, it is assumed that the structural deficit remains unchanged.

[2]Excludes one-off receipts from the sale of mobile telephone licenses equivalent to 2.5 percent of GDP in 2000 for Germany, 0.1 percent of GDP in 2001 and 2002 for France, 1.2 percent of GDP in 2000 for Italy, 0.1 percent of GDP in 2000 for Spain, 0.7 percent of GDP in 2000 for the Netherlands, and 0.2 percent of GDP in 2001 for Belgium, 0.4 percent of GDP in 2000 for Austria, 0.3 percent of GDP in 2000 for Portugal, and 0.2 percent of GDP in 2002 for Ireland. Also excludes one-off receipts from sizable asset transactions, in particular 0.5 percent of GDP for France in 2005.

[3]Excludes Luxembourg.

[4]Excludes commonwealth government privatization receipts.

[5]Excludes oil.

[6]Government balance is revenue minus expenditure plus balance of state-owned enterprises, excluding privatization receipts.

Table 15. Advanced Economies: Monetary Aggregates[1]

(Annual percent change)

	1998	1999	2000	2001	2002	2003	2004	2005
Narrow money[2]								
Advanced economies	**5.7**	**8.3**	**2.0**	**9.4**	**9.1**	**8.1**	**6.4**	**5.4**
United States	2.1	2.6	–3.2	8.7	3.1	7.0	5.2	–0.3
Euro area[3]	10.5	10.6	5.3	6.0	9.9	10.6	8.9	11.4
Japan	5.0	11.7	3.5	13.7	23.5	4.5	4.0	5.6
United Kingdom	6.0	11.5	4.6	7.6	6.4	7.4	5.7	4.7
Canada[4]	8.1	7.9	14.5	15.3	5.1	10.1	11.0	11.2
Memorandum								
Newly industrialized Asian economies	0.9	19.9	4.6	11.4	13.4	13.9	9.2	7.5
Broad money[5]								
Advanced economies	**6.8**	**5.9**	**4.9**	**8.1**	**5.6**	**5.3**	**5.5**	**5.6**
United States	8.7	6.0	6.0	10.4	6.3	4.9	5.7	4.0
Euro area[3]	5.0	5.7	4.1	8.0	6.9	7.1	6.6	7.4
Japan	4.0	2.7	1.9	3.3	1.8	1.6	1.8	2.0
United Kingdom	8.4	4.1	8.4	6.7	7.0	7.2	8.8	12.7
Canada[4]	0.8	5.2	6.7	6.1	5.1	6.1	6.1	5.4
Memorandum								
Newly industrialized Asian economies	20.0	17.3	14.5	7.3	5.7	6.8	3.4	4.5

[1]End-of-period based on monthly data.
[2]M1 except for the United Kingdom, where M0 is used here as a measure of narrow money; it comprises notes in circulation plus bankers' operational deposits. M1 is generally currency in circulation plus private demand deposits. In addition, the United States includes traveler's checks of nonbank issues and other checkable deposits and excludes private sector float and demand deposits of banks. Canada excludes private sector float.
[3]Excludes Greece prior to 2001.
[4]Average of Wednesdays.
[5]M2, defined as M1 plus quasi-money, except for Japan, and the United Kingdom, for which the data are based on M2 plus certificates of deposit (CDs), and M4, respectively. Quasi-money is essentially private term deposits and other notice deposits. The United States also includes money market mutual fund balances, money market deposit accounts, overnight repurchase agreements, and overnight Eurodollars issued to U.S. residents by foreign branches of U.S. banks. For the United Kingdom, M4 is composed of non-interest-bearing M1, private sector interest-bearing sterling sight bank deposits, private sector sterling time bank deposits, private sector holdings of sterling bank CDs, private sector holdings of building society shares and deposits, and sterling CDs less building society of banks deposits and bank CDs and notes and coins. For the euro area, M3 is composed of M2 plus marketable instruments held by euro-area residents, which comprise repurchase agreements, money market fund shares/units, money market paper, and debt securities up to two years.

Table 16. Advanced Economies: Interest Rates
(Percent a year)

	1998	1999	2000	2001	2002	2003	2004	2005	July 2006
Policy-related interest rate[1]									
United States	4.7	5.3	6.4	1.8	1.2	1.0	2.2	4.2	5.2
Euro area[2]	. . .	3.0	4.8	3.3	2.8	2.0	2.0	2.3	2.8
Japan	0.3	0.0	0.2	0.0	0.0	0.0	0.0	0.0	0.2
United Kingdom	6.3	5.5	6.0	4.0	4.0	3.8	4.8	4.5	4.5
Canada	5.0	4.8	5.8	2.3	2.8	2.8	2.5	3.3	4.3
Short-term interest rate[2]									
Advanced economies	**4.0**	**3.4**	**4.4**	**3.2**	**2.1**	**1.6**	**1.7**	**2.5**	**3.8**
United States	4.9	4.8	6.0	3.5	1.6	1.0	1.4	3.2	5.1
Euro area	3.7	3.0	4.4	4.3	3.3	2.3	2.1	2.2	3.1
Japan	0.2	0.0	0.2	0.0	0.0	0.0	0.0	0.0	0.4
United Kingdom	7.4	5.5	6.1	5.0	4.0	3.7	4.6	4.7	4.7
Canada	4.7	4.7	5.5	3.9	2.6	2.9	2.2	2.7	4.2
Memorandum									
Newly industrialized Asian economies	10.4	4.6	4.6	3.6	2.7	2.3	2.2	2.3	4.1
Long-term interest rate[3]									
Advanced economies	**4.5**	**4.6**	**5.1**	**4.4**	**4.1**	**3.6**	**3.7**	**3.6**	**4.3**
United States	5.3	5.6	6.0	5.0	4.6	4.0	4.3	4.3	5.1
Euro area	4.7	4.6	5.5	5.0	4.9	3.9	3.8	3.4	4.1
Japan	1.3	1.7	1.7	1.3	1.3	1.0	1.5	1.4	1.9
United Kingdom	5.1	5.2	5.0	5.0	4.8	4.5	4.8	4.3	4.6
Canada	5.3	5.6	5.9	5.5	5.3	4.8	4.6	4.1	4.4
Memorandum									
Newly industrialized Asian economies	9.6	7.3	7.0	5.5	5.0	3.9	3.7	3.8	5.2

[1]Annual data are end of period. For the United States, federal funds rate; for Japan, overnight call rate; for the euro area, main refinancing rate; for the United Kingdom, base lending rate; and for Canada, target rate for overnight money market financing.

[2]Annual data are period average. For the United States, three-month treasury bill market bid yield at constant maturity; for Japan, three-month bond yield with repurchase agreement; for the euro area, three-month EURIBOR; for the United Kingdom, three-month interbank offered rate; for the Canada, three-month treasury bill yield.

[3]Annual data are period average. For the United States, 10-year treasury bond yield at constant maturity; for Japan, 10-year government bond yield; for the euro area, a weighted average of national 10-year government bond yields through 1998 and 10-year euro bond yield thereafter; for the United Kingdom, 10-year government bond yield; and for Canada, 10-year government bond yield.

Table 17. Advanced Economies: Exchange Rates

	1998	1999	2000	2001	2002	2003	2004	2005	Exchange Rate Assumption 2006
	U.S. dollars per national currency unit								
U.S. dollar nominal exchange rates									
Euro	. . .	1.067	0.924	0.896	0.944	1.131	1.243	1.246	1.250
Pound sterling	1.656	1.618	1.516	1.440	1.501	1.634	1.832	1.820	1.821
	National currency units per U.S. dollar								
Japanese yen	130.4	113.5	107.7	121.5	125.2	115.8	108.1	110.0	115.6
Canadian dollar	1.482	1.486	1.485	1.548	1.569	1.397	1.299	1.211	1.132
Swedish krona	7.948	8.257	9.132	10.314	9.707	8.068	7.338	7.450	7.418
Danish krone	6.691	6.967	8.060	8.317	7.870	6.577	5.985	5.987	5.973
Swiss franc	1.447	1.500	1.687	1.686	1.554	1.346	1.242	1.243	1.254
Norwegian krone	7.544	7.797	8.782	8.989	7.932	7.074	6.730	6.439	6.360
Israeli new sheqel	3.786	4.138	4.077	4.205	4.735	4.548	4.481	4.485	4.518
Icelandic krona	70.94	72.30	78.28	96.84	91.19	76.64	70.07	62.94	71.94
Cyprus pound	0.517	0.542	0.621	0.643	0.609	0.517	0.468	0.464	0.470
Korean won	1,403.2	1,189.4	1,130.4	1,290.8	1,251.6	1,191.6	1,146.2	1,024.2	950.0
Australian dollar	1.589	1.550	1.717	1.932	1.839	1.534	1.358	1.309	1.335
New Taiwan dollar	33.434	32.263	31.216	33.787	34.571	34.441	33.418	32.156	32.415
Hong Kong dollar	7.745	7.757	7.791	7.799	7.799	7.787	7.788	7.777	7.765
Singapore dollar	1.674	1.695	1.724	1.792	1.791	1.742	1.690	1.664	1.589
	Index, 2000 = 100								*Percent change from previous assumption*[2]
Real effective exchange rates[1]									
United States	90.5	90.3	100.0	102.4	102.5	93.8	85.9	85.3	1.8
Euro area[3]	118.1	113.4	100.0	101.8	107.5	121.3	127.5	126.4	0.3
Germany	105.0	104.8	100.0	101.5	101.7	105.4	104.4	102.8	0.2
France	112.5	107.6	100.0	97.9	99.8	104.1	104.5	102.9	0.1
Italy	106.7	106.7	100.0	100.7	107.3	116.4	123.6	126.9	0.1
Spain	101.0	100.2	100.0	102.1	104.9	109.1	112.6	112.5	0.1
Netherlands	105.6	103.9	100.0	102.9	108.5	117.8	119.7	117.3	0.2
Belgium	106.1	106.5	100.0	102.0	103.0	107.5	110.9	110.9	0.1
Austria	116.0	110.5	100.0	96.4	97.4	100.4	101.5	100.0	0.1
Finland	114.7	110.3	100.0	105.2	104.8	109.9	113.8	112.9	0.1
Greece	103.8	104.6	100.0	99.4	102.5	107.4	115.4	118.2	0.2
Portugal	97.8	99.8	100.0	102.4	105.3	109.7	113.4	112.6	0.1
Ireland	131.0	117.8	100.0	98.8	93.6	101.1	109.0	109.2	0.2
Luxembourg	103.9	104.7	100.0	101.8	102.2	105.3	108.2	108.3	0.1
Japan	87.9	97.5	100.0	92.8	83.9	80.2	79.9	74.8	–2.9
United Kingdom	97.6	97.9	100.0	97.1	100.2	94.9	98.7	98.0	–0.5
Canada	106.6	103.9	100.0	101.5	99.0	108.6	113.9	120.5	–1.5
Korea	90.4	94.2	100.0	92.9	96.7	94.9	97.7	115.7	0.4
Australia	100.9	103.4	100.0	94.3	99.6	111.6	124.4	130.9	0.3
Taiwan Province of China	90.0	96.2	100.0	106.0	94.1	86.3	82.5	83.9	–1.4
Sweden	110.8	103.4	100.0	96.9	92.6	95.2	99.2	97.9	1.3
Switzerland	101.6	101.1	100.0	105.5	111.6	113.5	114.8	114.0	–0.8
Hong Kong SAR	108.2	102.9	100.0	103.4	98.5	86.1	77.3	73.0	0.9
Denmark	106.5	105.2	100.0	101.3	103.7	108.1	113.9	113.7	—
Norway	98.0	99.3	100.0	102.3	116.1	116.4	113.0	116.8	–1.7
Israel	91.9	89.5	100.0	101.6	89.3	82.4	83.2	85.9	1.9
Singapore	112.7	98.7	100.0	104.7	102.1	97.8	99.7	100.0	0.9
New Zealand	115.7	113.1	100.0	96.3	105.3	120.1	131.4	138.2	–0.5

[1]Defined as the ratio, in common currency, of the unit labor costs in the manufacturing sector to the weighted average of those of its industrial country trading partners, using 1999–2001 trade weights.

[2]In nominal effective terms. Average May 5–June 2, 2006 rates compared with July 5–August 2, 2006 rates.

[3]A synthetic euro for the period prior to January 1, 1999 is used in the calculation of real effective exchange rates for the euro. See Box 5.5 in the *World Economic Outlook*, October 1998.

Table 18. Other Emerging Market and Developing Countries: Central Government Fiscal Balances
(Percent of GDP)

	1998	1999	2000	2001	2002	2003	2004	2005	2006	2007
Other emerging market and developing countries	**–3.7**	**–3.8**	**–2.9**	**–3.1**	**–3.5**	**–2.8**	**–1.7**	**–0.9**	**–0.5**	**–0.3**
Regional groups										
Africa	–3.8	–3.4	–1.2	–2.1	–2.3	–1.4	–0.2	1.5	4.2	3.0
Sub-Sahara	–3.7	–3.8	–2.3	–2.5	–2.4	–2.4	–0.8	0.4	3.3	1.9
Excluding Nigeria and South Africa	–3.4	–4.9	–4.3	–2.8	–2.9	–2.9	–1.9	–0.9	3.5	0.1
Central and eastern Europe	–4.1	–5.4	–5.0	–7.3	–8.0	–6.3	–5.1	–3.2	–3.6	–2.8
Commonwealth of Independent States[1]	–5.2	–4.0	0.3	1.8	1.1	1.2	2.7	5.4	6.1	6.2
Russia	–5.9	–4.2	0.8	2.7	1.3	1.7	4.3	7.5	8.5	7.6
Excluding Russia	–3.2	–3.3	–1.3	–0.8	0.2	–0.2	–1.7	0.2	0.2	2.7
Developing Asia	–3.4	–4.2	–4.4	–3.9	–3.7	–3.2	–2.3	–2.1	–2.0	–1.8
China	–2.8	–3.7	–3.3	–2.7	–3.0	–2.4	–1.5	–1.3	–1.2	–1.1
India	–5.3	–6.5	–7.1	–6.6	–6.1	–5.3	–4.4	–4.2	–4.0	–3.6
Excluding China and India	–2.9	–2.9	–4.0	–3.8	–3.2	–2.7	–2.2	–1.9	–2.1	–1.9
Middle East	–5.1	–1.8	4.2	–0.5	–3.1	–1.0	1.6	6.2	8.1	8.4
Western Hemisphere	–3.3	–2.8	–2.4	–2.6	–3.6	–3.4	–2.1	–2.4	–2.3	–1.6
Brazil	–5.4	–2.7	–2.3	–2.1	–0.8	–4.0	–1.5	–3.8	–3.5	–2.2
Mexico	–1.7	–1.7	–1.5	–1.0	–2.2	–1.5	–1.3	–1.1	–1.9	–1.7
Analytical groups										
By source of export earnings										
Fuel	–5.7	–3.0	3.7	1.2	–0.3	1.4	4.2	8.4	10.4	10.8
Nonfuel	–3.4	–3.9	–3.9	–3.8	–4.0	–3.4	–2.6	–2.2	–2.1	–1.9
of which, primary products	–2.4	–3.9	–4.6	–3.0	–3.1	–2.7	–1.5	0.4	2.0	0.4
By external financing source										
Net debtor countries	–3.8	–4.1	–4.1	–4.2	–4.5	–3.9	–2.9	–2.6	–2.3	–1.9
of which, official financing	–3.3	–3.5	–4.1	–4.1	–5.2	–3.5	–3.0	–2.4	–2.3	–2.3
Net debtor countries by debt-servicing experience										
Countries with arrears and/or rescheduling during 1999–2003	–3.0	–3.1	–3.2	–3.4	–4.5	–3.0	–1.8	–1.0	–0.1	—
Other groups										
Heavily indebted poor countries	–3.7	–4.3	–4.9	–4.0	–4.2	–3.9	–3.2	–2.1	4.3	–2.1
Middle East and north Africa	–4.7	–1.8	3.7	–0.6	–2.6	–0.4	1.6	5.6	7.5	7.8
Memorandum										
Median										
Other emerging market and developing countries	–3.0	–3.2	–2.7	–3.7	–3.6	–3.2	–2.7	–2.0	–1.9	–1.7
Africa	–3.3	–3.3	–2.8	–3.4	–3.6	–3.1	–2.9	–1.9	–1.2	–1.9
Central and eastern Europe	–2.8	–2.9	–2.5	–4.2	–5.2	–3.9	–3.3	–2.7	–2.7	–2.2
Commonwealth of Independent States[1]	–5.0	–5.1	–1.2	–1.4	–0.4	–1.1	—	–0.2	–0.1	–1.2
Developing Asia	–2.2	–3.3	–3.8	–4.2	–4.1	–3.4	–2.0	–3.0	–3.0	–2.6
Middle East	–6.0	–1.5	7.2	1.6	–1.2	–0.1	–0.1	4.0	6.5	5.6
Western Hemisphere	–3.0	–3.0	–2.6	–4.2	–4.8	–3.8	–3.4	–2.5	–1.9	–1.7

[1]Mongolia, which is not a member of the Commonwealth of Independent States, is included in this group for reasons of geography and similarities in economic structure.

Table 19. Other Emerging Market and Developing Countries: Broad Money Aggregates
(Annual percent change)

	1998	1999	2000	2001	2002	2003	2004	2005	2006	2007
Other emerging market and developing countries	**18.5**	**17.6**	**16.5**	**15.4**	**15.9**	**16.2**	**17.1**	**19.2**	**18.0**	**14.4**
Regional groups										
Africa	18.0	19.3	19.9	20.8	21.0	21.9	18.7	22.7	19.3	17.8
Sub-Sahara	16.4	21.4	22.5	21.8	24.2	25.4	21.7	26.5	22.0	19.6
Central and eastern Europe	36.8	36.9	24.3	37.8	10.9	10.4	15.7	15.8	14.4	11.5
Commonwealth of Independent States[1]	44.1	53.2	57.5	37.9	34.0	38.7	34.8	35.2	35.3	28.2
Russia	50.2	48.1	57.2	35.7	33.9	39.4	33.7	35.5	37.8	29.8
Excluding Russia	24.8	70.3	58.2	43.2	34.2	36.7	37.8	34.0	27.1	22.6
Developing Asia	18.7	13.9	12.1	14.6	14.0	16.3	13.5	16.9	17.3	14.7
China	14.8	14.7	12.3	17.6	16.9	19.6	14.4	17.9	17.5	15.0
India	19.1	15.9	16.1	14.6	14.6	16.3	13.3	19.2	20.2	18.2
Excluding China and India	22.9	11.7	9.4	9.2	8.2	10.0	11.9	13.2	14.7	11.4
Middle East	8.5	10.6	12.6	13.1	16.8	13.2	18.5	21.3	18.6	14.2
Western Hemisphere	10.4	10.2	12.1	6.1	15.5	13.3	17.6	17.8	14.1	8.9
Brazil	4.1	6.9	15.5	12.6	23.2	3.7	18.6	18.9	4.5	4.0
Mexico	24.6	22.8	16.2	13.7	12.6	11.7	13.5	15.1	18.9	11.2
Analytical groups										
By source of export earnings										
Fuel	25.3	24.7	29.3	20.6	22.1	24.0	25.6	28.5	27.8	21.1
Nonfuel	17.1	16.2	14.2	14.5	14.8	14.7	15.3	17.2	15.7	12.7
of which, primary products	17.0	20.5	22.5	21.6	21.6	26.1	29.9	30.2	27.3	24.8
By external financing source										
Net debtor countries	17.8	16.6	15.2	14.0	14.5	13.0	15.7	17.0	15.4	12.0
of which, official financing	22.5	11.0	9.4	—	13.0	18.9	15.8	16.1	15.8	12.1
Net debtor countries by debt-servicing experience										
Countries with arrears and/or rescheduling during 1999–2003	24.2	12.6	13.8	2.1	17.4	23.7	19.7	21.6	19.8	17.5
Other groups										
Heavily indebted poor countries	18.0	24.0	30.6	19.1	18.5	17.4	15.0	15.0	14.4	13.0
Middle East and north Africa	11.0	11.1	12.7	13.9	16.2	13.2	17.4	20.0	17.7	14.1
Memorandum										
Median										
Other emerging market and developing countries	11.4	13.1	15.1	13.6	13.3	12.4	13.5	14.0	13.0	10.5
Africa	8.5	12.6	14.1	14.8	18.6	15.5	14.0	14.2	13.2	11.3
Central and eastern Europe	13.0	13.1	18.0	21.4	9.5	11.0	14.0	11.6	10.3	9.1
Commonwealth of Independent States[1]	25.3	32.1	40.1	35.7	34.1	30.7	32.3	25.2	25.5	19.7
Developing Asia	13.2	14.7	12.3	9.1	13.3	13.1	14.1	12.1	14.1	10.5
Middle East	8.1	10.6	10.2	11.6	10.9	8.2	12.1	17.0	14.1	12.0
Western Hemisphere	12.1	10.5	9.5	9.0	8.3	8.4	12.0	11.5	9.2	6.7

[1]Mongolia, which is not a member of the Commonwealth of Independent States, is included in this group for reasons of geography and similarities in economic structure.

Table 20. Summary of World Trade Volumes and Prices

(Annual percent change)

	Ten-Year Averages											
	1988–97	1998–2007	1998	1999	2000	2001	2002	2003	2004	2005	2006	2007
Trade in goods and services												
World trade[1]												
Volume	7.0	6.5	4.5	5.6	12.1	—	3.4	5.3	10.6	7.4	8.9	7.6
Price deflator												
In U.S. dollars	1.4	2.2	–5.7	–1.5	–0.4	–3.2	1.2	10.5	9.7	5.4	4.6	2.2
In SDRs	0.8	1.4	–4.3	–2.3	3.3	0.2	–0.5	2.2	3.7	5.6	5.2	1.0
Volume of trade												
Exports												
Advanced economies	7.1	5.4	4.1	5.5	11.6	–0.9	2.3	3.3	8.8	5.5	8.0	6.0
Other emerging market and developing countries	7.7	8.9	4.9	3.3	13.5	3.0	6.9	10.8	14.6	11.8	10.7	10.6
Imports												
Advanced economies	6.7	5.9	6.0	7.9	11.6	–0.9	2.6	4.0	9.1	6.0	7.5	6.0
Other emerging market and developing countries	7.5	8.7	0.1	0.6	14.3	3.3	6.1	10.2	16.4	11.9	13.0	12.1
Terms of trade												
Advanced economies	–0.1	–0.2	1.5	–0.4	–2.6	0.4	0.8	0.9	–0.2	–1.3	–0.9	—
Other emerging market and developing countries	–0.7	1.5	–6.2	4.4	6.5	–2.6	0.8	0.8	2.7	4.5	4.0	0.5
Trade in goods												
World trade[1]												
Volume	7.2	6.7	4.6	5.3	12.8	–0.5	3.7	6.3	10.9	7.5	9.4	7.8
Price deflator												
In U.S. dollars	1.3	2.1	–6.5	–1.1	0.3	–3.7	0.6	10.1	9.9	6.1	4.8	2.2
In SDRs	0.7	1.4	–5.2	–1.8	3.9	–0.2	–1.1	1.8	4.0	6.3	5.5	1.0
World trade prices in U.S. dollars[2]												
Manufactures	1.3	1.6	–4.1	–2.5	–5.9	–3.9	2.3	14.2	9.4	3.6	2.2	2.3
Oil	0.6	14.6	–32.1	37.5	57.0	–13.8	2.5	15.8	30.7	41.3	29.7	9.1
Nonfuel primary commodities	1.3	2.7	–14.3	–7.2	4.8	–4.9	1.7	6.9	18.5	10.3	22.1	–4.8
World trade prices in SDRs[2]												
Manufactures	0.7	0.8	–2.8	–3.2	–2.4	–0.4	0.5	5.6	3.5	3.8	2.9	1.2
Oil	—	13.8	–31.2	36.4	62.8	–10.7	0.8	7.1	23.6	41.6	30.5	7.8
Nonfuel primary commodities	0.7	1.9	–13.1	–7.9	8.6	–1.5	—	–1.2	12.1	10.5	22.9	–5.9
World trade prices in euros[2]												
Manufactures	1.5	0.4	–2.9	2.4	8.7	–0.8	–3.0	–4.7	–0.5	3.4	1.9	0.1
Oil	0.7	13.3	–31.3	44.4	81.3	–11.1	–2.8	–3.3	18.9	41.0	29.3	6.7
Nonfuel primary commodities	1.5	1.5	–13.3	–2.6	20.9	–1.9	–3.5	–10.8	7.8	10.0	21.7	–6.9

Table 20 *(concluded)*

	Ten-Year Averages											
	1988–97	1998–2007	1998	1999	2000	2001	2002	2003	2004	2005	2006	2007
Trade in goods												
Volume of trade												
Exports												
Advanced economies	7.1	5.4	4.3	4.9	12.5	–1.4	2.3	3.8	8.7	5.3	8.6	6.1
Other emerging market and developing countries	7.6	8.9	4.8	2.8	14.1	2.3	7.3	11.6	14.4	11.2	10.8	10.6
Fuel exporters	4.4	4.6	–1.8	–1.6	8.0	0.6	2.8	10.2	9.6	6.2	6.4	6.4
Nonfuel exporters	8.9	10.4	7.1	3.9	16.0	2.9	8.8	12.1	16.0	12.9	12.6	12.3
Imports												
Advanced economies	7.0	6.2	5.9	8.2	12.3	–1.6	3.0	4.9	9.4	6.3	8.0	6.0
Other emerging market and developing countries	7.6	9.1	1.2	–0.4	14.5	2.9	6.4	12.1	17.4	12.0	13.5	12.8
Fuel exporters	1.7	9.7	–2.6	–10.5	12.0	14.1	7.2	10.2	18.2	18.9	18.7	15.2
Nonfuel exporters	9.5	9.0	2.1	1.7	15.0	1.0	6.2	12.5	17.2	10.8	12.5	12.4
Price deflators in SDRs												
Exports												
Advanced economies	0.5	0.6	–3.8	–3.0	0.5	–0.2	–0.8	2.6	3.2	3.9	3.4	0.9
Other emerging market and developing countries	1.6	4.1	–10.4	4.7	14.4	–0.8	–0.1	1.9	7.4	13.2	11.6	1.5
Fuel exporters	1.7	10.4	–22.4	22.2	42.7	–6.9	0.5	5.6	16.2	31.1	25.2	5.1
Nonfuel exporters	1.7	1.8	–6.3	0.2	5.8	1.5	–0.3	0.7	4.5	7.0	6.0	—
Imports												
Advanced economies	0.2	0.8	–5.1	–2.8	3.7	–0.5	–1.8	1.3	3.3	5.6	4.4	1.0
Other emerging market and developing countries	2.4	2.0	–4.8	–0.7	6.5	1.7	–0.7	0.5	4.2	7.1	6.1	0.5
Fuel exporters	2.7	1.2	–3.4	–3.0	1.4	1.4	1.6	0.2	2.9	6.5	5.3	–0.2
Nonfuel exporters	2.2	2.1	–5.1	–0.2	7.4	1.7	–1.2	0.5	4.4	7.2	6.3	0.6
Terms of trade												
Advanced economies	0.3	–0.2	1.4	–0.2	–3.1	0.3	1.0	1.3	–0.1	–1.6	–0.9	–0.1
Other emerging market and developing countries	–0.7	2.1	–5.9	5.5	7.4	–2.5	0.7	1.4	3.1	5.7	5.1	1.0
Fuel exporters	–1.0	9.0	–19.7	26.1	40.8	–8.2	–1.0	5.3	12.9	23.2	19.0	5.3
Nonfuel exporters	–0.5	–0.3	–1.2	0.4	–1.5	–0.3	0.9	0.2	—	–0.2	–0.3	–0.6
Memorandum												
World exports in billions of U.S. dollars												
Goods and services	5,039	10,061	6,783	7,033	7,819	7,556	7,933	9,243	11,208	12,684	14,464	15,891
Goods	4,030	8,064	5,384	5,572	6,278	6,011	6,288	7,359	8,945	10,186	11,721	12,896

[1]Average of annual percent change for world exports and imports.

[2]As represented, respectively, by the export unit value index for the manufactures of the advanced economies; the average of U.K. Brent, Dubai, and West Texas Intermediate crude oil spot prices; and the average of world market prices for nonfuel primary commodities weighted by their 1995–97 shares in world commodity exports.

Table 21. Nonfuel Commodity Prices[1]
(Annual percent change; U.S. dollar terms)

	Ten-Year Averages											
	1988–97	1998–2007	1998	1999	2000	2001	2002	2003	2004	2005	2006	2007
Nonfuel primary commodities	**1.3**	**2.7**	**–14.3**	**–7.2**	**4.8**	**–4.9**	**1.7**	**6.9**	**18.5**	**10.3**	**22.1**	**–4.8**
Food	0.7	0.6	–11.1	–12.6	2.5	0.2	3.4	5.2	14.3	–0.3	7.9	–0.3
Beverages	1.8	–3.2	–13.2	–21.3	–15.1	–16.1	16.5	4.9	3.0	21.0	1.7	–4.2
Agricultural raw materials	2.6	–0.2	–16.7	1.2	4.4	–4.9	1.8	3.7	5.5	1.6	5.3	–1.9
Metals	1.3	7.4	–17.7	–1.1	12.2	–9.8	–2.7	12.2	36.1	26.4	45.2	–8.9
Advanced economies	**1.5**	**3.5**	**–15.8**	**–6.0**	**5.6**	**–6.1**	**1.9**	**8.1**	**20.6**	**12.2**	**27.7**	**–5.2**
Other emerging market and developing countries	**1.6**	**3.1**	**–16.1**	**–7.3**	**4.5**	**–7.0**	**2.2**	**8.4**	**20.8**	**12.3**	**26.7**	**–5.4**
Regional groups												
Africa	1.2	2.5	–14.7	–6.9	2.6	–6.9	4.4	8.1	14.7	10.8	22.6	–4.0
Sub-Sahara	1.2	2.6	–14.8	–6.7	2.6	–7.2	4.5	8.3	14.7	11.2	23.2	–4.1
Central and eastern Europe	1.6	4.2	–16.6	–4.6	6.5	–7.1	1.0	8.4	23.4	15.4	31.6	–6.4
Commonwealth of Independent States[2]	. . .	6.0	–17.9	–2.6	9.9	–8.5	–0.7	10.6	29.8	20.7	40.6	–7.8
Developing Asia	1.6	2.0	–13.6	–7.5	2.3	–6.3	2.8	6.7	16.6	9.1	19.6	–4.2
Middle East	1.3	3.8	–15.4	–7.1	6.4	–7.2	0.9	9.8	21.8	13.7	29.4	–5.7
Western Hemisphere	1.9	2.7	–18.4	–10.0	4.6	–7.1	2.5	9.2	22.8	11.1	26.4	–5.4
Analytical groups												
By source of export earnings												
Fuel	1.3	5.1	–17.0	–4.6	8.3	–8.4	–0.4	10.8	26.6	18.3	35.6	–7.0
Nonfuel	1.7	3.1	–16.1	–7.4	4.4	–7.0	2.3	8.3	20.7	12.1	26.4	–5.4
of which, primary products	1.2	4.3	–16.8	–7.7	4.6	–7.6	4.1	9.3	23.6	15.1	35.9	–6.7
By source of external financing												
Net debtor countries	1.7	2.8	–16.1	–8.1	3.9	–6.9	2.6	8.3	20.1	11.6	25.4	–5.1
of which, official financing	1.1	2.1	–12.9	–10.1	0.4	–7.1	4.5	8.1	15.7	10.9	21.0	–3.6
Net debtor countries by debt-servicing experience												
Countries with arrears and/or rescheduling during 1999–2003	1.5	2.4	–15.4	–9.6	2.6	–7.3	3.6	8.8	18.9	11.1	23.2	–4.8
Other groups												
Heavily indebted poor countries	0.6	1.8	–13.7	–12.4	–2.5	–7.6	9.7	9.5	12.3	10.0	20.3	–1.9
Middle East and north Africa	1.3	3.2	–14.9	–7.7	5.5	–6.3	1.6	8.9	19.7	11.6	26.0	–5.0
Memorandum												
Average oil spot price[3]	0.6	14.6	–32.1	37.5	57.0	–13.8	2.5	15.8	30.7	41.3	29.7	9.1
In U.S. dollars a barrel	18.36	37.33	13.08	17.98	28.24	24.33	24.95	28.89	37.76	53.35	69.20	75.50
Export unit value of manufactures[4]	1.3	1.6	–4.1	–2.5	–5.9	–3.9	2.3	14.2	9.4	3.6	2.2	2.3

[1]Averages of world market prices for individual commodities weighted by 1995–97 exports as a share of world commodity exports and total commodity exports for the indicated country group, respectively.
[2]Mongolia, which is not a member of the Commonwealth of Independent States, is included in this group for reasons of geography and similarities in economic structure.
[3]Average of U.K. Brent, Dubai, and West Texas Intermediate crude oil spot prices.
[4]For the manufactures exported by the advanced economies.

Table 22. Advanced Economies: Export Volumes, Import Volumes, and Terms of Trade in Goods and Services
(Annual percent change)

	Ten-Year Averages											
	1988–97	1998–2007	1998	1999	2000	2001	2002	2003	2004	2005	2006	2007
Export volume												
Advanced economies	**7.1**	**5.4**	**4.1**	**5.5**	**11.6**	**−0.9**	**2.3**	**3.3**	**8.8**	**5.5**	**8.0**	**6.0**
United States	9.2	3.9	2.4	4.3	8.7	−5.4	−2.3	1.3	9.2	6.8	8.3	7.1
Euro area	6.5	5.3	7.0	5.1	11.8	2.8	1.5	1.3	6.6	4.1	7.4	5.3
Germany	6.0	7.0	8.0	5.9	13.5	6.4	4.3	2.4	9.6	6.9	9.4	4.4
France	6.5	4.9	7.7	4.0	12.9	2.7	1.3	−1.1	3.3	3.2	8.7	7.0
Italy	5.9	1.3	1.1	−1.7	9.0	0.5	−4.0	−2.4	3.0	0.3	4.5	3.6
Spain	8.6	4.8	8.0	7.4	10.3	4.0	1.8	3.6	3.3	1.0	4.4	4.4
Japan	5.4	5.5	−2.3	1.5	12.2	−6.7	7.5	9.0	13.9	7.0	9.4	5.1
United Kingdom	5.5	5.5	3.0	3.8	9.1	2.9	1.0	1.7	4.9	6.5	15.1	7.7
Canada	6.9	3.7	9.1	10.7	8.9	−3.0	1.2	−2.4	5.2	2.1	2.6	3.9
Other advanced economies	8.4	7.2	2.3	8.4	14.8	−1.9	6.3	8.3	13.2	7.2	7.4	6.9
Memorandum												
Major advanced economies	6.8	4.7	3.8	4.1	10.6	−1.1	1.1	1.6	7.8	5.4	8.7	5.7
Newly industrialized Asian economies	10.9	9.0	1.3	9.3	17.3	−3.8	10.1	13.6	17.8	9.3	8.9	7.9
Import volume												
Advanced economies	**6.7**	**5.9**	**6.0**	**7.9**	**11.6**	**−0.9**	**2.6**	**4.0**	**9.1**	**6.0**	**7.5**	**6.0**
United States	6.9	6.8	11.6	11.5	13.1	−2.7	3.4	4.1	10.8	6.1	6.2	5.3
Euro area	5.7	5.6	9.9	7.2	10.8	0.9	0.2	2.8	6.5	5.2	7.2	5.4
Germany	5.5	6.0	9.4	8.6	10.2	1.2	−1.4	5.3	6.9	6.5	8.9	4.8
France	4.5	6.4	10.8	5.8	15.1	2.2	1.6	1.5	6.0	6.5	8.6	6.8
Italy	4.4	2.7	8.6	3.1	5.8	−0.2	−0.5	0.8	2.5	1.4	3.0	2.5
Spain	9.3	8.2	14.8	13.6	10.8	4.2	3.9	6.0	9.3	7.1	7.0	5.8
Japan	7.3	4.0	−6.7	3.6	8.5	1.0	0.8	4.0	8.5	6.3	7.7	7.7
United Kingdom	5.6	7.2	9.2	7.9	9.0	4.8	4.8	2.0	6.6	5.9	14.2	7.6
Canada	6.8	4.7	5.1	7.8	8.1	−5.1	1.7	4.5	8.2	7.1	4.9	5.0
Other advanced economies	8.8	6.3	−2.2	7.0	14.2	−3.9	6.4	7.2	13.9	7.4	7.4	6.9
Memorandum												
Major advanced economies	6.0	5.8	7.7	8.1	10.9	−0.3	1.9	3.5	8.0	5.9	7.6	5.7
Newly industrialized Asian economies	12.7	6.9	−8.2	8.4	17.7	−5.5	9.0	9.8	16.8	7.3	8.0	8.2
Terms of trade												
Advanced economies	**−0.1**	**−0.2**	**1.5**	**−0.4**	**−2.6**	**0.4**	**0.8**	**0.9**	**−0.2**	**−1.3**	**−0.9**	**—**
United States	0.4	−0.5	3.4	−1.2	−2.1	2.3	0.5	−1.0	−1.5	−2.6	−1.9	−0.9
Euro area	−0.5	−0.1	1.7	−0.2	−3.9	0.8	1.4	1.0	−0.4	−1.0	−0.6	−0.1
Germany	−1.8	−0.2	1.7	−0.7	−4.6	0.2	1.5	2.0	−0.2	−1.0	−0.4	−0.5
France	−0.8	−0.3	1.7	0.2	−3.6	0.9	0.9	0.4	−1.2	−1.2	−1.0	0.1
Italy	—	−0.1	3.7	−0.4	−7.1	1.0	2.3	1.7	0.1	−1.9	−0.8	0.3
Spain	0.9	0.6	2.5	−0.1	−2.8	2.4	3.1	1.3	−0.3	1.3	−1.3	—
Japan	−0.5	−1.7	3.4	−0.2	−5.3	—	−0.6	−1.8	−3.7	−5.6	−3.3	0.8
United Kingdom	0.7	0.4	2.2	0.7	−0.8	−0.6	2.5	1.0	0.4	−2.3	0.5	0.7
Canada	—	1.3	−3.9	1.4	4.0	−1.6	−2.4	6.0	4.1	4.0	1.1	0.7
Other advanced economies	0.3	−0.3	−0.4	−1.1	−0.8	−0.5	0.3	−0.1	0.2	0.2	−0.4	—
Memorandum												
Major advanced economies	−0.3	−0.2	2.2	−0.3	−3.2	0.5	0.9	1.5	−0.2	−2.1	−1.4	−0.1
Newly industrialized Asian economies	0.2	−1.5	0.3	−2.4	−3.2	−0.6	—	−1.7	−1.8	−2.3	−2.5	−0.2
Memorandum												
Trade in goods												
Advanced economies												
Export volume	7.1	5.4	4.3	4.9	12.5	−1.4	2.3	3.8	8.7	5.3	8.6	6.1
Import volume	7.0	6.2	5.9	8.2	12.3	−1.6	3.0	4.9	9.4	6.3	8.0	6.0
Terms of trade	0.3	−0.2	1.4	−0.2	−3.1	0.3	1.0	1.3	−0.1	−1.6	−0.9	−0.1

Table 23. Other Emerging Market and Developing Countries—by Region: Total Trade in Goods
(Annual percent change)

	Ten-Year Averages											
	1988–97	1998–2007	1998	1999	2000	2001	2002	2003	2004	2005	2006	2007
Other emerging market and developing countries												
Value in U.S. dollars												
Exports	9.3	13.8	–7.2	7.3	25.2	–2.1	8.8	22.8	29.4	25.0	22.2	13.2
Imports	9.8	11.9	–4.8	–1.1	17.4	0.8	7.4	21.5	29.2	19.6	19.5	14.4
Volume												
Exports	7.6	8.9	4.8	2.8	14.1	2.3	7.3	11.6	14.4	11.2	10.8	10.6
Imports	7.6	9.1	1.2	–0.4	14.5	2.9	6.4	12.1	17.4	12.0	13.5	12.8
Unit value in U.S. dollars												
Exports	2.3	4.9	–11.7	5.6	10.3	–4.3	1.7	10.2	13.5	13.0	10.8	2.7
Imports	3.0	2.8	–6.1	0.1	2.7	–1.8	1.0	8.7	10.2	6.9	5.4	1.6
Terms of trade	–0.7	2.1	–5.9	5.5	7.4	–2.5	0.7	1.4	3.1	5.7	5.1	1.0
Memorandum												
Real GDP growth in developing country trading partners	3.5	3.3	1.8	3.5	4.9	1.6	2.3	2.9	4.5	3.7	4.1	3.6
Market prices of nonfuel commodities exported by other emerging market and developing countries	1.6	3.1	–16.1	–7.3	4.5	–7.0	2.2	8.4	20.8	12.3	26.7	–5.4
Regional groups												
Africa												
Value in U.S. dollars												
Exports	4.9	13.3	–13.9	7.7	28.0	–6.4	2.8	25.6	29.1	27.8	23.5	18.7
Imports	5.5	10.8	–2.4	0.6	3.5	1.5	9.9	22.4	26.2	18.0	16.8	15.1
Volume												
Exports	4.5	5.3	2.4	1.7	10.5	1.6	1.8	6.6	7.2	5.2	4.3	12.2
Imports	4.5	7.3	4.5	2.3	1.6	6.9	8.2	7.2	9.0	10.7	10.5	13.1
Unit value in U.S. dollars												
Exports	0.6	7.7	–15.9	6.5	15.7	–7.9	1.1	18.0	20.5	21.6	18.8	6.2
Imports	1.5	3.6	–6.4	–1.4	2.6	–4.9	1.7	16.1	15.8	7.0	5.9	1.9
Terms of trade	–0.9	4.0	–10.1	8.0	12.7	–3.2	–0.6	1.7	4.1	13.7	12.1	4.2
Sub-Sahara												
Value in U.S. dollars												
Exports	4.5	13.1	–14.1	6.5	25.5	–6.6	3.2	26.3	30.3	27.1	22.0	21.3
Imports	5.4	10.5	–5.0	–0.5	3.2	1.4	9.3	25.1	26.2	21.1	16.7	12.5
Volume												
Exports	4.8	5.4	1.7	–0.4	11.9	1.5	0.8	7.3	7.5	5.5	4.5	15.2
Imports	4.4	7.1	2.6	1.9	0.8	5.9	8.4	8.6	9.1	12.4	11.4	10.4
Unit value in U.S. dollars												
Exports	–0.1	7.4	–15.7	7.5	11.9	–8.0	2.5	18.0	21.2	20.6	17.1	5.7
Imports	1.4	3.7	–7.2	–2.0	3.4	–4.2	1.1	17.8	15.6	8.2	4.9	2.1
Terms of trade	–1.5	3.6	–9.1	9.7	8.2	–3.9	1.4	0.1	4.8	11.4	11.6	3.5

Table 23 ***(continued)***

	Ten-Year Averages											
	1988–97	1998–2007	1998	1999	2000	2001	2002	2003	2004	2005	2006	2007
Central and eastern Europe												
Value in U.S. dollars												
Exports	7.0	14.4	6.4	–2.4	13.3	10.8	13.9	28.9	31.7	15.6	17.1	12.3
Imports	9.5	13.2	5.9	–4.3	16.1	–0.4	13.7	29.6	31.6	15.3	17.8	11.9
Volume												
Exports	5.4	10.4	9.5	1.4	16.0	9.4	7.5	12.2	16.9	9.9	11.7	10.0
Imports	9.3	9.3	11.2	–1.8	16.0	1.3	8.5	12.4	18.0	8.6	11.2	9.4
Unit value in U.S. dollars												
Exports	2.3	3.7	–2.9	–3.6	–2.4	1.8	6.0	15.0	13.0	5.3	4.9	2.0
Imports	2.6	3.6	–4.8	–2.5	0.1	–1.6	5.0	15.5	11.8	6.2	6.0	2.2
Terms of trade	–0.3	0.1	2.0	–1.2	–2.6	3.4	1.0	–0.4	1.1	–0.8	–1.1	–0.2
Commonwealth of Independent States[1]												
Value in U.S. dollars												
Exports	. . .	14.7	–14.0	0.1	36.9	–0.9	6.3	26.8	36.7	29.1	28.6	10.8
Imports	. . .	10.2	–15.9	–25.8	14.6	15.0	9.6	26.5	29.5	23.9	24.4	15.4
Volume												
Exports	. . .	5.8	0.1	–1.4	9.5	4.2	7.1	12.4	12.8	3.8	4.5	5.8
Imports	. . .	8.1	–12.3	–21.4	13.8	18.0	8.4	22.9	20.1	14.8	15.1	11.6
Unit value in U.S. dollars												
Exports	. . .	8.4	–13.4	1.2	24.3	–4.9	–0.8	12.9	21.6	24.3	22.4	4.1
Imports	. . .	2.0	–4.4	–5.6	0.9	–2.4	1.6	3.0	8.0	8.4	7.9	3.5
Terms of trade	. . .	6.3	–9.4	7.2	23.2	–2.5	–2.4	9.6	12.6	14.7	13.4	0.6
Developing Asia												
Value in U.S. dollars												
Exports	15.7	14.7	–2.3	8.3	22.1	–1.6	14.0	23.3	27.9	23.3	19.7	16.5
Imports	14.2	14.2	–13.7	11.8	26.0	–1.2	12.3	25.8	31.0	20.3	20.4	16.6
Volume												
Exports	13.3	12.9	7.2	5.2	21.0	0.4	13.1	16.0	18.8	17.3	16.4	15.7
Imports	11.8	11.4	–5.3	8.3	20.0	1.0	12.8	18.1	18.9	12.5	15.0	15.9
Unit value in U.S. dollars												
Exports	2.3	1.9	–8.7	4.8	0.9	–2.0	0.9	6.5	8.0	5.3	3.0	0.9
Imports	2.6	2.9	–9.1	6.2	5.8	–1.8	–0.3	6.8	10.3	6.9	4.9	0.9
Terms of trade	–0.2	–1.0	0.4	–1.3	–4.6	–0.1	1.3	–0.3	–2.1	–1.5	–1.7	—
Excluding China and India												
Value in U.S. dollars												
Exports	14.9	8.5	–4.0	10.0	18.5	–9.1	6.0	11.6	18.0	14.8	13.5	9.2
Imports	15.4	7.3	–23.3	11.5	21.2	–7.8	5.3	11.2	22.4	18.3	14.0	9.8
Volume												
Exports	12.2	5.8	9.2	3.1	17.0	–7.0	5.1	3.7	7.2	6.5	7.9	6.7
Imports	12.5	4.7	–14.5	4.7	19.0	–7.5	6.7	5.6	12.0	9.5	7.9	7.9
Unit value in U.S. dollars												
Exports	2.7	3.0	–11.9	10.2	1.3	–2.2	1.1	7.9	10.4	7.9	5.3	2.4
Imports	3.0	3.2	–10.4	12.2	2.6	0.1	–1.1	5.6	9.6	8.1	5.8	1.8
Terms of trade	–0.3	–0.2	–1.7	–1.7	–1.3	–2.3	2.3	2.1	0.8	–0.3	–0.4	0.5

Table 23 ***(concluded)***

	Ten-Year Averages											
	1988–97	1998–2007	1998	1999	2000	2001	2002	2003	2004	2005	2006	2007
Middle East												
Value in U.S. dollars												
Exports	8.8	15.8	–28.0	28.4	44.9	–9.2	6.4	25.5	32.6	37.5	32.0	10.8
Imports	6.5	11.4	–1.6	–4.8	7.4	6.3	9.0	16.7	28.6	23.7	20.8	13.0
Volume												
Exports	8.5	4.5	–4.9	1.1	6.3	1.4	3.1	10.8	9.1	5.9	8.7	4.0
Imports	4.2	9.0	2.8	–1.9	9.6	8.5	5.0	5.3	18.2	16.9	16.0	11.5
Unit value in U.S. dollars												
Exports	0.8	11.2	–24.4	27.0	37.5	–10.6	3.8	13.4	22.1	30.4	22.5	6.7
Imports	2.4	2.3	–4.2	–2.8	–1.9	–2.0	3.7	11.0	8.9	5.9	4.1	1.3
Terms of trade	–1.6	8.7	–21.1	30.7	40.1	–8.7	0.1	2.2	12.1	23.2	17.7	5.4
Western Hemisphere												
Value in U.S. dollars												
Exports	10.6	9.4	–3.9	4.1	19.6	–3.8	0.5	11.4	24.3	22.3	17.6	6.5
Imports	14.0	7.2	4.6	–6.8	14.8	–1.4	–8.5	4.4	22.8	19.0	17.3	10.8
Volume												
Exports	8.6	5.4	7.7	2.2	7.9	2.0	0.6	3.5	10.5	8.8	5.0	5.8
Imports	11.2	5.2	8.7	–4.3	12.2	–0.6	–7.3	0.5	15.1	11.2	11.2	8.2
Unit value in U.S. dollars												
Exports	3.2	4.0	–10.9	3.4	11.0	–5.7	0.1	7.8	12.4	12.5	12.2	0.8
Imports	3.6	1.9	–3.8	–2.6	2.3	–0.8	–1.4	4.0	6.8	7.2	5.6	2.5
Terms of trade	–0.3	2.1	–7.4	6.1	8.5	–4.9	1.5	3.6	5.2	4.9	6.3	–1.6

[1]Mongolia, which is not a member of the Commonwealth of Independent States, is included in this group for reasons of geography and similarities in economic structure.

Table 24. Other Emerging Market and Developing Countries—by Source of Export Earnings: Total Trade in Goods
(Annual percent change)

	Ten-Year Averages											
	1988–97	1998–2007	1998	1999	2000	2001	2002	2003	2004	2005	2006	2007
Fuel												
Value in U.S. dollars												
Exports	6.2	16.1	–24.8	20.5	48.2	–9.4	4.8	25.8	34.1	38.5	31.8	13.0
Imports	4.4	11.7	–7.0	–12.2	9.3	11.7	10.6	18.6	28.2	25.8	24.0	16.1
Volume												
Exports	4.4	4.6	–1.8	–1.6	8.0	0.6	2.8	10.2	9.6	6.2	6.4	6.4
Imports	1.7	9.7	–2.6	–10.5	12.0	14.1	7.2	10.2	18.2	18.9	18.7	15.2
Unit value in U.S. dollars												
Exports	2.3	11.2	–23.5	23.2	37.7	–10.1	2.3	14.2	22.8	30.8	24.4	6.3
Imports	3.3	2.0	–4.7	–2.3	–2.2	–2.1	3.3	8.4	8.8	6.2	4.6	1.0
Terms of trade	–1.0	9.0	–19.7	26.1	40.8	–8.2	–1.0	5.3	12.9	23.2	19.0	5.3
Nonfuel												
Value in U.S. dollars												
Exports	10.6	12.9	–1.2	3.9	18.2	0.7	10.2	21.8	27.8	20.2	18.3	13.3
Imports	11.5	11.9	–4.3	1.2	18.8	–1.1	6.8	22.0	29.3	18.4	18.6	14.0
Volume												
Exports	8.9	10.4	7.1	3.9	16.0	2.9	8.8	12.1	16.0	12.9	12.6	12.3
Imports	9.5	9.0	2.1	1.7	15.0	1.0	6.2	12.5	17.2	10.8	12.5	12.4
Unit value in U.S. dollars												
Exports	2.3	2.6	–7.6	0.9	2.1	–2.1	1.5	8.9	10.5	6.8	5.3	1.2
Imports	2.8	2.9	–6.4	0.6	3.6	–1.8	0.6	8.7	10.4	7.0	5.6	1.8
Terms of trade	–0.5	–0.3	–1.2	0.4	–1.5	–0.3	0.9	0.2	—	–0.2	–0.3	–0.6
Primary products												
Value in U.S. dollars												
Exports	5.3	8.8	–10.0	1.8	3.3	–5.2	4.9	16.9	39.2	19.2	24.0	3.0
Imports	5.8	6.8	–6.5	–11.6	6.4	–0.6	0.2	16.2	25.1	22.0	15.2	8.1
Volume												
Exports	6.0	4.4	1.8	5.9	1.3	4.9	0.8	4.1	14.1	3.3	3.4	5.5
Imports	4.8	4.7	2.9	–7.8	0.6	4.2	3.8	6.1	13.8	10.4	7.6	7.2
Unit value in U.S. dollars												
Exports	1.0	4.5	–11.3	–3.7	2.1	–9.6	5.3	12.5	21.9	15.5	20.1	–1.2
Imports	1.5	2.7	–9.0	–3.7	6.1	–4.3	–2.8	12.6	10.7	11.2	7.3	1.3
Terms of trade	–0.6	1.8	–2.6	—	–3.8	–5.5	8.4	–0.1	10.1	3.9	11.9	–2.4

Table 25. Summary of Payments Balances on Current Account

(Billions of U.S. dollars)

	1998	1999	2000	2001	2002	2003	2004	2005	2006	2007
Advanced economies	**18.5**	**–114.8**	**–267.1**	**–214.6**	**–229.5**	**–221.9**	**–267.2**	**–486.3**	**–571.1**	**–655.2**
United States	–213.5	–299.8	–415.2	–389.0	–472.4	–527.5	–665.3	–791.5	–869.1	–959.1
Euro area[1]	49.1	23.2	–40.9	3.6	42.4	34.4	82.5	–2.6	–9.6	–16.9
Japan	119.1	114.5	119.6	87.8	112.6	136.2	172.1	165.7	167.3	162.9
Other advanced economies[2]	63.8	47.4	69.3	83.0	87.9	134.9	143.5	142.1	140.3	157.9
Memorandum										
Newly industrialized Asian economies	64.6	57.2	38.9	47.9	55.3	80.0	88.7	86.2	78.5	80.1
Other emerging market and developing countries	**–113.4**	**–24.0**	**79.6**	**40.0**	**78.5**	**147.8**	**211.9**	**424.7**	**586.7**	**638.9**
Regional groups										
Africa	–19.4	–15.0	7.2	0.4	–7.8	–3.1	–0.4	18.4	33.1	44.5
Central and eastern Europe	–19.4	–26.5	–32.3	–16.2	–23.6	–36.4	–59.4	–63.3	–74.8	–76.9
Commonwealth of Independent States[3]	–7.4	23.7	48.2	33.1	30.2	35.9	62.5	87.7	127.1	138.8
Developing Asia	49.5	38.3	38.2	37.7	66.9	86.1	94.2	165.3	184.6	197.9
Middle East	–26.1	12.1	67.0	39.0	28.9	58.5	96.8	182.9	282.1	306.0
Western Hemisphere	–90.6	–56.6	–48.6	–54.1	–16.2	6.8	18.2	33.7	34.7	28.5
Memorandum										
European Union	35.8	–19.8	–86.6	–28.7	16.4	17.5	42.3	–47.9	–68.2	–76.4
Analytical groups										
By source of export earnings										
Fuel	–36.8	36.2	145.7	83.4	63.3	108.9	182.2	335.3	505.1	556.9
Nonfuel	–76.6	–60.2	–66.1	–43.4	15.2	38.9	29.7	89.4	81.5	82.1
of which, primary products	–7.4	–2.5	–2.7	–3.6	–3.8	–3.1	0.1	–0.6	2.5	1.2
By external financing source										
Net debtor countries	–129.4	–96.0	–87.8	–69.9	–39.1	–26.8	–57.8	–72.4	–80.5	–78.2
of which, official financing	–32.6	–18.0	–10.6	–7.0	8.3	10.0	–4.5	–8.7	–15.3	–19.3
Net debtor countries by debt-servicing experience										
Countries with arrears and/or rescheduling during 1999–2003	–35.5	–23.1	–4.6	–8.3	0.2	6.1	–2.8	2.8	8.1	21.3
Total[1]	**–95.0**	**–138.8**	**–187.4**	**–174.6**	**–151.0**	**–74.2**	**–55.3**	**–61.6**	**15.5**	**–16.3**
Memorandum										
In percent of total world current account transactions	–0.7	–1.0	–1.2	–1.1	–0.9	–0.4	–0.2	–0.2	0.1	–0.1
In percent of world GDP	–0.3	–0.5	–0.6	–0.6	–0.5	–0.2	–0.1	–0.1	—	—

[1]Reflects errors, omissions, and asymmetries in balance of payments statistics on current account, as well as the exclusion of data for international organizations and a limited number of countries. Calculated as the sum of the balance of individual euro area countries. See "Classification of Countries" in the introduction to this Statistical Appendix.

[2]In this table, "other advanced economies" means advanced economies excluding the United States, euro area countries, and Japan.

[3]Mongolia, which is not a member of the Commonwealth of Independent States, is included in this group for reasons of geography and similarities in economic structure.

Table 26. Advanced Economies: Balance of Payments on Current Account

	1998	1999	2000	2001	2002	2003	2004	2005	2006	2007
					Billions of U.S. dollars					
Advanced economies	**18.5**	**–114.8**	**–267.1**	**–214.6**	**–229.5**	**–221.9**	**–267.2**	**–486.3**	**–571.1**	**–655.2**
United States	–213.5	–299.8	–415.2	–389.0	–472.4	–527.5	–665.3	–791.5	–869.1	–959.1
Euro area[1]	49.1	23.2	–40.9	3.6	42.4	34.4	82.5	–2.6	–9.6	–16.9
Germany	–16.3	–26.9	–32.6	0.4	41.0	45.6	101.9	114.9	120.6	120.7
France	38.6	42.0	18.0	21.5	14.5	7.9	–7.0	–33.6	–38.6	–40.1
Italy	17.7	5.9	–6.1	–0.9	–8.1	–19.9	–15.6	–28.5	–25.6	–20.2
Spain	–7.0	–18.1	–23.2	–23.6	–22.5	–31.6	–54.9	–83.0	–100.6	–115.1
Netherlands	13.0	15.6	7.2	9.8	10.9	29.4	54.2	40.0	50.1	56.0
Belgium	13.3	20.1	9.4	7.9	11.7	12.7	12.2	10.1	10.9	10.9
Austria	–5.2	–6.7	–4.9	–3.7	0.7	–0.5	0.4	3.8	4.9	5.9
Finland	7.3	7.8	10.6	12.0	12.6	10.6	14.7	10.0	10.4	10.1
Greece	–5.9	–8.6	–9.9	–9.5	–9.7	–12.5	–13.0	–17.5	–19.7	–21.2
Portugal	–8.5	–10.4	–11.7	–11.4	–10.0	–9.2	–12.9	–17.0	–18.7	–19.6
Ireland	0.7	0.2	–0.4	–0.7	–1.2	—	–1.1	–5.2	–6.5	–7.8
Luxembourg	1.6	2.3	2.7	1.8	2.5	1.9	3.5	3.6	3.2	3.5
Japan	119.1	114.5	119.6	87.8	112.6	136.2	172.1	165.7	167.3	162.9
United Kingdom	–5.3	–35.1	–37.6	–31.5	–24.8	–24.4	–35.4	–48.3	–55.9	–58.0
Canada	–7.7	1.7	19.7	16.2	12.6	10.1	21.3	26.3	25.5	25.4
Korea	40.4	24.5	12.3	8.0	5.4	11.9	28.2	16.6	3.3	2.9
Australia	–18.4	–22.4	–15.2	–7.7	–16.2	–29.5	–40.1	–42.2	–41.4	–42.3
Taiwan Province of China	3.4	8.0	8.9	18.3	25.6	29.3	18.5	16.1	20.7	22.0
Sweden	9.7	10.6	9.9	9.8	12.5	22.4	23.9	21.6	21.9	22.8
Switzerland	26.1	29.4	30.7	20.0	23.0	43.0	50.5	50.7	50.7	52.9
Hong Kong SAR	2.5	10.3	7.0	9.8	12.4	16.5	15.7	20.3	16.4	15.7
Denmark	–1.5	3.3	2.3	5.0	4.3	7.0	5.6	7.7	6.0	6.9
Norway	0.1	8.5	26.1	26.2	24.4	28.9	34.6	49.7	66.0	79.3
Israel	–1.4	–1.6	–1.2	–0.7	–0.5	1.8	3.2	3.8	1.6	1.4
Singapore	18.3	14.4	10.7	11.8	11.9	22.3	26.3	33.3	38.0	39.5
New Zealand	–2.1	–3.5	–2.7	–1.4	–2.4	–3.4	–6.5	–9.6	–9.8	–9.3
Cyprus	0.3	–0.2	–0.5	–0.3	–0.5	–0.3	–0.9	–1.0	–0.8	–0.6
Iceland	–0.6	–0.6	–0.9	–0.3	0.1	–0.5	–1.3	–2.6	–2.0	–0.7
Memorandum										
Major advanced economies	–67.5	–197.7	–334.1	–295.5	–324.7	–371.9	–428.1	–595.1	–676.0	–768.4
Euro area[2]	23.0	–34.0	–91.7	–19.3	50.3	36.6	61.8	–28.8	–10.5	–12.6
Newly industrialized Asian economies	64.6	57.2	38.9	47.9	55.3	80.0	88.7	86.2	78.5	80.1

Table 26 ***(concluded)***

	1998	1999	2000	2001	2002	2003	2004	2005	2006	2007
					Percent of GDP					
Advanced economies	**0.1**	**–0.5**	**–1.1**	**–0.9**	**–0.9**	**–0.8**	**–0.8**	**–1.4**	**–1.6**	**–1.7**
United States	–2.4	–3.2	–4.2	–3.8	–4.5	–4.8	–5.7	–6.4	–6.6	–6.9
Euro area[1]	0.7	0.3	–0.7	0.1	0.6	0.4	0.9	—	–0.1	–0.2
Germany	–0.7	–1.3	–1.7	—	2.0	1.9	3.7	4.1	4.2	4.0
France	2.6	2.9	1.3	1.6	1.0	0.4	–0.3	–1.6	–1.7	–1.7
Italy	1.5	0.5	–0.6	–0.1	–0.7	–1.3	–0.9	–1.6	–1.4	–1.0
Spain	–1.2	–2.9	–4.0	–3.9	–3.3	–3.6	–5.3	–7.4	–8.3	–8.7
Netherlands	3.3	3.9	2.0	2.4	2.5	5.4	8.9	6.3	7.6	7.9
Belgium	5.2	7.9	4.0	3.4	4.6	4.1	3.4	2.7	2.8	2.7
Austria	–2.4	–3.2	–2.5	–1.9	0.3	–0.2	0.2	1.2	1.5	1.7
Finland	5.6	5.9	8.7	9.6	9.3	6.4	7.8	5.1	5.1	4.6
Greece	–4.9	–6.9	–8.5	–8.0	–7.1	–7.1	–6.2	–7.8	–8.1	–8.0
Portugal	–7.2	–8.6	–10.4	–9.8	–7.8	–5.9	–7.3	–9.3	–9.8	–9.6
Ireland	0.8	0.2	–0.4	–0.6	–1.0	—	–0.6	–2.6	–3.0	–3.2
Luxembourg	8.5	10.7	13.2	8.8	11.0	6.4	10.5	9.7	8.2	8.2
Japan	3.1	2.6	2.6	2.1	2.9	3.2	3.8	3.6	3.7	3.5
United Kingdom	–0.4	–2.4	–2.6	–2.2	–1.6	–1.3	–1.6	–2.2	–2.4	–2.3
Canada	–1.2	0.3	2.7	2.3	1.7	1.2	2.1	2.3	2.0	1.9
Korea	11.7	5.5	2.4	1.7	1.0	2.0	4.1	2.1	0.4	0.3
Australia	–4.9	–5.6	–3.9	–2.1	–3.9	–5.6	–6.3	–6.0	–5.6	–5.3
Taiwan Province of China	1.2	2.7	2.8	6.3	8.7	9.8	5.7	4.7	5.8	5.9
Sweden	3.9	4.2	4.1	4.4	5.1	7.3	6.8	6.0	5.8	5.6
Switzerland	9.7	11.1	12.4	8.0	8.3	13.3	14.1	13.8	13.3	13.3
Hong Kong SAR	1.5	6.3	4.1	5.9	7.6	10.4	9.5	11.4	8.7	7.8
Denmark	–0.9	1.9	1.4	3.1	2.5	3.2	2.3	3.0	2.2	2.3
Norway	—	5.4	15.6	15.4	12.8	13.0	13.6	16.8	19.9	22.2
Israel	–1.3	–1.4	–1.0	–0.6	–0.5	1.6	2.6	2.9	1.2	1.0
Singapore	22.2	17.4	11.6	13.8	13.4	24.1	24.5	28.5	28.5	27.3
New Zealand	–3.9	–6.2	–5.2	–2.8	–4.1	–4.3	–6.7	–8.9	–9.6	–9.1
Cyprus	3.1	–1.8	–5.3	–3.3	–4.5	–2.5	–5.7	–5.8	–4.6	–3.5
Iceland	–6.8	–6.8	–10.2	–4.4	1.6	–5.0	–10.1	–16.5	–12.5	–4.4
Memorandum										
Major advanced economies	–0.3	–1.0	–1.6	–1.4	–1.5	–1.6	–1.6	–2.2	–2.4	–2.6
Euro area[2]	0.3	–0.5	–1.5	–0.3	0.7	0.4	0.6	–0.3	–0.1	–0.1
Newly industrialized Asian economies	7.4	5.8	3.5	4.7	5.1	6.9	7.0	6.0	5.0	4.9

[1]Calculated as the sum of the balances of individual euro area countries.
[2]Corrected for reporting discrepancies in intra-area transactions.

Table 27. Advanced Economies: Current Account Transactions

(Billions of U.S. dollars)

	1998	1999	2000	2001	2002	2003	2004	2005	2006	2007
Exports	4,193.1	4,293.8	4,679.2	4,445.8	4,584.6	5,267.5	6,237.6	6,802.1	7,586.7	8,216.9
Imports	4,131.4	4,377.3	4,915.2	4,644.8	4,775.5	5,487.2	6,554.7	7,334.6	8,214.5	8,898.4
Trade balance	61.7	–83.4	–236.0	–199.1	–190.9	–219.7	–317.1	–532.5	–627.8	–681.4
Services, credits	1,128.8	1,201.3	1,254.8	1,253.3	1,332.4	1,526.9	1,812.4	1,966.0	2,140.2	2,316.5
Services, debits	1,051.2	1,119.5	1,176.2	1,184.3	1,244.0	1,418.8	1,663.0	1,786.8	1,948.5	2,108.8
Balance on services	77.6	81.8	78.6	69.0	88.4	108.1	149.3	179.2	191.7	207.8
Balance on goods and services	139.3	–1.6	–157.3	–130.0	–102.5	–111.6	–167.8	–353.3	–436.1	–473.7
Income, net	9.8	20.2	30.1	43.5	20.0	67.1	109.2	97.8	79.0	39.7
Current transfers, net	–130.6	–133.3	–139.8	–128.1	–147.1	–177.5	–208.6	–230.8	–214.0	–221.2
Current account balance	**18.5**	**–114.8**	**–267.1**	**–214.6**	**–229.5**	**–221.9**	**–267.2**	**–486.3**	**–571.1**	**–655.2**
Balance on goods and services										
Advanced economies	**139.3**	**–1.6**	**–157.3**	**–130.0**	**–102.5**	**–111.6**	**–167.8**	**–353.3**	**–436.1**	**–473.7**
United States	–164.6	–263.3	–377.6	–362.8	–421.1	–494.9	–611.3	–716.7	–799.6	–847.3
Euro area[1]	143.8	99.5	36.8	92.7	160.5	178.8	203.0	144.7	144.5	148.3
Germany	30.7	11.8	1.0	34.2	84.0	95.5	136.3	140.2	154.9	156.3
France	42.3	36.3	16.5	21.4	24.7	19.1	2.4	–22.2	–29.7	–30.6
Italy	37.5	22.4	10.4	15.3	11.7	8.3	12.2	–0.9	2.3	9.4
Spain	–1.7	–11.5	–17.7	–14.0	–13.1	–18.7	–39.7	–57.7	–76.2	–88.6
Japan	73.2	69.2	69.0	26.5	51.7	72.5	94.2	69.8	62.7	54.3
United Kingdom	–11.8	–25.0	–29.4	–38.6	–46.4	–48.1	–64.1	–80.5	–85.6	–88.6
Canada	11.8	23.8	41.3	40.6	31.9	31.8	40.6	42.2	41.2	41.8
Other advanced economies	87.0	94.2	102.5	111.5	120.8	148.3	169.7	187.3	200.7	217.9
Memorandum										
Major advanced economies	19.0	–124.9	–268.7	–263.4	–263.4	–315.8	–389.6	–568.3	–653.9	–704.7
Newly industrialized Asian economies	63.6	57.6	41.3	45.8	56.2	77.7	85.1	88.9	78.8	79.5
Income, net										
Advanced economies	**9.8**	**20.2**	**30.1**	**43.5**	**20.0**	**67.1**	**109.2**	**97.8**	**79.0**	**39.7**
United States	4.3	13.9	21.1	25.1	12.2	36.6	27.6	11.3	–4.6	–49.1
Euro area[1]	–44.3	–26.1	–30.4	–40.3	–67.7	–76.7	–42.5	–55.7	–65.1	–70.0
Germany	–16.9	–12.2	–7.7	–9.8	–17.0	–18.0	0.8	10.8	3.2	3.8
France	8.7	19.0	15.5	15.0	4.0	8.0	12.6	16.3	13.4	14.2
Italy	–12.4	–11.1	–12.1	–10.4	–14.5	–20.1	–18.3	–17.5	–18.3	–19.4
Spain	–8.6	–9.6	–6.8	–11.2	–11.6	–13.1	–15.1	–21.4	–20.7	–22.5
Japan	54.7	57.4	60.4	69.2	65.8	71.2	85.7	103.5	113.8	117.4
United Kingdom	20.4	2.1	6.9	16.8	35.2	40.3	48.7	54.4	54.4	57.9
Canada	–20.0	–22.6	–22.3	–25.4	–19.3	–21.4	–19.1	–15.5	–15.1	–16.0
Other advanced economies	–5.3	–4.4	–5.6	–1.9	–6.2	17.2	8.8	–0.2	–4.3	–0.5
Memorandum										
Major advanced economies	38.8	46.5	61.7	80.5	66.3	96.5	138.0	163.1	146.7	108.8
Newly industrialized Asian economies	2.0	2.6	2.4	8.2	6.3	10.9	13.0	7.5	11.1	12.6

[1]Calculated as the sum of the individual euro area countries.

Table 28. Other Emerging Market and Developing Countries: Payments Balances on Current Account

	1998	1999	2000	2001	2002	2003	2004	2005	2006	2007
	Billions of U.S. dollars									
Other emerging market and developing countries	**–113.4**	**–24.0**	**79.6**	**40.0**	**78.5**	**147.8**	**211.9**	**424.7**	**586.7**	**638.9**
Regional groups										
Africa	–19.4	–15.0	7.2	0.4	–7.8	–3.1	–0.4	18.4	33.1	44.5
Sub-Sahara	–17.7	–14.4	–0.6	–7.4	–12.9	–12.7	–11.9	–3.9	2.6	18.9
Excluding Nigeria and South Africa	–12.4	–10.6	–5.8	–9.7	–8.2	–9.0	–7.8	–6.1	–2.5	5.0
Central and eastern Europe	–19.4	–26.5	–32.3	–16.2	–23.6	–36.4	–59.4	–63.3	–74.8	–76.9
Commonwealth of Independent States[1]	–7.4	23.7	48.2	33.1	30.2	35.9	62.5	87.7	127.1	138.8
Russia	0.2	24.6	46.8	33.9	29.1	35.4	58.6	83.6	120.1	124.4
Excluding Russia	–7.7	–0.9	1.4	–0.8	1.1	0.4	3.9	4.1	6.9	14.5
Developing Asia	49.5	38.3	38.2	37.7	66.9	86.1	94.2	165.3	184.6	197.9
China	31.6	15.7	20.5	17.4	35.4	45.9	68.7	160.8	184.2	206.5
India	–6.9	–3.2	–4.6	1.4	7.1	8.8	1.4	–11.9	–17.6	–25.1
Excluding China and India	24.7	25.9	22.2	18.9	24.4	31.5	24.2	16.4	18.0	16.5
Middle East	–26.1	12.1	67.0	39.0	28.9	58.5	96.8	182.9	282.1	306.0
Western Hemisphere	–90.6	–56.6	–48.6	–54.1	–16.2	6.8	18.2	33.7	34.7	28.5
Brazil	–33.4	–25.3	–24.2	–23.2	–7.6	4.2	11.7	14.2	5.8	4.4
Mexico	–16.0	–13.9	–18.7	–17.7	–13.5	–8.6	–6.6	–4.8	–0.5	–1.6
Analytical groups										
By source of export earnings										
Fuel	–36.8	36.2	145.7	83.4	63.3	108.9	182.2	335.3	505.1	556.9
Nonfuel	–76.6	–60.2	–66.1	–43.4	15.2	38.9	29.7	89.4	81.5	82.1
of which, primary products	–7.4	–2.5	–2.7	–3.6	–3.8	–3.1	0.1	–0.6	2.5	1.2
By external financing source										
Net debtor countries	–129.4	–96.0	–87.8	–69.9	–39.1	–26.8	–57.8	–72.4	–80.5	–78.2
of which, official financing	–32.6	–18.0	–10.6	–7.0	8.3	10.0	–4.5	–8.7	–15.3	–19.3
Net debtor countries by debt-servicing experience										
Countries with arrears and/or rescheduling during 1999–2003	–35.5	–23.1	–4.6	–8.3	0.2	6.1	–2.8	2.8	8.1	21.3
Other groups										
Heavily indebted poor countries	–7.6	–9.0	–7.4	–7.7	–9.4	–8.2	–8.2	–9.0	–9.6	–9.8
Middle East and north Africa	–29.5	9.7	72.8	44.6	32.6	66.7	106.5	201.3	310.2	330.3

Table 28 *(concluded)*

	Ten-Year Averages 1988–97	1998–2007	1998	1999	2000	2001	2002	2003	2004	2005	2006	2007
	Percent of exports of goods and services											
Other emerging market and developing countries	**–7.3**	**4.9**	**–7.8**	**–1.6**	**4.2**	**2.2**	**3.9**	**6.0**	**6.7**	**10.8**	**12.4**	**11.9**
Regional groups												
Africa	–8.1	–0.5	–16.2	–11.7	4.6	0.3	–5.0	–1.6	–0.2	5.9	8.7	9.9
Sub-Sahara	–9.4	–6.4	–19.6	–15.0	–0.5	–6.8	–11.4	–8.9	–6.5	–1.7	0.9	5.6
Excluding Nigeria and South Africa	–20.8	–11.9	–27.5	–22.0	–10.7	–18.3	–14.2	–13.1	–8.8	–5.4	–1.8	2.9
Central and eastern Europe	–2.4	–10.5	–8.5	–12.4	–13.3	–6.2	–8.2	–9.9	–12.5	–11.5	–11.8	–10.8
Commonwealth of Independent States[1]	. . .	18.9	–5.8	19.2	29.3	20.0	16.9	16.0	20.5	22.5	25.6	25.3
Russia	. . .	27.5	0.3	29.1	40.9	29.9	24.1	23.3	28.8	31.2	34.4	32.8
Excluding Russia	. . .	0.3	–19.0	–2.2	2.7	–1.6	1.9	0.6	3.9	3.4	4.7	8.5
Developing Asia	–7.3	8.2	9.2	6.6	5.5	5.5	8.5	9.0	7.7	10.9	10.2	9.4
China	4.6	11.9	15.2	7.1	7.3	5.8	9.7	9.5	10.5	19.2	17.9	16.7
India	–19.4	–3.2	–15.1	–6.3	–7.7	2.3	10.0	10.3	1.2	–7.6	–8.9	–10.7
Excluding China and India	–11.3	5.8	8.7	8.5	6.3	5.8	7.0	8.2	5.3	3.1	3.0	2.6
Middle East	–6.8	19.0	–16.9	6.3	25.2	15.9	11.0	18.0	22.7	31.9	38.2	37.4
Western Hemisphere	–14.2	–6.3	–30.8	–18.6	–13.5	–15.6	–4.7	1.8	3.8	5.9	5.2	4.0
Brazil	–12.2	–15.2	–56.6	–45.9	–37.5	–34.4	–10.9	5.0	10.7	10.6	4.0	2.8
Mexico	–26.7	–9.2	–18.5	–14.3	–15.8	–15.5	–11.8	–7.3	–4.9	–3.1	–0.3	–0.8
Analytical groups												
By source of export earnings												
Fuel	–2.5	21.1	–13.3	11.1	31.0	19.3	13.9	19.1	24.0	32.3	37.2	36.4
Nonfuel	–9.0	–0.7	–6.5	–5.0	–4.7	–3.0	1.0	2.1	1.2	3.1	2.4	2.1
of which, primary products	–12.1	–4.4	–15.7	–5.3	–5.4	–7.7	–7.6	–5.4	0.2	–0.6	2.2	1.1
By external financing source												
Net debtor countries	–11.9	–6.0	–14.5	–10.6	–8.4	–6.7	–3.6	–2.1	–3.6	–3.7	–3.5	–3.1
of which, official financing	–16.3	–3.9	–16.8	–9.4	–4.8	–3.3	3.8	4.1	–1.5	–2.5	–3.9	–4.5
Net debtor countries by debt-servicing experience												
Countries with arrears and/or rescheduling during 1999–2003	–16.4	–2.9	–18.6	–12.0	–1.9	–3.7	0.1	2.3	–0.8	0.7	1.6	3.8
Other groups												
Heavily indebted poor countries	–29.2	–26.0	–31.9	–38.6	–28.9	–29.6	–34.7	–25.6	–20.2	–18.8	–16.5	–15.6
Middle East and north Africa	–7.4	17.9	–16.0	4.3	23.5	15.4	10.6	17.5	21.5	30.4	36.4	34.8
Memorandum												
Median												
Other emerging market and developing countries	–12.7	–10.3	–15.9	–10.9	–9.8	–9.5	–9.5	–8.3	–8.0	–9.8	–11.1	–10.4

[1]Mongolia, which is not a member of the Commonwealth of Independent States, is included in this group for reasons of geography and similarities in economic structure.

Table 29. Other Emerging Market and Developing Countries—by Region: Current Account Transactions

(Billions of U.S. dollars)

	1998	1999	2000	2001	2002	2003	2004	2005	2006	2007
Other emerging market and developing countries										
Exports	1,190.5	1,277.7	1,599.1	1,565.6	1,703.9	2,092.0	2,707.3	3,383.5	4,133.8	4,678.6
Imports	1,209.8	1,196.3	1,404.1	1,414.8	1,520.0	1,846.6	2,384.9	2,852.2	3,409.1	3,899.0
Trade balance	–19.3	81.4	195.0	150.8	183.8	245.4	322.5	531.3	724.7	779.6
Services, net	–46.6	–47.4	–59.3	–65.1	–65.5	–69.4	–69.8	–79.6	–109.3	–122.6
Balance on goods and services	–65.9	34.0	135.7	85.6	118.3	176.0	252.6	451.7	615.4	657.0
Income, net	–98.8	–120.3	–125.1	–123.8	–132.9	–148.0	–179.2	–192.8	–205.9	–198.7
Current transfers, net	51.4	62.3	69.1	78.1	93.1	119.7	138.5	165.8	177.2	180.6
Current account balance	**–113.4**	**–24.0**	**79.6**	**40.0**	**78.5**	**147.8**	**211.9**	**424.7**	**586.7**	**638.9**
Memorandum										
Exports of goods and services	1,461.4	1,538.0	1,884.8	1,856.9	2,016.2	2,448.1	3,158.4	3,916.1	4,737.3	5,357.4
Interest payments	140.1	139.7	140.0	132.2	125.6	138.7	151.0	173.0	206.7	217.0
Oil trade balance	99.2	146.3	234.0	191.7	200.1	257.1	340.4	508.5	671.7	774.6
Regional groups										
Africa										
Exports	98.2	105.7	135.3	126.7	130.2	163.5	211.2	270.0	333.5	396.0
Imports	100.9	101.5	105.1	106.7	117.2	143.5	181.2	213.7	249.8	287.4
Trade balance	–2.8	4.2	30.3	20.0	13.0	20.1	30.0	56.2	83.7	108.6
Services, net	–11.6	–11.0	–11.2	–11.7	–12.0	–13.1	–17.0	–20.5	–24.7	–30.8
Balance on goods and services	–14.4	–6.9	19.1	8.3	1.0	7.0	13.1	35.7	59.0	77.8
Income, net	–16.2	–18.2	–23.3	–20.8	–22.8	–28.2	–35.8	–42.6	–53.0	–61.8
Current transfers, net	11.1	10.1	11.5	13.0	14.0	18.2	22.3	25.3	27.1	28.5
Current account balance	**–19.4**	**–15.0**	**7.2**	**0.4**	–7.8	**–3.1**	**–0.4**	**18.4**	**33.1**	**44.5**
Memorandum										
Exports of goods and services	119.6	128.0	157.5	149.9	154.6	194.4	248.6	313.3	382.7	450.3
Interest payments	14.9	14.4	13.6	11.9	10.6	11.5	12.0	12.9	12.9	14.3
Oil trade balance	19.8	26.8	45.9	39.5	38.4	54.2	74.2	111.5	142.6	185.3
Central and eastern Europe										
Exports	161.5	157.6	178.5	197.7	225.2	290.1	382.1	441.6	517.0	580.5
Imports	208.8	199.9	232.1	231.2	262.8	340.7	448.5	517.1	608.9	681.5
Trade balance	–47.3	–42.3	–53.6	–33.5	–37.6	–50.6	–66.5	–75.5	–91.9	–101.0
Services, net	21.5	11.1	16.6	14.1	12.5	15.1	19.2	22.6	24.6	27.5
Balance on goods and services	–25.8	–31.2	–37.1	–19.4	–25.2	–35.5	–47.2	–52.8	–67.2	–73.5
Income, net	–6.4	–6.6	–7.2	–8.1	–10.8	–14.8	–29.1	–31.0	–31.6	–32.0
Current transfers, net	12.8	11.3	11.9	11.3	12.4	13.9	17.0	20.5	24.0	28.6
Current account balance	**–19.4**	**–26.5**	**–32.3**	**–16.2**	**–23.6**	**–36.4**	**–59.4**	**–63.3**	**–74.8**	**–76.9**
Memorandum										
Exports of goods and services	227.6	213.6	242.6	259.8	288.7	367.9	475.9	549.7	635.9	713.1
Interest payments	11.4	11.7	12.6	13.7	13.7	16.6	25.7	27.5	30.7	33.0
Oil trade balance	–12.2	–14.2	–23.3	–21.5	–22.0	–27.4	–33.7	–48.1	–61.5	–67.6

Table 29 *(concluded)*

	1998	1999	2000	2001	2002	2003	2004	2005	2006	2007
Commonwealth of Independent States[1]										
Exports	107.5	107.5	147.3	145.9	155.1	196.7	268.7	346.9	446.0	494.1
Imports	99.4	73.8	84.6	97.3	106.7	135.0	174.8	216.6	269.4	311.0
Trade balance	8.0	33.7	62.7	48.6	48.4	61.7	94.0	130.3	176.6	183.2
Services, net	–3.8	–3.9	–7.0	–10.8	–11.8	–13.1	–17.6	–20.0	–22.9	–22.3
Balance on goods and services	4.2	29.9	55.6	37.8	36.7	48.6	76.4	110.3	153.7	160.8
Income, net	–13.0	–8.5	–9.8	–6.9	–9.1	–16.1	–17.6	–27.0	–32.5	–29.2
Current transfers, net	1.3	2.4	2.4	2.1	2.6	3.4	3.7	4.4	5.9	7.2
Current account balance	**–7.4**	**23.7**	**48.2**	**33.1**	**30.2**	**35.9**	**62.5**	**87.7**	**127.1**	**138.8**
Memorandum										
Exports of goods and services	127.2	123.6	164.7	165.9	178.6	224.1	304.1	389.4	496.0	548.8
Interest payments	17.4	13.1	13.3	12.4	13.4	25.1	25.4	35.8	46.4	49.1
Oil trade balance	13.4	19.6	38.4	36.7	43.2	57.3	84.7	130.3	180.7	211.7
Developing Asia										
Exports	455.6	493.4	602.5	592.8	675.7	832.9	1,065.0	1,313.5	1,572.7	1,831.9
Imports	388.6	434.5	547.4	540.6	607.3	764.0	1,001.1	1,204.5	1,449.9	1,690.9
Trade balance	67.0	58.9	55.1	52.2	68.5	68.9	63.9	109.0	122.8	141.1
Services, net	–12.1	–6.9	–13.0	–14.1	–11.6	–15.7	–6.7	–2.7	–1.9	0.9
Balance on goods and services	54.9	52.1	42.1	38.1	56.8	53.2	57.2	106.3	120.9	142.0
Income, net	–27.7	–44.9	–39.9	–41.5	–39.7	–30.8	–31.2	–22.1	–18.6	–19.9
Current transfers, net	22.3	31.1	36.0	41.1	49.8	63.7	68.2	81.1	82.3	75.8
Current account balance	**49.5**	**38.3**	**38.2**	**37.7**	**66.9**	**86.1**	**94.2**	**165.3**	**184.6**	**197.9**
Memorandum										
Exports of goods and services	538.6	577.1	694.7	688.6	785.0	951.7	1,231.5	1,516.9	1,815.5	2,115.8
Interest payments	33.6	33.3	32.3	28.6	28.1	27.5	28.6	34.0	40.8	45.8
Oil trade balance	–12.6	–19.3	–37.2	–34.7	–38.7	–50.4	–80.9	–115.1	–152.8	–173.8
Middle East										
Exports	125.9	161.7	234.4	212.8	226.5	284.3	377.0	518.3	684.4	758.3
Imports	128.2	122.0	131.1	139.3	151.9	177.2	227.8	281.9	340.5	384.7
Trade balance	–2.2	39.7	103.4	73.5	74.5	107.0	149.2	236.4	344.0	373.6
Services, net	–25.5	–25.2	–32.2	–27.9	–33.0	–34.3	–39.3	–46.5	–66.0	–75.8
Balance on goods and services	–27.8	14.6	71.1	45.6	41.5	72.8	109.9	189.9	277.9	297.8
Income, net	16.0	10.6	10.5	9.4	3.2	1.7	3.1	9.2	21.7	27.3
Current transfers, net	–14.3	–13.1	–14.7	–15.9	–15.8	–16.0	–16.2	–16.2	–17.6	–19.1
Current account balance	**–26.1**	**12.1**	**67.0**	**39.0**	**28.9**	**58.5**	**96.8**	**182.9**	**282.1**	**306.0**
Memorandum										
Exports of goods and services	154.1	191.8	265.8	246.2	262.3	325.8	426.3	573.9	739.1	817.4
Interest payments	11.9	11.6	9.5	9.2	8.9	7.2	8.5	10.1	16.9	18.9
Oil trade balance	74.6	108.3	169.5	140.8	145.7	185.6	245.9	355.2	465.8	513.7
Western Hemisphere										
Exports	241.9	251.7	301.0	289.6	291.1	324.5	403.3	493.1	580.1	617.8
Imports	283.9	264.6	303.8	299.7	274.2	286.2	351.4	418.3	490.7	543.7
Trade balance	–42.0	–12.9	–2.8	–10.1	17.0	38.3	51.8	74.8	89.5	74.1
Services, net	–15.1	–11.6	–12.3	–14.7	–9.5	–8.4	–8.5	–12.5	–18.3	–22.1
Balance on goods and services	–57.1	–24.5	–15.1	–24.7	7.4	29.9	43.3	62.3	71.1	52.1
Income, net	–51.6	–52.7	–55.5	–55.9	–53.8	–59.7	–68.6	–79.3	–92.0	–83.1
Current transfers, net	18.1	20.5	22.0	26.6	30.1	36.5	43.5	50.7	55.5	59.5
Current account balance	**–90.6**	**–56.6**	**–48.6**	**–54.1**	**–16.2**	**6.8**	**18.2**	**33.7**	**34.7**	**28.5**
Memorandum										
Exports of goods and services	294.1	303.9	359.5	346.5	347.0	384.3	472.0	572.9	668.1	711.9
Interest payments	50.9	55.8	58.6	56.5	50.9	50.8	50.8	52.6	59.0	55.9
Oil trade balance	16.2	25.1	40.7	30.9	33.4	37.8	50.1	74.5	96.9	105.4

[1]Mongolia, which is not a member of the Commonwealth of Independent States, is included in this group for reasons of geography and similarities in economic structure.

Table 30. Other Emerging Market and Developing Countries—by Analytical Criteria: Current Account Transactions
(Billions of U.S. dollars)

	1998	1999	2000	2001	2002	2003	2004	2005	2006	2007
By source of export earnings										
Fuel										
Exports	246.3	296.7	439.7	398.2	417.3	524.8	703.9	974.7	1,284.8	1,451.5
Imports	209.6	184.0	201.1	224.7	248.4	294.7	377.9	475.5	589.8	684.6
Trade balance	36.6	112.7	238.6	173.5	168.9	230.1	326.0	499.2	695.0	766.9
Services, net	–46.2	–48.5	–58.3	–57.6	–62.9	–69.0	–84.7	–99.6	–121.6	–141.1
Balance on goods and services	–9.6	64.2	180.3	115.9	105.9	161.1	241.3	399.6	573.3	625.8
Income, net	–9.1	–11.1	–15.5	–11.4	–22.0	–33.0	–40.1	–45.7	–47.8	–48.0
Current transfers, net	–18.1	–16.9	–19.0	–21.0	–20.6	–19.2	–19.0	–18.6	–20.4	–20.9
Current account balance	**–36.8**	**36.2**	**145.7**	**83.4**	**63.3**	**108.9**	**182.2**	**335.3**	**505.1**	**556.9**
Memorandum										
Exports of goods and services	277.8	325.0	469.8	432.0	456.1	570.9	758.9	1,039.2	1,357.9	1,529.9
Interest payments	36.2	32.0	30.1	27.6	27.2	37.6	39.4	51.4	69.7	74.8
Oil trade balance	128.6	181.7	296.4	253.2	262.7	334.7	456.0	669.8	878.0	1,008.6
Nonfuel exports										
Exports	944.2	981.0	1,159.4	1,167.4	1,286.6	1,567.2	2,003.4	2,408.8	2,849.1	3,227.2
Imports	1,000.2	1,012.3	1,203.0	1,190.1	1,271.6	1,551.9	2,006.9	2,376.7	2,819.4	3,214.5
Trade balance	–55.9	–31.3	–43.6	–22.7	15.0	15.3	–3.5	32.1	29.7	12.7
Services, net	–0.4	1.1	–0.9	–7.5	–2.6	–0.4	14.8	20.0	12.4	18.6
Balance on goods and services	–56.4	–30.2	–44.6	–30.2	12.4	14.9	11.3	52.1	42.1	31.3
Income, net	–89.7	–109.2	–109.6	–112.4	–110.9	–115.0	–139.1	–147.1	–158.2	–150.7
Current transfers, net	69.5	79.2	88.1	99.2	113.7	139.0	157.5	184.4	197.6	201.5
Current account balance	**–76.6**	**–60.2**	**–66.1**	**–43.4**	**15.2**	**38.9**	**29.7**	**89.4**	**81.5**	**82.1**
Memorandum										
Exports of goods and services	1,183.6	1,213.0	1,415.1	1,424.9	1,560.0	1,877.2	2,399.4	2,876.9	3,379.4	3,827.5
Interest payments	103.9	107.8	109.9	104.6	98.4	101.1	111.6	121.6	137.0	142.2
Oil trade balance	–29.4	–35.4	–62.4	–61.6	–62.6	–77.6	–115.6	–161.4	–206.3	–233.9
Nonfuel primary products										
Exports	39.3	40.0	41.3	39.2	41.1	48.0	66.8	79.6	98.7	101.7
Imports	40.9	36.2	38.5	38.3	38.3	44.6	55.7	68.0	78.4	84.8
Trade balance	–1.7	3.8	2.8	0.9	2.7	3.5	11.1	11.6	20.3	16.9
Services, net	–4.0	–4.0	–3.7	–3.7	–4.1	–4.3	–5.3	–5.5	–6.9	–7.5
Balance on goods and services	–5.6	–0.2	–0.9	–2.7	–1.4	–0.8	5.8	6.1	13.5	9.4
Income, net	–4.9	–5.3	–5.0	–4.5	–6.7	–7.6	–12.9	–15.7	–21.2	–18.9
Current transfers, net	3.1	3.0	3.3	3.7	4.3	5.3	7.3	9.0	10.2	10.8
Current account balance	**–7.4**	**–2.5**	**–2.7**	**–3.6**	**–3.8**	**–3.1**	**0.1**	**–0.6**	**2.5**	**1.2**
Memorandum										
Exports of goods and services	47.1	47.6	48.9	47.1	49.4	57.6	78.4	93.2	113.4	116.7
Interest payments	4.1	3.9	4.2	3.9	3.5	3.3	3.4	3.5	4.0	4.1
Oil trade balance	–1.7	–2.0	–3.0	–3.2	–4.1	–3.9	–3.6	–4.5	–5.0	–5.1

Table 30 ***(continued)***

	1998	1999	2000	2001	2002	2003	2004	2005	2006	2007
By external financing source										
Net debtor countries										
Exports	690.1	713.3	840.8	834.5	886.8	1,050.7	1,316.3	1,575.9	1,857.5	2,071.6
Imports	805.3	791.6	909.5	888.4	918.9	1,079.4	1,369.0	1,641.9	1,921.5	2,141.7
Trade balance	−115.2	−78.3	−68.7	−53.9	−32.2	−28.7	−52.7	−66.0	−64.0	−70.1
Services, net	−5.9	−0.8	−2.5	−10.4	−7.4	−3.7	8.6	9.2	2.6	2.3
Balance on goods and services	−121.0	−79.2	−71.1	−64.3	−39.5	−32.5	−44.2	−56.8	−61.4	−67.8
Income, net	−77.3	−93.8	−101.5	−98.5	−103.5	−118.5	−152.1	−180.3	−201.5	−206.4
Current transfers, net	68.9	77.0	84.8	92.9	103.9	124.1	138.5	164.7	182.5	196.0
Current account balance	**−129.4**	**−96.0**	**−87.8**	**−69.9**	**−39.1**	**−26.8**	**−57.8**	**−72.4**	**−80.5**	**−78.2**
Memorandum										
Exports of goods and services	890.9	904.7	1,049.9	1,041.7	1,102.2	1,296.3	1,625.8	1,942.0	2,269.1	2,531.3
Interest payments	98.6	102.6	105.1	96.9	89.2	91.8	100.6	109.1	120.7	123.9
Oil trade balance	−4.9	−1.0	−0.9	−6.2	−5.4	0.9	−1.4	1.0	4.2	33.2
Official financing										
Exports	157.8	155.3	182.2	172.3	177.2	200.6	236.7	281.6	326.6	357.5
Imports	169.5	156.1	173.3	164.6	156.2	180.8	227.0	277.4	324.2	358.2
Trade balance	−11.7	−0.8	8.9	7.7	21.0	19.9	9.7	4.2	2.4	−0.7
Services, net	−21.9	−12.5	−17.2	−17.0	−14.8	−16.3	−15.1	−18.1	−26.8	−28.1
Balance on goods and services	−33.6	−13.3	−8.3	−9.3	6.2	3.5	−5.4	−13.9	−24.3	−28.8
Income, net	−18.1	−25.8	−27.2	−26.0	−28.9	−29.7	−39.3	−41.8	−44.0	−47.0
Current transfers, net	19.1	21.1	24.9	28.3	31.1	36.2	40.2	47.0	52.9	56.5
Current account balance	**−32.6**	**−18.0**	**−10.6**	**−7.0**	**8.3**	**10.0**	**−4.5**	**−8.7**	**−15.3**	**−19.3**
Memorandum										
Exports of goods and services	193.8	190.8	219.7	210.8	216.4	243.0	292.5	345.1	392.2	428.2
Interest payments	29.7	30.4	31.3	26.1	24.7	24.0	24.5	25.7	27.6	28.7
Oil trade balance	3.4	5.0	5.8	1.9	1.1	1.6	0.2	−2.3	−8.0	−11.3
Net debtor countries by debt-servicing experience										
Countries with arrears and/or rescheduling during 1999–2003										
Exports	157.3	160.7	201.6	189.1	194.6	229.6	279.6	351.1	422.8	491.1
Imports	161.8	152.8	168.5	162.9	163.5	191.5	239.4	299.1	352.7	394.7
Trade balance	−4.5	7.9	33.1	26.2	31.1	38.0	40.2	52.0	70.1	96.4
Services, net	−26.5	−17.8	−22.6	−24.5	−22.3	−25.7	−27.2	−35.3	−44.5	−50.1
Balance on goods and services	−31.0	−9.9	10.5	1.7	8.8	12.3	13.0	16.7	25.6	46.2
Income, net	−22.8	−32.1	−38.2	−34.2	−36.7	−40.1	−53.1	−58.4	−67.4	−77.0
Current transfers, net	18.3	18.8	23.1	24.2	28.1	33.8	37.4	44.5	49.9	52.0
Current account balance	**−35.5**	**−23.1**	**−4.6**	**−8.3**	**0.2**	**6.1**	**−2.8**	**2.8**	**8.1**	**21.3**
Memorandum										
Exports of goods and services	191.0	193.2	236.8	224.5	231.7	269.2	332.1	411.6	489.6	564.0
Interest payments	32.5	33.3	33.8	27.6	25.0	24.4	24.7	25.6	26.7	28.3
Oil trade balance	15.0	20.9	33.7	27.6	26.4	37.8	51.6	73.5	90.2	124.5

Table 30 *(concluded)*

	1998	1999	2000	2001	2002	2003	2004	2005	2006	2007
Other groups										
Heavily indebted poor countries										
Exports	18.4	17.4	19.2	19.6	20.2	24.0	31.3	36.9	45.8	49.7
Imports	24.1	25.0	25.2	26.3	29.2	32.6	40.2	47.7	54.9	60.1
Trade balance	–5.8	–7.6	–6.0	–6.6	–9.0	–8.6	–9.0	–10.8	–9.1	–10.4
Services, net	–3.6	–3.1	–3.0	–3.4	–3.5	–4.0	–4.7	–5.1	–6.3	–6.1
Balance on goods and services	–9.3	–10.8	–9.0	–10.0	–12.5	–12.6	–13.6	–15.9	–15.3	–16.5
Income, net	–3.2	–3.4	–4.2	–4.5	–4.2	–4.7	–5.7	–6.6	–8.7	–8.4
Current transfers, net	4.9	5.1	5.9	6.8	7.3	9.1	11.1	13.5	14.4	15.1
Current account balance	**–7.6**	**–9.0**	**–7.4**	**–7.7**	**–9.4**	**–8.2**	**–8.2**	**–9.0**	**–9.6**	**–9.8**
Memorandum										
Exports of goods and services	23.9	23.4	25.4	26.1	27.1	32.0	40.8	48.1	57.9	62.9
Interest payments	3.5	3.1	2.9	2.8	2.6	2.8	3.0	3.2	3.2	3.5
Oil trade balance	–0.2	–0.4	—	–0.8	–1.6	–0.9	0.4	0.8	2.2	2.0
Middle East and north Africa										
Exports	150.0	188.6	271.6	247.8	262.2	328.5	433.1	591.3	781.0	870.2
Imports	156.4	151.0	161.4	170.7	186.6	217.3	279.1	340.3	409.0	469.3
Trade balance	–6.4	37.6	110.1	77.1	75.6	111.2	154.0	251.0	372.0	400.8
Services, net	–24.6	–24.4	–31.5	–26.7	–31.6	–32.4	–37.5	–44.5	–64.1	–75.7
Balance on goods and services	–31.1	13.2	78.7	50.4	44.0	78.7	116.5	206.5	307.9	325.2
Income, net	10.9	5.1	4.2	4.3	–2.0	–4.3	–4.2	0.2	8.5	12.0
Current transfers, net	–9.4	–8.5	–10.1	–10.1	–9.4	–7.8	–5.9	–5.4	–6.2	–6.9
Current account balance	**–29.5**	**9.7**	**72.8**	**44.6**	**32.6**	**66.7**	**106.5**	**201.3**	**310.2**	**330.3**
Memorandum										
Exports of goods and services	184.7	225.6	309.9	289.2	306.6	380.2	494.7	661.4	852.5	948.1
Interest payments	–16.6	–16.2	–14.1	–13.0	–12.1	–10.2	–11.8	–13.2	–20.0	–22.3
Oil trade balance	84.6	120.1	189.9	159.3	163.6	209.3	277.1	399.9	530.6	590.5

Table 31. Other Emerging Market and Developing Countries—by Country: Balance of Payments on Current Account
(Percent of GDP)

	1998	1999	2000	2001	2002	2003	2004	2005	2006	2007
Africa	**–4.5**	**–3.4**	**1.6**	**0.1**	–1.6	**–0.5**	**–0.1**	**2.3**	**3.6**	**4.2**
Algeria	–1.9	—	16.7	12.8	7.6	13.0	13.1	21.3	24.8	19.1
Angola	–28.8	–27.5	8.7	–14.8	–2.7	–5.1	3.5	12.8	12.2	17.4
Benin	–5.4	–7.3	–7.7	–6.4	–8.4	–8.3	–7.3	–6.6	–7.0	–6.7
Botswana	3.9	11.0	8.8	9.9	3.3	5.6	3.0	15.4	14.7	13.5
Burkina Faso	–8.4	–11.0	–12.2	–11.0	–10.0	–8.2	–9.0	–10.2	–10.0	–10.2
Burundi	–6.4	–5.0	–8.6	–4.6	–3.5	–4.6	–8.1	–10.5	–17.5	–16.2
Cameroon	–2.3	–3.6	–1.5	–3.6	–5.2	–2.0	–3.4	–1.5	—	0.3
Cape Verde	–11.0	–12.4	–11.2	–10.1	–11.4	–11.1	–14.4	–4.6	–6.9	–10.0
Central African Republic	–6.1	–1.6	–3.0	–2.5	–3.4	–4.7	–4.5	–2.9	–3.2	–3.3
Chad	–8.1	–11.3	–15.4	–33.7	–100.4	–47.4	–4.8	0.9	—	0.6
Comoros	–8.4	–6.8	1.7	3.0	–0.6	–2.7	–4.1	–4.6	–4.6	–5.8
Congo, Dem. Rep. of	–9.0	–2.6	–4.6	–4.9	–3.2	–1.8	–5.7	–4.9	–4.2	–0.2
Congo, Rep. of	–20.6	–17.2	7.9	–5.6	0.6	1.0	2.2	11.7	19.3	18.0
Côte d'Ivoire	–2.7	–1.4	–2.8	–0.6	6.7	2.1	1.6	–0.1	1.8	3.1
Djibouti	–1.3	2.0	–3.4	2.7	4.5	5.3	–1.2	–4.1	–4.1	–17.0
Equatorial Guinea	–89.3	–29.9	–16.4	–49.0	–13.5	–43.8	–24.2	–12.7	–5.0	9.3
Eritrea	–23.8	–17.9	0.5	4.2	3.6	5.1	5.7	–0.8	–2.4	–4.5
Ethiopia	–1.4	–6.7	–4.3	–3.0	–4.7	–2.2	–5.1	–9.1	–10.1	–7.1
Gabon	–13.8	8.4	19.7	11.0	6.8	9.5	10.9	15.9	22.3	24.0
Gambia, The	–2.4	–2.8	–3.1	–2.6	–2.8	–5.1	–11.8	–13.0	–11.0	–6.1
Ghana	–5.0	–11.6	–8.4	–5.3	–3.2	–2.2	–2.7	–7.7	–7.6	–7.9
Guinea	–8.5	–6.9	–6.4	–2.7	–4.3	–3.4	–5.6	–4.9	–4.3	–4.4
Guinea-Bissau	–14.3	–13.3	–5.6	–22.1	–10.7	–2.8	3.1	–7.1	–5.1	–8.0
Kenya	–4.0	–1.8	–2.3	–3.1	2.2	–0.2	–2.7	–2.2	–3.8	–5.8
Lesotho	–25.0	–22.7	–18.8	–14.1	–18.0	–10.8	–2.7	–1.6	–3.4	–8.3
Liberia	. . .	. . .	–17.5	–14.9	3.5	–11.4	–2.8	–1.6	–5.4	–15.1
Madagascar	–7.5	–5.6	–5.6	–1.3	–6.0	–4.9	–9.3	–10.8	–10.5	–10.7
Malawi	–0.4	–8.3	–5.3	–6.8	–11.2	–7.6	–9.3	–5.9	–5.0	–2.6
Mali	–6.6	–8.5	–10.0	–10.4	–3.1	–6.2	–8.4	–7.2	–6.1	–5.8
Mauritania	–1.4	–2.5	–9.0	–11.7	3.0	–13.6	–34.6	–49.9	–6.9	1.8
Mauritius	–2.8	–1.6	–1.5	3.4	5.7	2.4	0.8	–3.5	–4.5	–4.1
Morocco	–0.4	–0.5	–1.4	4.8	4.1	3.6	1.9	1.8	0.5	–0.1
Mozambique, Rep. of	–14.4	–22.0	–18.2	–19.4	–19.3	–15.1	–8.6	–10.8	–11.8	–11.8
Namibia	2.8	7.3	10.9	3.2	5.4	5.1	10.2	5.7	9.0	7.9
Niger	–6.9	–6.5	–6.2	–4.8	–6.5	–5.6	–7.0	–6.6	–10.7	–7.3
Nigeria	–8.9	–8.4	11.7	4.5	–11.7	–2.7	4.6	12.4	15.7	18.9
Rwanda	–9.6	–7.7	–5.0	–5.9	–6.7	–7.8	–3.0	–3.1	–10.8	–10.0
São Tomé and Príncipe	–30.8	–32.8	–31.4	–22.3	–24.1	–22.3	–23.1	–29.5	–63.0	–61.2
Senegal	–3.9	–4.8	–6.6	–4.4	–5.6	–6.2	–6.1	–8.1	–9.7	–9.5
Seychelles	–16.5	–19.8	–7.3	–23.5	–16.3	6.4	5.3	–14.4	–3.4	–3.1
Sierra Leone	–2.6	–11.0	–15.1	–16.2	–4.8	–7.6	–4.9	–7.1	–7.0	–6.7
South Africa	–1.8	–0.5	–0.1	0.1	0.6	–1.3	–3.4	–4.2	–5.5	–4.7
Sudan	–15.3	–15.9	–14.9	–15.8	–9.8	–7.8	–6.3	–10.6	–5.9	–2.8
Swaziland	–6.9	–2.6	–5.4	–4.5	4.8	1.9	1.7	–1.4	–1.6	–2.7
Tanzania	–11.0	–9.9	–5.3	–5.0	–6.8	–4.7	–3.9	–5.2	–8.3	–9.8
Togo	–8.8	–8.1	–11.8	–12.7	–9.5	–9.4	–13.2	–14.9	–13.9	–12.2
Tunisia	–3.4	–2.2	–4.2	–4.2	–3.5	–2.9	–2.0	–1.3	–1.6	–1.4
Uganda	–7.5	–9.4	–7.0	–3.8	–4.9	–5.8	–1.0	–1.6	–5.0	–7.1
Zambia	–16.7	–13.7	–18.2	–19.9	–15.3	–14.8	–10.3	–7.8	–6.4	–7.6
Zimbabwe	–4.7	2.5	0.4	–0.3	–0.6	–2.9	–8.3	–11.1	0.5	–0.5

Table 31 *(continued)*

	1998	1999	2000	2001	2002	2003	2004	2005	2006	2007
Central and eastern Europe	**–3.1**	**–4.4**	**–5.2**	**–2.7**	**–3.4**	**–4.3**	**–5.7**	**–5.2**	**–5.7**	**–5.4**
Albania	–3.3	2.3	–3.6	–2.8	–7.1	–5.5	–3.8	–6.9	–6.7	–5.8
Bosnia and Herzegovina	–8.4	–9.1	–17.5	–20.0	–26.5	–22.4	–24.4	–26.6	–23.0	–22.8
Bulgaria	–0.5	–5.0	–5.6	–7.3	–2.4	–5.5	–5.8	–11.8	–12.4	–12.2
Croatia	–6.7	–7.0	–2.6	–3.7	–8.3	–6.1	–5.4	–6.3	–6.8	–6.8
Czech Republic	–2.1	–2.4	–4.7	–5.3	–5.7	–6.3	–6.0	–2.1	–1.9	–1.6
Estonia	–8.7	–4.4	–5.5	–5.6	–10.2	–12.1	–13.0	–11.0	–12.0	–11.7
Hungary	–7.2	–7.8	–8.5	–6.1	–7.1	–8.7	–8.6	–7.4	–9.1	–8.0
Latvia	–9.0	–8.9	–4.8	–7.6	–6.6	–8.1	–12.9	–12.4	–14.0	–13.7
Lithuania	–11.7	–11.0	–5.9	–4.7	–5.2	–6.9	–7.7	–6.9	–7.5	–7.4
Macedonia, FYR	–8.7	–2.7	–1.9	–7.2	–9.5	–3.4	–7.7	–1.3	–3.1	–3.9
Malta	–6.1	–3.3	–12.4	–4.2	0.3	–5.6	–9.6	–13.1	–12.5	–12.0
Poland	–4.0	–7.4	–5.8	–2.8	–2.5	–2.1	–4.2	–1.4	–1.7	–1.9
Romania	–7.1	–4.1	–3.7	–5.5	–3.3	–5.8	–8.5	–8.7	–10.9	–11.1
Serbia	–5.1	–8.0	–3.9	–4.6	–9.5	–9.3	–12.5	–9.6	–10.0	–9.7
Slovak Republic	–9.6	–4.8	–3.4	–8.3	–7.9	–0.8	–3.6	–8.6	–7.7	–5.9
Slovenia	–0.6	–3.3	–2.8	0.2	1.5	–0.3	–2.1	–1.1	–2.0	–2.3
Turkey	1.0	–0.7	–5.0	2.4	–0.8	–3.3	–5.2	–6.4	–6.7	–5.8
Commonwealth of Independent States[1]	**–1.9**	**8.2**	**13.6**	**8.0**	**6.5**	**6.3**	**8.1**	**8.8**	**10.1**	**9.4**
Russia	0.1	12.6	18.0	11.1	8.4	8.2	9.9	10.9	12.3	10.7
Excluding Russia	–6.8	–0.9	1.4	–0.8	1.0	0.3	2.1	1.8	2.5	4.5
Armenia	–22.1	–16.6	–14.6	–9.5	–6.2	–6.8	–4.6	–3.3	–4.4	–4.6
Azerbaijan	–31.9	–13.1	–3.5	–0.9	–12.3	–27.8	–29.8	1.3	26.0	44.8
Belarus	–6.7	–1.6	–2.7	–3.2	–2.1	–2.4	–5.2	1.6	0.2	–1.1
Georgia	–12.8	–10.0	–7.9	–6.4	–5.9	–7.3	–8.4	–5.4	–9.9	–11.5
Kazakhstan	–5.5	–0.2	3.0	–5.4	–4.2	–0.9	1.1	–0.9	2.3	2.1
Kyrgyz Republic	–22.3	–15.0	–4.3	–1.5	–5.0	–4.1	–3.4	–8.1	–7.9	–7.7
Moldova	–19.7	–5.8	–7.6	–1.7	–4.0	–6.6	–2.0	–8.3	–10.5	–6.8
Mongolia	–7.8	–6.7	–5.7	–7.6	–9.6	–7.7	1.7	1.6	4.3	0.6
Tajikistan	–7.3	–5.6	–6.0	–4.9	–3.5	–1.3	–4.0	–3.4	–4.2	–4.8
Turkmenistan	–32.7	–14.8	8.2	1.7	6.7	2.7	0.6	5.1	7.6	8.0
Ukraine	–3.1	5.3	4.7	3.7	7.5	5.8	10.6	3.1	–2.2	–3.8
Uzbekistan	–0.7	–1.0	1.7	–1.0	1.2	8.7	10.0	13.1	12.0	11.9

Table 31 *(continued)*

	1998	1999	2000	2001	2002	2003	2004	2005	2006	2007
Developing Asia	**2.5**	**1.8**	**1.7**	**1.6**	**2.5**	**2.9**	**2.7**	**4.2**	**4.1**	**3.9**
Afghanistan, Rep. of	. . .	. . .	. . .	. . .	–3.7	3.0	1.4	–1.0	–1.5	–4.5
Bangladesh	–1.1	–0.9	–1.4	–0.8	0.3	0.2	–0.3	–0.5	–0.3	–0.7
Bhutan	9.8	2.2	–9.4	–5.3	–9.1	–8.1	–23.8	–15.2	–3.1	–4.2
Brunei Darussalam	44.9	33.7	48.6	47.6	39.4	46.2	44.9	53.3	69.9	70.9
Cambodia	–5.9	–5.2	–2.8	–1.1	–2.4	–3.7	–2.3	–4.3	–5.6	–6.4
China	3.1	1.4	1.7	1.3	2.4	2.8	3.6	7.2	7.2	7.2
Fiji	–0.3	–3.8	–5.8	–3.3	–1.6	–4.7	–5.0	–4.5	–4.2	–3.4
India	–1.7	–0.7	–1.0	0.3	1.4	1.5	0.2	–1.5	–2.1	–2.7
Indonesia	3.8	3.7	4.8	4.3	4.0	3.5	0.6	0.3	0.2	0.6
Kiribati	35.2	13.3	12.6	1.9	–1.8	6.5	–11.1	–21.1	–16.5	–15.5
Lao PDR	–4.6	–4.0	–10.6	–8.3	–7.2	–8.2	–14.3	–19.9	–14.6	–24.9
Malaysia	13.2	15.9	9.4	8.3	8.4	12.7	12.6	15.2	15.6	15.7
Maldives	–4.1	–13.4	–8.2	–9.4	–5.6	–4.6	–16.0	–36.5	–37.6	–21.4
Myanmar	–14.3	–5.9	–0.8	–2.4	0.2	–1.0	2.3	4.0	4.1	2.7
Nepal	–1.0	4.3	3.2	4.8	4.5	2.6	3.0	2.2	3.3	4.5
Pakistan	–2.2	–2.6	–0.3	0.5	3.9	4.9	1.8	–1.4	–3.9	–4.6
Papua New Guinea	0.9	2.8	8.5	6.5	–1.0	4.4	2.1	3.3	6.8	–1.3
Philippines	2.3	–3.8	–2.9	–2.5	–0.5	0.4	1.9	2.4	2.4	1.7
Samoa	9.5	2.0	1.0	0.1	–1.1	5.8	8.3	11.9	–4.5	–5.6
Solomon Islands	–1.6	3.1	–10.6	–12.8	–7.1	1.3	12.2	–10.8	–15.8	–15.9
Sri Lanka	–1.4	–3.6	–6.5	–1.1	–1.4	–0.4	–3.2	–2.8	–4.9	–4.1
Thailand	12.8	10.2	7.6	5.4	5.5	5.6	4.2	–2.1	–0.8	–1.3
Timor-Leste, Dem. Rep. of	. . .	2.1	14.6	13.2	10.2	5.8	40.4	88.3	123.5	167.3
Tonga	–10.9	–0.6	–6.2	–9.5	5.1	–3.1	4.2	–4.8	–6.2	–5.2
Vanuatu	2.5	–4.9	2.0	2.0	–9.0	–10.2	–9.5	–7.1	–8.8	–7.7
Vietnam	–3.9	4.5	2.3	1.6	–1.9	–4.8	–3.1	0.1	0.1	–1.1
Middle East	**–5.1**	**2.2**	**10.7**	**6.2**	**4.6**	**8.3**	**11.9**	**18.5**	**23.2**	**22.5**
Bahrain	–12.6	–0.3	10.6	3.0	–0.4	2.3	4.0	11.7	20.6	18.9
Egypt	–2.9	–1.9	–1.2	—	0.7	2.4	4.3	3.3	2.0	1.2
Iran, I.R. of	–2.2	6.3	13.0	5.2	3.1	0.6	0.9	7.3	10.0	8.9
Iraq	. . .	. . .	. . .	. . .	. . .	. . .	. . .	. . .	. . .	. . .
Jordan	0.3	5.0	0.7	–0.1	5.6	11.6	–0.2	–18.2	–20.7	–19.7
Kuwait	8.5	16.8	38.9	23.9	11.2	20.4	31.1	43.3	52.5	51.9
Lebanon	–29.5	–18.8	–17.1	–19.2	–15.5	–15.2	–18.2	–11.9	–12.8	–16.2
Libya	–1.2	9.2	22.5	13.8	2.9	21.5	24.2	40.2	47.9	51.4
Oman	–22.3	–2.9	15.5	9.3	6.6	4.0	1.7	14.2	19.4	19.6
Qatar	–21.5	6.8	18.0	23.4	19.4	24.3	26.5	20.6	49.1	48.4
Saudi Arabia	–9.0	0.3	7.6	5.1	6.3	13.1	20.7	29.3	32.9	31.9
Syrian Arab Republic	0.5	1.6	5.2	5.7	7.2	4.7	—	–2.2	–1.8	–1.8
United Arab Emirates	2.0	1.6	17.4	9.6	4.1	8.1	10.2	14.7	21.0	21.3
Yemen	–2.8	2.7	13.2	5.3	5.4	–0.1	1.9	4.7	–1.4	–5.6

Table 31 ***(concluded)***

	1998	1999	2000	2001	2002	2003	2004	2005	2006	2007
Western Hemisphere	**–4.5**	**–3.2**	**–2.5**	**–2.8**	**–1.0**	**0.4**	**0.9**	**1.4**	**1.2**	**1.0**
Antigua and Barbuda	–10.8	–8.8	–9.7	–3.2	–16.2	–15.7	–18.7	–15.9	–21.1	–19.8
Argentina	–4.8	–4.2	–3.2	–1.2	8.9	6.3	2.2	1.9	1.0	0.6
Bahamas, The	–23.2	–5.1	–10.4	–11.6	–7.8	–8.6	–5.3	–8.9	–11.4	–13.5
Barbados	–2.6	–5.9	–5.7	–4.3	–6.8	–6.3	–12.0	–12.2	–12.0	–11.3
Belize	–6.0	–10.4	–20.6	–22.4	–20.1	–22.1	–14.4	–14.3	–10.6	–11.8
Bolivia	–7.8	–5.9	–5.3	–3.4	–4.1	1.0	3.9	5.0	5.0	4.8
Brazil	–4.2	–4.7	–4.0	–4.5	–1.7	0.8	1.9	1.8	0.6	0.4
Chile	–5.0	0.1	–1.2	–1.6	–0.9	–1.3	1.7	0.6	1.8	0.9
Colombia	–4.9	0.8	0.9	–1.3	–1.7	–1.2	–1.0	–1.6	–1.2	–1.7
Costa Rica	–3.5	–3.8	–4.3	–4.4	–5.6	–5.5	–4.3	–4.7	–4.9	–4.8
Dominica	–8.7	–17.2	–19.7	–18.7	–13.7	–13.0	–17.2	–24.6	–20.4	–20.3
Dominican Republic	–2.1	–2.4	–5.1	–3.4	–3.7	6.0	6.1	–0.3	–2.4	–2.9
Ecuador	–9.3	4.6	5.3	–3.2	–4.8	–0.6	–0.9	–0.3	4.4	3.7
El Salvador	–0.8	–1.9	–3.3	–1.1	–2.8	–4.7	–4.0	–4.6	–4.5	–4.6
Grenada	–23.5	–14.1	–21.5	–26.6	–32.0	–33.2	–13.5	–37.1	–32.8	–28.0
Guatemala	–5.3	–5.5	–5.4	–6.0	–5.3	–4.2	–4.4	–4.5	–4.2	–4.1
Guyana	–13.7	–11.4	–15.3	–19.2	–15.2	–11.9	–8.9	–19.9	–28.8	–24.7
Haiti	0.3	–0.7	–1.1	–1.9	–1.4	–1.6	–1.3	0.8	–0.1	–1.6
Honduras	–2.5	–4.5	–4.0	–4.1	–3.1	–3.7	–5.4	–0.4	–0.6	–0.7
Jamaica	–2.3	–4.1	–5.2	–11.0	–10.8	–9.9	–5.8	–10.0	–10.5	–14.4
Mexico	–3.8	–2.9	–3.2	–2.8	–2.1	–1.4	–1.0	–0.6	–0.1	–0.2
Netherlands Antilles	–3.9	–5.1	—	–5.7	–1.8	–0.3	–3.2	–2.4	–2.3	–2.9
Nicaragua	–19.3	–24.9	–31.6	–31.2	–30.6	–30.9	–30.4	–26.2	–25.2	–24.7
Panama	–9.3	–10.1	–5.9	–1.5	–0.7	–3.9	–8.0	–5.3	–4.0	–3.9
Paraguay	–2.0	–2.3	–2.3	–4.1	1.8	2.3	0.8	–2.7	–2.5	–2.0
Peru	–6.4	–3.4	–2.8	–2.1	–1.9	–1.5	—	1.3	0.7	0.2
St. Kitts and Nevis	–16.5	–22.4	–21.0	–31.8	–37.9	–34.1	–24.4	–21.0	–19.0	–14.6
St. Lucia	–9.5	–16.6	–14.1	–16.2	–15.4	–20.4	–13.0	–25.2	–16.8	–10.6
St. Vincent and the Grenadines	–29.7	–20.6	–7.1	–10.4	–11.5	–20.8	–25.1	–24.0	–24.3	–24.4
Suriname	–14.3	–19.0	–3.8	–15.2	–6.3	–13.8	–5.1	–15.8	–11.9	–8.1
Trinidad and Tobago	–10.6	0.4	6.7	4.7	0.8	8.0	13.2	24.4	25.7	15.7
Uruguay	–2.1	–2.4	–2.8	–2.9	3.2	–0.5	0.3	–0.5	–4.3	–3.2
Venezuela	–4.9	2.2	10.1	1.6	8.2	13.7	12.5	19.1	17.5	17.6

[1]Mongolia, which is not a member of the Commonwealth of Independent States, is included in this group for reasons of geography and similarities in economic structure.

Table 32. Summary of Balance of Payments, Capital Flows, and External Financing

(Billions of U.S. dollars)

	1998	1999	2000	2001	2002	2003	2004	2005	2006	2007
Other emerging market and developing countries										
Balance of payments[1]										
Balance on current account	–113.4	–24.0	79.6	40.0	78.5	147.8	211.9	424.7	586.7	638.9
Balance on goods and services	–65.9	34.0	135.7	85.6	118.3	176.0	252.6	451.7	615.4	657.0
Income, net	–98.8	–120.3	–125.1	–123.8	–132.9	–148.0	–179.2	–192.8	–205.9	–198.7
Current transfers, net	51.4	62.3	69.1	78.1	93.1	119.7	138.5	165.8	177.2	180.6
Balance on capital and financial account	136.3	51.6	–56.6	–5.3	–65.7	–150.3	–251.2	–392.8	–572.4	–627.5
Balance on capital account[2]	6.4	9.5	23.5	5.6	1.8	12.4	18.6	19.2	44.3	33.8
Balance on financial account	129.9	42.1	–80.0	–10.9	–67.5	–162.7	–269.8	–412.0	–616.6	–661.3
Direct investment, net	159.2	157.6	151.0	168.8	156.2	147.1	185.8	239.3	240.7	228.0
Portfolio investment, net	9.0	3.0	–37.0	–53.0	–47.0	–21.9	8.8	–28.8	–165.6	–130.1
Other investment, net	–42.7	–77.0	–105.8	–33.3	–19.8	3.0	–31.8	–85.4	–92.8	–62.7
Reserve assets	4.3	–41.4	–88.2	–93.3	–157.0	–290.9	–432.6	–537.1	–599.0	–696.5
Errors and omissions, net	–22.9	–27.6	–23.1	–34.7	–12.7	2.6	39.3	–31.9	–14.3	–11.5
Capital flows										
Total capital flows, net[3]	125.5	83.5	8.2	82.4	89.4	128.2	162.7	125.1	–17.6	35.2
Net official flows	37.7	31.0	–36.1	8.4	–0.1	–38.8	–50.7	–136.6	–223.2	–153.0
Net private flows[4]	87.8	52.5	44.3	74.0	89.6	167.1	213.4	261.7	205.6	188.3
Direct investment, net	159.2	157.6	151.0	168.8	156.2	147.1	185.8	239.3	240.7	228.0
Private portfolio investment, net	14.0	–0.6	–17.2	–44.7	–39.8	11.0	47.5	42.4	14.3	27.5
Other private flows, net	–85.4	–104.5	–89.6	–50.1	–26.9	9.0	–19.9	–20.0	–49.4	–67.2
External financing[5]										
Net external financing[6]	265.9	222.8	231.6	174.3	158.0	294.7	449.2	566.0	584.0	631.0
Non-debt-creating flows	185.7	187.1	203.0	177.9	167.0	189.7	287.9	378.3	397.7	385.7
Capital transfers[7]	6.4	9.5	23.5	5.6	1.8	12.4	18.6	19.2	44.3	33.8
Foreign direct investment and equity security liabilities[8]	179.3	177.6	179.5	172.3	165.2	177.4	269.3	359.1	353.4	351.8
Net external borrowing[9]	80.2	35.7	28.5	–3.6	–8.9	105.0	161.3	187.7	186.3	245.4
Borrowing from official creditors[10]	42.7	27.5	–16.2	16.7	7.1	–6.0	–12.0	–65.5	–43.3	4.5
of which, credit and loans from IMF[11]	14.0	–2.4	–10.9	19.0	13.4	1.7	–14.9	–39.9	. . .	. . .
Borrowing from banks[10]	9.4	–12.4	–12.4	–12.0	–18.1	14.1	31.3	46.5	50.5	44.7
Borrowing from other private creditors[10]	28.1	20.5	57.2	–8.4	2.1	96.8	142.0	206.6	179.2	196.1
Memorandum										
Balance on goods and services in percent of GDP[12]	–1.1	0.6	2.1	1.3	1.8	2.4	2.9	4.3	5.1	4.9
Scheduled amortization of external debt	247.3	289.7	333.1	312.9	329.3	369.1	380.8	428.4	468.2	409.6
Gross external financing[13]	513.1	512.4	564.7	487.2	487.3	663.7	830.0	994.4	1,052.1	1,040.6
Gross external borrowing[14]	327.4	325.3	361.7	309.3	320.3	474.0	542.1	616.1	654.5	654.9
Exceptional external financing, net	40.6	28.7	10.4	27.9	50.0	33.0	13.7	–36.9	9.8	6.1
Of which,										
Arrears on debt service	21.8	8.0	–30.3	0.3	9.6	18.4	9.0	–22.1	. . .	. . .
Debt forgiveness	1.7	2.3	1.9	2.9	3.2	2.1	1.7	5.7	. . .	. . .
Rescheduling of debt service	7.5	14.1	2.5	7.4	10.6	6.4	6.8	4.8	. . .	. . .

[1]Standard presentation in accordance with the 5th edition of the International Monetary Fund's *Balance of Payments Manual* (1993).

[2]Comprises capital transfers—including debt forgiveness—and acquisition/disposal of nonproduced, nonfinancial assets.

[3]Comprise net direct investment, net portfolio investment, and other long- and short-term net investment flows, including official and private borrowing. In the standard balance of payments presentation above, total net capital flows are equal to the balance on financial account minus the change in reserve assets.

[4]Because of limitations on the data coverage for net official flows, the residually derived data for net private flows may include some official flows.

[5]As defined in the *World Economic Outlook* (see footnote 6). It should be noted that there is no generally accepted standard definition of external financing.

[6]Defined as the sum of—with opposite sign—the goods and services balance, net income and current transfers, direct investment abroad, the change in reserve assets, the net acquisition of other assets (such as recorded private portfolio assets, export credit, and the collateral for debt-reduction operations), and the net errors and omissions. Thus, net external financing, according to the definition adopted in the *World Economic Outlook*, measures the total amount required to finance the current account, direct investment outflows, net reserve transactions (often at the discretion of the monetary authorities), the net acquisition of nonreserve external assets, and the net transactions underlying the errors and omissions (not infrequently reflecting capital flight).

[7]Including other transactions on capital account.

[8]Debt-creating foreign direct investment liabilities are not included.

[9]Net disbursement of long- and short-term credits, including exceptional financing, by both official and private creditors.

[10]Changes in liabilities.

[11]Comprise use of IMF resources under the General Resources Account, Trust Fund, and Poverty Reduction and Growth Facility (PRGF). For further detail, see Table 36.

[12]This is often referred to as the "resource balance" and, with opposite sign, the "net resource transfer."

[13]Net external financing plus amortization due on external debt.

[14]Net external borrowing plus amortization due on external debt.

Table 33. Other Emerging Market and Developing Countries—by Region: Balance of Payments and External Financing[1]

(Billions of U.S. dollars)

	1998	1999	2000	2001	2002	2003	2004	2005	2006	2007
Africa										
Balance of payments										
Balance on current account	–19.4	–15.0	7.2	0.4	–7.8	–3.1	–0.4	18.4	33.1	44.5
Balance on capital account	4.1	4.6	3.5	4.4	4.8	3.6	5.4	6.9	20.5	11.0
Balance on financial account	16.5	11.3	–10.4	–4.2	1.6	–3.2	–15.7	–27.3	–54.9	–54.8
Change in reserves (– = increase)	3.5	–0.4	–12.8	–9.7	–5.6	–11.5	–32.8	–42.2	–62.0	–75.2
Other official flows, net	3.9	1.8	0.6	–2.7	3.0	1.6	1.0	–14.4	–17.8	–1.3
Private flows, net	9.2	9.9	1.7	8.2	4.1	6.8	16.1	29.4	24.9	21.7
External financing										
Net external financing	27.6	29.1	14.6	19.8	17.3	22.4	32.1	31.9	35.9	41.1
Non-debt-creating inflows	20.1	23.1	15.8	23.5	17.5	21.8	33.2	42.6	55.8	47.5
Net external borrowing	7.5	6.0	–1.2	–3.8	–0.2	0.6	–1.1	–10.7	–19.9	–6.4
From official creditors	3.9	1.8	0.7	–2.7	3.1	1.5	1.0	–14.4	–17.7	–1.2
of which, credit and loans from IMF	–0.4	–0.2	–0.2	–0.4	–0.1	–0.8	–0.7	–1.0	. . .	. . .
From banks	–1.0	1.2	–0.9	—	0.6	0.9	2.2	1.6	2.3	0.9
From other private creditors	4.6	3.1	–0.9	–1.0	–3.9	–1.8	–4.3	2.1	–4.5	–6.0
Memorandum										
Exceptional financing	9.4	8.7	6.7	5.5	19.1	6.9	3.8	–0.3	8.7	3.5
Sub-Sahara										
Balance of payments										
Balance on current account	–17.7	–14.4	–0.6	–7.4	–12.9	–12.7	–11.9	–3.9	2.6	18.9
Balance on capital account	4.0	4.3	3.4	4.2	4.6	3.6	5.3	6.8	20.4	10.8
Balance on financial account	15.5	10.6	–2.6	4.3	7.2	6.5	–3.8	–6.0	–22.7	–29.7
Change in reserves (– = increase)	2.4	–0.7	–6.1	0.5	–1.2	–2.2	–21.0	–23.2	–36.6	–49.1
Other official flows, net	5.7	4.3	3.5	0.5	5.9	4.5	4.7	–10.6	–10.1	–0.7
Private flows, net	7.4	7.1	—	3.2	2.5	4.2	12.5	27.8	24.0	20.1
External financing										
Net external financing	26.2	27.2	13.5	16.2	16.2	21.3	30.5	32.6	40.1	37.2
Non-debt-creating inflows	18.5	21.1	14.2	19.0	15.1	18.3	30.2	38.8	52.6	44.2
Net external borrowing	7.7	6.1	–0.6	–2.8	1.1	3.1	0.3	–6.2	–12.5	–6.9
From official creditors	5.7	4.3	3.6	0.5	6.0	4.5	4.7	–10.5	–10.0	–0.6
of which, credit and loans from IMF	–0.3	–0.1	—	–0.2	0.2	–0.4	–0.3	–0.4	. . .	. . .
From banks	–1.0	–0.3	–1.3	–0.6	–0.2	0.1	1.3	1.2	2.2	1.2
From other private creditors	3.1	2.1	–3.0	–2.8	–4.7	–1.6	–5.7	3.1	–4.7	–7.5
Memorandum										
Exceptional financing	8.3	8.0	6.6	5.4	19.0	6.9	3.8	–0.3	8.7	3.5
Central and eastern Europe										
Balance of payments										
Balance on current account	–19.4	–26.5	–32.3	–16.2	–23.6	–36.4	–59.4	–63.3	–74.8	–76.9
Balance on capital account	0.4	0.4	3.0	4.2	5.0	5.1	12.7	16.4	21.1	20.8
Balance on financial account	18.8	22.5	35.0	13.5	25.0	33.7	49.1	58.7	66.8	65.5
Change in reserves (– = increase)	–9.4	–12.0	–6.5	–4.4	–20.4	–12.5	–14.6	–46.3	–18.8	–17.1
Other official flows, net	1.0	–2.5	1.7	6.1	–7.8	–5.2	–6.7	–8.5	–3.2	–2.2
Private flows, net	27.1	36.9	39.8	11.8	53.2	51.4	70.4	113.5	88.8	84.8
External financing										
Net external financing	34.0	47.2	54.7	31.5	49.2	60.1	109.9	143.1	130.4	127.7
Non-debt-creating inflows	21.3	21.4	26.9	28.6	30.6	24.1	53.6	75.6	64.8	56.6
Net external borrowing	12.7	25.8	27.8	2.8	18.6	36.0	56.4	67.5	65.6	71.1
From official creditors	1.0	–2.5	1.8	6.2	–7.6	–5.2	–6.6	–8.5	–3.2	–2.2
of which, credit and loans from IMF	–0.5	0.5	3.3	9.9	6.1	—	–3.8	–5.9	. . .	. . .
From banks	2.7	2.1	4.2	–7.4	3.5	13.2	15.8	19.5	17.5	16.9
From other private creditors	9.0	26.1	21.8	4.0	22.7	28.1	47.2	56.5	51.3	56.4
Memorandum										
Exceptional financing	0.2	1.1	4.8	11.0	7.0	–0.3	–3.6	–4.9	–3.2	–2.1

Table 33 ***(continued)***

	1998	1999	2000	2001	2002	2003	2004	2005	2006	2007
Commonwealth of Independent States[2]										
Balance of payments										
Balance on current account	−7.4	23.7	48.2	33.1	30.2	35.9	62.5	87.7	127.1	138.8
Balance on capital account	−0.3	−0.4	10.7	−9.6	−12.5	−1.0	−1.6	−12.7	−1.2	−1.3
Balance on financial account	5.5	−21.7	−53.7	−12.2	−9.8	−23.9	−54.8	−61.4	−126.4	−138.2
Change in reserves (− = increase)	12.6	−6.3	−20.3	−14.5	−15.1	−32.9	−55.0	−76.6	−115.0	−139.2
Other official flows, net	1.5	−2.0	−5.7	−5.0	−10.4	−8.8	−7.3	−22.5	−30.2	−4.5
Private flows, net	−8.6	−13.3	−27.7	7.2	15.7	17.7	7.5	37.6	18.8	5.4
External financing										
Net external financing	8.2	0.3	−1.2	−2.3	−0.6	40.8	61.2	81.4	76.1	101.0
Non-debt-creating inflows	4.6	4.1	14.1	−5.6	−7.4	9.5	20.8	9.9	27.3	28.2
Net external borrowing	3.6	−3.7	−15.2	3.3	6.8	31.3	40.4	71.5	48.8	72.8
From official creditors	1.5	−2.0	−5.7	−3.7	−10.4	−3.3	−2.7	−19.5	−23.5	−1.0
of which, credit and loans from IMF	5.8	−3.6	−4.1	−4.0	−1.8	−2.3	−2.1	−3.8	. . .	. . .
From banks	−2.9	3.5	1.6	4.1	−1.4	2.3	1.6	8.5	−1.6	−0.7
From other private creditors	5.0	−5.2	−11.1	2.9	18.6	32.3	41.5	82.5	73.9	74.4
Memorandum										
Exceptional financing	7.9	7.4	2.3	−0.1	−0.3	0.8	0.4	0.7	—	—
Developing Asia										
Balance of payments										
Balance on current account	49.5	38.3	38.2	37.7	66.9	86.1	94.2	165.3	184.6	197.9
Balance on capital account	1.0	0.8	0.9	0.9	0.9	2.3	1.0	6.8	2.6	2.3
Balance on financial account	−28.3	−27.2	−28.9	−29.7	−72.9	−103.3	−120.9	−147.6	−180.3	−197.6
Change in reserves (− = increase)	−20.7	−28.9	−16.4	−57.0	−110.0	−165.2	−259.7	−233.1	−283.9	−282.2
Other official flows, net	18.2	19.5	−5.8	−2.5	7.4	−4.3	6.2	6.9	12.7	11.7
Private flows, net	−25.8	−17.9	−6.7	29.9	29.7	66.1	132.6	78.6	90.9	72.9
External financing										
Net external financing	55.6	60.3	65.1	48.1	72.7	101.9	167.5	238.2	240.2	227.5
Non-debt-creating inflows	68.3	64.7	71.6	55.2	69.4	84.9	109.7	162.4	153.9	160.0
Net external borrowing	−12.6	−4.4	−6.5	−7.1	3.4	17.0	57.9	75.8	86.2	67.5
From official creditors	18.2	19.5	−5.8	−2.5	7.4	−4.3	6.2	6.9	12.7	11.7
of which, credit and loans from IMF	6.6	1.7	0.9	−2.2	−2.7	−0.6	−1.9	−1.6	. . .	. . .
From banks	−12.1	−11.7	−13.0	−5.9	−2.9	1.4	16.6	10.8	18.9	15.7
From other private creditors	−18.7	−12.3	12.3	1.3	−1.1	19.9	35.1	58.1	54.6	40.2
Memorandum										
Exceptional financing	12.6	7.3	7.1	3.5	3.6	3.4	0.2	4.3	−0.2	0.1
Excluding China and India										
Balance of payments										
Balance on current account	24.7	25.9	22.2	18.9	24.4	31.5	24.2	16.4	18.0	16.5
Balance on capital account	1.0	0.8	1.0	1.0	0.9	2.4	1.1	2.7	2.7	2.3
Balance on financial account	−20.2	−30.0	−24.6	−16.5	−22.8	−29.8	−23.3	−10.6	−13.5	−16.3
Change in reserves (− = increase)	−11.6	−14.3	0.2	−1.0	−15.6	−22.5	−29.8	−11.6	−31.0	−33.2
Other official flows, net	12.6	12.5	−5.4	−3.4	6.2	0.4	−5.0	−9.0	−5.0	−1.9
Private flows, net	−21.2	−28.2	−19.4	−12.0	−13.4	−7.7	11.5	10.0	22.6	18.8
External financing										
Net external financing	13.1	6.2	−3.7	−2.8	9.1	16.1	39.9	60.8	74.4	75.7
Non-debt-creating inflows	25.4	23.7	15.9	5.8	16.7	23.6	37.6	48.3	57.4	62.1
Net external borrowing	−12.2	−17.6	−19.5	−8.6	−7.6	−7.5	2.3	12.5	17.0	13.7
From official creditors	12.6	12.5	−5.4	−3.4	6.2	0.4	−5.0	−9.0	−5.0	−1.9
of which, credit and loans from IMF	7.0	2.1	0.9	−2.2	−2.7	−0.6	−1.9	−1.6	. . .	. . .
From banks	−15.0	−9.8	−6.4	−6.0	−5.0	−5.1	2.3	−4.3	−1.4	0.1
From other private creditors	−9.7	−20.3	−7.7	0.8	−8.8	−2.7	5.0	25.8	23.4	15.5
Memorandum										
Exceptional financing	12.6	7.3	7.1	3.5	3.6	3.4	0.2	4.3	−0.2	0.1

Table 33 ***(concluded)***

	1998	1999	2000	2001	2002	2003	2004	2005	2006	2007
Middle East										
Balance of payments										
Balance on current account	–26.1	12.1	67.0	39.0	28.9	58.5	96.8	182.9	282.1	306.0
Balance on capital account	–0.5	0.9	2.4	3.1	1.5	1.3	—	0.4	0.3	0.2
Balance on financial account	22.9	–2.5	–65.4	–31.2	–30.5	–51.7	–96.5	–185.5	–282.1	–303.1
Change in reserves (– = increase)	10.2	–1.5	–30.7	–11.2	–3.7	–32.9	–47.3	–106.1	–79.4	–133.5
Other official flows, net	–0.9	8.2	–20.6	–12.8	–9.9	–26.6	–34.9	–68.1	–172.2	–154.4
Private flows, net	13.6	–9.2	–14.2	–7.3	–16.9	7.8	–14.3	–11.4	–30.5	–15.1
External financing										
Net external financing	18.0	–11.0	22.5	–9.6	–14.7	25.5	40.0	44.2	44.2	59.3
Non-debt-creating inflows	6.8	6.2	3.1	8.1	6.9	9.4	14.4	17.7	30.1	28.1
Net external borrowing	11.1	–17.2	19.4	–17.7	–21.6	16.1	25.5	26.5	14.1	31.2
From official creditors	3.9	3.8	–0.3	–3.4	–0.8	–0.2	–0.7	–0.9	–0.6	–1.7
of which, credit and loans from IMF	0.1	0.1	–0.1	0.1	—	–0.1	–0.1	–0.1	. . .	. . .
From banks	5.3	0.9	–0.5	–2.0	–4.7	1.7	1.6	8.3	7.2	5.0
From other private creditors	2.0	–21.9	20.1	–12.3	–16.1	14.6	24.7	19.0	7.4	28.0
Memorandum										
Exceptional financing	0.4	0.2	0.3	0.3	0.6	2.5	0.3	0.4	0.3	0.2
Western Hemisphere										
Balance of payments										
Balance on current account	–90.6	–56.6	–48.6	–54.1	–16.2	6.8	18.2	33.7	34.7	28.5
Balance on capital account	1.7	3.4	3.0	2.6	2.2	1.0	1.2	1.5	1.0	0.8
Balance on financial account	94.5	59.6	43.4	52.9	19.1	–14.3	–31.0	–48.9	–39.8	–33.1
Change in reserves (– = increase)	8.1	7.6	–1.6	3.5	–2.2	–36.0	–23.1	–32.8	–39.9	–49.3
Other official flows, net	14.0	5.9	–6.3	25.3	17.5	4.5	–9.0	–30.1	–12.6	–2.2
Private flows, net	72.3	46.1	51.3	24.1	3.8	17.3	1.1	14.0	12.7	18.5
External financing										
Net external financing	122.5	96.9	75.7	86.8	34.0	43.9	38.4	27.2	57.1	74.3
Non-debt-creating inflows	64.7	67.7	71.4	68.0	49.9	40.1	56.2	70.1	65.7	65.2
Net external borrowing	57.8	29.2	4.3	18.8	–15.9	3.9	–17.7	–42.9	–8.6	9.1
From official creditors	14.2	6.8	–6.8	22.8	15.4	5.5	–9.2	–29.2	–11.1	–1.0
of which, credit and loans from IMF	2.5	–0.9	–10.7	15.6	11.9	5.6	–6.3	–27.6	. . .	. . .
From banks	17.3	–8.3	–3.8	–0.8	–13.2	–5.4	–6.4	–2.2	6.1	7.0
From other private creditors	26.3	30.7	14.9	–3.2	–18.1	3.9	–2.1	–11.6	–3.6	3.2
Memorandum										
Exceptional financing	10.2	3.9	–10.8	7.6	19.9	19.8	12.6	–37.2	4.3	4.4

[1]For definitions, see footnotes to Table 32.
[2]Mongolia, which is not a member of the Commonwealth of Independent States, is included in this group for reasons of geography and similarities in economic structure.

Table 34. Other Emerging Market and Developing Countries—by Analytical Criteria: Balance of Payments and External Financing[1]

(Billions of U.S. dollars)

	1998	1999	2000	2001	2002	2003	2004	2005	2006	2007
By source of export earnings										
Fuel										
Balance of payments										
Balance on current account	−36.8	36.2	145.7	83.4	63.3	108.9	182.2	335.3	505.1	556.9
Balance on capital account	0.3	1.1	13.6	−6.1	−10.6	—	−1.3	−12.1	−2.2	−1.7
Balance on financial account	31.0	−24.9	−149.9	−56.6	−47.7	−89.1	−180.5	−310.5	−502.5	−553.9
Change in reserves (− = increase)	28.6	−1.0	−67.5	−28.6	−16.2	−71.4	−120.6	−208.0	−244.6	−343.7
Other official flows, net	−0.4	3.5	−24.9	−14.8	−19.7	−29.7	−37.7	−97.6	−199.8	−152.1
Private flows, net	2.8	−27.4	−57.5	−13.2	−11.7	12.0	−22.2	−4.8	−58.0	−58.1
External financing										
Net external financing	34.3	−5.7	22.3	−11.0	−20.7	57.9	75.7	72.1	80.7	131.4
Non-debt-creating inflows	17.1	13.1	23.4	10.4	7.2	27.9	45.3	34.5	59.5	61.8
Net external borrowing	17.2	−18.8	−1.1	−21.4	−28.0	30.0	30.3	37.6	21.2	69.6
From official creditors	4.1	−1.4	−4.2	−5.5	−9.9	−2.7	−3.1	−30.9	−28.5	0.5
of which, credit and loans from IMF	4.7	−4.1	−3.5	−4.1	−1.8	−2.4	−2.2	−4.3	. . .	. . .
From banks	−0.9	3.7	0.2	1.4	−6.8	3.7	2.1	18.2	5.7	5.4
From other private creditors	14.0	−21.0	2.8	−17.3	−11.3	29.0	31.3	50.3	44.0	63.7
Memorandum										
Exceptional financing	14.8	12.7	4.6	2.2	2.6	3.3	−0.3	−3.5	1.0	0.9
Nonfuel										
Balance of payments										
Balance on current account	−76.6	−60.2	−66.1	−43.4	15.2	38.9	29.7	89.4	81.5	82.1
Balance on capital account	6.1	8.5	9.8	11.7	12.4	12.3	19.9	31.3	46.5	35.5
Balance on financial account	98.8	66.9	69.9	45.7	−19.9	−73.6	−89.4	−101.5	−114.2	−107.4
Change in reserves (− = increase)	−24.3	−40.4	−20.7	−64.7	−140.8	−219.5	−312.0	−329.0	−354.4	−352.8
Other official flows, net	38.1	27.5	−11.2	23.2	19.6	−9.1	−13.0	−39.0	−23.4	−0.9
Private flows, net	85.1	79.9	101.8	87.2	101.3	155.1	235.6	266.5	263.6	246.4
External financing										
Net external financing	231.5	228.4	209.2	185.2	178.8	236.8	373.6	493.9	503.3	499.7
Non-debt-creating inflows	168.6	174.0	179.6	167.4	159.7	161.8	242.6	343.8	338.1	323.9
Net external borrowing	63.0	54.4	29.6	17.8	19.0	75.0	131.0	150.0	165.1	175.7
From official creditors	38.5	28.9	−12.1	22.3	17.0	−3.3	−8.9	−34.6	−14.9	4.0
of which, credit and loans from IMF	9.3	1.7	−7.4	23.1	15.2	4.1	−12.7	−35.6	. . .	. . .
From banks	10.3	−16.0	−12.6	−13.4	−11.2	10.4	29.2	28.3	44.8	39.3
From other private creditors	14.2	41.6	54.4	8.9	13.3	67.9	110.7	156.3	135.2	132.4
Memorandum										
Exceptional financing	25.8	15.9	5.8	25.6	47.4	29.7	14.1	−33.4	8.8	5.3
By external financing source										
Net debtor countries										
Balance of payments										
Balance on current account	−129.4	−96.0	−87.8	−69.9	−39.1	−26.8	−57.8	−72.4	−80.5	−78.2
Balance on capital account	6.7	9.2	10.1	12.0	13.0	12.4	20.4	27.7	45.6	35.1
Balance on financial account	128.1	86.9	78.6	66.5	38.1	14.0	24.9	41.1	46.3	51.4
Change in reserves (− = increase)	−13.1	−25.6	−18.0	−16.7	−58.1	−90.7	−93.5	−124.7	−130.5	−134.8
Other official flows, net	37.0	23.7	−6.4	22.7	18.4	−2.3	−18.5	−60.8	−33.1	−10.5
Private flows, net	104.3	88.8	103.0	60.6	77.7	107.0	136.9	226.7	210.0	196.6
External financing										
Net external financing	213.0	189.3	147.8	140.7	119.7	162.2	236.8	295.8	319.1	321.1
Non-debt-creating inflows	119.7	135.7	121.3	130.6	111.2	110.7	170.4	226.8	234.3	215.1
Net external borrowing	93.4	53.6	26.5	10.1	8.5	51.5	66.5	69.0	84.8	106.0
From official creditors	37.5	25.1	−7.3	21.8	15.8	−0.5	−17.5	−56.4	−27.6	−5.6
of which, credit and loans from IMF	8.8	1.4	−6.9	23.3	15.5	4.3	−12.5	−35.1	. . .	. . .
From banks	5.2	−14.8	−6.7	−14.9	−13.4	4.0	14.3	11.6	27.9	26.7
From other private creditors	50.7	43.3	40.4	3.2	6.1	48.0	69.7	113.8	84.5	84.9
Memorandum										
Exceptional financing	31.5	20.9	7.8	28.0	50.4	32.4	13.4	−37.7	9.8	6.1

Table 34 *(continued)*

	1998	1999	2000	2001	2002	2003	2004	2005	2006	2007
Official financing										
Balance of payments										
Balance on current account	–32.6	–18.0	–10.6	–7.0	8.3	10.0	–4.5	–8.7	–15.3	–19.3
Balance on capital account	4.6	5.8	5.7	7.1	5.9	5.2	5.7	8.7	13.6	8.8
Balance on financial account	27.7	13.5	–1.0	5.6	–7.4	–10.4	2.1	—	7.7	13.4
Change in reserves (– = increase)	–6.0	–3.4	–1.3	11.8	–1.9	–23.0	–13.3	–14.5	–12.4	–17.2
Other official flows, net	12.2	20.1	2.1	12.0	15.7	11.9	–1.2	–12.8	–20.0	–2.3
Private flows, net	21.4	–3.3	–1.8	–18.3	–21.2	0.7	16.6	27.2	40.2	32.9
External financing										
Net external financing	45.3	35.7	14.5	8.8	6.5	27.2	32.2	43.8	46.6	51.9
Non-debt-creating inflows	20.4	17.3	9.6	13.2	15.2	14.7	21.1	34.2	43.4	37.3
Net external borrowing	24.9	18.4	4.8	–4.4	–8.7	12.5	11.1	9.6	3.2	14.6
From official creditors	11.9	20.7	2.5	13.6	14.1	12.4	–0.1	–11.3	–18.3	–0.9
of which, credit and loans from IMF	5.4	0.8	1.7	8.2	—	0.5	–3.3	–4.8	. . .	. . .
From banks	1.5	1.9	2.0	–2.1	–4.2	–0.5	1.7	–2.9	1.7	3.6
From other private creditors	11.5	–4.2	0.4	–15.8	–18.7	0.6	9.4	23.9	19.8	11.9
Memorandum										
Exceptional financing	15.8	10.2	9.2	5.4	25.6	23.2	15.2	–8.4	9.1	6.1
Net debtor countries by debt-servicing experience										
Countries with arrears and/or rescheduling during 1999–2003										
Balance of payments										
Balance on current account	–35.5	–23.1	–4.6	–8.3	0.2	6.1	–2.8	2.8	8.1	21.3
Balance on capital account	3.9	6.7	5.5	5.8	5.7	4.2	4.7	7.2	16.2	10.3
Balance on financial account	31.1	18.7	–4.8	9.3	0.4	–3.3	–1.9	–9.5	–21.2	–29.5
Change in reserves (– = increase)	–5.4	–1.7	–8.0	10.6	–2.0	–17.1	–23.6	–29.7	–44.1	–61.0
Other official flows, net	13.2	20.4	2.0	10.5	11.6	9.1	–1.2	–21.9	–22.8	–4.5
Private flows, net	23.2	—	1.1	–11.7	–9.2	4.7	22.9	42.1	45.6	36.0
External financing										
Net external financing	51.4	43.6	18.2	12.5	17.3	25.5	36.3	41.9	54.3	54.3
Non-debt-creating inflows	22.8	20.9	16.9	19.2	22.1	25.6	35.9	45.1	60.1	53.5
Net external borrowing	28.7	22.6	1.4	–6.7	–4.7	–0.1	0.3	–3.2	–5.8	0.7
From official creditors	13.3	20.4	2.2	10.5	11.7	9.1	–1.2	–21.9	–22.7	–4.3
of which, credit and loans from IMF	5.3	1.1	1.9	8.1	–1.5	–0.2	–3.8	–5.4	. . .	. . .
From banks	–0.8	—	—	–2.9	–4.7	–2.2	1.4	–1.4	5.2	5.4
From other private creditors	16.2	2.2	–0.8	–14.3	–11.7	–7.0	—	20.1	11.7	–0.3
Memorandum										
Exceptional financing	21.9	16.5	12.8	9.9	31.4	25.6	20.2	–10.4	10.1	7.9
Other groups										
Heavily indebted poor countries										
Balance of payments										
Balance on current account	–7.6	–9.0	–7.4	–7.7	–9.4	–8.2	–8.2	–9.0	–9.6	–9.8
Balance on capital account	4.3	5.2	3.6	4.3	3.3	3.5	5.0	6.6	21.5	10.8
Balance on financial account	4.2	3.2	2.6	3.9	6.8	4.3	3.4	3.2	–11.1	–0.7
Change in reserves (– = increase)	0.5	–0.3	–0.3	—	–1.4	–2.3	–2.3	–1.9	–1.4	–1.4
Other official flows, net	1.5	1.6	1.6	–0.3	4.6	4.4	4.4	–5.1	–10.9	–1.6
Private flows, net	2.2	2.0	1.3	4.2	3.6	2.1	1.3	10.3	1.2	2.3
External financing										
Net external financing	8.6	8.9	6.5	8.0	11.2	10.2	10.5	10.9	11.2	11.4
Non-debt-creating inflows	6.5	8.6	6.6	7.3	7.9	7.7	9.4	11.0	26.2	15.9
Net external borrowing	2.1	0.3	—	0.8	3.4	2.5	1.2	—	–15.0	–4.6
From official creditors	1.5	1.6	1.7	–0.3	4.7	4.4	4.4	–5.0	–10.8	–1.5
of which, credit and loans from IMF	0.2	0.3	0.2	—	0.2	–0.2	–0.1	–0.2	. . .	. . .
From banks	–0.1	0.1	–0.5	0.3	0.6	0.4	1.0	0.7	0.7	0.7
From other private creditors	0.7	–1.4	–1.2	0.7	–1.9	–2.3	–4.3	4.3	–4.9	–3.7
Memorandum										
Exceptional financing	2.6	2.9	3.0	3.1	14.2	3.6	1.8	4.5	7.3	5.4

Table 34 *(concluded)*

	1998	1999	2000	2001	2002	2003	2004	2005	2006	2007
Middle East and north Africa										
Balance of payments										
Balance on current account	–29.5	9.7	72.8	44.6	32.6	66.7	106.5	201.3	310.2	330.3
Balance on capital account	–0.4	1.2	2.5	3.2	1.6	1.3	0.1	0.5	1.6	0.5
Balance on financial account	25.7	–0.4	–71.9	–38.0	–35.1	–59.7	–106.9	–203.2	–313.1	–326.8
Change in reserves (– = increase)	11.2	–1.2	–37.4	–21.2	–8.3	–42.4	–60.0	–125.9	–106.0	–161.1
Other official flows, net	–1.6	6.8	–22.3	–15.2	–12.2	–29.1	–38.1	–71.3	–180.0	–154.2
Private flows, net	16.1	–6.1	–12.2	–1.5	–14.6	11.8	–8.9	–6.0	–27.1	–11.5
External financing										
Net external financing	21.2	–7.9	24.9	–4.7	–12.4	28.3	44.0	47.5	43.3	65.7
Non-debt-creating inflows	9.2	8.4	5.0	13.3	10.0	14.1	19.4	24.8	36.9	33.3
Net external borrowing	11.9	–16.3	19.9	–18.0	–22.4	14.1	24.6	22.7	6.4	32.5
From official creditors	3.2	2.4	–2.1	–5.9	–3.1	–2.6	–3.9	–4.1	–8.4	–1.5
of which, credit and loans from IMF	–0.1	—	–0.3	–0.2	–0.3	–0.6	–0.6	–0.8	. . .	. . .
From banks	5.3	2.3	–0.2	–1.5	–3.8	2.5	2.5	8.7	7.3	4.7
From other private creditors	3.5	–21.0	22.2	–10.6	–15.4	14.3	26.0	18.0	7.5	29.3
Memorandum										
Exceptional financing	2.8	2.3	1.8	1.4	1.5	3.2	1.0	1.2	1.1	1.0

[1]For definitions, see footnotes to Table 32.

Table 35. Other Emerging Market and Developing Countries: Reserves[1]

	1998	1999	2000	2001	2002	2003	2004	2005	2006	2007
					Billions of U.S. dollars					
Other emerging market and developing countries	**690.9**	**717.0**	**807.5**	**903.0**	**1,082.9**	**1,408.5**	**1,861.9**	**2,399.0**	**2,998.0**	**3,694.6**
Regional groups										
Africa	41.4	42.1	54.3	64.5	72.2	90.6	126.7	168.9	230.9	306.2
Sub-Sahara	27.9	29.3	35.4	35.7	36.3	40.3	62.8	86.0	122.6	171.7
Excluding Nigeria and South Africa	16.2	17.3	19.1	18.9	22.7	26.5	32.5	38.9	50.7	65.4
Central and eastern Europe	89.7	93.7	95.9	97.4	130.9	160.3	183.5	229.8	248.6	265.7
Commonwealth of Independent States[2]	15.1	16.5	33.2	44.2	58.3	92.8	149.2	225.7	340.7	479.9
Russia	8.5	9.1	24.8	33.1	44.6	73.8	121.5	186.3	288.9	420.9
Excluding Russia	6.6	7.4	8.4	11.0	13.7	19.0	27.7	39.4	51.9	59.0
Developing Asia	274.6	307.7	321.9	380.5	497.1	670.4	934.4	1,167.5	1,451.4	1,733.6
China	149.8	158.3	168.9	216.3	292.0	409.2	615.5	822.6	1,062.6	1,302.6
India	27.9	33.2	38.4	46.4	68.2	99.5	127.2	141.7	154.5	163.5
Excluding China and India	96.8	116.2	114.6	117.8	136.9	161.8	191.7	203.3	234.3	267.5
Middle East	116.8	113.5	146.1	157.2	163.1	198.2	246.7	352.8	432.1	565.7
Western Hemisphere	153.4	143.4	156.1	159.2	161.3	196.2	221.4	254.3	294.2	343.5
Brazil	34.4	23.9	31.5	35.8	37.7	49.1	52.8	53.6	73.3	90.2
Mexico	31.8	31.8	35.5	44.8	50.6	59.0	64.1	71.3	72.8	82.1
Analytical groups										
By source of export earnings										
Fuel	129.5	125.7	190.4	214.0	229.5	306.0	428.5	636.5	881.2	1,224.9
Nonfuel	561.4	591.3	617.1	688.9	853.4	1,102.5	1,433.4	1,762.5	2,116.9	2,469.7
of which, primary products	27.4	26.4	27.0	26.6	28.9	30.7	33.3	36.8	46.9	57.0
By external financing source										
Net debtor countries	394.7	411.2	434.7	459.2	538.8	656.8	767.8	892.5	1,023.0	1,157.8
of which, official financing	85.7	94.0	94.3	87.1	95.3	118.9	130.8	145.3	157.7	174.9
Net debtor countries by debt-servicing experience										
Countries with arrears and/or rescheduling during 1999–2003	75.0	82.9	90.8	84.0	89.4	105.5	128.0	157.7	201.8	262.8
Other groups										
Heavily indebted poor countries	8.5	9.3	10.0	10.7	13.2	16.0	19.1	21.1	22.5	23.9
Middle East and north Africa	130.6	126.7	165.6	186.5	200.0	249.8	312.7	438.6	544.6	705.7

Table 35 *(concluded)*

	1998	1999	2000	2001	2002	2003	2004	2005	2006	2007
	Ratio of reserves to imports of goods and services[3]									
Other emerging market and developing countries	**45.2**	**47.7**	**46.2**	**51.0**	**57.1**	**62.0**	**64.1**	**69.2**	**72.7**	**78.6**
Regional groups										
Africa	30.9	31.2	39.2	45.5	47.0	48.3	53.8	60.9	71.3	82.2
Sub-Sahara	27.2	28.7	33.7	33.3	31.4	28.1	34.9	39.7	48.6	60.4
Excluding Nigeria and South Africa	28.4	30.2	33.4	31.1	35.6	34.7	34.3	34.0	37.6	42.8
Central and eastern Europe	35.4	38.3	34.3	34.9	41.7	39.8	35.1	38.1	35.4	33.8
Commonwealth of Independent States[2]	12.3	17.6	30.5	34.5	41.1	52.9	65.5	80.9	99.5	123.7
Russia	11.5	17.2	40.6	44.6	52.9	71.5	92.7	113.1	140.8	179.2
Excluding Russia	13.6	18.2	17.5	20.6	23.8	26.2	28.6	34.4	37.8	38.5
Developing Asia	56.8	58.6	49.3	58.5	68.3	74.6	79.6	82.8	85.7	87.8
China	91.6	83.3	67.4	79.7	89.0	91.1	101.5	115.5	120.9	122.8
India	47.0	52.9	52.6	65.0	90.0	107.1	95.8	76.4	66.1	58.8
Excluding China and India	37.1	42.7	34.8	38.3	42.2	45.4	44.1	39.6	40.3	42.1
Middle East	64.2	64.0	75.0	78.3	73.9	78.3	78.0	91.9	93.7	108.9
Western Hemisphere	43.7	43.7	41.7	42.9	47.5	55.4	51.7	49.8	49.3	52.1
Brazil	45.4	37.6	43.5	49.2	61.1	77.2	65.9	54.8	62.3	68.2
Mexico	33.4	30.3	27.6	35.2	40.1	45.8	43.5	42.7	38.0	38.7
Analytical groups										
By source of export earnings										
Fuel	45.1	48.2	65.8	67.7	65.5	74.7	82.8	99.5	112.3	135.5
Nonfuel	45.3	47.6	42.3	47.3	55.1	59.2	60.0	62.4	63.4	65.1
of which, primary products	52.1	55.2	54.2	53.3	57.0	52.5	45.8	42.2	47.0	53.1
By external financing source										
Net debtor countries	39.0	41.8	38.8	41.5	47.2	49.4	46.0	44.7	43.9	44.5
of which, official financing	37.7	46.1	41.4	39.6	45.3	49.7	43.9	40.5	37.9	38.3
Net debtor countries by debt-servicing experience										
Countries with arrears and/or rescheduling during 1999–2003	33.8	40.8	40.1	37.7	40.1	41.1	40.1	39.9	43.5	50.8
Other groups										
Heavily indebted poor countries	25.5	27.3	29.0	29.7	33.4	35.8	35.1	32.9	30.7	30.1
Middle East and north Africa	60.5	59.7	71.6	78.1	76.1	82.9	82.7	96.4	100.0	113.3

[1]In this table, official holdings of gold are valued at SDR 35 an ounce. This convention results in a marked underestimate of reserves for countries that have substantial gold holdings.
[2]Mongolia, which is not a member of the Commonwealth of Independent States, is included in this group for reasons of geography and similarities in economic structure.
[3]Reserves at year-end in percent of imports of goods and services for the year indicated.

Table 36. Net Credit and Loans from IMF[1]

(Billions of U.S. dollars)

	1997	1998	1999	2000	2001	2002	2003	2004	2005
Advanced economies	**11.3**	**5.2**	**–10.3**	**—**	**–5.7**	**—**	**—**	**—**	**—**
Newly industrialized Asian economies	11.3	5.2	–10.3	—	–5.7	—	—	—	—
Other emerging market and developing countries	**3.3**	**14.0**	**–2.4**	**–10.9**	**19.0**	**13.4**	**1.7**	**–14.5**	**–39.9**
Regional groups									
Africa	–0.5	–0.4	–0.2	–0.2	–0.4	–0.1	–0.8	–0.7	–1.0
Sub-Sahara	–0.5	–0.3	–0.1	—	–0.2	0.2	–0.4	–0.3	–0.4
Excluding Nigeria and South Africa	–0.1	0.1	–0.1	—	–0.2	0.2	–0.4	–0.3	–0.4
Central and eastern Europe	0.4	–0.5	0.5	3.3	9.9	6.1	—	–3.8	–5.9
Commonwealth of Independent States[2]	2.1	5.8	–3.6	–4.1	–4.0	–1.8	–2.3	–2.1	–3.8
Russia	1.5	5.3	–3.6	–2.9	–3.8	–1.5	–1.9	–1.7	–3.4
Excluding Russia	0.5	0.5	—	–1.2	–0.2	–0.3	–0.4	–0.5	–0.4
Developing Asia	5.0	6.6	1.7	0.9	–2.2	–2.7	–0.6	–1.9	–1.6
China	—	—	—	—	—	—	—	—	—
India	–0.7	–0.4	–0.3	–0.1	—	—	—	—	—
Excluding China and India	5.7	7.0	2.1	0.9	–2.2	–2.7	–0.6	–1.9	–1.6
Middle East	0.2	0.1	0.1	–0.1	0.1	—	–0.1	0.3	–0.1
Western Hemisphere	–4.0	2.5	–0.9	–10.7	15.6	11.9	5.6	–6.3	–27.6
Brazil	—	4.6	4.1	–6.7	6.7	11.2	5.2	–4.4	–23.8
Mexico	–3.4	–1.1	–3.7	–4.3	—	—	—	—	—
Analytical groups									
By source of export earnings									
Fuel	1.4	4.7	–4.1	–3.5	–4.1	–1.8	–2.4	–1.8	–4.3
Nonfuel	1.9	9.3	1.7	–7.4	23.1	15.2	4.1	–12.7	–35.6
of which, primary products	–0.1	0.2	–0.1	–0.2	–0.2	0.1	–0.3	–0.3	–0.3
By external financing source									
Net debtor countries	1.3	8.8	1.4	–6.9	23.3	15.5	4.3	–12.0	–35.1
of which, official financing	2.6	5.4	0.8	1.7	8.2	—	0.5	–3.3	–4.8
Net debtor countries by debt-servicing experience									
Countries with arrears and/or rescheduling during 1999–2003	3.1	5.3	1.1	1.9	8.1	–1.5	–0.2	–3.4	–5.4
Other groups									
Heavily indebted poor countries	—	0.2	0.3	0.1	—	0.2	–0.2	–0.1	–0.2
Middle East and north Africa	0.3	–0.1	—	–0.3	–0.2	–0.3	–0.6	–0.1	–0.8
Memorandum									
Total									
Net credit provided under:									
General Resources Account	14.355	18.811	–12.856	–10.741	13.213	12.832	1.741	–14.276	–39.798
PRGF	0.179	0.374	0.194	–0.148	0.106	0.567	0.009	–0.179	–0.714
IMF credit outstanding at year-end under:[3]									
General Resources Account	62.301	84.541	69.504	55.368	66.448	85.357	95.323	84.992	40.637
PRGF[4]	8.037	8.775	8.749	8.159	7.974	9.222	10.108	10.421	8.978

[1]Includes net disbursements from programs under the General Resources Account and Poverty Reduction and Growth Facility (formerly ESAF—Enhanced Structural Adjustment Facility). The data are on a transactions basis, with conversion to U.S. dollar values at annual average exchange rates.

[2]Mongolia, which is not a member of the Commonwealth of Independent States, is included in this group for reasons of geography and similarities in economic structure.

[3]Data referring to disbursements at year-end correspond to the stock of outstanding credit, converted to U.S. dollar values at end-of-period exchange rates.

[4]Includes outstanding SAF and Trust Fund Loans.

Table 37. Summary of External Debt and Debt Service

	1998	1999	2000	2001	2002	2003	2004	2005	2006	2007
					Billions of U.S. dollars					
External debt										
Other emerging market and developing countries	**2,407.5**	**2,447.6**	**2,366.9**	**2,380.6**	**2,450.7**	**2,674.6**	**2,918.8**	**3,012.3**	**3,150.6**	**3,352.1**
Regional groups										
Africa	283.1	281.7	271.6	260.8	273.8	298.1	311.9	289.4	244.1	243.2
Central and eastern Europe	271.1	287.6	308.8	316.8	366.9	459.9	561.6	604.7	664.4	722.7
Commonwealth of Independent States[1]	222.8	218.9	200.4	189.0	199.3	239.3	279.6	334.0	363.7	418.1
Developing Asia	694.7	692.4	656.1	676.1	681.0	713.7	769.9	808.3	892.9	954.8
Middle East	163.1	169.0	165.4	161.3	162.2	174.2	200.2	221.8	243.4	255.7
Western Hemisphere	772.7	798.0	764.6	776.7	767.6	789.5	795.6	754.1	742.0	757.5
Analytical groups										
By external financing source										
Net debtor countries	1,823.7	1,863.8	1,817.6	1,809.1	1,871.9	2,029.2	2,177.2	2,168.8	2,211.9	2,306.1
of which, official financing	570.3	577.8	565.8	573.9	574.0	608.5	633.9	606.0	588.7	592.7
Net debtor countries by debt-servicing experience										
Countries with arrears and/or rescheduling during 1999–2003	585.6	590.2	571.1	574.4	568.6	598.4	620.5	574.7	547.7	549.8
Debt-service payments[2]										
Other emerging market and developing countries	**370.8**	**403.7**	**455.4**	**435.0**	**422.4**	**478.1**	**490.1**	**597.8**	**628.5**	**595.5**
Regional groups										
Africa	26.1	25.5	27.0	26.1	21.2	26.0	29.4	34.3	37.7	31.3
Central and eastern Europe	54.7	58.6	63.6	73.6	74.2	95.7	106.8	121.4	136.4	146.5
Commonwealth of Independent States[1]	29.5	27.0	61.9	40.1	47.1	63.2	74.2	106.1	123.7	92.8
Developing Asia	97.1	92.7	93.9	100.0	109.8	109.3	98.1	107.5	114.7	123.3
Middle East	19.0	19.2	19.5	22.8	15.4	19.5	22.5	28.2	29.7	31.4
Western Hemisphere	144.5	180.6	189.6	172.3	154.6	164.4	159.0	200.3	186.2	170.2
Analytical groups										
By external financing source										
Net debtor countries	289.0	324.0	342.5	338.1	323.6	355.9	351.3	415.9	419.0	415.4
of which, official financing	79.9	76.4	85.0	89.4	75.8	76.2	69.8	92.3	76.0	68.3
Net debtor countries by debt-servicing experience										
Countries with arrears and/or rescheduling during 1999–2003	78.3	74.4	83.7	89.1	70.9	72.7	68.9	95.3	78.6	72.0

Table 37 *(concluded)*

	1998	1999	2000	2001	2002	2003	2004	2005	2006	2007
				Percent of exports of goods and services						
External debt[3]										
Other emerging market and developing countries	**164.7**	**159.1**	**125.6**	**128.2**	**121.6**	**109.2**	**92.4**	**76.9**	**66.5**	**62.6**
Regional groups										
Africa	236.6	220.0	172.4	173.9	177.2	153.4	125.5	92.4	63.8	54.0
Central and eastern Europe	119.1	134.7	127.3	122.0	127.1	125.0	118.0	110.0	104.5	101.3
Commonwealth of Independent States[1]	175.2	177.2	121.7	113.9	111.6	106.8	91.9	85.8	73.3	76.2
Developing Asia	129.0	120.0	94.4	98.2	86.8	75.0	62.5	53.3	49.2	45.1
Middle East	105.8	88.1	62.2	65.5	61.8	53.4	47.0	38.6	32.9	31.3
Western Hemisphere	262.7	262.6	212.7	224.2	221.2	205.4	168.6	131.6	111.1	106.4
Analytical groups										
By external financing source										
Net debtor countries	204.7	206.0	173.1	173.7	169.8	156.5	133.9	111.7	97.5	91.1
of which, official financing	294.3	302.8	257.5	272.2	265.3	250.4	216.7	175.6	150.1	138.4
Net debtor countries by debt-servicing experience										
Countries with arrears and/or rescheduling during 1999–2003	306.6	305.5	241.2	255.9	245.4	222.3	186.8	139.6	111.9	97.5
Debt-service payments										
Other emerging market and developing countries	**25.4**	**26.2**	**24.2**	**23.4**	**21.0**	**19.5**	**15.5**	**15.3**	**13.3**	**11.1**
Regional groups										
Africa	21.8	19.9	17.1	17.4	13.7	13.4	11.8	10.9	9.9	6.9
Central and eastern Europe	24.0	27.4	26.2	28.3	25.7	26.0	22.4	22.1	21.4	20.5
Commonwealth of Independent States[1]	23.2	21.9	37.6	24.2	26.4	28.2	24.4	27.3	24.9	16.9
Developing Asia	18.0	16.1	13.5	14.5	14.0	11.5	8.0	7.1	6.3	5.8
Middle East	12.3	10.0	7.3	9.3	5.9	6.0	5.3	4.9	4.0	3.8
Western Hemisphere	49.1	59.4	52.7	49.7	44.6	42.8	33.7	35.0	27.9	23.9
Analytical groups										
By external financing source										
Net debtor countries	32.4	35.8	32.6	32.5	29.4	27.5	21.6	21.4	18.5	16.4
of which, official financing	41.2	40.0	38.7	42.4	35.0	31.4	23.9	26.7	19.4	16.0
Net debtor countries by debt-servicing experience										
Countries with arrears and/or rescheduling during 1999–2003	41.0	38.5	35.3	39.7	30.6	27.0	20.8	23.2	16.0	12.8

[1]Mongolia, which is not a member of the Commonwealth of Independent States, is included in this group for reasons of geography and similarities in economic structure.
[2]Debt-service payments refer to actual payments of interest on total debt plus actual amortization payments on long-term debt. The projections incorporate the impact of exceptional financing items.
[3]Total debt at year-end in percent of exports of goods and services in year indicated.

Table 38. Other Emerging Market and Developing Countries—by Region: External Debt, by Maturity and Type of Creditor
(Billions of U.S. dollars)

	1998	1999	2000	2001	2002	2003	2004	2005	2006	2007
Other emerging market and developing countries										
Total debt	**2,407.5**	**2,447.6**	**2,366.9**	**2,380.6**	**2,450.7**	**2,674.6**	**2,918.8**	**3,012.3**	**3,150.6**	**3,352.1**
By maturity										
Short-term	351.6	327.4	306.7	348.7	342.5	418.2	511.2	605.7	679.1	745.4
Long-term	2,056.0	2,120.2	2,060.2	2,031.9	2,108.3	2,256.3	2,407.6	2,406.6	2,471.5	2,606.6
By type of creditor										
Official	922.4	922.4	881.4	876.7	912.5	949.3	949.5	854.6	778.2	779.7
Banks	699.3	697.6	642.6	616.3	615.7	646.3	724.6	753.8	828.1	920.8
Other private	785.8	827.7	842.9	887.6	922.5	1,079.0	1,244.7	1,403.9	1,544.3	1,651.6
Regional groups										
Africa										
Total debt	**283.1**	**281.7**	**271.6**	**260.8**	**273.8**	**298.1**	**311.9**	**289.4**	**244.1**	**243.2**
By maturity										
Short-term	34.8	36.4	15.9	14.7	17.8	18.7	20.6	18.8	18.0	17.9
Long-term	248.2	245.3	255.7	246.1	256.1	279.4	291.2	270.6	226.1	225.3
By type of creditor										
Official	207.9	205.0	204.2	202.3	215.3	232.1	238.9	212.0	161.2	157.1
Banks	48.2	47.3	41.2	38.2	37.8	42.8	46.2	47.8	51.6	53.6
Other private	27.0	29.4	26.2	20.3	20.8	23.3	26.7	29.7	31.3	32.6
Sub-Sahara										
Total debt	**220.4**	**221.8**	**216.8**	**210.4**	**221.7**	**241.7**	**257.1**	**241.2**	**202.1**	**200.9**
By maturity										
Short-term	33.0	34.6	14.0	12.8	15.4	16.3	17.8	14.6	14.1	14.5
Long-term	187.4	187.2	202.8	197.5	206.3	225.4	239.3	226.5	188.0	186.5
By type of creditor										
Official	161.4	161.1	163.6	164.6	175.0	188.0	196.1	174.8	130.4	126.2
Banks	37.2	35.1	29.8	27.2	26.7	30.4	34.4	36.7	40.4	42.2
Other private	21.9	25.6	23.4	18.5	20.0	23.3	26.7	29.7	31.3	32.6
Central and eastern Europe										
Total debt	**271.1**	**287.6**	**308.8**	**316.8**	**366.9**	**459.9**	**561.6**	**604.7**	**664.4**	**722.7**
By maturity										
Short-term	56.5	60.2	66.0	57.0	63.7	93.3	120.2	137.5	147.4	158.6
Long-term	214.5	227.4	242.9	259.8	303.1	366.6	441.5	467.2	517.0	564.1
By type of creditor										
Official	79.5	75.8	77.5	83.2	76.5	74.3	69.9	61.3	58.6	56.0
Banks	102.6	110.3	121.7	109.5	139.4	177.5	215.9	230.0	253.0	280.1
Other private	89.0	101.5	109.6	124.2	151.0	208.0	275.9	313.4	352.7	386.6
Commonwealth of Independent States[1]										
Total debt	**222.8**	**218.9**	**200.4**	**189.0**	**199.3**	**239.3**	**279.6**	**334.0**	**363.7**	**418.1**
By maturity										
Short-term	23.8	14.4	13.6	16.1	18.8	30.8	36.2	48.3	50.4	52.1
Long-term	199.1	204.5	186.8	172.8	180.5	208.5	243.4	285.7	313.3	366.0
By type of creditor										
Official	113.9	113.4	102.8	90.8	85.2	86.6	85.0	56.6	33.5	32.2
Banks	49.9	49.8	18.1	22.3	21.1	23.0	29.7	48.3	62.2	100.0
Other private	59.1	55.8	79.5	76.0	92.9	129.6	165.0	229.1	268.0	285.9

Table 38 ***(concluded)***

	1998	1999	2000	2001	2002	2003	2004	2005	2006	2007
Developing Asia										
Total debt	**694.7**	**692.4**	**656.1**	**676.1**	**681.0**	**713.7**	**769.9**	**808.3**	**892.9**	**954.8**
By maturity										
Short-term	85.3	66.8	54.7	107.6	108.2	130.0	168.7	221.7	269.9	307.2
Long-term	609.4	625.6	601.4	568.5	572.8	583.6	601.2	586.6	623.1	647.6
By type of creditor										
Official	289.5	295.3	279.5	272.6	280.2	285.1	293.4	302.1	318.5	334.2
Banks	201.0	195.5	179.9	174.7	167.6	160.1	176.2	188.4	209.4	226.1
Other private	204.2	201.6	196.7	228.7	233.2	268.5	300.3	317.7	365.1	394.5
Middle East										
Total debt	**163.1**	**169.0**	**165.4**	**161.3**	**162.2**	**174.2**	**200.2**	**221.8**	**243.4**	**255.7**
By maturity										
Short-term	51.8	53.9	52.1	55.6	55.6	67.4	84.4	96.1	104.6	113.4
Long-term	111.3	115.0	113.3	105.6	106.6	106.7	115.8	125.7	138.9	142.3
By type of creditor										
Official	54.9	53.6	50.6	48.7	52.9	57.8	58.9	57.9	56.9	54.6
Banks	62.8	65.0	62.7	57.7	51.7	53.6	67.8	78.4	87.1	91.7
Other private	45.5	50.3	52.0	54.9	57.5	62.8	73.5	85.6	99.5	109.4
Western Hemisphere										
Total debt	**772.7**	**798.0**	**764.6**	**776.7**	**767.6**	**789.5**	**795.6**	**754.1**	**742.0**	**757.5**
By maturity										
Short-term	99.3	95.7	104.4	97.6	78.4	78.0	81.1	83.3	88.9	96.2
Long-term	673.3	702.3	660.1	679.1	689.2	711.4	714.5	670.8	653.1	661.3
By type of creditor										
Official	176.8	179.3	166.7	179.1	202.4	213.3	203.4	164.7	149.4	145.6
Banks	234.8	229.7	219.0	214.0	198.2	189.2	188.8	161.0	164.8	169.3
Other private	361.1	389.0	378.9	383.5	367.1	386.9	403.4	428.4	427.8	442.7

[1]Mongolia, which is not a member of the Commonwealth of Independent States, is included in this group for reasons of geography and similarities in economic structure.

Table 39. Other Emerging Market and Developing Countries—by Analytical Criteria: External Debt, by Maturity and Type of Creditor
(Billions of U.S. dollars)

	1998	1999	2000	2001	2002	2003	2004	2005	2006	2007
By source of export earnings										
Fuel										
Total debt	**456.3**	**453.8**	**422.2**	**402.4**	**409.4**	**454.0**	**507.7**	**557.9**	**577.7**	**640.9**
By maturity										
Short-term	79.9	72.2	50.4	54.8	56.5	76.2	96.2	113.0	121.4	127.9
Long-term	376.4	381.6	371.9	347.6	352.9	377.8	411.4	445.0	456.2	513.0
By type of creditor										
Official	207.0	202.5	190.8	176.9	180.3	189.2	190.1	139.8	95.8	95.6
Banks	118.1	119.6	85.0	83.6	74.4	78.6	98.3	128.9	150.4	193.0
Other private	131.1	131.7	146.4	141.9	154.6	186.2	219.3	289.2	331.5	352.3
Nonfuel										
Total debt	**1,951.2**	**1,993.8**	**1,944.7**	**1,978.2**	**2,041.4**	**2,220.5**	**2,411.1**	**2,454.3**	**2,572.9**	**2,711.2**
By maturity										
Short-term	271.6	255.2	256.4	293.9	285.9	342.0	415.0	492.7	557.7	617.6
Long-term	1,679.6	1,738.7	1,688.3	1,684.3	1,755.4	1,878.5	1,996.2	1,961.7	2,015.2	2,093.6
By type of creditor										
Official	715.4	719.9	690.6	699.8	732.2	760.1	759.4	714.8	682.4	684.1
Banks	581.1	578.0	557.6	532.7	541.3	567.6	626.3	624.8	677.7	727.8
Other private	654.7	695.9	696.5	745.7	767.9	892.8	1,025.4	1,114.7	1,212.8	1,299.3
Nonfuel primary products										
Total debt	**97.3**	**101.8**	**103.7**	**106.6**	**114.7**	**121.2**	**125.5**	**123.4**	**108.3**	**105.6**
By maturity										
Short-term	6.8	6.0	7.9	6.7	7.5	9.6	10.3	10.0	11.7	12.3
Long-term	90.6	95.8	95.8	99.9	107.2	111.5	115.2	113.4	96.6	93.3
By type of creditor										
Official	63.2	63.1	62.5	63.8	71.3	75.3	76.6	69.9	52.4	47.0
Banks	21.4	22.6	23.4	23.3	23.1	24.8	23.5	5.0	5.2	4.8
Other private	12.8	16.2	17.8	19.5	20.2	21.0	25.3	48.5	50.7	53.8
By external financing source										
Net debtor countries										
Total debt	**1,823.7**	**1,863.8**	**1,817.6**	**1,809.1**	**1,871.9**	**2,029.2**	**2,177.2**	**2,168.8**	**2,211.9**	**2,306.1**
By maturity										
Short-term	259.1	249.9	236.0	220.4	206.7	239.6	279.5	307.7	325.5	353.5
Long-term	1,564.5	1,613.9	1,581.7	1,588.7	1,665.3	1,789.6	1,897.6	1,861.1	1,886.4	1,952.6
By type of creditor										
Official	710.9	717.2	698.7	706.8	741.6	769.1	760.6	686.0	624.1	616.6
Banks	542.6	532.6	512.5	486.8	493.1	519.9	568.0	555.6	594.3	634.4
Other private	570.2	614.0	606.5	615.5	637.2	740.1	848.6	927.2	993.5	1,055.1
Official financing										
Total debt	**570.3**	**577.8**	**565.8**	**573.9**	**574.0**	**608.5**	**633.9**	**606.0**	**588.7**	**592.7**
By maturity										
Short-term	67.4	64.6	67.9	66.1	52.0	59.5	69.1	74.8	77.6	80.5
Long-term	502.9	513.2	497.9	507.8	521.9	548.9	564.8	531.3	511.2	512.2
By type of creditor										
Official	261.6	270.8	265.1	270.7	291.6	311.1	313.4	296.0	258.2	255.0
Banks	99.7	98.1	92.4	92.7	86.9	87.7	92.9	92.1	97.4	102.2
Other private	209.1	208.9	208.3	210.5	195.4	209.6	227.6	217.9	233.1	235.5

Table 39 *(concluded)*

	1998	1999	2000	2001	2002	2003	2004	2005	2006	2007
Net debtor countries by debt-servicing experience										
Countries with arrears and/or rescheduling during 1999–2003										
Total debt	**585.6**	**590.2**	**571.1**	**574.4**	**568.6**	**598.4**	**620.5**	**574.7**	**547.7**	**549.8**
By maturity										
Short-term	61.8	59.7	39.6	34.5	26.5	29.7	34.1	32.9	32.5	33.0
Long-term	523.9	530.5	531.5	540.0	542.1	568.7	586.3	541.8	515.2	516.9
By type of creditor										
Official	323.3	333.3	329.9	330.2	339.5	361.6	365.9	332.2	287.5	284.6
Banks	96.2	93.8	82.8	84.9	77.7	77.2	82.2	79.6	86.7	91.9
Other private	166.1	163.1	158.4	159.4	151.5	159.6	172.4	162.8	173.6	173.3
Other groups										
Heavily indebted poor countries										
Total debt	**107.0**	**106.7**	**106.5**	**107.1**	**112.1**	**120.2**	**124.2**	**115.3**	**84.2**	**81.5**
By maturity										
Short-term	2.7	2.9	3.0	3.5	3.2	3.1	3.3	3.4	3.0	3.0
Long-term	104.2	103.8	103.5	103.6	108.9	117.1	120.8	111.9	81.2	78.4
By type of creditor										
Official	101.1	99.8	101.1	99.6	104.8	111.5	114.0	106.9	75.1	72.3
Banks	4.6	4.7	2.8	6.0	6.0	6.5	7.4	5.3	6.1	6.6
Other private	1.2	2.1	2.6	1.5	1.3	2.2	2.8	3.1	2.9	2.6
Middle East and north Africa										
Total debt	**250.3**	**253.9**	**242.4**	**234.9**	**240.1**	**258.7**	**283.6**	**300.6**	**316.1**	**330.8**
By maturity										
Short-term	53.7	55.8	54.0	57.6	57.9	69.8	87.3	100.4	108.6	117.0
Long-term	196.6	198.1	188.5	177.4	182.2	188.8	196.3	200.1	207.5	213.8
By type of creditor										
Official	120.5	117.2	110.1	106.0	115.2	125.7	126.0	121.0	113.7	113.2
Banks	78.0	81.3	76.7	71.4	65.7	69.4	83.3	93.1	101.8	107.0
Other private	51.8	55.4	55.5	57.5	59.2	63.5	74.3	86.5	100.5	110.5

Table 40. Other Emerging Market and Developing Countries: Ratio of External Debt to GDP[1]

	1998	1999	2000	2001	2002	2003	2004	2005	2006	2007
Other emerging market and developing countries	**40.5**	**42.1**	**37.4**	**37.0**	**37.2**	**35.8**	**33.1**	**28.9**	**26.2**	**25.2**
Regional groups										
Africa	65.5	64.8	60.8	58.6	58.1	52.2	45.2	35.9	26.2	23.1
Sub-Sahara	67.2	67.2	63.9	62.7	62.1	55.6	48.7	38.6	28.1	24.4
Central and eastern Europe	42.9	47.7	50.1	52.8	52.7	53.7	54.0	49.6	50.8	50.7
Commonwealth of Independent States[2]	58.2	75.2	56.4	45.7	43.0	41.9	36.3	33.6	29.0	28.3
Developing Asia	35.2	32.3	28.4	27.9	25.8	23.8	22.2	20.3	19.7	19.0
Middle East	32.1	30.4	26.4	25.6	25.6	24.6	24.5	22.4	20.1	18.8
Western Hemisphere	38.5	44.8	38.8	40.6	45.4	44.8	39.4	31.0	26.6	25.5
Analytical groups										
By source of export earnings										
Fuel	50.5	51.7	40.4	36.1	35.7	33.9	30.1	26.2	21.6	20.8
Nonfuel	38.7	40.4	36.8	37.2	37.5	36.2	33.8	29.6	27.5	26.5
of which, primary products	58.7	64.0	67.1	70.2	67.2	72.1	63.5	53.6	39.5	34.9
By external financing source										
Net debtor countries	45.9	48.9	44.8	45.6	47.2	45.5	42.2	35.8	32.4	31.0
of which, official financing	65.7	65.1	62.8	65.1	76.6	71.4	65.4	54.4	45.9	42.1
Net debtor countries by debt-servicing experience										
Countries with arrears and/or rescheduling during 1999–2003	74.7	72.6	67.4	68.0	76.3	70.3	63.9	50.4	40.3	35.6
Other groups										
Heavily indebted poor countries	103.0	102.9	105.9	103.5	102.5	96.5	87.6	71.6	46.5	41.2
Middle East and north Africa	40.0	37.7	32.4	31.2	31.4	29.9	28.2	25.0	21.6	20.1

[1]Debt at year-end in percent of GDP in year indicated.
[2]Mongolia, which is not a member of the Commonwealth of Independent States, is included in this group for reasons of geography and similarities in economic structure.

Table 41. Other Emerging Market and Developing Countries: Debt-Service Ratios[1]
(Percent of exports of goods and services)

	1998	1999	2000	2001	2002	2003	2004	2005	2006	2007
Interest payments[2]										
Other emerging market and developing countries	**9.7**	**8.9**	**7.6**	**7.4**	**6.2**	**5.8**	**4.7**	**4.4**	**4.3**	**4.0**
Regional groups										
Africa	10.4	9.2	7.2	6.9	5.0	4.7	3.6	3.1	2.5	2.2
Sub-Sahara	6.9	6.6	5.7	5.7	3.6	4.0	3.0	2.9	2.1	2.0
Central and eastern Europe	10.2	10.2	9.8	9.9	8.9	8.5	7.2	6.9	6.6	6.5
Commonwealth of Independent States[3]	13.3	10.2	8.2	7.5	7.5	11.0	8.4	9.1	9.3	8.9
Developing Asia	6.3	5.5	4.7	4.2	3.5	2.9	2.3	2.2	2.3	2.2
Middle East	3.3	2.6	2.1	1.9	1.6	2.3	1.9	1.6	1.4	1.4
Western Hemisphere	17.0	17.7	15.8	16.1	13.7	11.3	9.1	8.4	8.1	7.2
Analytical groups										
By source of export earnings										
Fuel	10.4	7.5	5.3	5.5	4.7	6.4	4.9	4.6	4.5	4.3
Nonfuel	9.5	9.2	8.4	8.0	6.7	5.7	4.6	4.4	4.2	3.9
of which, primary products	4.9	5.1	7.1	6.2	4.5	3.8	2.9	2.6	2.2	1.8
By external financing source										
Net debtor countries	11.7	11.5	10.5	10.1	8.4	7.3	6.0	5.7	5.4	5.0
of which, official financing	14.2	13.6	13.4	11.5	9.1	6.5	5.4	5.4	5.3	5.1
Net debtor countries by debt-servicing experience										
Countries with arrears and/or rescheduling during 1999–2003	14.3	13.5	12.4	11.4	7.9	5.7	4.6	4.5	4.0	3.7
Other groups										
Heavily indebted poor countries	7.4	6.7	7.5	6.6	3.9	4.9	3.8	3.7	2.2	1.9
Middle East and north Africa	6.1	4.6	3.3	3.1	2.6	2.9	2.3	1.8	1.6	1.6
Amortization[2]										
Other emerging market and developing countries	**15.7**	**17.4**	**16.6**	**16.0**	**14.7**	**13.7**	**10.8**	**10.8**	**9.0**	**7.1**
Regional groups										
Africa	11.4	10.7	9.9	10.5	8.8	8.7	8.3	7.8	7.4	4.7
Sub-Sahara	10.7	9.7	9.0	10.2	7.2	7.4	6.9	7.2	6.1	5.0
Central and eastern Europe	13.8	17.3	16.5	18.5	16.8	17.6	15.3	15.2	14.8	14.1
Commonwealth of Independent States[3]	9.9	11.6	29.4	16.6	18.9	17.2	16.0	18.1	15.7	8.0
Developing Asia	11.8	10.6	8.8	10.3	10.5	8.6	5.6	4.9	4.1	3.7
Middle East	9.0	7.5	5.3	7.3	4.3	3.7	3.4	3.3	2.6	2.4
Western Hemisphere	32.1	41.7	36.9	33.6	30.9	31.5	24.5	26.6	19.8	16.7
Analytical groups										
By source of export earnings										
Fuel	11.3	10.1	14.3	11.5	10.5	9.7	9.0	9.3	7.5	4.1
Nonfuel	16.7	19.3	17.3	17.4	15.9	14.9	11.4	11.4	9.6	8.4
of which, primary products	9.9	12.3	15.0	15.1	16.5	14.3	13.7	8.9	9.2	8.0
By external financing source										
Net debtor countries	20.7	24.3	22.1	22.3	20.9	20.2	15.6	15.7	13.1	11.4
of which, official financing	27.0	26.4	25.3	30.8	25.9	24.9	18.5	21.4	14.1	10.9
Net debtor countries by debt-servicing experience										
Countries with arrears and/or rescheduling during 1999–2003	26.7	25.0	22.9	28.4	22.7	21.4	16.2	18.7	12.1	9.1
Other groups										
Heavily indebted poor countries	15.4	12.1	13.4	14.8	8.8	7.5	9.8	5.5	17.6	13.7
Middle East and north Africa	9.7	8.4	6.3	7.9	5.4	4.9	4.6	4.1	3.6	2.6

[1]Excludes service payments to the International Monetary Fund.
[2]Interest payments on total debt and amortization on long-term debt. Estimates through 2005 reflect debt-service payments actually made. The estimates for 2006 and 2007 take into account projected exceptional financing items, including accumulation of arrears and rescheduling agreements. In some cases, amortization on account of debt-reduction operations is included.
[3]Mongolia, which is not a member of the Commonwealth of Independent States, is included in this group for reasons of geography and similarities in economic structure.

Table 42. IMF Charges and Repurchases to the IMF[1]

(Percent of exports of goods and services)

	1998	1999	2000	2001	2002	2003	2004	2005
Other emerging market and developing countries	**0.6**	**1.2**	**1.2**	**0.7**	**1.1**	**1.2**	**0.7**	**0.5**
Regional groups								
Africa	1.1	0.5	0.2	0.3	0.4	0.3	0.2	0.2
Sub-Sahara	0.8	0.2	0.1	0.1	0.2	—	0.1	—
Excluding Nigeria and South Africa	0.5	0.4	0.3	0.3	0.4	0.1	0.1	—
Central and eastern Europe	0.4	0.4	0.3	0.8	2.7	0.8	1.3	1.7
Commonwealth of Independent States[2]	1.7	4.9	3.2	3.1	1.2	1.1	0.7	0.9
Russia	1.9	5.9	3.1	3.8	1.4	1.3	0.9	1.3
Excluding Russia	1.2	2.9	3.4	1.4	0.7	0.6	0.5	—
Developing Asia	0.2	0.2	0.2	0.6	0.6	0.3	0.2	—
Excluding China and India	0.2	0.3	0.4	1.2	1.4	0.8	0.5	0.1
Middle East	—	0.1	0.1	0.1	—	—	—	—
Western Hemisphere	1.1	3.2	4.2	0.6	2.0	5.3	2.6	0.9
Analytical groups								
By source of export earnings								
Fuel	1.0	1.9	1.0	1.1	0.5	0.5	0.3	0.4
Nonfuel	0.5	1.0	1.3	0.6	1.3	1.4	0.9	0.5
By external financing source								
Net debtor countries	0.6	1.3	1.6	0.8	1.8	2.0	1.3	0.7
of which, official financing	0.7	0.9	1.1	1.9	2.2	3.6	2.9	1.4
Net debtor countries by debt-servicing experience								
Countries with arrears and/or rescheduling during 1999–2003	0.9	1.1	1.1	1.9	2.1	3.3	2.5	1.1
Other groups								
Heavily indebted poor countries	0.4	0.2	0.1	0.3	0.9	0.1	—	—
Middle East and north Africa	0.4	0.3	0.1	0.2	0.2	0.2	0.1	0.1
Memorandum								
Total, billions of U.S. dollars[3]								
General Resources Account	8.809	18.531	22.863	13.849	22.352	29.425	23.578	46.393
Charges	2.510	2.829	2.846	2.638	2.806	3.020	3.384	3.253
Repurchases	6.300	15.702	20.017	11.211	19.546	26.405	20.193	43.144
PRGF[4]	0.881	0.855	0.835	1.042	1.214	1.225	1.432	1.358
Interest	0.040	0.042	0.038	0.038	0.040	0.046	0.050	0.048
Repayments	0.842	0.813	0.798	1.005	1.174	1.179	1.382	1.310

[1]Excludes advanced economies. Charges on, and repurchases (or repayments of principal) for, use of IMF credit.
[2]Mongolia, which is not a member of the Commonwealth of Independent States, is included in this group for reasons of geography and similarities in economic structure.
[3]The data are converted to U.S. dollar values at annual average exchange rates.
[4]Poverty Reduction and Growth Facility (formerly ESAF—Enhanced Structural Adjustment Facility).

Table 43. Summary of Sources and Uses of World Saving

(Percent of GDP)

	Averages										Average
	1984–91	1992–99	2000	2001	2002	2003	2004	2005	2006	2007	2008–11
World											
Saving	22.9	21.9	22.3	21.2	20.3	20.7	21.3	21.8	22.7	23.1	23.6
Investment	23.7	22.5	22.4	21.4	20.7	21.0	21.6	22.2	22.7	23.2	24.0
Advanced economies											
Saving	22.3	21.5	21.6	20.4	19.1	19.0	19.3	19.2	19.6	19.6	19.9
Investment	23.0	21.8	22.1	20.8	19.8	19.9	20.3	20.8	21.2	21.4	21.8
Net lending	–0.6	–0.3	–0.4	–0.4	–0.7	–0.9	–1.0	–1.6	–1.6	–1.7	–1.9
Current transfers	–0.3	–0.5	–0.6	–0.5	–0.6	–0.6	–0.6	–0.7	–0.6	–0.6	–0.6
Factor income	–0.2	–0.3	0.7	0.6	0.2	0.1	0.2	0.1	0.2	0.1	–0.1
Resource balance	–0.1	0.5	–0.6	–0.5	–0.4	–0.4	–0.5	–1.0	–1.2	–1.3	–1.2
United States											
Saving	17.3	16.4	18.0	16.4	14.2	13.3	13.2	12.9	13.7	13.5	13.9
Investment	19.9	19.0	20.8	19.1	18.4	18.4	19.3	19.7	20.2	20.4	20.8
Net lending	–2.6	–2.6	–2.7	–2.8	–4.2	–5.1	–6.1	–6.8	–6.6	–6.9	–6.8
Current transfers	–0.4	–0.6	–0.6	–0.5	–0.6	–0.6	–0.7	–0.7	–0.5	–0.5	–0.5
Factor income	—	–0.6	1.7	1.3	0.5	—	–0.2	–0.3	—	–0.4	–0.9
Resource balance	–2.2	–1.5	–3.8	–3.6	–4.0	–4.5	–5.2	–5.8	–6.0	–6.1	–5.5
Euro area											
Saving	. . .	20.9	21.3	21.1	20.6	20.4	21.0	20.7	21.0	21.2	21.6
Investment	. . .	21.2	22.0	21.1	20.0	20.0	20.3	20.8	21.0	21.2	21.8
Net lending	. . .	–0.3	–0.7	—	0.5	0.4	0.7	–0.1	—	–0.1	–0.2
Current transfers[1]	–0.5	–0.7	–0.8	–0.8	–0.7	–0.8	–0.8	–0.9	–0.9	–0.9	–0.9
Factor income[1]	–0.5	–0.8	–0.5	–0.6	–1.0	–0.9	–0.5	–0.6	–0.6	–0.6	–0.6
Resource balance[1]	1.0	1.6	0.6	1.5	2.3	2.1	2.1	1.5	1.4	1.3	1.2
Germany											
Saving	24.0	21.0	20.1	19.5	19.3	19.3	20.9	21.3	21.6	21.8	21.9
Investment	21.2	21.9	21.8	19.5	17.3	17.4	17.1	17.1	17.4	17.8	18.6
Net lending	2.8	–1.0	–1.7	—	2.0	1.9	3.7	4.1	4.2	4.0	3.4
Current transfers	–1.6	–1.5	–1.4	–1.3	–1.3	–1.3	–1.3	–1.3	–1.3	–1.3	–1.3
Factor income	0.8	–0.1	–0.4	–0.5	–0.8	–0.7	—	0.4	0.1	0.1	0.2
Resource balance	3.5	0.6	0.1	1.8	4.1	3.9	5.0	5.0	5.4	5.1	4.5
France											
Saving	20.9	20.0	21.8	21.6	20.0	19.3	19.1	18.6	18.5	18.4	18.3
Investment	21.2	18.5	20.5	20.0	19.0	18.9	19.4	20.2	20.3	20.1	19.8
Net lending	–0.3	1.5	1.3	1.6	1.0	0.4	–0.3	–1.6	–1.7	–1.7	–1.5
Current transfers	–0.6	–0.7	–1.1	–1.1	–1.0	–1.1	–1.1	–1.3	–1.0	–1.0	–1.0
Factor income	–0.3	0.1	1.2	1.1	0.3	0.4	0.6	0.8	0.6	0.6	0.6
Resource balance	0.6	2.2	1.2	1.6	1.7	1.1	0.1	–1.0	–1.3	–1.3	–1.1
Italy											
Saving	19.8	18.7	20.2	20.5	20.4	19.4	19.8	19.3	20.1	20.7	22.1
Investment	22.5	19.6	20.8	20.6	21.1	20.7	20.7	20.9	21.5	21.8	22.9
Net lending	–2.7	–0.9	–0.6	–0.1	–0.7	–1.3	–0.9	–1.6	–1.4	–1.0	–0.8
Current transfers	–0.1	–0.5	–0.4	–0.5	–0.4	–0.5	–0.6	–0.6	–0.5	–0.5	–0.5
Factor income	–2.7	–3.3	–1.1	–0.9	–1.2	–1.3	–1.1	–1.0	–1.0	–1.0	–1.0
Resource balance	0.2	3.0	0.9	1.4	1.0	0.6	0.7	–0.1	0.1	0.5	0.8
Japan											
Saving	33.3	30.7	27.8	26.9	25.9	26.2	26.4	26.9	27.6	27.8	27.7
Investment	30.5	28.2	25.2	24.8	23.0	23.0	22.7	23.2	23.9	24.3	24.6
Net lending	2.8	2.5	2.6	2.1	2.9	3.2	3.7	3.6	3.7	3.5	3.2
Current transfers	–0.1	–0.2	–0.2	–0.2	–0.1	–0.2	–0.2	–0.2	–0.2	–0.2	–0.2
Factor income	0.6	1.1	1.3	1.7	1.7	1.7	1.9	2.3	2.5	2.6	2.7
Resource balance	2.3	1.6	1.5	0.6	1.3	1.7	2.1	1.5	1.4	1.2	0.7
United Kingdom											
Saving	17.0	15.7	14.9	15.0	15.2	15.1	15.3	14.9	15.2	15.5	16.1
Investment	19.4	16.9	17.5	17.2	16.8	16.5	16.9	17.1	17.5	17.8	18.7
Net lending	–2.3	–1.2	–2.6	–2.2	–1.6	–1.3	–1.6	–2.2	–2.4	–2.3	–2.5
Current transfers	–0.7	–0.8	–1.1	–0.7	–0.9	–0.9	–0.9	–1.0	–1.0	–1.1	–1.1
Factor income	—	0.4	0.5	1.2	2.2	2.2	2.3	2.4	2.3	2.3	2.2
Resource balance	–1.6	–0.7	–2.0	–2.7	–2.9	–2.7	–3.0	–3.6	–3.6	–3.5	–3.6
Canada											
Saving	18.9	17.4	23.6	22.2	21.0	21.2	22.9	23.8	23.9	24.2	24.9
Investment	21.3	19.1	20.2	19.2	19.3	20.0	20.7	21.5	21.9	22.3	23.0
Net lending	–2.5	–1.7	3.4	3.0	1.7	1.2	2.1	2.3	2.0	1.9	1.9
Current transfers	–0.2	—	0.1	0.1	—	—	—	—	—	—	—
Factor income	–3.2	–3.6	–2.4	–2.8	–2.6	–2.5	–1.9	–1.4	–1.2	–1.1	–1.1
Resource balance	0.9	1.9	5.7	5.7	4.3	3.7	4.1	3.7	3.2	3.1	3.0

Table 43 ***(continued)***

	Averages 1984–91	Averages 1992–99	2000	2001	2002	2003	2004	2005	2006	2007	Average 2008–11
Newly industrialized Asian economies											
Saving	35.1	33.8	31.9	29.9	29.6	31.4	33.0	31.8	30.6	30.6	30.6
Investment	28.7	31.1	28.4	25.3	24.6	24.5	26.1	25.6	25.6	25.7	26.1
Net lending	6.4	2.7	3.5	4.6	5.1	6.9	7.0	6.2	5.0	4.9	4.5
Current transfers	0.1	–0.2	–0.4	–0.6	–0.7	–0.7	–0.7	–0.7	–0.7	–0.7	–0.7
Factor income	1.0	0.8	0.2	0.8	0.6	0.9	1.0	0.7	0.7	0.8	0.8
Resource balance	5.3	2.1	3.8	4.5	5.1	6.7	6.7	6.2	5.1	4.8	4.4
Other emerging market and developing countries											
Saving	24.6	23.7	24.8	24.3	25.3	27.3	28.7	30.4	32.0	32.9	33.2
Investment	26.2	25.4	23.7	23.9	24.2	25.5	26.4	26.7	27.3	28.2	29.8
Net lending	–1.6	–1.7	1.1	0.4	1.1	1.8	2.2	3.7	4.7	4.6	3.4
Current transfers	0.4	0.8	1.1	1.2	1.4	1.6	1.6	1.6	1.5	1.4	1.3
Factor income	–1.8	–1.6	–2.1	–2.1	–2.2	–2.1	–2.2	–2.2	–1.9	–1.6	–1.1
Resource balance	–0.1	–0.9	2.1	1.3	1.8	2.4	2.9	4.3	5.1	4.9	3.2
Memorandum											
Acquisition of foreign assets	0.6	3.4	4.6	3.1	3.3	5.7	6.9	8.9	9.1	8.9	7.1
Change in reserves	—	1.1	1.4	1.5	2.4	3.9	4.9	5.2	5.0	5.2	4.1
Regional groups											
Africa											
Saving	18.5	17.0	21.3	20.4	18.7	20.7	21.8	23.5	25.3	26.3	26.3
Investment	21.2	19.9	19.5	20.2	19.2	20.9	21.8	21.3	21.8	22.1	22.9
Net lending	–2.7	–2.8	1.7	0.2	–0.5	–0.2	—	2.2	3.5	4.2	3.4
Current transfers	2.0	2.6	2.6	2.9	3.0	3.2	3.2	3.1	2.9	2.7	2.6
Factor income	–5.1	–4.2	–5.1	–4.6	–3.7	–4.6	–5.2	–5.4	–5.7	–5.9	–4.3
Resource balance	0.4	–1.2	4.3	1.9	0.2	1.2	1.9	4.4	6.3	7.4	5.2
Memorandum											
Acquisition of foreign assets	0.4	1.1	4.7	5.1	2.1	3.0	3.9	5.9	7.1	7.8	7.2
Change in reserves	0.3	0.4	2.9	2.2	1.2	2.0	4.8	5.2	6.7	7.1	6.5
Central and eastern Europe											
Saving	27.6	21.0	19.8	19.3	18.9	18.5	18.9	18.8	19.6	20.8	22.2
Investment	27.4	23.3	25.0	22.0	22.4	22.9	24.5	23.8	24.9	25.6	26.6
Net lending	0.2	–2.3	–5.2	–2.7	–3.5	–4.3	–5.6	–5.1	–5.3	–4.8	–4.4
Current transfers	1.4	1.8	1.9	1.9	1.8	1.6	1.6	1.7	1.8	2.0	2.0
Factor income	–0.8	–1.1	–1.1	–1.4	–1.7	–1.8	–2.7	–2.4	–2.0	–1.7	–1.4
Resource balance	–0.4	–3.1	–6.0	–3.2	–3.6	–4.1	–4.5	–4.3	–5.1	–5.2	–5.1
Memorandum											
Acquisition of foreign assets	0.9	2.5	3.5	2.3	3.4	2.4	4.3	5.9	3.8	3.2	2.4
Change in reserves	–0.5	2.0	1.1	0.7	2.9	1.5	1.4	3.8	1.4	1.2	0.7
Commonwealth of Independent States[2]											
Saving	. . .	23.5	31.9	29.4	26.3	27.1	28.7	29.5	30.4	30.0	28.5
Investment	. . .	22.4	17.9	21.1	19.8	20.9	21.1	20.9	20.5	20.8	22.5
Net lending	. . .	1.1	14.0	8.3	6.6	6.2	7.7	8.6	9.9	9.2	6.0
Current transfers	. . .	0.7	0.7	0.5	0.6	0.6	0.5	0.4	0.5	0.5	0.5
Factor income	. . .	–1.6	–2.3	–1.4	–1.9	–2.9	–2.7	–3.0	–2.8	–2.1	–1.3
Resource balance	. . .	2.0	15.6	9.1	7.9	8.5	9.9	11.1	12.3	10.9	6.9
Memorandum											
Acquisition of foreign assets	. . .	2.7	12.4	6.8	5.5	11.6	14.3	15.7	15.1	15.3	11.5
Change in reserves	. . .	0.3	5.7	3.5	3.3	5.8	7.1	7.7	9.2	9.4	6.4

Table 43 *(continued)*

	Averages 1984–91	Averages 1992–99	2000	2001	2002	2003	2004	2005	2006	2007	Average 2008–11
Developing Asia											
Saving	27.0	31.8	30.0	30.5	32.2	34.9	36.0	38.3	40.2	41.8	43.0
Investment	29.9	32.4	28.2	29.0	29.8	32.0	33.4	34.8	36.3	37.9	39.5
Net lending	–2.9	–0.6	1.7	1.6	2.5	2.9	2.7	3.5	4.0	3.9	3.5
Current transfers	0.7	1.2	1.6	1.7	1.9	2.1	2.0	2.0	1.8	1.5	1.3
Factor income	–1.9	–1.4	–1.7	–1.7	–1.6	–1.0	–1.0	–1.2	–0.5	–0.5	–0.4
Resource balance	–1.8	–0.4	1.8	1.6	2.2	1.8	1.6	2.7	2.7	2.8	2.6
Memorandum											
Acquisition of foreign assets	1.2	6.1	4.2	3.1	5.0	6.2	7.3	9.7	8.9	8.0	6.4
Change in reserves	0.5	1.6	0.7	2.4	4.2	5.5	7.5	5.9	6.3	5.6	4.5
Middle East											
Saving	16.7	22.8	29.4	26.3	25.7	29.2	33.2	40.6	45.1	44.6	41.1
Investment	22.8	23.5	20.0	21.9	23.2	23.1	22.5	22.5	23.1	23.6	25.6
Net lending	–6.1	–0.7	9.4	4.4	2.5	6.1	10.7	18.1	22.0	21.0	15.5
Current transfers	–3.3	–3.0	–2.3	–2.5	–2.5	–2.3	–2.0	–1.6	–1.4	–1.4	–1.2
Factor income	1.1	2.8	0.4	–0.3	–1.6	–1.9	–0.8	0.5	0.5	0.5	2.2
Resource balance	–3.9	–0.5	11.3	7.2	6.6	10.3	13.4	19.2	22.9	21.9	14.5
Memorandum											
Acquisition of foreign assets	–0.7	2.6	14.1	4.8	2.4	12.7	16.1	22.5	25.7	25.7	20.1
Change in reserves	–1.3	0.7	4.9	1.8	0.6	4.6	5.8	10.7	6.5	9.8	8.2
Western Hemisphere											
Saving	19.8	18.1	18.5	17.1	18.5	20.0	21.5	22.0	21.8	22.0	21.3
Investment	20.6	21.3	21.1	20.1	19.4	19.5	20.7	20.7	20.7	21.1	21.7
Net lending	–0.7	–3.2	–2.7	–3.0	–0.9	0.4	0.8	1.2	1.1	0.9	–0.3
Current transfers	0.7	0.9	1.1	1.4	1.8	2.1	2.2	2.1	2.0	2.0	2.0
Factor income	–4.1	–2.7	–3.0	–3.1	–3.1	–3.3	–3.5	–3.4	–3.5	–2.9	–2.5
Resource balance	2.6	–1.4	–0.8	–1.3	0.4	1.7	2.1	2.6	2.6	1.8	0.2
Memorandum											
Acquisition of foreign assets	0.6	1.9	1.0	1.5	0.8	2.5	2.0	1.8	2.7	2.9	1.8
Change in reserves	0.4	0.8	0.1	–0.2	0.1	2.0	1.1	1.3	1.4	1.7	1.0
Analytical groups											
By source of export earnings											
Fuel											
Saving	27.9	23.2	33.3	29.2	26.8	29.7	32.1	37.1	39.8	39.3	36.2
Investment	29.2	23.4	20.2	22.7	22.5	22.7	22.1	21.7	21.7	22.1	23.8
Net lending	–1.3	–0.3	13.1	6.5	4.3	7.0	10.0	15.4	18.1	17.1	12.4
Current transfers	–1.3	–2.1	–1.8	–1.9	–1.8	–1.4	–1.1	–0.9	–0.8	–0.7	–0.6
Factor income	–0.4	–0.8	–2.3	–2.0	–3.1	–3.6	–3.2	–2.5	–2.6	–2.4	–0.8
Resource balance	0.4	2.6	17.2	10.4	9.2	12.0	14.3	18.8	21.5	20.3	13.8
Memorandum											
Acquisition of foreign assets	0.2	2.3	15.5	6.2	3.3	11.8	13.8	18.0	20.6	21.1	16.4
Change in reserves	–0.4	0.1	6.5	2.6	1.4	5.3	7.1	9.8	9.2	11.1	8.6
Nonfuel											
Saving	23.2	23.8	23.2	23.2	25.0	26.8	27.8	28.7	29.8	30.9	32.2
Investment	24.9	25.8	24.4	24.1	24.6	26.1	27.4	28.0	28.9	30.1	31.6
Net lending	–1.7	–2.0	–1.2	–0.9	0.4	0.7	0.4	0.8	0.9	0.9	0.6
Current transfers	1.1	1.4	1.7	1.9	2.1	2.3	2.2	2.2	2.1	2.0	1.8
Factor income	–2.4	–1.8	–2.1	–2.2	–1.9	–1.8	–2.0	–2.1	–1.7	–1.4	–1.2
Resource balance	–0.4	–1.7	–0.8	–0.6	0.2	0.2	0.2	0.6	0.5	0.3	—
Memorandum											
Acquisition of foreign assets	0.7	3.7	2.5	2.4	3.3	4.3	5.2	6.5	5.8	5.2	4.3
Change in reserves	0.2	1.3	0.4	1.2	2.6	3.6	4.4	4.0	3.8	3.4	2.7

Table 43 *(concluded)*

	Averages										
	1984–91	1992–99	2000	2001	2002	2003	2004	2005	2006	2007	Average 2008–11
By external financing source											
Net debtor countries											
Saving	20.5	20.1	19.5	18.8	19.8	21.2	21.8	21.8	22.1	22.7	23.1
Investment	23.2	23.0	21.7	20.7	20.7	21.7	23.0	23.1	23.3	23.7	24.6
Net lending	–2.7	–2.9	–2.2	–1.8	–0.9	–0.5	–1.2	–1.3	–1.3	–1.0	–1.5
Current transfers	1.3	1.8	2.1	2.3	2.6	2.8	2.7	2.7	2.7	2.6	2.5
Factor income	–3.6	–3.6	–2.5	–2.6	–2.5	–2.6	–3.0	–3.1	–3.1	–2.8	–2.3
Resource balance	–0.5	–2.5	–1.8	–1.6	–1.0	–0.7	–0.9	–0.9	–0.9	–0.9	–1.7
Memorandum											
Acquisition of foreign assets	0.4	1.9	1.2	1.6	1.8	2.8	2.8	3.2	3.1	2.8	2.2
Change in reserves	0.1	1.0	0.4	0.4	1.5	2.0	1.8	2.1	1.9	1.8	1.2
Official financing											
Saving	16.8	19.4	17.3	17.4	20.0	22.1	20.5	20.5	20.4	21.0	21.4
Investment	22.3	23.1	18.9	18.6	18.6	20.9	20.9	21.4	21.8	22.4	23.0
Net lending	–5.5	–3.7	–1.6	–1.2	1.3	1.2	–0.4	–0.9	–1.4	–1.4	–1.6
Current transfers	1.7	2.0	2.8	3.2	4.1	4.2	4.2	4.2	4.1	4.0	3.7
Factor income	–5.3	–5.3	–3.4	–3.4	–3.6	–3.5	–4.0	–3.8	–3.6	–3.4	–2.6
Resource balance	–1.8	–3.3	–0.9	–1.1	0.8	0.4	–0.6	–1.3	–1.9	–2.0	–2.7
Memorandum											
Acquisition of foreign assets	0.6	2.1	0.2	0.1	1.9	4.5	2.6	2.5	2.3	2.2	1.4
Change in reserves	0.2	0.8	0.1	–1.3	0.3	2.7	1.4	1.3	1.0	1.2	1.0
Net debtor countries by debt-servicing experience											
Countries with arrears and/or rescheduling during 1999–2003											
Saving	16.1	19.1	18.5	17.8	19.5	22.1	21.0	21.4	21.8	22.7	22.8
Investment	21.8	23.2	19.3	19.1	18.5	21.1	21.2	21.1	21.3	21.3	22.1
Net lending	–5.7	–4.1	–0.9	–1.2	1.0	1.0	–0.2	0.3	0.5	1.4	0.8
Current transfers	1.2	2.0	2.7	2.9	3.8	4.0	3.8	3.9	3.7	3.4	3.1
Factor income	–5.9	–5.9	–4.8	–4.3	–3.9	–4.4	–5.4	–5.1	–5.0	–5.0	–3.7
Resource balance	–0.9	–2.7	1.2	0.2	1.2	1.4	1.3	1.5	1.9	3.0	1.4
Memorandum											
Acquisition of foreign assets	–0.3	1.8	1.3	0.2	2.3	3.7	2.8	3.4	4.2	4.5	3.7
Change in reserves	0.2	0.7	0.9	–1.3	0.3	2.0	2.4	2.6	3.2	4.0	3.5

Note: The estimates in this table are based on individual countries' national accounts and balance of payments statistics. Country group composites are calculated as the sum of the U.S dollar values for the relevant individual countries. This differs from the calculations in the April 2005 and earlier *World Economic Outlooks*, where the composites were weighted by GDP valued at purchasing power parities (PPPs) as a share of total world GDP. For many countries, the estimates of national saving are built up from national accounts data on gross domestic investment and from balance-of-payments-based data on net foreign investment. The latter, which is equivalent to the current account balance, comprises three components: current transfers, net factor income, and the resource balance. The mixing of data source, which is dictated by availability, implies that the estimates for national saving that are derived incorporate the statistical discrepancies. Furthermore, error omissions and asymmetries in balance of payments statistics affect the estimates for net lending; at the global level, net lending, which in theory would be zero, equals the world current account discrepancy. Notwithstanding these statistical shortcomings, flow of funds estimates, such as those presented in these tables, provide a useful framework for analyzing development in saving and investment, both over time and across regions and countries.

[1]Calculated from the data of individual euro area countries.

[2]Mongolia, which is not a member of the Commonwealth of Independent States, is included in this group for reasons of geography and similarities in economic structure.

Table 44. Summary of World Medium-Term Baseline Scenario

	Eight-Year Averages		Four-Year Average					Four-Year Average
	1988–95	1996–2003	2004–07	2004	2005	2006	2007	2008–11
			Annual percent change unless otherwise noted					
World real GDP	**3.2**	**3.7**	**5.0**	**5.3**	**4.9**	**5.1**	**4.9**	**4.8**
Advanced economies	2.9	2.6	2.9	3.2	2.6	3.1	2.7	2.7
Other emerging market and developing countries	3.7	5.1	7.4	7.7	7.4	7.3	7.2	6.7
Memorandum								
Potential output								
Major advanced economies	2.6	2.5	2.5	2.5	2.5	2.5	2.5	2.5
World trade, volume[1]	**6.6**	**6.0**	**8.6**	**10.6**	**7.4**	**8.9**	**7.6**	**6.9**
Imports								
Advanced economies	6.4	5.8	7.1	9.1	6.0	7.5	6.0	5.5
Other emerging market and developing countries	6.7	6.9	13.3	16.4	11.9	13.0	12.1	10.2
Exports								
Advanced economies	6.8	5.3	7.1	8.8	5.5	8.0	6.0	5.5
Other emerging market and developing countries	7.0	7.8	11.9	14.6	11.8	10.7	10.6	9.0
Terms of trade								
Advanced economies	—	—	–0.6	–0.2	–1.3	–0.9	—	0.1
Other emerging market and developing countries	–1.2	0.6	2.9	2.7	4.5	4.0	0.5	–0.6
World prices in U.S. dollars								
Manufactures	3.3	–1.7	4.3	9.4	3.6	2.2	2.3	1.2
Oil	–0.7	6.7	27.1	30.7	41.3	29.7	9.1	–2.1
Nonfuel primary commodities	2.2	–2.4	11.0	18.5	10.3	22.1	–4.8	–6.1
Consumer prices								
Advanced economies	3.7	1.9	2.3	2.0	2.3	2.6	2.3	2.2
Other emerging market and developing countries	65.2	9.3	5.3	5.6	5.3	5.2	5.0	4.2
Interest rates (in percent)								
Real six-month LIBOR[2]	3.4	2.7	1.4	–1.0	0.7	2.4	3.5	3.5
World real long-term interest rate[3]	4.2	2.9	1.9	1.8	1.3	1.8	2.7	3.1
				Percent of GDP				
Balances on current account								
Advanced economies	–0.1	–0.4	–1.4	–0.8	–1.4	–1.6	–1.7	–1.9
Other emerging market and developing countries	–1.5	0.0	4.0	2.4	4.1	4.9	4.8	3.5
Total external debt								
Other emerging market and developing countries	32.4	37.6	28.3	33.1	28.9	26.2	25.2	23.4
Debt service								
Other emerging market and developing countries	4.5	6.3	5.2	5.6	5.7	5.2	4.5	4.1

[1]Data refer to trade in goods and services.
[2]London interbank offered rate on U.S. dollar deposits less percent change in U.S. GDP deflator.
[3]GDP-weighted average of 10-year (or nearest maturity) government bond rates for the United States, Japan, Germany, France, Italy, the United Kingdom, and Canada.

Table 45. Other Emerging Market and Developing Countries—Medium-Term Baseline Scenario: Selected Economic Indicators

	Eight-Year Averages		Four-Year Average					Four-Year Average
	1988–95	1996–2003	2004–07	2004	2005	2006	2007	2008–11
			Annual percent change					
Other emerging market and developing countries								
Real GDP	3.7	5.1	7.4	7.7	7.4	7.3	7.2	6.7
Export volume[1]	7.0	7.8	11.9	14.6	11.8	10.7	10.6	9.0
Terms of trade[1]	–1.2	0.6	2.9	2.7	4.5	4.0	0.5	–0.6
Import volume[1]	6.7	6.9	13.3	16.4	11.9	13.0	12.1	10.2
Regional groups								
Africa								
Real GDP	1.8	3.7	5.5	5.5	5.4	5.4	5.9	5.1
Export volume[1]	5.0	5.2	7.5	7.1	6.2	4.9	11.8	5.0
Terms of trade[1]	–2.7	1.7	7.9	3.7	13.3	11.1	4.0	–0.9
Import volume[1]	4.0	5.6	11.5	8.9	12.3	10.9	13.8	6.1
Central and eastern Europe								
Real GDP	—	3.4	5.6	6.5	5.4	5.3	5.0	4.7
Export volume[1]	4.7	9.0	11.1	15.0	9.4	10.4	9.7	7.7
Terms of trade[1]	0.5	—	–0.8	0.5	–1.0	–2.1	–0.5	0.1
Import volume[1]	6.7	9.4	10.4	15.9	8.0	9.2	8.8	7.7
Commonwealth of Independent States[2]								
Real GDP	. . .	3.4	7.0	8.4	6.5	6.8	6.5	5.7
Export volume[1]	. . .	5.0	7.4	13.1	5.1	6.1	5.7	5.6
Terms of trade[1]	. . .	3.0	9.2	10.7	14.5	10.8	1.1	–2.5
Import volume[1]	. . .	5.6	14.6	19.8	15.5	13.4	10.0	7.2
Developing Asia								
Real GDP	8.0	6.8	8.8	8.8	9.0	8.7	8.6	8.0
Export volume[1]	13.0	10.9	17.4	19.9	17.8	16.3	15.7	12.7
Terms of trade[1]	0.1	–1.1	–1.6	–1.8	–1.9	–2.0	–0.6	0.2
Import volume[1]	13.1	7.9	15.2	18.7	12.7	14.5	15.1	13.5
Middle East								
Real GDP	3.9	4.2	5.6	5.5	5.7	5.8	5.4	5.4
Export volume[1]	9.0	4.1	7.4	10.1	8.0	7.5	4.2	4.4
Terms of trade[1]	–3.1	4.9	12.7	9.3	18.8	18.3	4.9	–1.7
Import volume[1]	2.4	6.5	14.7	14.4	15.0	18.2	11.3	7.8
Western Hemisphere								
Real GDP	2.5	2.3	4.7	5.7	4.3	4.8	4.2	3.7
Export volume[1]	7.8	5.6	7.2	9.2	8.9	5.3	5.7	6.1
Terms of trade[1]	–0.9	0.3	3.1	6.5	3.5	4.5	–2.0	–1.5
Import volume[1]	9.8	4.4	10.8	14.7	10.7	10.4	7.4	6.9
Analytical groups								
Net debtor countries by debt-servicing experience								
Countries with arrears and/or rescheduling during 1999–2003								
Real GDP	3.8	3.2	6.6	6.8	7.1	6.1	6.5	5.6
Export volume[1]	7.7	5.6	7.8	6.0	8.0	6.1	11.2	6.0
Terms of trade[1]	–0.4	–1.0	4.0	3.6	6.0	4.8	1.8	–0.8
Import volume[1]	6.3	2.7	11.2	11.0	14.5	9.8	9.7	7.0

Table 45 ***(concluded)***

	1995	1999	2003	2004	2005	2006	2007	2011
	Percent of exports of goods and services							
Other emerging market and developing countries								
Current account balance	–7.1	–1.6	6.0	6.7	10.8	12.4	11.9	6.9
Total external debt	152.0	159.1	109.2	92.4	76.9	66.5	62.6	56.8
Debt-service payments[3]	20.6	26.2	19.5	15.5	15.3	13.3	11.1	9.9
Interest payments	8.7	8.9	5.8	4.7	4.4	4.3	4.0	3.6
Amortization	11.9	17.4	13.7	10.8	10.8	9.0	7.1	6.3
Regional groups								
Africa								
Current account balance	–13.0	–11.7	–1.6	–0.2	5.9	8.7	9.9	7.3
Total external debt	247.6	220.0	153.4	125.5	92.4	63.8	54.0	55.0
Debt-service payments[3]	26.0	19.9	13.4	11.8	10.9	9.9	6.9	5.0
Interest payments	15.1	9.2	4.7	3.6	3.1	2.5	2.2	2.0
Amortization	10.9	10.7	8.7	8.3	7.8	7.4	4.7	3.0
Central and eastern Europe								
Current account balance	–3.8	–12.4	–9.9	–12.5	–11.5	–11.8	–10.8	–9.8
Total external debt	113.5	134.7	125.0	118.0	110.0	104.5	101.3	95.6
Debt-service payments[3]	19.2	27.4	26.0	22.4	22.1	21.4	20.5	20.3
Interest payments	6.0	10.2	8.5	7.2	6.9	6.6	6.5	5.7
Amortization	13.2	17.3	17.6	15.3	15.2	14.8	14.1	14.6
Commonwealth of Independent States								
Current account balance	2.9	19.2	16.0	20.5	22.5	25.6	25.3	15.7
Total external debt	117.3	177.2	106.8	91.9	85.8	73.3	76.2	109.0
Debt-service payments[3]	9.5	21.9	28.2	24.4	27.3	24.9	16.9	23.3
Interest payments	6.1	10.2	11.0	8.4	9.1	9.3	8.9	11.4
Amortization	3.4	11.6	17.2	16.0	18.1	15.7	8.0	11.9
Developing Asia								
Current account balance	–9.0	6.6	9.0	7.7	10.9	10.2	9.4	6.9
Total external debt	125.7	120.0	75.0	62.5	53.3	49.2	45.1	33.1
Debt-service payments[3]	15.6	16.1	11.5	8.0	7.1	6.3	5.8	4.4
Interest payments	6.0	5.5	2.9	2.3	2.2	2.3	2.2	1.6
Amortization	9.5	10.6	8.6	5.6	4.9	4.1	3.7	2.7
Middle East								
Current account balance	2.2	6.3	18.0	22.7	31.9	38.2	37.4	28.0
Total external debt	78.5	88.1	53.4	47.0	38.6	32.9	31.3	31.4
Debt-service payments[3]	11.5	10.0	6.0	5.3	4.9	4.0	3.8	2.8
Interest payments	4.4	2.6	2.3	1.9	1.6	1.4	1.4	1.4
Amortization	7.1	7.5	3.7	3.4	3.3	2.6	2.4	1.4
Western Hemisphere								
Current account balance	–15.1	–18.6	1.8	3.8	5.9	5.2	4.0	–3.5
Total external debt	252.6	262.6	205.4	168.6	131.6	111.1	106.4	96.7
Debt-service payments[3]	40.8	59.4	42.8	33.7	35.0	27.9	23.9	20.8
Interest payments	16.9	17.7	11.3	9.1	8.4	8.1	7.2	6.5
Amortization	23.8	41.7	31.5	24.5	26.6	19.8	16.7	14.3
Analytical groups								
Net debtor countries by debt-servicing experience								
Countries with arrears and/or rescheduling during 1999–2003								
Current account balance	–16.7	–12.0	2.3	–0.8	0.7	1.6	3.8	—
Total external debt	282.7	305.5	222.3	186.8	139.6	111.9	97.5	85.5
Debt-service payments[3]	28.4	38.5	27.0	20.8	23.2	16.0	12.8	10.3
Interest payments	11.5	13.5	5.7	4.6	4.5	4.0	3.7	3.0
Amortization	16.9	25.0	21.4	16.2	18.7	12.1	9.1	7.3

[1]Data refer to trade in goods and services.
[2]Mongolia, which is not a member of the Commonwealth of Independent States, is included in this group for reasons of geography and similarities in economic structure.
[3]Interest payments on total debt plus amortization payments on long-term debt only. Projections incorporate the impact of exceptional financing items. Excludes service payments to the International Monetary Fund.

WORLD ECONOMIC OUTLOOK AND *STAFF STUDIES FOR THE WORLD ECONOMIC OUTLOOK*, SELECTED TOPICS, 1995–2006

I. Methodology—Aggregation, Modeling, and Forecasting

	World Economic Outlook
The Difficult Art of Forecasting	October 1996, Annex I
World Current Account Discrepancy	October 1996, Annex III
Alternative Exchange Rate Assumptions for Japan	October 1997, Box 2
Revised Purchasing Power Parity Based Weights for the *World Economic Outlook*	May 2000, Box A1
The Global Current Account Discrepancy	October 2000, Chapter I, Appendix II
How Well Do Forecasters Predict Turning Points?	May 2001, Box 1.1
The Information Technology Revolution: Measurement Issues	October 2001, Box 3.1
Measuring Capital Account Liberalization	October 2001, Box 4.1
The Accuracy of *World Economic Outlook* Growth Forecasts: 1991–2000	December 2001, Box 3.1
On the Accuracy of Forecasts of Recovery	April 2002, Box 1.2
The Global Current Account Discrepancy and Other Statistical Problems	September 2002, Box 2.1
The Global Economy Model	April 2003, Box 4.3
How Should We Measure Global Growth?	September 2003, Box 1.2
Measuring Foreign Reserves	September 2003, Box 2.2
The Effects of Tax Cuts in a Global Fiscal Model	April 2004, Box 2.2
How Accurate are the Forecasts in the *World Economic Outlook*?	April 2006, Box 1.3
Drawing the Line Between Personal and Corporate Savings	April 2006, Box 4.1

	Staff Studies for the World Economic Outlook
How Accurate Are the IMF's Short-Term Forecasts? Another Examination of the World Economic Outlook Michael J. Artis	December 1997
IMF's Estimates of Potential Output: Theory and Practice Paula R. De Masi	December 1997
Multilateral Unit-Labor-Cost-Based Competitiveness Indicators for Advanced, Developing, and Transition Countries Anthony G. Turner and Stephen Golub	December 1997

II. Historical Surveys

	World Economic Outlook
The Rise and Fall of Inflation—Lessons from Postwar Experience	October 1996, Chapter VI
The World Economy in the Twentieth Century	May 2000, Chapter V
The Monetary System and Growth During the Commercial Revolution	May 2000, Box 5.2
The Great Depression	April 2002, Box 3.2
Historical Evidence on Financial Crises	April 2002, Box 3.3

A Historical Perspective on Booms, Busts, and Recessions	April 2003, Box 2.1
Institutional Development: The Influence of History and Geography	April 2003, Box 3.1
Long-Term Interest Rates from a Historical Perspective	April 2006, Box 1.1
Recycling Petrodollars in the 1970s	April 2006, Box 2.2

	Staff Studies for the World Economic Outlook
Globalization and Growth in the Twentieth Century *Nicholas Crafts*	May 2000
The International Monetary System in the (Very) Long Run *Barry Eichengreen and Nathan Sussman*	May 2000
External Imbalances Then and Now	April 2005, Box 3.1

III. Economic Growth—Sources and Patterns

	World Economic Outlook
Saving in a Growing World Economy	May 1995, Chapter V
North-South R&D Spillovers	May 1995, Box 6
Long-Term Growth Potential in the Countries in Transition	October 1996, Chapter V
Globalization and the Opportunities for Developing Countries	May 1997, Chapter IV
Measuring Productivity Gains in East Asian Economies	May 1997, Box 9
The Business Cycle, International Linkages, and Exchange Rates	May 1998, Chapter III
The Asian Crisis and the Region's Long-Term Growth Performance	October 1998, Chapter III
Potential Macroeconomic Implications of the Year 2000 Computer Bug	May 1999, Box 1.2
Growth Divergences in the United States, Europe, and Japan: Long-Run Trend or Cyclical?	October 1999, Chapter III
How Can the Poorest Countries Catch Up?	May 2000, Chapter IV
Trends in the Human Development Index	May 2000, Box 5.1
Productivity Growth and IT in the Advanced Economies	October 2000, Chapter II
Transition: Experience and Policy Issues	October 2000, Chapter III
Business Linkages in Major Advanced Countries	October 2001, Chapter II
How Do Macroeconomic Fluctuations in the Advanced Countries Affect the Developing Countries?	October 2001, Chapter II
Confidence Spillovers	October 2001, Box 2.1
Channels of Business Cycle Transmission to Developing Countries	October 2001, Box 2.2
The Information Technology Revolution	October 2001, Chapter III
Has the IT Revolution Reduced Output Volatility?	October 2001, Box 3.4
The Impact of Capital Account Liberalization on Economic Performance	October 2001, Box 4.2
How Has September 11 Influenced the Global Economy?	December 2001, Chapter II
The Long-Term Impact of September 11	December 2001, Box 2.1
Is Wealth Increasingly Driving Consumption?	April 2002, Chapter II
Recessions and Recoveries	April 2002, Chapter III
Was It a Global Recession?	April 2002, Box 1.1
How Important Is the Wealth Effect on Consumption?	April 2002, Box 2.1
A Household Perspective on the Wealth Effect	April 2002, Box 2.2
Measuring Business Cycles	April 2002, Box 3.1
Economic Fluctuations in Developing Countries	April 2002, Box 3.4

IV. Inflation and Deflation; Commodity Markets

V. Fiscal Policy

Effects of Increased Government Debt: Illustrative Calculations	May 1995, Box 13
Subsidies and Tax Arrears	October 1995, Box 8
Focus on Fiscal Policy	May 1996
The Spillover Effects of Government Debt	May 1996, Annex I
Uses and Limitations of Generational Accounting	May 1996, Box 5
The European Union's Stability and Growth Pact	October 1997, Box 3
Progress with Fiscal Reform in Countries in Transition	May 1998, Chapter V
Pension Reform in Countries in Transition	May 1998, Box 10
Transparency in Government Operations	May 1998, Annex I
The Asian Crisis: Social Costs and Mitigating Policies	October 1998, Box 2.4
Fiscal Balances in the Asian Crisis Countries: Effects of Changes in the Economic Environment Versus Policy Measures	October 1998, Box 2.5
Aging in the East Asian Economies: Implications for Government Budgets and Saving Rates	October 1998, Box 3.1
Orienting Fiscal Policy in the Medium Term in Light of the Stability and Growth Pact and Longer-Term Fiscal Needs	October 1998, Box 5.2
Comparing G-7 Fiscal Positions—Who Has a Debt Problem?	October 1999, Box 1.3
Social Spending, Poverty Reduction, and Debt Relief in Heavily Indebted Poor Countries	May 2000, Box 4.3
Fiscal Improvement in Advanced Economies: How Long Will It Last?	May 2001, Chapter III
Impact of Fiscal Consolidation on Macroeconomic Performance	May 2001, Box 3.3
Fiscal Frameworks in Advanced and Emerging Market Economies	May 2001, Box 3.4
Data on Public Debt in Emerging Market Economies	September 2003, Box 3.1
Fiscal Risk: Contingent Liabilities and Demographics	September 2003, Box 3.2
Assessing Fiscal Sustainability Under Uncertainty	September 2003, Box 3.3
The Case for Growth-Indexed Bonds	September 2003, Box 3.4
Public Debt in Emerging Markets: Is It Too High?	September 2003, Chapter III
Has Fiscal Behavior Changed Under the European Economic and Monetary Union?	September 2004, Chapter II
Bringing Small Entrepreneurs into the Formal Economy	September 2004, Box 1.5
HIV/AIDS: Demographic, Economic, and Fiscal Consequences	September 2004, Box 3.3
Implications of Demographic Change for Health Care Systems	September 2004, Box 3.4
Impact of Aging on Public Pension Plans	September 2004, Box 3.5
How Should Middle Eastern and Central Asian Oil Exporters Use Their Oil Revenues?	April 2005, Box 1.6
Financial Globalization and the Conduct of Macroeconomic Policies	April 2005, Box 3.3
Is Public Debt in Emerging Markets Still Too High?	September 2005, Box 1.1
Improved Emerging Market Fiscal Performance: Cyclical or Structural?	September 2006, Box 2.1

VI. Monetary Policy; Financial Markets; Flow of Funds

	World Economic Outlook
Saving in a Growing World Economy	May 1995, Chapter V
Saving and Real Interest Rates in Developing Countries	May 1995, Box 10
Financial Market Turmoil and Economic Policies in Industrial Countries	October 1995, Chapter III
Financial Liberalization in Africa and Asia	October 1995, Box 4

Policy Challenges Facing Industrial Countries in the Late 1990s	October 1996, Chapter III
Using the Slope of the Yield Curve to Estimate Lags in Monetary Transmission Mechanism	October 1996, Box 2
Financial Repression	October 1996, Box 5
Bank-Restructuring Strategies in the Baltic States, Russia, and Other Countries of the Former Soviet Union: Main Issues and Challenges	October 1996, Box 7
Monetary and Financial Sector Policies in Transition Countries	October 1997, Chapter V
Dollarization	October 1997, Box 6
Interim Assessment (Focus on Crisis in Asia—Regional and Global Implications)	December 1997
Financial Crises: Characteristics and Indicators of Vulnerability	May 1998, Chapter IV
The Role of Hedge Funds in Financial Markets	May 1998, Box 1
International Monetary System: Measures to Reduce the Risk of Crises	May 1998, Box 3
Resolving Banking Sector Problems	May 1998, Box 6
Effective Banking Prudential Regulations and Requirements	May 1998, Box 7
Strengthening the Architecture of the International Monetary System Through International Standards and Principles of Good Practice	October 1998, Box 1.2
The Role of Monetary Policy in Responding to Currency Crises	October 1998, Box 2.3
Summary of Structural Reforms in Crisis Countries	October 1998, Box 3.2
Japan's Liquidity Trap	October 1998, Box 4.1
How Useful Are Taylor Rules as a Guide to ECB Monetary Policies?	October 1998, Box 5.1
The Crisis in Emerging Markets	December 1998, Chapter II
Turbulence in Mature Financial Markets	December 1998, Chapter III
What Is the Implied Future Earnings Growth Rate that Would Justify Current Equity Prices in the United States?	December 1998, Box 3.2
Leverage	December 1998, Box 3.3
The Near Collapse and Rescue of Long-Term Capital Management	December 1998, Box 3.4
Risk Management: Progress and Problems	December 1998, Box 3.5
Supervisory Reforms Relating to Risk Management	December 1998, Box 3.6
Emerging Market Banking Systems	December 1998, Annex
International Financial Contagion	May 1999, Chapter III
From Crisis to Recovery in the Emerging Market Economies	October 1999, Chapter II
Safeguarding Macroeconomic Stability at Low Inflation	October 1999, Chapter IV
The Effects of a Zero Floor for Nominal Interest Rates on Real Output: Selected Simulation Results	October 1999, Box 4.2
Asset Prices and Business Cycle	May 2000, Chapter III
Global Liquidity and Asset Prices	May 2000, Box 3.2
International Capital Flows to Emerging Markets	October 2000, Chapter II
Developments in Global Equity Markets	October 2000, Chapter II
U.S. Monetary Policy and Sovereign Spreads in Emerging Markets	October 2000, Box 2.1
Impact of the Global Technology Correction on the Real Economy	May 2001, Chapter II
Inflation Targeting in Emerging Market Economies: Implementation and Challenges	May 2001, Box 4.3
Financial Market Dislocations and Policy Responses After the September 11 Attacks	December 2001, Box 2.2
Investor Risk Appetite	December 2001, Box 2.3
Monetary Policy in a Low Inflation Era	April 2002, Chapter II

VII. Labor Market Issues

Labor Markets—An Analytical Framework	May 1999, Box 4.3
The OECD Jobs Study	May 1999, Box 4.4
The Effects of Downward Rigidity of Nominal Wages on (Un)employment: Selected Simulation Results	October 1999, Box 4.1
Unemployment and Labor Market Institutions: Why Reforms Pay Off	April 2003, Chapter IV
Regional Disparities in Unemployment	April 2003, Box 4.1
Labor Market Reforms in the European Union	April 2003, Box 4.2

	Staff Studies for the World Economic Outlook
Evaluating Unemployment Policies: What Do the Underlying Theories Tell Us? *Dennis J. Snower*	September 1995
Institutional Structure and Labor Market Outcomes: Western Lessons for European Countries in Transition *Robert J. Flanagan*	September 1995
The Effect of Globalization on Wages in the Advanced Economies *Matthew J. Slaughter and Phillip Swagel*	December 1997
International Labor Standards and International Trade *Stephen Golub*	December 1997
EMU Challenges European Labor Markets *Rüdiger Soltwedel, Dirk Dohse, and Christiane Krieger-Boden*	May 2000

VIII. Exchange Rate Issues

	World Economic Outlook
Exchange Rate Effects of Fiscal Consolidation	October 1995, Annex
Exchange Rate Arrangements and Economic Performance in Developing Countries	October 1997, Chapter IV
Asymmetric Shocks: European Union and the United States	October 1997, Box 4
Currency Boards	October 1997, Box 5
The Business Cycle, International Linkages, and Exchange Rates	May 1998, Chapter III
Evaluating Exchange Rates	May 1998, Box 5
Determining Internal and External Conversion Rates for the Euro	October 1998, Box 5.4
The Euro Area and Effective Exchange Rates	October 1998, Box 5.5
Recent Dollar/Yen Exchange Rate Movements	December 1998, Box 3.1
International Financial Contagion	May 1999, Chapter III
Exchange Rate Crashes and Inflation: Lessons for Brazil	May 1999, Box 2.1
Recent Experience with Exchange-Rate-Based Stabilizations	May 1999, Box 3.1
The Pros and Cons of Dollarization	May 2000, Box 1.4
Why Is the Euro So Undervalued?	October 2000, Box 1.1
Convergence and Real Exchange Rate Appreciation in the EU Accession Countries	October 2000, Box 4.4
What Is Driving the Weakness of the Euro and the Strength of the Dollar?	May 2001, Chapter II
The Weakness of the Australian and New Zealand Currencies	May 2001, Box 2.1
How Did the September 11 Attacks Affect Exchange Rate Expectations?	December 2001, Box 2.4
Market Expectations of Exchange Rate Movements	September 2002, Box 1.2
Are Foreign Exchange Reserves in Asia Too High?	September 2003, Chapter II
How Concerned Should Developing Countries Be About G-3 Exchange Rate Volatility?	September 2003, Chapter II

Reserves and Short-Term Debt	September 2003, Box 2.3
The Effects of a Falling Dollar	April 2004, Box 1.1
Learning to Float: The Experience of Emerging Market Countries Since the Early 1990s	September 2004, Chapter II
How Did Chile, India, and Brazil Learn to Float?	September 2004, Box 2.3
Foreign Exchange Market Development and Intervention	September 2004, Box 2.4
How Emerging Market Countries May Be Affected by External Shocks	September 2006, Box 1.3

	Staff Studies for the World Economic Outlook
Multilateral Unit-Labor-Cost-Based Competitiveness Indicators for Advanced, Developing, and Transition Countries *Anthony G. Turner and Stephen Golub*	December 1997
Currency Crises: In Search of Common Elements *Jahangir Aziz, Francesco Caramazza and Ranil Salgado*	May 2000
Business Cycle Influences on Exchange Rates: Survey and Evidence *Ronald MacDonald and Phillip Suragel*	May 2000

IX. External Payments, Trade, Capital Movements, and Foreign Debt

	World Economic Outlook
Trade Among the Transition Countries	October 1995, Box 7
World Current Account Discrepancy	October 1996, Annex III
Capital Inflows to Developing and Transition Countries—Identifying Causes and Formulating Appropriate Policy Responses	October 1996, Annex IV
Globalization—Opportunities and Challenges	May 1997
Moral Hazard and IMF Lending	May 1998, Box 2
The Current Account and External Sustainability	May 1998, Box 8
Review of Debt-Reduction Efforts for Low-Income Countries and Status of the HIPC Initiative	October 1998, Box 1.1
Trade Adjustment in East Asian Crisis Countries	October 1998, Box 2.2
Are There Dangers of Increasing Protection?	May 1999, Box 1.3
Trends and Issues in the Global Trading System	October 1999, Chapter V
Capital Flows to Emerging Market Economies: Composition and Volatility	October 1999, Box 2.2
The Global Current Account Discrepancy	October 2000, Chapter I, Appendix II
Trade Integration and Sub-Saharan Africa	May 2001, Chapter II
Sustainability of the U.S. External Current Account	May 2001, Box 1.2
Reducing External Balances	May 2001, Chapter I, Appendix 2
The World Trading System: From Seattle to Doha	October 2001, Chapter II
International Financial Integration and Economic Performance: Impact on Developing Countries	October 2001, Chapter IV
Potential Welfare Gains From a New Trade Round	October 2001, Box 2.3
Critics of a New Trade Round	October 2001, Box 2.4
Foreign Direct Investment and the Poorer Countries	October 2001, Box 4.3
Country Experiences with Sequencing Capital Account Liberalization	October 2001, Box 4.4

Contagion and Its Causes	December 2001, Chapter I, Appendix
Capital Account Crises in Emerging Market Countries	April 2002, Box 3.5
How Have External Deficits Adjusted in the Past?	September 2002, Box 2.2
Using Prices to Measure Goods Market Integration	September 2002, Box 3.1
Transport Costs	September 2002, Box 3.2
The Gravity Model of International Trade	September 2002, Box 3.3
Vertical Specialization in the Global Economy	September 2002, Box 3.4
Trade and Growth	September 2002, Box 3.5
How Worrisome Are External Imbalances?	September 2002, Chapter II
How Do Industrial Country Agricultural Policies Affect Developing Countries?	September 2002, Chapter II
Trade and Financial Integration	September 2002, Chapter III
Risks to the Multilateral Trading System	April 2004, Box 1.3
Is the Doha Round Back on Track?	September 2004, Box 1.3
Regional Trade Agreements and Integration: The Experience with NAFTA	September 2004, Box 1.4
Globalization and External Imbalances	April 2005, Chapter III
The Ending of Global Textile Trade Quotas	April 2005, Box 1.3
What Progress Has Been Made in Implementing Policies to Reduce Global Imbalances?	April 2005, Box 1.4
Measuring a Country's Net External Position	April 2005, Box 3.2
Global Imbalances: A Saving and Investment Perspective	September 2005, Chapter II
Impact of Demographic Change on Saving, Investment, and Current Account Balances	September 2005, Box 2.3
How Will Global Imbalances Adjust?	September 2005, Appendix 1.2
Oil Prices and Global Imbalances	April 2006, Chapter II
How Much Progress Has Been Made in Addressing Global Imbalances?	April 2006, Box 1.4
The Doha Round After The Hong Kong SAR Meetings	April 2006, Box 1.5
Capital Flows to Emerging Market Countries: a Long-Term Perspective	September 2006, Box 1.1
How Will Global Imbalances Adjust?	September 2006, Box 2.1

	Staff Studies for the World Economic Outlook
Foreign Direct Investment in the World Economy *Edward M. Graham*	September 1995
Trade and Financial Integration in Europe: Five Years After the Euro's Introduction	September 2004, Box 2.5

X. Regional Issues

	World Economic Outlook
Adjustment in Sub-Saharan Africa	May 1995, Annex II
Macroeconomic and Structural Adjustment in the Middle East and North Africa	May 1996, Annex II
Stabilization and Reform of Formerly Centrally Planned Developing Economies in East Asia	May 1997, Box 10
EMU and the World Economy	October 1997, Chapter III
Implications of Structural Reforms Under EMU	October 1997, Annex II

The European Union's Stability and Growth Pact	October 1997, Box 3
Asymmetric Shocks: European Union and the United States	October 1997, Box 4
Interim Assessment (Focus on Crisis in Asia—Regional and Global Implications)	December 1997
The Asian Crisis and the Region's Long-Term Growth Performance	October 1998, Chapter III
Economic Policy Challenges Facing the Euro Area and the External Implications of EMU	October 1998, Chapter V
Economic Policymaking in the EU and Surveillance by EU Institutions	October 1998, Chapter V, Appendix
Chronic Unemployment in the Euro Area: Causes and Cures	May 1999, Chapter IV
Growth in Sub-Saharan Africa: Performance, Impediments, and Policy Requirements	October 1999, Chapter VI
The Regional Economic Impact of the Kosovo Crisis	October 1999, Box 1.5
Counting the Costs of the Recent Crises	October 1999, Box 2.6
Africa and World Trends in Military Spending	October 1999, Box 6.1
The Economic Impact of HIV/AIDS in Southern Africa	October 2000, Box 1.4
Accession of Transition Economies to the European Union: Prospects and Pressures	October 2000, Chapter IV
The IMF and the Transition Economies	October 2000, Box 3.1
Previous EU Enlargements	October 2000, Box 4.2
The Enhanced HIPC Initiative in Africa	May 2001, Box 1.4
Large Current Account Deficits in EU Accession Countries	May 2001, Box 1.5
Africa's Trade and The Gravity Model	May 2001, Box 2.2
The Implications of the Japanese Economic Slowdown for East Asia	October 2001, Box 1.4
Relative Euro-Area Growth Performances: Why Are Germany and Italy Lagging Behind France?	October 2001, Box 1.5
Economic Growth, Civil Conflict, and Poverty Reduction in Sub-Saharan Africa	October 2001, Box 1.7
Information Technology and Growth in Emerging Asia	October 2001, Box 3.3
The IT Slump and Short-Term Growth Prospects in East Asia	October 2001, Box 3.5
The Effects of the September 11 Attacks on the Caribbean Region	December 2001, Box 3.3
Debt Crises: What's Different About Latin America?	April 2002, Chapter II
Foreign Direct Investment in Africa	September 2002, Box 1.6
Promoting Stronger Institutions and Growth: The New Partnership for Africa's Development	April 2003, Box 3.3
How Can Economic Growth in the Middle East and North Africa Region Be Accelerated?	September 2003, Chapter II
Gulf Cooperation Council: Challenges on the Road to a Monetary Union	September 2003, Box 1.5
Accounting for Growth in the Middle East and North Africa	September 2003, Box 2.1
Is Emerging Asia Becoming an Engine of World Growth?	April 2004, Box 1.4
What Works in Africa	April 2004, Box 1.5
Economic Integration and Structural Reforms: The European Experience	April 2004, Box 3.4
What Are the Risks of Slower Growth in China?	September 2004, Box 1.2
Governance Challenges and Progress in Sub-Saharan Africa	September 2004, Box 1.6
The Indian Ocean Tsunami: Impact on South Asian Economies	April 2005, Box 1.1
Workers' Remittances and Emigration in the Caribbean	April 2005, Box 2.1
What Explains Divergent External Sector Performance in the Euro Area?	September 2005, Box 1.3
Pressures Mount for African Cotton Producers	September 2005, Box 1.5

Is Investment in Emerging Asia Too Low?	September 2005, Box 2.4
Developing Institutions to Reflect Local Conditions: The Example of Ownership Transformation in China Versus Central and Eastern Europe	September 2005, Box 3.1
How Rapidly Are Oil Exporters Spending Their Revenue Gains?	April 2006, Box 2.1

	Staff Studies for the World Economic Outlook
The Design of EMU *David Begg*	December 1997
The Great Contraction in Russia, the Baltics and Other Countries of the Former Soviet Union: A View from the Supply Side *Mark De Broeck and Vincent Koen*	May 2000

XI. Country-Specific Analyses

	World Economic Outlook
Factors Behind the Financial Crisis in Mexico	May 1995, Annex I
New Zealand's Structural Reforms and Economic Revival	May 1995, Box 3
Brazil and Korea	May 1995, Box 5
The Output Collapse in Russia	May 1995, Box 8
Foreign Direct Investment in Estonia	May 1995, Box 9
September 1995 Economic Stimulus Packages in Japan	October 1995, Box 1
Uganda: Successful Adjustment Under Difficult Circumstances	October 1995, Box 3
Changing Wage Structures in the Czech Republic	October 1995, Box 6
Resolving Financial System Problems in Japan	May 1996, Box 3
New Zealand's Fiscal Responsibility Act	May 1996, Box 4
Deindustrialization and the Labor Market in Sweden	May 1997, Box 7
Ireland Catches Up	May 1997, Box 8
Foreign Direct Investment Strategies in Hungary and Kazakhstan	May 1997, Box 12
China—Growth and Economic Reforms	October 1997, Annex I
Alternative Exchange Rate Assumptions for Japan	October 1997, Box 2
Hong Kong, China: Economic Linkages and Institutional Arrangements	October 1997, Box 9
Russia's Fiscal Challenges	May 1998, Box 9
Japan's Economic Crisis and Policy Options	October 1998, Chapter IV
Brazil's Financial Assistance Package and Adjustment Program	December 1998, Box 1.1
Recent Developments in the Japanese Financial System	December 1998, Box 1.2
Malaysia's Capital Controls	December 1998, Box 2.1
Hong Kong's Intervention in the Equity Spot and Futures Markets	December 1998, Box 2.2
Is China's Growth Overstated?	December 1998, Box 4.1
Measuring Household Saving in the United States	May 1999, Box 2.2
Australia and New Zealand: Divergences, Prospects, and Vulnerabilities	October 1999, Box 1.1
The Emerging Market Crises and South Africa	October 1999, Box 2.1
Structural Reforms in Latin America: The Case of Argentina	October 1999, Box 2.3
Malaysia's Response to the Financial Crisis: How Unorthodox Was It?	October 1999, Box 2.4
Financial Sector Restructuring in Indonesia, Korea, Malaysia, and Thailand	October 1999, Box 2.5
Turkey's IMF-Supported Disinflation Program	May 2000, Box 2.1
Productivity and Stock Prices in the United States	May 2000, Box 3.1

India: Reinvigorating the Reform Process	May 2000, Box 4.2
Risky Business: Output Volatility and the Perils of Forecasting in Japan	October 2000, Box 1.2
China's Prospective WTO Accession	October 2000, Box 1.3
Addressing Barter Trade and Arrears in Russia	October 2000, Box 3.3
Fiscal Decentralization in Transition Economies: China and Russia	October 2000, Box 3.5
Accession of Turkey to the European Union	October 2000, Box 4.3
Japan's Recent Monetary and Structural Policy Initiatives	May 2001, Box 1.3
Japan: A Fiscal Outlier?	May 2001, Box 3.1
Financial Implications of the Shrinking Supply of U.S. Treasury Securities	May 2001, Box 3.2
The Growth-Poverty Nexus in India	October 2001, Box 1.6
Has U.S. TFP Growth Accelerated Outside of the IT Sector?	October 2001, Box 3.2
Fiscal Stimulus and the Outlook for the United States	December 2001, Box 3.2
Argentina: An Uphill Struggle to Regain Confidence	December 2001, Box 3.4
China's Medium-Term Fiscal Challenges	April 2002, Box 1.4
Rebuilding Afghanistan	April 2002, Box 1.5
Russia's Rebounds	April 2002, Box 1.6
Brazil: The Quest to Restore Market Confidence	September 2002, Box 1.4
Where Is India in Terms of Trade Liberalization?	September 2002, Box 1.5
How Important Are Banking Weaknesses in Explaining Germany's Stagnation?	April 2003, Box 1.3
Are Corporate Financial Conditions Related to the Severity of Recessions in the United States?	April 2003, Box 2.2
Rebuilding Post-Conflict Iraq	September 2003, Box 1.4
How Will the U.S. Budget Deficit Affect the Rest of the World?	April 2004, Chapter II
China's Emergence and Its Impact on the Global Economy	April 2004, Chapter II
Can China Sustain Its Rapid Output Growth?	April 2004, Box 2.3
Quantifying the International Impact of China's WTO Accession	April 2004, Box 2.4
Structural Reforms and Economic Growth: New Zealand's Experience	April 2004, Box 3.1
Structural Reforms in the United Kingdom During the 1980s	April 2004, Box 3.2
The Netherlands: How the Interaction of Labor Market Reforms and Tax Cuts Led to Strong Employment Growth	April 2004, Box 3.3
Why Is the U.S. International Income Account Still in the Black, and Will This Last?	September, 2005, Box 1.2
Is India Becoming an Engine for Global Growth?	September, 2005, Box 1.4
Saving and Investment in China	September, 2005, Box 2.1
China's GDP Revision: What Does It Mean for China and the Global Economy?	April 2006, Box 1.6

Staff Studies for the World Economic Outlook

How Large Was the Output Collapse in Russia? Alternative Estimates and Welfare Implications *Evgeny Gavrilenkov and Vincent Koen*	September, 1995

World Economic and Financial Surveys

This series (ISSN 0258-7440) contains biannual, annual, and periodic studies covering monetary and financial issues of importance to the global economy. The core elements of the series are the *World Economic Outlook* report, usually published in April and September, and the semiannual *Global Financial Stability Report*. Other studies assess international trade policy, private market and official financing for developing countries, exchange and payments systems, export credit policies, and issues discussed in the *World Economic Outlook*. Please consult the IMF *Publications Catalog* for a complete listing of currently available World Economic and Financial Surveys.

World Economic Outlook: A Survey by the Staff of the International Monetary Fund

The *World Economic Outlook*, published twice a year in English, French, Spanish, and Arabic, presents IMF staff economists' analyses of global economic developments during the near-and medium term. Chapters give an overview of the-world economy; consider issues affecting industrial countries, developing countries, and economies in transition to the market; and address topics of pressing current interest.

ISSN 0256-6877.

$57.00 (academic rate: $54.00); paper.

April 2006 ISBN 1-58906-549-2. **Stock #WEOEA2006001.**
September 2005 ISBN 1-58906-454-2. **Stock #WEOEA2005002.**
April 2005 ISBN 1-58906-429-1. **Stock #WEOEA2005001.**
September 2004 ISBN 1-58906-406-2. **Stock #WEOEA2004002.**

Global Financial Stability Report: Market Developments and Issues

The *Global Financial Stability Report*, published twice a year, examines trends and issues that influence world financial markets. It replaces two IMF publications—the annual *International Capital Markets* report and the electronic quarterly *Emerging Market Financing* report. The report is designed to deepen understanding of international capital flows and to explore developments that could pose a risk to international financial market stability.

$57.00 (academic rate: $54.00); paper.

April 2006 ISBN 1-58906-504-2. **Stock #GFSREA2006001.**
September 2005 ISBN 1-58906-450-X. **Stock #GFSREA2005002.**
April 2005 ISBN 1-58906-418-6. **Stock #GFSREA2005001.**
September 2004 ISBN 1-58906-378-3. **Stock #GFSREA2004002.**
April 2004 ISBN 1-58906-328-7. **Stock #GFSREA0012004.**

Emerging Local Securities and Derivatives Markets

by Donald Mathieson, Jorge E. Roldos, Ramana Ramaswamy, and Anna Ilyina

The volatility of capital flows since the mid-1990s has sparked an interest in the development of local securities and derivatives markets. This report examines the growth of these markets in emerging market countries and the key policy issues that have arisen as a result.

$42.00 (academic rate: $35.00); paper.

2004. ISBN 1-58906-291-4. **Stock #WEOEA0202004.**

Official Financing: Recent Developments and Selected Issues

by a staff team in the Policy Development and Review Department led by Martin G. Gilman and Jian-Ye Wang

This study provides information on official financing for developing countries, with the focus on low-income countries. It updates the 2001 edition and reviews developments in direct financing by official and multilateral sources.

$42.00 (academic rate: $35.00); paper.

2003. ISBN 1-58906-228-0. **Stock #WEOEA0132003.**
2001. ISBN 1-58906-038-5. **Sto ck #WEOEA0132001.**

Exchange Arrangements and Foreign Exchange Markets: Developments and Issues

by a staff team led by Shogo Ishii

This study updates developments in exchange arrangements during 1998–2001. It also discusses the evolution of exchange rate regimes based on de facto policies since 1990, reviews foreign exchange market organization and regulations in a number of countries, and examines factors affecting exchange rate volatility.

ISSN 0258-7440

$42.00 (academic rate $35.00)

March 2003. ISBN 1-58906-177-2. **Stock #WEOEA0192003.**

World Economic Outlook Supporting Studies

by the IMF's Research Department

These studies, supporting analyses and scenarios of the *World Economic Outlook*, provide a detailed examination of theory and evidence on major issues currently affecting the global economy.

$25.00 (academic rate: $20.00); paper.

2000. ISBN 1-55775-893-X. **Stock #WEOEA0032000.**

Exchange Rate Arrangements and Currency Convertibility: Developments and Issues

by a staff team led by R. Barry Johnston

A principal force driving the growth in international trade and investment has been the liberalization of financial transactions, including the liberalization of trade and exchange controls. This study reviews the developments and issues in the exchange arrangements and currency convertibility of IMF members.

$20.00 (academic rate: $12.00); paper.

1999. ISBN 1-55775-795-X. **Stock #WEOEA0191999.**

Available by series subscription or single title (including back issues); academic rate available only to full-time university faculty and students. For earlier editions please inquire about prices.

The IMF *Catalog of Publications* is available on-line at the Internet address listed below.

Please send orders and inquiries to:
International Monetary Fund, Publication Services, 700 19th Street, N.W.
Washington, D.C. 20431, U.S.A.
Tel.: (202) 623-7430 Telefax: (202) 623-7201
E-mail: publications@imf.org
Internet: http://www.imf.org